D0072649

CONGRESS AND MONEY

CONGRESS AND MONEY

Budgeting, Spending and Taxing

Allen Schick

The Urban Institute
2100 M Street, N.W.
Washington, D.C. 20037

Printed in the United States of America

LC 80-53322
ISBN 87766-278-9
UI 1002

Please refer to URI 29400 when ordering

THE URBAN INSTITUTE is a nonprofit research organization established in 1968 to study problems of the nation's urban communities. Independent and nonpartisan, the Institute responds to current needs for disinterested analyses and basic information and attempts to facilitate the application of this knowledge. As part of this effort, it cooperates with federal agencies, states, cities, associations of public officials, and other organizations committed to the public interest.

The Institute's research findings and a broad range of interpretive viewpoints are published as an educational service. The interpretations or conclusions are those of the authors and should not be attributed to The Urban Institute, its trustees, or to other organizations that support its research.

Contents

List of Tables

Page

Page

Foreword

This book is the first study of legislative behavior issued under the auspices of The Urban Institute. Yet it is squarely within the scope of interests that have animated the Institute since its inception a dozen years ago. Congress, and legislative bodies at all levels of American government, are vital and influential participants in the policy-making process. Efforts to improve the quality of public programs must take into account the institutional competence and capacities of the legislatures which formulate public policies and allocate public funds. Housing programs, health care, urban financing—indeed all programmatic concerns of the Institute—owe much of their design and performance to congressional enactments and appropriations. Policy analysis cannot flower into a full-fledged influence on public policy if it is restricted to executive suites and fails to penetrate legislative committees and chambers.

The Congressional Budget Act of 1974 was heralded at the time of enactment as a major advance in the practice and accountability of the American government. The budget process established by the 1974 Act serves as an integrating mechanism for the separate tax, appropriations, and authorizations processes which continue to function on Capitol Hill. The process purports to give Congress a comprehensive and consistent means of making fiscal choices and setting national priorities.

After the new process had been in operation for several years, the Institute commissioned Allen Schick to undertake an examination of its effects on congressional behavior. As a senior specialist at the Congressional Research Service, Schick had served as one of the framers of the Budget Act and participated in its early implementation. During two years as a visiting scholar at the Institute, Schick expanded the scope of the study to encompass tax measures, appropriations, and authorizing legislation. *Congress and Money* is a comprehensive account of the congressional budget process and of its effects on related legislative activities.

William Gorham
President
The Urban Institute

Foreword

Acknowledgments

In the course of studying congressional budgeting, I accumulated considerable data and many debts. From start to finish, my research and writing were facilitated by William Gorham and Robert Harris, who encouraged me to undertake the project, provided a stimulating environment and financial support at The Urban Institute, and refused to let my interest flag or my pen slow down. At the Institute, Helen Burnett and James Abrams effectively assisted with data collection and research. Almost 100 Members and staff of Congress shared their knowledge in interviews which expanded my understanding of congressional budgeting. My commitment to preserve the anonymity of these people requires me to thank them *en bloc.*

The completed manuscript was carefully reviewed by the following experienced congressional staff leaders: John McEvoy, Sidney Brown, and Ira Tannenbaum of the Senate Budget Committee; Bruce Meredith and Wendell Belew of the House Budget Committee; and Robert Reischauer, John Ellwood, and Jim Verdier of the Congressional Budget Office. James Storey of The Urban Institute, formerly a staff member of the Senate Budget Committee, also reviewed the entire manuscript.

The final product benefited from Priscilla Taylor's editorial care and skill.

Allen Schick
June 1980

Chapter I.

INTRODUCTION

Overview of the Congressional Budget Process

Congress and the Budget

Is It Working?

Plan of the Book

I Introduction

SINCE 1975, Congress has been making budgetary war and peace within the budget process it established in the previous year. The Congressional Budget Act of 1974 altered budgetary roles and relationships within Congress, bringing new participants into the process and compelling older participants to function within new procedural and substantive rules. This book examines the congressional budget process in its political habitat: the United States Congress. Although it gives some attention to relationships with the executive branch, its main focus is on the legislative participants, on how their behavior differs from pre-Budget Act practices, and on the patterns of conflict and cooperation that have developed in the early years of the new process. The scope of inquiry thus extends to the tax, appropriations, and authorizations work of Congress, as these are inextricably intertwined with the activities that constitute the budget process.[1]

OVERVIEW OF THE CONGRESSIONAL BUDGET PROCESS

The congressional budget process is centered on two concurrent resolutions on the budget—resolutions agreed upon by both Houses of Congress. The first must be adopted by May 15 of each year, prior to House and Senate consideration of budget-related legislation. The second is to be adopted by September 15, shortly before the start of the next federal fiscal year (see table 1). Each resolution specifies the total amount of revenues, new budget authority, outlays, surplus or deficit, and public debt of the federal government. Each subdivides the spending totals among 19 "functions"—budgetary terminology for functional areas of spending such as

1. Many specialized terms are used in the budgetary process, and throughout this book. The terms are defined in the appendix.

Table 1

CONGRESSIONAL BUDGET TIMETABLE

Deadline	*Action to be Completed*
15th day after Congress convenes	President submits his budget, along with current services estimates.[1]
March 15	Committees submit views and estimates to Budget Committees.
April 1	Congressional Budget Office submits report to Budget Committees.[2]
April 15	Budget Committees report first concurrent resolution on the budget to their Houses.
May 15	Committees report bills authorizing new budget authority.
May 15	Congress adopts first concurrent resolution on the budget.
7th day after Labor Day	Congress completes action on bills providing budget authority and spending authority.
September 15	Congress completes actions on second required concurrent resolution on the budget.
September 25	Congress completes action on reconciliation process implementing second concurrent resolution.
October 1	Fiscal year begins.

[1] Current service estimates are estimates of the dollar levels that would be required next year to support the same level of services in each program as this year's budget. The Budget Act originally required submission of the current services estimates by November 10 of the previous year. Since the President was still in the midst of developing his budget proposals for the next year, Congress later agreed to permit simultaneous submission of the current services and executive budgets in January.

[2] The Budget Committees and CBO have found April 1 too late in the budget process to be useful; hence CBO submits its report(s) in February, although April 1 remains the date required by law.

health or defense. Prior to consideration of the first budget resolution, each House and Senate committee with jurisdiction over the authorization of expenditures, the appropriations of funds, or raising of revenues formulates its recommendations concerning matters within its domain. The first budget resolution establishes targets to guide Congress and its committees during subsequent consideration of money legislation. As the House and Senate take up individual revenue, spending, and debt measures, Members are kept informed (by means of scorekeeping procedures) of the current status of the budget as well as of the budgetary impact of pending legislation. After action has been completed on specific appropriations and other spending bills, Congress adopts a second resolution which reflects all of the actions taken. If necessary, Congress also passes a reconciliation bill to assure that existing tax, spending, and debt statutes are consistent with the total congressional budget. The revenue and spending totals in the second resolution must be adhered to in subsequent legislation, but Congress has the option to revise its budget resolution during the fiscal year. Table 1 summarizes the steps in the process and dates required by law for specific actions.

Primary responsibility for the new process is assigned to House and Senate Budget Committees, each of which has a sizable professional staff. A Congressional Budget Office (CBO) also has been organized to provide information and analysis. As part of the congressional budget process, a comprehensive timetable synchronizes the activities of the various legislative participants (in particular, the budget, appropriations, and authorizing committees) and sets deadlines for the completion of various congressional actions. The 1974 law also contains numerous provisions to improve the quality and availability of budget information, encourage program evaluation by congressional committees, and restrict "backdoor" spending practices (expenditure measures considered outside the normal appropriations process).

A separate title of the Act prescribes new legislative controls over the impoundment of funds by the executive branch. Two types of impoundments are defined, and distinct procedures are established for each. *Deferrals* are executive actions to delay the obligation or expenditure of funds appropriated by Congress; *rescissions* are proposals to repeal appropriations or other spending laws. A deferral can remain in effect until the end of the fiscal year unless it is disapproved by either the House or the Senate. But a rescission ceases—and impounded funds must be released—unless it is approved by both Houses of Congress within 45 days.

If the new procedures survive, 1974 will be marked as the year in which Congress created a budget process. But the Congressional Budget Act lacks many key elements of a budget process. It prescribes rules for making budget resolutions, but not a single dollar can be spent by federal agencies pursuant to such resolutions, nor a dollar of revenue raised. By itself, the process ordained in 1974 would be incomplete, lacking the statutory base and legislative procedures for authorizing the collection and disbursement of federal money.

The Budget Act constitutes a complete process only because it continues and integrates the various money-deciding processes that antedate it. Congressional budget decisions did not begin in 1974. Congress has three other such processes: the appropriations power bequeathed to it by the Constitution, the power to tax, and authorizations requirements provided for in various statutes and in the rules of the House and Senate. These processes continue to exist, and the committees responsible for their operation continue with much the same jurisdiction as they had before the Budget Act. Table 2 inventories the main budget responsibilities of the participants in the complete congressional budget process.

CONGRESS AND THE BUDGET

What happens to a budget process when it confronts Congress, and what happens to Congress when it must attend to new budget functions? This twofold question is the central concern of this study. In establishing a budget process, Congress sought to preserve its essential character as a legislative body while creating an integrated process that makes it responsible for the budget policies of the United States.

Congressional structure and budget practice do not fit easily with one another. Congress is an institution in which power is widely shared. Within Congress there are multiple points of access and influence, and important decisions often are made piecemeal and inconsistently. These characteristics are political imperatives for a legislature whose distinctive feature is the diffusion of power. In its traditional budget-making activities, Congress has pursued this imperative by separating tax from spending decisions, setting up parallel authorizing and appropriating processes, and splitting its spending business among more than a dozen appropriation bills (and subcommittees) and other bits of legislation.

While legislative norms propel Congress toward the fragmentation of power, budgeting invites the concentration of power. Budgeting necessarily involves the pulling together of disparate interests and perspectives in a reasonably comprehensive and consistent decisional process. Budgeting demands attention to the relationship of the parts and the whole, to the linkage of tax and spending policies, as well as to the priorities accorded to the competing claims for public resources. Hence, budgeting has generally been regarded as an executive rather than a legislative function, not only at the national level, but in most American cities and states as well. "To be a budget, it must be prepared by the executive" was the persuasive message of budgeting experts more than a half-century ago when they led a movement that culminated in the 1921 Budget and Accounting Act and the concentration of federal budget responsibilities in the presidency.

The critical test for congressional budgeting is the extent to which it harmonizes the legislative imperative for fragmentation with the drive for integrated budget outcomes. The process cannot succeed if it concentrates legislative power over money in a few hands. Even as it empowers new budget functionaries on Capitol Hill, the congressional budget process must maintain a broad division of budgetary labors among virtually all committees. In fact, the Congressional Budget Act has expanded the budgetary roles of the tax, appropriations, and authorizations committees, but at the price of trying to compel them to function within the discipline of the new process. In this way, the 1974 Act tries to accommodate both the budget's need for fiscal cohesion and Congress's need for legislative collegiality and diffusion of power. But this blueprint for budgetary reform is strained by a clash of interests within Congress, between pressures to guard the treasury and pressures to open the coffers to favored interests.

As noted, the Budget Committees must continually interact with three sets of participants: the tax committees (House Ways and Means, and Senate Finance), the House and Senate Appropriations Committees, and the various authorizing committees in each chamber. The broad scope of the process also requires interaction with the House and Senate leaderships. Each relationship opens the possibility of conflict and alliance. Conflict cannot be avoided because the budget process inevitably redistributes legislative power and has the potential to alter budget outcomes. Alliances are necessary because the Budget Committees cannot challenge all other power holders simultaneously. One can expect that coalitions of convenience, many of them transitory and oriented to specific issues and opportunities, will be formed by participants striving to ward off new threats to their established power and by newcomers intent on enhancing their nascent budget status.

IS IT WORKING?

Perhaps the most frequently asked question about the budget

Table 2

PRINCIPAL DUTIES AND FUNCTIONS OF PARTICIPANTS IN THE CONGRESSIONAL BUDGET PROCESS

President	*Authorizing Committees*	*Appropriations Committees*	*Revenue Committees*	*Budget Committees*	*Congressional Budget Office*
—Submits executive budget and current services estimates. —Updates budget estimates in April and July. —Signs or vetoes revenue, appropriations, and other budget-related legislation. —May propose the deferral or rescission of appropriated funds.	—Prepare views and estimates on programs within jurisdiction. —Report authorizing legislation for the next fiscal year. —Include CBO cost estimates in reports accompanying their legislation. *Limitations:* 1. Legislation providing contract or borrowing authority is effective only as provided in appropriations.	—Report regular and supplemental appropriations bills. —After adoption of a budget resolution, allocate budget authority and outlays among their subcommittees. —Provide five-year projections of outlays in reports accompanying appropriations, and compare budget authority with amounts provided in latest budget resolution.	—Submit views and estimates on budget matters in their jurisdiction. —Can be directed by second resolution to report legislation changing tax laws. *Limitation:* Legislation cannot cause revenues to fall below level set in the second resolution.	—Report two or more concurrent resolutions on the budget each year. —Allocate new budget authority and outlays among House and Senate committees. —Monitor congressional actions affecting the budget. —Advise Congress on the status of the budget.	—Issues reports on annual budget. —Estimates cost of bills reported by House and Senate committees. —Issues periodic scorekeeping reports on status of the congressional budget. —Assists the budget, revenue, appropriations, and other committees. —Issues five-year budget projections.

2. Entitlements cannot become effective before next fiscal year.	—Can be directed by second budget resolution to report reconciliation bill repealing new or existing budget authority. —Review rescission and deferrals proposals of the President. *Limitation:* After second resolution is adopted, spending cannot exceed amount set by Congress.

process is, "Is it working?" This is an understandable starting point for an inquiry about the 1974 change in congressional practice. The question has two quite different dimensions, procedural and substantive. First, is the process working in terms of the routines and requirements laid down in the Budget Act? Do congressional participants adhere to the timetable laid down in the Act for dealing with budget resolutions, tax bills, authorizing legislation, and appropriations? Are committees and Members of Congress adequately informed with regard to the budgetary consequences of their decisions? Has the Congressional Budget Office (CBO) supplied timely and useful cost estimates, scorekeeping reports, and budget analyses? Procedure is the bedrock of budgeting, and the successful implementation of a new procedure must be a first concern of every budget reform.

"Is it working?" also relates to the substantive impact of the budget process on congressional decisions. Has the budget process made a difference in terms of the levels of revenue and expenditure? Do the Budget Committees come to grips with the fiscal implications of congressional action when they mark up a budget resolution? Do the fiscal policy and spending priorities voted by Congress differ much in amount or in kind from those presented in the President's budget? When they prepare a budget resolution, do the Budget Committees try to make independent judgments, or do they merely accommodate to the preferences of others?

It is much easier to get procedural than substantive answers. One can track the number of times that Congress operates within the budget timetable and the number of times it misses deadlines. CBO's production of budgetary data and the timeliness of its reports can be computed. One cannot be so confident, however, with regard to substantive outcomes. New procedures can yield the same results as before. Even if the outcome appears to be different, one cannot be sure that the change is attributable to the budget process. If, for example, Congress cuts defense spending more than in previous years, to what factor or factors ought this action be credited: the activism of the Budget Committees, changes in public opinion in the United States, newspaper headlines, or international events? Congress actually made a sizable cut in defense spending for fiscal 1976, its first year under the budget process, and many people hailed this feat as a great success for the budget process. In subsequent years, defense spending was hardly cut at all, and once again the budget process was credited (or blamed) for the outcome.

In this study of the budget process, the primary focus is on how Congress makes money decisions. Because budgetary power is so widely diffused within Congress, this study must consider all the parts, including the tax, appropriations, and authorizations work of Congress. It would be incomplete if it reviewed only the work of the Budget Committees, the budget resolutions, CBO reports, and the other activities that make up the formal budget process. Only after a careful review of the entire range of processes leading to money decisions can the questions posed above about the impact of the budget process be addressed. They will be considered in the last chapter.

PLAN OF THE BOOK

This study covers the first five years in the operation of the congressional budget process, 1975 through 1979. During these years, Congress completed a "trial" budget cycle, three full cycles, and most of a fifth. It took hundreds of budget-related actions, passing a dozen budget resolutions, eight major tax bills, almost a hundred appropriations measures, and more than that number of authorizations. Each action carved a documentary trail of its own. In the course of these five years, congressional committees issued hundreds of budget-related reports, and CBO produced hundreds of cost projections and analytic studies. Because the budget extends to so much of what Congress does, the trails cross the congressional scene in disorderly lines. One of the main reasons why the House and Senate Budget Committees built large staffs (more than 70 in each committee, in addition to CBO) was to keep track of all budget developments in Congress. This study follows as many of the trails as possible, sifting through countless thousands of pages of committee reports, floor debates, and transcripts. But some important developments undoubtedly have been missed, left out, or slighted.

In addition to the published records, the Senate Budget Committee made available the transcripts of its business sessions and markups, many thousands of pages in all. The House Budget Committee does not keep a transcript of its meetings, but some of its deliberations are accessible through a journal (which records roll calls during markup) and the transcripts of conference committee meetings. Finally, 30 Members of Congress and more than 60 staff members, including most of those active in the fiscal decision-making process, were interviewed for this study.[2]

2. Most of the interviews were tape-recorded, with the understanding that remarks would not be attributed. When interview material appears in the text, therefore, such comments are quoted but not footnoted.

The findings of this research are presented in three parts of several chapters each. Each part presents the data developed in the course of the study on an important aspect of how Congress deals with money.

Part One reviews the budgetary conflicts of the 1960s and early 1970s that convinced Congress of the need for new budgetary processes, and describes the new institutions created to meet that need. Budgeting and deciding how money shall be spent inherently involve conflict. All participants in the process of developing budgets, including political constituency groups, have an interest in protecting or expanding their share of the pie. Thus, when federal budgets are being developed and debated, conflict and competition for funds exist within and between executive agencies, within Congress, between Congress and the President, and among recipients of the funds: states, counties, cities, and groups interested in particular programs.

From 1921 to 1974 the President had responsibility for initiating the annual process of resolving these conflicts. The President played a dominant role throughout the process, even though Congress was responsible for appropriations. The President began the process each year by submitting a budget to Congress. Various congressional committees then acted on parts of the budget—enacting separate bills to authorize or appropriate monies to be spent on specific programs or to provide tax relief to various groups. By the end of a legislative session, many bills had been acted upon piecemeal in committees and on the floors of both Houses of Congress, and federal agencies began another year of collecting and spending sums of money. The amounts usually differed from the amounts the President originally proposed, but throughout the process, the President played major role, maintaining control of much of the information necessary for congressional deliberation.

The system was untidy, complex, cumbersome, and sometimes apparently irrational, but it worked, primarily because acceptable and necessary conflict-resolving processes were built into the process by statute, tradition, and understandings among the many participants.

Between 1966 and 1973, conflict over budgetary issues intensified, and the mechanisms for resolving conflicts proved increasingly ineffective. One symptom was steadily growing deficits in the federal budget, which almost everyone decried but which Congress seemed increasingly unable to control. Precipitating factors included power struggles among congressional committees, between new

Members of Congress and old-timers, and ultimately between the President and Congress. Another significant factor was the growth in the participation of interested outside parties in the political process.

Conflict was so protracted and so intense that the period can legitimately be characterized, as in Chapter II, as a Seven-Year Budget War. The outcome of that war was the Congressional Budget and Impoundment Control Act of 1974. This act can be viewed as a treaty that sought to bring equilibrium to the annual budget cycle by redefining power relationships among the old participants and creating new participants to develop better information and to control and channel the inevitable budgetary conflicts. Chapter III analyzes the process by which the treaty was negotiated, and describes its general terms and the new participants: the House and Senate Budget Committees and the Congressional Budget Office. Chapter IV analyzes the roles and characteristics of the new committees as originally envisaged and as they have evolved over their first five years of functioning in the congressional arena. Chapter V does the same for the Congressional Budget Office.

Part Two details the way in which the new institutions have functioned to produce congressional budget resolutions, and how they have interacted with the preexisting institutions with strong roles in taxing and spending policies. It also reviews efforts to enforce budgetary discipline under the new procedures.

The starting point of any budget process is a claim for limited resources. In the congressional environment, the main claimants are committees themselves, principally the authorizing committees with jurisdiction over the programs and agencies of the federal government. Chapter VI deals with the claims and claimants in the budget process. Long before the Budget Act was formulated, Congress had an authorizing process through which committees recommended and it approved substantive legislation authorizing particular public programs. This chapter examines the processes by which authorizing committees consider and develop legislation, their role in the budget process, and the interaction between them and the Budget Committees in legitimizing claims.

The budget resolution is a misleadingly simple document—consisting of a few pages of tables with little text. It embodies, however, many of the political conflicts of the nation. Creating a resolution that can be approved by vote in both Houses is a political exercise rather than a purely technical procedure. Chapter VII outlines the development of the resolutions by each Budget Committee, and the political forces that shape them in each House. Chapter VIII outlines the processes of accommodation to the interests of other members and committees that the Budget Committees have adopted in order to pass their budgets.

A budget is designed to be a restraint. To restrain requires enforcement mechanisms and rules. Chapter IX discusses the enforcement of decisions.

Part Three focuses on relations between the budget process and committees and the major preexisting budgetary power centers—the Appropriations Committees of both Houses, the House Ways and Means Committee, and the Senate Finance Committee. The Budget Committees have forged budget resolutions that both Houses will accept, and other legislative committees have been willing—some reluctantly—to conform to the overall budget process. But budget resolutions do not directly lead to expenditures and revenues. Decisions on specific money bills are still made by Appropriations Committees in both bodies, and by the House Committee on Ways and Means and the Senate Finance Committee, just as before passage of the Budget Act. Behavior of those committees, as they deal with specific pieces of legislation, determines both the extent to which the budget process is followed and whether the Budget Committees can stake out a significant role in the shaping of policy—setting spending priorities and distributing the tax burden.

Part Three reviews in some retail the relationships that have developed between the Budget Committees and the four money committees. Chapters X and XI review the performance and behavior of the Appropriations Committees before and after enactment of the Budget Act. Chapters XII and XIII review the performance and behavior of the tax-writing committees.

A concluding chapter sums up the findings and returns to the basic question "Does it work?"

PART ONE

II The Seven-Year Budget War: 1966-73

ON OCTOBER 18, 1972, the last day of the 92nd Congress, the House and the Senate approved a bill raising the statutory limit on the public debt of the United States. Section 201(a) of the legislation (P.L. 92-599) established a $250 billion ceiling on federal outlays for fiscal 1973, the fiscal year then underway. Section 201(b), however, provided that the spending limitation would cease to have effect one day after the bill became law and that any action taken pursuant to the limitation would be null and void. These contradictory provisions were the product of heated, election-year controversy between the President and Congress, and conflict within the legislative branch over the budget policies and powers of the two Houses.

Although the conflict over spending limitations ended in stalemate, it did spur a search for new methods of budget control. As part of the legislation containing the self-destructing limitation, Congress established a 32-member Joint Study Committee on Budget Control to devise procedures for "improving Congressional control of budgetary outlay and receipt totals." Over the next 20 months, congressional budget procedures were examined by the Joint Committee, two Senate committees, one House committee, an *ad hoc* legislative staff group, and a conference committee. On July 12, 1974, less than one month before his resignation, President Nixon signed the Congressional Budget and Impoundment Control Act, bringing to a close nearly two years of controversy within Congress over the form and scope of budget control.

The Congressional Budget Act thus was born in conflict. The precipitating clash was over President Nixon's demand that Congress enact a $250 billion ceiling on fiscal 1973 outlays and his wholesale impoundment of funds appropriated for social programs; but intense budgetary battles between the President and Congress, and within Congress itself, had raged for a number of years. Although many Members of Congress had misgivings over various facets of the budget—for example, the size and persistence of deficits, the growth of uncontrollable expenditures, and the failure to enact appropriations by the beginning of the fiscal year—Congress probably would not have revamped its budget procedures if it had enjoyed budgetary tranquillity in the years preceding the 1974 Act.

The purpose of this chapter is to introduce the contestants and the stakes in congressional budget reform and the fiscal conditions that stimulated budgetary conflict. The relationships among the appropriations, tax, and authorizations committees, as well as the relationships between Congress and the President are described in terms of the battles they fought and the interests they sought to advance or protect. The story concentrates on the period between 1966 and 1973, years bounded by Vietnam escalation and Watergate turmoil. At the beginning of this period, the federal government began to experience financial difficulty, only a brief time after it had programmed itself for continuing economic growth. At the end of this period, Congress was vigorously seeking a new process to stem its loss of budget power and to bring a measure of peace to its legislative institutions. In between were years of budgetary warfare much more intensive and divisive than the usual budget fights. To put this seven-year conflict into perspective, this chapter begins with a general consideration of why participants fight over budget, and why conflict increased in the years prior to the Budget Act. It then discusses in some detail both the internal congressional struggle and the struggle between the President and the Congress for budgetary power. These events together laid the groundwork for Congress to develop new budgetary procedures.

FIGHTING OVER BUDGETS

The budget is a perennial battleground of American politics. Everybody fights. Agencies strive for more money, budget offices for more control over spending. The President announces one set of budget priorities, Congress enacts another. Within Congress, it is House versus Senate, authorizations versus appropriations committees, spenders versus savers. The battle sprawls across the full landscape of American politics. States and cities lobby together for more federal assistance and against one another for division of the largesse. Interest groups campaign for programs that benefit their constituents; taxpayers demand lower tax bills even as the interests with which they are associated clamor for more public benefits.

It could hardly be otherwise. With hundreds of billions of dollars included in the budget each year and with vital interests and policies hinging on the outcome, there appears to be virtually boundless potential for conflict. The budget could be a routine, settled affair only if disadvantaged interests were suppressed or if the United States possessed sufficient resources to satisfy all politically attractive claims. Because neither condition prevails, conflict is a universal feature of budgeting.

Yet in American budgeting, almost everything gets settled. Despite the potential for open and protracted strife, the federal budget is decided each year, sometimes after little more than ritualistic disagreement, sometimes after great struggle. Among the factors working to limit conflict are the budget's one-year-at-a-time approach, concentrating on the increment rather than on the total budget, avoiding explicit determination of budget priorities, and tolerating second-best—or worse—outcomes.[1] The budget ordinarily is peacefully negotiated because the price of extended disagreement is unacceptably high to the major participants. A budget in deadlock threatens payless paydays for public employees, a halt to government activities, the suspension of favored programs, and the abandonment of new ones. Almost everyone enters the budget fray expecting to reach agreement, committed not to push a view beyond the point of prudent dispute. Budget makers are schooled in the necessities of accommodation. They reach agreement because they believe that protracted discord is improper. Reinforcing this attitude are the visible risks of blame for holding up appropriations, pressure from affected interests, and banishment from the political mainstream.

The practice of budgeting itself has a good deal to do with the containment and resolution of conflict. A budget process is the routinization of choice; it consists of a repertoire of strategies to nudge the participants toward consent. Budget participants have stable roles and relationships that help move matters along an expected course. The President knows that Congress will reduce some parts of his budget; yet he also understands that Congress will boost spending for its favored programs. Members of Congress

1. Some budget reforms can exacerbate budgetary conflict. Thus, the planning-programming-budgeting (PPB) system heralded in the 1960s probably heightened budget conflict by giving more attention to program objectives, future-year impacts, and cost-effectiveness.

know that some contentious issues must be deferred as the price for obtaining agreement on more vital matters. Most participants understand that for the budget to be settled, the number of issues must be limited and old sores must not be reopened. They must be comfortable with the pace of incremental change and willing to ignore big questions of national priorities.

Budgetary warfare escalated in the years prior to the Congressional Budget Act. Some indications were the impoundment battles between the White House and Congress, a new requirement for Senate confirmation of the director and deputy director of the President's Office of Management and Budget (OMB),[2] huge disparities between the amounts authorized and the amounts appropriated by Congress, pressures from interest groups and research organizations, and increased use of continuing resolutions to fund federal programs and agencies.

The question of budgetary conflict cannot be divorced from the overall political context in which budget decisions are made. A nation cannot have budgetary peace when it is torn by political strife. Inevitably, the political cleavages opened by Watts, Vietnam, and Watergate spilled over into the budgetary arena. Legislative distrust of the President emboldened Congress to challenge executive budget recommendations. Widespread concern over national purposes sparked conflict over budget priorities. Even more direct provocations for budgetary conflict occurred in the late 1960s and early 1970s, when the number and variety of budgetary participants significantly expanded and, as a consequence, the diversity of interests that had to be satisfied increased. During the same period, the United States slipped from vigorous economic growth to "stagflation," a combination of high unemployment and high inflation. Both the more open budget process and the unexpected fiscal stringency strained the conflict-resolution capacity of the existing system.

Increased Participation in Budget Policy

Before the 1970s, the budget process was closed to outside scrutiny by its inherent complexity, the obscurantism of budget

2. For more than 50 years—from 1921 when the position was created—the director of the budget was appointed by the President without Senate confirmation. In 1973, Congress passed a bill requiring Senate confirmation of both the director and deputy director of the Office of Management and Budget, and applied this new procedure to the incumbents in those two positions. President Nixon vetoed the bill and after it failed to override, Congress, in 1974, passed a new bill applying the requirement to future directors and deputy directors.

documents, the impenetrability of the tax laws, and the failure of affected interests to invest in budget research and data. There is much truth in the observation that the House Appropriations subcommittees gained budgetary power by long hours of hard work, mastery over the details of expenditures, and markups behind closed doors.[3] On the tax side, the privileged status of the Ways and Means Committee was protected for many years by a monolithic committee structure (no subcommittees), closed rules (barring amendments) for floor consideration of tax measures, and exclusive access to expert staff. For most outsiders, the budget was an intimidating document, a curtain of numbers that inhibited them from knowing what was going on. The privileged insiders did little to improve the readability of the basic documents or the supply of information to outsiders. After all, the ignorance of others augmented their own budget power.

In terms of budgetary conflict, probably the most relevant data are those that expand or restrict the consideration of alternatives. It is not surprising that conventional budget practices precluded or hid data on alternatives. Regardless of the options it developed in the course of preparing its budget, an agency normally submitted only one set of estimates. The President gave only his recommendations to Congress; these were defended by agency spokesmen at appropriation hearings, and any discrepancy between an agency's original request and the President's budget was shielded by executive secrecy. Relying on its interpretation of the Budget and Accounting Act of 1921, OMB (like its predecessor, the Bureau of the Budget) resisted congressional demands for the publication of agency requests.[4] The House Appropriations Committee actively discouraged legislative consideration of alternatives to its recommendations. By tradition, committee members did not file dissenting reports, and the committee generally united against floor amendments.[5]

---

3. "Hard work" was one of the traditional norms of the House Appropriations Committee according to Richard C. Fenno in *The Power of the Purse: Appropriations Politics in Congress* (Boston, Mass.: Little, Brown and Co., 1966). The role and behavior of the Appropriation Committees are detailed in chapter X.
4. The OMB policy was based on Section 206 of the Budget and Accounting Act of 1921 which barred agencies from forwarding their budget requests directly to Congress except at the request of either the House or Senate. See OMB Circular A-10 for application of the policy.
5. These traditions were not so firmly implanted in the Senate Appropriations Committee. Since Senators serve on more committees than House members do, Senators were cross-pressured by conflicting loyalties to their other committees.

In the 1970s, however, there was more widespread and explicit attention to budget alternatives. Congress began to chip away at executive secrecy by requiring certain agencies to submit their raw estimates to Congress at the same time that they are given to OMB.[6] Legislative committees became more persistent and successful in prying such information from recalcitrant (and, sometimes, not so recalcitrant) officials. It no longer was difficult for Congress and interest groups to obtain agency alternatives to the President's budget.

Of even greater importance was the availability of independent, readable analyses of the federal budget. One milestone was the 1970 initiation of the annual *Setting National Priorities* series of the Brookings Institution. Numerous interest organizations now issue their own budget studies each year. Shortly after the President's budget goes to Congress, mayors, governors, county officials, and many interest groups release analyses of what the budget means for their governments or their clients. In addition, countless groups now monitor budget activity throughout the year; many effectively intervene to protect their interests during executive or legislative consideration.

Change has been even more dramatic with regard to taxation, if only because tax policy once was the most cloistered part of the budget. The political breakthrough of defining and publicizing "tax expenditures" (subsidies provided through the tax system) has focused legislative and public attention on provisions of the Internal Revenue Code that benefit various interests.[7] With expansion of the membership of the House Ways and Means Committee, its establishment of subcommittees, and relaxation of the closed rule, congressional participation in tax policy has been significantly widened.

The scope of budgetary participation also has been broadened by the trend toward limited-term—annual or multiyear—authori-

6. For example, the Consumer Product Safety Commission Act of 1972 requires the Commission to submit its budget estimates concurrently to OMB and Congress. 86 *Stat.* 1229. The Postal Service's own request must be included by the President in the budget "with his recommendation but without revision." 88 *Stat.* 288. The request of the International Trade Commission is included in the President's budget "without revision." 88 *Stat.* 2011.

7. Tax expenditures are defined in Section 3(a) of the Congressional Budget Act as "revenue losses attributable to provisions of the Federal tax laws" which provide special deductions, exclusions, credits, or preferential tax rates. For an examination of the change in the behavior of the Ways and Means and Finance Committees, see chapter XII.

zations.[8] The reasons for and effects of this trend are explored in chapter VI. At this point, it suffices to note that most of the authorizing committees have become active participants in the congressional budget process.

More varied participation, wider access to budgetary information, and relaxation of restrictive procedures all have enlarged the circle of budget participants on Capitol Hill. This "socialization" of budgetary conflict—the term is adapted from E. E. Schattschneider—is contagious and difficult to reverse.[9]

An increase in the number and diversity of participants is apt to mean an increase in the claims on the budget as well. Previously excluded interests now are armed with access and information, and can press their claims in a more vigorous and timely manner. Whether these pressures are for tax breaks, cash subsidies, or preferential loans, they can be satisfied only at the expense of other claims on the budget (if the total is deemed to be fixed) or by drawing on unencumbered resources, such as might be provided by economic growth. If satisfaction comes at the expense of others, budgetary conflict will rise unless the disadvantaged interests are too weak to protest, are ignorant of what is happening, or are duped into believing that they will gain from the outcome. But with the expansion of budgetary participation, it is harder to deprive an affected interest without a fight.

The Lost Increment

The second reason for the escalation in budgetary conflict is that incremental resources to satisfy new budget claims no longer are conveniently available because much of the increment has already been encumbered by past commitments.

The standard method for easing budget strife is the now familiar incremental strategy applauded by Aaron Wildavsky in *The Politics of the Budgetary Process.*[10] Wildavsky distinguishes be-

8. More than half of the budget, primarily older agencies and mandatory entitlements, still is permanently authorized. Most of the programs established since World War II have limited-term authorizations.

9. E. E. Schattschneider wrote of politics in *The Semisovereign People* (New York: Holt, Rinehart, and Winston, 1960), p. 2, "the outcome of every conflict is determined by the *extent* to which the audience becomes involved in it. . . . The number of people involved in any conflict determines what happens."

10. First published in 1964 (Boston, Mass.: Little, Brown and Co.) and reissued with additional material a decade later, this probably has been the most influential work on budgeting during the postwar era.

tween the "base" and the "increment," with different decision rules applied to each. The base consists of the continuation costs of current programs; the increment provides for new and expanded programs. The base tends to be a conflict-free zone. Once a program has been established, it usually is continued in future budgets, although there are notable exceptions, such as the Office of Economic Opportunity. Because most past decisions are not reviewed annually, it is possible to quarantine budget conflict to incremental choices. The process of budgeting comes to be "whose ox is to be fattened," a much more agreeable task than deciding "whose ox is to be gored." But an obvious *sine qua non* for any incremental strategy is an increment available for distribution. Otherwise, new claims could be satisfied only by invading the base, that is, by taking from programs and agencies funded in previous budgets.[11] In federal budgeting, increments derive from three sources: economic growth, new taxes, and deficit financing. Only the first of these assures a comparatively calm resolution of the annual budget contest.

In the years since Wildavsky's influential work first appeared, the economy has experienced zigzagging fortunes. During the mid-1960s, many economists foresaw a rosy future in which the federal government would have an ample "fiscal dividend" to devote to Great Society initiatives and tax reduction. Spurred by the quick success of the "new economics" (in particular, the 1964 tax cut), these economists anticipated a future in which the normal rise in federal revenues would outpace the incremental growth in program costs. The economy was approaching full employment, inflation still was moderate, and economists were confident that they possessed the "fine-tuning" skills to maintain a productive growth rate.[12]

The dividend vanished with the Vietnam War, in the wake of which the United States was buffeted by the twin ills of unemployment and inflation. With increments no longer available in sufficient amounts to cover both the built-in increases in the budget

---

11. For an elaboration of why conflict expanded during these years, see Allen Schick, "The Battle of the Budget," in Harvey C. Mansfield, ed., *Congress Against the President* (New York: Academy of Political Science, 1975), pp. 51-70.

12. For an optimistic statement of the "new economics" written by one of its foremost practitioners, see Walter W. Heller, *New Dimensions of Political Economy* (New York: W.W. Norton & Co., 1967).

and the pressures of new programs,[13] much of the budget battle revolved around future increments. Inasmuch as current resources were precommitted by the time the new year arrived, the normal increment was already encumbered by past decisions and it was necessary to buy budget peace by eating into another year's share. In the absence of strong economic growth or a revenue windfall from new taxes, this predicament became self-perpetuating.

For several years in the late 1960s, the Johnson Administration straddled a "guns and butter" policy that tolerated high military and domestic spending. This policy was predicated on two assumptions, one economic, the other political. It was expected that after the Vietnam War, the "peace dividend" would assure sufficient funds for the many claims upon the government. Moreover, it was deemed prudent to avoid the political conflicts that might ensue from deciding between Vietnam and domestic priorities. "Guns and butter" was a policy to buy time and budget peace, but it was founded on fiscal unreality, because inflation and stagnation took their tolls.

Shortly after the military escalation in Vietnam began to affect the budget, President Johnson confidently affirmed the ability of the United States to spend on both military and domestic needs without trading off one against the other. Thus, his 1967 budget message (issued in January 1966) asserted:

> Both of these commitments involve great costs. They are costs we can and will meet. . . . The struggle in Vietnam must be supported. The advance toward a Great Society at home must continue unabated.[14]

Just one year later—in his budget message for fiscal 1968—President Johnson acknowledged the budget tensions facing the nation as he proposed both deficit spending and a tax surcharge:

---

13. In its study of the 1973 budget, the Brookings Institution devoted a chapter to "What Happened to the Fiscal Dividend?" "In summary, the answer is simple. First, in the space of 10 short years, federal civilian expenditures as a percentage of GNP almost doubled; even if no new programs are added, the annual growth in existing expenditure programs now absorbs a much larger fraction of the growth in revenues than was the case 10 years ago. Second, the American people and their political representatives have accepted a greatly broadened concept of the appropriate role of the federal government in dealing with the nation's social problems. Third, paradoxically, over the same decade the nation has chosen to reduce federal income and excise taxes in a number of successive steps and by a large amount. "Charles L. Schultze and others, *Setting National Priorities: The 1973 Budget* (Washington, D.C.: The Brookings Institution, 1972), pp. 397-98.
14. *The Budget of the United States Government, Fiscal Year 1967*, p. 35.

This program will require a measure of sacrifice as well as continued work and resourcefulness. . . . This budget represents a careful balance of our abundant resources and our awesome responsibilities.[15]

The next year, the President sought an even larger deficit and surtax, and spoke of the need for hard choices:

. . . faced with a costly war abroad and urgent requirements at home, we have to set priorities. And "priority" is but another word for "choice." We cannot do everything we would wish to do. And so we must choose carefully among the many competing demands on our resources.[16]

Budget pressures did not abate after the Vietnam War. There was no peace dividend, in large part because Vietnam did not conform to the budgetary patterns of previous American wars. Without exception, each previous war had produced a steep rise in federal spending followed by a sharp postwar decline, though to a trough well above the prewar level. However, in no year following the Vietnam War has spending been lower than in the peak war years. As table 3 shows, the wind-down in Vietnam did not yield even a one-year drop in spending.

Part of the reason for this deviation from past patterns was a radical change in the composition of the federal budget. As shown in table 4, before the Vietnam conflict, most of the budget was spent on the operations of government agencies. As measured in the national income accounts, 55 percent of the fiscal 1964 outlays (the last year before significant Vietnam escalation) went for purchases of goods and services, with 25 percent for transfer payments, and less than 10 percent for grants to state and local governments. The distribution was quite different in fiscal 1975, the last year before implementation of the congressional budget process. Forty percent of the 1975 budget was spent on transfer payments to individuals, and another 15 percent was granted to states and localities.

Most transfer payments are mandatory entitlements over which Congress is extremely reluctant to exercise control. The amounts spent on a particular benefit program usually are determined by external factors such as the number of people receiving Social Security, public assistance, or unemployment compensation. As

15. *The Budget of the United States Government, Fiscal Year 1968*, pp. 8 and 38.

16. *The Budget of the United States Government, Fiscal Year 1969*, p. 7.

Table 3

BUDGET OUTLAYS, DEFICIT SPENDING, THE FEDERAL DEBT, AND UNCONTROLLABLE EXPENDITURES, 1965-74

(dollars in billions)

Year	*Total Receipts*	*Total Outlays*	*Budget Deficit*	*Federal Debt*	*Uncon-trollable Outlays*	*Percent Uncon-trollable*
1965	$116.8	$118.4	$ 1.6	$323.2	NA	NA
1966	130.9	134.7	3.8	329.5	NA	NA
1967	149.6	158.3	8.7	341.3	93.5	59.1
1968	153.7	178.8	25.2	369.8	107.3	60.0
1969	187.8	184.5	+3.2	367.1	116.4	63.1
1970	193.7	196.6	2.8	382.6	125.7	64.0
1971	188.4	211.4	23.0	409.5	140.4	66.4
1972	208.6	232.0	23.4	437.3	153.5	66.2
1973	232.2	247.1	14.9	468.4	173.1	70.0
1974	264.9	271.1	6.1	486.2	194.5	72.2

Note: Outlay and deficit figures for 1973 and 1974 include off-budget agencies.
Source: *The Budget of the United States Government, Fiscal Year 1976.*

the beneficiary populations increase, they generate automatic rises in federal payments. Moreover, most of the transfer programs are indexed so that the level of benefits automatically adjusts in response to changes in the cost of living or some other index. Civilian and military retirement pay are linked to the consumer price index, as are Social Security benefits. Railroad retirement payments; benefits for disabled coal miners; Supplemental Security Income for the aged, disabled, and blind; food stamps; and child nutrition programs also are indexed.

As a consequence of this growth in entitlements and transfer payments, the portion of the budget that is "uncontrollable" climbed from 60 percent in fiscal 1968 to 72 percent in the 1974 budget.[17] During this period, more than 90 percent of the increase in total outlays was accounted for by uncontrollable spending.

---

17. OMB distinguishes between outlays which are "relatively uncontrollable under existing law" and those which are "relatively uncontrollable." Most "uncontrollables" can be brought under budgetary control by a change in law. For a consideration of the concept of control, see House Committee on the Budget, *Congressional Control of Expenditures*, January 1977, especially chapter 1.

Table 4

TRANSFER PAYMENTS AND GRANTS: A GROWING SHARE OF THE FEDERAL BUDGET
(in billions of dollars)

Fiscal Year	*Purchases of Goods and Services*	*Transfer Payments*	*Grants to States and Localities*	*Net Interest*	*Total Budget*
1964	$ 65.9 (56.2%)	$ 29.6 (25.3%)	$ 9.8 (8.4%)	$ 7.7 (6.6%)	$117.2
1965	64.6 (54.5)	30.6 (25.8)	10.9 (9.2)	8.2 (6.9)	118.5
1966	72.4 (54.6)	34.1 (25.7)	12.7 (9.6)	8.7 (6.6)	132.7
1967	86.0 (55.5)	39.4 (25.4)	14.8 (9.6)	9.6 (6.2)	154.9
1968	95.0 (55.2)	44.8 (26.0)	17.8 (10.3)	10.5 (6.1)	172.2
1969	98.0 (53.1)	50.9 (27.6)	19.2 (10.4)	12.1 (6.6)	184.7
1970	97.0 (49.6)	57.0 (29.1)	22.6 (11.6)	13.6 (6.7)	195.6
1971	94.8 (44.6)	70.0 (32.9)	26.8 (12.6)	14.2 (6.3)	212.7
1972	100.9 (43.3)	78.9 (33.9)	32.6 (14.0)	14.1 (6.1)	232.9
1973	101.7 (39.7)	89.8 (35.1)	40.4 (15.8)	15.9 (6.2)	256.2
1974	104.8 (37.6)	104.7 (37.5)	41.6 (14.9)	19.8 (7.1)	278.9
1975	119.0 (36.1)	134.1 (40.7)	48.3 (14.7)	21.9 (6.6)	329.5

Note: The amounts in this table reflect federal transactions in the National Income Accounts. Figures in parentheses are percentages of the total, and do not add to 100 percent because certain transactions are not shown.

Source: *The Budget of the United States Government, Special Analyses, Fiscal Year 1977.*

These figures suggest that most incremental resources are committed before Congress has an opportunity to make current budget decisions. As a result, budget conflict cannot be contained merely by tapping the incremental resources of the federal government.

This problem has been complicated by the sluggish performance of the economy and periodic reductions in income tax rates. The combination of spiraling expenditures, lowered tax rates, and revenue shortfalls has resulted in chronic and sizable budget deficits. Throughout the 1960s, deficit spending averaged about $5.5 billion a year; during the first half of the 1970s, it averaged about $14 billion a year. Deficit spending was a political "safety valve," making it possible to soften the harsh choices of program cutbacks or tax increases. It was a convenient conflict-abatement strategy, provided that budget makers were willing to bear the political onus of high deficits.[18]

Yet, despite—perhaps because of—deficit spending, budgetary conflict heated up during the pre-Budget Act years. There were repeated efforts to terminate or curtail programs, in disregard of the incremental strategy of assuring budget tranquillity by continuing programs. Most of the attempted cutbacks were concentrated in four domestic categories: agriculture, health, education, and housing and community development. President Nixon waged periodic battles to purge the budget of programs he did not want. Although many of his aims were thwarted by Congress, his cutback drives precipitated intense budget strife.[19]

—In the 1971 budget, President Nixon proposed 57 program terminations, reductions, and restructurings. First-year outlay savings were estimated at $2.1 billion.

—The 1972 budget listed 36 cutbacks that could be implemented without legislation and another 15 requiring substantive legislation. The combined outlay reduction for the fiscal year was targeted at almost $3 billion.

—The 1974 budget proposed more than a hundred actions, almost all of which the President proposed to implement without prior legislative approval. The budget targeted about $17 billion in first-year savings.[20]

---

18. President Nixon's endorsement of the "full-employment budget" concept in 1972 was an example of deficit politics. This concept enabled the President to claim a hypothetical balance, though the budget had a cash deficit.

19. The savings estimated for each of these fiscal years were the amounts reported by the Administration, not necessarily the amounts that would be computed on the basis of other assumptions.

20. After President Ford took office, he continued his predecessor's budget-cutting drives, proposing major reductions in the fiscal 1975-78 budgets.

As a consequence of these retrenchment drives, there was much more fighting over the base than over the increment. This shift in budgetary focus came from one basic fact: because much of the increment was uncontrollable, it was less amenable to budget discretion than the controllable portion of the base. As a consequence, controllable programs—even those funded in previous budgets—were given more attention than some incremental items. But when budgeting deals with base rather than incremental issues, conflict inevitably rises.

At the same time the White House was campaigning for budget cutbacks, the federal budget process was—as noted earlier—becoming more open and accessible to outside influence. Organized groups were more informed of the effects of the budget on their interests and more vigilant in combating adverse policies. It was becoming more difficult to implement budget cuts.

The budgetary confrontations summarized above had a direct impact on the course of budget reform. But these were not the only relevant conflicts in the late 1960s and early 1970s. In the division of budgetary labors that prevailed before passage of the Budget Act, two sets of relationships invited conflict: (1) those between the revenue committees (House Ways and Means and Senate Finance) and the Appropriations Committees, and (2) those between Congress and the President. Each set of conflicts had its particular issues: the revenue and Appropriations Committees battled over spending ceilings, while the President affronted Congress by refusing to spend appropriated funds. Each of these conflicts spurred congressional interest in budget reform.

APPROPRIATIONS VERSUS TAX COMMITTEES: FIGHTING OVER SPENDING CEILINGS

In the past, the spending and revenue sides of the budget had little to do with one another in Congress. Each had its own committees; the House Ways and Means and Senate Finance Committees were responsible for tax legislation, while the two Appropriations Committees had jurisdiction over expenditures. Until 1974, Congress lacked a formal procedure for assessing the combined impact of tax and spending legislation on budget surpluses or deficits. Each year's surplus or (more likely) deficit happened as a consequence of dozens of separate revenue and spending decisions. No congressional entity was responsible for the budget's "bottom line." Taxes could be cut and spending raised, and each side would ritualistically complain about the red ink. This "no fault" situation was disturbed by massive federal deficits, reaching $25 billion in fiscal 1968. Moreover, during the early 1960s, the President requested, and Congress enacted, a substantial tax cut; during the last years of that decade, the President called upon Congress to impose a surtax.

With the shift in fiscal fortunes, the issue of responsibility for the budget totals could no longer be avoided. As Congress became more sensitive to the deficit, the Appropriations Committees found themselves being blamed for the unsatisfactory condition of the budget. But the tax committees could not avoid being implicated in the issue because they had jurisdiction over debt legislation. The recurring budget deficits necessitated frequent boosts in the legal limit on the public debt.[21] When required by budget conditions, the House Ways and Means and Senate Finance Committees had no choice but to report this unpopular type of legislation. The tax committees became convinced that the federal government was incapable of controlling expenditures—that in any year, it would manage to spend just about all that it took in or more. Accordingly, in their view, the best way to hold down expenditures was to keep a lid on revenues. Even if this meant chronic deficits, at least spending would be lower than would be likely with higher revenues.

Concern over the budget deficit posed considerable difficulty for the Appropriations Committees. They were accustomed to operating as clusters of semiautonomous subcommittees, each of which had its own appropriations bill. The full committees considered individual appropriations bills, not spending as a whole. Moreover, the Appropriations Committees lacked jurisdiction over a substantial and growing portion of federal expenditures as other committees promoted a variety of "backdoor" schemes. Significantly, the Ways and Means and Finance Committees were expanding their spending jurisdictions in addition to their role in tax and debt matters. Most entitlements (such as Social Security, public assistance, Medicare and Medicaid, and Supplemental Security Income) were under the jurisdiction of the Ways and Means and Finance Committees. For example, the revenue-sharing legisla-

---

21. The statutory limit on the public debt consists of a permanent limit substantially below the actual indebtedness of the United States and a temporary limit pegged at the current debt. This arrangement compels frequent adjustments in the debt limit.

tion enacted in 1972 was reported by these committees.[22] In response to charges that they were culpable for the big deficits, the Appropriations Committees argued that although they had regularly cut appropriations below the level requested by the President, Congress had habitually increased backdoor spending beyond their control. Many of the increases were in the entitlement programs sponsored by the two tax committees.

Another problem facing the Appropriations Committees was that, although budget watchers are primarily interested in federal outlays, the appropriations process deals almost exclusively with budget authority, the amount of funds provided for obligation. The Appropriations Committees do not take action with regard to the amounts expended in a fiscal year. Rather they provide authority to obligate funds, with much of the outlay occurring in later years.[23] As a result, a cut in appropriations rarely is matched dollar for dollar by a reduction in outlays. Depending on the spending rate of a program, it might take as much as a $5 billion cut in budget authority to achieve a $1 billion reduction in outlays during the budget year. Moreover, outlays for some programs with long lead times (such as major construction projects) cannot be immediately reduced through cuts in budget authority.

The 1967 Expenditure Limitation

On five occasions between 1967 and 1973, Congress acted on proposals to limit total federal spending. The first of these occurred during 1967, shortly after the new fiscal year started. On April 3, 1967, President Johnson asked for a 10 percent tax increase (he had previously requested a 6 percent surtax); he warned that the deficit might reach $29 billion if Congress failed to act. The President estimated that federal spending might be as high as $143.5 billion, some $8.5 billion above the original budget request submitted in January of that year.[24] President Johnson's proposal

22. In 1974, the House transferred jurisdiction over revenue sharing from its Ways and Means to its Government Operations Committee. In the Senate, jurisdiction still is lodged in the Finance Committee.
23. An appropriation is a form of budget authority, defined in the Congressional Budget Act as "authority provided by law to enter into obligations which will result in immediate or future outlays involving government funds." Sometimes an appropriation provides funds to "liquidate" an obligation. In such instances, the appropriation is not counted as budget authority.
24. For an informative and detailed account of tax and spending conflicts in 1967 and 1968, see Lawrence C. Pierce, *The Politics of Fiscal Policy Formation* (Pacific Palisades, Calif.: Goodyear Publishing Company, 1971), pp. 148-72.

triggered a Republican attempt to attach a spending ceiling to a continuing resolution providing interim funding for federal agencies which had not yet received their regular appropriations for the fiscal year. Rep. Frank Bow offered an amendment to limit total administrative budget expenditures to $131.5 billion, billions of dollars below both the original and the later estimates for the fiscal year. However, the Bow amendment was ruled out of order on the ground that it was not germane to the continuing resolution.[25] During the floor debate, Chairman George H. Mahon issued a statement defending the performance of the Appropriations Committee (he claimed that $4 billion had already been cut from budget requests and that another $1 billion probably would be cut in the remaining appropriation bills) and promising that:

> The Committee will carefully review the appropriation actions of the session and determine whether or not it may, prior to adjournment, recommend rescissions of appropriations previously made . . .[26]

Mahon also warned that adoption of the proposed spending limitation would expand the impoundment powers of the President and mean the abdication of budget responsibility by Congress. In a vote that split the normally nonpartisan Appropriations Committee along party lines, however, the House decided 202 to 182 to recommit the continuing resolution.[27]

The issue was renewed one week later (October 3, 1967) when the House reversed itself and passed a resolution continuing the funding of federal agencies through October 10 without the Bow amendment.[28]

Immediately after this, Rep. John Byrnes, ranking Republican on the Ways and Means Committee, announced that the Committee

> has just met in executive session and has adopted a motion that the committee temporarily lay the matter of the tax matter on the table, and that further consideration of the tax increase be deferred until such time as the President and the Congress reach an understanding on a

25. 113 *Congressional Record* 26960 (September 27, 1967).
26. *Ibid.*, 26963.
27. The recommittal was supported by all voting Republicans, as well as by 34 Democrats, including the chairman of the House Ways and Means Committee.
28. The key vote was on adoption of the rule under which the continuing resolution was to be considered. By a 213-205 vote, the House adopted a rule that precluded consideration of the Bow amendment.

means of implementing more effective expenditure reduction and control as an essential corollary to further consideration of a tax increase. . . .[29]

Here was a direct confrontation between two House committees. Ways and Means was putting Appropriations on notice that the *quid pro quo* for a surtax would have to be a ceiling on expenditures. The conflict was cooled for a brief period when the Senate adopted a continuing resolution with interim funding,[30] a device which was twice extended. On October 18, 1967, the House Appropriations Committee reported a new resolution that would have cut federal spending $1.5 billion, but this "compromise" was rejected on the floor in favor of a substitute that combined a rollback of most fiscal 1968 spending to the 1967 level with the $131.5 billion ceiling proposed earlier by Representative Bow.[31]

The strife was not over, however, because the Senate refused to go along with any spending limitation. The Senate Appropriations Committee insisted that spending cuts "should be made in the appropriation bills and not by across-the-board reductions in a continuing resolution."[32] This position was upheld by the Senate on October 25.[33] The stalemate was finally broken when the Administration proposed that personnel costs be reduced by 2 percent and other obligational authority (the term then used for budget authority) be trimmed by 10 percent. Significantly, the Administration did not openly involve itself in the congressional battle until months of deadlock had demonstrated that the House and Senate could not resolve the dispute by themselves. Significantly, also, the Administration's proposal was made at a hearing before the Ways and Means Committee, not to either of the Appropriations Committees.

The spending limitation enacted in P.L. 90-218 did not impose a ceiling on total expenditures for fiscal 1968. Rather it directed that certain actions (the 2 percent and 10 percent cuts) be taken to reduce obligations and expenditures, $9 billion and $4 billion respectively, below the amounts in the President's budget. In other words, the savings were estimates, not statutorily fixed amounts. Moreover, uncontrollable programs as well as trust funds and

29. 113 *Congressional Record* 27659 (October 3, 1967).
30. P.L. 90-102.
31. The rollback was proposed by Rep. Jamie Whitten, a leading member of the Appropriations Committee. The Bow amendment was attached to it by a vote of 192-131.
32. S. Rept. No. 90-672.
33. 113 *Congressional Record* 30109 (October 25, 1967).

permanent appropriations were exempted from the mandatory "2 plus 10 percent" formula. In effect, the limitation was applied only to controllable items within the scope of the appropriations process. Congress thus established a double standard in which items subject to appropriations control were less favorably treated than other spending programs.

It is difficult to assess the effectiveness of this limitation, although total spending certainly was below the amount that it would have been in the absence of the mandated reductions. However, it is doubtful that the reductions reached the targeted levels, because uncontrollables constituted a sizable portion of the budget.

The Revenue and Expenditure Control Act of 1968

Enactment of the continuing resolution provided only a brief respite in the battle over budget cuts, because Congress still had to deal with the President's request for a surtax. The 1967 spending cutback still did not satisfy the demand of the Ways and Means Committee that the President come up with a spending control proposal before the committee would consider his tax legislation. During floor debate in February 1968 on an excise tax bill, Chairman Wilbur Mills reiterated his insistence that the two sides of the budget be linked:

> It might be well . . . for me at this time to restate my position with respect to the surcharge proposal although I believe my position is clear. I believe that any income tax increase should be coupled with actions evidencing firm control over the expenditure side of the budget both in spirit and deed. There have been some improvements taken in this regard but in my estimation not sufficient to justify final consideration of tax increases.[34]

In accord with this statement, the Ways and Means Committee refused to consider the tax legislation. There was, however, a formidable obstacle to the linkage of a surtax and a spending ceiling: The surtax was under one committee's jurisdiction, the ceiling was under another committee's control. The Ways and Means Committee feared that if it reported a surtax, the surtax might be adopted without any concomitant reduction in expenditures. For its part, the House Appropriations Committee took the position that spending control should be considered separately from tax matters, when the various appropriations measures were acted on, not through a meat-ax approach.

34. 114 *Congressional Record* 4704 (February 29, 1968).

This difficulty was finally surmounted by an unusual tactic during Senate action on an excise tax bill. Senators Harrison A. Williams, Jr. and George Smathers sponsored a floor amendment adding both a surtax and a spending limitation to the bill. Senator Russell Long, Chairman of the Finance Committee, moved to strike the limitation on the ground that the issue should be considered as part of the appropriations process:

> The Committee on Appropriations has not considered the first appropriation bill for fiscal year 1969, and yet this amendment would dictate to that committee the amount it could appropriate and what it could appropriate for.[35]

A plea on behalf of the Appropriations Committee was made by Senator Warren N. Magnuson, who warned that

> the effect of the pending proposal would be to say to the Appropriations Committee, "Let's forget about you people meeting and going over these items one by one and looking at them and shaping them at least within the framework of the fiscal condition of the Nation," and their work would go for naught.[36]

Nevertheless, the Senate rejected Senator Long's motion by a vote of 33 to 56, with most of the Democrats on the Appropriations Committee voting for it and all of the Republicans lined up against it. The Senate then passed the excise tax bill with both the surcharge and the spending limitation.

In conference, extensive negotiations among Administration and congressional leaders produced a package that could satisfy both the House Appropriations and Ways and Means Committees, and attract majority support on the floor. As part of the maneuvering, the House Appropriations Committee adopted a "sense of the Committee" resolution committing its support to substantial budget reductions.[37] This helped pave the way for resolution of the protracted conflict in June 1968, but it could not detract from the fact that enactment of a spending reduction entirely bypassed the regular appropriations process.[38]

---

35. *Ibid.*, 7712 (March 26, 1968).
36. *Ibid.*, 7719 (March 26, 1968).
37. The text of the resolution is reprinted in 114 *Congressional Record* 18059 (June 20, 1968).
38. For a justification of the procedure used in this case, see the remarks of Rep. George Mahon in *ibid.*, 18058. For an opposing view by another leading member of the Appropriations Committee, see the remarks of Rep. Jamie Whitten in *ibid.*, 17975.

The Revenue and Expenditure Control Act of 1968 (P.L. 90-364) imposed ceilings on both outlays and new obligational authority for fiscal 1969. The amount of the reduction was decided by tax conferees, although a different amount had previously been negotiated with the Administration. Four categories were exempted from these limits: Vietnam War costs, interest payments, veterans' benefits, and Social Security expenses. Two exemptions were added in later legislation: $900 million in farm price supports and $560 million in public assistance above the amounts estimated in the budget. To hold spending within the prescribed ceiling, the President was authorized to withhold from obligation "such amounts as may be necessary to effectuate" the limitations.

Actual outlays for fiscal 1969 were $4.5 billion above the limitations enacted in P.L. 90-364. Failure to meet the ceiling was due to uncontrollable increases in exempted programs; despite an $8.4 billion reduction in spending for programs covered by the limitation, the goal of $6 billion in expenditure cuts was not achieved.[39] This spending pattern was to become familiar in subsequent years; uncontrollables soared above their budgeted levels while the portion of the budget subject to control was held below the budget estimates. Moreover, congressional action rather than the spending limit accounted for virtually all of the reduction in budget authority and for approximately half of the outlay reduction.[40]

Spending Limitations in 1969 and 1970

Once an overall spending limitation had been adopted, the Appropriations Committees decided to go along with this method of budget control. The Second Supplemental Appropriations Act of 1969 (P.L. 91-47), which provided for spending limitations, did not attract the controversy of previous years. During floor debate, Chairman Mahon explained this new position:

39. As explained in the fiscal 1971 budget, "outlays excepted from the limitation increased by $6.9 billion over original estimates, with Vietnam costs and interest on the debt accounting for three-fifths of the overrun. Programs covered by the ceiling were reduced by $8.4 billion below initial budget estimates, a cut of about 9 percent. However, because of the expenditure increases excepted from the ceiling, total budget spending was reduced by only $1.5 billion." *The Budget of the United States Government, Fiscal Year 1971*, p. 46.

40. See the scorekeeping reports for the 1969-73 fiscal years summarized in the *Interim Report* of the Joint Study Committee (February 7, 1973), p. 21.

> For a long time, I fought along with others the so-called Bow amendment fixing a ceiling on expenditures, and I do not apologize for that. But, I have come to the conclusion that an expenditure ceiling can be meaningful, and that it will encourage greater focus of attention by Congress and the country and the press upon spending. But in embracing this idea of an expenditure ceiling as here proposed, I do not want us for any means to delude ourselves. The best means and most appropriate and effective way to reduce Government spending is to hold the line on authorizations and appropriations.[41]

P.L. 91-47 imposed a $191.9 billion limit on outlays for fiscal 1970 but set no ceiling on obligations. Once again, the ceiling was to be adjusted if certain uncontrollable costs exceeded the budget estimates, but such adjustments were limited to $2 billion. In addition, the ceiling was to be adjusted to the extent that congressional action varied from the revised budget estimates.[42]

It was not possible to contain spending within the limits. Two problems were particularly troublesome: first, uncontrollable expenses rose by more than twice the $2 billion allowance provided in the law; second, because the ceiling was automatically lowered in response to congressional cuts in appropriations, it was difficult for the Administration to secure sufficient savings in controllable programs.[43] Faced with an overrun in uncontrollable programs, Congress was compelled to raise the limitation on 1970 outlays to almost precisely the amount requested by the Administration in its own estimates.[44]

Nevertheless, Congress established a ceiling for the next fiscal year, pegging 1971 outlays at $200.8 billion, an amount equal to the President's budget request for that year. Once again the limitation was indexed to congressional actions; the President was authorized to add as much as $4.5 billion for uncontrollable spending on Social Security, interest, farm price supports, and other items. Actual outlays for fiscal 1971 were more than $10 billion

41. 115 *Congressional Record* 13125 (May 20, 1969).
42. The revised estimates are printed in *ibid.*, 9351-56 (April 16, 1969). The limitation was $3.4 billion below the amount estimated when the budget was first sent to Congress, but only $1 billion below the revised estimates submitted by President Nixon in April 1969.
43. These problems were explained in the 1971 Budget. "Current estimates for 1970 indicate that the ceiling will be exceeded by $2.2 billion. All of the overrun is attributable to increases in designated uncontrollable payments. Thus, the $2 billion allowance for designated uncontrollable increases is proving to be extremely inadequate. *The Budget of the United States Government, Fiscal Year 1971*, p. 47.
44. Title IV, P.L. 91-305.

above the limitation, with the overrun due both to uncontrollable costs and to congressional actions.[45] The spending ceiling had no significant impact on final expenditure ceilings for the fiscal year.

When spending limitations were first proposed in 1967, Chairman Mahon cautioned that they might be exploited by the President to justify the impoundment of funds. This apprehension was realized during the Nixon Administration.[46] In order to avert further impoundments grounded on spending ceilings, Congress did not enact any limitation for fiscal 1972.[47]

The 1972 Spending Dispute

Congress was compelled to reconsider the issue of expenditure limitations in 1972 when President Nixon challenged it to enact a $250 billion limit on fiscal 1973 outlays and threatened to take unilateral action if Congress failed to vote the ceiling. The battle began on July 26, 1972, when the President castigated "the hoary and traditional procedure of the Congress, which now permits action on the various spending programs as if they were unrelated and independent actions."[48] He demanded a $250 billion outlay limitation for the fiscal year that had just begun, some $3.7 billion above the original budget total but billions of dollars below the amount that he warned would be spent in the absence of a ceiling on expenditures.

In September 1972, the request for a spending limit was attached to a bill raising the statutory limit on the public debt. Once again, the appropriations process was bypassed; once again, there was open controversy between congressional committees over this practice. Although there was virtually no public controversy over the $250 billion level (1972 was a presidential election year), Members of Congress were divided over how the limitation should be enforced. The President wanted unrestricted discretion to reduce expenditures and Administration spokesmen refused to specify in

45. The 1972 budget estimated that $4 billion of the overrun was due to increases in uncontrollable programs and the remainder to congressional action on spending bills. *The Budget of the United States Government, Fiscal Year 1972*, p. 56.

46. House Committee on Appropriations, Hearings on *Public Works for Water and Power Development and Atomic Energy Appropriations*, 92nd Cong., 1st Sess. 1971, p. 4, statement by Casper Weinberger.

47. Congress failed to stem presidential impoundments, as the account in the next section of this chapter shows. The Administration used multiple justifications for its actions, so that it continued to impound even in the absence of a spending limitation.

48. 8 *Weekly Compilation of Presidential Documents* (1972), p. 1176.

advance which programs might be cut.[49] This position was upheld in the debt ceiling bill (H.R. 16810) reported by the House Ways and Means Committee on September 27, 1972,[50] which would have authorized the President "notwithstanding the provisions of any other law" to withhold such amounts as may be necessary to maintain the $250 billion limit.

When the bill was considered by the House, Representative Mahon proposed a substitute that would have rejected the discretionary power sought by the President. Mahon argued that the measure approved by the Ways and Means Committee would be a dangerous transfer of legislative power to the executive branch. The Mahon substitute provided instead for the President to propose specific reductions which would take effect only if approved by Congress. During floor debate, the accumulated frustrations could not be held back any longer and Chairman Mahon abandoned the usual courtesies as he sought to defend his committee by placing the blame for budget deficits on Ways and Means:

> The chairman of the Committee on Ways and Means says that the Mahon substitute is cotton candy. . . . it surprises me a bit that my good friend from Arkansas would speak so fervently about economy and a balanced budget when he has led the fight to bring about the condition with which we are confronted today. Yet he talks about economy and points the finger at the Appropriations Committee, and yet the gentleman from Arkansas has led the fight over the last 10 years that has reduced the revenues of this Government by the equivalent of $50 billion for the forthcoming fiscal year. Except for those reductions, we would be in the black, provided the economy would have behaved as it has.
>
> Yet the gentleman points his finger at the Appropriations Committee. This is not where the problem is. The cutting of revenues and the increasing of spending through the Committee on Ways and Means, through the leadership of the gentleman from Arkansas, have helped bring us to this day of crisis.
>
> Why would he point the finger at the Appropriations Committee with respect to the problem of expenditures when the gentleman led the fight for the $30 billion revenue sharing which has to a very large extent brought us to this moment of distress?
>
> The President has tried to keep the Congress from providing a 20-percent increase in social security, but he was overridden with the help

49. House Committee on Ways and Means, Hearings on *Administration Request to Increase Debt Ceiling,* 92nd Cong., 2nd Session, (1972).
50. H. Rept. No. 92-1456.

of the economy-minded chairman of the Committee on Ways and Means and the 20 percent prevailed.[51]

Despite his impassioned plea, however, Mahon's substitute lost by a vote of 167 to 216. The House then passed H.R. 16810 with the spending ceiling by a vote of 221 to 163.[52] The debt-ceiling bill then moved to the Senate where it again emerged from committee with full authority for the President to curtail programs in accord with his preferences.[53] However, the Senate, voting 46 to 28, adopted a floor amendment requiring the President to make proportional cuts in programs and barring reduction of more than 10 percent in any activity or item. The amendment also exempted nine enumerated spending categories from any presidential cuts. The bill with this provision passed by a 61-11 margin.

In conference, the Senate requirement that program cuts be proportional was dropped, and the President was given authority to reduce individual programs by as much as 20 percent.[54] The House approved the conference report on October 17, 1972, but on the same day the Senate rejected the report by a 27-39 vote. The Senate then approved an amendment that had the effect of nullifying the spending limitation.[55] On October 18—the last day of the 92nd Congress—the conferees accepted the Senate amendment and both Chambers passed the bill.[56] It was this measure which had the contradictory provisions establishing and voiding a ceiling on expenditures as well as a provision for a Joint Study Committee on Budget Control.

Congressional Ineffectiveness in Controlling Expenditures

The periodic drives for spending limitations had a number of adverse side effects on the ability of Congress to control federal expenditures. For one thing, the preferential treatment of uncontrollable costs gave Congress additional incentive to protect favored programs by making them uncontrollable. Congress also shielded certain programs against spending limitations by placing

51. 118 *Congressional Record* 34599 (October 10, 1972).
52. *Ibid.*, 34636.
53. S. Rept. No. 99-1292 (1972).
54. S. Rept. No. 92-1606 (1972).
55. See 118 *Congressional Record* 36854 (Oct. 17, 1972) for an explanation by Senator Long concerning the reason for this amendment.
56. This is the law referred to in the opening paragraph of this chapter. See Title II, P.L. 92-599.

them "off-budget," a status that excluded their expenditures from the budget totals and, therefore, from any limitation on spending.[57]

The five attempts to impose ceilings on expenditures between 1967 and 1972 demonstrated a lack of congressional procedures for the consideration of spending limitations. Four different legislative instruments were used during these years:

—In 1967, the spending reduction was attached to a continuing resolution.

—In 1968, spending limits were combined with tax legislation.

—In 1969 and 1970, limitations were written into supplemental appropriations.

—In 1972, outlay limits were added to a debt ceiling bill.

These *ad hoc* procedures were not effective in limiting federal outlays. Although it is impossible to pin down the exact effects of each year's limitation, a year-by-year summary suggests the following:

—The 1967 law did not set a maximum level of expenditures, but exempted uncontrollable costs and applied a formula for across-the-board percentage cuts in controllable programs. Some reductions were achieved but not the amounts specified in the law.

—The 1968 law exempted six categories of expenditure, and reductions were achieved more by congressional action on individual spending bills than by the overall ceiling.

—The 1969 law exempted both uncontrollable and congressional actions; the ceiling was later passed to accommodate these exemptions.

—The 1970 law also exempted uncontrollable and congressional actions, the two categories accounting for virtually all nonbudgeted increases in outlays.

—The 1972 law nullified its own spending limitation.

Legislative conflict and budgetary impotence—the twin results of congressional grasping for spending control—were powerful spurs in the quest for a new budget process. While leading Members of Congress were divided on the type of system that should

57. During the 1971-74 years, off-budget status was accorded to the Environmental Financing Authority, the Export-Import Bank, Federal Financing Bank, Rural Electrification and Telephone Revolving Fund, Rural Telephone Bank, and United States Railway Association.

be installed, they were united in their determination to find a way out of their budgetary malaise.

PRESIDENT VERSUS CONGRESS: FIGHTING OVER SPENDING PRIORITIES

Mere discontent with its own procedures would not, by itself, have been sufficient stimulus to cause Congress to devise a budget process. Congress needed a firm indication that the legislative branch would lose power and esteem if it persisted without a budget process of its own. The necessary provocation came from the White House after Richard Nixon assumed office. In part because of political divisions between the Republican Administration and the Democratic Congress, in part because Nixon wanted to rearrange national priorities by undoing many of the program initiatives of his predecessors, friction between the legislative and executive branches increased. But Nixon's early budget battles with Congress were tame, at least by comparison with those he waged in 1972 and 1973. The President proposed some program curtailments—as he did for fiscal 1971 and 1972—most of which were rejected by Congress. Nixon vetoed only a few appropriations bills, in the aftermath of which he usually managed to negotiate a compromise with Congress. For example, after the appropriations bill for the Departments of Labor and Health, Education, and Welfare for fiscal 1970 was vetoed, Congress passed another bill limiting obligations to 98 percent of the amount appropriated. Relying on some of the spending ceilings then in force as well as on claims of presidential power, Nixon withheld sizable amounts of money, but he stopped short of deploying impoundment as an all-out weapon against Congress.

Warfare escalated sharply in 1972, however, as the President turned the budget into one of the major issues of his 1972 election campaign. The opening salvo was Nixon's demand for a $250 billion spending limitation, to which he coupled an attack on congressional fiscal procedures and priorities. The President warned that he would not "sit by and silently watch" Congress raise spending above the levels he wanted. He would act "with or without the cooperation of the Congress," and he threatened to veto bills "calling for excessive spending."[58] But as was detailed earlier,

58. 8 *Weekly Compilation of Presidential Documents* (1972), p. 1177.

Congress refused to establish the spending limitation; it also passed various appropriations and authorizations above the levels requested by the Administration.

Throughout the campaign, Nixon openly attacked Congress for its "budget-busting" actions. In a nationwide radio address less than one month before the election, he decried the lack of a budget process in Congress:

> . . . the Congress suffers from institutional faults when it comes to Federal spending . . . Congress not only does not consider the total financial picture when it votes on a particular spending bill, it does not even contain a mechanism to do so if it wished. . . . The Congress, thus, has no sure way of knowing whether or when its many separate decisions are contributions to higher prices, or possibly to higher taxes.[59]

When Congress did not accede to Nixon's demands, he embarked on a "second line of defense," widespread use of his veto power.

The Nixon Vetoes

Presidents ordinarily are reluctant to veto appropriations bills, preferring to take the bad along with the good and necessary rather than go to the brink on dollars-and-cents disputes. But on some 1972 bills, the differences between Nixon and Congress were so large as to rule out orderly budget compromise. Nixon vetoed the 1973 Labor-HEW appropriation bill, charging that the $1.8 billion added by Congress "is a perfect example of that kind of reckless spending that just cannot be done without more taxes or more inflation."[60] When Congress proved unable to override the veto, it passed instead a second Labor-HEW appropriation bill which retained the levels in the original version but authorized the President to impound up to $1.2 billion, about two-thirds of the amount in dispute. Nixon pocket-vetoed the second bill on October 27, 1972, only one week before the election and after Congress had adjourned for the year. Congress then abandoned its efforts to enact a regular appropriations bill for Labor and HEW, and decided to fund the two agencies for all of fiscal 1973 by continuing resolution. However, in a departure from usual practice, Congress continued these agencies at levels substantially above either the previous year's level or the President's budget.[61]

---

59. *Ibid.*, p. 1498.
60. *Ibid.*, p. 1240.
61. The continuing resolution provided (with some exceptions) that each program of the Departments of Labor and Health, Education, and Wel-

Nixon's veto of the second Labor-HEW appropriation was one of nine vetoes packaged into a single presidential message. By grouping the vetoes together, the President hoped to emphasize his budgetary differences with Congress. All told, Nixon vetoed 16 bills during 1972, 12 of them after Congress had adjourned and, therefore, too late for any override. Most of the bills were conventional authorizations that could be spent only as provided by subsequent appropriations. In the heat of the election campaign, Nixon was unwilling to compromise by accepting high authorizations in expectation of lower appropriations.

Yet the battle of the budget was much more than a campaign ploy. As things turned out, conflict intensified after the election as Nixon signaled a shift in strategy in his October 17 veto of the Federal Water Pollution Control Act Amendments of 1972. Nixon anticipated a successful override of his veto but announced that he would nonetheless refuse to spend all of the funds:

> Even if this bill is rammed into law over the better judgment of the Executive—even if the Congress defaults its obligations to the taxpayers —I shall not default mine. Certain provisions of S. 2770 [the vetoed bill] confer a measure of spending discretion and flexibility upon the President, and if forced to administer this legislation, I mean to use those provisions to put the brakes on budget-wrecking expenditures as much as possible.[62]

After Congress overrode the veto, Nixon impounded $6 billion of water pollution control funds, an amount later increased to $9 billion. He also withheld more than $10 billion provided for other domestic programs and took other unilateral steps to prevent the expenditure of appropriations. More than any of the other budget disputes that racked Congress between 1967 and 1973, the impoundment controversy incited Congress to devise its own budget process.

The Nixon Impoundments

During its first years, the Nixon Administration generally used impoundment to defer expenditures rather than to rearrange national priorities to suit its policy preferences. Thus in a May 17,

---

fare shall be continued at the lower of the amounts contained in the original appropriation bills passed by the House and Senate for fiscal 1973. These lower amounts, however, totaled as much as $1.9 billion above the amount requested by the President.

62. 8 *Weekly Compilation of Presidential Documents* (1972), p. 1532.

1971, report, OMB listed $12.2 billion in reserve, most of which was scheduled for later release. OMB estimated that—

—$1.36 billion was being set aside for contingencies,

—$7.14 billion would be released by June 30, 1972,

—$1.13 billion would be released after June 30, 1972,

—$1.38 billion was withheld in compliance with congressional requirements, and

—$1.2 billion was reserved, without any scheduled release date.

Some of these impoundments were justified by the Administration as necessary to comply with the spending limitation enacted by Congress. As already described, Congress refused to extend the spending ceiling for another fiscal year in order to discourage future impoundments. Under the guise of merely restraining expenditures, the Nixon Administration undoubtedly was trying to curtail some programs that were at variance with its own priorities. Nevertheless, OMB took the position that most of the impoundments were for financial and administrative—not policy—reasons. Referring to the $12.3 billion then withheld, the May 17, 1971, report averred:

> Quite the opposite of a freeze, what we have here is a flow, and the regulation of the flow, which is the prudent management of the funds made available by the Congress. . . . Thus it is a continuous process of funds coming into the tank and funds going out.[63]

After he lost the spending limitation battle in 1972 but won the election, President Nixon embarked on a large-scale effort to overturn the priorities established by Congress. Far from administrative routine, Nixon's impoundments in late 1972 and 1973 were designed to rewrite national policy at the expense of congressional power and intent. Rather than the deferment of expenses, Nixon's aim was the cancellation of unwanted programs. Agriculture was a prime target as five rural development programs were halted. Impoundment took $225 million from the rural environmental assistance program, $10 million from the water bank program, $120 million from rural water and sewer grants, and undeterminable amounts from the emergency loan and the rural electrification pro-

63. U.S. Office of Management and Budget, "Statement of Withholding of Funds," May 17, 1971.

grams. In the latter two programs, the Administration ordered a moratorium on the processing of new loan applications, thereby cutting off funds at their administrative source. The Administration used a similar tactic on January 5, 1973, when it halted all subsidized housing programs. No new administrative reservations (the procedure used for committing funds to subsidized housing) were to be made for homeownership assistance, rental housing assistance, rent supplements, and other assistance programs. New enrollments in federal manpower training programs were also temporarily halted.

On February 5, 1973, OMB reported that $8.7 billion was being reserved, substantially less than the amount reported in May 1971. However, OMB's list was woefully incomplete and misleading. It did not include the $6 billion of water pollution control funds already impounded by presidential order. OMB acknowledged that the funds had been impounded, but it excluded them from the list on questionable technical grounds.[64] OMB also failed to account for $1.9 billion appropriated by continuing resolution to the Departments of Labor and HEW, again relying on narrow technical grounds.[65] With these and other excluded items added to the $8.7 billion reported by the Administration, the real level of impoundment reached about $18 billion, far above the amounts withheld by any previous President.

Dollars tell only a part of the Nixon impoundment story; another part relates to the purpose, duration, and distribution of the impoundments—their impact on federal policies and priorities. A key question in assessing any impoundment is whether the funds will lapse before they are released for expenditure. OMB skirted this issue by stating that "the period of time during which funds are to be in reserve is dependent in all cases upon the results of such later review." Nevertheless, firm indications of Nixon's in-

64. These funds were excluded on a narrow technicality. The contract authority for water pollution control programs involved a two-stage administrative procedure: First, funds were allotted to each state in accord with a statutory formula; second, states entered into obligations pursuant to their allotments. Since the President ordered the funds withheld from allotment, the states were unable to enter into obligations. Hence, OMB argued, no budget authority was being withheld.

65. Funds appropriated in continuing resolutions generally are exempted from provisions of the Antideficiency Act which requires the apportionment of funds over the course of the fiscal year in order to avoid a deficiency later in the year. But a continuing resolution normally provides stopgap funds until the regular appropriation is enacted. For this reason, the apportionment process is not applied to such resolutions.

tentions were evident in his fiscal 1974 budget, issued shortly before the impoundment report was released. The budget contained a long list of savings anticipated from program reductions and terminations, including savings estimated for fiscal 1973, the year then in progress. The only way many of those savings could be achieved was through the impoundment actions of the President. Thus, the programs scheduled for termination or reduction in 1973 included water and sewer grants, rural environmental assistance, and rural electrification direct loans, programs that also appeared prominently in the impoundment report. Significantly, all of the impoundments listed for defense were temporary—the routine deferment of construction and procurement expenditures until the funds were needed. Domestic programs took the full brunt of the President's impoundment policy. The aim of impoundment was to change the mix, not merely the level, of expenditures.

When a President disagrees with Congress on budget priorities, he can recommend a budget that reflects his preferences and resist efforts by Congress to deviate from them. He can veto spending bills that do not conform to his priorities and he can take his case against Congress to the people. Nixon did all of these things and he also impounded appropriated funds. Impoundment differed from the other tactics in two ways, both of which exacerbated Nixon's relationship with Congress. First, impoundment was a unilateral action, taken without any involvement of Congress whatsoever.[66] When Nixon impounded for policy reasons, he in effect told Congress, "I don't care what you appropriate; I will decide what will be spent." Second, impoundment offered no clear-cut procedure for resolving budgetary impasses between the two branches. If Congress overrides a presidential veto, its budget priorities prevail; if it cannot muster a two-thirds vote, the President's priorities win. Impoundments, by contrast, invited stalemate and protracted conflict.[67]

---

66. An impoundment also has the characteristic of an item veto; it is targeted to specific programs rather than to an entire bill.

67. In the case of impoundment, as in other conflicts, the issue often was decided by the courts. In the aftermath of Nixon's impoundments, dozens of court suits were brought, most of which were decided against the President. In February 1975, a unanimous Supreme Court ruled against Nixon's impoundment of $9 billion of water pollution control funds. This first impoundment decision by the Supreme Court was based on statutory interpretation, not constitutional principles.

CONCLUSION

In impoundment battles, the President had the advantage *vis-à-vis* Congress. Although policy impoundments were not recognized in law, inaction meant that the President's priorities would triumph. The longer the dispute dragged on, the greater the loss of congressional control over the purse. Congress could not permit the impasse to continue on such unfavorable terms. Thus, in early 1973, about the same time that it commenced work on designing a budget process for its own decisions, Congress also set about establishing an impoundment control procedure to govern its relations with the executive branch. Impoundment, however, was only one of the problems that Congress had to deal with in devising new budget procedures. The battles chronicled in this chapter show internal congressional conflict as heated and protracted as that which racked the two branches. In developing budget reform legislation, Congress gave much more attention to the redistribution of power among its taxing, appropriating, and authorizing committees than to its relationships with the executive branch. The story of this redistribution is the next chapter in the emergence of the congressional budget process.

III The Congressional Budget Treaty of 1974

By 1973 the wearying budget battles and the chronic budget deficits (25 in the previous 32 years) had persuaded Congress that it could no longer make financial decisions without a budget process of its own.[1] During the early months of 1973, dozens of bills were introduced to establish a congressional budget process and to control impoundments. But although Congress was determined to act, it would not be rushed to action. The concepts and procedures of budget reform were sifted through five legislative units before a final version was adopted. Yet in view of the potential impact on congressional procedures and committee jurisdictions, the road to enactment was traversed with remarkable speed. The Congressional Budget Act was signed into law on July 12, 1974, less than two years after agitation for reform had begun.

In its quest for a budget process, Congress was inhibited by knowledge of past failures and awareness of current legislative realities. Since 1921, when the Budget and Accounting Act established the presidential budget process, most efforts at budgetary improvements had been concentrated in the executive branch and taken without much congressional involvement.[2] Perhaps the most

1. "The Joint Study Committee believes that failure to arrive at congressional budgetary decisions on an overall basis has been a contributory factor in the size of these deficits. . . . The fact that no legislative committee has the responsibility to decide whether total outlays are appropriate in view of the current situation appears to be responsible for much of the problem." Joint Study Committee on Budget Control, *Report*, April 18, 1973, p. 8.
2. Over the years, modifications in executive budget processes have been achieved through executive orders (in particular, Executive Order 8248 which spelled out the functions of the Bureau of the Budget shortly after its transfer to the Executive Office of the President), reorganizations (such as Reorganization Plan No. 2 of 1970 which established the Office of Management and Budget as successor to the Bureau of the Budget), and administrative action (such as Budget Bureau Bulletin 66-3 promulgating the planning-programming-budgeting [PPB] system for federal agencies).

ambitious attempt by Congress to improve its own budget operations was the provision in the Legislative Reorganization Act of 1946 for congressional determination of the maximum amount to be appropriated each year.[3] The legislative budget, unsuccessfully tried in 1947 and 1948, was subsequently abandoned.[4] Congress improvised a more modest approach in 1950, consolidating all appropriations into a single bill. However, the omnibus approach was discarded because the Appropriations subcommittees feared that it would concentrate power in the full committee.[5]

Congress was aware that any significant overhaul of its budgetary methods inevitably would redistribute power and position within the legislative branch. A new budget process might enhance legislative power *vis-à-vis* the executive, but it also would have an adverse impact on some committees and interests. The tension between the goal of enlarging and the inevitability of redistributing legislative power was omnipresent during development of the budget control legislation. The new process would have to bring substantial improvement without openly depriving established power holders of the advantages they derived from the status quo. Congress had to seek coordination, but avoid centralization. It had to continue giving many interests a part of the budget power, but also it had to harmonize these interests into a reasonably consistent budget policy. The task was complicated by the sure knowledge that no reform could be truly neutral in its impact on future budgetary outcomes. The debate would be waged over rules and procedures, but at stake would be the programs and interests for which funds were to be allocated in the budget process.

Committees always are a crucial arena for legislation; they were particularly decisive in budget reform. Members of Congress must have an interest in budgeting, even if they shy away from its technical and accounting details. Their constituencies, program interests, and committee assignments all are related to budgetary decisions. In 1973-74, it was not politically attractive to oppose budget

---

3. Section 138; 60 Stat. 812, Section 138, provided that the members of the House and Senate Appropriations and the tax committees were to constitute a joint committee each year and recommend a legislative budget. Section 138 did not provide for a permanent budget committee or staff; nor did it provide a means for enforcing the legislative budget.
4. See Avery Leiserson, "Coordination of Federal Budgetary and Appropriations Procedures Under the Legislative Reorganization Act of 1946," *National Tax Journal* 1 (June 1948): 118.
5. See Dalmas H. Nelson, "The Omnibus Appropriations Act of 1946," *Journal of Politics* 15 (1953): 274-88.

reform; nor was it likely that major decisions about the new process would be made on the floor of the House or Senate. Those who wanted to protect their interests or to influence the particulars had to work through the committees responsible for developing the legislation. The multiplicity of committees actively engaged in fashioning the congressional budget process provided abundant opportunity for diverse legislative interests to participate in designing the final product. At each stage, the shape of the budget legislation was strongly influenced by the committee environment in which it was drafted.

This chapter traces the passage of budget reform through five congressional committees in terms of the major actions taken by each, summarizes the principles of budget reform which these committees implicitly adopted during their deliberations, and sketches the new terms of conflict resolution that emerged. The legislative history of the Congressional Budget and Impoundment Control Act is outlined in table 5.

DEVELOPMENT OF BUDGET REFORM

The drive for budget reform was started by the Joint Study Committee on Budget Control, a special group convened specifically for the purpose of recommending new means of legislative control over the budget. In the House, budget reform legislation was referred to the Rules Committee; this move was facilitated by the wording of the title of H.R. 7130.[6] Senate consideration commenced in the Government Operations Committee whose chairman, Sen. Sam Ervin, filed his own budget reform measure (S. 1541). The bill was sequentially referred to the Rules and Administration Committee,[7] ostensibly for an examination of the impact of budget reform on the operation of Congress, although the committee extended its review to all features of the legislation. Final develop-

6. The title is a brief description of the bill placed immediately before the enacting clause. It often guides the Parliamentarian in deciding which committee should have jurisdiction over a bill. The original title of H.R. 7130 began with the phrase: "To amend the Rules of the House of Representatives and the Senate." Immediately after the House approved H.R. 7130, this phrase was struck from the title.

7. "Sequential procedure" means that after the first committee reports a bill, it is referred to a second committee which can propose its own version. Floor consideration of the measure occurs after the second committee has reported.

Table 5

LEGISLATIVE HISTORY OF CONGRESSIONAL BUDGET AND IMPOUNDMENT CONTROL ACT

Date	*Action*	*Citation*
October 27, 1972	Joint Study Committee established	Title IV, P.L. 92-599
April 11, 1973	S. 1541 introduced	
April 17, 1973	S. 373 (Impoundment Control) reported by Senate Government Operations Committee	S. Rept. No. 93-121
April 18, 1973	Joint Study Committee report issued	*Recommendations for Improving Congressional Control over Budgetary Outlay and Receipt Totals. (H.R. 7130 and S. 1641)*
May 10, 1973	Senate passed S. 373	
June 27, 1973	House Rules Committee reported H.R. 8480 (Impoundment Control)	H. Rept. No. 93-336
July 25, 1973	House passed H.R. 8480	
November 20, 1973	House Rules Committee reported H.R. 7130	H. Rept. No. 93-658
November 28, 1973	Senate Government Operations Committee reported S. 1541	S. Rept. No. 93-579
December 4-5, 1973	House debated and passed H.R. 7130	
February 21, 1974	Senate Committee on Rules and Administration reported S. 1541	S. Rept. No. 93-688
March 19-22, 1974	Senate debated and passed S. 1541	
June 11-12, 1974	Conference Committee reported	H. Rept. No. 93-1101; S. Rept. No. 93-924
June 18, 1974	House adopted conference report	
June 21, 1974	Senate adopted conference report	
July 12, 1974	President signed Congressional Budget and Impoundment Control Act	P.L. 93-344

ment of the Budget Act came in a conference committee which reconciled the differences between House and Senate versions.

Joint Study Committee on Budget Control: Reconciling Tax and Appropriations Interests

Because the creation of this committee was occasioned by intramural strife between the appropriations and the revenue committees over a spending limitation, these two sets of stake holders dominated the Joint Study Committee (JSC). Twenty-eight of the 32 members of JSC were drawn from the House and Senate Appropriations, House Ways and Means, and Senate Finance Committees. Only 4 were from the rest of the House and Senate, and none specifically from the party leaderships. Moreover, the cochairmen and entire staff of the Joint Study Committee were from the spending and revenue committees.[8]

Its composition dictated that JSC would not have to consider the potential effects of budget reform on all the relevant interests in Congress. Rather, its primary mission was to devise a coordinating procedure acceptable to both the spending and revenue committees. JSC thus tried to end budgetary warfare between these committees by dividing budgetary power between them. Understandably, the easiest path to budgetary peace was one that protected and even augmented the powers of the appropriations and the tax committees at the expense of other congressional interests underrepresented in JSC.

The first thing JSC had to do was to build a case for reform that would persuade Congress to embrace its recommendations. In both of its reports, JSC issued a bill of particulars against the prevailing budget methods in Congress: the failure to consider the budget as a whole; the splintering of the appropriations process; the rising uncontrollable expenditures; the lack of coordination between tax and expenditure policies; and the delaying effects of tardy authorizations on congressional appropriations action. These arguments were buttressed by a statistical appendix which showed huge budget deficits and carryover balances, appropriations cuts and backdoor increases by Congress, growth in uncontrollable spending, disparities between the amounts authorized and appropriated, and other budget data.

8. The cochairmen were Rep. Jamie Whitten and Rep. Al Ullman, the ranking Democrats on the House Appropriations and Ways and Means Committees. Three of the four staff persons came from the tax committee, and one came from the spending committee.

Both the appropriations and the tax committees wanted to assure that a new congressional budget process would not impair their existing jurisdictions. Yet the drive for budget reform posed a direct and obvious threat to them. New budget committees would undoubtedly deal with various spending, debt, and tax issues—the primary interests of the Appropriations, Ways and Means, and Finance Committees. The surest way to avert this problem would have been to make do without any budget committees or with committees that functioned on an *ad hoc* basis during the budget season in Congress. Neither alternative was attractive. The recent budget struggles had persuaded JSC that Congress needed an institutional mechanism for coordinating the revenue and spending sides of the budget. Without budget committees, the tax and spending committees would have protected their turf only to invite continuing budget strife between themselves in the future. Moreover, the lack of permanent budget committees was widely regarded as a principal defect of the 1946 legislative budget scheme.[9]

The next best thing, therefore, was to assure that any new budget committees would always be under the dominion of the appropriations and the tax committees. Early in its work, JSC considered the possibility of patterning new House and Senate budget committees in its own image; each committee would have had 16 members, only 2 of whom would have been drawn from the memberships at large. But the JSC later decided to give one-third of the budget committee seats to "outsiders," reserving the other two-thirds plus the chairmanships for the appropriations and the tax committees.[10]

The legislation that emerged from the Joint Study Committee reflected the domination of the appropriations and the tax committees. The JSC's basic recommendation was to layer a new budget process over the existing revenue and appropriations processes of Congress. A concurrent resolution on the budget would set limitations on total new budget authority and outlays, and would allocate these spending totals among congressional committees and appropriations subcommittees. The budget resolution also would fix the overall levels of revenue, debt, and budget surplus or defi-

9. During the 1960s, bills were repeatedly introduced to establish a joint (House-Senate) budget committee. The Senate approved several of the bills, but the House consistently rejected the joint committee concept.
10. Under this proposal, the chairman of each budget committee would alternate between a tax and appropriations committee member each year. When the House Budget Committee was chaired by an Appropriations Committee member, the Senate Budget Committee would be headed by a person from the Senate Finance Committee, and vice versa.

cit. Floor debate on the budget resolution would be regulated by a "rule of consistency" requiring all proposed floor amendments to maintain the mathematical consistency of the resolution at every stage of consideration. Thus, an amendment proposing increases in one budget category also would have had to propose an increase in the budget totals or an equivalent reduction in another category. After its adoption, the budget resolution would function as a constraint on individual spending measures.

The budget process proposed by JSC had the potential to bolster the control of the appropriations committees over floor action. The House Appropriations Committee wanted to dampen independent floor action such as amendments, and JSC responded to its interests by recommending a number of provisions that would have affected the floor consideration of appropriations measures. JSC suggested, for example, that amendments proposing to reduce appropriations be considered first; only after these were decided would proposals to raise appropriations be considered. Moreover, amendments proposing appropriations in excess of the amounts allocated in the concurrent resolution on the budget would be subject to a point of order. Neither provision survived later developments in the budget reform legislation.

Although they were the most potent stake holders in congressional budgeting, the two pairs of committees had reason to be displeased with fiscal trends within Congress. The Appropriations Committees had suffered an erosion of their spending jurisdiction; an end to "backdoors" was accordingly their prime objective in the JSC. But this goal ran counter to the jurisdictional claims of the Ways and Means and Finance Committees which handled all Social Security legislation as well as other "backdoor" programs. The Appropriations Committees were thus circumscribed in what they could win from the JSC; some limitations might be placed on backdoors promoted by authorizing committees, but the backdoor jurisdiction of the tax committees would continue to be protected. A second major concern of the Appropriations Committees was the late enactment of authorizing legislation which in turn delayed congressional action on appropriations bills. Here the Appropriations representatives were able to advance their cause with no overt opposition from the affected authorizing committees. JSC recommended that Congress require enactment of authorizations in the fiscal year prior to the one in which they would take effect.

While the budgetary power of Appropriations had waned during the previous decade, the House Ways and Means and Senate Finance Committees had strengthened their position, especially with regard to backdoor programs and spending limitations. The leaders of these committees were concerned about the steep deficits that had plagued recent budgets. The revenue committees tended to favor tough control over expenditures—a position they had advanced during earlier battles over spending limitations. Once again, the two sets of committees had opposite viewpoints, but once again the preferences of the tax committees prevailed. The treaty forged in JSC had a pronounced tilt toward tough spending controls. The rule of consistency and the early establishment of spending ceilings in a budget resolution manifested the determination of JSC to write strong controls into the new process.

But perhaps the most pointed indication of the tilt in JSC was its recommendation with regard to control over specific parts of the budget. Although it was set up to recommend procedures for fixing budget totals, JSC decided early in its deliberations that the new controls would have to reach the various spending components of the budget as well. In the view of many Members of Congress, the abortive legislative budgets of 1947 and 1948 offered telling evidence that ceilings could not be effective unless Congress also specified the maximum allocation for each spending category in the budget. The problem, however, was that controls over budget subtotals would trespass on the jurisdiction of the Appropriations Committees and their subcommittees. Nevertheless, JSC unanimously recommended that Congress set ceilings for each budget category by May 1 of each year.

As conceived by JSC, the budget resolution would have allocated outlays and budget authority among the programs or subcommittees of each committee. To soften this limitation on the Appropriations Committees, JSC proposed that some funds be set aside in an emergency reserve, to be allocated by these committees, as well as a contingency reserve for new programs. JSC also recommended another change in appropriations practice, a procedure under which each appropriations bill would limit the outlays that could ensue from it during the fiscal year. This procedure would have had the effect of holding the Appropriations Committees responsible for actual outlays, not just for the new budget authority provided in each bill.

Why did Appropriations accede to these constraints on its traditional mode of operations? As noted, JSC's recommendations were unanimous and there was no public indication of dissent at this stage of budget reform legislation. A partial explanation is that the

House Appropriations Committee (which was more active in JSC than was its Senate counterpart) gained certain advantages in return for these concessions. It got deadlines on authorizations and limits on new backdoor and permanent appropriations. In the give and take within JSC, all money committees had to surrender some prerogative. The revenue committees also gave up something—though not as much as Appropriations—for JSC recommended a procedure which could have forced Congress to vote on tax increases.[11]

Despite their possession of almost half the membership in JSC, the Appropriations Committees were weaker in this forum than they would be at later stages when participation in the development of budget legislation was expanded to take a broader range of interests into account. In JSC, it was the spenders versus the taxers, two competing power centers which had tangled many times in the past decade. As in the previous encounters, the tax committees were again dominant. At least two factors accounted for their success in JSC: First, it was easier to blame budget deficits on excessive spending than on inadequate taxation; to many legislators, budget control meant spending control and this view was reflected in the reform package that emerged from JSC. Second, when JSC was formulating its proposals, the Ways and Means Committee was at the peak of its legislative power, while the Appropriations Committees were suffering a severe erosion in their status.[12]

Two fundamental decisions of the Joint Study Committee shaped the future of budget reform. One was the decision to "layer" a new congressional budget process over the existing revenue and appropriations processes of Congress. JSC did not even consider the possibility of merging the authorizations and appropriations processes.[13] Whatever disadvantages might derive from an added

11. The JSC bill would have required the tax committees to report surtax legislation if the expected deficit (or surplus) was above (or below) the level set in the second budget resolution. This feature was not included in later versions of the budget legislation.

12. The weakening of the Appropriations Committees is discussed in Allen Schick, "The Appropriations Committees versus Congress," presented at the 1975 Annual Meeting of the American Political Science Association. The erosion of the appropriations process was reflected in the growth of backdoor programs, permanent appropriations, and uncontrollable expenditures.

13. Charles L. Schultze, an economist who served as Director of the Bureau of the Budget in the Johnson Administration and an acknowledged federal budget expert, proposed such a scheme in House Committee on Rules, *Hearings on Budget Control Act of 1973*, 93rd Cong., 1st Sess. (1973), p. 319ff.

layer of budget procedures and institutions, the JSC scheme had one overriding virtue: no congressional committee would suffer a loss of its basic jurisdiction.[14] The road to congressional budget reform would be through the creation of a new process, not through a contraction of the old ones. This feature remained in almost all later proposals and was preserved in the Congressional Budget Act.

A second determination of JSC was to create a process independent of the President and dependent solely on congressional action. The linchpin of the new process was to be a concurrent resolution, a legislative measure which is not submitted to the President for his review. After years of battling the President on budget priorities and economic policies, Congress would have its own procedures, unconstrained by presidential preferences. This feature, too, remained in all later versions of the budget reform legislation.

The charter of the Joint Study Committee did not authorize it to report legislation and, as a consequence, the bills introduced pursuant to its report (H.R. 7130 and S. 1641) were referred to standing committees of the House and Senate.[15]

House Rules Committee: The View From the Leadership

H.R. 7130 was handled in the House by the Rules Committee, which differs from most congressional committees in several ways that bear on its consideration of the budget bill. Rules does not often have original jurisdiction over legislation; it ordinarily serves as the "traffic" coordinator for the House, determining the conditions under which legislation is considered on the floor.[16] When it reviewed the budget control legislation in 1973, Rules had had little experience with the detailed markup of legislation, although earlier in that year it developed and reported an impoundment control bill.

14. Of course, some committees inevitably would lose jurisdiction or status because of ancillary features of the legislation such as the restrictions on backdoor programs.

15. Rep. John B. Anderson introduced a resolution enabling JSC to report legislation but no action was taken on it. H. Con. Res. 178, 93rd Cong. (1973). However, the JSC recommendations were drafted into bills (H.R. 7130 and S. 1641) and introduced in the House and Senate.

16. Certain types of legislation are "privileged"; they can be considered by the House without clearance from the Rules Committee. Most legislation, however, requires a "rule" before the House takes it up. The rule, which is approved before the House proceeds to consider the substantive measure itself, ordinarily specifies the terms under which amendments may be considered (if at all) and the amount of time allowed for debate. It frequently also provides for a waiver of House rules with which the pending legislation might conflict.

Over the previous decade, the Rules Committee had become an arm of the House Democratic leadership, surrendering its role as an independent checkpoint for legislation. As an agent of the majority party, Rules had to formulate a budget bill that represented the interests of more than a single committee, a bill that could attract support from major factions within the Democratic Party and would not provoke serious challenge on the floor. Thus, the Rules bill had to satisfy the interests of committees other than House Appropriations and Ways and Means, but without incurring the displeasure of these two power centers.

As a committee, Rules was not in a position to canvass and balance the various interests of the House. Rules was an exclusive committee; most of its members served on no other legislative committee. Any interests other committees may have had in budget reform could not be effectively channeled through overlapping memberships. Moveover, Rules had no subcommittees and almost no staff of its own. It was accustomed to considering bills "whole" rather than section by section.

In its revision of H.R. 7130, the Rules Committee's conduit to the outside was Rep. Richard Bolling, its third-ranking Democrat and a leading advocate of institutional reform in the House of Representatives. During the period that he worked on the budget legislation, Representative Bolling also headed a select committee established to recommend changes in the jurisdiction and operation of House committees.

Bolling tilted the budget reform bill toward the interest of the Appropriations Committee and away from that of the Ways and Means Committee. This reversal of the orientation of JSC derived from (1) Bolling's own position (his select committee sought to divest Ways and Means of some of its jurisdiction),[17] (2) his possible antagonism to Ways and Means leaders, and (3) a confluence of interests of liberal Democrats and the Appropriations Committee. Even before it began to examine H.R. 7130, the Rules Committee was put on notice that the JSC version was not acceptable to liberal Democrats in the House. In a detailed and caustic attack on

---

17. Bolling's Select Committee on Committees proposed to strip Ways and Means of jurisdiction over revenue sharing, public debt, maternal and child care, renegotiation legislation, and the work incentive program. Ways and Means, under this scheme, would have gained jurisdiction over food stamps, but overall it would have lost much more than it would have gained. H. Res. 988 as passed by the House took away revenue sharing, but not the other programs recommended by the Bolling group.

the Joint Study Committee's report, the Democratic Study Group —composed of liberal members of the House—charged that the proposed budget would "lock the congressional budgetary process into a conservative mold for generations to come and wipe out reform progress made in recent years toward democratizing House and Senate procedures and strengthening the leadership and caucus."[18] The group severely criticized many of the features of the JSC plan, concentrating much adverse comment on the new budget committees: "The proposed House Budget Committee and its Senate counterpart would be the most powerful committee in Congress—a super elite. . . . the committee makeup would be unrepresentative of the House as a whole. . . . the committee would be dominated by conservatives.[19]

Led by Representative Bolling, the Rules Committee was able to meld liberal opposition and Appropriations Committee apprehension into broad support for an alternative approach. Liberal Democrats who preferred minimal new spending controls were able to make common cause with the Appropriations Committee even though they had long regarded that committee as a bastion of fiscal conservatism. From the liberal point of view, it would be better to fund their programs through a weak appropriations process than to run the gamut of two tough layers of control—appropriations and budget.

While the House Appropriations members of JSC had endorsed the original H.R. 7130, their interest was concentrated in selected provisions rather than in the bill as a whole. In appearances before the House Select Committee on Committees during June and before the Rules Committee in August, Chairman Mahon applauded the work of the Joint Study Committee but singled out the few items that he really wanted. Chief among these were an end to backdoors and a deadline on authorizing legislation.[20] Mahon's support was critical for the budget legislation. Had he come out in open opposition to new committees or a separate process, the whole idea might have been scuttled in JSC or in the Rules Committee. But this was not Mahon's way. Not only did he shy away from confrontation (as he had on many other occasions while chairman of the Appropriations Committee), but he really wanted to do

18. Democratic Study Group, "Recommendations of the Joint Study Committee on Budget Control," May 10, 1973, p. 17.
19. *Ibid.*, p. 18.
20. Mahon testified before the Rules Committee in *Hearings on Budget Control Act of 1973*, 93rd Cong., 1st Sess. (1973), pp. 125-46.

something about federal spending and budget deficits. As a fiscal conservative, Mahon believed that a budget process was the right approach for Congress, and it would have been unthinkable for him to try to block the reform effort with a jurisdictional protest.

Some of Mahon's colleagues, however, were troubled by the prospects for reform. Liberal Rep. David Obey worried about the possible capture of new budget committees by conservatives.[21] Obey proposed that a reconstructed budget process be centered in the existing Appropriations Committees rather than in new budget committees. He advocated a more cohesive process within Appropriations, including expanded overview hearings, more input from the authorizing committees, concentrated floor action on the individual appropriation bills, and reconsideration of the various bills by the committee after all had been approved by the House. The net effect would have been a transfer of some power from the appropriations subcommittees to the full committee.

While Obey's position might have represented the optimal outcome for some House Appropriations Committee members and liberal Democrats, sentiment in favor of new budget committees was quite strong. Appropriations itself could not supply the macroeconomic guidance, integration of spending and tax policy, and consideration of national priorities sought by those who favored a distinct budget process. Appropriations would have to accept new budget committees, though not with the scope specified by the original H.R. 7130.

The preference of some Appropriations members was unveiled in a bill introduced on October 16, 1973, by Rep. Jamie Whitten, ranking member of the House Appropriations Committee and co-chairman of the Joint Study Committee. The Whitten bill, H.R. 10961, would have confined the budget committees to a macroeconomic advisory role, a capability which Appropriations clearly lacked. The budget committees would report a resolution dealing only with spending totals; these would guide but not limit subsequent action on the individual appropriations bills. The Whitten bill was introduced as the Rules Committee began its markup of the budget legislation. Rules had prepared its own draft of a budget bill which was substantially similar to Whitten's except for the

21. Representative Obey also served as head of the DSG task force whose report criticized the Joint Study Committee. In a joint statement with Rep. William A. Steiger of Wisconsin, Obey noted the irony "that a budget reform which is designed to reduce fragmentation winds up creating another committee," *ibid.*, p. 288.

lack of suballocations in the latter.[22] Yet for Rules to report a bill commanding wide support, it had to reconcile three versions of budget reform: its own draft bill, H.R. 10961, and the Joint Study Committee bill which had undergone some modification.[23]

Inasmuch as the primary differences were between Whitten and the JSC bill, any agreement between these two parties that did not abandon concessions already made to the liberals (such as a revision in budget committee makeup) was likely to be acceptable to the Rules Committee. At this stage of negotiations, the JSC position was defended by Ways and Means because Appropriations had staked out its own position. The compromise that was worked out tilted toward Whitten. In the give and take, it was necessary to defer to the primary interest of the Appropriations Committee in preserving its jurisdiction over spending matters and, as a consequence, the less affected parties bowed to its claims. Moreover, with a solid majority in the Rules Committee backing the Appropriations position, Ways and Means could not dictate the terms of the legislation.

Although the Rules Committee retained the basic JSC formulation, it modified many of the particulars. It proposed a reduction in Appropriations/Ways and Means membership on the House's budget committee from two-thirds to less than 45 percent. Moreover, the budget committee was to have rotating membership, with no member serving on the committee for more than 4 years during any 10-year period. The first budget resolution was to be a target rather than a ceiling, with no "consistency" limitation on floor amendments. Allocations in the budget resolution were to be by budget function rather than by appropriation category. The reconciliation of spending legislation with the congressional budget was to take place in the fall, at which time a second resolution would be adopted. At the instigation of Representative Bolling, a previously passed impoundment control bill (H.R. 8480) was attached to the budget legislation.

As revised, H.R. 7130 was unanimously reported by the Rules Committee, but several members reserved the right to offer floor amendments. In two days of floor debate, however, the compromise bill withstood a number of attempts to change its provisions. Only

22. Rules, like other committees, refined its draft legislation through a succession of committee prints, so that the Committee itself marked up a bill which had undergone substantial revision on the basis of discussion among interested Members and staff.

23. Since Representative Whitten now had his own bill, the JSC position, in effect, was that of its other cochairman, Representative Ullman.

two comparatively minor amendments (concerning the layover period between committee report and floor consideration of the budget resolution) were adopted. The main parties to the compromise—in particular, Representatives Bolling, Ullman, and Whitten —committed themselves in advance not to accept any other amendments, not even those they favored, lest the whole package come apart on the floor. When the final vote was taken, many members who may have had misgivings about particular provisions voted in favor of H.R. 7130. With only 23 votes in opposition, budget control legislation had cleared one of the formidable obstacles to enactment.

Senate Government Operations Committee: Reconciling Liberal and Conservative Views

The road to budget reform was somewhat different in the Senate where the Government Operations Committee had original jurisdiction over the legislation. Although it is not one of the major committees of the Senate,[24] Government Operations nonetheless had a number of leading Senators among its members. For almost two decades, its chairman had been John McClellan, who relinquished that post in 1972 to become chairman of Senate Appropriations. Although he maintained an interest in budget reform during the 1950s and 1960s, Senator McClellan did not actively participate in the consideration of the new legislation. The chairman of Government Operations in 1973 was Sen. Sam Ervin who introduced S. 1541, the bill marked up by the committee.[25] Although he was then actively engaged in the Watergate investigation, Senator Ervin was intent on capping his congressional career with legislation restoring to Congress its control over the purse. First consideration of S. 1541 was in the Subcommittee on Budgeting, Management, and Expenditures, headed by Sen. Lee Metcalf.

All Senators on Government Operations served on at least one additional Senate committee; thus they were aware of some of the potential effects of budget reform on other Senate interests. This

24. The Legislative Reorganization Act of 1970 classified Government Operations as a major Senate committee, thereby limiting its members to only one other major committee post (but exempting those already on Government Operations from this two-committee limitation). However, *de facto*, Government Operations does not have the status of other major Senate committees.

25. S. 1541 was introduced one week before JSC reported, but it copied some of the features of the JSC bill, though in skeletal form. By getting S. 1541 into the hopper first, Senator Ervin was able to make it the vehicle for Government Operations action.

broader perspective accounted for some of the departures of the Metcalf subcommittee from the recommendations of the Joint Study Committee. For example, the Metcalf group voted to remove all quotas in determining the membership of the new Senate Budget Committee, thereby expanding the opportunities for appointment of Senators not on the Finance or Appropriations Committees.

Despite its agreement on how the new budget power should be distributed within Congress, the Metcalf subcommittee was deeply divided on the substance of that power. Conservatives looked to the new budget process as an opportunity to impose strong controls over spending and to curb federal deficits. Liberals, however, preferred a process that would not prevent Congress from appropriating the amounts it wanted for government programs. The subcommittee was split 5 to 4 between those who favored an early adoption of ceilings and subceilings on expenditures (as the JSC had proposed) and those who insisted that the initial budget determination be in the form of a target that would not limit later congressional action. The majority sought a budget process that would make it difficult for Congress to enact spending programs at variance with the determinations in its first budget resolution. The minority were concerned that a binding process would prove to be unworkable and unacceptable to Congress.

In spite of the wide difference between their positions, both sides had reasons to seek a compromise. A 5-to-4 division in subcommittee does not augur well for the legislation in full committee or on the floor. Moreover, throughout congressional consideration of budget reform, efforts were made to get broad support for the legislation. This was one bill that members did not want stamped as a partisan or controversial measure. Accordingly, when the full committee took up S. 1541 in September 1973, it was presented with an accommodation worked out by Senators Muskie and Percy, the main spokesmen for the liberal and conservative points of view. As it finally emerged from Government Operations, the bill provided for a complicated process combining ceilings and targets. Congress would be able to adopt appropriations in excess of the levels in its budget resolution, but no spending bill could take effect until Congress enacted special "triggering" legislation. Such legislation could be considered, however, only if the amounts in spending bills were within the limits of the resolution.

The Government Operations Committee bill also had procedures for backdoor legislation and a deadline on authorizations. It added provisions dealing with budgetary information, program authorizations, and the pilot testing of new programs. A number of these provisions were "member" amendments, in which only a single Senator was interested. These amendments, much more common in Senate than in House bills, substantially expanded the scope of budget reform legislation beyond that conceived by either JSC or the House Rules Committee.

Senate Rules and Administration Committee: The View From the Senate

When S. 1541 was reported by the Government Operations Committee, Majority Whip Robert G. Byrd moved that it be referred to the Committee on Rules and Administration (on which he served and whose Subcommittee on the Rules of the Senate he chaired) for the purpose of reviewing its effects on the rules and operations of the Senate.[26] However, once it obtained jurisdiction, the Rules and Administration Committee examined and modified the entire bill, formulating a version that was much closer to the one already approved by the House than to the Government Operations bill.

Senator Byrd was aware that although budget reform affected the interests of every committee and Member, few Senators other than those on Government Operations had substantive knowledge of the pending legislation. Most were prepared to treat S. 1541 as they would legislation coming out of any committee outside their jurisdiction, and would limit their participation to the comparatively few issues opened up on the floor. But because of the popularity of budget reform, Byrd preferred that major modifications be made before floor consideration. Byrd had an additional concern. For several years, he had worked to expedite floor action in the Senate, and he had only recently succeeded in forging unanimous consent into an effective device for moving the Senate to orderly disposition of most of its legislative business.[27] But the bill pre-

26. The Senate practices sequential referral much more than the House does, in part because it considers most legislation under unanimous consent agreements. If a Senator's request to have a measure referred to his committee is denied, he can put a "hold" on the bill and jeopardize its prospects for floor consideration.

27. Every unanimous consent agreement represents a waiver of one or more Senate rules. Although unanimous consent is almost as old as the Senate itself, during the 1970s, Senator Byrd extended its use considerably. Now, time-limit agreements are negotiated for almost all legislation before floor debate commences.

pared by Government Operations had numerous potential blockage points, instances in which Senate consideration of certain measures might be halted because of the new budget rules.[28] Byrd thus had to do two things to mobilize support for a major revision of the bill by Rules and Administration: (1) draw the attention of leading Senators to S. 1541 and (2) demonstrate that the bill received by Rules and Administration was not in "go" condition. Both aims were achieved through a two-pronged approach. First, a letter (signed by Rules and Administration Chairman Howard Cannon) was dispatched to the chairmen of all Senate committees. After reviewing some features of S. 1541, the letter noted: "It does not appear that any committee chairman was specifically asked for his views on them and no committee chairman testified about them before the [Metcalf] Subcommittee." The letter concluded with a warning that "since this bill directly affects the work of the Senate and many of its committees, it is important that each committee carefully consider the impact of all of its provisions on their operations." In response, five Senate chairmen joined together in a letter which raised numerous questions about S. 1541 and suggested that the bill required "very detailed study and further legislative refinement."[29]

The second tactic was a one-day hearing which, though brief, vigorously challenged the work of the Government Operations Committee. Senator Byrd read the name of each member of the Senate Finance and Appropriations Committees, fewer than 10 percent of whom were also on the Government Operations Committee, to hammer home his point that the latter had not adequately consulted with the rest of the Senate. With letters from apprehensive chairmen and adverse comment at a public hearing, the Rules and Administration Committee succeeded in establishing its jurisdiction over all of S. 1541.[30]

---

28. The more restrictive the budget control process is, the more likely it is to provide for points of order against money legislation. Thus, because the Government Operations bill provided relatively tight controls, it also erected numerous rules for the enforcement of the controls.
29. The letter, dated December 19, 1973, has not been printed in any of the documents associated with the Congressional Budget Act. However, the responses from various committee chairmen are appended to Senate Committee on Rules and Administration, *Hearings on Federal Budget Control by the Congress*, 93rd Cong., 2nd Sess. (1974), pp. 149-56.
30. Actually, Rules and Administration gave the Government Operations Committee the option of reworking its bill, but the latter demurred, probably because a revised version still would have to be processed through the Rules and Administration Committee.

Once it was committed to serve as the guardian of all the Senate's interests, the Rules and Administration Committee had to provide a forum for bringing all the interests together. As described in its report on S. 1541, the committee convened a working group to which

> All standing committees were invited to designate representatives. The resulting staff effort to produce a "consensus" bill is probably without precedent in the Senate. In all, 45 staff members took part. . . . They came from ten standing committees of the Senate, four joint committees, the House Appropriations Committee, the Congressional Research Service, and the Office of Senate Legislative Counsel. . . .
>
> The working group met for about 90 hours in twenty-five sessions during sixteen days.[31]

The group functioned informally, allowing the discussion to move from one topic to another as mood or opportunity dictated. No votes were taken, but by the time it was done, the group had produced a bill that was certain of Senate approval. Some committees participated throughout the proceedings, others hardly at all. Committee involvement generally was governed by the extent to which the committee's interests were impinged upon by S. 1541. Among the authorizing committees, those with backdoor legislation tended to be the most active. The Finance Committee vigilantly defended its interest in tax and entitlement legislation, and the final outcome was substantially swayed by its attentiveness to the precise details of the bill. Senate Appropriations opted for an observer role, only occasionally expressing its own views and preferences. In an extraordinary act of bicameral cooperation, however, representatives of the House Appropriations Committee effectively participated in the working group, protecting the interests of its Senate counterpart and assuring that S. 1541 was modified in ways that brought it into closer alignment with the House version.

Rules and Administration converted the first budget resolution to a target and added an optional reconciliation procedure to the second resolution. Changes were made in the treatment of backdoor programs, distinguishing between contract and borrowing authority on one hand and entitlements on the other. Titles dealing with pilot testing of new programs and a time limit on authorizations were removed in favor of provisions strengthening the role of Congress in program evaluation.

31. S. Rept. No. 93-688.

Rules and Administration reported its "consensus" bill on February 21, 1974, and the full Senate took up the measure one month later. No attempt was made to bind Senators to the accommodations negotiated in the working group, and approximately 20 floor amendments were adopted. Most were comparatively minor and did not disturb the balance worked out in committee. Several substantial changes, however, had the effect of tightening the budget controls over appropriations and entitlements, confirming that those Members who preferred less control had to work their will in committee rather than on the floor. After four days of debate, the Senate passed S. 1541 by a vote of 80 to 0.[32]

Conference Committee: Reconciling Impoundment Control and Budget Reform

With most of the differences between the various viewpoints on budget reform substantially narrowed by the House and Senate actions, one might have expected an easy time in conference. Such was not the case, however. At their very first meeting, the conferees deadlocked on the issue of impoundment control, thereby threatening to stalemate budget reform with a dispute that had persisted for almost a full year. In May 1973, the Senate passed S. 373, an impoundment bill introduced by Senator Ervin. Two months later, the House passed H.R. 8480, its own version of impoundment control, the substance of which was then incorporated into H.R. 7130, the budget reform legislation. The two bills diverged substantially over the form of congressional impoundment control. S. 373 would have required that an impoundment cease unless it was approved by Congress within 60 days. H.R. 8480, however, provided for the termination of any impoundment disapproved by either the House or Senate during a 60-day period. If Congress failed to act on an executive impoundment, the Senate bill would have compelled release of the funds while the House bill would have permitted the impoundment to continue in effect.

The conferees decided to deal separately with impoundment control and budget reform, although they recognized that final agreement could not be reached on the latter until the former also was worked out. The impasse was broken by dividing impoundments into two categories—rescissions and deferrals—and combining elements of S. 373 and H.R. 8480 into the Congressional Budget

32. The Senate devoted four days to consideration of S. 1541—March 19-22, 1974.

and Impoundment Control Act. The procedure for rescission conforms to the concept of S. 373 in that a rescission requires approval by both Houses of Congress. Withheld funds must be released unless Congress passes a rescission bill within 45 days after it has been notified by the President. In the case of deferrals, the procedure is in accord with that formulated in H.R. 8480; that is, a deferral continues unless disapproved by either the House or Senate. The conferees also approved an amendment to the Antideficiency Act restricting the purposes for which budgetary reserves could be established.

As for the congressional budget procedure, the conference committee provided for a targeting resolution in the spring and a reconciliation process in the fall. It settled for a deadline on the reporting rather than the passage of authorizing legislation. It provided for the new budget process to commence with the 1977 fiscal year but with optional implementation for fiscal 1976.

Final passage of the legislation occurred in the House on June 18, 1974, by a vote of 401 to 6, and in the Senate on June 21 by a 75-0 vote. After the bill was signed into law on July 12, 1974, some provisions (such as impoundment control) took effect at once, but most of the provisions became effective at the beginning of 1975 or later.

PRINCIPLES OF BUDGET REFORM

No legislative interest got all that it wanted from the Congressional Budget Act; nor was any interest completely thwarted. In the legislative process, ambition checked ambition, and the end product was an accommodation to the main interests of the affected parties. Conservatives who sought strong budget committees and a restrictive budget process had to settle for a process that does not prevent Congress from spending as it sees fit. Liberals who were apprehensive about the possible effect of any budget process on domestic programs had to accept new budget controls. Authorizing committees were able to shelter existing backdoors, but not most new ones. They successfully resisted the imposition of deadlines on the enactment of authorizations, but could not avert deadlines for the reporting of such legislation. The Appropriations Committees avoided the allocation of budget amounts among appropriations categories but had to accept allocations among broad budget functions. The tax committees blocked proposals to specify tax expenditures in the congressional budget, but they acceded to provisions which substantially increase attention to tax expenditures in the federal budget.

The fact that committees protected their most vital interests does not mean that the Budget Act merely ratified the status quo. There were winners and losers in the legislative struggle, but no party gained all it wanted or lost everything. Nor were the power shifts spelled out in the Act; rather they were inherent in the striving of new budget committees for a place in congressional policy making. One could not read the Budget Act and be sure of which committees would come out ahead and which would suffer a loss of legislative status; but neither could one read the Act without feeling that change was sure to come.

In retrospect, it should be clear that the Budget Act took more from the powerful than the weak, more, that is, from the tax committees than from the Appropriations Committees. This finding does not rest on the bare terms of the Act but on the simple realization that the Appropriations Committees had already suffered great blows to their status and were unlikely to be threats to the new process, while Ways and Means and Finance, though near the apogee of their power, would face new rivals in the making of tax policy. Yet the tax committees could not oppose this harbinger of change because the threat to their jurisdiction was implied rather than overt.

Hardly a single provision of the Congressional Budget Act escaped the attention of legislative compromisers. Even as it embraced the overall structure devised by the Joint Study Committee, Congress engineered the details in ways which deviated significantly from the original purpose. But even though the compromises were motivated by the interests of the affected parties and the pressures of legislative bargaining, it is possible to discern a number of principles which influenced Congress in its development of the Budget Act.

Neutrality of the Process

The Joint Study Committee version was loaded in favor of those who wanted less federal spending and smaller budget deficits. In view of the background of budget reform and the composition of JSC, this preference was to be expected. But Congress could not subscribe to a biased process, that is, to an arrangement which explicitly favored spending cuts over increases. To have done so would have curbed the legislative power of Congress by making future outcomes dependent on budget procedures rather than on majority will. What has emerged, therefore, is a process that is neutral on its face. It can be deployed in favor of higher or lower spending, bigger or smaller deficits. Its effects on budget outcomes will depend on congressional preferences rather than on procedural limitations.

The chief means of neutralizing the budget process was a shift from ceilings to targets in the first budget resolution. If the first resolution were to function as a limitation—with Congress barred from considering legislation in excess of the ceiling—it inevitably would be biased against proposed increases in expenditures. The bias probably would be strongest against new programs not endorsed in previous budgets. Existing programs would have a clear advantage in the competition for legislative support, as they do in any budget process. The conversion to targets does not by itself eliminate budgetary bias against program innovation, but it at least removes some of the procedural impediments in the legislative process.

The conversion from ceilings to targets preserved budgetary neutrality by removing the explicit preference for budget committee decisions over those of the Appropriations Committees. If ceilings were to be set early, the inevitable effect would have been to erode the power of the Appropriations Committees. The Act itself would have resolved that spending preferences of the budget committees were always to have primacy over those of the appropriations groups. As mentioned earlier, the Budget Act does not spell out its power shifts; to do so would be a breach of the neutrality principle. By shifting the first resolution to a target, the Act veiled its effect on budget outcomes and on the future conduct and relationships of congressional committees.

The commitment to balance also is reflected in the development of the second budget resolution as a floor on revenues. When the second budget resolution was originally conceived, it was limited to the expenditure side of the budget. But the enacted version applies to the revenue side as well. After Congress has adopted its second resolution for a fiscal year, it cannot take action that would raise spending above, or lower revenues below, the amounts fixed in the resolution. By treating tax and expenditure legislation in the same way, Congress signified its intent to establish a process which would not foreordain any of its outcomes.

In assessing the neutrality of the Budget Act, two important reminders are in order. First, the Act was neutral in terms of the issues and alternatives considered in the course of developing the legislation. In terms of the fundamental biases of the American political system, the Act could not possibly be neutral. Congress was bent on doing something about spending and deficits because it shared the prevailing bias that federal spending was too high and that deficits are not to be desired. Congress was neutral within the boundaries of the legislative process, not in terms of basic political values. Were it not constrained by "mainstream" politics, Congress might have fashioned a different process, for example, one that might have favored claims for higher spending. To speak of Budget Act neutrality is merely to state that Congress did not markedly tilt in favor of one of the options presented to it.

Second, any significant change in budgetary procedure can be expected to affect budgetary outcomes. Congress voted a Budget Act because it wanted things to be different in the future. But in opting for change, Congress preserved its neutrality by allowing the play of legislative interests to prevail.

Congress's Discretion To Act According to Its Budgetary Preferences

Along with a "ceiling" resolution, the Joint Study Committee proposed numerous special rules to restrict congressional discretion on budget-related legislation. Some of the rules pertained to the timing of the budget process; others related to the substance of legislative decisions. Congress could not consider appropriations before a certain date, or authorizations for the next fiscal year after another date. In acting on appropriations, Congress would have been compelled to consider proposed reductions first, and could not consider any proposed increases in excess of the congressional budget. All told, the JSC proposed more than a dozen stoppage points in the legislative process, circumstances under which action could be halted by a point of order. And to assure that these special rules were not brushed aside by legislative expediency, JSC recommended that a two-thirds approval be required for waiving any of the new congressional budget rules.

Many of the restrictive procedures were discarded by the House Rules Committee in its version of H.R. 7130; others were removed or modified by the Senate. The Rules Committee was convinced that Congress would sooner break its own budget process than abide intolerable restraints on its legislative power:

> Not everything that carries the label of a legislative budget can be made to work. . . . the new process must be in accord with the realities of congressional budgeting. . . . budget reform must not become an instrument for preventing Congress from expressing its will on spending policy. . . . The constant objective of budget reform should be to make Congress informed about and responsible for its budget decisions, not to take away its power to act.[33]

This view prevailed in the Budget Act. Gone was the requirement for a two-thirds vote to waive the rules. Gone was the ironclad "rule of consistency" which would have barred any floor amendments to the budget resolution that failed to preserve a consistent relationship between all totals and subtotals. A number of special rules were retained, mostly to expedite—not to stop—the legislative process.

Substitution of Information for Control

The Congressional Budget Act retains a number of controls essential to the functioning of the budget process. For example, Congress cannot—with some exceptions—consider spending, revenue, or debt legislation for a fiscal year before it has passed the first budget resolution. Nor can it cut revenues below, or raise expenditures above, the levels fixed in its second (or later) budget resolution. Without these controls, the budget process would have little muscle or meaning. Congress would be able to evade the process by passing appropriations before the first resolution has been adopted and ignore the process by deviating from the marks after its second resolution.

Nevertheless, the process attempts to make do with far fewer controls than were suggested by the Joint Study Committee. But what it traded away in the form of controls, Congress tried to recoup partly in the form of comprehensive and timely budget information. A case in point is the treatment of outlay limitations. JSC proposed that, under certain conditions, appropriations bills be required to limit the amount of outlays permitted under both new and carryover budget authority. This requirement was to apply only to the extent that the first budget resolution prescribed the inclusion of outlay limits in spending bills. Congress also would have been required to impose outlay limitations on permanent appropriations, funds that become available without current action by Congress.

33. H. Rept. No. 93-658, p. 29.

In the course of developing the budget reform legislation, Congress opted for outlay information in committee reports in lieu of statutory limitations. Thus, Section 308 of the Budget Act requires committees to estimate the five-year outlays deriving from new budget authority. Section 308 also directs the Congressional Budget Office (CBO) to issue periodic scorekeeping reports on the status of the congressional budget. Other provisions of the Budget Act provide for reports on how the functional amounts in each budget resolution are to be distributed among congressional committees and subcommittees (Section 302), a House Appropriations Committee summary report on all regular appropriation bills (Section 307), reports on tax expenditure legislation (Section 308), and CBO reports on authorizing legislation (Section 403).

The purpose of this avalanche of budget information is to assure that Congress is aware of what it is doing whenever it takes an action that impacts on the budget. In line with the assumption that it is futile to try to stop Congress from doing what it wants to do, the Budget Act strives to make Congress responsible for its actions.

Broad Representation and Participation in the Process

As was discussed earlier, the Joint Study Committee initially proposed identical percentage quotas for the House and Senate budget committees. Under the original formula, one-third of the positions of each committee would have gone to Appropriations, one-third to Ways and Means and Finance, and one-third to the membership at large. In addition, the chairmanships of the two committees would have alternated between the spending and tax committee members. From the start, however, committee composition was among the most controversial features of the budget legislation. The main complaint was that House and Senate interests—and particularly liberals—would be denied effective participation and influence in the new process. Rep. Al Ullman, cochairman of the Joint Study Committee, argued for "coordinative" budget committees on the ground that "the functions of the Budget Committee—to the extent they are performed by House and Senate committees at all—are now performed by the appropriations and tax committees."[34]

Both of the budget committees were established on a more representative basis than JSC preferred. The House committee's seats

34. House Committee on Rules, *Hearings on Budget Control Act of 1973*, p. 57.

were to be allocated by formula among the principal budget interests in the House (Appropriations, Ways and Means, at-large member, and the party leaderships); Senate Budget Committee was to be made representative by the normal committee assignment processes of the two parties.

The emphasis on broad participation was reflected in other features of the Budget Act. In preparing the first resolution, the budget committees must know the views and preferences of other legislative interests. There is no way for a single committee to be informed of all the particulars and issues involved in each year's budget cycle. Even if they conducted hearings prior to formulating the first resolution, the budget committees would be able to tap only a limited range of views within the available time. The JSC bill sought to remedy this problem by providing for the tax and appropriations committees to submit their own budget views early each year. The House bill added a clause permitting (but not requiring) any other congressional committee to report its views and estimates to the budget committee of its House. The Senate Rules and Administration Committee went a big step further by requiring each legislative committee to advise the budget committee each year with regard to all budget-related matters in its jurisdiction. The budget committees thus receive a broad and diverse set of views before they mark up the first resolution.

Broad participation was not deemed to be an end in itself but a necessary precondition for a workable process. The budget process would be of no avail if Congress proved unable to marshal majority support for its resolutions. By giving access and voice to all legislative interests, Congress facilitated the process of gathering support for its budget determinations.

Congressional Responsibility for Budgetary Decisions

From the outset, the main purpose of budget reform was to establish fiscal responsibility in Congress. However, in the course of developing the Budget Act, Congress transformed the concept of responsibility from a substantive to a procedural test.

At the start, fiscal responsibility was associated with smaller budget deficits and less government spending. The first operative paragraph of the Joint Study Committee's report opened with an indictment of recurring and growing budget deficits. The JSC bill, as already noted, would have imposed strict controls on legislative spending action, but these controls were relaxed in favor of a process permitting Congress to act according to its preferences. Congress redefined, but did not abandon, the notion of fiscal responsibility. As enacted, budget responsibility meant that Congress would make financial decisions in the context of, rather than outside, its budget process. Congress could take whatever tax or spending action it deemed appropriate, provided that it acted in accordance with the procedure laid out in the Budget Act.

Foremost among the procedural rules is the requirement that Congress defer revenue and spending legislation until it has adopted the first budget resolution for a fiscal year. The Budget Act extended this prohibition to entitlement legislation, one of the few instances in which the final version was more stringent than the JSC proposal. Congress also barred new entitlements from taking effect before the start of the next fiscal year. The purpose of these prohibitions is to assure that entitlements, no less than other fiscal actions, are subject to the discipline of the budget process.

Budgetary responsibility, however, was framed in the one-year cycle of the congressional budget. Congress was not limited in the actions that it could take affecting future budgets, although it is informed of the five-year costs of its actions. This one-year-at-a-time procedure accords with the normal routine of federal budgeting, but complicates the task of securing longer-term budgetary responsibility.

Protection of Existing Interests

In Congress, as in other institutions, it is very difficult to reform by taking power away from those who hold it. If provoked by over-reaching change, powerful interests can block not only intrusions on their own position but overall reform as well. The surer way to institute change, therefore, is to accept existing arrangements and not try to divest powerholders of their special advantages. New rules would be applied to new matters, for which interests have not yet been vested.

The Budget Act illustrates this principle in operation. Budget power is not directly taken from the authorizing, appropriating, or taxing committees. No direct change is made in their jurisdiction; each committee can proceed pretty much as it has in the past. Change is concentrated, however, in the new budget process, with regard to which none of the existing committees had a vested interest. Of course, the budget process might turn into a trespass on the work and discretion of the other committees, but this would be determined by later practices, not by the bare terms of the Act.

Virtually every effort to withdraw existing advantages was thwarted in the course of developing the budget legislation. The Joint Study Committee proposed to bring guaranteed loans within the scope of the budget process, but such loans were later excluded on the ground that they are contingent rather than direct liabilities of the United States. The House Rules Committee bill also would have controlled existing backdoor programs, but the Budget Act applies the new procedures only to new backdoors. The Government Operations Committee added a title limiting all authorizations (including existing ones) to three years, but this was deleted in subsequent action on the legislation. Senate Rules and Administration tried to terminate the off-budget status of a half-dozen agencies, but the Budget Act settled for a study of the off-budget agencies. Existing privileges were "grandfathered," the term used on Capitol Hill for exempting past practices from changes in the rules.

Benefits for All Major Participants in Congressional Budgeting

If the road to reform is paved by the protection of existing interests, it also is facilitated by according specific benefits to each such interest. In order for existing committees to accept the new rules, they had to get some concrete gains to compensate for the risk of future losses.

The Appropriations Committees got half of the loaves they wanted. New contract and borrowing authority was placed under their jurisdiction and they gained a limited role with regard to entitlements. These committees did not succeed in establishing a deadline on the enactment of authorizing legislation, but they got a deadline on the reporting of authorizations. The tax committees achieved their primary objective, a legislative procedure for limiting federal expenditure. They also secured a second advantage, some alleviation of the political onus for periodic legislation raising the statutory limit on the public debt. Authorizing committees gained some opportunity to influence budget outcomes before the Appropriations Committees have acted.

The benefits were not equally distributed among the various participants. The authorizing committees which had risked the least also gained the least. The Appropriations Committees, however, had put their jurisdiction over federal spending on the line and they were rewarded with expanded jurisdiction.

AN UNCERTAIN PEACE

The Congressional Budget Act did not put an end to budgetary strife any more than the introduction of presidential budgeting brought perfect peace a half-century ago. The Budget Act was a respite and a redirection. While it could not assure budgetary tranquillity, it at least provided new conditions under which future battles would be fought.

Not the least of the reasons why Congress was able to accommodate diverse interest in the Budget Act was the ambiguous and permissive process that it established. While some matters such as scheduling were precisely decided, others were left to future implementation. The budget committees, for example, might turn into the strongest congressional committees, stamping their mark on all program and policy decisions that cost money to implement. Or they might function as feeble participants, lacking genuine legislative jurisdiction of their own and dependent on other budget parties for support. The Budget Act ordains neither outcome. Nor does it spell out the effects of the new process on the appropriating, authorizing, and taxing committees. No one can foretell the future by examining the Budget Act alone. It all depends on how the parties interact with one another in the congressional arena.

For this reason alone, the Budget Act promotes an augmentation of budgetary conflict. The Act provides license and opportunity, threats, and possibilities. Every party to the 1974 treaty has been compelled to jockey for advantage, to assert prerogatives and ward off intrusion by others. In fact, the new process enlarges the potential for conflict within Congress because it expands the scope of participation and compels Congress to make more explicit budget choices than before. Priorities have to be decided; the parts must be consistent with the whole; Congress must go on record with regard to the size of the budget and the deficit; tax expenditures are displayed and can be challenged; the cost of legislation and its impact on the congressional budget are identified.

The Budget Act fuels conflict in yet another critical way. Prior to the Act, the parts of the budget were cordoned off from one another. Tax policy was made by a single set of committees; appropriations went through their own process; authorizations had their own committee roots and routes. The Budget Act means that there is hardly a single financial decision that can be made via one set of committees alone. Revenue decisions involve both the tax and the budget committees. The budget committees share spending power with the Appropriations Committees. The wills of all these committees have to be concerted in the development of the congressional budget.

In this new environment, the budget committees can have only the power they grab. They must take the initiative and stake their own claims, often against those of the older committees. Neither the budget committees nor the budget process can be effective if the prerogatives and work of the other committees are not disturbed. The new process marks the institutionalization of budget conflict within Congress.

Yet the congressional budget, no less than executive budgets, has to be decided each year. The Budget Act directs Congress to make peace through the channels and procedures of its new budget process. The Act facilitates the search for peace by enabling a congressional majority to do whatever it wants to do. It can peg the budget's numbers at any level it prefers and change them as often as it wishes. Whenever Congress can organize a majority in support of any budget position, it will be well on the road to budget peace. But what happens when Congress is so split and individual Members cross-pressured that a majority cannot be mustered behind any overall course of action? We pose this question now to suggest that political strife within Congress rather than the "Rube Goldberg" design of the 1974 Budget Act represents the greatest threat to the hopes and survival of congressional budget reform. Congress did no more than negotiate a treaty in 1974.

The next two chapters describe the functions and structure of the new actors injected into the process by that treaty (the budget committees and the CBO) before turning to a consideration of how all parties to the treaty have operated under its terms.

IV The Budget Committees

CONGRESS decided in 1974 that it must have its own budget specialists—committees dedicated to the success of the process, and staff possessing the expertise and data necessary to make sound fiscal decisions. It therefore institutionalized budgetary power in new House and Senate Budget Committees and established the Congressional Budget Office (CBO). This chapter considers the structure and composition of the Budget Committees, the socialization and roles of their members and chairmen, and some of the operational differences between the House and Senate committees.

POWERFUL, BUT NOT TOO POWERFUL

Congress had good reason for wanting its own Budget Committees. It knew that a budget is not a self-made or self-enforcing decision, that in order for the new process to take hold and discipline congressional behavior, it would not suffice merely to decree the process into being. Congress would have to post budgetary guardians within its ranks, committees whose purpose would be to see that the dictates of the budget are heeded. The Budget Committees would vigilantly protect the new process because their own interests also would be at stake.

Much of the early controversy over the Budget Committees was tinged with apprehension that they might become elite or super-committees, dominating the legislative process and overriding the interests of other committees. Part of this fear stemmed from the centralizing tendency of any budget process. Because it would reach to all corners of congressional activity, a budget process might give the new committees undue leverage over other legislative participants.

Various provisions of the budget reform legislation could have enhanced this natural advantage. The JSC proposal would have made it exceedingly difficult to amend budget resolutions on the floor and would have compelled all committees to live with the ceilings in the first budget resolution. Yet the committees actually established are assured less power than was originally envisaged for them. The rigorous floor rules proposed by JSC were abandoned or substantially relaxed, and the Act poses no special encumbrance to the consideration of amendments. With the conversion of the first resolution from a ceiling to a target, greater reliance was placed on the second resolution, which largely reflects the actions of the appropriations and the revenue committees.

The most far-reaching dilution of Budget Committee power came as a by-product of the shift from coordinative to representative committees. If the JSC version had prevailed, the Budget Committees would have operated as agents of the revenue and Appropriations Committees, not as independent power centers. The preferred position of the Budget Committees would have been augmented by the status of these powerful committees. But by making the Budget Committees somewhat independent, the Budget Act assured that they would have rivals in the contest for budgetary power. The Act did not create weak committees, but neither did it launch them with an assured supply of power. The committees might yet turn into supercommittees by vanquishing their tax and appropriations rivals, but a much more likely arrangement would be temporary alliances in which the Budget Committees would be restrained by their need to maintain favorable relationships with potential adversaries.

The Budget Committees were activated during the last months of the 93rd Congress, shortly after the Budget Act was signed into law. Nine Democrats and six Republicans were appointed to the Senate Budget Committee (SBC) during the summer of 1974; a tenth Democrat was added to the committee at the start of the 95th Congress; and the committee was expanded to 12 Democrats and 8 Republicans in the 96th Congress. Only 5 of the Democrats and 2 of the Republicans had been on SBC since the 94th Congress. Most of the departing Democrats no longer were Members of the Senate; most of the Republicans were replaced because of party rules concerning committee assignments. Sen. Edmund Muskie was the committee's only chairman during the five years covered by this study. Sen. Henry Bellmon was designated ranking minority member by the Republicans.

The House Budget Committee (HBC) was formed in August 1974, with Rep. Al Ullman elected as its first chairman. Ullman vacated this position a few months later in order to assume the chairmanship of the House Ways and Means Committee. He was succeeded as HBC chairman by Rep. Brock Adams, who served two years in that post. Rep. Robert Giaimo was selected chairman at the beginning of the 95th Congress and continued in this post during the 96th Congress. Rep. Delbert Latta was the ranking Republican during the 94th, 95th, and 96th Congresses. HBC was enlarged from 23 to 25 members in 1975 to give the Democrats a 17-8 margin in the committee. Only 5 of the HBC Democrats were on the committee during the three Congresses covered by this study, while half of the Republicans were on the committee throughout the period. HBC turnover has been due both to departures from Congress and to the Budget Act's limitation on the duration of HBC membership.

POLITICAL DEMOGRAPHY OF THE BUDGET COMMITTEES

In rejecting domination by the tax and appropriations committees, Congress, in 1974, opted for Budget Committees which cover the spectrum of political interests within each chamber. This striving for balance was written into the formula for the House Budget Committee: 5 members each from Ways and Means and House Appropriations; 13 from other House committees; and 2 from the Democratic and Republican leaderships.[1] The desire for balance was also reflected in the Budget Act's stipulation that appointments to HBC "shall be made without regard to seniority." Senate Budget Committee members were to be selected by normal party process, without any statutory formula for their selection. Less than a week after the Budget Act became law, Majority Leader Mike Mansfield urged the Senate Democratic Conference not to "proceed as though we are dealing with a routine matter of committee assignments":

> . . . there is an imperative need for balance as among geographic areas and ideological nuances. . . . The Democrats who sit on the Budget Committee should . . . reflect an accurate cross-section of the Democratic members of the Senate.[2]

---

1. As enacted in 1974, the House Budget Committee was to have 23 members, including 11 "at-large" members. At the beginning of the 94th Congress (1975), HBC's membership was increased to 25, of whom 13 were to come from House committees other than Appropriations or Ways and Means.
2. Mansfield's statement appears in 120 *Congressional Record* (daily ed., July 22, 1974) S12974.

In the legislative environment, geography, seniority, political ideology, and other committee assignments are the most relevant criteria for apportioning positions among Members with different interests. Each of these is discussed in turn, with special attention paid to shifts in Budget Committee composition during the three Congresses (94th, 95th, and 96th) that they have been in existence.[3]

Geography

The two Budget Committees are remarkably balanced in terms of the percentage of Southern Democrats on each. In the 94th Congress, the North-South split on these committees was virtually identical to the divisions within the House and Senate. Five of the 17 Democrats (29 percent) on HBC and 3 of the 10 (30 percent) on SBC were from Southern states, compared with Southern Democratic ratios of 31 and 29 percent in the House and Senate, respectively. This closeness of fit was due to Democratic efforts to establish geographic balance on the two committees. When two Southern Democrats (Gibbons and Landrum) left HBC at the start of the 95th Congress, they were replaced by two other Southerners (Lehman and Mattox). Because it was difficult to attract Democrats to the Senate Budget Committee in 1977, new members were those who could be persuaded to accept the position. SBC lost one Southern Democrat (Nunn) in the 95th Congress, but added two others (Johnston and Sasser). The four Southerners constituted one-third of SBC's Democrats when the committee was enlarged in 1979.

Seniority

At the outset, the Budget Committees were "free" committees—Representatives and Senators joining them did not have to forgo any of their other legislative positions[4]—and were regarded as

3. As noted, the Budget Committees were set up in the summer of 1974, near the end of the 93rd Congress. They performed few legislative functions prior to the 94th Congress; hence this chapter does not consider their pre-1975 existence except when it is directly relevant to a matter under discussion.

4. However, if a Representative is a member of two other House committees when he is appointed to HBC, one of those memberships is suspended, without loss of seniority, during the period that he is on the Budget Committee. Senator Muskie paid a price for the SBC chairmanship. Under a "grandfather" arrangement, he was one of the Senators still holding three major committee posts. Thus, SBC would have been his fourth major committee. Under pressure from Senator Mansfield, Muskie left the Foreign Relations Committee. He subsequently resigned from the Government Affairs Committee and returned to Foreign Relations.

prize assignments when the budget process was launched. Accordingly, these committees could have quickly become the domains of senior Members of Congress.

This has not happened. Congressional notables and power holders do not dominate either of the Budget Committees. Two party leaders are on HBC, as prescribed by the Budget Act, but few other senior Members serve on it. No chairman of a House committee or of an Appropriations or Ways and Means subcommittee has been appointed to HBC. Despite the "without regard to seniority rule," both parties tended to appoint relatively senior Members. Five of the original Democrats had completed three or fewer terms in the House, but 10 had been in the House for more than six terms. The Republican contingent was less balanced between junior and senior Members; all but two had served in the House for eight or more terms.

The Democrats aimed for balanced membership in their original appointments to SBC. Although two committee chairmen were appointed to it, 4 of the 10 Democrats were still serving their first term in the Senate and another 5 were in their second or third terms. The Republican Members in the 94th Congress consisted of 4 first-termers and 2 second-termers. Overall, SBC members averaged significantly fewer years in Congress than their House counterparts (8 years for SBC versus 13 for HBC), suggesting either the Senate's greater success in awarding Budget Committee appointments to junior Members, or senior Senators' success in avoiding SBC.

Several institutional factors could account for this difference between the two committees. First, although Senators are permitted to serve on only two "major" committees (as classified in the Senate rules), the Budget Act (as originally passed) permitted SBC members to hold three committee posts during the 94th Congress. Accordingly, Senators joining SBC faced the prospect of having to leave either the Budget Committee or one of their other major committees in little more than two years. Senators who had accumulated seniority on other committees were understandably more reluctant to put themselves in this predicament than were members who had not gained positions of authority in the Senate. Second, senior Senators generally have numerous committee and subcommittee assignments; many, therefore, were unwilling to take on additional work responsibilities. A third reason applies to SBC Republicans. The Senate Republican Conference has grouped the Budget Committee with four other Senate committees on which a Republican may have no more than one membership. The other committees are Appropriations, Armed Services, Finance, and Foreign Relations—committees to which senior Members gravitate. There is one exception to this rule: the Republicans on Appropriations and Finance designate one member of each committee to serve on the Budget Committee. But the overall effect of the rule is to bias SBC toward junior Republicans.

Shifts in the allocation of positions among junior and senior Members of Congress provide clues as to how Members assess a committee's attractiveness. Table 6 compares the service records of Budget Committee members in the 94th to 96th Congresses. In the 94th Congress, the Budget Committees were brand new and lacked

Table 6

YEARS IN CONGRESS, BUDGET COMMITTEE MEMBERS

	Congress		
House Budget Committee	*94th*	*95th*	*96th*
	(Average Years in House)		
All Members	13.0	10.0	8.2
Democrats	12.9	10.2	7.4
Leaving Committee	—	14.0	11.0
Joining Committee	—	6.0	2.8
Republicans[a]	13.3	9.3	9.8
Leaving Committee[b]	—	13.7	9.7
Joining Committee[c]	—	6.5	5.3
	Congress		
Senate Budget Committee	*94th*	*95th*	*96th*
	(Average Years in Senate)		
All Members	7.6	7.0	6.6
Democrats	9.6	8.6	8.2
Leaving Committee	—	9.3	6.0
Joining Committee	—	1.3	2.0
Republicans	4.3	4.3	4.3
Leaving Committee	—	4.0	5.0
Joining Committee	—	0	3.0

[a] Based on original membership as of the beginning of the 94th Congress.

[b] Includes Hastings and Clawson, who left the committee at the beginning of the 2nd session of the 94th Congress.

[c] Includes Holt and Rousselot, who joined the committee at the beginning of the 2nd session of the 94th Congress.

Source: Tabulated from committee rosters.

a record on which Members could appraise their performance or potential. By the next Congress, the Budget Committees had shown some of their strengths and limitations. If Members judged them to be productive and rewarding, there probably would have been an increase in senior Members on these committees. Exactly the opposite occurred in the 95th Congress. There was a pronounced drop in the number of long-term Members of Congress on both committees. The average House service of HBC's members dropped from 13 to 10 years; SBC's average declined from 7.6 to 7 years. Both committees experienced a further drop in the 96th Congress, with the decline concentrated among Budget Committee Democrats.

These statistics do not fully show the growing reliance on junior Members. Among the eight Democrats joining HBC in 1977, three were in their second terms and one was a freshman; the new Democrats in 1979 included two freshmen, two in their second term, three in their third term, and no one who had served in the House more than six years. In 1977, the added Democrats averaged 6 years in the House compared with the 14 years of congressional service by the Democrats whom they replaced. In 1979, the departing Democrats averaged 11 years of House service while the entering ones had less than 3 years. A similar shift has occurred among HBC Republicans, with the new appointees in the 95th and 96th Congresses having only half as much tenure in Congress as the replaced Members.

Five positions were shifted on SBC in the 95th Congress. Four of the new members were just beginning their Senate careers, while the fifth was still in his first term. Thus, not a single "reelected" Senator opted for SBC membership. Eleven Senators joined SBC in 1979, all but one of whom was still in his first term, and five of whom were commencing their Senate careers.

These statistics strongly suggest that within two years after they were inaugurated, the House and Senate Budget Committees had already lost much of their allure for senior Members. If the operational definition of a popular committee is one for which a Representative or Senator would sacrifice a seat on another committee, the Budget Committees do not fill the bill. Nobody leaves another committee to get on Budget. Nor do senior Members of Congress use their congressional status to wrangle seats on the Budget Committees. Since 1975, there have been approximately 40 membership changes and additions to the two Budget Committees; only 4 of these assignments went to Members ranking in the upper half of their party's seniority.

Party leaders in the House and Senate do not regard it as important to place older Members on these committees. Indeed, Republican Conference restrictions in the Senate assure that most SBC members from the minority will be first-termers. When the Budget Committees were established, Democratic congressional leaders were unsure of their power and impact. To relieve their uncertainty, they named senior Members to the Budget Committees, people whom they could trust and who could restrain and guide the new committees. Thus, a good deal of arm twisting was exerted to get Senator Magnuson to take an SBC post. In the House, Democratic leaders sought mature members who were not committee or (in most cases) subcommittee chiefs. But once the new budget process went through a cycle or two, party leaders knew what to expect from it, and they no longer had to rely on senior Members. Moreover, Democratic leaders in the House became increasingly dependent on young Members for interest in, and support of, the new process. As a result of high turnover in the 1974 and 1976 congressional elections, by 1977 more than 100 House Democrats were in only their first or second terms. The new power center in the Democratic Party was the freshman and sophomore classes. Without their support, the leadership could not have passed the budget resolutions. As a "representative" committee, HBC grew younger to reflect the changing age composition of the House.

Political Ideology

To be balanced, the Budget Committees would have to span the full range of ideological viewpoints within Congress. They would have conservative and liberal members in approximately the same proportion as these political tendencies are found in the House and Senate and in each political party. Tables 7 and 8 combine two standard measures of voting ideology (the ratings issued by the liberal Americans for Democratic Action and the conservative Americans for Constitutional Action) to show the ideological leanings of House and Senate Budget Committee members,[5] compared with the full membership of each House. In this combined rating, the higher the score, the more liberal it is.

Democrats and Republicans have pursued different objectives in determining the ideological makeup of the Budget Committees.

5. ADA and ACA base their ratings on a small number of key votes in the House and Senate. The conservative coalition score covers all votes on which a majority of Southern Democrats and Republicans were on one side and the majority of Northern Democrats took the other side.

Table 7

COMPARISON OF POLITICAL IDEOLOGY RATINGS, SENATE MEMBERSHIP, AND SENATE BUDGET COMMITTEE MEMBERS, 94th AND 95th CONGRESSES

	94th Congress		*95th Congress*	
Category	*Senate*	*Budget Committee*	*Senate*	*Budget Committee*
Average Political Ideology Score				
All Members	55.4	53.3	54.4	55.3
Democrats	68.8	72.8	68.8	69.6
Republicans	33.6	20.8	33.6	26.1
Distribution of Political Ideology Scores				
All Members				
0-40	36.0%	43.8%	34.0%	38.0%
40-60	10.0	12.5	12.0	12.0
60-75	12.0	0.0	17.0	12.0
75-100	42.0	43.8	37.0	38.0
	100.0	100.0	100.0	100.0
Democrats				
0-40	17.7%	10.0%	16.0%	10.0%
40-60	9.7	20.0	16.0	20.0
60-75	14.5	0.0	14.0	10.0
75-100	58.1	70.0	53.0	60.0
	100.0	100.0	100.0	100.0
Republicans				
0-40	65.8%	100.0%	63.0%	83.0%
40-60	10.5	0.0	5.0	0.0
60-75	7.9	0.0	21.0	17.0
75-100	15.8	0.0	10.0	0.0
	100.0	100.0	100.0	100.0

Source: Gordon L. Weil, *Political Intelligence Newsletter.* Weil's scale combines the ratings of Americans for Democratic Action and Americans for Constitutional Action into a single score. It also bases the scores on a Member's voting record for six years (less, for Members who have not served that long in Congress).

Senate Democrats have heeded Mansfield's admonition to give the various political shadings within their party seats on SBC. SBC Democrats include a contingent of liberals, as well as a fair share of moderates and conservatives. On the Democratic side, SBC comes quite close to reflecting the distribution of viewpoints within

Table 8

COMPARISON OF POLITICAL IDEOLOGY RATINGS, HOUSE MEMBERSHIP AND HOUSE BUDGET COMMITTEE MEMBERS, 94th AND 95th CONGRESSES

Category	94th Congress		95th Congress	
	House	Budget Committee	House	Budget Committee
Average Political Ideology Score				
All Members	52.3	49.9	49.6	55.0
Democrats	66.2	66.5	62.9	73.8
Republicans	22.3	14.5	23.6	15.0
Distribution of Political Ideology Scores				
All Members				
0-40	40.3%	44.0%	41.3%	36.0%
40-60	10.7	12.0	15.2	12.0
60-75	13.3	4.0	16.2	8.0
75-100	35.7	40.0	27.7	44.0
	100.0	100.0	100.0	100.0
Democrats				
0-40	20.8%	17.6%	21.4%	5.9%
40-60	9.5	17.6	16.1	17.6
60-75	16.9	5.9	21.8	11.8
75-100	52.8	58.8	40.7	64.7
	100.0	100.0	100.0	100.0
Republicans				
0-40	78.6%	100.0%	79.7%	100.0%
40-60	13.1	0.0	13.5	0.0
60-75	6.2	0.0	5.4	0.0
75-100	2.1	0.0	1.4	0.0
	100.0	100.0	100.0	100.0

Source: *See table 7.*

the Senate. In the 94th Congress, SBC Democrats averaged only five points more liberal (higher) on the combined ADA/ACA scale; in the 95th Congress, the spread was less than one point between SBC Democrats and the entire Democratic membership of the Senate. Moreover, the distribution of SBC Democrats came close to the overall distribution of Democrats within the Senate. In the 94th Congress, 27 percent of all Democrats and 30 percent of

SBC's Democrats had political ideology scores below 60. In the 95th Congress, 32 percent of the Senate's Democrats and 30 percent of those on SBC rated below 60 in political ideology.

In the House, the Democrats initially sought ideological balance, but they were later impelled to establish a liberal preponderance. About two-thirds of HBC's Democrats in the 94th Congress were liberals or moderates, about the same as the incidence in the House. Overall, the mean political ideology scores for HBC and House Democrats were virtually identical, with only three-tenths of a percentage point separating the two groups.

The Republican pattern on the two committees was markedly different. All HBC Republicans in both the 94th and 95th Congresses were in the most-conservative political ideology category; only one of the Republicans placed on SBC during that period scored higher than 60 in the ADA/ACA ratings. This difference between Budget Committee Democrats and Republicans cannot be accounted for solely by the ideological compositions of the two parties. The Republicans on the Budget Committees have not been representative of the Republican Party in either the House or the Senate. As measured by their ADA and ACA ratings, HBC and SBC Republicans have been significantly more conservative than their party colleagues. In the 94th Congress, SBC Republicans scored 13 points less on the combined scale than did all Senate Republicans; in the 95th Congress, they were 7 points lower. A similar condition prevailed in the House where HBC Republicans were 8 points below the party average in the 94th and 95th Congresses.

The conservative preponderance on the Budget Committees was not an accident but a design by Republicans to thwart what they feared would be a liberal majority on the two committees. Republican leaders were concerned that if each party filled its seats with a balanced membership, the Budget Committees would be disposed toward high government spending and big budget deficits. To counter this possibility, they stacked the two committees with conservative Republicans. As a Republican leader in the House explained: "The Committee has been tilted in one direction on the Democratic side, so we move in the other direction to counterbalance it. . . . If you look down the line on the Republican side, almost without exception our members are fiscal conservatives."

Democratic balance and Republican imbalance led to committees which were not ideologically representative of the House or Senate. In the 94th Congress, both committees were more conservative than their parent bodies. In both, a coalition of Republicans and conservatives came close to commanding a majority. The six Republicans plus the three Southern Democrats on SBC often outvoted the liberal bloc. The 17-8 Democratic margin in HBC assured a liberal-moderate majority on most issues, but there were a number of close calls and the budget resolutions were not so liberal in spending policy as some Democrats wanted.

In the 95th Congress, House Democrats countered the Republican strategy by replacing moderates and conservatives with liberals. Inasmuch as HBC's limited term assures high turnover, it was possible to replace 8 of the 17 Democrats on the committee. Democrats leaving HBC had an average political ideology score of 63; the added Democrats averaged 83 on the combined ADA/ACA scale. A matchup of the departing and new Democrats reveals the liberal tilt on HBC. One Appropriations Committee slot was shifted from a moderate (Smith) to a liberal (Obey); two Ways and Means Democrats (Gibbons and Landrum) were replaced by congressmen (Fisher and Pike) with more liberal voting records. Of the 11 Democrats competing for at-large seats on HBC, the most conservative contender (Runnels) was the only one rejected by the party caucus.

These changes resulted in a Budget Committee which was no longer representative of House Democrats. HBC Democrats scored 12 points higher in political ideology than all House Democrats, and the bias was especially pronounced in the most liberal group (political ideology scores above 75). Two-thirds of HBC's Democrats now were in this most liberal category, compared with only 40 percent for the House. This Democratic tactic had a further effect of sharply polarizing the two parties in the Budget Committee. The spread between HBC Democrats and Republicans averaged almost 60 points in the 95th Congress, compared with 40 points for the House as a whole.

Conservative strength has been potentially more troublesome for SBC Democrats because they have only a four-seat edge on the committee. Nevertheless, the Democrats have persisted with ideological balance, avoiding the polarization that has beset the budget process in the House. As a consequence, a bipartisan working relationship encompassing all but the most liberal Democrats and the most conservative Republicans has managed to submerge ideological differences. A broad majority on the committee has become accustomed to considering budget issues as "How much?" disputes, not as matters of great ideological portent. With SBC able to garner overwhelming support for its budget resolutions, Senate Democratic leaders were not inclined to alter its makeup. Senator Muskie tried to recruit some liberals in the 95th Congress, but at the time it was exceedingly difficult to attract Senators to SBC and hardest of all to get liberals with years of service to join the committee. SBC had to settle for those who could be cajoled into membership on the committee. The Budget Committee was a more alluring assignment in the 96th Congress, partly as a result of rules changes to be discussed later. Because of competition for membership, the committee was enlarged from 16 to 20 members, and 4 of the new Democrats were moderates or liberals.

Committee Representation

Budgeting intrudes on the legislative interests of most congressional committees. It directly affects the tax and Appropriations Committees but also impinges on the work of the authorizing committees. This sprawl of the congressional budget process suggests a final aspect to balance, giving a diversity of House and Senate committees' "membership" on the Budget Committees. Table 9 displays the number of Budget Committee members on each of the other standing committees of the House and Senate.

Even though it has more members than SBC, the House Budget Committee overlaps with fewer committees. In the 95th Congress, only one Senate Committee (Rules and Administration) lacked representation on SBC. In the House, by contrast, nine standing committees had no members on HBC. The gap narrowed in the 96th Congress, with a half-dozen House and two Senate committees unrepresented on the Budget Committees. The chief reason for the disparity between the two chambers is that 10 of HBC's members are drawn from just two committees, while all of SBC's members are selected from the entire Senate membership. Another reason is that all Senators sit on at least two standing committees (in addition to Budget) while most Representatives have only a single other committee assignment. Thus, in the 95th Congress, the 16 SBC Senators held 33 other committee posts, while the 25 HBC members had only 27 other positions. Inasmuch as 10 of the HBC slots are reserved for Appropriations and Ways and Means, there are not enough remaining seats to cover all of the other House committees. With many committees not represented at all, and most of the others represented either by a majority or minority member, HBC cannot routinely use its members as conduits to other House committees. Within HBC, the linkages tend to be hit or miss, de-

Table 9

NUMBER OF BUDGET COMMITTEE MEMBERS ON HOUSE AND SENATE STANDING COMMITTEES, 95th AND 96th CONGRESSES

Committee	95th Congress	96th Congress
House:		
Agriculture	0	1
Appropriations	5	5
Armed Services	2	1
Banking, Finance, and Urban Affairs	5	2
District of Columbia	0	1
Education and Labor	1	1
Government Operations	0	0
House Administration	0	1
Interior and Insular Affairs	0	0
International Relations [2]	1	2
Interstate and Foreign Commerce	1	2
Judiciary	1	1
Merchant Marine and Fisheries	2	1
Post Office and Civil Service	2	0
Public Works and Transportation	1	2
Rules	1	1
Science and Technology	0	1
Small Business	0	0
Standards of Official Conduct	0	0
Veterans' Affairs	0	0
Ways and Means	5	5
Senate:		
Agriculture, Nutrition, and Forestry	3	1
Appropriations	6	6
Armed Services	1	2
Banking, Housing, and Urban Affairs	2	3
Commerce, Science, and Transportation	2	7
Energy and Natural Resources	4	4
Environment and Public Works	4	5
Finance	1	2
Foreign Relations	1	2
Governmental Affairs	4	2
Human Resources [1]	2	4
Judiciary	2	3
Rules and Administration	0	0
Veterans Affairs	1	0

[1] Renamed Labor and Human Resources in the 96th Congress.

[2] Renamed Foreign Affairs in the 96th Congress.

Source: Tabulated from committee rosters.

pending on whether a particular committee has anyone on HBC and on the extent to which members are inclined to function as brokers or representatives for their committees.

Because no chairman of an Appropriations or Ways and Means subcommittee has been elected to HBC, the substantial overlap in membership has not been the main channel for dealings with the Budget Committee. HBC Chairman Giaimo is one of the Democrats on Appropriations, but he cannot speak for the autonomous subcommittees. Barber Conable uses his position as ranking Republican on Ways and Means to communicate some of that committee's interests to HBC, but his minority status limits his role as a link to the tax committee. Most of the others who serve concurrently on Budget and Appropriations or Ways and Means are either too conservative or too junior to function as unofficial spokesmen for their committees, though they have been influential on matters closely related to their particular spheres of interest.

Although they have been drawn from all but a few Senate committees, SBC members do not cover all committees equally. Some committees have only one SBC member, one has had as many as seven, and in both the 95th and 96th Congresses, Appropriations had six Senators who also held SBC positions. Finance and Armed Services have been two of the most underrepresented committees on SBC. Despite its broad involvement in budgetary matters, Finance did not have a single SBC Democrat in the 95th Congress and only one in the 96th. Armed Services has sent only junior Democrats to the Budget Committee. When Sam Nunn was selected for the new committee in 1974, he was the lowest-ranking Democrat on Armed Services, and when he left SBC in 1977, his place was taken by Wendell Anderson, the newest Democrat on Armed Services in the 95th Congress. Armed Services' representation increased in the 96th Congress, but the two new appointees were still in their first Senate terms.

GETTING ON AND OFF THE BUDGET COMMITTEES

Every Member of Congress is a potential Budget Committee member, but the methods and criteria for making the appointments effectively narrow the prospect of being selected. The "balanced" Democratic slate on HBC in the 94th Congress, its liberal bias in the 95th Congress, and the Republican preference for conservatives all point to a selection process in which members do not get on the Budget Committees merely by wanting to. Liberal Republicans face a "don't bother to apply" situation; for conservative Democrats, the same unwritten rule might be emerging in the House. When SBC was provisionally organized in 1974, Sen. Charles H. Percy, who had been the most active Republican in the drafting of the Congressional Budget Act, was denied a seat, even though he expressed an interest in it. In 1977, Rep. Harold Runnels was turned down for a second two-year term on HBC, even though he originally had been appointed for four years.

The Role of the Leadership

The pattern just described suggests an active role by Democratic and Republican leaders in the selection process. In the House, Democratic candidates are nominated by the party's Steering and Policy Committee (an arm of the leadership) and approved by the caucus. The procedure is similar to that used for Democratic appointments to other House committees, but it partly deviates from the method used for the first HBC selections in 1974 and 1975. Initially, the chairmen of Ways and Means and Appropriations each nominated three Democrats from their committees, but in 1977 the Steering and Policy Committee made all Democratic nominations. This shift bolstered the leadership's role in making appointments and facilitated the addition of liberals to HBC. The caucus votes separately for Appropriations, Ways and Means, and at-large members, so that candidates within each of these groups compete against one another for HBC positions. In the Senate, Democratic nominations are made by a steering committee with approval by the Democratic Conference.

Republican selections in the House and Senate are made by party leaders, acting through their Committee on Committees. Although this arrangement gives them a dominant voice, congressional leaders do not always get their way. In 1974, the six nominated Republican Senators all came from Appropriations and Finance, but rank-and-file Republicans voted in conference to substitute two members from other committees.

In making their selections, party leaders are guided by two considerations: the desired composition of the Budget Committees, and expressions of interest by Members. The leaders usually pick interested Members of Congress unless an appointment would unbalance the committee or deviate from the preferred ideological makeup. Expressions of interest have been decisive in years when there has been little or no competition for the available slots. In 1974, three Democratic contenders for HBC were defeated in the caucus; there were two losers in 1975 and another two in 1977. However, interest in the Budget Committee perked up significantly in 1979. In the House, the Democrats had more than 20 applicants, three times the number of vacancies; in the Senate, four seats were added to SBC in order to satisfy Senators seeking Budget assignments. The Budget Committees, like many other committees, are not equally alluring in every legislative season.

Expressions of interest account for some of the unevenness in the distribution of Budget Committee memberships among congressional committees. Particularly in the Senate, committees with a concentration of members interested in the new process tend to have more Budget Committee positions than do committees on which the budget process is regarded with hostility or indifference. Several members of the Senate Governmental Affairs Committee (which had primary jurisdiction over the Budget Act) expressed interest in the budget process and this interest was translated into four 95th Congress placements on SBC. Similarly, Senate Appropriations has developed a working relationship with SBC, on which it has six positions. But most Senators on Armed Services and Finance have been wary of the budget process, and not eager to serve on the Budget Committee. This is the main reason why each of these committees has only one SBC seat.

Occasionally, congressional leaders have tried to thwart the ambition of a Member of Congress by keeping him off a Budget Committee. Before the 95th Congress opened, Rep. Fortney H. (Pete) Stark announced his intention to seek the chairmanship of HBC, although he was not yet a member of the committee. To be eligible for chairman, Stark had to win one of the three HBC slots available to Ways and Means Democrats. But as the low vote-getter in a four-candidate race, Stark was eliminated from the competition. Two years later, House leaders tried to thwart the interests of another Ways and Means Democrat but failed. Rep. Jim Jones was nominated for HBC by Ways and Means Democrats, but passed over by the party's Steering and Policy Committee in favor of a more liberal Member. Jones challenged the rejection and was awarded a seat by the caucus.

Perhaps the most significant denial of expressed interest occurred in 1977 when, according to persons interviewed, Senator Long privately indicated that he would like an SBC position, but it was not forthcoming. However, his Louisiana colleague, Bennett Johnston, joined the Budget Committee, reportedly at Long's behest.

Duration of Membership

Members become attached to committees because they expect to spend their legislative careers on them. The seniority system encourages Members to regard their committees as permanent assignments. Legislative mobility usually is concentrated in a Member's early years in Congress as less preferred positions are vacated in favor of choice assignments.

From this standpoint, HBC is an anomaly on Capitol Hill: it is a permanent committee with a permanent mission, but with rotating membership. The Budget Act limited members to no more than four years on HBC within any 10-year period, but at the instigation of the Democratic Caucus, the limit was raised to 6 years in 1979. The arguments in favor of a lengthened term included the contention that members would have an opportunity to function more effectively on the committee if they could remain on it after becoming educated in budgetary issues and techniques. But there has been little support for making HBC membership permanent. As a consequence, representatives joining HBC know that their affiliation will last for a maximum of six years, and that no matter how earnest their commitment, they cannot build seniority on it. While on HBC, they continue on their permanent committees, where they can exercise the legislative influence accumulated from past service or do the work which might pay off in future recognition. In their permanent posts, Members of Congress can acquire standing as legislative specialists; on HBC, they work with little prospect of future reward.

HBC's unique limitation means that Members of Congress do not have to consider the long-term effects of budget service on their congressional careers. They can take their turns on the committee and then leave when the time is reached. Most HBC members take this rotation for granted and even see it as a desirable arrangement, though not one they would want applied to their permanent committee assignments. In interviews, a number of Members scheduled to leave HBC at the end of the 95th Congress suggested that rotating service is an excellent way of exposing many members to the budget process and giving them a broader view of the federal government than can be obtained from work on a regular committee. Because they had not formed permanent attachments to HBC, most saw their departure as simply going on to other things rather than breaking with their budgetary interests.

In the interviews conducted for this study, only one HBC member deviated from this pattern; he was a young Democrat who professed, "I don't allow myself to think about leaving the committee; I'm really going to miss it. When I think about that time, it makes me very sad. The Budget Committee is where I really have had an opportunity to become part of the process and make a contribution." This member differed from his HBC colleagues in a fundamental way: the budget process had become his principal legislative interest, the yardstick by which he measured his legislative worth. He was more than just a temporary Budget Committee member. He was one of the few whose legislative behavior was significantly influenced by the budget process. Nevertheless, when an opportunity opened on another committee in which he had a career interest, this Member abandoned HBC in favor of his new appointment. Because of the rules change mentioned above, he could have remained on HBC for another two years, but this enticement was not sufficient to keep him on the Budget Committee.

The transitory character of HBC membership contrasts with the permanence of the staff. The staff provides the committee with continuity, a departure from congressional reliance on seniority to transmit group roles and expectations to new members. Although members of the Budget Committee generally have high regard for their staff, they are uneasy about dependence on these people. One Member of Congress argued that the combination of permanent staff with transitory members has been "to divorce the decision-making process from elected members and give it to sort of a shadow staff."

The difficulty of getting members to accept SBC assignments forced the Senate to retreat from its rule limiting Senators to two "major" committees. The Budget Act allowed SBC members to sit on a third committee during the 94th Congress. It would have required these Senators to drop either SBC or one of their other committees in 1977, when the 95th Congress organized. In the summer of 1976, Senator Muskie's budget staff estimated that if the two-committee limitation were activated, SBC might lose all of the other Democrats on the committee. Nevertheless, it advised Muskie not to seek a delay in the two-committee rule but to concentrate on pressing a few members to stay on and to fill the other slots with junior Members.[6] This approach was grounded on a number of assumptions, including the expectation that new Members would be more committed to the budget process and more responsive to Muskie's leadership than would experienced Members who had built up seniority and expertise on other committees.

Muskie realized that protracted uncertainty about the two-committee rule was an impediment to full acceptance of SBC by its members. As long as their status was clouded by delay in deciding whether or not to make SBC a permanent third committee, most members, understandably, hedged their identification with the committee. They would not remain if the limitation were enforced, but, while the possibility existed that SBC would be established as a third committee, Members had an interest in strengthening its role. Although group ties have been stronger in SBC than on the House committee, Senators prudently restrained their investment in a committee which they might have had to abandon in a few years.

It proved impossible to induce junior Members to commit themselves to SBC as one of their two major committees. An embarrassing situation resulted in which the Senate adopted one set of rules for SBC early in the 95th Congress but had to violate the rules one week later in making committee assignments. As part of the reorganization of its committee structure, the Senate, in February 1977, voted to "grandfather" Senators previously appointed to the Budget Committees for another two years, but to count SBC as one of the major committees for Senators newly appointed to it. A few days later, bowing to what Majority Leader Byrd described as "extenuating circumstances to meet a temporary situation," the Senate placed five members on SBC, allowing each two other major posts.[7]

But the "extenuating circumstances" would not disappear. The Senate faced the issue again in 1979, when, as already noted, interest in budget work was rising. Senators on SBC wanted to retain it as a third committee; others wanted to get onto it without surrendering any other post. Of necessity, therefore, SBC was made a permanent third committee; for some, it was a fourth major assignment. With permanence now assured, SBC can become an important part of the legislative careers of its members.

When Members sense a common destiny with a committee on which they serve, they have a stake in building its institutional

6. "Committee Membership and Reorganization," Memorandum for Senator Muskie, August 23, 1976. The memorandum was prepared by the four top Democratic staff members of SBC.

7. 123 *Congressional Record* (daily ed., February 11, 1977) S2648.

position in Congress. They become more receptive to cues from the committee in determining how to vote on matters affecting its interests. They stand together with it when the committee is threatened by other power holders on Capitol Hill. It is to their advantage for the committee to perform effectively as a group, even if this sometimes requires the subordination of their own preferences to the group's. If, however, members expect no enduring relationship with the committees on which they serve, they will behave on the basis of individual interest and respond to cues from sources other than their committees. They will subordinate the group's interests to their own, and they will not fight to make their committee into a power center.

These considerations help to explain some of the behavioral differences between the two Budget Committees. Temporariness on HBC does not make its members indifferent to budgetary outcomes or indolent about their legislative responsibilities. Rather, it affects the extent to which these Members of Congress perceive their own legislative status as intertwined with the fortunes of the Budget Committee. HBC is a limited investment because it can yield only a limited return to its members. The Senate Budget Committee offers the prospect of rising in legislative prominence as its own fortunes improve. The committee can reward its members if they act in ways that enhance the committee's position in Congress. (Significantly, even during the period of uncertainty over SBC's status, most of its members expected to retain their seats on it, if only because of the Senate's historic reluctance to take away committee assignments. Accordingly, they had reason to act as if they were permanent members.)

The various differences between the two committees will be elaborated in the course of this study. The key operational distinctions that flow from those differences can be summarized as follows: HBC is split into partisan factions; SBC often submerges partisanship in favor of a unified position. HBC members go their separate ways when budget resolutions are debated in the House; SBC members overwhelmingly support their resolutions on the floor. HBC has been hesitant to fight other committees in the open; SBC has waged a number of public battles with various Senate committees. HBC is increasingly dependent on party leaders; SBC is substantially independent from the leadership. On each of these counts, SBC extracts more group loyalty from its members; on each, HBC maintains weaker control over its members.

But differences between the two committees are a matter of degree. SBC has not been welded into a perfectly unified group, and HBC has not been splintered into an assemblage of 25 members, each going his or her own way. Moreover, duration of membership is only one of the factors influencing the behavior of the Budget Committees and their members. The character of budget work—to be examined shortly—also diminishes the attachments of members to these committees.

Leaving the Committees

Turnover on the Budget Committees has been quite high. Only 5 of the 16 Senators on SBC in 1975, and 8 of HBC's 25 members, were still on these committees four years later. Half of those who left the Budget Committees did so by reason of departure from Congress; the others were either bumped by rivals for their seats or traded in Budget for a preferred assignment. Because SBC membership is costless for the Democrats, they can continue on the committee even if they are displeased with its status or performance. A notable exception was Sen. Sam Nunn, who voluntarily resigned his SBC seat in 1977. Nunn's move was significant because of his reputation as one of the Senate's most promising junior Members, intelligent, hard working, and likely to become chairman of the Armed Services Committee at a young age.[8] "He was bored," one SBC staff aide speculated, while another suggested that Nunn's aversion to big budget deficits prompted his disassociation from the budget process. Other Senators have manifested their lack of interest by not participating in SBC meetings, a practice addressed in the next section.

The incentives are different for SBC Republicans because of their party's rule denying them seats on some of the most prestigious Senate committees. Few Senators can be expected to forgo assignment to Finance, Appropriations, Armed Services, or Foreign Relations in order to remain on the Budget Committee. In 1979, three Republicans gave up their SBC seats in order to take prestigious assignments on other committees. They were replaced by freshmen who lacked the seniority to secure more coveted positions. For upwardly mobile Republicans, the Senate Budget Committee might turn out to be merely the first stop rather than the permanent stage on which legislative aspirations are fulfilled.

---

8. Don Winter, "Hard Work Is Paying Off for Georgia's Sam Nunn," in *National Journal*, (November 26, 1977), pp. 1850-52.

In the House, the limited duration of membership makes for substantial turnover among Members continuing in Congress. But even there, a number of Members of Congress left the committee before their terms had expired. Rep. Richard Bolling, who had been the floor manager of the Budget Act in the House, left HBC after only a brief stint on it, preferring to concentrate on the Joint Economic Committee of which he had recently become cochairman. In the 95th Congress, Rep. John Rhodes dropped HBC in order to give more attention to his responsibilities as minority leader. Other high-ranking Republicans (Elford A. Cederberg and Del Clawson, for example) left the committee claiming that other legislative work demanded their time.

When the limitation on membership was stretched to six years in 1979, most of those who had previously been scheduled to leave opted to remain. The two added years were a "free good" for these members and they willingly accepted it. But there were a couple of exceptions. Butler Derrick yielded HBC in order to get on the Rules Committee, and Parren Mitchell obtained seats on the Small Business and Joint Economic Committees. Both had been active and important HBC Democrats: Derrick had headed a task force organized by the Speaker to shepherd the budget resolutions through the House; Mitchell had been the committee's foremost spokesman for social programs. Neither saw his long-term congressional goals enhanced by two more years.

BEING A BUDGET COMMITTEE MEMBER

When Members of Congress join an established committee, they become part of an ongoing social system. They learn its ways of doing business, its traditions and group norms, the unwritten rules that pattern its members into a functioning social unit. There is nothing sinister about this socialization process; it is mostly a matter of Members' embracing the habits of the committees on which they spend their legislative careers. Socializing influences are not equally powerful on all committees or equally effective for all Members of Congress. Some committees have a strong sense of tradition; others are breaking away from their past. Some Members "go along to get along"; others make their mark by challenging established practices. But most Members come to define their careers and shape their legislative interests in terms of their committee identification. For most, status and power are by-products of their committee attachments. The recognition accorded them as specialists in particular legislative areas ordinarily derives from the committees on which they serve.

The Budget Committees began with no past or traditions, no repertoire of expectations and behaviors into which recruits could be socialized. The committees had to learn along with their members; they had to improvise written and unwritten rules of conduct as they went along. Members had to come to grips, for example, with the issue of whether the Budget Committees would be ones on which partisanship would be rampant or muted; both patterns coexist on Capitol Hill, and both are acceptable, but each committee had to carve out its own path.

Newness alone did not prevent the socialization of members. Rather, it meant that each Budget Committee had to weld its members together on a basis other than tradition and transmitted norms. The sense of excitement and high purpose and the great expectations of the budget process could have bonded the members of the House and Senate Budget Committees into political units in which group identifications strongly shaped legislative interests.

It has not happened that way. Attachments to the Budget Committees for most members have been limited and weak. Few members have altered their legislative interests or behavior in any significant way. Few perceive themselves as members of a committee with a common purpose and spirit. By 1977, the novelty and excitement were gone and what animated the committees was a bundle of routines, the cyclical business of processing budget resolutions, the busywork of operating a budget process. The ease with which most members would leave the Budget Committees if any price were exacted for remaining indicates that these committees have not been important influences on members' legislative careers. There have been some exceptions: the chairmen and SBC's ranking Republican, who have received notice and applause for their budgetary roles, and perhaps a few others. For most members, service on the committee has turned into a grind or, at best, an opportunity to protect some of their other legislative interests.

Members have learned that it is all right to go their separate ways even while coming together on the Budget Committees. This separateness is understandably more pronounced on HBC because of its temporary membership. The committee tolerates each member's use of the budget process to protect or advance his or her favorite programs. Except on certain procedural questions, there is little group loyalty or shared purpose. This HBC behavior was commented on by a principal staff aide on the Senate Budget Committee: "When you have statutory representation from the major power centers and everybody has a parent committee to which they will return within a few years, the Budget Committee is unlikely to take dramatic new initiatives not directed by the places to which the members will return." A somewhat similar statement was made by a top HBC staffer: "I think the members of the House see the Budget Committee as representative of the whole House rather than as a separate identifiable interest." Unlike the House Appropriations Committee, which has a tradition (though not so effective as it once was) against public dissent within the committee, HBC reports spawn a diversity of dissenting and separate opinions.

There is definitely more group loyalty on SBC. Members band together in support of their resolutions and defend the Budget Committee against floor attack. But this common purpose yields to competing objectives formed by attachments to other committees. Several of the floor amendments offered by SBC members to the first resolution for fiscal 1980 attest to the comparative strength of SBC and competing loyalties. Sen. Howard N. Metzenbaum won increased funds for nutrition programs benefiting older Americans. He was supported by two SBC colleagues who also served on the Labor and Human Resources Committee which has jurisdiction over the nutrition program. Sen. Lawton Chiles sought restoration of money for Social Security, a program in which he had great interest as chairman of the Senate's Special Committee on Aging. Senator Magnuson got additional funds for food stamps, an issue on which the Appropriations Committee, of which he was chairman, was ready to act. SBC loyalties usually cannot withstand the other legislative interests of members.

The Budget Committees have done an effective job of educating their members about fiscal policy and budgeting. When the committees were established, few of their members were familiar with the techniques, nomenclature, or analytic methods of budgeting. Members were given "cram courses" by staff—seminars and briefings were common during the first year—but even more important, they learned on the job by working with budgetary data and marking up budget resolutions. From resolution to resolution, one could sense the growing confidence with which members conversed about the numbers. Active Budget Committee members have acquired a command of the language and procedures of budgeting. Federal budgeting is a complicated process, and in the beginning, members of the Budget Committees were befuddled by it. In markup, they constantly had to be advised by staff as to what they really intended to say or do. Members habitually confused outlays (the cash spent by government) with budget authority (the obligations authorized by Congress). They frequently talked about authorizations (legislation establishing a program) while intending to deal with appropriations (legislation financing the program). Within a year, most of the members were able to converse on budgetary matters without mistaking one for the other. Sen. Pete V. Domenici displayed his education the second time that SBC marked up a budget resolution:

> I have begun to put a difference in my mind between the words authorization and budget authority. I am not sure that six months ago I did, but I am now. I think I am talking about budget authority and not authorization.[9]

The budget process also has educated committee members concerning a range of federal programs beyond their specialized legislative interests. As a result of budgetary service, they have a broader view of how programs relate to one another and add up to a federal budget. They have received a general education—not intensive enough to make them experts about all federal programs, but sufficient to enable them to make reasoned judgments about the financing of such programs. HBC members have this sensitizing effect of the budget process in mind when they speak of the advantages of rotating membership. They believe that Congress would benefit from a more comprehensive perspective.

Budget Committee members have become more knowledgeable with regard to the economic implications of budget policy. Most members came to the Budget Committees with preconceived notions about budget deficits, inflation, and unemployment. Few understood much about how the figures in the budget affect (and are affected by) economic performance. Through the congressional budget process, many have developed a working understanding of economic tools and concepts; some have become proficient in interpreting economic data and relating them to budget issues. Economics training appears to be more effective on SBC than the House committee, perhaps because the latter's members tend to be locked into ideological positions and because HBC has less of a "macro" perspective on budgetary issues.

---

9. SBC markup of second budget resolution for fiscal 1976, transcript, p. 205.

Economics education has proceeded on two levels: an enhanced understanding of the "arithmetic" of budgeting, and, for some, changed views on fiscal policy. Before the budget process was introduced, it was convenient for members to think that a reduction in federal expenditures would produce an equivalent drop in the budget deficit. Now many Budget Committee members recognize that during periods of high unemployment, an expenditure cut can lead to a decline in revenues as well, so that there would not be a dollar-for-dollar reduction in the budget deficit. For some members, new understanding has induced a change in thinking about fiscal policy. The following exchange occurred after Sen. Henry L. Bellmon, a fiscal conservative, supported additional spending for public service jobs with the claim that they would lower the costs of the unemployment compensation and food stamp programs:

Chiles: Do you really believe that?
Hollings: Do you really believe that?
Bellmon: Yes, I believe it.
Chiles: You sound like an economist now.
Bellmon: At this point, I am.[10]

Education, however, is not a substitute for socialization. One relates to the substantive skills of committee members, the other to group behavior. As they have become more adept at budgeting, members have not become more attached to the process or more oriented to their committees. Budget Committee members are buffeted by various disincentives against developing strong ties to the process. One of these has already been considered, the temporary and uncertain tenure of Budget Committee positions. Another derives from the peculiarities of budget work in Congress. The Budget Committees do not have normal legislative agendas; they do not develop legislation in the same manner as other congressional committees. To understand the Budget Committees, one must look at the kinds of work that they perform.

WORKING ON THE BUDGET COMMITTEES

The committee system is Congress's way of dividing legislative work and power among its Members. The system gives everybody a part of the action but assures that no one dominates all areas of

10. SBC markup of first budget resolution for fiscal 1976, transcript, p. 635.

legislation. The system also bonds members to their committees because, for most Members of Congress, power and status are a function of the committees on which they serve. With appointment to a committee, a Member becomes part of a group with custody over a designated field of legislation. Members tend to concentrate on matters within the jurisdiction of their committees, acquiring the expertise, position, and control of staff by means of which power is exercised on Capitol Hill. For committees and Members alike, specialization is the surest road to legislative success.

Specialization

A problem of the Budget Committees is that they have few exclusive areas of specialization. Almost everything they do spills over into the substantive jurisdictions of other committees. Because they have no unchallenged "turf," no aspect of public policy walled off from anybody else's business, they cannot reward their members in the currency in which careers are built in Congress: the opportunity to develop one's specialty. Rather, the Budget Committees and their members are often perceived as dilettantes and meddlers, not as experts who have earned standing as legislative experts. Even worse, the overlapping of membership and substantive interests with other committees deters Budget Committee members from compartmentalizing their loyalties, disregarding their other legislative interests as they work on budgetary issues. They neither forget nor ignore the fact that one of their colleagues is on Armed Services, another on Education and Labor, a third on Judiciary, on down the membership list. The members of the Budget Committees are brought together to deal with matters on which they are divided in their everyday legislative work. All bring their particular specialties into the meeting room, and throughout the process of budgeting most exhibit their identities as members of the other committees on which they sit. Merely by watching the markup of a budget resolution, an observer can ascertain the legislative interests of many Budget Committee members.

Budgetary procedure is the domain of the Budget Committees, their main opportunity to gain clear recognition as the specialists for Congress. These committees are the custodians of the process, the experts in putting together the numbers and monitoring budget-related developments. It is in the interest of the Budget Committees to band together in support of the procedures prescribed for the conduct of budgetary business in Congress. If they cannot safeguard the methods established for making budget decisions, the committees would lose purpose and place on Capitol Hill. When they act on procedural issues, Budget Committee members can put aside their substantive concerns—the matters that divide them—and unite behind a common position. But procedure can almost never be wholly divorced from substance. A Budget Act deadline, for example, can stop action on a bill dearly wanted by its committee of jurisdiction. What cues does a Member of Congress serving on both the Budget Committee and the "legislative" committee take: the Budget Committee's enforcement of the budget process or the legislative committee's advancement of its program?

Because substance divides while procedure unites, it makes sense for the Budget Committees to portray such issues in process terms. Not only will a procedural matter ordinarily be more successful in unifying the Budget Committees; it also is more likely to attract support from the House and Senate at large. The Budget Committees have behaved differently in staking out their roles as procedural specialists. HBC has cautiously stressed fidelity to the deadlines and technical requirements of the Budget Act, only rarely venturing beyond these to substantive issues. SBC, however, has tried to cast various substantive questions as matters affecting the viability of the budget process. On occasion, tax and spending legislation at variance with the amounts adopted in the budget resolutions has been vigorously challenged by SBC as a violation of the process. The procedural and substantive differences between the two committees are the subject of later chapters dealing with the formulation and enforcement of congressional budget decisions.

The most "socialized" members of the Budget Committees have been those whose activity has focused primarily on procedural matters. Rather than viewing the process as a means for advancing their program interests, they have perceived it as a mechanism for bringing budgetary discipline to Congress. Rep. Butler Derrick's case offers a clear example of this behavior in the House. Derrick was assigned to HBC as a freshman, before he had established legislative interests on other committees. Although he lacked seniority, Derrick was one of HBC's most active members, chairing a task force on the budget process, sponsoring a series of publications on problems of budgetary control, and heading a drive to secure floor passage of the budget resolutions. As a new Member from a conservative state (South Carolina), Derrick voted against the first budget resolution in 1975. But his commitment to the budget process spurred a turnaround in his voting record and he subsequently supported the budget resolutions.

Derrick, however, has been one of the few Budget Committee members to put procedural interests above substantive results. Most others measure their commitment to their committee in terms of the outcomes of the budget process.

Fiscal Policy

The Budget Committees have a second area of specialization, national economic policy. Although the Joint Economic Committee (JEC) was organized for this purpose after World War II, it lacks legislative jurisdiction and functions in an advisory or research role. Congress does not have to take any action pursuant to a JEC report or recommendation. It does, however, have to act on the "macro" numbers presented by the Budget Committees and, in so doing, Congress participates in shaping national policy with respect to economic growth, employment, and inflation. In jurisdictional terms, it would appear advantageous for the Budget Committees to stake their claim as the fiscal policy experts of Congress.

These committees recognize that fiscal policy involves some of the most contentious political issues of our times: the appropriate size of the federal government, trade-offs between jobs and inflation, the size of the deficit. A budget process that accentuates these issues would sharpen cleavages within the Budget Committees and Congress. Moreover, in casting the budget debate in fiscal terms, these committees might be assuming more responsibility for economic performance than they can deliver. They might be deemed culpable for shortfalls in economic results, or for budget targets that tolerated high unemployment or inflation.

Although the Budget Committees have been forthright about the economic assumptions underlying their recommendations, they have not encouraged a wide-open debate on national economic objectives. Fiscal policy has been a derivative concern, and the talk has centered on budget numbers rather than jobs, economic growth, or prices. At no time do the members of the Budget Committees vote on economic policy directly; nor do such votes occur when the budget is debated in the House or Senate. JEC has not intervened with its own economic assumptions or objectives, and the Budget Committees have rebuffed proposals to stress economic matters. Thus, HBC Democrats have warded off Republican attempts to divide floor debate into a macroeconomic stage at which the budget aggregates would be decided, and a functional stage at which spending would be allocated among the budget categories.

The fiscal role of the Budget Committees was considered muted in 1978 when Congress acted on the Humphrey-Hawkins legislation setting full employment as an economic goal of the United States. When the legislation reached the House in March 1978, it contained a procedure for explicit congressional determination of national economic objectives. As proposed, JEC would formulate an "economic objectives" resolution which would be adopted two weeks before the first budget resolution. JEC would have gained a significant role in making fiscal policy at the expense of the Budget Committees and its work would have upstaged the annual budget process.

HBC Republicans, who had been campaigning for a two-stage budget process with an opportunity to vote first on the aggregates, backed away from explicit fiscal targets, while committee liberals, who had opposed the "macro" procedure, now embraced the economic objectives approach. Barber Conable led the opposition, arguing that the new scheme would reduce "the Budget Committee to largely an arithmetic function." HBC's ranking Republican Delbert Latta protested "a major attack . . . on the procedures and on the jurisdiction of the Budget Committee" while the junior Republican Ralph Regula urged the House "to avoid destroying . . . an effective way to deal with budget problems."[11]

This stalwart opposition by HBC Republicans had little to do with the jurisdiction of the Budget Committee and much to do with dislike for the social policies embedded in Humphrey-Hawkins. If the Republicans voted to defend their political interests rather than their Budget Committee, HBC liberals behaved in the same manner, abandoning their committee in order to advance competing objectives. David Obey argued for the new JEC procedure because it would provide "a direct vote on items like unemployment, like employment growth. . . . I did not want to lose the ability of the House to vote on those specific targets." HBC colleague Parren Mitchell noted that without the new emphasis on fiscal policy, information on employment "would, at best, appear as a kind of appendage to the budget resolution." A third HBC Democrat, Donald Fraser, explained how fiscal policy issues get submerged in the budget process:

> On the Committee on the Budget we deal with all kinds of problems: with defense spending, with welfare spending, with the problems

11. 124 *Congressional Record* (daily ed., March 16, 1978) H2137, H2138.

affecting health, and how much we are going to do for education. The Humphrey-Hawkins objectives will simply disappear in the morass of considerations that the Committee on the Budget has to take into account unless we first fix those goals, talk about them, decide upon them, and then try to get the budget process to effectively account for those objectives as we go into the budget process itself.[12]

With HBC members unwilling to regard the issue as a test of their committee's jurisdiction, voting on Conable's motion to remove the JEC procedure split along political lines. All of the Republicans and most of the moderate and conservative Democrats supported the Conable amendment; seven HBC Democrats, including Chairman Giaimo, opposed it.[13]

In the Senate, the Humphrey-Hawkins bill posed a different challenge to SBC's fiscal policy role. One proposal would have limited the budget of the federal government to no more than 20 percent of the gross national product. Another would have required the Budget Committees to set a new date for reducing unemployment to 4 percent if the President determined that that goal could not be met by the 1983 deadline set in the legislation. Senator Muskie won adoption of an amendment eliminating precise arithmetical targets from the first provision; Senator Bellmon followed with an amendment giving the Budget Committees discretion with respect to unemployment objectives. Both SBC leaders framed the issue in terms of Budget Committee flexibility to deal with different fiscal needs and conditions.[14] But most SBC rank-and-filers voted in accord with their political preferences. In fact, 8 of the 12 SBC members who voted on both amendments flip-flopped on Budget Committee jurisdiction. SBC liberals supported Muskie's motion to eliminate a ceiling on the federal budget, but against Bellmon's proposal to get the Budget Committees off the hook with respect to employment goals. The conservatives voted for Bellmon, but against Muskie, venting their desire for a limit on the federal budget but their opposition to a rigid full employment goal. Only Muskie, Bellmon, and a couple of moderates sided with the Budget Committee on both votes.

---

12. *Ibid.*, H2139.
13. Giaimo reportedly voted to give JEC a dominant role in fiscal policy in exchange for a commitment to extend his term as HBC chairman for another two years.
14. See 124 *Congressional Record* (daily ed., October 13, 1978) S18898, remarks of Senator Muskie, and S18914, remarks of Senator Bellmon.

Workload

Members of Congress face many conflicting demands on their time. Committee business is only one of the things they have to attend to. A committee with a heavy agenda does not always attract the attention of its members, but a committee with a light workload does not ordinarily play a significant role in its members' legislative careers.

The Budget Committees have seasonal work, the preparation of spring and fall budget resolutions. Their other activities, such as the year-round tracking of legislation and updating of budget numbers, can be performed by staff, without the involvement of the rank-and-file members. Because they have an externally mandated agenda, the members of the Budget Committees do not have to come together for the purpose of deciding what it is that they will try to accomplish. The statutory requirement simplifies the problem of establishing group objectives but also lowers the demands made on members for group support.

Because their members go long stretches of time without being engaged in budget work, both committees have sought means of attracting attention during the interval between resolutions. HBC conducts "early warning" briefings for its members at which staff review the budgetary implications of pending legislation. Attendance at these meetings is low, primarily because it is not an "actionable" use of members' time. The members talk about budgetary issues, but rarely are they called upon to take any action. SBC has been more vigorous in developing "nonresolution" activity. Shortly after it was created, SBC claimed joint jurisdiction (with Appropriations) over impoundment proposals. In 1974 and 1975, it held a number of meetings on impoundment measures, but this business diminished as impoundments became more routinized and the number of policy impoundments declined. SBC has tried to take advantage of its Budget Act jurisdiction over certain waivers (regarding the statutory deadline for reporting authorizations and the period during which budget-related legislation may be considered), but, despite a steep rise in the number of waivers, this activity also has declined. At the beginning, SBC convened its members to discuss waiver requests, but by 1977 most waivers were being processed—and approved—routinely via a telephone poll, without a committee meeting.

Participation

Workload is a necessary condition for a committee to engage

the interests of its members, but being busy does not always suffice. In order to command attention, a committee's work must have a legislative purpose that warrants priority on a crowded schedule. Members of Congress do not usually resign from a committee when they lose interest in its work; they just stop participating in its activities. Some committees regularly have a full house when they meet; others have difficulty getting a quorum. On some, members habitually make it their business to be present when votes are taken; on others, members make extensive use of proxies to record their votes.

Table 10 summarizes the voting participation rates of Budget Committee members for all roll calls on budget resolutions between 1976 and 1979.[15] Without comparative data, there is no basis for judging whether these rates are in line with those of other House and Senate committees. Comparisons, however, can be made among Budget Committee members as well as between SBC and HBC. As might be expected, Budget Committee members differ widely in their voting practices. About one-third of the members have high participation rates; they are present for 90 percent of the roll calls and they rarely vote by proxy. This category includes the chairmen of the Budget Committees who have the highest participation scores. At the other extreme, somewhat fewer than one-third are frequently absent and make extensive use of proxies. One member, Sen. James Abourezk, was present for only a handful of the more than one hundred roll calls during his four years on the Budget Committee.

Because Senators have more committee (and subcommittee) assignments than Representatives do, one would expect voting participation to be lower on SBC than on the House committee. This pattern was not borne out in 1976. Senate Budget Committee members had a slightly higher rate of participation than HBC members (77 percent versus 75 percent). Although all SBC members had at least two other major committee assignments, most gave prominence to budget work in arranging their work schedules. This participation reflected the sense of importance and promise with which the budget process was inaugurated. But overall SBC participation dropped 20 percentage points in 1977 and further in 1978. SBC participation was substantially below the rate for the House Budget Committee. The drop in participation occurred among all groupings

15. The data here refer to calendar years. Thus, the committee votes during calendar 1976 were for the fiscal 1977 budget resolutions. The 1979 votes were for the first 1980 resolution.

Table 10

VOTING PARTICIPATION RATES, HOUSE AND SENATE BUDGET COMMITTEES, 1976-79 CALENDAR YEARS

Budget Committee	Present and Voting	Non-voting
House		
1976		
All Members	75.4%	6.5%
Democrats	73.3	8.6
Republicans	79.8	1.9
1977		
All Members	77.8	4.3
Democrats	79.5	4.9
Republicans	73.9	3.1
1978		
All Members	65.0	4.4
Democrats	61.1	5.0
Republicans	73.5	3.3
1979 [a]		
All Members	79.7	0.8
Democrats	78.9	0.6
Republicans	81.4	1.4
Senate		
1976		
All Members	77.2%	14.5%
Democrats	68.5	20.3
Republicans	91.7	20.3
1977		
All Members	58.2	19.8
Democrats	55.0	23.8
Republicans	63.5	13.1
1978		
All Members	50.5	19.0
Democrats	43.6	20.4
Republicans	63.5	16.7
1979 [a]		
All Members	80.1	19.9
Democrats	77.9	22.1
Republicans	83.3	16.7

[a] Includes only the first budget resolution for fiscal 1980.

Source: Tabulated from House Budget Committee Journal and Senate Budget Committee reports on budget resolutions.

within SBC: Democrats and Republicans, liberals and conservatives. The newly appointed members did not start with a surge of enthusiasm; they participated at about the same rate as the old ones. Only two years old, the budget process had already slipped in legislative esteem and importance. It became a grind for some members, an act of futility for others. Many Senators on the Budget Committee no longer were moved to accord priority to their budget work; "another engagement" was sufficient cause for missing an SBC markup.

But in 1979 a remarkable turnaround occurred, as participation by SBC members soared above the peak rates of the first years. SBC members averaged more than 80 percent attendance at roll calls, and although participation was higher among Republicans than Democrats, every carryover Senator had a higher participation rate than in the previous year. The comparison, however, is tainted by the adoption of a no-proxy rule in 1979. In previous years, proxy voting was available to absentee members. With this option now eliminated, SBC members faced a loss of their votes if they were absent during roll calls. When the no-proxy rule was proposed by Senator Chiles, Chairman Muskie argued against it, fearing that some of his colleagues would withdraw from SBC participation rather than attend the long and arduous markups. But his apprehension was unwarranted, at least during the first year without proxies.

It should be noted that the nonvoting percentage was constant between 1977 and 1979. This means that the elimination of proxies did not lead to any increase in nonvoting. As a consequence, the investment in committee work by SBC members rose sharply in 1979. By itself, this behavioral change would not be significant, but it is consistent with other changes affecting the budget process in 1979, such as the increased interest in serving on the Budget Committees which has already been discussed.

HBC's participation experience has varied with the makeup of the committee and congressional interest in budgeting. Its participation rate rose in 1977, primarily because of the voting performances of its new members, particularly the liberal Democrats who had been added to the committee. These newcomers took their appointment as an opportunity to sway the congressional budget to a more liberal direction. But interest declined in their second year on the committee (1978), as did the interest of the other committee members. The 1979 upsurge in participation matched rising congressional interest in the budget process.

THE REWARDS OF BUDGETING

Members of Congress have various reasons for wanting legislative office, but whatever their purposes, most of the rewards come through committee service. On some committees, the prizes of membership are concentrated in a few hands, usually those of the chairman and the few other power holders who set the legislative agenda and control the staff. On other committees, power and opportunity are widely dispersed and staff is permanently assigned to subcommittees. On both these counts, the Budget Committees offer limited benefits to their rank-and-file members.

No Subcommittees

Both Budget Committees made early decisions against subcommittees. Each has a single legislative product—a comprehensive and consistent budget resolution. Quite understandably, neither wanted to divide the production of its resolutions among many competing subcommittees, each stocked with members striving to advance their favorite programs. Each budget resolution is supposed to be a financial determination of the nation's priorities; the Budget Committees did not want to invite subunits to compose "wish lists" that would then be pasted together by logrolling members. The responsibility for establishing the fiscal objectives to be realized through the budget suggests the need for a holistic perspective, not just program-by-program determinations.

In lieu of subcommittees, each Budget Committee established *ad hoc* task forces with "study" rather than "legislative" functions. In the 94th Congress, SBC had four such groups: three (energy, tax policy and expenditures, and capital needs) cut across the functional lines in the budget and one (defense) encompassed a single expenditure category. HBC set up seven task forces, four of which (national security, human resources, physical resources, and community resources) blanketed all of the functions in the budget, two (tax expenditures and economic projections) covered revenues and fiscal policy, and one (budget process) was concerned with the effectiveness of congressional budget controls.

HBC task forces have been moderately active, though less so than most subcommittees authorized to report legislation. SBC's task forces were generally inactive in the 94th Congress and they all but disappeared in the 95th. Because they are structured into the categories by which Congress makes budget decisions, HBC's task forces have been relevant to the work of the committee and, consequently, rather successful in attracting the interest of members. Through task force participation, HBC members could try to expand their influence over particular areas of the budget and have been able to relate HBC work to their other legislative activities. Representative Giaimo, for example, chaired the national security task force while he was also active on the Defense Appropriations subcommittee. Representative Mitchell's chairmanship of the human resources group dovetailed with his leadership of the Black Caucus in Congress. The SBC task forces were not (with the exception of defense) directly related to budgetary decisions and Senators did not have much prospect for legislative advantage by participating in them.

But there is a more compelling explanation for the failure of SBC task forces. Every Democrat on SBC in the 94th Congress was the chairman of one or more Senate committees or subcommittees. Most of the Republicans had ranking minority status on their own committees or subcommittees. SBC members already had opportunities to be heard and to promote their legislative interests. They gained little by having a task force without legislative purpose or staff. The situation was different for HBC Democrats, few of whom had their own subcommittees. Their ability to draw media attention and to influence the course of legislation could be augmented by investing in task force activities.

Within a few months after the task forces were organized, some SBC staffers realized that the task forces were poor substitutes for subcommittees. In a February 21, 1975, staff memorandum, John McEvoy (then the committee's chief counsel and later its staff director) argued that "in terms of the prominence of the Committee, the publicity it gets, and the amount of ground it can cover, it was a significant mistake not to establish subcommittees with clearly defined jurisdiction."[16] McEvoy referred to "a considerable amount of frustration on the part of members" and to demands by SBC Democrats for "a larger role on the Committee." Nothing was done, however, because SBC leaders (members and staff) still believed that the task forces were adequate substitutes for permanent subcommittees. The issue was revived in the summer of 1976, as Chairman Muskie considered the prospect of losing most of the Democrats if the two-committee limitation were activated. By this time, the task forces were beyond salvage and SBC needed some

16. Senate Budget Committee files.

bait with which to retain members or recruit new ones. He was advised by top staffers:

Task force chairmanships are indefinite and their charter relatively unclear. They are purposely designed to have less permanence and authority than subcommittees and are not a sufficient substitute. . . . the subcommittees could study, debate, publish, and hold hearings. . . . they could provide a forum which would not involve the full manpower and time (including yours) of the Committee for public debate of all important issues.[17]

Chairman Muskie espoused the subcommittee plan at an SBC meeting, early in the 95th Congress:

. . . the principal reason I am more receptive to the idea of subcommittees is that I have a feeling that the members of the committee may feel there is not sufficient challenge for them on a year-round basis in the work of the Budget Committee. . . . I just don't want this committee to become a one-man show or a two-man show; I want it to become a 13- or 16-man show. So if we can do it with subcommittees, if that is the strong inclination of members, if it would stimulate them to get more deeply involved in the work of the committee, then on that ground alone, I would feel disposed to experiment with it.[18]

The offer of subcommittees was too late; most SBC members had already lost interest in budget work. It also was too little, for Muskie made it clear that funds would not be available for additional staff. Subcommittees were neither rejected nor accepted by SBC in 1977; nobody cared enough to put up a fight and the idea faded without any action either way.

Staff

When Muskie withheld the prospect of additional staff, he took away one of the incentives for subcommittees. Although some Senate committees have centralized staffs, they tend to be powerful ones (such as Armed Services and Finance) where the benefit of having a say on important legislation suffices to attract members to the committee. As already noted, the prizes of membership are meager when a committee lacks legislative importance and its subcommittees lack staffs of their own.

---

17. Staff memorandum for Senator Muskie, August 23, 1976, p. 4.
18. SBC markup of the third budget resolution for fiscal 1977, transcript, p. 7.

Each Budget Committee had more than 75 staff members (including staff assigned to individual members) in 1979. These staffs are larger than the numbers authorized for most congressional committees. Approximately three-quarters of each committee's staff are organized into a core group of program specialists, economists, budget experts, and support personnel. SBC's core staff consists of majority, minority, and nonpartisan persons. The members of the majority staff are controlled by the chairman, while the minority staffers are responsible to the ranking Republican on SBC. All of HBC's core staff members are responsible to the chairman; a small minority group serve the Republican members. SBC entitles each of its Senators to one professional and one clerical aide; HBC had no staff entitlement for its members until 1977 when it authorized a professional staff assistant for each.

The "core" and "member" staffs are substantially divorced from one another on both committees. SBC's majority and minority "core" work in adjacent offices and have frequent contact with one another; the members' staffs once sprawled into other office buildings, and although they have been united with the central staff, they still have only intermittent dealings with the core group. Most of the HBC staff members work in their employer's offices, not at the Senate Budget Committee's headquarters. In both committees, relationships between the two sets of staff are strained and limited. Core staff members complain that Member aides are not well informed or interested in the details of budgeting. "They just want to grandstand for their boss" is a common complaint. Those who work for individual Members have a different view of the problem. They complain about being kept in the dark on committee business, of not getting invited to sessions of the core group at which important staff-level decisions are made, and of obtaining staff documents only a short time before the committee meets. Democratic staff employees on SBC are particularly resentful that Muskie's core group consults regularly with Bellmon's minority staff but not so frequently with them.

Unlike the core staffs which are busy policing the budget process, those staff members who work for Members go long periods without much budget work. The problem is more serious on SBC because it does not have operative task forces to which staff members can devote their time. To keep active and useful to their employers, staff aides spend a considerable portion of their time on nonbudget work.

Publicity and Influence

Subcommittees and staff are not ends in themselves but means of attracting attention and influencing legislative outcomes. Although a portion of the media's early interest in the budget process accrued to committee members, many of whom advertised their budget roles in press releases and newsletters to constituents, the lion's share of publicity has gone to the chairmen of the Budget Committees. Now that much of the excitement has passed, Members draw little notice for their budget work.

Nor do they see themselves gaining much program influence by being on the Budget Committees. One might expect that the federal budget would offer ample opportunity for committee members to tilt the outcomes in favor of the things they want. The give and take of budgeting should produce resolutions that honor the program interests of committee members. When little money is available for program expansion, committee members should be in a favorable position to channel funds to the programs they care about. Moreover, the pervasive reach of the budget to all federal programs should dictate bargaining in which members defer to one another's interests. In short, the Budget Committees should at least reward their members with a larger say over how federal dollars are spent.

These expectations seem to be borne out by the activity of committee members during the markup of budget resolutions. Although the decision-making styles of the two committees differ, their members frequently intervene on behalf of particular programs. Because HBC makes "line-item" decisions, its members try to assure that funds are included in the functional targets for specific programs. SBC members usually settle for "legislative history" which indicates that the amount provided for a function suffices for a particular program.

Despite these interventions, Budget Committee members perceive themselves as having little effect on programs. In interviews, they speak of the hard choices faced by the Budget Committee, of having to subordinate their own program interests in order to get agreement on a manageable budget. One member compared his behavior on Budget with an authorizing committee on which he also serves. "There, we can decide what is good and worthwhile and give it money; here, we have to say 'No' to many good causes." A leading SBC member pointed to "there's nothing in it for us" as a principal explanation for reluctance to serve on the committee:

We have no goodies to hand out; all we have is discipline. You can't do much for constituents through the Budget Committee so Senators do not like to give up another committee which they perceive as having some special interests for their constituents.

How can the observed interventions of Budget Committee members be reconciled with their own sense of impotence? Part of the answer lies in the need of committee members to believe that they are conforming to the expectations of Congress. The budget process was established, most Members of Congress believe, to control federal spending. The Budget Committees were empowered to act as a discipline against the spending pressures within Congress; they were not supposed to function as the promoters of new spending schemes. Other committees were expected to continue their role as program advocates, so that the division of labor within Congress would have the Budget Committees acting as controls and checkpoints. For members to define budgetary success in terms of the program initiatives they sponsored would violate a key purpose of the budget process.

With some notable exceptions, members practice "defensive" budgeting, a strategy based on the notion that the budget process can do more harm than good for favored programs. Defensive budgeting occurs when members act to protect a program against cuts below its current level of service or when they try to prevent the setting of targets at levels that might preclude later congressional funding of established programs. When it comes to adding money for program starts or expansions, defensive budget makers usually do not take the initiative. The most aggressive Budget Committee members are those trying to assure that the Budget Committees do not obstruct the program objectives they are pursuing via other committees. For example, when Senator Magnuson pushes SBC to increase the allocation for the health function substantially above the amount requested by the President, he is merely arguing for the level that his Appropriations subcommittee expects to report.

Listening to members of the Budget Committees discount their program accomplishments is reminiscent of the proverbial definition of budgeting as "the uniform distribution of discontent."[19] Virtually all participants come away from the annual budget encounter with less than they want. Even before markup, Budget

19. This statement is generally attributed to Maurice Stans, Director of the Budget in 1959-60.

Committee members are confronted with work sheets showing huge deficits. The message they get is that this year's margin has already been eaten up, that the deficit is going to be much higher than they want it to be, that funds for new programs will only add to the deficit, and that they must restrict their own program objectives in order to obtain agreement on a budget.

These committees school their members in the frustrations of budgeting. They learn that each budget is so much a product of past decisions that there is little that can be accomplished in one year's installment. No members of either Budget Committee have been able to reshape the budget into their preferred configuration of program priorities and economic policies. All have discovered that the budget excels as a maintenance process, as the means for continuing government agencies and programs at or near their current level of operations. The frustrations of budgeting are greatest for the most ideologically committed members, those who have sought to dislodge the budget from its incremental path. As we shall see, liberals and conservatives rail against the priorities registered in the budget resolutions; middle-of-the-roaders are more likely to abide the budget's constraints against change.

Two factors detract from a sense of budgetary accomplishment. First, budget decisions are made at a higher level of aggregation than the appropriations or authorizations voted by Congress. Second, a budget decision does not suffice to achieve program objectives; it must be implemented through other legislative means. Accordingly, members do not have so much certainty regarding the effects of their actions as when they add a provision to an appropriation bill or raise the level authorized for a program.

THE REWARDS OF BEING CHAIRMAN

Senator Muskie opened the first organization meeting of SBC at the start of the 94th Congress with a statement of the kind of committee he did not want: "I would not like to see this committee become simply a question of the chairman and the ranking member carrying the workload on the Senate floor and being the only ones pressing for our policy decisions on the Senate floor."[20]

Things have not turned out that way. On each committee, the

20. Senate Budget Committee Organizational Meeting, January 28, 1975, transcript, p. 8.

chairman has done the bulk of the work and reaped the bulk of the advantages. The chairman controls the core staffs and remains active on budget matters during the intervals between resolutions. He commands the process which produces the sole legislative output of his committee. Unlike appropriations which are splintered into more than a dozen separate bills, each one of which has its own subcommittee and its own floor manager, the budget resolutions are developed and defended under the leadership of the chairman.

Nevertheless, in assessing the role and potency of the chairmen, one must draw a sharp distinction between the chairmen's performance within committee and their external relations with other congressional actors and the media. In committee, the resolutions have not been rammed down the throats of recalcitrant members by a chairman wielding the powers of his office. Both chairmen have tried to steer the resolutions toward their preferred results. On any particular matter, the chairman might lose out to a colleague who has the votes or a more pressing stake in the issue; but on the budget as a whole, the chairman is likely to have more say than any other member.

Outside the Budget Committees, the chairman's role has been magnified in image and importance. Brock Adams and Edmund Muskie received an extraordinary amount of media exposure during the start-up years. They were featured in news accounts and in journalistic assessments of the new process. They supplied personalized explanations for why Congress was regaining control over the federal budget. If the process was working, it was because of Adams's caution, Muskie's persistence, each one's skill and hard work. The attentiveness of the media to the budget process has waned somewhat, but the image of two chairmen, each single-handedly bringing the process to life within his committee, remains.

The chairmen also dominate dealings with other congressional participants, though in different ways. They monitor the budget activities of other committees and tend to the busywork of the process. Other members have been willing to permit the chairman to take charge, ceding to him the credit and the burden:

> It has been very time consuming with an enormous amount of detail plus some disorganization. Many of the Senators just haven't bothered to put in the time. There hasn't been cooperation but a willingness to have Muskie take on the work. He has been perfectly willing to do that and has done it well.

As is often the case in conference, the chairmen take the lead in negotiations, both in the public sessions and in the equally important private dealings at which most House-Senate differences are reconciled. Despite the fact that Muskie missed some conferences because of illness, he was, in the words of one House conferee, "the Budget Committee in the Senate. He carries to a very large degree the rhetoric of the Senate in the conference. . . ."

Muskie's work included a blizzard of floor statements commenting on the relationship between pending legislation and the congressional budget. He made floor appearances on more than 150 bills during the first four years of the budget process, informing the Senate on whether the funds provided in appropriation, entitlement, or authorizing legislation accord with the latest budget resolution. From time to time, Muskie challenged legislation reported by other committees as violations of the budget process. These public appearances and confrontations spotlighted Muskie's role as Budget Committee chairman.

HBC has preferred private diplomacy, with its chairman advising other committees when their bills do not conform to the budget. The chairman usually counsels the affected committee on how to remedy the problem, and the issue often is resolved without public notice and without involving other Budget Committee members.

Along with the rewards of chairmanship come the costs. The chairmen bear the brunt of congressional displeasure and chafing at the constraints of budgeting. Precisely because they are the most visible members and the ones who conduct the "external relations," the chairmen become targets for attacks on the budget process. "Muskie is covered with scars," a close adviser confided in explaining why Muskie had adopted a lower profile in the 95th Congress. One of the HBC chairmen acknowledged that "a good Budget chairman would burn himself out after X number of years. I'm not sure that two years is the magic number, maybe four." Over time, a chairman's utility can be weakened by the accumulation of antagonisms he has built up.

The chairmen are the "Lone Rangers" of congressional budgeting, not in the *ad hominem* sense of being solely responsible for the achievements and shortcomings of the process, but in their institutional role as representatives of and combatants for the Budget Committees. The role is more controlling than the Member of Congress who plays it. Giaimo succeeded Adams as HBC chairman, with few significant changes in the conduct of congressional budgeting in the House. When Muskie was ill during a major confrontation between SBC and the Senate Finance Committee on energy legislation, Senator Hollings was vigorous and visible as acting chairman. As long as a comprehensive budget resolution is their single product, the Budget Committees are likely to be perceived by others through their chairmen. The stress on this role might be alleviated somewhat by establishing subcommittees with their own staffs, but the chairmen still will be the dominant figures.

There appear to be few signs that other Budget Committee members are eager to share in the burdens. During a protracted floor controversy with Senator Long over Finance's tax bill, Muskie pleaded with his colleagues at a special SBC meeting:

> I would like to have you join me on this. This is so critical that we have to make sure we are understood. It has to be understood that it is no longer a Muskie-Long feud but it is something on which you all feel strong. If you all do that, it would help. I am afraid I strike sparks. . . .[21]

When no colleagues directly responded to his suggestion, the discussion wandered off into other matters and the chairman was left to continue as the point man for the budget process.

STATUS OF THE BUDGET COMMITTEES

Members of Congress adhere to group norms because they perceive some advantage in going along with the group. If a committee has legislative power and esteem on Capitol Hill, its members gain from their association with it. Weak committees can demand little of their members because they have little to offer in return. Nor can they impose sanctions on recalcitrants who deviate from group norms.

During a tense debate in the Senate on Social Security legislation, Senator Morgan (not a member of SBC) offered his own explanation for why Senators did not want to be on the Budget Committee:

> Yesterday at the luncheon table [presumably in the Senate dining room], I heard it stated, "We cannot get anybody to serve on the Budget Committee; so and so wants to get off the committee, and we cannot get anybody to serve." Why? Because in the short span of two years, it has

21. Senate Budget Committee meeting on Amendments to H.R. 14114, Temporary Debt Ceiling Act, June 29, 1976, transcript, p. 20.

become meaningless, because we continue to bypass it. Mr. President, I would not want to serve on a committee that is not going to have any real effect on legislation.[22]

Morgan may have been moved to overstatement by his pique at not being able to get the Social Security bill returned to committee, but his statement should not be dismissed as merely a spur-of-the-moment reaction to legislative frustrations.

Yet within a year after Morgan's outburst, the Budget Committees were showing renewed signs of life, as measured by interest in getting on the Budget Committees and in the participation rates during markup. If in 1977, the Budget Committees seemed on a downhill course, in 1979 they were the place to be. Paradoxically, as budget work became more arduous, members seemed more attracted to it. During the first years of the budget process, the order of the day was stimulus, and Budget Committee members had a say in allocating the spending increases. Yet during these years, participation in committee work dipped, as did competition for seats on the Budget Committees. But when demands for belt tightening grew at the end of the decade, Members campaigned for the few open places on the House and Senate Budget Committees, and voting participation increased. One might surmise that during periods of budget scarcity, Members of Congress have more incentive to practice the kind of defensive budgeting for which membership on the Budget Committees is suited. From their vantage points on the Budget Committees, Members could try to assure that their programs are spared budget cuts.

But this is not the whole explanation. There does not appear to have been a rise in defensive behavior on either of the Budget Committees. In fact, the new arrivals have been more vigorous in pushing for budgetary savings and efficiency. There is another explanation that relates to the place of budgeting in the American political system. Budgeting is not equally vital or interesting every year. Although the routines continue from one cycle to the next with little change, the importance of budgeting varies from year to year. In the late 1970s, the movement for a balanced budget and for fiscal parsimony increased the importance of budgeting within Congress. As one new member who successfully competed for a seat on it in 1979 said, "the Budget Committee is where the action is going to be. There is not much appetite for new legislation or big, costly programs, but all eyes are on the budget. Everything

22. 123 *Congressional Record* (daily ed., November 2, 1977) S18608.

that comes through Congress will have its price tag closely examined."

Working on the Budget Committees means something different in such an environment from what it means when the budget is just one of the decision-making processes available to Congress. Members equate legislative success with being in the center of things; as national attentiveness to budget issues grows, so too do the ardor and commitment of Budget Committee members.

The Budget Committees therefore should expect to experience periodic ups and downs in their legislative fortunes. They will have good years and bad years; they will not be listened to every year. Sometimes, the committee room will be jammed during markup of the budget resolutions; sometimes members will be elsewhere. In some years, it will be necessary to draft reluctant members into service on the Budget Committees; in other years, the leadership will have a tough time deciding among the candidates. In sum, the prizes of budgeting are not always equally regarded or coveted. Perhaps the most valued prize is to be part of a vital process. That was the payoff for Budget Committee members in the beginning and in 1979, when balanced budget fever besieged Washington.

V The Budget's New Analysts

CONGRESS got its own budget agency in 1975 when the Congressional Budget Office (CBO) commenced operations.[1] Although the functions of this new staff agency were specified in the Budget Act, Congress was not sure what it wanted or what it was getting. Like many other provisions of the Act, CBO was forged in compromise, with enough ambiguity on key questions to enable the various sides to reach agreement.

Everybody wanted a budget staff for Congress. During years of budgetary warfare, Congress had perceived itself at a great disadvantage in challenging the executive branch. The President had his own Office of Management and Budget (OMB), along with legions of budget experts and policy analysts in executive agencies. All versions of congressional budget reform, therefore, called for a new staff, but differences emerged over the type of unit that should be established, whom it should work for, and the functions it should perform. Although most justifications for the budget staff pointed to mismatches between executive and legislative information and resources, Members of Congress were concerned as much about the distribution of power within Congress as with the relationship between the two branches. They recognized that in budgeting, power follows information, and that if the many are kept in the dark about budgetary alternatives and outcomes, the knowledgeable few would have a substantial advantage. Conversely, if budgetary information were widely shared, financial power also would be dispersed.

As part of its scheme to concentrate power in the Budget Committees, the Joint Study Committee (JSC) wanted a legislative budget unit to function solely as the joint staff for the two new committees, neither of which would have a staff of its own. The budget staff's congressional role would have been similar to that of the Joint Committee on Taxation which serves the House Ways

1. Section 905(b) of the Budget Act provided for CBO to come into existence on the day that its first director was appointed. This occurred on February 24, 1975.

and Means and Senate Finance Committees. The new staff would have been primarily a "numbers" operation, producing the data and reports necessary for the budget process. This limited concept was incorporated in H.R. 7130 by the House Rules Committee. The Senate version of budget reform, however, had a much more ambitious scope. It provided for a relatively independent budget office, in addition to the separate staffs of the two Budget Committees. This office would assist other congressional clients and produce an annual report for Congress on budget priorities and alternatives.

Members who wanted a budget staff beholden to the Budget Committees sought to vest these committees with the advantages accruing from superior information; those who wanted the staff to serve all of Congress preferred a wide distribution of budgetary power. The Congressional Budget Office was an artful compromise, tilting toward the Senate position in structure and potential, but sufficiently restricted to satisfy the House. The Budget Committees were given first claim on CBO's time and resources, but other committees and members also were entitled to assistance in accord with an explicit order of priorities: (1) It is the duty of CBO to assist the Budget Committees on all matters within their jurisdiction. (2) The Appropriations, House Ways and Means, and Senate Finance Committees are to be assisted on matters within their jurisdiction. (3) Other committees are entitled to assistance only "to the extent practicable," that is, after the requirements of the primary clients have been met. (4) Members are entitled to available information, implying that special studies are not to be initiated on their behalf.

Tension between the House and Senate over CBO also was etched in the statutory functions assigned to the new agency. These functions fall into three categories: budgetary assistance, economic analysis, and policy analysis. The strictly budgetary activities prescribed by the Act include cost estimates on pending legislation, scorekeeping reports, and five-year budget projections. CBO is charged to produce an annual report "with respect to fiscal policy . . . taking into account projected economic factors."[2]

In sum, the Budget Act gave CBO four sets of masters, three distinct tasks, a legacy of House and Senate disagreements over

---

2. Section 202(f) of the Budget Act. The Senate version of the budget legislation provided for CBO to report to Congress; as part of the compromise, the Budget Act provides for the annual report to go to the Budget Committees.

its purpose and scope, and license to grow into either a small budget unit or a major analytic agency.

House and Senate conflict over CBO carried into appointment of its first director, a precondition for activating the new agency. HBC preferred someone with extensive budgetary experience, an insider who could provide technical support to the budget process. Its leading candidate was Philip S. Hughes of the General Accounting Office, a former career official of the Bureau of the Budget who rose from the ranks to deputy director of that agency. SBC's Muskie agreed that Hughes "could do a competent administrative job," but he wanted "somebody who can grasp the dimensions of the global problem that this committee is going to be struggling with."[3] SBC's choice was Alice Rivlin, a Brookings Institution economist who had previously held the highest analytic position in the Department of Health, Education, and Welfare, and had written a well-known book on the use of analytic knowledge by the federal government.[4] The Senate ultimately prevailed in this contest between "budgeting" and "analysis," and Rivlin was named director of CBO on February 24, 1975, more than seven months after the Budget Act was signed into law.

STAFFING THE BUDGET PROCESS

This delay in the choice of director had a telling effect on the early role of CBO and its relationship to the Budget Committees. When CBO came into existence, Congress already had two sizable budget staffs in place. Given the need to produce a congressional budget before CBO was able to offer substantive assistance, each of the Budget Committees had recruited an array of fiscal and program specialists. HBC favored persons with budgetary and technical skills; its top staff included an individual who had served as a key aide to the chairman of the House Appropriations Committee and an economist who had worked in the Bureau of the Budget and had experience with budget numbers. The Senate committee se-

3. Senate Budget Committee, transcript of committee meeting, December 19, 1974, p. 2.

4. Dr. Rivlin was a member of the senior staff of the Brookings Institution prior to and after her years at HEW. At Brookings, she was coauthor of several of the annual *Setting National Priorities* publications. For her view on policy analysis, see *Systematic Thinking for Social Action* (Washington, D.C.: The Brookings Institution, 1971).

lected persons with political backgrounds, as well as fiscal and budget experts. Yet it would be misleading to overstate the differences between the two staffs. Each committee had individuals experienced in congressional politics as well as persons skilled in budgetary techniques. Moreover, it did not take long for the politically oriented people to become knowledgeable about budgetary practices and for the budgetary technicians to learn about the political environment of Congress.

Shortly after they were organized, the committee staffs had to begin production of a congressional budget for fiscal 1976, using some (but not all) of the new budget procedures for the first time. They relied on OMB data, assistance from other congressional staffs, and their own budgetary capabilities. Although CBO started operations before the first resolution was completed, it prudently refrained from getting involved in that work. It concentrated, instead, on building its own staff and informational resources.

When Congress was writing the Budget Act, it did not specifically consider the size of the new budget office. House members generally had a small group in mind, certainly one with no more than 50 to 100 employees. Senators with more ambitious expectations for the office looked for a somewhat larger organization. An SBC memorandum prepared before Rivlin was appointed projected a staff of 118; Muskie at a January 1975 meeting of his committee guessed that CBO would have perhaps 100 to 200 professional and clerical staff members.[5]

Rivlin, however, was not bound by these estimates. The Budget Act authorized the CBO director to appoint "such personnel as may be necessary to carry out the duties and functions of the Office."[6] The Act also allowed CBO to start hiring at once, before it received a regular appropriation from Congress.[7] As a consequence, CBO was able to recruit a large staff without specific guidelines from the Appropriations Committees, although it reviewed its staff plans with the Budget Committees at formal oversight

5. Senate Budget Committee, transcript of committee meeting, January 28, 1975, p. 25.

6. Section 201(b). The managers' statement on this section was appropriately vague: "The managers expect that the growth and development of the Budget Office will be consonant with the requirements of the congressional budget process and with the needs of committees and members for assistance."

7. CBO was permitted to pay its expenses out of the contingency fund of the Senate for a period not to exceed one year. Because the year would have expired before CBO could receive its first regular appropriation, it had to request a supplemental appropriation for fiscal 1976.

hearings as well as in consultations with committee leaders.[8] By the time CBO faced its first appropriations hearing in October 1975, it had already hired or made job commitments to 193 persons, and it requested funds for 259 positions, a level it considered appropriate for the full array of services contemplated by the Budget Act.

CBO's staff plans ran into a storm of opposition from the House Appropriations Committee, especially from Republicans who wanted a much smaller organization. In a two-day hearing, Rivlin was repeatedly forced to justify the purpose and work of CBO. After barely defeating efforts to trim CBO's staff to less than half of the requested level, the House Appropriations Committee approved funds for the 193 positions already filled or committed. The House went along with this number, but it adopted a Republican amendment to specify the 193 positions as a limitation in the appropriations act, thereby barring CBO from using available funds for temporary personnel.[9] Pleading staff imbalances and inability to fulfill its statutory responsibilities, CBO appealed to the Senate Appropriations Committee for the restoration of 35 positions, and the committee (as well as the Senate) acceded to this request. However, the House refused to budge and Congress funded only 193 positions, placing this ceiling in the appropriations act. CBO asked for and received 15 additional positions in fiscal 1977, but it pledged not to request further staff increases unless Congress were to add significantly to its workload.[10] (Increased staff was provided

8. At CBO's first appropriations hearing, Rivlin assured the committee that she had discussed the staff plans with the Budget Committees. However, Representative Coughlin quoted a statement by Representative Latta (ranking minority member of the House Budget Committee) that CBO "never requested the approval of this member at least on their hiring practices." Rivlin responded with an unusually blunt comment: "Mr. Latta is, with all due respect, in error on that. I have discussed our plans with Mr. Latta. I know he doesn't agree with them. There has been nothing secretive about it." This exchange suggests the strained relationship between Rivlin and conservative Republicans. See House Committee on Appropriations, *Hearings on Supplemental Appropriations for Fiscal Year 1976*, Part 1, p. 109, 94th Cong., 1st Sess. (1975). Hereafter cited as *House Supplemental Apprcpriations.*

9. Normally, the Appropriations Committees specify staff limitations in their committee reports, if at all. The inclusion of a limitation on CBO staff size in the text of the appropriation act is a departure from the usual practice. The limitation written into the 1976 appropriation has been modified in subsequent appropriation acts.

10. The House Appropriations Committee took the unusual step of reprinting Rivlin's pledge in its report on the 1977 legislative branch appropriation bill. H. Rept. No. 94-1225, p. 18.

in fiscal 1979 at the initiative of Members who wanted CBO to analyze the inflationary impact of federal actions.)

The heated dispute over staff size was much more than a numbers game. It was not a matter of CBO's inflating its request in expectation of a cut by the Appropriations Committees. At the appropriations hearings, Members voiced concern about duplications of staff and services, the creation of legislative bureaucracy with its own work priorities and standards, the scope and sponsorship of the studies CBO intended to undertake, and CBO's relationships with the Budget Committees and other congressional units. To add to these concerns, press accounts made it appear that CBO (in its reports and statements by the director) was advocating its own views on policy questions.

CBO's troubles were compounded as a result of distrust of Rivlin by conservatives on the Budget and Appropriations Committees. Rivlin's liberal, policy-advocacy background triggered fears that she would try to make CBO into a "think tank" for expansionist government. CBO's ambitious work plans and its first studies of the economy seemed to confirm these anxieties. Conservatives who were not comfortable with the role provided for CBO in the Budget Act or with Rivlin's appointment as director exploited the request for 259 positions to launch a broad attack on the new organization. A conservative leader warned the House that "under the direction of Dr. Rivlin the CBO is getting into political and policy questions at every level," and he accused Rivlin of establishing CBO "as an institute for policy studies (which happens to be the name of a left-wing research organization) and recommendations."[11]

Much more was involved than pique over the CBO director. CBO was a lightning rod for legislative worries about the new budget process. When the budget process was established, the Appropriations Committees were directly threatened with a potential loss of legislative jurisdiction. By attacking the ambitions of CBO, these committees were raising a red flag about the ambitions of the budget process as well. They were sending both CBO and the Budget Committees a message about the scope and reach of budgeting in Congress.

At its core, however, the fight was a battle for control of the Congressional Budget Office. CBO's early moves stamped it as an

---

11. 121 *Congressional Record* (daily ed., November 13, 1975) H11095, remarks of Representative Bauman.

organization reaching for substantial independence from Congress and the Budget Committees. The Appropriations-based attack was a maneuver to make CBO more responsive to congressional interests.

WORKING FOR THE BUDGET COMMITTEES

Although CBO was born in controversy, it might have settled into a routine, tranquil existence by permitting itself to be cast as the staff arm of the Budget Committees. It could have thus acquired a role similar to that of the Joint Committee on Taxation as a quiet, behind-the-scenes, little-known but respected group of budget experts. The chances are that even SBC—or at least its staff—would have approved of a budget office on call to perform assignments and studies in its behalf. But with Rivlin's appointment, this limited role was no longer a likely option; the new director intended a more ambitious, independent scope for her organization.

Rivlin had good reason for not wanting CBO to be tied so closely to the Budget Committees, although she recognized that its relationships with these committees would be much more vital and continuous than those with any other congressional unit. If CBO had been beholden to the Budget Committees, it would have become little more than a committee staff, or, worse yet, it might have developed into a staff for the committees' staffs. In view of the fact that the Budget Committee staffs were established before CBO was organized, it is quite likely that CBO would have been treated as a support agency programmed to do the bidding of the staffs of the committees. The staffs of the Budget Committees would have guarded their relationships with their members and would have tried to keep CBO at a distance. "Many of the Committee staff," an SBC memorandum reported in July 1975, "believe that the CBO should be more in the posture of an 'employee' with respect to the Budget Committee."[12] As an employee, CBO (and Rivlin) would have had limited access to members of Congress and would have been required to handle the things that the staffs of the Budget Committees were too busy, or not interested enough, to do. CBO would have had little opportunity to decide which studies to un-

12. Memorandum from Mark Lackritz to John McEvoy, July 8, 1975, SBC files.

dertake. Representative Giaimo described the relationship in responding to a question about whom he would turn to to get budget information: "I primarily and almost totally depend on my House Budget Committee staff, but my House committee staff deals directly with CBO every day of the year."[13]

CBO had a difficult time satisfying the two committees because they did not see eye to eye on what CBO should do and be. The staff of the House Budget Committee viewed itself as essentially self-sufficient, with little need of analytic assistance from CBO. It wanted CBO to handle the specialized backup work of the budget process, information systems, scorekeeping, cost estimates, and the like. Because of its own perceived proficiency in these areas, HBC was not satisfied by CBO's performance. HBC's staff incessantly complained that CBO's technical work was inadequate and its analytic work irrelevant.

The staff of the Senate Budget Committee was easier to please because it wanted analytic studies, viewing them as a means of directing attention to the financial and program choices facing Congress. But SBC staff persons were enraged by Rivlin's direct contacts with the chairman and other committee members. They wanted to control CBO by controlling its access to Members of Congress. If CBO could deal directly with Members, the special status of the Senate Budget Committee staff would be threatened.

Thus, for somewhat different reasons, the staffs of the two committees saw CBO "as a rival rather than collaborator,"[14] as an organization with a purpose and striving of its own, not just as an appendage of the committees. The staffs were apprehensive about CBO's independence but uncertain of exactly what the relationship between the two groups should be. They did not perceive CBO as vital to their own success and effectiveness; yet they were compelled to support it in public. As a result, they sniped at CBO in private but showed support when CBO was attacked by other congressional committees. In this tense environment, CBO tried to edge toward independence from the Budget Committees and the budget process.

13. *House Supplemental Appropriations*, p. 78.

14. The phrase and the conclusion are from the House Commission on Information and Facilities, *Congressional Budget Office: A Study of Its Organizational Effectiveness*, H. Doc. No. 95-20 (1977), p. 19. The Commission suggests that this was the "initial" relationship, but that this start-up problem has subsequently diminished.

ANALYTIC INDEPENDENCE

Shortly after her appointment Alice Rivlin told an interviewer, "CBO is an independent organization that has responsibilities to the whole Congress."[15] The two parts of this equation were interrelated: independence from the Budget Committees was deemed to be a precondition for CBO's independence within Congress. By claiming responsibility to all of Congress, CBO would be able to maintain some freedom from these committees.

Rivlin presented this formula for independence in her early appearances on Capitol Hill. The new organization, she bravely notified the Senate Budget Committee at an October 1975 hearing, "was not set up to work solely for the Budget Committees. I work for the whole Congress and have responsibilities to all committees and indeed to all members."[16] Rivlin repeated this claim to the House Appropriations Committee later that month: "We work for the whole Congress. I stress that because I think there is an impression that we work only for the budget committees."[17]

Independence was valued as a precondition for serving Congress with analytic integrity and competence. While CBO did not define what it intended by independence, its early actions were clear enough. CBO wanted substantial discretion to decide what to study (in addition to the activities mandated by statute); it wanted to select the assumptions used in its studies, and the alternatives considered. It did not want its analytic work tainted by subservience to congressional masters who would dictate the terms of inquiry. The trappings of independence included issuance of CBO reports under its own label (rather than as committee prints) and public statements by the director. In Rivlin's view, independence of thought—the *sine qua non* of analytic work—could thrive only if CBO had an identity apart from the Budget Committees.

Rivlin rejected all of the organizational models available in Congress: "It is a unique animal, the CBO. It is not like anything that Congress has done before really. . . . It isn't exactly like a committee staff, it isn't exactly like anything. It is a new kind of thing on Capitol Hill."[18]

---

15. *Challenge*, July/August 1975, p. 28.
16. U.S. Congress, Senate Committee on the Budget, *Congressional Budget Office Oversight*, October 6, 1975, p. 4.
17. *House Supplemental Appropriations*, p. 45.
18. U.S. Congress, Senate Committee on the Budget, *Congressional Budget Office Oversight*, October 6, 1975, p. 4.

From an analytic standpoint, the problem with committee staffs is their closeness to the legislative process and their employers. These staffs are a critical part in the continuing flow of legislative business; relevance and loyalty are more important for them than thoughtfulness and objectivity. CBO was able to strive for independence because the House and Senate Budget Committees had previously set up their own staffs. If it had been called upon to perform the everyday work of the Budget Committees, CBO might not have been able to maintain any analytic distance from them. It would have been compelled to function as a staff arm of these committees, responsive at all times to their immediate needs and interests.

If CBO did not want to become a committee staff, neither did it want to become another congressional support agency, molded into the traditional service roles of the General Accounting Office and the Congressional Research Service. CBO wanted to be its own boss, deciding what to do and what not to do. The old-line support agencies were viewed by CBO as sources of routine assistance to Congress, responsive to specific inquiries but without long-range vision and perspective. In declaring its independence, CBO was telling Congress that it wanted to be treated differently from the other agencies.

Rivlin's model for CBO was a combination of a strong analytic organization (such as the one she once headed in HEW) and a think tank (such as Brookings where she had spent much of her career). In other words, CBO was to be an amalgam of Rivlin's successful career as a policy analyst. It would be "plugged into the system," but with sufficient analytic vigor and objectivity to call the shots as it saw them. Rivlin selected individuals with analytic skills—economists predominated—for most of CBO's top positions. Of the 24 persons in the highest administrative posts, three-quarters had executive branch experience, 9 had worked in think tanks, a half-dozen had been in both types of organizations, and only 1 had had prior congressional service. CBO's staff, a sympathetic observer wrote, "is said by some to have been created very much in Alice Rivlin's own image."[19]

The shortage of persons with congressional experience suggests a view of Congress which pushed CBO to reach for independence.

---

19. William M. Capron, "The Congressional Budget Office," in U.S. Congress, Commission on the Operation of the Senate, *Congressional Support Agencies*, 94th Cong., 2nd Sess. (1976), p. 80.

The analyst's view of Congress is of an institution inhospitable to analysis, given to partisanship in policy making, and exploitive in its use of data to serve predetermined ends. The place of analysis in Congress is discussed later in this chapter. For the present, it suffices to note that many CBO analysts came to their jobs with a great deal of skepticism and naivete about Congress. They saw Congress as a disorderly institution, accustomed to bargains of convenience, not to the systematic consideration of the evidence. This analytic bias reinforced CBO's desire for independence. Among those who came to CBO with this bias, some departed quickly, more convinced than ever that Congress cannot be a faithful consumer of their analytic wares. But among those who remained, there grew an appreciation of Congress as a political institution in which analysis, although important, is but one of the considerations that go into the making of legislative decisions.

If CBO had been constrained to work according to the spasms of the legislative calendar or in response to the interests of Members of Congress, CBO would have been denied the freedom to set its own research agenda. It would have faced a problem familiar to executive branch analysts—how to shelter long-range thinking from daily work demands. Only this time, the demands would have come from dozens of discrete committees and Members within Congress, not from just a handful of clients. CBO also might have been denied the freedom to study matters which Congress preferred to leave untouched. Its research could have become fixed in the safe and narrow legislative politics, to the exclusion of venturesome departures from the status quo. CBO wanted to avoid congressional dictation of its analytic boundaries. When Sen. Robert Dole asked whether SBC members would have an opportunity to say that certain matters were not proper subjects of CBO research, Rivlin firmly responded: "If you wanted to veto our looking into something, I would want to resist that. The report is our report. . . ."[20]

Independence had another purpose for CBO: to free it from the routines and limitations of budgeting. Rivlin believed that CBO had to be independent of the congressional budget process in order to serve that process. She did not want CBO's work or its perspective bounded by the pressures of budgeting. A CBO confined to the routines of budgeting could adequately perform its statutory

---

20. U.S. Congress, Senate Committee on the Budget, *Congressional Budget Office Oversight*, October 6, 1975, p. 35.

chores—estimating the cost of legislation reported by committees, keeping score of congressional actions, and projecting future budget levels. But it could not engage in the creative policy analysis that Rivlin wanted to be the essence of CBO. Through independence, Rivlin wanted to assure that CBO would be much more than Congress's bookkeeper, merely recording the cost of past decisions rather than exploring alternatives to them.

Rivlin saw the annual budget process as anti-analytic, driven by incremental routines, eschewing serious program evaluation, and narrowing the range of options open to decision makers. She had a vision of budgeting different from this incremental version and she hoped, through the work of CBO, to inch Congress toward it. Several years before the CBO was established, Rivlin espoused the view that Congress should abandon annual budgeting in favor of multiyear budget plans. She regarded the one-year-at-a-time approach as providing the appearance of control but preventing Congress (or the President) from exercising meaningful discretion with regard to each year's budget choices.[21] Only days before her appointment as CBO director, she gave the Senate Budget Committee (in a closed-door interview that clinched the committee's support of her) her view of an *analytic* budget process, that is, a process in which fiscal decisions could be made with critical use of analytic intelligence:

> If I may venture a prediction, that if this process succeeds, you will eventually begin thinking more and more ahead, and looking at two-year and three-year budgets in trying to make decisions. I think that's the only way you really get control of what the federal government spends.[22]

As long as Congress budgets within a one-year framework, CBO needs some distance from the budget process in order to conduct its analytic work. Even as the Budget Committees go through their incremental paces, CBO would be looking beyond the current numbers for opportunities to redirect federal programs and priorities. Independence thus welled up from a conviction that, in order for CBO to assist Congress, it must be positioned outside the never-ending stream of budget work.

Rivlin saw CBO as a change agent for Congress—not for any

21. Some of those views are reflected in Congressional Budget Office, *Advance Budgeting: A Report to the Congress*, February 24, 1977.
22. Senate Budget Committee, executive session, interview with Dr. Alice Rivlin, February 20, 1975, p. 23.

particular change (she admirably upheld CBO's claim of neutrality in the face of disbelief by some Members of Congress) but for the proposition that Congress should search for more efficient and effective alternatives to its current programs. The bias for change is inherent in policy analysis, but it runs counter to budgeting's bias for continuity. The analyst intervenes in order to change policy outcomes; the budget maker puts a high value on stability and order. CBO would serve the maintenance functions of budgeting by means of its scorekeeping and other "numbers" activities, but analytic independence would enable the same organization to participate in the change process as well.

CBO's claim of independence meant that Members of Congress could not form expectations about it by comparing the Congressional Budget Office to familiar organizations. If CBO had no role models, neither did it offer any role comparisons for Members apprehensive about its early performance. At oversight and appropriations hearings during CBO's first year, Rivlin was repeatedly asked whether her staff was duplicating the work of other organizations. One after another, Members of Congress tried to compare CBO with other legislative staffs: the Budget Committees, the Joint Economic Committee, the General Accounting Office, and the Congressional Research Service. Comparisons also were drawn with outside organizations such as the President's Office of Management and Budget and the Brookings Institution. Some of the questioning was a transparent attempt to show that CBO did not need a large staff; much, however, was rooted in genuine confusion over CBO's role. "Members of Congress," Representative Giaimo remarked at an oversight session, "are asking what the role of the CBO is to be."[23] Rivlin's answers, though articulate and consistent, only added to the confusion. At every turn, she patiently insisted that CBO was different, not doing the jobs already being performed by others.

Uncertainty about CBO's role was combined with alarm about its independence as in this meandering comment by Rep. John J. McFall, a member of the Appropriations Committee as well as Democratic Whip in the House:

> We are feeling our way to find out what this organization that you are heading—and you can call it a monster if it doesn't work, but you can call it a wonderful body if it works—is all about. . . .

---

23. U.S. Congress, House Committee on the Budget, *Congressional Budget Office Oversight*, 94th Cong., 1st Sess., December 17, 1975, p. 10.

What could happen here is that we have created a bureaucracy which generates its own purpose, not run by anybody in either House or the Senate, taking over the functions not only of the Appropriations Committee, but also the policy determination functions of the legislative committees. That is one of the concerns behind all of these questions we are asking you. We are not sure we have the answers yet.

Maybe I don't sound very coherent, but it is because I am not sure that any of us are coherent in our understanding of just exactly what you do, and since this committee is one of the few that are looking at your operation, we feel we must get some answers. That is one of the reasons our questions may seem to be repetitious, and give the impression of a lack of complete understanding of what the process actually is. . . . I want to make sure that somebody from the House and the Senate is really in charge of what is going on in your organization. . . .[24]

Rivlin responded with fresh claims that Congress was "intentionally creating something that isn't like what you had before," along with assurances that oversight by the Budget Committees would "make sure it (CBO) doesn't get out of hand, and it makes us responsive, not only to the budget committees, but to others." Representative Giaimo, a member of both the Budget and Appropriations Committees, provided the answer that Members of Congress were looking for, explicit assurance that CBO would not be independent of congressional control. The discussion of CBO's role ended with Rivlin's conceding the point and McFall's satisfaction that control would be exercised by Congress:

Mr. Giaimo. The House committee members are aware of this problem. They are very much aware of it. The fact that you could be setting up a unique entity, this Congressional Budget Office, which is really different from any other kind of staff that we have had, and it could get out of hand, it could begin to enunciate its own policies and statements. This is a danger.

I can tell you for certain that both the committee members on the House committee and also the House staff people are very much aware of what the CBO is doing and are watching carefully. In fact, the chairman has set up a task force which has jurisdiction to supervise and see what is going on in the Congressional Budget Office for this very purpose, to make sure that it remains a creature of the House committee, and I suspect the same is true on the Senate side. Is that right?

Dr. Rivlin. Yes.

Mr. Giaimo. So that there is concern that this could happen, and the committees are seeing to it that it does not happen.

24. *House Supplemental Appropriations*, pp. 91-92.

Mr. McFall. If the gentleman would yield for a reply, I am glad that this is true, because so long as members of Congress are in charge of this office, then other members of Congress can get response to whatever wishes they may have, and they can get some kind of determination by the House, either for or against whatever they believe.[25]

SBC members generally were less concerned than HBC members about CBO's claim of independence. "We expect you to be independent but cooperative,"[26] Muskie advised Rivlin at the conclusion of an oversight hearing, a statement that suggests the continuing tension between CBO's independence and its service to Congress.

THE STRATEGY OF INDEPENDENCE

Independence was more than mere rhetoric for Rivlin and CBO. It was an operational guide for important decisions concerning the organization's structure and work; several of these became flashpoints for conflict between CBO and the Budget and Appropriations Committees.

Separation of Budgeting and Policy Analysis

Rivlin's conviction that analysis requires institutional independence was reflected in CBO's structure. CBO's organization plan provided for a budget division to handle the scorekeeping, bill costing, and five-year projections, as well as several program divisions to conduct analytic studies. Under this arrangement, the work of estimating the cost of an agriculture bill would be handled by the budget staff; in-depth studies of agricultural policy would be done by program analysts.

This separation between CBO's budget and analytic functions drove CBO to seek a large staff. Because the first claim on its resources would be for budget work, Rivlin realized that the smaller the organization, the fewer would be the number of people available for policy analysis. The plan for 259 positions contemplated about 50 slots for the budget division, less than half of the number slated for the analysis divisions and about equal to the combined size of the tax and fiscal policy staffs.

25. *Ibid.*, p. 93.
26. U.S. Congress, Senate Committee on the Budget, *Congressional Budget Office Oversight*, October 6, 1975, p. 43.

The separation between the two functions cast the budget staff as second-class citizens within CBO, the "numbers crunchers" who handled the details of budgeting but lacked the analytic skills to deal with the "interesting" questions. This is the way Rivlin characterized the budget division at an oversight hearing:

> . . . it is really the most busy. It will be staffed with people who are good at budget numbers and familiar with the technicalities of costing and projecting and how government programs work. . . .
>
> We see that partly as an entry level job, as a way to train some people who come out of, say, master degree programs in public administration.[27]

The analysts, by contrast, would be drawn predominantly from economics, would have advanced training and executive branch experience, and would have most of the high-paying slots in CBO. Muskie, however, was uneasy with the emerging structure, preferring to view both staffs as engaged in analytic work: The budget division, he suggested in response to Rivlin's characterization, "might be described as the short-term analysis people, people who are concerned with this year's budget, 5 years at the outside. And the other divisions, six in number, are more concerned with long-term analysis. Is that a fair statement?"[28]

Rivlin would have nothing of the notion that the budget crew might conduct analysis:

> I don't think that short-term/long-term is exactly the right distinction to be drawn here. It is really a distinction between the costing and projecting operation—a pretty technical, numerical operation—and analysis of alternatives and options.[29]

But members and staff of both Budget Committees widely regarded the separation of the budget and analytic staffs as a blunder, a "misallocation of resources." The committees came to perceive CBO as really two distinct organizations, one responsive to their needs and relevant to the congressional budget process, the other "doing its own thing" and of little use to congressional budget makers.

The two committees, however, did not share the same reasons for their disgruntlement about the budget/analysis split. House

27. *Ibid.*, p. 11.
28. *Ibid.*, p. 13.
29. *Ibid.*, p. 14.

members and their staff took the view that CBO should be exclusively—some would say, predominantly—a budget office. The prospect of a big organization with its own analytic agenda "is a legislative mistake. . . . They do nothing for us that we can't do with five more people." A Democrat on HBC replied to an interview question about CBO's analytic work with: "I don't know what they do; you tell me." In the same measure that they disparage CBO's analytic work, Members of Congress have come to appreciate its "numbers" service. "I think the CBO does a marvelous job," a key staff person on House Appropriations remarked, adding at once, "I am speaking of the budget staff." Nevertheless, Rivlin refused to concede that budgeting was CBO's main function, as the following exchange during the 1975 Appropriations hearings shows:

> Mr. Coughlin. This is the guts of your operation, isn't it?
> Dr. Rivlin. I think it is a very important part of it.
> Mr. Coughlin. Budget analysis is what the whole thing is about.
> Dr. Rivlin. That is part of it.
> Mr. Coughlin. That is what it is supposed to be about.
> Dr. Rivlin. These are the people who do the quite technical work that is required under the law, the costing and projecting, mainly. These are cost analysts and the statisticians and experts on projecting the cost of government programs.[30]

SBC members and staff also were troubled by the budget/analysis separation. They felt that budgeting and analysis, rather than being distinct operations requiring different skills, are complementary activities that would benefit from interaction. Bill costing would improve if it were performed by people with substantive program knowledge; program analysis would be more relevant if budget staff participated in it.

Nevertheless, the separation between CBO's two faces has persisted, largely because of Rivlin's belief that CBO would lose its analytic impulse and key staff if its policy analysts were absorbed in budget work. But CBO has been compelled to allocate a much larger portion of its staff to the budget division than it originally intended. In reducing CBO from 259 to 193 positions, the House Appropriations Committee insisted that CBO

> must follow very carefully the priorities set forth in the Congressional Budget Act; in particular, the priorities given to scorekeeping, cost

---

30. *House Supplemental Appropriations*, p. 131.

analyses, and other reports to support the Budget Committees in preparation and revision of concurrent resolutions on the budget. . . .[31]

A similar admonition was conveyed by the Senate Appropriations Committee,[32] which also took a hard line one year later in a report on CBO's budget request for fiscal 1977. After listing scorekeeping reports, costs estimates, and requested assistance to the financial committees of Congress as CBO's highest priority tasks, Senate Appropriations instructed CBO "to take adequate measures, including the reallocation and the reorganization of resources, if necessary,"[33] to assure satisfactory performance of these budget functions.

CBO got the message and increased the size of its budget division, even though its overall size was cut sharply below the projected level. Of the permanent staff of 208, CBO gave the budget unit 67 slots. Many of the reassigned positions came from the program analysis divisions, which dropped from a projected 45 percent of CBO's staff to about 35 percent.

An equally important development has been a softening of the distinction between analysis and budgeting. The policy analysis divisions have become heavily involved in budget work, although in a distinctively more analytic way than is customarily practiced by the budget group. The analysts' interest in budget numbers has been stimulated by a desire to be appreciated and to be relevant. The deliberate, though private, bad-mouthing of the analysis divisions (chiefly by the Budget Committees) had its effect, as did the analysts' preference to be involved in policy making. Analysts do not like to be told that their studies are of no value to Congress in making its budget decisions; many, therefore, have been willing to accommodate their work to the topical interests of Congress.

The program analysis divisions have been able to contribute a more sophisticated analysis of data than the "nuts and bolts" scorekeeping competence of the budget unit. CBO scored a success, for example, with a model of the poverty population which enabled it to produce timely estimates of various proposals to change the Food Stamp Program. These estimates were extensively used by the

31. H. Rept. No. 94-645 (November 7, 1975), p. 32.
32. The Senate Appropriations Committee "totally agrees with the report of the House Appropriations Committee with regard to the work priorities of the Congressional Budget Office. . . . CBO must follow very carefully the priorities set forth in the Congressional Budget Act." S. Rept. No. 94-511 (December 5, 1975).
33. S. Rept. No. 94-1201, p. 28.

Agriculture Committees in marking up food stamp legislation. When CBO boasts of its accomplishments, it is more likely to refer to this type of budget-related work than to its widely circulated analytic reports. Thus, the respected head of one of CBO's program analysis divisions admitted: "If I had to point to the marked success of my division, I am going to point to the numbers types of things. The stuff that we have done in this division that has been found to be most useful has at its core budget numbers. It has a budget question as its central interest."

CBO has become more of a budget office and less of an analytic shop than Rivlin intended. As a consequence, disquiet over CBO's role and performance has diminished, and the organization has become part of the budgetary routine of Capitol Hill. This does not mean, however, that CBO has completely abandoned its analytic strivings. Its ultimate success may be the integration, rather than the separation, of analysis and budgeting.

Setting the Agenda

For CBO, independence meant discretion to pursue its own analytic interests and priorities. Rivlin recognized, of course, that CBO would have to undertake numerous studies at the request of Congress, but she also wanted CBO to initiate its own research activities. When Rivlin made her initial appearances before the Budget and Appropriations Committees in 1975, she presented a list of some three dozen analytic studies, more than half of which had been commenced without any specific request from a committee or Member. But rather than being applauded for its initiative, CBO was castigated for going off on its own without direction from Congress. "It is my understanding," Senator Dole protested, that "the primary purpose of the CBO is to be responsible to congressional needs and directions. But it appears that more than half of these are self-initiated." He wondered that there "may not be resources available to the committees in the House or Senate for studies by CBO. You have them all wrapped up in your own studies. Then you really are not responsive to the Congress and the Budget Committees." Rivlin retorted that although CBO "is trying to be as responsive as we can to all committees, I don't think the way to do that is to have a staff that is unemployed until somebody asks them a question."[34]

---

34. U.S. Congress, Senate Committee on the Budget, *Congressional Budget Office Oversight*, October 6, 1975, p. 35.

Stronger objections were voiced by House members. Representative Evans, a moderate Democrat on the Appropriations Committee, asked for the language of the Budget Act that would authorize a particular transportation study. Rivlin replied that "the law is not specific about the subject of the studies," but she referred to CBO's responsibility for an annual report on budget priorities and alternatives. This answer, suggesting that all of CBO's analytic work might be justified by its need to produce an annual report, worried Rep. Robert R. Casey, chairman of the Legislative Branch Appropriations Subcommittee. Since "everything that goes on in this country affects our economy someway or somehow, that means you can get into everything." Rivlin saw matters differently, arguing that "we are not proposing to study everything that goes on in this country, but to help the Congress and the committee to study the major issues of allocations among the major functions of the Government."[35] She acknowledged, however, that a particular study had been undertaken without any request from the committee of jurisdiction. This admission brought Rep. Frank E. Evans back into the debate:

> Would you also on your own study whether or not other possibilities were seriously considered by an authorizing committee? . . . are you going to be studying the things that the legislative or appropriations committee really isn't seriously considering?

Rivlin stood her ground, assuring the Members that CBO did not want to get into matters that nobody is interested in, but upholding the Budget Office's right to look at program issues:

> It clearly says so in the law: It is a judgment question on our part and a question of interacting with the Congress to choose some alternatives which have some real support, which are of interest to the Congress.[36]

But the Appropriations Committees were not content to leave issue selection to CBO. They were concerned that self-initiated studies might prove embarrassing to legislative committees. Yet they were unwilling to flatly cut off all initiative, because such action could have been a crippling blow to the new organization. Instead they fell back to the formula written into the Budget Act for determining CBO's work priorities. The House Appropriations Committee

35. *House Supplemental Appropriations*, p. 61.
36. *Ibid.*, p. 74.

cautioned that assistance "to individual members should be strictly construed as relating primarily to information compiled for the committees listed in the act."[37] Almost identical language was placed in the report of the Senate Appropriations Committee.

These strictures compelled CBO to recede from its announced independence to study whatever it wanted. CBO, in consultation with the Budget Committees, drafted a set of guidelines for determining what to study, and Rivlin, testifying about the change in policy, said, "I think we have learned something in the last few months . . . about the nature of our responsibility; that is, that the law was very carefully drafted when it created a hierarchy of customers for CBO to respond to."[38]

The data in table 11 reflect a shift from self-initiated studies to work for the budget committees and other congressional clients. CBO, in fact, now avoids labeling any of its studies as "self-initiated"; it discreetly classifies such work as a statutory requirement of the Budget Act or as a component of the annual report. These two categories accounted for one-quarter of all completed CBO research projects from its inception until March 1979, but only 2 percent of the studies still under way in 1979. CBO research for the Senate Budget Committee has climbed from 20 percent of the total (for completed work) to more than 40 percent of the studies in progress. The House Budget Committee has been less interested in CBO's analyses, and has sponsored fewer than half the number requested by SBC. Nevertheless, the data portray a Congressional Budget Office hard at work to meet the requests of the Budget Committees and, to a much lesser extent, those of other committees. This is precisely the image that CBO wishes to foster.

But this image is not entirely accurate. CBO has learned how to solicit committee sponsorship of studies it has decided to undertake. In the pluralist environment of Capitol Hill, it has not been hard for CBO to veil its initiatives by getting committees to commission the work it wants to do. CBO also has learned how to redefine—unilaterally or in negotiations with its clients—requests for assistance from congressional committees. CBO almost never says "no" to a request from the Budget Committees, but it often recasts the work to suit its own research objectives. Committees frequently submit narrow, itemized requests for assistance, and it is not diffi-

37. H. Rept. No. 94-645 (1975), p. 32.
38. U.S. Congress, Senate Committee on Appropriations, *Supplemental Appropriations Fiscal Year 1976*, October 1975, p. 641.

Table 11
SPONSORSHIP OF CONGRESSIONAL BUDGET OFFICE STUDIES, COMPLETED AND IN PROGRESS
Cumulative, February 1975-March 1979

	Completed Studies		*Studies in Progress*	
Sponsor	*Number*	*Percent*	*Number*	*Percent*
Senate Budget Committee	90	29	21	41
House Budget Committee	64	20	7	14
Appropriations and Tax Committees				
House	14	4	1	2
Senate	11	3	1	2
Authorizing Committees				
House	30	10	9	18
Senate	23	7	10	20
Joint Congressional Committees	3	1	1	2
Statutory Requirement	29	9	1	2
Annual Report	49	16	0	0
Total	313 [a]	100	51 [b]	100

Note: Percentages may not add to 100 because of rounding.
[a] Because of the multiple requests for some CBO reports, these 313 requests represent 279 reports.
[b] These 51 requests represent 45 reports.

Source: Congressional Budget Office.

cult for CBO to broaden them to fit its research agenda. Some requests are overdrawn and vague; CBO can preserve its independence by contracting or redirecting them. The finished product sometimes bears little resemblance to the original inquiry, but at least CBO cannot be accused of flagrant unresponsiveness to congressional needs.

The question of for whom CBO works is no longer an issue. CBO gives priority to its budget and cost-estimating duties, does not officially conduct research at the request of Members, lists few studies as undertaken on its initiative, and has figures to show that most of what it does is for the Budget Committees. Like the other congressional staff agencies, it has learned how to maintain a measure of independence without seeming to be independent. Budget Committee and staff members are aware of what is going on, but as long as CBO keeps out of trouble, they have no firm basis for challenging the arrangement.

Publicizing the Budget Office

The third prop of CBO's independence has been the active publicizing of its studies and leadership. CBO has successfully carved out for itself an identity apart from that of the Budget Committees. Within a very short period of time, CBO was making news and winning public recognition. By contemporary political standards, the things that CBO has done to attract notice do not appear to be exceptional. It distributed studies and press releases, called press conferences to announce some of its newsworthy reports, and established an information office to handle inquiries from the public for documents and other available material. Rivlin was accessible for interviews, gave occasional lectures, and made public statements. CBO did not have to exert itself much to get publicity. The news media were interested in CBO and its articulate director. CBO was a good story and most of the coverage was favorable. One might have expected Congress to welcome the focus on CBO as an indication that the new budget process was a political success.

But the torrent of publicity that put CBO on the map and aided its recruitment of skilled analysts also got it into trouble with the Budget Committees. One problem—considered in the next section—was that CBO's public appearances cast it as an advocate for particular viewpoints, not as a neutral budget agency. Even more seriously, CBO's public actions were at variance with the normal conduct by congressional staff. The usual practice is for congressional staff agencies to submit their reports to the Member or committee which requested the study, leaving release of the report to the discretion of its sponsor. Staff agencies do not ordinarily hold press conferences or actively publicize their work. They function behind the scenes and do not try to draw attention to their activities. By violating these congressional norms, CBO was in effect asserting that it was not to be regarded just as a staff group, but that it was to have status and recognition of its own. It also was garnering a good deal of the political credit and media attention that would otherwise have accrued to the committees or Members requesting the study.

The protests came at once, mainly from the House. While key members of the House Budget Committee were enraged, SBC members were somewhat less perturbed. "Maybe it is because Senators can get publicity more easily than House members can," one budget aide suggested; "perhaps Senators are more accustomed to giving their staffs some discretion." An early blow-up occurred at an HBC oversight hearing in December 1975. Portions of a CBO report on oil policy were discussed in the news media before the report was officially released. Another report on unemployment received widespread press coverage in a way that offended some conservative Members. Chairman Adams urged Rivlin to be more careful in distributing CBO reports and working papers:

> . . . this is an area which has personally caused me a considerable amount of agony in the last month. I'm not blaming you personally for it, or any one member of the CBO, but . . . portions of a report that had never been issued were being used by advocates of positions up here for or against one side.[39]

The House Appropriations Committee warned CBO that "in the legislative branch, debate over public policy must be conducted by elected officials," and it set the following guideline for public relations:

> While the Congressional Budget Office must respond to inquiries about its operations and about individual reports, its public information function should be strictly informational in nature, and not promote the Congressional Budget Office or take a position on any particular policy.[40]

The strongest attack on CBO's public activities came in an assessment of CBO's organizational effectiveness by the House Commission on Information and Facilities. In an otherwise favorable appraisal of CBO's rapid development and analytic competence, the House Commission railed against the manner in which the Congressional Budget Office released and promoted its studies. The Commission's report opened with a complaint that CBO "maintains too high a profile." It went on to elaborate this "central conclusion":

> Its willing visibility, unique among the Legislative Branch support agencies, threatens seriously to impair the usefulness and integrity of a highly promising and productive policy research agency. . . . [CBO] is not an independent agency, nor does it have any policy-making authority. It provides information and analysis to the committees and members of

39. U.S. Congress, House Committee on the Budget, *Congressional Budget Office Oversight*, December 17, 1975, p. 17.
40. H. Rept. No. 94-645 (1975), p. 32.

the House and Senate, to those who are constitutionally empowered to make decisions.

Too often, however, CBO appears to forget or ignore its proper relationship to the Congress. Members of Congress frequently read in the daily press reports of CBO views on the state of the economy before those views are distributed through official channels. While this phenomenon may reflect media fascination with a new and expert body of opinion, it also appears to be a result of CBO preoccupation with a public relations mission. Press conferences, press briefings and news releases are designed to reach the public through the media. They are not conventional means of communication with congressional clients.[41]

Despite these admonitions, disputes over CBO's public pronouncements continued to flare up from time to time. One such instance occurred in 1977 when Rivlin held a briefing in conjunction with CBO's publication of an assessment of President Carter's energy program. The session was held just one day before a hearing scheduled by the committee which had requested the report. Rivlin's blunt statement that the program could not achieve the Administration's energy goals was given wide coverage by the news media. Several days later, Rivlin was sharply questioned by Chairman Giaimo, at an HBC task force meeting. "Do you consider it your function, as head of CBO," he asked, "to have a press conference on that report and to issue conclusions?" Rivlin responded to part of the question: "I didn't issue any conclusions." Giaimo would not drop the issue, quoting from a news account of Rivlin's comments: "Now, are you speaking for the Congress in this instance?"[42] Rivlin explained that she was only going over the conclusions of the report. The questioning continued with Giaimo calling for ground rules to govern the release of CBO reports and two HBC members—a liberal Democrat and a conservative Republican—coming to Rivlin's defense. The session ended with Rivlin's expressing a desire to get guidance from Congress but insisting "that it is very important to get maximum exposure of a study where it is useful and to let people see what the conclusions are and how they were arrived at."[43]

CBO has become somewhat cautious in its public relations. It often consults with a committee which requests a study before de-

41. U.S. Congress, House Commission on Information and Facilities, *Congressional Budget Office: A Study of its Organizational Effectiveness,* H. Doc. 95-20, January 4, 1977, pp. 1-2.
42. U.S. Congress, House Committee on the Budget, Task Force on Budget Process, *Congressional Budget Office Oversight,* June 2, 1977, p. 19.
43. *Ibid.,* p. 24.

ciding how the report is to be released. It conducts fewer press conferences, but this drop is probably due as much to CBO's loss of newness as to avoidance of press contacts. CBO, however, continues to regard public recognition as vital to staff morale and institutional status. It must have a public face if it is to avoid becoming just another behind-the-scenes, subservient staff agency of Congress. It therefore regards the occasional tiffs over its public activities as welcome signs that the Congressional Budget Office has not succumbed to that fate.

In fact, CBO regards public notice as essential to the performance of its analytic mission. Press coverage of its reports often are the only means by which Members and key staff would even be aware of CBO's work. As defended by CBO officials, the seeking out of media is not just a way of building up its institutional ego but recognition that Members of Congress get perhaps the bulk of their information from newspapers and television reports.

THE PROBLEMS OF BEING ANALYTIC

"If the analysts have something relevant and useful to say," Alice Rivlin wrote a few years before the CBO post, "they will be listened to."[44] But by whom? By other analysts or by policy makers? The analytic community has been attentive to CBO and its analytic products since the start. Fellow analysts have applauded CBO's accomplishments and the quality of its analytic output. They often seem to regard the Congressional Budget Office, and not the budget process, as the really important story. Thus, from a keen observer of the analytic scene: "*CBO is pivotal. . . . CBO must not only be highly skilled but powerful, influential, and large if the budget act is to work.*"[45] This prescription, written only weeks after the Budget Act was passed, seems to have been a blueprint for organizing the new Congressional Budget Office.

Rivlin's confidence and the conception of CBO as the central issue reflect an "analycentric bias,"[46] the conviction that the surest

44. Alice M. Rivlin, *Systematic Thinking for Social Action* (Washington, D.C.: The Brookings Institution, 1971), p. 6.
45. Walter Williams, *The Congressional Budget Office: A Critical Link in Budget Reform* (Seattle: Institute of Governmental Research, University of Washington, July 1974), p. 4, emphasis in original.
46. See Allen Schick, "Beyond Analysis," in *Public Administration Review* 37 (May/June 1977): 258-63.

way to improve the quality of public decisions is to have more analysts producing more analyses. To a considerable degree, CBO's growing pains were due to its "analycentric" view of public policy, a bias that has been substantially overcome by the realities of congressional budgeting.

Policy analysts have mixed feelings about Congress. They perceive, correctly, that Congress has not been a major consumer of analysis, certainly much less so than executive agencies. Some analysts write off Congress as a hopeless case; others see it as an institution whose operations can be radically transformed by a massive infusion of analysts and analyses. The first view assumes that because analysis cannot become the dominant consideration for Congress, it cannot have a significant role in the legislative process. The latter assumes that analysis can become more than one of a number of inputs for Congress. Neither view is tenable. Congressional use of analysis increased markedly in the 1970s, but it is unlikely that an analytic institution, whether it be one oriented to the budget process or one more broadly linked to the legislative process, could yield more than a slight increment in analytic activity on Capitol Hill. Those who have looked to CBO for a massive upgrading of Congress's disposition to use analysis have been woefully disappointed. But the disappointment is due to a misunderstanding of the place of analysis in the legislative process.

There is a legislative market for analysis, and its conditions vary over time and policy areas.[47] For Congress, policy analysis can be at most a sometime thing, selective and spasmodic, never a wholesale commitment to support, let alone use, the fruits of this booming industry. Congress functions as a massive scanning machine, sucking in data and arguments from a bewildering variety of sources, and refining them into legislative material. In this process, Congress treats analysis much as it treats news, constituency mail, interest-group handouts, the local newspaper, and the like. Everything is grist for the congressional mill, and analysis enjoys no preferred position by virtue of its esteem in intellectual circles. For this reason, the legislative product will be a compound of analysis (usually in a "translated" or bastardized version) and numerous other inputs. Some of that input will be of analytic caliber; much will not. All of it, however, is potentially relevant to the legisla-

47. For an elaboration of these views, see Allen Schick, "The Supply and Demand for Policy Analysis on Capitol Hill," in *Policy Analysis* 2 (Spring 1976): 215-34.

tive process. The limitations on analytic work are rooted in the representative role of Congress. When it has a window to the outside, Congress can best fulfill that role because it is not restricted in what it takes for evidence. If Congress were blessed with a sufficiency of analytic resources, it might be tempted to live by its own wits and data. That would be a costly loss for representative democracy.

Measured against the great expectations of those who hoped that CBO would turn Congress into an avid customer for analytic studies, the record of the first years has been disappointing. The quality of CBO's analytic work has been quite good in its strong areas, such as welfare policy. Yet the production of solid analyses has not by itself influenced many legislative outcomes or evoked much congressional interest, though "numbers" work addressed to the immediate concerns of the budget has made an impact. CBO's main problem is endemic throughout the "knowledge industry": analysis done is not equivalent to analysis used. The production of policy studies in the United States is much greater than the consumption. Rivlin was sensibly aware of this imbalance when she launched CBO on an analytic course. In one of her first appearances before the House Budget Committee she confessed that "the worst thing that could happen to the CBO would be that it would be ignored and not used."[48] This "worst case" scenario came close to describing CBO's early predicament. After giving CBO high marks for the quality of its analyses, a sympathetic observer concludes, "I uncovered no clear evidence that CBO's formal products have yet had a direct, identifiable impact on outcomes."[49] In interviews, CBO's leaders did not challenge this conclusion, although a few throught that the situation was improving and that as Congress became more familiar and comfortable with the policy studies, it would be more willing to use them. A less optimistic view was expressed by a highly regarded CBO official who has been in the forefront of its analytic work:

> We're still peripherally related to the budget process except for technical support and the tax and fiscal analysis. It is unfortunate but the 50 to 60 percent of CBO that really is tied into policy and program evaluation relates very peripherally to the budget process. I'm not sure there is an

---

48. U.S. Congress, House Committee on the Budget, hearings on *Organization and Activities of the Congressional Budget Office*, 94th Cong., 1st Sess., July 23, 1975, p. 5.
49. Capron, *op. cit.*, p. 81.

interest in that kind of thing on the Hill. I don't think I came here with any illusions that there was going to be a great surge of interest in this kind of thing. I think the market for CBO's work in these areas is not on the Hill at all. The question is whether policy analysis, laying out broad options, is something we can continue to do if there is no true interest in having CBO as a creative arm of Congress to do that.

CBO's analytic problems are reflected in the difficulty of producing a useful annual report. The first effort, a 400-page volume on *Budget Options for Fiscal Year 1977*, was criticized by staff members of both Budget Committees. The complaints were not exactly consistent: The report was little more than a costing out of alternative program levels and had failed to consider policy issues and priorities; the report dealt with program issues not genuinely relevant to that year's budget choices; the report tried to cover the whole budget without focusing on the small number of germane issues.

CBO tried a different approach the next time around: a series of budget issues papers (about 20 in all) plus a briefer and earlier (February) annual report. The idea was to discuss particular issues in the individual papers and to deal with the overall budget outlook in the report. The issue papers were acclaimed in analytic circles but were used only sparingly by the Budget Committees. Adverse comment on the report diminished, but by then the committees had scaled down their expectations of what they could get out of the annual document. CBO further revised the process for fiscal 1979 and 1980, retaining its series of issue papers and substituting two quite brief reports (about 40 pages each) for the annual report. The two reports dealt with the long-term budget outlook and current fiscal policy. CBO abandoned its effort to produce an analytic report on the major program areas in the budget.

CBO has made earnest efforts to target its issue papers to the budget issues being considered by Congress, and it resents unilateral demands from the Budget Committees telling it what to do without prior consultation and negotiation. SBC staffers think that the utility of the analytic products would improve if it could dictate CBO's research agenda. "We have not achieved a way to integrate what they want to do with what we need on the analytic side," a senior SBC official complained. CBO "does not integrate its analytic work with the actual choices confronting Congress." But the overall tenor of SBC comments is upbeat: CBO is getting better and more responsive.

While the situation is improving on the Senate side, HBC's conception of the budget process and of CBO's role rules out the ambitious analytic perspective that Rivlin wants to bring to the budgetary consideration of federal programs. After two years of having something to say and not being listened to, Rivlin openly pleaded with HBC for guidance and input into the analytic process. "As I look at our relationship with this committee, and its staff," she professed at an HBC oversight hearing in June 1977,

> the place where we can use the most help is in the development of budget issue papers and our annual report. If we can have more sense of what would be useful to this committee, what kinds of issues you are interested in, what formats would be useful, we would appreciate it very much.
>
> Insofar as the numbers work and the budget estimates and the costing, we get very good direction, and there isn't a problem. But we would like to communicate more, both with members and staff, on the development of issues.[50]

This plea fell on deaf ears. HBC knows what it wants to get from CBO and the type of budget control it wants to exercise. It is interested in (1) keeping track of appropriations, (2) guarding against backdoors, (3) enforcing the procedures in the Budget Act, and (4) preventing end runs and irregularities in financing. It is not interested in trying to shape future policy outcomes by examining program options and priorities. HBC's sponsorship of CBO studies has declined sharply. In March 1979, while CBO was in the thick of preparing issue papers for the next year's budget cycle, HBC accounted for only 7 research projects in progress, compared with the 21 studies being conducted for the Senate Budget Committee. HBC's share of CBO's workload dropped from 20 percent for completed projects to 14 percent for studies under way.

CBO decided in 1977 to solicit authorizing committee interest in its analytic services. Using the lines of communications to these committees opened up by its bill-costing activities, CBO increased the proportion of its work targeted to authorizing clients. The statistics (in table 11, already presented) do not adequately reveal this trend because CBO has been adept at securing Budget Committee (usually SBC) sponsorship for research intended for authorizing

50. U.S. Congress, House Committee on the Budget, Task Force on Budget Process, hearings on *Congressional Budget Office Oversight*, 95th Cong., 1st Sess., June 2, 1977, p. 17.

committees. This "tilt"—the same term is used by Budget Committee and CBO staffers—not only enhances the Congressional Budget Office's independence but also enables it to do work which is not bounded by the immediate concerns of the budget process. In line with Rivlin's strong view that the annual process is not an effective means of considering priorities issues, CBO has gambled that analytic research on behalf of the authorizing committees might have a greater long-term impact on budget outcomes than work which is specifically targeted to current budget issues. This strategy was cogently justified by a high CBO official:

> If we are really trying to influence the outcomes and have any kind of impact on the congressional decision process when it comes to major items that are going to affect budget priorities over the next several years, we've got to do it with the authorizing committees. You can write a nifty analytical study for the Senate Budget Committee, but that doesn't mean that anything happens. It may even influence the budget resolution, but if it doesn't influence the authorizing process where the main stream of decisionmaking in the Senate is, then we haven't had an impact.

The tilt has been a matter of concern to the House Budget Committee staff which is skeptical about the utility of CBO activities not closely linked to the annual budget process and apprehensive that service to authorizing committees might detract from CBO's budget work. SBC staffers generally welcome this development, seeing it as a maturation of CBO's legislative capability, a sensitizing of its analysts to congressional needs and interests.

The opening to the authorizing committees might enable CBO to pursue a more analytic course, but it is unlikely that these committees will displace the Budget Committees as the principal overseers and controllers of CBO, or that analysis will displace budgeting as CBO's main service to Congress.

CBO suffers not only from analysis being done and not used but also from analysis being misused. Members of Congress who know CBO primarily through the news media have an image of an overreaching, partisan agency that makes recommendations and advocates its own preferences on controversial issues. This perception is partly an outgrowth of CBO's publicizing of its work, but the perception also stems from a chronic and perhaps irremediable confusion of analysis and advocacy. Rivlin's best efforts to distinguish between the laying out of options and the taking of sides has been in vain. "Let me say strongly and loudly," she proclaimed to the Senate Budget Committee in 1975, "that CBO wants to be fair and nonpartisan, and to be perceived as and to be an analytically straightforward professional organization that calls issues as we see them, without any bias in any political direction."[51]

Although CBO wants to be perceived as nonpartisan, it also wants to remain free to call the shots without inhibition. It cannot have it both ways, professing to be neutral while finding that one option is more costly or less efficient than another. When it forecasts that the unemployment rate will be higher if the budget deficit is lower, CBO is seen by some Members of Congress as an advocate for a particular economic theory of government. When it reports that the federal budget provides for real growth in defense spending, not just for an inflation increase, it is seen as favoring less spending for national security. But when it suggests that more funds might be required to match the Soviet buildup in defense forces, CBO is seen as arguing for more spending in this controversial area. Statements that CBO eschews policy recommendations cannot surmount the plain fact that analysis is inseparable from advocacy in Congress.

The strongest demands for policy analysis in Congress are from policy advocates, not from neutrals who have not yet made up their minds and are waiting for the evidence to come in. Whether from CBO or any one of the countless nonlegislative producers of analysis, Congress excels in taking objective findings and applying them to partisan purposes. CBO thus faces a dismal prospect—the more it is used, the more its neutrality will be abused. CBO can avoid accusations of partiality only by retreating to bland statements or to the technical work of budgeting. If CBO want to present bold analyses, it must either build supportive relationships with legislative clients who may exploit and misuse its work, or be sheltered by the Budget Committees. The latter option simply is not now viable on the House side; the former is a possible by-product of CBO's work for the authorizing committees.

The inherent difficulty of maintaining a neutral stance while producing data that support program advocacy has been complicated by CBO's public posture. While Rivlin disavows policy recommendations, the media often report CBO's findings as if they were recommendations. In addition, the controlled language of CBO reports sometimes yields in the give and take of press conferences and in-

51. U.S. Congress, Senate Committee on the Budget, hearings on *Congressional Budget Office Oversight*, 94th Cong., 1st Sess., October 6, 1975, p. 25.

terviews to less carefully balanced words. Sometimes, quotable comments from the director steal the headlines from the text of the reports. Moreover, although Rivlin vouches for CBO's neutrality, she also sees the Congressional Budget Office as having a responsibility to call public and congressional attention to the hard fiscal choices that lie ahead. On numerous occasions, Rivlin has gone on record concerning the need to choose among competing priorities, the slim margin available for program initiatives, and the incompatibility of valued objectives (such as a balanced budget and low unemployment). She has prodded Congress to face up to the future consequences of current decisions, to take a longer view than that afforded by one-year-at-a-time budgeting. This kind of talk makes Rivlin appear to be taking sides even when she does not endorse any particular outcome.

THE MATURING OF CBO

"Your statement and the justifications are so well laid out that the questions have been almost nil,"[52] Chairman George E. Shipley of the House's Legislative Branch Appropriations Subcommittee complimented Alice Rivlin at the conclusion of a hearing on CBO's appropriation request for fiscal 1978. At the hearing, Rep. R. Lawrence Coughlin, one of CBO's harshest critics in previous years, commended Rivlin for developing "a highly professional operation and a tough, lean agency."[53] During the Senate appropriations hearings for the same year, only the subcommittee chairman was present for the 50-minute session. These two hearings were in marked contrast to the tumultuous and angry confrontations when CBO made its initial appropriations appearances, seeking funds for fiscal 1976. More than $4 million was sliced from CBO's appropriation request for fiscal 1976;[54] nothing was cut from the next year's request, and hardly any in subsequent years.

While CBO was settling into a stable relationship with the Appropriations Committees, it also was developing closer ties to the

52. U.S. Congress, House Committee on Appropriations, hearings on *Legislative Branch Appropriations for 1978*, 95th Cong., 1st Sess., February 1977, p. 422.
53. *Ibid.*, p. 418.
54. CBO requested $10.2 million for a 12-month period (covering 9 months of fiscal 1976, and the 3-month transition quarter); Congress appropriated $5.9 million for 9 months (6 months of the fiscal year plus the transition quarter).

Budget Committees. A key official who has had a high post in the budget office since its inception explained why:

> The CBO role has become much more defined, less a cause for anxiety for the committees. There are functions we perform now for them which are relatively routinized. The tension about where the line of demarcation is and where we are going to have our next fight are a lot more settled.

In equilibrium, CBO is not quite the analytic organization that Rivlin had in mind, nor the numbers operation that HBC wanted to restrict it to. Nobody got quite the Budget Office that he or she wanted, but neither did anyone lose out altogether. From HBC's standpoint, as one observer commented, "the numbers-crunching operation has been proven sufficiently useful that the other functions are tolerated in order to get the technical support." Rivlin has preserved an analytic core within CBO, although she has not been able to make analysis the definitive activity of the organization. SBC has not been able to make up its mind about the type of budget agency it wants; most likely, it wants CBO to be all things: an independent analytic group and a responsive service agency, a budget office that handles the technical details of this year's budget, and a staff that looks beyond current concerns to future issues and opportunities. CBO probably comes closest to SBC's version, an organization that constantly has to satisfy its disparate clients.

On the numbers side, CBO is performing with increasing competence and confidence. Its cost estimates cover most spending legislation, and the committees of jurisdiction accept the CBO role as legitimate and the numbers as reliable. CBO estimates are routinely used in legislative discourse, and Members frequently solicit these numbers when they prepare amendments for committee or floor consideration. CBO has become adept at hedging the numbers with protective assumptions, sometimes supplying different sets of estimates to disputing Members who want their own assumptions built into the process.

CBO's scorekeeping activities also have become technically proficient and accepted. The bugs that haunted the first crops of scorekeeping reports have been eradicated, and CBO has used its data base as an effective bridge to the Appropriations Committees, neither of which was self-sufficient in tracking the budget numbers before the new process was established. CBO's outlay estimates generally have proved more accurate than have those of the executive branch (in part, because they are published later) and its economic forecasts have tended to be closer to the mark.

Thus, in the course of a few years, CBO has moved from blueprint to an ongoing, effective budget organization. It has, in the official language of a House report, "established itself as a full-fledged, competent, and respected member of the congressional support family."[55]

As it has become accepted, CBO has lost its novelty, excitement, and newness. It no longer lives under the threat of possible extinction, but neither does it live as a venturesome, go-for-broke staff. One of CBO's "old hands" summed up the change:

> It is now a more routine, bureaucratic kind of environment. I think this is sort of a pervasive qualty of institutions as they grow older. The bureaucratization of CBO is 90 percent internal, not a response to external factors. It is the aging of an institution, and what surprises me is how rapidly that occurs.

CBO is here to stay, and although its role is not yet completely defined, the first years of its life offer telling clues, both as to the type of organization that it must be and the type that it cannot become.

55. U.S. Congress, House Commission on Information and Facilities, *op. cit.*, p. 5.

PART TWO

THE NEW RULES IN OPERATION: MAKING AND ENFORCING BUDGET RESOLUTIONS

VI Claims and Claimants

GOVERNMENTS have budgets because they do not possess sufficient funds to satisfy the demands of all interests on their resources. In this respect, there is no difference between a legislative and an executive budget: both have to cope with excess demand for public funds. Because Congress is a political institution in which power is widely shared, it requires multiple and varied opportunities through which interest groups, government agencies, and its committees and members can express their budgetary preferences.

If Congress had a single process through which all budgetary claims were channeled, some important interests almost certainly would be prevented from presenting their demands. The "gatekeepers" of budgeting would be able to suppress the articulation of preferences by certain interests. In establishing a budget process of its own, Congress neither closed off the points of access already available through its Members and committees, nor increased its reliance on the President's budget recommendations. Rather, it added a new process for the expression of budgetary wants while preserving all of the old lines of communication.

As a consequence, budgetary claims now press upon Congress from diverse sources. Some come from (or are filtered through) the executive branch.[1] The President's budget remains an influential, perhaps the dominant, factor in congressional budgeting.[2] But in view of this study's focus on congressional practices, the claims and claimants considered in this chapter are those within Congress itself.

---

1. Section 206 of the 1921 Budget and Accounting Act barred agencies from going directly to Congress with their budget claims; rather, they must first be screened through the executive budget process. However, during the 1970s, Congress chipped away at this wall of secrecy. For example, the Consumer Product Safety Commission is directed by its 1972 law to give its budget requests simultaneously to the President and Congress.
2. The House Appropriations Committee, in particular, is highly sensitive to the President's budget recommendations, and (along with the Senate Appropriations Committee) compares its every action to the President's numbers.

Congress has two main processes for generating budgetary claims: (1) authorizing legislation promoted by its committees and (2) annual reports on budgetary views and estimates. The first of these is a long-established process, though it has undergone major changes during the past 30 years. The second is a requirement of the 1974 Budget Act, which compels congressional committees to behave as claimants for federal dollars.

THE AUTHORIZATIONS PROCESS

Under the rules of Congress, a program or agency must be authorized before funds can be appropriated for it. Clause 2 of Rule XXI of the House provides that no "appropriation shall be reported in any general appropriation bills, or be in order as an amendment thereto, for any expenditure not previously authorized by law." Paragraph 2 of Senate Rule XVI precludes "an appropriation bill containing amendments proposing new or general legislation." The chief purpose of this two-step authorizations/appropriations procedure is to separate program decision making from financial decision making within Congress. The rules prescribe a division of labor which is essential to prevent the Appropriations Committees from swallowing up the legislative business of other committees and to prevent legislative committees from making appropriations decisions. To avoid an excessive concentration of legislative power, therefore, the rules purport to limit the Appropriations Committees to financial issues while barring them from substantive policy.

But the rules are not so clear-cut as they appear to be. A complicated body of precedents in each House governs the definition of what constitutes legislation in appropriation bills.[3] Moreover, the rules come into play only if a Member of Congress raises an objection (in the form of a point of order). In fact, substantive legislation frequently is incorporated into appropriation bills because no one objects when the bill is on the floor. In addition, both Houses

3. *Deschler's Procedure,* the most recent compilation of rulings by the House Parliamentarian, devotes more space to legislation and limitation in appropriation bills than to any other issue. Although it is difficult to offer a succinct statement covering all circumstances, as a general rule, if restrictive language imposes new duties or requirements, it is likely to be ruled out of order; if it merely limits the use of an appropriation, the provision is likely to be upheld.

have formal procedures for waiving or bypassing their restrictions against legislation in appropriations bills. If Congress appropriates money for an "unauthorized" program, the funds become available for expenditure, even when an authorization is required by law (rather than only by House and Senate rules). Nevertheless, most appropriations are made pursuant to authorizations.

Authorizing Legislation and Pressures To Appropriate

Over the past 30 years, the authorizations process has evolved into a means for legislative committees and Congress to periodically express their budgetary objectives for particular programs and agencies by specifying a desired level of funding in authorizing legislation. This was not always the case, however. Until the end of World War II, virtually all of the federal budget (exclusive of nonrecurring construction projects) was covered by permanent authorizations. When Congress set up an agency, it usually authorized the new organization to continue in operation indefinitely. The usual formula, authorizing "such sums as may be necessary," meant that the authorization committees would not be involved in the annual budget process except when they proposed new programs or revisions of existing ones. The Appropriations Committees, lacking specific financial guidelines from Congress, normally used the President's budget as their benchmark.

Permanent authorizations still account for well over half of the federal budget, but they are concentrated in three categories: interest on the public debt, mandatory entitlements (such as Social Security, veterans' benefits, and public assistance), and the basic operations of most Cabinet departments. Many of the major programs and agencies established since the 1950s, however, have temporary (annual or multiyear) authorizations. Congress also has converted the authorizations for some of the oldest federal agencies from permanent to limited terms. As a result, an increasing number of agencies now must appear periodically before their authorizing committees in order to secure funds from Congress. By limiting the terms of authorizations, virtually every House and Senate committee has gained some role in budget policy.

Annual authorizations add up to 10 percent to 15 percent of federal expenditures. In dollar terms, the largest annual authorizations apply to certain programs of the Defense Department. A major step in this direction was taken in 1959 with enactment of legislation requiring annual authorization for the procurement of aircraft, missiles, and naval vessels. At present, military procurement, construction, research, development, testing and evaluation, and civil defense are reauthorized each year. In the 1977 military authorization bill, the House proposed annual authorization for the entire Defense Department budget, but this proposal was dropped in conference.

The State Department, the Justice Department, and intelligence activities are now subject to annual authorizations. The Foreign Assistance Act of 1971 stipulated that no appropriation bill shall be made to the State Department or the U.S. Information Agency (now called the U.S. International Communications Agency) "unless previously authorized by legislation hereafter enacted by the Congress." Although this language did not mandate annual authorization, it was implemented by means of one-year-at-a-time legislation. State thus became the first Cabinet department subject to annual authorization for its entire appropriation. The Justice Department was placed on annual authorization by a 1976 rider to Law Enforcement Assistance Administration legislation which terminated the permanent authorization that the department had held ince 1870. The permanent authorization of intelligence programs also ended in 1976, when a Senate resolution barred the appropriation of funds for the Central Intelligence Agency, the National Security Agency, the Defense Intelligence Agency, and various intelligence activities of the State and Defense Departments and the Federal Bureau of Investigation "unless such funds shall have been previously authorized by a bill or joint resolution passed by the Senate during the same or preceding fiscal year." This "simple" resolution applies only to the Senate, but in 1977 the House adopted a companion requirement. The House resolution prohibited appropriations, except for temporary funding under continuing resolutions, for intelligence activities that have not been authorized by Congress.

Congress sometimes opts for a two- to five-year authorization period when it establishes a new program or terminates the permanent authorization of an existing one. In any single year, the multiyear authorizations scheduled for renewal amount to less than 10 percent of the budget, but the annual outlays for all new programs on a multiyear cycle amount to more than $100 billion. The multiyear programs include revenue sharing, economic development, highway construction, water pollution control, most education programs, and various health programs. This time framework is also popular for grant-in-aid programs, especially those established since the 1960s. In setting two- to five-year terms, Congress has both indicated unwillingness to accord permanent status to new and untried assistance programs, and demonstrated its sensitivity to the need of state and local governments for some advance indication of the amounts of federal aid they might receive.

Legislative committees have two distinct motives in seeking limited-term authorizations. One is to enhance congressional oversight and control of executive agencies; the other is to enable the committees to serve as advocates for favored programs. The oversight role was uppermost in the conversion of the State and Justice Departments and the intelligence community to limited-term authorization. Thus in 1976 Chairman Peter W. Rodino, Jr., of the House Judiciary Committee urged the termination of the permanent authorization for the Justice Department because

> our citizens require a responsible and vigilant oversight by the Congress. . . . The [Judiciary] committee believes that a thorough and orderly authorization scrutiny of Justice Department functions and activities will better serve the interests of Congress. . . .[4]

Congress also can use its authorization power to control executive activities by writing specific conditions or limitations into authorizing legislation. This has frequently been the case in legislation dealing with the conduct of foreign policy.[5]

When Congress no longer believes it necessary to scrutinize a program, it rarely reverts to permanent authorization. Rather, the periodic reauthorization becomes a *pro forma* exercise, processed through Congress without debate or controversy. A good illustration is the multibillion-dollar authorization for defense-related atomic energy programs. Once a controversial issue, the bill did not

---

4. 122 *Congressional Record* (daily ed., August 31, 1976) H9277.
5. For example, the fiscal 1976 Foreign Relations Authorization Act barred the State Department from developing a machine-readable passport system; declared that political contributions should not be criteria in the award of ambassadorial positions; urged the reopening of a consulate at Gothenburg, Sweden; instructed the Arms Control and Disarmament Agency to study the effects of arms limitations on military expenditures; modified statutory requirements with regard to security investigations for contractors; limited U.S. contributions to certain international organizations and activities; called for the temporary assistance of Foreign Service officers to congressional, state, local, and public organizations; established grievance procedures for Foreign Service personnel; and authorized certain employees to carry firearms. This was just one law's list of congressional concerns which piggybacked the annual authorizations process to enactment.

attract a single floor amendment when the Senate considered it in May 1977. The chairman of the authorizing committee was the only Senator to speak on the measure. His brief remarks noted the lack of interest in the legislation: "I thought something should be said about the bill, as it is important. There is nothing to say, except it has been considered and unanimously recommended for passage."[6]

Limited-term authorizations have a second purpose: They give legislative committees an opportunity to influence budgetary outcomes. Permanent authorizations ordinarily do not specify the amount of money available for appropriation. Accordingly, the Appropriations Committees make their expenditure decisions for permanent programs without guidance or pressure from the authorizing committees. But if an authorizing committee wants more money appropriated for its programs, it can seek an annual or multiyear authorization that fixes the maximum amount that may be appropriated for the year (or years) covered by the legislation. This was the principal motive for the conversion of military procurement from permanent to annual status some 20 years ago. A more recent case involved an effort by the House Post Office and Civil Service Committee to convert the intergovernmental personnel program from "such sums as may be necessary" to a definite authorization. Appropriations for the program were about $15 million a year, but the committee wanted a much higher level. It therefore proposed to substitute a $40 million authorization for fiscal 1976 and $50 million for fiscal 1977 for the "such sums" provision of law. The Post Office and Civil Service Committee acknowledged that the change was intended "to indicate its concern for more adequate funding of this program," but the proposal ran into opposition from Members of Congress who wanted to shield the Appropriations Committees from pressure for higher spending levels.[7]

Regardless of the motive for limited-term authorizations, these legislative actions become claims for federal dollars. Before enactment of the Congressional Budget Act, these claims were addressed primarily to the Appropriations Committees; under the new process, claims are presented to the Budget Committees as well.

---

6. 123 *Congressional Record* (daily ed., May 23, 1977) S8372, remarks of Senator Stennis.
7. Supporters of the specific authorization were forced to argue that the committee was proposing a limitation on appropriations, not an expectation of higher future expenditures. See 121 *Congressional Record* (daily ed., September 3, 1975), remarks of Representatives Ford and Rousselot, H8255.

The Authorizations-Appropriations Gap

In assessing the potency of authorizations as claims on the budget, one must make a distinction between annual and multiyear legislation. In the case of an annual cycle, Congress usually decides the authorization and appropriation amounts during the same year. Often, the appropriations bill is taken up only weeks after passage of the companion authorization. As a result, the authorization is likely to exert a direct influence on the subsequent appropriation. For most annual authorizations, the amount appropriated is more than 90 percent of the authorized level. This pattern is especially persistent when the authorizing committees and Appropriations Committees share similar program objectives. The correlation between authorizations and appropriations for defense programs has been strengthened by overlapping memberships on the Armed Services and Appropriations Committees in the Senate and by strong support for defense programs in the House Appropriations Committee.[8] But when the two sets of committees do not share the same attitudes about a program, authorizations and appropriations will tend to diverge. This partly explains why authorizations for foreign assistance sometimes have been substantially higher than appropriations.

Even though an authorization is a congressional decision, it can be a weaker signal to the Appropriations Committees than is the President's budget. These committees meticulously compare each of their actions with the President's request. So long as the authorized level does not significantly exceed the budget, the appropriation is likely to be close to it. But if the authorization is substantially above the budget request, the Appropriations Committees are apt to use the President's numbers as their benchmark, with a resulting discrepancy between the authorized and appropriated amounts. This gap between the two congressional actions sometimes occurs when annual authorizations are introduced as a means of enabling the authorizing committees to advance the interests of their programs. However, once the authorizations committee's role becomes routinized, the budget request, the authorization, and the appropriation tend to converge.

---

8. Senator Stennis, the chairman of the Armed Services Committee, was for many years a leading member of the Defense Appropriations subcommittee. In 1978, he became chairman of the subcommittee, thus heading both the authorizations and appropriations units with jurisdiction over defense programs.

In the case of multiyear authorizations, the link to the appropriations process frequently is much looser. Multiyear authorizations, as noted, are concentrated in grant programs in which state and local governments and interest groups usually exert strong pressure for increased federal assistance. In response to these pressures, the authorizing committees often schedule annual increases in the amount authorized for each year covered by the legislation. This strategy has a dual advantage for the authorizing committees: (1) It shows interest groups that the committees are sympathetic to their aims, but in a manner that defers the bulk of the increase to future budgets; and (2) it pressures the Appropriations Committees to provide more funds for these programs.

But the Appropriations Committees do not have to honor these claims. A standard authorization has no legal effect—funds cannot be spent pursuant to it—unless it is "validated" by an appropriation. The Appropriations Committees can continue to appropriate at levels more responsive to the President's budget than to legislative authorizations.

During the past decade, there has been a wide "authorizations-appropriations" gap for many grant programs stemming from steep increases in authorizations without a corresponding rise in appropriations. This gap began to open during the mid-1960s when (in the face of Vietnam War spending pressures) Congress appropriated less than the amounts authorized for Great Society programs. In a 1970 report, the Advisory Commission on Intergovernmental Relations calculated that the gap between authorizations and appropriations for 169 grant programs had risen from $2.7 billion in 1966 to $8.5 billion in 1970. "Expressed in percentage terms, Federal aid appropriations fell from approximately 80 percent of authorizations in 1966 to an estimated 65 percent by 1970."[9] The gap continued to widen during the first half of the 1970s, as authorizing committees tried to mobilize support for progressively higher appropriations. They took the position that an authorization should reflect the financial needs of a program, not the budgetary condition of the government. Thus, for fiscal 1975, Congress authorized $14.8 billion for HEW education programs but it appropriated $6.2 billion, only 42 percent of the authorized level.[10]

An illustration of how the gap develops can be drawn from the regional medical program. Annual increases raised the amount au-

9. U.S. Advisory Commission on Intergovernmental Relations, *The Gap Between Federal Aid Authorizations and Appropriations*, June 1970.
10. 121 *Congressional Record* (daily ed., June 3, 1975) S9456.

thorized from $65 million in fiscal 1969 to $250 million in fiscal 1973. During the first of these years, the appropriation was $56.2 million, or 90 percent of authorizations. For 1973, the appropriation had tripled to $159 million, but it had slipped to 64 percent of authorizations.[11]

ENTER THE BUDGET PROCESS

Authorization issues were high on the agenda during the negotiations that culminated in the Budget Act. The Appropriations Committees wanted to retrieve some of the power they had lost as a consequence of limited-term authorizations and backdoor spending. In the end, they settled for constraints on backdoor legislation, a deadline on the reporting of authorization bills, and a few provisions linking the authorizations committees to the new budget process. The basic structure of the authorizations process was not touched; rather, it was made to operate within the context of the new budget routines.

As a result of the budget process, authorizing comimttees have been sensitized to the fiscal status of their programs. Before the Budget Act, many committees were uncertain of how much was being requested or appropriated for their programs; some also were unsure of exactly which programs fell under their jurisdiction. Part of the problem was that some committees (such as those with permanent authorizations) did not need to know. A complicating factor was the structural differences between authorizations and appropriations. There are many more federal programs than there are appropriation accounts; most appropriations lump numerous separate authorizations into a single account. Often, a new program is folded into an existing appropriation; such action makes it difficult for the authorizing committee to keep track of financial developments.

When the President presented his budget to Congress each year, few authorizing committees had sure knowledge of how much was proposed to be spent for programs within their jurisdiction. Many did not even try to find out. Only committees with annual authorizations had a continuing incentive to monitor the budgets of the programs for which they were responsible. This situation was sub-

11. House Committee in Interstate and Foreign Commerce, *Fiscal Data for Health Authorities Expiring in 1973*, Committee Print No. 1, March 1973, p. 13.

stantially changed by the Budget Act's requirement that each committee report its views and estimates with respect to all budget matters within its jurisdiction. In practice, committees have been compelled to recommend spending levels for authorizations enacted in prior years as well as for anticipated new legislation. But to fulfill this annual requirement, committees must be much better informed about the budgetary status of their programs than once was necessary. They must be in a position to advise Congress as to how much should be budgeted and appropriated for all their programs. They cannot be lax about this responsibility because failure to make an effective claim for funds may prejudice their programs.

Most authorizing committees have added budget specialists to their staffs to monitor all phases of the congressional budget process and to maintain year-round contact with the Budget Committees and the CBO. Awareness of the budgetary implications of authorizations has been sharpened by the CBO cost estimates that now accompany committee reports on authorizing legislation. Although this procedure got off to a slow start, the CBO's cost estimates have become an accepted fixture in Congress. Both CBO and the General Accounting Office (GAO) have developed information systems linking authorizations and appropriations to each other. The CBO and GAO lists are used by a number of authorizing committees in preparing their March 15 reports.

One cannot be certain whether heightened budgetary awareness has significantly affected the behavior of authorizing committees. There seems to be little reason for change in the handling of permanent and annual authorizations. Committees do not have to take any legislative action for their permanent authorizations to be covered by the budget and appropriations processes. They have only to estimate the amount that will be available (or required) for expenditure on the basis of laws already in effect. With regard to annual authorizations, the President's budget has long served as a benchmark for committee action, and it continues to have this status under the congressional budget process. In interviews, several members and staff of authorizing committees argued that the budget process has brought a sense of realism to the determination of authorization levels. Pie-in-the-sky authorizations, some suggested, have been curbed by an awareness that such actions are likely to be futile and invite charges of budgetary irresponsibility. Others insisted, however, that committees continue to authorize in accord with their perceptions of program needs, even if this practice means authorizations substantially in excess of budget and appropriation levels.

Although the gap has probably been narrowed somewhat, it has not been eliminated. For example, in fiscal 1978, Office of Education programs were funded at slightly more than 50 percent of authorization,[12] a better record than in pre-Budget Act years, but factors other than the budget process might have been responsible. More conservative attitudes toward government spending and the same conditions that impelled Congress to accept budget controls also have constrained its appetite for costly programs. Moreover, the levels authorized for some programs have been affected by presidential action. Between 1972 and 1976, Presidents Nixon and Ford vetoed a number of authorization bills; they refused to accept high authorizations in expectation of much lower appropriations. In response, Congress then scaled down the authorizations for certain vetoed bills. For example, after Ford successfully vetoed two health authorization bills in 1974, Congress, in 1975, passed a new authorization 30 percent below the amount fixed in the earlier bills, a reduction from $1.2 billion to about $800 million for fiscal 1976 alone.[13] When Ford once again used his veto power on this bill, however, Congress overrode his action by a wide margin. Even Republicans deserted their party leader and defended the new bill as fiscally sound. Republican Congressman James T. Broyhill argued for an override by pointing to the relatively modest level of authorization, saying that if we "compare these authorization levels to prior-year authorizations, they are very much in line, and in fact, less than the authorizations of prior years."[14]

Members of Congress respond to two sets of pressure when they act on authorizations and appropriations. Through the authorizations process, Congress demonstrates its responsiveness to particular interests; through its appropriations decisions, Congress deals with the financial limitations of the federal government. The basic political conditions that led in the past to different authorization and appropriation outcomes have not been fundamentally altered

---

12. This percentage covers programs which have a fixed (definite) authorization, not those with indefinite authorizations. See U.S. Office of Education, *Justifications of Appropriation Estimates for Committee on Appropriations, Fiscal Year 1979.*
13. Ford vetoed two health authorization bills in 1974, H.R. 14214 and H.R. 17085. These bills were combined into S. 66 which was passed by Congress in 1975 over Ford's veto, but with significantly lower authorizations than the predecessor bills.
14. 121 *Congressional Record* (daily ed., July 29, 1975) H7729.

by the budget process. The continuing gap reflects the ambivalence within Congress on spending policy as well as tension between the two sets of committees. The conflict is strained by the budgetary role of Congress as both a claimant for funds and an adjudicator of budgetary claims. Through authorizations, Congress goes on record in support of specific programs; through appropriations, it decides the extent to which these claims are to be satisfied.

Committees campaign for escalating multiyear authorizations by suggesting that more favorable fiscal circumstances in the future may permit Congress to increase appropriations well above the current level. Committees continue to win high authorizations by assuring Congress that the real spending decisions will be made at the appropriations stage. In 1975, for example, Congress approved a conference report progressively raising the authorization for education of the handicapped from $100 million to $3.2 billion over a seven-year period. In House debate, members were assured that the actual funding level would be decided annually through the appropriations process. "I do not know," one of the bill's managers told the House, "whether we will appropriate at those levels or not." He added,

> I think what we are doing here is laying out the goal. Ignoring other Federal priorities, we thought it acceptable if funding reaches that level. However, there will be another Congress by that time, as well as many appropriations processes, and at that later time if it is felt too high a level has been set and false promises have been made, we could be making the change at that time.[15]

The introduction of a budget process therefore has provided fresh incentives to mobilize support for programs by pushing for higher authorizations. To the extent that congressional budget constraints are perceived as effective, the authorization committees might want to stake their claims on future budgets. They can couple assurances that the authorization does not bind future appropriations with similar words regarding budget levels.

An example of this behavior occurred in 1975, when the Senate Interior Committee developed a bill (S. 327) to increase the authorization for the Land and Water Conservation Fund from $300 million to $1 billion per year. The floor manager of the bill assured the Senate that it should not consider the proposed authorization

15. 121 *Congressional Record* (daily ed., November 18, 1975) H11349, remarks of Representative Quie.

to be a firm commitment to future appropriations: ". . . we realize that the full $1 billion called for by this bill cannot be funded this year. We understand that, we realize it, and we take the language of this bill to be an authorization and not an automatic appropriation."[16]

Senator Muskie was not satisfied by this statement. He foresaw pressure on the Budget Committees from those who would maintain that Congress had already voted increased spending for the program. He wanted explicit assurance that "passage of S. 327 does not amount to a prejudgment of what that funding will be following consideration by the budget process and the appropriation process."[17] The issue was resolved through an exchange of letters between the chairmen of the Budget and Interior Committees, a floor colloquy, and acknowledgment that "The actual funding for this legislation will be the result of the process through which the Budget Committee evaluates economic and fiscal policy [and] considers requests for Federal spending."[18]

Although Muskie vigorously intervened in debate on the Land and Water Conservation Fund, the Budget Act provides no clear guidelines as to the role of the Budget Committees in the authorizations process. The charter of these committees includes "studies of the effect on budget outlays of relevant existing and proposed legislation." But inasmuch as the budget resolutions deal with budget authority and not with authorizations, there is no compelling need for the Budget Committees to get involved.

As has happened on many other budgetary issues, the Budget Committees have taken different positions. The House Budget Committee does not ordinarily comment on authorization bills, although in its "early warning" examination of spending bills prior to floor action it considers such measures along with appropriations and entitlements. HBC publicly considers an authorization bill only if it misses the May 15 reporting deadline or if it has a backdoor or entitlement provision or some other questionable financial arrangement. This tactic comports with the committee's overall view of its role as a behind-the-scenes guardian of the budget process, intervening only when necessary to uphold the requirements of the Budget Act. HBC justifies its limited role on authorizations by

16. 121 *Congressional Records* (daily ed., October 29, 1975) S18901, remarks of Senator Johnston.
17. *Ibid.*, S18904.
18. *Ibid.*, S18905, statement of Senator Jackson, read into the record by Senator Muskie.

noting that the real spending decisions are made in the appropriations process. Even if Congress passes unrealistic authorizations, there is, in the committee's view, no loss of budget control as long as the appropriations conform to congressional budget determinations.

Occasionally, the HBC chairman has broken his silence on authorization bills to support the congressional budget process. This has occurred, for example, when the budget process has been threatened by a presidential veto. HBC Chairman Adams argued for an override of President Ford's veto of the 1975 health authorization bill. The bill, he advised the House, does not "blow the budget up." If the House passed this bill and if Congress stayed on its current course, Adams predicted, the budget figures would be more than $3 billion below those in the budget resolution.[19]

Yet there is a big difference between intervening on the side of the authorizing committee, as Adams did in the health legislation, and intervening in opposition to committee action. From the beginning, the Senate Budget Committee has actively opposed authorizations that might lead to appropriations in excess of the budget targets. SBC staffers prepare detailed memoranda on major authorization bills pending before the Senate, many of which are converted into floor statements for use by SBC leaders. Together, these SBC leaders have commented on dozens of authorization bills during the first years of the budget process. SBC also maintains careful watch over the authorizations business of the Senate through the scorekeeping process. Estimates for selected authorizations which might lead to higher than budgeted (or expected) appropriations are included in the scorekeeping materials distributed to Senate committees and Members.[20]

SBC takes the position that if it were to withdraw from the authorizations process, it would (by silence) be acquiescing in legislation that exceeded the congressional budget levels or which effectively foreclosed future budget options. It thus regards authorizations not merely as wishful expressions of legislative aspirations but as real influences on appropriation decisions. In its view, if authorization control were to slip away, the committee's ability to hold the line on appropriations would be weakened.

19. 121 *Congressional Record* (daily ed., July 29, 1975) H7728.

20. CBO not only prepares periodic scorekeeping reports for Congress; it also prepares separate scorekeeping data for the House and Senate Budget Commiittees. HBC's scorekeeping reports do not cover authorizations.

SBC scored a signal success in its first year by challenging a conference report on the annual military procurement authorization bill. Although that authorization covered less than one-third of the amount allocated in the budget resolution to the national defense function, Muskie (supported by most of his Democratic and Republican colleagues on the committee) argued that it would cause total defense spending to exceed the level targeted in the budget resolution. This computation was based on assumptions about what Congress would do with the portion of defense spending that does not go through the authorizations process. Sen. John L. McClellan, chairman of the Appropriations Committee, asked for approval of the conference report because "everything in this bill, if it does exceed the budget, will have a review." He noted,

> It still has to be appropriated and anything in the appropriation bill that exceeds what the Budget Committee thinks is proper is subject to amendment, subject to change, subject to debate, and the issue can be resolved.[21]

Muskie, for his part, admitted "that we are considering here an authorization bill, which does not provide budget authority directly." But, he warned the Senate, this bill "sets the pattern for spending bills that follow. . . . In my judgment, if we accept these numbers, we will have to live with the consequences."[22] Muskie's argument carried the day, as the Senate rejected the conference report by a 42-48 vote, an extraordinary rebuff to one of the Senate's most powerful committees. One month later, the military authorization bill was returned from conference with a lower spending level.

More than any other, this victory established the Senate Budget Committee as a vigilant protector of the new budget process. But it also left the committee with a dilemma. It could not attack every authorization bill that breached congressional budget targets; to do so would set the committee on a collision course with virtually every other Senate committee. But neither could it play favorites, opposing above-budget authorizations if it did not like the program, but ignoring the matter if the legislation happened to be supported by its members. The problem did not surface at once because SBC's opposition to the defense bill was coupled with opposition to a pending conference report on a school lunch pro-

21. 121 *Congressional Record* (daily ed., August 1, 1975) S14723.
22. *Ibid.*, S14722.

gram.[23] Not only did this tandem strategy enable SBC to forge bipartisan and near-unanimous agreement among its members, but also it projected SBC as a group that even-handedly considered spending bills, regardless of their liberal or conservative tint.

SBC could not, however, long ignore the fact that authorizations differ. First, a clear distinction has to be maintained between conventional authorizations and entitlements. Second, some authorizations strongly influence the amount appropriated by Congress while others have little impact. Moreover, a distinction must be drawn between annual authorizations, which relate entirely to the current (or next year's) budget process, and multiyear authorizations, which chiefly affect future budgets. SBC is on firmer budgetary ground when it intervenes with respect to an annual than to a multiyear bill. These considerations set defense authorizations apart from much of the authorizing legislation acted on by Congress. Military procurement and construction are authorized annually, and the amount appropriated rarely diverges more than a few percentage points from the authorization. It was with this fact in mind that SBC challenged the defense authorization bill in 1975. The situation is much different, however, in health and education programs for which the authorization usually extends several years into the future, and the appropriation usually is far below the authorized level.

SBC also has had to take into account the difference between authorizations and appropriations. The committee cannot treat every authorization bill as if it provides the actual funds for expenditures; to do so would erase the congressional distinction between the two sets of committees. SBC was confronted with these issues during its markup of the second budget resolution for fiscal 1976. The markup occurred shortly after the committee's double success with the defense and school lunch bills. Despite these successes, SBC was faced with a need to raise some of the functional allocations above the amounts set in the first budget resolutions for the

23. When the conference report on the school lunch bill reached the floor in September 1975, one month after the Senate had rejected the military authorization bill, Muskie urged that it be recommitted: "Today we have the opportunity to show the breadth of our commitment to fiscal discipline. On August 1 we voted to keep military spending close to the congressional budget. Today we can apply that same sense of constraint to spending on domestic programs by voting to recommit the child nutrition bill to conference." 121 *Congressional Record* (daily ed., September 5, 1975) S15396. The recommittal was given unanimous approval 76 to 0.

fiscal year. Sen. Sam Nunn could not "understand how we get this far over the target in a category with no real fundamental challenge."[24] In response, Senator Muskie explained the differences between authorizations, entitlements, and appropriations, and admitted "in all candor that in June [before the defense and school lunch bills] we were much more tenderfooted about what kind of clout we had, or what kind of credibility we had, or what kind of case we could make than we became later on as we were more sure of ourselves and had harder facts."[25]

Senator Nunn raised another problem, that by challenging "realistic" authorizations, the Budget Committee might stimulate authorizing committees to propose still costlier measures:

If the reward for making the authorization and the appropriation bills close like defense does is to have both of them challenged by the Budget Committee every year, then I would say that the authorizing committee would move in the same direction the other authorizing committees are in, and sort of paint the picture as to where the goal ought to be rather than having an all-out effort to cut.[26]

Despite Muskie's declaration that authorizations and appropriations have to be treated differently, some of his early statements did not always indicate recognition of the differences between the two processes. In floor remarks during Senate consideration of the first budget resolution for fiscal 1977, Muskie promised the same vigilance over appropriations and authorizations:

Spending bills in excess of the budget targets will raise the deficit. Authorizations which put pressure on the Appropriations committee to exceed the targets will equally jeopardize our success with the budget.

The Budget Committee and its Chairman will be examining both the spending and authorization bills closely throughout the rest of the session for compliance with the targets in the budget resolution. We will not hesitate to make very clear to the Senate when those targets are being jeopardized by either spending or authorization bills. We will not hesitate to oppose those bills, amendments, and even conference reports which pose a threat to these targets.[27]

This tough pronouncement put Muskie in an untenable position. He could not mount a campaign against every authorization that

24. Senate Budget Committee, markup of the second concurrent resolution on the budget for fiscal 1976, transcript, p. 316.
25. *Ibid.*, p. 322.
26. *Ibid.*, p. 325.
27. 122 *Congressional Record* (daily ed., May 12, 1976) S7070.

exceeded the budget; nor could he deploy the budget process against the proclivity of committees to authorize in accord with their assessment of program needs. In a letter to Muskie dealing with a health authorization bill, Sen. Edward M. Kennedy argued for restraint in the application of budget control to authorization bills:

> Authorization levels set by our [Labor and Public Welfare] committee historically have reflected the need in a particular program area, and the capacity of the Executive agencies involved or the affected institutions to move ahead. They do not necessarily reflect the amount that should be appropriated given necessary tradeoffs and ceilings within the budget and appropriations processes. At the very least, authorizations should allow enough flexibility so that decisions can be made to cut back on one health program and expand another above its budgeted figure in response to a special need or opportunity. If the authorization levels were the same as the budgeted figures, this type of tradeoff would be impossible since any increase in the appropriation would exceed the authorization amount. Indeed, if the authorization level simply represented the amount set in the budget, we would be reducing the appropriations process to nothing more than a review of what the Budget Committee and authorizing committees have done.[28]

In addition to sympathizing with Kennedy's arguments, Muskie and SBC had reasons of their own for not opposing all authorizations in excess of budget levels. Given the tendency of Congress to "overauthorize" for many social programs, a no-exception rule would have compelled SBC to wage continuing warfare against popular legislation. As a habitual nay-sayer, SBC would have risked offending almost everyone in the Senate, and its own credibility would have been impaired. Rather than being seen as a fair-minded and balanced committee, SBC would have quickly become typed as a biased and obdurate outpost of fiscal conservatism. Its advice would become suspect, even in instances involving a genuine breach of budgetary discipline. Moreover, SBC members sat on other committees and supported higher spending for favored programs. Their own legislative effectiveness therefore would have been damaged by unbending fidelity to budget control.

In practice, Muskie and SBC were carefully picking their fights, challenging very few authorizations that exceeded the budget. Muskie's staff advised him to take "a *highly* selective approach to authorizations," and proposed three standards by which to decide

28. Quoted in Memorandum from John McEvoy to Senator Muskie, May 25, 1976. Senate Budget Committee files.

SBC's posture. The basic rule was opposition to any authorization "which is so large in amount that it is unreasonable to believe that it can be accommodated within the functional target together with other legislation known to be necessary in the session if appropriations for these can be reasonably anticipated."[29] This rule was more easily stated than applied, and SBC staff produced a stream of memos seeking to clarify the committee's position and to develop consistency in practice.[30] It is relatively simple for SBC to take a stand when a budget category contains a small number of authorization bills and virtually all spending is covered in a single appropriation. National defense has these characteristics, but most of the other functions in the budget are spread among a multiplicity of authorizations and appropriations. In such cases, SBC must make a string of subjective judgments about what Congress might do in the future.

This problem arose in June 1976, for example, only a month after Muskie had announced that SBC would intervene against excessive authorizations. The Senate was considering authorizations for the Federal Energy Agency (FEA), one of perhaps nine or more authorization bills expected during the session for energy programs. By itself, the FEA bill did not exceed budget targets, but together with the other anticipated legislation, authorizations might have totaled $1 billion more than was allocated in the budget for energy activities.

Muskie could not make a winning case against the bill, or even a convincing argument that it threatened the budget. Instead, he decided simply to lay the facts before the Senate and use the data to counter amendments that would boost energy authorizations above the amounts reported by committee. He began with a retreat from the contention that authorizations and appropriations should meet the same budget test, noting that "this is an authorization bill and not an appropriation bill, and we do not try to impose the same kind of budgetary disciplines upon authorization bills as we do on appropriations bills with some exceptions."[31]

He then went on to caution the Senate that there would not be room in the budget for all the energy proposals being advanced by various committees:

---

29. *Ibid.*
30. In addition to the May 25, 1976, memo, the issue is discussed in memos dated October 1, 1975, and May 17, 1976.
31. 122 *Congressional Record* (daily ed., June 15, 1976) S9411.

I realize that the FEA bill before us today . . . is only a small part of this [energy] total. And I also realize that many of the authorizations may not be fully funded. But we do know that high authorizations put pressure on the Committee on Appropriations to increase funding levels. I must therefore advise the Senate that the Appropriations Committee, in several instances, will have to fund energy programs at well below the level of authorizations if we are to stay within the budget resolution targets.[32]

This kind of statement became Muskie's—and SBC's—characteristic response to authorizing legislation that threatened the budget targets or called for much steeper spending in the future. Instead of opposing an authorization bill on the floor, Muskie usually endorsed legislation with a warning about pressures on the budget and an expression of skepticism as to whether it would be possible to fund the authorization fully. This strategy enabled SBC to function as guardian of the budget without offending the authorizing committees.[33]

The "for, but with a warning" tactic was used by Muskie in 1975 when the Senate took up the bill to authorize education for the handicapped. Although it was unlikely that the program would be fully funded, Muskie realized that the bill would pave the way for steep increases in future spending. But rather than making a frontal assault on this highly popular legislation, Muskie opted for a warning about the bill's impact on future budgets.

. . . this legislation creates what is known in budget parlance as a "wedge." That is, we appear to be establishing a program that may not look like a big commitment now but may soon become a very substantial one.

It is the task of the authorizing committees to identify the needs for programs such as this, and I am especially appreciative of the Labor and Public Welfare Committee's efforts to translate such needs with the clarity that has been exhibited in this legislation.

However, the probability that we will fully meet these needs seems small. Unless we forfeit on commitments to other important priorities

32. *Ibid.*

33. This is the way Muskie explained his committee's role during the debate within SBC over its approach to authorization bills: ". . . we have tried, especially in the last two or three months in the statements we have put in the record to raise warning flags, red flags, in functions where we could see some dangers coming down the line, even though we could not at that point prove that a target had been breached. We tried to raise warning flags . . ." Markup of the second concurrent resolution on the budget for fiscal 1976, transcript, p. 323.

in the Federal budget, it strikes me as unlikely that we will be able to fund this program at the full authorization in the near future.

Mr. President, I am of two minds on this bill. I applaud the specificity of the out-year authorizations in this bill; yet I have reservations about this first step toward committing ourselves to authorizations for such large spending in the future.[34]

Muskie also has resorted to cautionary statements rather than outright opposition because standard authorizations can be spent only to the extent provided in appropriations. He thus has adopted the same argument that authorizing committees use to promote unrealistically costly programs. This was Muskie's approach to a $5.6 billion multiyear authorization for mass transit programs passed by the Senate in 1977, but almost all of which was for future years. Muskie announced that he would vote for the bill because "the Senate will not be forfeiting its opportunity to control the level of funding of the capital grant program through future budget resolutions and appropriation bills." Rather, the bill "gives the Appropriations Committee the flexibility to fund whatever specific types and mix of capital grants finally are determined to be most appropriate."[35]

The dozens of floor statements Muskie has issued on authorizing legislation add up to a clear picture of a chairman intent on avoiding open conflict with authorizing committees but still determined to remind the Senate again and again of the need for budgetary discipline.

Although authorizing committees would be happy to do without Budget Committee comments on their legislation, they are not averse to using the budget process for their own purposes. This occurred, for example, when a $2.5 billion authorization for energy programs attracted a flurry of floor amendments during Senate debate in 1977. Rather than opposing them directly on substantive grounds, Sen. Frank Church (the floor manager of the bill) waved the banner of budget control. "I do not know why we pass budget resolutions if we are then going to ignore them with every major bill that comes up afterwards."[36] Still, the Senate approved seven floor amendments raising the authorizations for designated energy activities, although it rejected the most costly proposals.

At best, the Budget Committees and the authorizing committees

34. 121 *Congressional Record* (daily ed., November 19, 1975) S20436.
35. 123 *Congressional Record* (daily ed., June 23, 1977) S10578.
36. 123 *Congressional Record* (daily ed., June 13, 1977) S9593.

have been fleeting allies, joining together when their interests converge but going their separate ways on most issues. As claimants in the budget process, authorizing committees have not ordinarily shared the same perspective or interests as those who must cope with excess demands. In the specialized world of Congress, the authorizing committees and the Budget Committees move in separate spheres, and it is only the outreach of the budget process that forces them into frequent contact with one another. The authorizing committees prefer peaceful coexistence with the new budget makers, not only because this is the way of Congress, but also because they do not want to be regarded as irresponsible on budget matters. Thus far, the authorizing committees have been able to live under a budget regimen that has not substantively affected their behavior. In fact, the main impact of the budget process has been on the timing of their legislative operations, an issue that deeply troubles many authorizing committees.

SPEEDING UP THE AUTHORIZATIONS PROCESS

"The Budget Act treats the authorizations process almost as an afterthought," the staff director of one of the most powerful authorizing committees complained. His ire was directed at the requirement that all committees report their authorizing legislation for the next fiscal year by May 15, which is also the date for completion of congressional action on the first budget resolution. The Appropriations Committees campaigned for a deadline on the ground that delays in the authorizations process had prevented Congress from completing action on appropriation bills by the beginning of the fiscal year. The Appropriations Committees wanted a deadline on the enactment of authorizations, but Congress could not accept a deadline that would have put basic legislation beyond its reach for most of the year.

Although the May 15 deadline was devised to accommodate the appropriations process, that date is equally relevant to congressional budget making. A budget process must operate within a timetable, not necessarily a formal one or one applicable to all events, but certainly one that covers most key milestones. Financial decisions can be made without budget routines—Congress managed to operate in this way for almost 200 years—but a budget process could not be effective if claimants were free to levy demands whenever they wanted and decisions were made whenever the deciders got around to them. Deadlines are important because they notify the participants of what they must do in the course of the cycle.

As claims on the budget, authorizations normally might be submitted before the budget is decided. If authorizations could be developed at any time during the year, Budget Committees would have a difficult time ascertaining the legislative intentions of the authorizing committees before they prepared the first budget resolution. Yet perfect synchronization of the budget and authorization processes would have required a reporting deadline much earlier than May 15. The May 15 authorizing deadline was a compromise between the Appropriations Committees' demand for an earlier cutoff date and the authorizing committees' preference for no time restriction. Understandably, authorizing committees cluster much of their output near the deadline, with the result that most of the first budget resolution's decisions have been made by the time the authorizations are reported. For example, House committees reported more than 40 public bills, mostly authorizations, on May 14 and 15, 1976. In the same year, Senate committees reported about 75 bills in the last days before the deadline, and on May 17, Majority Leader Mike Mansfield announced that 94 legislative matters remained on the Senate calendar. A similar logjam near the May 15 reporting date has been an annual occurrence since then.

Continuing contact between the Budget Committees and the authorizing committees enables the former to avoid being surprised by unexpected legislation. By the time that preparation of the first budget resolution enters the homestretch, the Budget Committees have a pretty solid idea of the authorization bills that will be forthcoming. Sometimes, however, rapidly changing conditions impel authorizing committees to veer from their expected course. This happened in 1977, when the Senate Agriculture Committee reported legislation substantially above the amount targeted for agriculture programs in the recently adopted budget resolution. The resulting clash between the Budget Committees and the authorizations committees (considered in a later chapter) might have been mitigated if the farm legislation had cleared the Agriculture Committee before the numbers were hardened in the budget resolution.

Routine does not come easily to Congress; it is a notoriously spasmodic institution and the calendar by which it works has few fixed intervals. Often months pass with no movement on legislation, only to be followed by a rush to get a measure through.

Nevertheless, the deadlines in the Budget Act have brought some order to Congress as a whole. Work periods and recesses are scheduled with the budget process in mind. Congressional leaders have welcomed the scheduling discipline provided by the May 15 deadline and have encouraged authorizing committees to develop work plans that enable them to clear legislation by that date. When the Budget Act took effect, Speaker Carl Albert convened several meetings of House committee chairmen at which the budget procedures were explained and the committees were asked to work within the new time framework. In the Senate, Robert Byrd has suported the timetable and urged committees to report their legislation by May 15.

Committees have adapted to the May 15 deadline by tackling major legislative issues during the first months of the session rather than putting them off until late in the year. The defense authorization bill, which customarily lingered in Congress long after the fiscal year had started, now marches through Congress before the beginning of the fiscal year; the military construction authorization bill, which once was treated as "hostage" legislation (i.e., it was held up until late in the session in order to induce members to cooperate on other legislation), now is processed earlier in the year. Staff members of authorizing committees have attested to the potency of the deadline: "If you don't have deadlines," said one, "there is a tendency for all organizations, especially committees, to wander afield and spend time, energy, and resources on less essential matters and less time on the essential. It has forced this committee to concentrate and establish its own priorities." The staff director of a House committee which handles a number of annual authorizations was pleased that "right now [early summer of 1977] all of our authorizing legislation is down at the White House and that hasn't happened before. The discipline it establishes is damn good."

All has not been roses, however. The relationship between the authorizations and appropriations processes definitely has been affected and, according to a number of experienced congressional aides, the quality of legislation has been impaired. Because the Budget Act calls for completion of action on regular appropriation bills by the end of the summer, Congress has not been able to liquidate the backlog of authorizations before it turns to appropriations business. The House generally begins considering appropriations bills in June, before many of the prerequisite authorizations have been enacted. In 1976, for example, the House began its appropriations phase with almost $40 billion in expected appropriations lacking authorization. But instead of waiting until the authorizations were enacted, the Appropriations Committees laid aside the unauthorized items and proceeded with the rest. In instances involving an item which had cleared the House but on which congressional action had not been completed, the committee obtained a rule waiving the prohibition against appropriating without prior authorization. More than half of the regular appropriation bills for the 1977-79 fiscal years were considered in the House with waivers of clause 2 of Rule XXI. In one case (the 1979 appropriation for the State, Justice, and Commerce Departments) the Appropriations subcommittee chairman refused to seek a waiver, and his bill was stripped of most provisions by points of order.

The House Appropriations Committee has always had these options, but the Budget Act put that committee in a more favorable position *vis-à-vis* the authorizing committees. An appropriation without an authorization is a trespass on the purpose and power of the authorizing committees. It violates the division of labor prescribed for the two sets of committees and enables the appropriators to fix spending levels before Congress has decided the substantive issues. An Appropriations Committee would face severe challenges from threatened authorizing committees if it tried to proceed before their handiwork was done. In the past, therefore, the House Appropriations Committee frequently deferred its own work until the authorization had been enacted or at least had been passed by the House. If necessary, the committee waited months before reporting regular appropriation bills; even if the fiscal year had started, it would accord priority to authorizing legislation.

The Budget Act encourages the Appropriations Committees to proceed without waiting for authorizations. These committees can claim that unless they move ahead on appropriations, the tight schedule laid out in the Act will not be met. For example, the 1977 appropriation bill for the Justice Department provided funds for the Law Enforcement Assistance Administration even though the LEAA authorization for that year had not been enacted. After enactment of the LEAA appropriations, Congress was faced with the anomaly of being asked to authorize more for fiscal 1977 than had already been appropriated.[37]

---

37. On July 26, 1976—two weeks after the LEAA appropriation for fiscal 1977 had been enacted into law—the Senate passed an LEAA authorization. The authorization was for $1 billion in fiscal 1977; the appropriation was $247 million below the authorized amount.

The accelerated schedule can affect the substance and quality of legislation when committees meet the May 15 deadline by ignoring matters that might be pursued if more time were available. This problem is greatest for committees that have a heavy authorization load, and (because of multiple committee assignments) it has been more troublesome in the Senate than in the House. The staff chief of a leading Senate committee dramatized the problem this way:

> May 15 has forced a tremendous compression of the workload. It creates a . . . scheduling problem with Senators having two to three authorizing markups at the same time. The month before May 15 is a hell of a month; the budget resolution is on the floor; authorizing committees are marking up; the appropriating committees are marking up. It's hard to keep track of everything that's going on.

Staff members from various committees have complained about the deadline's impact on their work. "We marked up nine bills in two days in order to meet the May 15 date. More of our members knew less about what we were doing than any time in memory." A staff member of a committee with an even heavier workload commented:

> This committee reported 36 bills in three executive sessions. In effect, no bill got more than two minutes. In previous years we reported the same number of bills over the course of six to eight months, and each one may have gotten half an hour. The deadline results in much less scrutiny of legislation, a much shorter time period for holding hearings and consolidating views, and a much briefer opportunity for the committee to go through the bills.

Some committees have evaded the problem by reporting skeletal legislation before May 15 and fleshing it out later. They sometimes offer committee amendments on the floor for matters whose consideration was not completed by the deadline. In some instances, the committee produces a substitute bill to replace the original version. Authorizing committees also have the option of seeking a waiver of the deadline in the House through the Rules Committee, in the Senate through the Budget Committee.[38] Although the Budget Act does not give the House Budget Committee a formal role, HBC has insisted that it be consulted before a waiver is

38. Section 402(b) of the Congressional Budget Act provides for waivers in the House; Section 402(c) specifies the procedures for waivers in the Senate.

granted,[39] and in the normal course of events Rules will not approve a waiver unless HBC has endorsed it. In line with its strict fidelity to the procedural specifications of the Budget Act, HBC has taken a generally tough stance on waivers of the May 15 deadline, although its posture has become more relaxed as the budget process has matured into a congressional routine. According to committee records, the deadline was waived for 19 bills during 1977. Seven of these were granted for "technical" reasons; five were for "emergency" purposes; and seven others were granted for new legislation made possible by congressional adoption of a third budget resolution for fiscal 1977.[40] In its report on the resolution, HBC announced that it would support waivers for legislation contemplated by the increased budget levels.[41]

The procedure in the Senate is more open than that in the House because the Budget Act provides for waivers of the May 15 deadline to be proposed by the committee of original jurisdiction, with review by the Budget Committee before floor action. While this procedure appears to give SBC a strong role, the opposite is true. Every waiver represents a formal request from another committee for an opportunity to bring its legislation to the floor. The waiver usually is requested when floor consideration is imminent. In this circumstance, SBC has been forced to go along with virtually every requested waiver. In 1976, it approved 21 of the 22 waivers applied for by other committees; in subsequent years, it endorsed perhaps twice that number. SBC practice is to resist waivers only when the affected legislation has a substantive problem.

The fact that numerous waivers have been granted does not mean that the May 15 deadline has been ineffective; most committees have made honest efforts to clear their legislation by that date. Rather, it indicates that Congress will not allow itself to be stopped by budget-induced deadlines. It appears that Congress has both accelerated its action on authorization bills and kept a door open for committees unable (or unwilling) to complete their work by May 15.

39. In some cases, the chairman (or representative) of HBC appears before the Rules Committee to discuss the Budget Committee's position on the waiver; in most instances, the HBC chairman sends a letter to Rules stating his committee's position.

40. See House Committee on the Budget, Hearings before the Task Force on Budget Process, *Oversight of the Congressional Budget Process*, 95th Cong., 1st Sess.

41. H. Rept. No. 95-12 (1977), p. 9.

The long-term issues are vexing for Congress. It has an annual appropriations process; it has been moving toward annual authorizations; and it now has an annual budget process. The lines between these activities are not precisely drawn; hence conflict has arisen over the respective roles of the three sets of committees, and time pressures on members and committees have intensified.

THE CLAIMS OF MARCH

Authorizations are official expressions of legislative interests. Even when they are inflated by wishful expectations about future spending levels, these enactments represent stronger claims on federal resources than do the thousands of bills introduced each year and the thousands of statements made by Members of Congress. If time were no problem, Congress might be able to arrange its calendar to consider budget levels and allocations after it had cleared all the authorizations for a fiscal year. Because this ideal condition is beyond reach, Congress must approach its annual budget routine with a great deal of uncertainty about the prospects of the many authorizing bills being prepared by its legislative committees.

The Budget Committees can fill some of the gaps with solid staff work and hearings on selected aspects of the budget. But they cannot try to cover all budgetary issues in annual hearings; nor can they be confident that their own staffs are adequately informed about all the interests at stake in the budget. The Budget Act partly compensates for this problem by requiring each congressional committee to report its "views and estimates" on all budgetary matters within its jurisdiction to the Budget Committees by March 15, long before Congress or the relevant committees have acted on many of the important authorizations for the next fiscal year.

The March 15 Process

The Budget Act offers no guidance on how the reports are to be prepared. Both Budget Committees, however, issue letters indicating the kinds of information the reports are to present. Understandably the standing committees of the House and Senate have performed their March 15 chores in a variety of ways. The main thing the reports have in common is that all have satisfied the formal requirement set by the Budget Act. Some reports have consisted of a brief letter sent by a chairman with no formal consultation with other committee members; others have been elaborate documents marked up by the full committee on the basis of drafts prepared by subcommittees or staff. Generally, the smaller a committee's stake in the budget, the less formal have been its March 15 procedures. The House Administration Committee, with only a handful of small programs under its care, entrusts the March 15 submission to the chairman. The report of the Senate Governmental Affairs Committee is a joint product of the chairman and ranking minority member, with no formal input from rank-and-file committee members. The House Ways and Means and Senate Finance Committees, by contrast, have full markups with briefing documents distributed in advance to the members.

Because of pressure from rank-and-file members, among other reasons, the trend has been toward increasingly formal and extensive consideration of reports by committees. In 1976, Chairman Rodino of the House Judiciary Committee circulated a three-page letter to satisfy the requirement. This unilateral action drew a sharp protest from 10 committee Republicans who complained that the Budget Act contemplates views and estimates from committees, not just statements from the chairman.[42] Rep. Robert W. Edgar brought his complaint about the March 15 report to the House Budget Committee:

> In the two committees that I served on [Public Works and Veterans' Affairs], the operation was identical. The chairman passed around a document prepared by staff, getting the nod of the ranking majority and minority member of each of the subcommittees, but it was not even shared with members of the full committee until it was presented to the Budget Committee.[43]

By 1979, most committees had at least one markup session of the report by the full committee. Veterans' Affairs, one of the targets of Representative Edgar's protest, modified its procedures in 1977. A staff officer described the process adopted at that time:

> What we do is meet with the chairman and the subcommittee chairmen and we review with them what they consider to be the legislative

---

42. House Committee on the Budget, *Views and Estimates . . . on the Congressional Budget for Fiscal Year 1977*, Committee Print, 94th Cong., 2nd Sess., March 22, 1976, pp. 407-9.

43. House Committee on the Budget, Task Force on Budget Process, *Oversight of the Congressional Budget Process*, 95th Cong., 1st Sess., p. 19.

issues and the oversight functions of the committees for the coming year. Then we put this in draft form and once it is refined, they sign off on it. We then schedule a meeting of the full committee and the chairman and ranking minority member will go in with a proposed program which the full committee considers. Once that is amended to take care of the full committee's desires, we submit it by the March 15 deadline. In other words, the report that goes in from this committee is truly a committee report because we actually vote on it.

House committees have tended to issue more detailed reports than Senate committees, although there have been exceptions to this pattern. As an extreme case, the House Armed Services Committee itemized dozens of defense issues and programs in its reports for fiscal years 1977 and 1978; its Senate counterpart, in contrast, issued two-page letters to cover the total amount of defense spending. This difference between the two chambers has stemmed from two factors: House committees usually are more advanced in their processing of authorizing legislation by March 15, and House members serve on fewer committees and can therefore devote more time to the preparation of budget views and estimates.

Party relationships within congressional committees vary considerably and these relationships inevitably influence the March 15 process. Even though it deals with controversial issues the Senate's Labor and Human Resources Committee has had a bipartisan tradition. Majority and minority members and staff together prepare the committee's budget views and estimates, which are issued without public dissent. The House Education and Labor Committee members, however, have often been divided along party lines and this division has carried over into work on the March 15 report:

Majority staff from each of the subcommittees meet with the committee chairman and review the President's request. They arrive at what they feel would be a good number for each program. This is then compiled and a meeting is held with the chairman of the full committee and the subcommittee chairman. This is still all on the majority side; the minority has not been involved so far. In the meeting, they look at the numbers, make a few changes, and then out comes a committee print. This is the chairman's mark. This is all again among the majority side.

Although the full committee then marks up the March 15 report, the process never loses its partisanship, as most of the Republicans on the committee file dissenting or additional views.

The role of subcommittees in the process is apt to depend on their overall status. In House Appropriations, where subcommittee autonomy has been enshrined for decades,

> the subcommittees provide the views and estimates which are consolidated at the full committee level. The report itself is then approved by the full committee and we send it to the Budget Committee. Theoretically, we mark it up at the full committee level, but there isn't a lot that is going to be done at that point since the subcommittees have had an opportunity to mark up their own individual pieces of it. At the full committee level, there is no substance added.

Rep. Robert W. Edgar suggested that committees be required to conduct open hearings before submitting their reports, but few committees have resorted to this traditional congressional method for gathering information and testing interest in legislative proposals. Nevertheless, as the budget process has become established, federal agencies and interest groups have become increasingly cognizant of the advantages of making their budget preferences known to the appropriate committees. The Defense Department monitors the March 15 work of the Armed Services Committees and advises them on budget and program issues. Veterans' groups lobby members and staff of the Veterans' Affairs Committees. The traditionally close relationship between the Labor and Human Resources Committee and its clients has extended to the March 15 process:

> The interest groups recognize that this is their first shot at the budget, so I think it has substantially accelerated their approach to us on a regular basis, as compared to every two or three or four years when the legislation they are most interested in is expiring. This gives them a more intense feeling, "we've got to get to the authorizing committee in January or February so that the March 15 report will take us into account in an adequate way."

Because hearings are few and markups (if any) are often truncated, committees must rely heavily on their staffs in drafting the report and determining its content. Although each committee has its particular member-staff relationships, the experience of the House Agriculture Committee is common:

> A great deal of [the work] is done by staff. We have held necessary meetings of the committee to approve our budget recommendations as such but it is a hurry-up type of job because quite frankly members do not want to spend that much time listening to all the budget requests of various agencies. The reports have been done in a hurry; the staff

has had to work like mad to get something to put in front of the members, but very few of the members actually participate.

In an age of burgeoning staffs on Capitol Hill, there is nothing exceptional about staff influence. What is unusual is that many committees' staffs appear to have broad scope in deciding what goes into the March 15 report. Whether because of time pressures, disdain for budgetary routines, the perceived prematurity of the March 15 reports, or some other factor, Members (with some truly notable exceptions) have not scrutinized the estimates prepared by staff with the same care given to legislation being marked up by their committees.

Policy and Content

Committees have free rein in deciding what to ask for in their March 15 reports. The Budget Committees have devised standard formats for the reports, but neither has sought to impose substantive limits on committee views and estimates.

The March 15 reports, in the words of a letter from Senators Muskie and Bellmon to the chairmen of Senate committees, are "the primary means by which your committee informs the Budget Committee of the Senate of its intended actions which may affect the budget."[44] The reports can fulfill this purpose, however, only if committees submit realistic estimates that inform the Budget Committees concerning the legislative prospects of pending proposals. If committees were to chronically inflate their estimates, the reports would not present real claims on the budget; nor would they be reliable indicators of intended actions. The Budget Committees would be misled if they tried to base their resolutions on the pseudo-claims of congressional committees.

As things have turned out, the reports have been neither concrete estimates of the costs of prospective legislation nor unrealistic "wish lists." A budget process is not a passive recipient of claims made by interested parties. The routines of budgeting prompt claimants to search for new demands to lay upon the government. Without the congressional budget process, those who want more money would have to go outside channels and make a special case for their interest. The availability of the March 15 procedure provides an authoritative channel for the promotion of new interests. The budget process thus invites claimants to ask for more funds and legitimizes new demands, although it generally does not accord

44. Letter dated February 3, 1978, Senate Budget Committee files.

them the same protection enjoyed by old ones. That which might be regarded as improper when a government lacks a regular procedure for handling claims becomes an expected part of the process when budget routines are in place. In response to (or in anticipation of) a "call for estimates," claimants canvass their operations and consult with interested parties to decide what should be added to their demands.

In congressional budgeting, the March 15 process is a powerful stimulant to claims by legislative committees. In this process, committees are not merely called upon to estimate next year's cost of current legislation or the budget level necessary for maintaining programs at their current level. They are invited to identify and promote the legislative initiatives which they might seek during the year. In a manner quite similar to executive agency behavior, congressional committees have responded to this "call" by undertaking their own search for bigger budgets.

The March 15 process forces committees to behave as program advocates, not merely presenting their estimates but marshaling arguments and support in behalf of legislation they favor. Some of the tactics usually associated with agency budgeting have been incorporated into the legislative process. Thus, committees defend their requests for increased spending with statistics showing that their programs' share of the federal budget is declining. The Senate Committee on Veterans' Affairs prefaced its report for fiscal 1977 with the argument that despite an increase in the veteran population, spending on veterans' programs had dropped from 7 percent to 5 percent of the federal budget over the past 20 years. The Senate Agriculture Committee noted that funds earmarked for agriculture programs had slipped from 3.7 percent of federal spending in 1968 to only 1.2 percent a decade later. "The Committee is . . . distressed that the decline in support has come even though Congress has given new responsibilities to the Department of Agriculture, and the Nation and the world are faced with serious and intensifying agricultural problems." The Senate Labor and Human Resources Committee took a similar approach, noting that spending for its programs would decline as a percentage of federal outlays even if all of its recommendations were approved by Congress. "The Committee . . . stresses that investment in the human resources programs under our jurisdiction is an exceedingly valuable one. The economic and social return for so modest a proportion of Federal resources is viewed as a critically important policy by the Committee."

One might expect committees to be less inhibited in their March 15 claims than they are in the promotion of authorizing legislation. After all, in their regular legislative work, committees must limit their objectives in order to get congressional approval for their programs. A committee alert to the overall interests of the House or Senate cannot merely report out every good or appealing idea which comes its way. It must choose from among the array of possibilities if it is to have a high success rate on the floor. No such constraint bears on committees in deciding their March 15 numbers. Their unilateral action does not have to be approved by the full House or Senate; committees might therefore consider it advantageous to inflate their claims to build a case for higher spending.

Moreover, the timing of the reports effectively prevents most committees from submitting claims strictly limited to their expected budget allocations. By March 15, few authorizing committees have made final decisions. Most have barely launched their legislative activities for the year, and (especially during the first year of a Congress) much important legislation is still in the early development stage. The March 15 requirement, coupled with the May 15 deadline, has encouraged some committees to organize more quickly and to accelerate their legislative timetables. In 1976, for example, the House Armed Services Committee advanced its hearings and markup of the military procurement authorization bill so that most of this work was completed by March 15. As a result, the committee was able to incorporate many of its final decisions in the March 15 report. The process broke down in 1977, however, because a new Congress had convened and a changeover in administration had occurred. President Carter submitted a new budget one month after taking office, leaving less than another month before the views and estimates had to be submitted. Accordingly, Armed Services was still in the preliminary stages of its annual authorizations process when it issued its March 15 report.

Committees have coped with the forced prematurity of their reports by cautioning that the views and estimates are subject to revision, and by withholding firm decisions on pending legislation. Many committees have called attention to the tentativeness of their recommendations. The Senate Commerce Committee has prefaced its reports with the notice that the estimates are "subject to further review and should . . . not be construed to represent the views of any individual member." The House Agriculture Committee has advised that its silence with regard to many items in the budget "should not be construed in any way as reflecting consent to the budget authority or outlay figures proposed by the President." The Senate Armed Services Committee has depicted its recommendation "as a target which may require additional adjustment as a result of . . . review or supplemental requests from the President." The House Appropriations Committee has emphasized "that this report identifies some of the major contingencies and areas of the budget that need further examination and that the report should not be interpreted as recommendations from the Committee."

A few committees have hedged their views and estimates by submitting brief statements that address total spending levels without going into program specifics. This approach has been favored by the Senate Armed Services and Finance Committees, both of which have avoided locking themselves into positions on prospective legislation. Chairman John C. Stennis of the Armed Services Committee forthrightly objected to the effects of the budget timetable on program decisions in a letter transmitting his committee's first March 15 submission:

> . . . the timing of the Congressional Budget Act may force Congress to choose between establishing figures on the overall Federal budget and determining which specific programs within the overall figure are best for the country. We should not have to make this choice.

Committees also have hedged in precisely the opposite way. They have avoided premature commitments by submitting a "shopping list" of spending proposals and setting the estimates at a sufficiently high level to accommodate more legislative initiatives than were likely to pass Congress. The House Armed Services Committee admitted to this ploy in its comments on the 1978 budget: "The Committee is still in the process of examining in detail the rationale underlying all of the budget revisions requested by the President. Thus the Committee is recommending budget authority for some accounts significantly above the President's request pending further hearings and study." In advance of firm decisions on spending legislation, committees have proved particularly reluctant to endorse program cuts proposed by the President. It is almost always difficult to get legislative support for program reductions; when committees are rushed to judgment long before they have been able to take a hard look at the issue or marshal support for the move, reductions are virtually impossible.

The need to hedge their recommendations has made committees

dubious about the value of the March 15 process. Referring to his experience as chairman of the Senate Committee on Banking, Housing, and Urban Affairs, Sen. William Proxmire admits that his committee

> . . . has never been able to provide a definitive and realistic report on its expected authorizing bills by March 15. In many cases, hearings were not completed. In most cases, the Committee had not met in markup session to discuss the authorization bills before it. Certain members of the Committee have been especially interested in particular authorizing legislation and have sought to have the full funding levels included in the March 15 report. Even though the full Committee may, at a later date, cut back in the authorization, it is difficult to deny a member his "day in court" until the Committee has formally voted on the legislation. Moreover, decisions on funding may depend to a large extent on program details that have yet to be agreed upon by the Committee. For these reasons, our March 15 report has tended to include all pending proposals before the Committee with little or no indication as to the probability that any individual item will be approved.
>
> That means that the estimates can be unusually high. They can contain everything, including the kitchen sink.[45]

Proxmire's view is widely shared by persons close to the authorizations process in Congress. A few selections from interviews with members of different committees should suffice. From the Senate Energy and Natural Resources Committee:

> When we start this thing off three weeks after the Congress comes in, we have got a thousand bills before this committee and we're going to have another thousand bills the following month. I couldn't tell you which of these bills are serious bills by March 1st. If I have five bills and know that three of them will get through, I don't know which three at the outset. I don't know what the controversies are going to be; I don't know how strong the proponents are for it. I got to put them all in. I can't choose. If I guess wrong, I am going to be in trouble.

The House Post Office and Civil Service Committee:

> The committee would not disapprove of anything. All of them are political gamists. You don't want to make any selection in the March 15 report. Why say that you are not going to pass a bill that benefits the widows? We can pass the responsibility on [to] the House Budget Committee, and why not? They will cut it out. You will find someone down the line who will act responsibly.

45. Senate Committee on the Budget, Hearings on *Can Congress Control the Power of the Purse?* 95th Cong., 2nd Sess., March 6, 1978, p. 22.

An examination of the more than one hundred March 15 reports submitted by House and Senate committees suggests that with only few exceptions (none of them significant) the committees ask for more than the President has recommended for their programs. Moreover, each year's estimates add up to tens of billions of dollars more than Congress is likely to budget. Committees commonly request more funds than they expect to receive, and they avoid making final decisions at this early date. But it would be erroneous to regard the reports as lacking in substantive value to the Budget Committees. The record shows that committees have not behaved in an unrestrained fashion. The March 15 requests of all committees have totaled approximately 10 percent more than the amount targeted in each year's budget resolution, not an extraordinarily large overestimate. Some of the committees which have been most expansive in their authorizing actions have been comparatively moderate in their March 15 objectives. The House Education and Labor Committee and the Senate Labor and Human Resources Committee have not sought full funding for all of their authorized programs; often they have been willing to settle for substantially less than the amount already authorized in law.

Why would an authorizing committee exercise self-restraint in its March 15 views and estimates when it has already succeeded in winning much more from Congress as a whole? One explanation lies in the effect of budgeting on committee behavior. As noted, a budget process invites claimants to request more, but it also moderates their demands. The incremental pace of budgeting, its strong links to current and past actions, its emphasis on stability and continuity in government policy all constrain the aspirations of claimants. Committees act as incrementalists, constructing their March 15 estimates with careful attention to current budget levels, the President's request, and the credibility of their demands. Committees can generally be expected to ask for somewhat more than the amount they got for the current year or the amount the President recommended for the next year, but not for so much more as to prejudice their interests. When they want more than incremental increases for their programs, committees often pursue policies independent of the budget process. They can, for example, develop new authorizing legislation with spending levels far above the amounts that they expect to be budgeted or appropriated.

Committees have another reason for being somewhat restrained in their March 15 statements. They have not wanted to raise the legislative expectations of interest groups by pegging their budget estimates at unattainable levels. If committees were to cram every legislative proposal into their views and estimates, they would run the risk of losing control over their legislation, or of being regarded as failures for not delivering on their earlier promises.

There is still another impetus toward moderation by authorizing committees. A March 15 report that asks for everything and fails to signal the authorizing committees' real intentions may enhance the power of the Budget Committees. An authorizing committee that makes unrealistic demands in its report invites the Budget Committees to decide which of the proposals should be funded and which should not. Conversely, if the views and estimates represent reasonably firm and realistic intentions, the Budget Committees have significantly fewer options with regard to the program mix for a targeted level of expenditure.

It should not be surprising, therefore, that the Budget Committees have welcomed March 15 claims in excess of realistic budget levels. Such claims not only permit the Budget Committees to act as budget controllers; they also somewhat expand their voice in deciding which programs actually get funded. Nevertheless, a committee cannot be excessively permissive in its views and estimates. The credibility of its claims influences budgetary outcomes. Even as it reaches for higher levels, an authorizing committee cannot afford to establish a reputation of being unrealistic in its budget aspirations.

In perceiving the March 15 reports as more inflated than they actually are, authorizing committee participants seem to have been voicing uneasiness about the process rather than making an assessment of the reports. They do not like to make early decisions, but have been compelled to do so. They do not like to have the pace of committee work dictated by a budget calendar. They do not want views and estimates to substitute for actual legislation as expressions of their program interests. Most of all, they do not like the idea of having their work reviewed by other congressional committees.

In evaluating the usefulness of the March 15 reports, one must keep in mind that the Budget Committees have other sources of information and baselines for making decisions. If all they had were the pile of March 15 documents, the Budget Committees would find it difficult to anticipate the spending actions likely to be acceptable to Congress. Yet the Budget Committees have managed to gain adoption of their resolutions, though not without floor amendments in some cases. By examining the March 15 reports in the context of past spending decisions, the President's budget, and current policy estimates, the Budget Committees get a good idea of the likely spending outcomes for the next fiscal year. Moreover, through informal contacts with authorizing committees they monitor the progress of legislation and ascertain which of the matters included in the March 15 reports are most likely to win congressional approval, which are window dressing, and which are serious. These contacts are an essential part of the process of developing a congressional budget that is responsive to interests of affected committees.

In addition to signaling prospective budgetary desires, the March 15 process has various important side benefits. Foremost is the provision to Congress of a basis for making budget decisions. Without the March 15 reports (or some compensatory changes in the budget process) Congress would lack its own source of claims covering the whole budget. The legitimacy and acceptance of the recommendations of the budget committees depend in good part on the belief that they reflect the full array of congressional interests and not merely executive branch requests. Second, the March 15 process has spurred committees to speed up and organize their legislative work. Committees now get an early start as well as a broad picture of the matters that they will face during the session. The views and estimates serve as informal agendas for some committees, although the reports do not commit committees in advance to take up any matter.

Finally, committees have become better informed about programs within their jurisdiction. As discussed early in this chapter, committees dealing with permanent authorizations have enjoyed the greatest benefit; the gain has been less for committees that already reviewed authorized programs periodically.

CLAIMANTS IN THE BUDGET PROCESS

Every budget claim is represented by claimants, that is, individuals or groups whose interest would be benefited by certain budgetary outcomes. Budget requests are not just numbers on a piece of paper, but the aspirations and demands of politically active committees and Members of Congress. Thus, an authorization bill is not only a claim on federal resources but also an expression of the amount of funds a legislative committee deems necessary or appropriate for a desired program. The disposition of a claim on the budget is greatly affected by the standing and actions of the interests that benefit from it. Therefore, budgetary claims presented to Congress must be considered in the context of the behavior and interests of the claimants as well. In the congressional context, committees are the principal claimants. Their behavior is considered in terms of their approach to the March 15 exercise.

At least three factors have influenced the March 15 behavior of congressional committees. First is the type of legislation for which they are responsible. A committee that specializes in annual authorizations can be expected to function differently from the way a committee that produces multiyear authorizations functions. A committee whose main interest is the formulation of new entitlement programs might approach the March 15 process differently from the way a committee whose chief concern is the protection of benefits already accorded by law would act. Second, committees differ in their degree of inclination to serve as program advocates and innovators. Some committees habitually view themselves as advocates for interests which might be disadvantaged in the competition for public funds if they did not have strong representation within Congress. These tend to be committees in which the authorizations-appropriations gap is largest. Hence, their claims already have been inflated through the authorizations process, and they have little incentive to levy still higher demands in the March 15 views and estimates. Other committees, however, are hold-the-line operations, unaccustomed to campaigning for annual increases in expenditures. In the long run, these committees might be dramatically affected by the March 15 pressures.

Third, the procedures used in formulating the March 15 reports affect the claims on the budget process. A committee that formulates its views and estimates under closed procedures (the chairman makes the decisions without full committee participation) may be able to head off demands that would be difficult to oppose in an open vote. A principal reason for the pressure to democratize the March 15 process was to give rank-and-file members an opportunity to gain committee consideration of pet ideas that had been pigeon-holed in the past. The trend toward open markup of the March 15 reports is likely to produce more ambitious claims because many members will find it hard to vote openly against proposals beneficial to their clients.

Four types of legislative claimants—each representing a different type of congressional committee—are discussed in this section: (1) committees which handle annual authorizations; (2) committees in which multiyear authorizations predominate; (3) committees with jurisdiction over entitlements; and (4) committees responsible for permanent programs. This list does not include committees that have "housekeeping" jurisdiction over the continuing and generally noncontroversial operations of government, or the Appropriations Committees which are considered in later chapters.

"Just a Little Bit More": Annual Authorizations

Although annual authorizations are reconsidered every year, the actions are not unpredictable. These recurring events have a pattern, although fluctuating political moods and conditions occasionally lead to wide swings in congressional behavior. The "normal" incremental pattern in which the President asks for more than has been provided for the current year, the authorizing committees add to the President's request, and Congress appropriates somewhat less than has been authorized veils the intense, recurring fights over some of the major annual authorizations, principally for national defense and international programs. In recent years, the conflict usually has been over the amount of the increase, and in particular, whether the programs should be permitted a real rise in spending or should be required to absorb some increased cost due to inflation.

This pattern has continued under congressional budgeting. The March 15 statements for most annually authorized programs have not varied substantially from the President's numbers. The same committees which are composing views and estimates for the next fiscal year also are working on authorizing legislation for the same period; these two actions should be in alignment with one another. Moreover, as discussed at the outset of this chapter, authorizations and appropriations ordinarily do not normally vary more than a few percentage points, except when the former differ substantially from the President's recommendations.

Annual authorizations dominate three budget categories. The general science, space, and technology category is currently noncontroversial; in their March 15 statements, the authorizing committees ask for perhaps 1 percent above the amount of the President's budget request. The pattern has been remarkably similar in the defense category. With the President seeking sizable annual increases in real spending, the Armed Services Committees have estimated defense requirements at about 1 percent more than his amount. The only deviations from the expected pattern have occurred in the views and estimates of the House International Relations Committee and the Senate Foreign Relations Committee. In the aftermath of the Vietnam War these committees did not support some military assistance programs; hence, in some years, their March 15 estimates were lower than the President's. But now that the budgetary effects of the war have dissipated, these authorizing committees seem to be falling into line.

"Somewhere over the Rainbow": Multiyear Authorizations

One might expect programs which are authorized for several years at a time to be more secure in their funding than those which must return to Congress for a new authorization each year. This is not the case, however. Because they diverge so much from current spending levels and are not constrained by incremental norms, multiyear authorizations offer ample opportunity for sharp swings in their spending patterns.

Committees that schedule steep increases in future authorizations openly serve as advocates for the programs in their care. This role has not been disturbed by the advent of congressional budgeting. As a staff leader of one such committee explained, these committees "feel very strongly about the programs under their jurisdiction; the March 15 report gives them another opportunity to serve as advocates." A review of the views and estimates of the House Education and Labor and Senate Labor and Human Resources Committees shows advocacy in full bloom. These committees regularly peg their estimates more than 50 percent above the President's budget, far above the amounts they expect to be appropriated. The House committee has defended its recommendations as "targets for expenditures that are not unreasonable in light of the need of the disadvantaged, the handicapped and the unemployed." The Senate committee has been more strident in its advocacy. "We regard the report," it declared in 1977, "as an instrument by which this Committee urges that room be made for the national priorities and goals under our jurisdiction." It described the purpose of the report as "to estimate and not to legislate. Consequently, our recommendations are advanced to make budgetary room for legislative actions . . . without pre-determining the source and content of exact legislation required."

Even advocacy-oriented committees have a desire to maintain budgetary respectability, but this task is not easy in the face of their overreaching views and estimates. For fiscal 1978, Education and Labor requested almost $9 billion in new budget authority above the amount recommended by President Carter for education, training, employment, and social service programs. The House Budget Committee eliminated most of the proposed increase from its first budget resolution. It provided only 75 percent of the amount requested for these programs, a much lower percentage than it approved for most other functions. HBC explained its steep cut in social programs by suggesting that Education and Labor had advocated "funding of most education programs at their full authorization level."[46] This statement provoked an angry response from Rep. Carl Perkins, chairman of Education and Labor, who listed various programs for which the March 15 recommendations were significantly below their authorized levels. "In setting targets much lower than proposed in the authorizing committee's views," Perkins complained, "it is of dubious value for the Budget Committee to state that full funding had been suggested for most education programs."[47] Education and Labor not only wanted to set the record straight but to avoid being tagged as a high spending committee which habitually produces unrealistic budget estimates.

Walking on a Tightrope: Entitlement Programs

Like the committees that deal in multiyear authorizations, the entitling committees, such as the House and Senate Veterans' Affairs Committees, are beneficiary-centered. But the legislative actions of these committees are similar to annual authorizations in that the amounts enacted closely influence actual appropriation levels. In effect, Congress must appropriate money for entitlements at 100 percent of their authorizations.

These two characteristics generate a great deal of budgetary tension. Because entitling committees are client-oriented, they are pressed to legislate additional benefits. The Veterans' Affairs Committees have little legislative business of consequence other than the provision of additional entitlements to beneficiaries, and they regularly deal with demands for new and expanded entitlements. But these committees cannot yield to all the pressures they face; to do so would mean spending far in excess of acceptable levels. In the past, the standard way for coping with these pressures was to

46. H. Rept. No. 95-189, p. 51.
47. Representative Perkins wrote to Representative Giaimo on April 29, 1977; Giaimo responded on July 12, 1977, but did not deal with the full authorization issue.

bottle up attractive but costly proposals in committee. The entitlement committees were where the buck had to stop because once the legislation was reported out, it was hard to stop on the floor.

The March 15 process has complicated the problem of the entitlement committees. What was once a wish list has become actionable through the March 15 process. The leader of the drive to democratize this process in the House Veterans' Affairs Committee made no bones about his aim to force committee action on proposals that had been buried in the past.[48] In these first years of the budget process, the Veterans' Affairs Committees have not rubber-stamped every idea brought to a vote. In 1977, for example, the Senate committee rejected an appealing liberalization of the GI bill on the ground that additional funds for this program would require either an increase in the budget for veterans or a diversion of money from other programs.

In the 1976-79 fiscal years, the Veterans' Affairs Committees' March 15 estimates averaged about 10 percent above those of the President's budget; such increases were much greater than those sought by annual authorizing committees, but also very much below the targets of the multiyear committees. A sizable portion of these increases was for cost-of-living adjustments rather than for new programs. Yet it is doubtful whether the entitlement committees will always be able to rebuff the pressures from beneficiaries. An entitlement committee that defers to budgetary constraints runs the risk of having the proposals it pigeon-holed added to budget resolutions on the floor. This has already happened in the House; in response, the Veterans' Affairs Committees have generally tilted toward their clients in their March 15 report.

Protecting the Base: The Power of Being Permanent

The committees considered in the foregoing paragraphs have only a small fraction of the entitlements in the federal budget. Most entitlements are in the custody of the House Ways and Means and Senate Finance Committees. The budgetary behavior of these committees, however, is not similar to that of the two Veterans' Affairs Committees. Unlike the Veterans' Affairs Committees, Ways and Means and Finance have a diversified jurisdiction that blankets almost the entire tax side of the budget, all Social Security

48. See House Committee on the Budget, Task Force on Budget Process, *Oversight of the Congressional Budget Process*, 95th Cong., 1st Sess., testimony of Representative Edgar, pp. 18-27.

programs, major health and welfare legislation, and international trade. Their legislative purpose has not been limited to the production of new entitlements. Although they annually file March 15 claims for program increases, the main concern of Finance and Ways and Means has been to protect existing programs against reductions advocated by the President. In each year of the congressional budget process, the President has proposed substantial cutbacks in various welfare and health benefits, and each year these committees have rebuffed most of his proposals.

Because their entitlements have been established as permanent programs, these two committees can get their way merely by doing nothing. With few exceptions, doing nothing, in fact, has been their favorite March 15 tactic. The Senate Finance Committee has one of the most elaborate processes in Congress for putting together its views and estimates, but little of the process appears in its official report. The staff prepares a briefing book for two to three days of markups at which the committee thoroughly reviews various budget issues. All this activity yields a letter (with no more than a handful of pages devoted to expenditures) summarizing the committee's decisions in budgetary aggregates. "The members," a staff official explained, "are very picky about the fact that they are not making legislative decisions. They are making decisions on budget levels. These are budgetary level decisions to accommodate legislation." The Finance Committee also firmly rejects most program reductions sought by the President. Its 1976 report "reflects the Committee's opinion that much of the legislation assumed by the President's budget will not be enacted or will not be enacted in sufficient time to have the fiscal impact shown in the budget." Similar language has been incorporated in subsequent March 15 letters.

The Ways and Means Committee has been more specific in its pronouncements, listing the proposed program reductions it has rejected. In its report for fiscal 1978, however, the committee backed away from outright rejection of all of the President's recommendations. The Subcommittee on Social Security advised that "it would be unrealistic and impractical" to anticipate some $800 million in program cuts budgeted by the President. Nevertheless, the full committee endorsed the President's action (Chairman Ullman reportedly wanted to demonstrate cooperation with the new administration), but it "agreed to put the Budget Committee on notice that it shares the subcommittee's concern over the expectation that these proposals will meet with congressional approval. . . ." Ways and Means was thus able to have the best of both worlds—accommodating to the President's wishes, but not committing itself to legislative action.

SOME CLAIMS ARE MORE EQUAL THAN OTHERS

In a depoliticized budget process, all claimants would simply ask for what they want, and the form in which the claim was presented would not bias the outcome one way or the other. This situation cannot exist in the real world of budgeting. Getting money from Congress is too important for claimants to allow the process to run its course in a completely neutral fashion. Claimants who want satisfaction in the budget do not merely deposit their claims at the congressional doorstep and leave the rest to the good sense of the decision makers. They try to sway the outcome in many ways, one of which is to cast their requests in a form that gives them some advantage. Just as some claimants are more advantageously positioned than others, so too some claims have preferential status, while others are prejudiced by the manner in which their case is presented.

A complete catalog of the different kinds of budget claims would run for many pages. Claimants striving for advantage can be expected to devise special ways of giving their programs an edge in the budgetary competion. The standard ways of according preference to programs include financing them through dedicated trust funds, giving them backdoor status, or establishing a mandatory claim on the federal treasury. Although some claims are given preference by being excluded from the congressional budget process, they may be subject to other forms of legislative review. This preferential status is held by off-budget agencies (agencies whose transactions are excluded by law from the budget), guaranteed loans (contingent liabilities in which the government bears a cost only in the event of default by the borrower), and certain government-sponsored corporations that are deemed for budgetary purposes to be private organizations.[49]

A budget claim can be structured in such a way as to narrow or eliminate discretionary action. A trust fund narrows discretion; a

49. For a discussion of contingent liabilities and related budget issues, see House Committee on the Budget, *Congressional Control of Expenditures*, Committee Print, January 1977, pp. 87-96.

mandatory entitlement takes it away. The Budget Act moved in the direction of expanding congressional choice by barring "preemptive" claims (expenditure decisions prior to adoption of the first budget resolution) and by restricting backdoor programs. The Act also tried to alter the perceptions of budget makers by introducing new definitions for certain transactions. The status and potency of the types of special claims examined below were affected by the Budget Act. They are a sample—and not a representative one—of the diversity of budget claims, but they should suffice to illustrate that the form in which a budget claim is cast can affect the decision on it.

Backdoor Spending

To give their claims preferential status, various authorizing committees have, over the years, fashioned techniques to evade the appropriations process. The use of backdoor spending practices had been significantly curtailed by the Congressional Budget Act. There are three main types of "backdoors":

1. Authority to borrow from the Treasury or the public is known as borrowing authority. When an agency has this authority, it can spend borrowed funds without going through the appropriations process. When the Budget Act was passed, about $200 billion in borrowing authority was available to federal agencies.

2. Authority to enter into contracts or obligations prior to an appropriation is known as contract authority. Although the Constitution requires that an appropriation precede payment of funds from the Treasury—"No money shall be drawn from the Treasury but in consequence of appropriations made by law"—it does not bar agencies from incurring obligations in advance of appropriations. In the case of backdoor contract authority, the usual sequence of events is reversed: first comes the obligation, then the appropriation to "liquidate" (pay off) the obligation.[50] In such cases, the Appropriations Committees have no effective control over their actions; they must pay the claims made upon the federal government. Yet before the Budget Act, contract authority marshaled popular support in Congress, sometimes in the face of stiff opposition from the Appropriations Committees. Thus, in 1972, Congress provided $18 billion in contract authority for water pollution control

50. When contract authority is established through this backdoor method, the liquidating appropriation is not computed as budget authority. Rather, the budget authority is deemed to be created by the legislation authorizing the program.

programs despite strong opposition from Chairman Mahon of House Appropriations.[51]

3. A third type of backdoor spending occurs when Congress entitles eligible persons or governments to payments from the federal government. In the decade before the Budget Act, entitlements were the fastest-growing portion of the federal budget as well as the single most important factor in the year-to-year rise in federal spending. Mandatory entitlements usually are open-ended, with the actual level of expenditure determined by factors over which Congress has no direct control. In some entitlement programs (such as Social Security), Congress establishes a permanent appropriation and no subsequent legislative action is necessary to keep the program going. In other instances (such as veterans' benefits and public assistance), annual appropriations are necessary to finance the entitlements, but Congress has little or no discretion when the appropriation is voted. The effective congressional decision is made at the time the entitlement is authorized. Thus, entitlements always transfer effective power from the Appropriations Committees to authorizing committees, even when formal appropriations actions are required each year.

It is easy to understand why backdoors are popular. Not only do they bolster the money powers of authorizing committees (on which most Members sit), but also they secure more favorable legislative treatment for programs graced with backdoor status. According to the Joint Study Committee on Budget Control, between 1969 and 1973, Congress appropriated $30 billion less than the President requested. But during these years, Congress approved $30 billion in backdoor spending above the budgeted amounts. If appropriations are regularly reduced while backdoor spending is increased, authorizing committees will be tempted to seek preferential status for their claims by converting them into backdoor spending. This is precisely what happened in the contentious years before the Budget Act.

The Act, however, limited the preferences accorded to backdoors. While existing legislation was not affected, new contract and borrowing authority can be enacted only as conventional authorizations for which funds can be spent only to the extent provided in

51. Mahon's "Dear Colleague" letter to House Members asking them to vote against the contract authority is in 118 *Congressional Record* 10775 (March 29, 1972).

appropriation acts.[52] New entitlement legislation can be considered by Congress only after the first budget resolution has been adopted and (in most circumstances) cannot become effective until the beginning of the next fiscal year. Moreover, when a new entitlement would exceed the amount available in the latest budget resolution, the legislation is referred to the Appropriations Committee, which can offer an amendment to reduce the amount of entitlement. In sum, contract and borrowing authority no longer possess preferential status; entitlements, however, continue to be accorded special treatment, but they must be considered in the context of congressional budget decisions. In theory at least, new entitlements must compete with other claims on the budget for limited congressional budget allocations.

The "Current Services" Baseline

The Budget Act introduced a new presidential budget submission, an estimate of expenditures "if all programs and activities were carried on during . . . [the] ensuing fiscal year at the same level as the fiscal year in progress and without policy changes in such programs and activities."[53] The "current services" budget can be conceived of as a neutral claim, which is unbiased by the program preferences of the Administration and which allows all agencies to compete for appropriations on an equal footing. In the context in which the current services budget has been used, however, it has been anything but a neutral baseline. It has influenced budgetary outcomes by sheltering programs from the budget-cutting drives of the White House as well as from the ravages of inflation.

It will be recalled that during the years of budgetary strife that preceded the Budget Act, President Nixon repeatedly sought to cut back domestic programs, sometimes by impoundment, sometimes by holding proposed expenditure increases below the rate of inflation. In response to this threat to the incremental stability of the budget process, Congress institutionalized incrementalism in the form of the current services budget. This new submission carries the implicit norm that programs and agencies should be held harmless from inflation. The current services budget thus complicates

---

52. Section 401 of the Budget Act exempts self-financed trust funds and several other categories from these controls on borrowing authority, contract authority, and entitlements.
53. Section 605 of the Budget Act.

doing that which is difficult to do under even the most favorable of circumstances—cutting into the base. This is a significant bias because the difference between "current expenditures" and "current services" often is the effective margin of choice for congressional decision makers. That is, when they cut programs, they frequently do so by holding the dollar increase below the rate of inflation.

For ambitious claimants, the current services level becomes the base upon which they build a case for higher future spending. Both the House Education and Labor Committee and the Senate Labor and Human Resources Committee have tried to moderate the reaction to their requests for very large dollar increases by casting their March 15 reports in current service terms rather than in relation to the President's budget. In fact, the Labor and Human Resources Committee eliminated all tabular comparisons with the President's budget from its fiscal 1978 report. This committee describes its approach as a "current services plus" concept; its views and estimates concentrate on selected add-ons to current program levels.

Perfect neutrality would be difficult to achieve even if it were sought by the various participants. Adjusting programs for inflation is no simple matter. Some programs (such as Social Security) are indexed by law to the rate of inflation or to some other measure; some (revenue sharing, for example) have fixed sums appropriated for a number of years; others (defense and many federal grant programs) have annual appropriations. Since the inception of congressional budgeting, OMB has fought with CBO over the proper method for handling inflation in the current services estimates. OMB differentiates among different types of programs, but CBO tries to apply the same rules to all. CBO generally allows a higher inflation adjustment for certain domestic programs than OMB does. But this is not just a technical issue. As will be examined in the next chapter, the Senate Budget Committee uses current services baselines in preparing its budget resolutions, so differences in adjustments for inflation can affect budgetary decisions.

The current services data can diminish the status of the President's request as a claim on the congressional budget. Although Congress always has been alert to what it would cost to maintain existing programs at a constant level, availability of these data not only makes Congress more independent of a President bent on cutting programs but also exposes Congress to more pressure from interest groups who want their programs protected against inflation.

The wants of congressional committees invariably exceed the

resources available to Congress. Since it cannot accede to every request, Congress needs a process for deciding among the various claims presented to it. The core of this process is the budget resolution, which sets revenue and expenditure levels and allocates new budget authority and outlays among a small number of functions. The manner in which Congress formulates its budget resolutions is the subject of the next chapter.

VII Making Budget Resolutions

IN THE chronology of budgeting, after claims have been submitted, budgetary resources are allocated among the various claimants. This step is the core of the congressional budget process, the annual formulation of two (or more) concurrent resolutions on the budget.

A budget resolution appears to be a rather simple measure. In printed form, it is usually only two pages long. Each resolution is formatted into the five fiscal aggregates prescribed by the Budget Act (total revenues, total new budget authority, total outlays, the budget surplus or deficit, and the public debt) and budget authority and outlay allocations for 19 functional categories.[1] Yet drawing up a budget resolution can be a complex undertaking. Each resolution requires more than 40 separate, but arithmetically consistent, decisions. The functional parts have to add up to the spending totals; the budget authority allocated to each function must be coordinated with estimated outlays; the difference between total revenues and outlays must equal the projected deficit.

The complications, as this chapter shows, are essentially political. At each of the five stages of congressional action—in the two Budget Committees, the House, the Senate, and the conference—differing political interests, spanning the full scope of governmental concerns, must be accommodated in a budget resolution. As might be expected, the House, the Senate, and their relevant committees go about their budget work differently. The two chambers have different political conditions, traditions, and rules. This chapter traces the movement of the budget resolutions through the various stages of consideration, concentrating on the decision-

1. The functional categories can be changed by the Office of Management and Budget in consultation with the Appropriations and Budget Committees of the two Houses. OMB expanded the number of functions in the fiscal 1979 budget, establishing separate categories for energy and transportation programs. This action increased the number from 17 to 19.

making methods and voting patterns in each. It focuses on the "first" resolutions, the ones adopted in the spring of each year, because they are more influential in shaping congressional policy than are the "second" resolutions adopted each September.

HBC'S BUDGET: DEMOCRATIC RULE AND REPUBLICAN OPPOSITION

With a 17-8 majority in the House Budget Committee and a comparable margin in the House, HBC Democrats regularly strive for a resolution that satisfies the interests of the majority party. Little attempt has been made to produce a resolution that would draw support from all quarters or to offer concessions that might soften Republican opposition. Reinforced by a sharp liberal-conservative schism, the distance between the two parties has been too great to be bridged by marginal adjustments.

HBC's formulation of a budget resolution occurs in two stages, the mark and the markup. In legislative parlance, the mark refers to recommendations formally presented to a committee to serve as a starting point in its deliberations. The markup is the process by which committee members work their way through a measure, revising some parts and adding or dropping others, until they are ready to report it to the House.

The Mark: Formulating Democratic Expectations

A markup usually begins with a concrete proposal, a draft bill in the typical legislative situation. Because Members of Congress perceived the new budget process as a declaration of independence from executive dominance, the Budget Committees did not want to use the President's budget as their mark. Moreover, when the process was initiated, a Republican President was calling for severe cutbacks in social programs, but committee Democrats wanted to start with their own numbers. This procedural independence continued after a Democratic President succeeded to the White House in 1977.

The starting point for HBC's markup of a budget resolution has been a "Democratic mark," a set of specific recommendations for each aggregate and functional category. In the first years of the budget process, the recommendations were issued by the chairman, but since 1979 they have been prepared by Democratic Members.

The marks for the fiscal 1980 resolutions were drafted by a caucus of committee Democrats, and the chairman opposed some of the key recommendations. In most respects, the caucus mark has been prepared in the same manner as the chairman's mark, and has had the same structure. It begins with a review of economic conditions followed by an analysis of the budget aggregates, and then by a consideration of each budget function. For each recommendation, the document explains the derivation of the numbers and compares them with the President's request. Within each function, selected issues are examined and major recommendations justified.

Although the report recommends budget authority and outlay totals for each function, it assumes a specific spending level for each account in the budget. HBC staff constructs the Democratic mark by adding to or subtracting from the amount requested for each function by the President. The staff also makes specific assumptions for program changes and legislative actions. In effect, therefore, the mark represents a line-item budget, although only the totals and a small number of issues are discussed in the report. This attention to program details persists through HBC markup of each budget resolution. If the committee changes a functional allocation, a corresponding adjustment is made in one or more programs, so that the program assumptions are always arithmetically consistent with the totals. Thus, even though the committee formally limits its decisions to the totals, it does so with program specifics in mind.

With its account-by-account inventory, HBC staff does most of the spadework for the mark. When the staff begins the task, it has little guidance from the chairman, perhaps only an indication of what he wants the deficit to be, plus some understanding of his position on the few issues in which he is strongly interested. Thus, without having to be told, HBC staffers sensed that Chairman Robert N. Giaimo would favor less spending for defense than what the President had proposed. Each staff analyst defends his mark for the programs in his jurisdiction at intensive review sessions which last several days. HBC analysts are challenged to justify recommended deviations from the President's budget, to show why they expect certain legislation to pass or fail, and to explain why they have singled out particular issues for special attention. These "adversary proceedings" (as several participants have referred to them) focus on what Congress is expected to do, not on the substantive merits of legislation. The purposes of these arduous sessions are to purge the numbers of the analysts' biases and to fix on levels that realistically anticipate congressional expectations.

As markup approaches, the chairman and other committee Democrats become more involved in the process. The chairman solicits the views of notables from other committees as well as of Democratic leaders in the House. He consults with the heads of HBC's task forces and with other Democrats on the committee. The chairman and HBC colleagues use chance get-togethers, for example, meeting other Members on the House floor, to discuss budget prospects and issues. Although any Democrat can influence the numbers by expressing an interest in a particular matter, House Republicans have had virtually no input into the process.

In the years in which his mark was used, the chairman's objective was to produce a budget that could garner sufficient Democratic support in committee and on the floor to overcome expected Republican opposition. Thus, although the recommendations bore his imprimatur and were his responsibility, the chairman was not really a free agent in selecting the numbers. His were anticipatory recommendations, tempered in some instances by his own preferences as well as by tactical considerations. Both Adams and Giaimo sensed that liberal Democrats on HBC would try to raise the spending level for social programs, no matter how high it had been pegged by the chairman. Therefore both leaders tended to offer relatively low figures for those programs.

Most HBC members did not resent the chairman's initiative, because they saw no difference between his recommendations and the draft legislation that forms the basis for conventional markups. As long as they remained free to propose changes, most HBC rank-and-filers welcomed the chairman's lead. "There is nothing sacred about it," a Democratic committeeman noted. "You have got to start somewhere because a markup without a mark would be frightful. It would take days or weeks just to arrive at a starting point."

Moreover, most Members knew that except for the few matters in which the chairman expressed personal interest, the document reflected House—almost exclusively Democratic—expectations rather than the individual views of the chairman. With the mark as a starting point, HBC members have had an opportunity to add their own expectations and preferences. They, too, have become cognizant of the need to secure House approval of the budget resolution.

Some committee liberals felt that by forcing them to propose spending increases in public the mark put a burden on committee members who preferred higher spending for social programs. The extent to which this problem existed depended on whether the chairman could accommodate committee Democratts without abandoning his own strong interests or jeopardizing the floor prospects of the resolution. The shift from a chairman's mark to a caucus mark for fiscal 1980 resulted, in part, from a growing divergence between committee and House Democrats. As HBC Democrats became more liberal than their House colleagues, it grew increasingly difficult for the chairman to devise a mark that satisfied both his liberal committee members and the House.

At this writing it is too early to tell whether HBC Democrats will continue with a caucus mark or revert to one prepared by the chairman. But as long as the committee is sharply divided between Democrats and Republicans on key budget issues, it is likely that the mark will continue to reflect the majority party's views.

The Democratic Markup

The Democratic mark has structured HBC's deliberations and has always served as the point of departure for amendments offered by committee members. But the committee has not docilely accepted the recommendations in the mark or its program assumptions. During HBC's markup of the first resolution for fiscal 1977, more than 40 amendments were offered, and that level was equaled for the 1978 and 1979 fiscal years. The fact that the fiscal 1980 resolution occasioned more than 60 proposed amendments indicates the contentiousness with which that budget was debated in HBC.

In the first years of the budget process, proposals to raise the spending targets outnumbered proposed decreases, but in fiscal 1980, 37 of the 62 proposals were for decreases in the mark presented to the committee. The quest for budget reductions was but one of many indications of a change in budgetary politics following the adoption in June 1978 of Proposition 13, which lowered property taxes, in California. HBC members proved sensitive to the changing political climate and were reluctant to adopt proposals that would add to the spending and deficit totals.

Nevertheless, proposed increases have always stood a better chance of winning committee approval than have reductions. In fiscal 1977, 10 of 21 proposed increases were adopted, compared with only 5 of the 19 decreases. In fact, the disparity was even greater than these numbers suggest because three of the approved increases were later reversed when the committee took a second round of votes on the resolution. The pattern was even more pronounced in the fiscal 1978 and 1979 actions. In these two years, HBC approved 27 increase amendments, while adopting only 5 reductions. In fiscal 1980, the margin of success for program increases was narrowed considerably by the budgetary restraint that prevailed. More reductions (12) were approved then than in the three previous years combined, and the number almost equaled the 13 approved increases.

The support for increases has reflected the domination of HBC markups by the Democratic majority. Between 1977 and 1980, Democrats sponsored more than 130 amendments during markup of the first resolution, compared with about 60 offered by the Republicans. Moreover, Democratic amendments had a much higher success rate, better than 50 percent compared with less than 25 percent for Republican amendments. The Republicans lost even though they sided together in committee more than the Democrats. During markup of the first resolution for fiscal 1977, the Republicans voted in unison on all 12 roll calls, while committee Democrats held ranks only once, in opposition to a Republican move to adopt President Ford's spending levels. Republican and Democratic majorities took opposite sides on all but one of the roll calls. Nevertheless, because of defections by several conservative Democrats, the Republicans won a few close votes in the 1977 markup.

The liberalization of Democratic membership in the 95th Congress (discussed in chapter IV) sharpened the partisan cleavages and strengthened the Democratic majority. Republicans maintained unanimity on 16 of the 25 roll calls for the first 1978 resolution and on 18 of the 25 votes on the 1979 resolution, but were outvoted time and again. The Democrats carried all but 2 of the 22 "party line" votes (roll calls in which half or more of the members of the two parties were on different sides) in fiscal 1978 and on 16 of the 22 such votes in the following year. But the Republicans were more successful in the fiscal 1980 markup, winning 14 of the 36 contested votes. Overall, the Democrats prevailed on more than 80 percent of the party line votes in 1978 and 1979, but on barely 60 percent of such votes in fiscal 1980.

The change in fiscal 1980 is evident when voting patterns are compared with the previous years. Table 12 displays the party cohesion records and winning scores for every HBC member between

Table 12

PARTY COHESION AND SUCCESS SCORES OF HOUSE BUDGET COMMITTEE MEMBERS, MARKUP OF FIRST RESOLUTION FOR FISCAL YEARS 1977-79

	Voted With or Against Party Majority			*Voted With or Against Committee Majority*		
Member	*Number With*	*Number Against*	*Percent With*	*Number With*	*Number Against*	*Percent With*
Democrats						
Adams	13	0	100.0%	9	4	69.2%
O'Neill	13	0	100.0	9	4	69.2
Smith	10	0	100.0	7	3	70.0
O'Hara	12	0	100.0	9	3	75.0
Ashley	63	5	92.6	54	6	90.0
Mink	12	1	92.3	10	3	76.9
Giaimo	64	6	91.4	63	9	87.5
Obey	51	5	91.1	50	8	86.2
Stokes	59	7	89.4	53	15	77.9
Simon	51	7	87.9	47	13	78.3
Lehman	49	7	87.5	49	9	84.5
Mitchell	61	10	85.9	55	18	75.3
Minetta	47	8	85.5	48	12	80.0
Fraser	47	8	85.5	39	18	68.4
Leggett	57	10	85.1	53	16	76.8
Holtzman	58	11	84.1	51	20	71.8
Fisher	44	9	83.0	43	12	78.2
Wright	56	12	82.4	56	14	80.0
Mattox	40	17	70.2	39	20	66.1
Derrick	38	24	61.3	41	23	64.1
Pike	31	23	51.4	32	24	57.1
Burleson	15	28	34.9	21	24	46.7
Gibbons	4	9	30.8	8	5	61.5
Landrum	2	8	20.0	4	6	40.0
Runnels	1	7	12.5	4	4	50.0
Total	898	222	80.2%	854	293	74.5%
Republicans						
Cederberg	13	0	100.0%	5	8	38.5%
Schneebeli	13	0	100.0	5	8	38.5
Clawson	13	0	100.0	5	8	38.5
Shriver	12	0	100.0	4	8	33.3
Latta	72	1	98.6	23	50	31.5
Broyhill	69	1	98.6	23	47	32.9
Duncan	54	2	96.4	17	39	30.4
Rousselot	51	2	96.2	15	38	28.3

(Continued)

PARTY COHESION AND SUCCESS SCORES OF HOUSE BUDGET COMMITTEE MEMBERS, MARKUP OF FIRST RESOLUTION FOR FISCAL YEARS 1977-79 (Cont.)

	Voted With or Against Party Majority			*Voted With or Against Committee Majority*		
Member	*Number With*	*Number Against*	*Percent With*	*Number With*	*Number Against*	*Percent With*
Burgener	55	4	93.2	20	39	33.9
Regula	53	4	93.0	21	36	36.8
Holt	67	5	93.0	24	48	33.3
Conable	67	6	91.8	24	49	32.9
Total	539	25	95.6%	186	378	33.0%

Source: Tabulations of roll call votes of the House Budget Committee for the first, second, and third budget resolutions of fiscal 1977, the first and second budget resolutions of fiscal 1978, and the first resolution for fiscal 1979.

fiscal 1977 and 1979. The table shows remarkable unity on the minority side, with 4 of the 12 Republicans who served on HBC during these years having perfect scores and all of the others scoring above 90 percent. Only 4 of the 25 Democrats voted with their party majority all of the time, and a number defected on more than half of the votes. The least partisan Republican (Conable) exhibited more party loyalty than all but one Democrat who served on the committee throughout those years. Nevertheless, even the most maverick Democrat (Runnels) had a higher success rate than any of the Republicans. As a group, the Democrats voted with the majority 75 percent of the time, the Republicans only 33 percent.

In addition, the more loyal the Democrat, the more likely he was to be on the winning side. Disaffected Democrats did not hold "swing votes" in committee after HBC was liberalized and the Democratic advantage was stretched to 17 to 8. As a result, liberal Democrats on the committee were able to tailor the budget resolutions to their own expectations and preferences rather than to those of the entire membership.

There was, however, a pronounced erosion in Democratic cohesion and strength in the fiscal 1980 markup. Table 13 shows that

Table 13

PARTY COHESION AND SUCCESS SCORES OF HOUSE BUDGET COMMITTEE MEMBERS, MARKUP OF FIRST RESOLUTION FOR FISCAL 1980

	Voted With or Against Party Majority			*Voted With or Against Committee Majority*		
Member	*Number With*	*Number Against*	*Percent With*	*Number With*	*Number Against*	*Percent With*
Democrats						
Giaimo	32	5	86.5%	27	10	73.0%
Wright	31	4	88.6	27	8	77.1
Ashley	30	4	88.2	26	8	76.5
Stokes	34	2	94.4	24	12	66.7
Holtzman	31	6	83.8	22	15	59.5
Obey	29	8	78.4	23	14	62.2
Simon	30	7	81.1	21	16	56.8
Minetta	32	4	88.9	23	13	63.9
Mattox	9	28	24.3	18	19	48.6
Jones	14	22	38.9	24	12	66.7
Solarz	35	2	94.6	24	13	64.9
Brodhead	34	3	92.0	25	12	66.6
Wirth	24	12	66.7	28	8	77.8
Panetta	23	13	63.9	24	12	66.7
Gephardt	18	19	48.6	23	14	62.2
Nelson	14	23	37.8	23	14	62.2
Gray	34	3	91.9	25	12	67.6
Total	454	165	73.3%	407	212	65.8%
Republicans						
Latta	34	1	97.1%	16	21	43.2%
Broyhill	34	0	100.0	15	20	42.9
Conable	34	1	97.1	16	21	43.2
Holt	34	1	97.1	15	21	41.1
Regula	33	1	97.0	13	23	36.1
Shuster	32	3	91.1	17	20	45.9
Frenzel	35	0	100.0	14	23	37.8
Rudd	34	1	97.1	16	21	43.2
Total	270	8	97.0%	122	170	41.8%

Source: Tabulations of roll call votes of the House Budget Committee for the first resolution of fiscal 1980.

the Democrats voted together less than 75 percent of the time, compared with 80 percent between 1977 and 1979. As a consequence, Democratic members' average success score fell from 75 to 65. New Democrats on HBC were generally the most disaffected; Democrats who had just joined the committee accounted for five of the six lowest party loyalty scores. Unlike the previous Congress when liberal Democrats got their way on the committee, in the fiscal 1980 markup disaffections by moderate or conservative Democrats sometimes enabled the Republicans to win.

The shifting voting pattern also resulted in a modification of the strategy for nailing down liberal Democratic support, that is, increased funding for programs favored by these Members. Between 1977 and 1979, liberals used the markup to enhance the resolution's appeal to the majority party—usually by allocating more funds for certain domestic programs than had been proposed by the President or the HBC chairman. In fact, the committee's line-item practices encouraged members (almost always Democrats) to try to add funds for specific programs. Members rarely sponsored amendments to shift funds within functions; to do so probably would have provoked opposition from committee colleagues who had their own program favorites. The safer course was to raise the functional totals while designating the programs to which funds were to be added.

HBC members have strongly defended the committee's line-item review, although they have readily acknowledged that the House is not bound by its program assumptions. "If you don't talk details," one Democrat insisted, "then you are just picking figures out of the air":

> To make decisions about education priorities, we almost have to be talking about impact aid; we're going to have to talk about aid to the handicapped. You can't talk about the defense budget without talking about the B-1 bomber.

Committee members also believe that their program assumptions should be made known to the House so that it is aware of the implications of its decisions. "It is our feeling," one declared, "that we have an obligation to inform the House as accurately as we can what our assumptions were in arriving at the numbers."

Yet there is another reason for dabbling in line items. Line-item additions seem to have become the price for garnering sufficient liberal Democratic support to overcome Republican and conservative Democratic opposition. Even with their commanding majority on the committee, the Democrats risk the possibility of having the resolution whipsawed by defections of conservatives who are distressed by the high deficits and of liberals who dislike the program priorities. This happened in the spring of 1975, the first time HBC produced a budget resolution. The resolution was rejected by a coalition of Republicans, conservative Democrats, and liberal Democrats. Only the switch of two Republican votes saved the resolution from possible defeat, and the new budget process from serious embarrassment.

Sometimes the line-item increases are promoted by Democratic leaders who want to make the resolution attractive enough to win majority support in committee and on the floor. One such instance occurred on the last day of HBC's extended markup of the first resolution for 1977. At that time, Majority Leader Thomas P. O'Neill, Jr., successfully added $4.2 billion for job stimulus programs and another $100 million previously cut by the committee from start-up funds for national health insurance and the Humphrey-Hawkins full employment legislation, both of which were of great symbolic importance to liberal Democrats.

Sometimes line-item sweeteners have been sponsored by members who brought to the markup some program attachments developed through their primary committee attachments. Rep. James G. O'Hara, a senior Democrat on the Education and Labor Committee, won a $358 million increase for three education programs, while Rep. Patsy Mink obtained $37 million for five territorial programs in which she was interested. In the most extreme case, one program won a $1 million increase during a line-item review. In fact, raising the spending level is a process in which most HBC Democrats participate. During markup of the first resolution for fiscal 1978, more than half the committee's Democrats won adoption of amendments earmarking more money for designated programs.

HBC members understand that line itemization biases the committee in favor of spending increases. "It is hard to vote for reductions," a Democratic member commented, "because we know which programs would be hurt. It is hard not to vote for the increases because we know which programs would benefit." Committee members also exploit the ambiguous status of the budget resolutions to argue for increases and against reductions. Sponsors of proposed increases argue that approval would merely assure that Congress has an opportunity to decide the issue when it later considers appropriations bills. Conversely, members oppose program reductions by arguing that approval would prevent Congress from having its say when it acts on spending legislation.

Although HBC continued line-item review in marking up the first resolution for fiscal 1980, it exercised restraint in adding to the budget. In a series of amendments near the end of markup, funds were added for local economic development, aid to the handicapped, rural assistance, regional development commissions, discretionary health programs, retirement benefits for Panama Canal employees, and aeronautical research and development. Without these last-minute additions, the committee's budget would have been lower than the mark recommended by HBC Democrats.

Nevertheless, the committee could not escape the budget-reduction mood affecting Congress, and in a number of cases Members had to settle for words rather than money for their favorite programs. Rep. Paul Simon won a promise that funding for an international wheat reserve would be considered in the second resolution if legislation were submitted for this purpose; Rep. Louis Stokes was promised a fresh examination of the fiscal needs of states and cities in the event of a downturn in the economy; Rep. James Mattox added language urging highest priority for job programs to assist the structurally unemployed; and Rep. William Brodhead extracted a reaffirmation of the committee's concern for Vietnam War veterans. In a time of parsimony, words became the currency through which support was purchased for the budget resolution.

The Resolution: Agreement with Dissent

The budget resolution that has emerged from HBC has borne a Democratic stamp of approval. With the one exception noted, involving a vote switch by two Republicans in 1975, Democrats have supplied the votes necessary to report the resolution while Republicans have steadfastly united in opposition. It has not been possible to buy Republican support with line-item concessions. Not only have HBC Republicans found overall expenditures and the deficit much too high for their taste, but also they have opposed many of the line-item increases voted in committee. The changes that make the resolution more satisfactory to liberal Democrats aggravate Republican unhappiness over the outcome. Like virtually all members of Congress, however, HBC Republicans have their program favorites, and they are not averse to using the markup to enhance the budgetary prospects for such programs. But although they sometimes sponsor line-item increases, their usual role is that of the outvoted opposition.

Although HBC makes numerous line-item changes during markup, it has not had open-ended discretion to load the resolution with all the increases that committee members might prefer. If too much were added to the functional allocations, the spending totals might become unacceptably high for some members and the resolution would be endangered. During markup, budget totals are prominently displayed on a blackboard in the committee room. When a change is made in an individual function, the budget totals also are visibly adjusted. Thus, the committee always has an up-to-date tally of its actions and their effect on total spending and the deficit. The mark of the chairman or of the Democratic leadership has served as a guide for the committee and the final totals have strayed only marginally from the mark. Table 14 compares the chairman's (or Democratic) recommendation and the committee's first resolutions for the 1976-80 fiscal years. The third resolution for fiscal 1977 also is included in this and the two succeeding tables, because Congress made new program decisions in it. (Second resolutions usually only confirm previous decisions.)

Although HBC always raises the outlay level, the increase has never exceeded 0.4 percent of the total. Increases in budget authority have been somewhat higher but still have averaged less than 1 percent for the period covered in this study. These marginal adjustments have provided room in the resolutions for comparatively small increases in the functions. Between 1976 and 1980, HBC made 88 functional allocations (excluding interest, allowances, and offsetting receipts) of new budget authority and an equal number of outlay decisions in developing the first resolutions (and the third for fiscal 1977). As shown in table 15, half of the functional outcomes were identical to the chairman's mark. Although 30 percent of the budget authority and outlay decisions were above the chairman's recommendations, in most cases the increase was slight. The HBC allocation exceeded the chairman's mark by 2 percent or more in only 9 percent of the functional decisions.

If the adjustments in the spending totals and the functions have bought majority support, they have not brought budgetary peace to the committee. If one can judge from the plethora of additional and dissenting views appended to the HBC reports, few members have been genuinely satisfied with the outcome. Table 16 discloses that each report has averaged almost 10 such statements and that

Table 14

COMPARISON OF MARK AND HOUSE BUDGET COMMITTEE REPORT, FIRST BUDGET RESOLUTION AGGREGATES, FISCAL YEARS 1976-80
(millions of dollars)

Budget Category	*Recommendation in Mark*	*Committee Report*	*Difference*	*Percent Difference*
Fiscal 1976				
Revenues	$290,264	$295,000	$4,736	1.6%
Budget Authority	388,991	386,493	−2,498	−0.6
Outlays	366,783	368,236	825	0.2
Deficit	76,519	73,236	−3,283	−4.2
Fiscal 1977				
Revenues	363,000	363,000	0	0.0
Budget Authority	445,700	452,261	6,561	1.5
Outlays	412,800	413,625	825	0.2
Deficit	49,800	50,625	825	1.6
Fiscal 1977[a]				
Revenues	348,500	348,500	0	0.0
Budget Authority	481,986	482,306	320	0.1
Outlays	418,755	418,815	60	—[b]
Deficit	70,255	70,315	60	0.1
Fiscal 1978				
Revenues	398,159	398,094	−65	—[b]
Budget Authority	498,473	500,764	2,291	0.5
Outlays	460,553	462,349	1,796	0.4
Deficit	62,394	64,255	1,861	2.9
Fiscal 1979				
Revenues	443,279	443,279	0	0.0
Budget Authority	561,134	568,152	7,018	1.2
Outlays	500,849	501,358	509	0.1
Deficit	57,570	58,079	509	0.8
Fiscal 1980				
Revenues	505,600	507,800	2,200	0.4
Budget Authority	607,680	608,418	718	0.1
Outlays	532,617	532,730	113	—[b]
Deficit	27,017	24,930	−2,087	−7.7

[a] For purposes of this table, the third budget resolution for fiscal 1977 is treated as if it were a first resolution.
[b] Less than 0.05 percent.

Source: Tabulated from House Budget Committee documents.

60 percent of the members have endorsed one or more statements. Dissent has not been limited to HBC's Republican minority; almost half of the Democrats have expressed additional or dissenting views.

Although statistical comparisons with other committees are lacking, the numbers of dissents and dissenters appear to be extraordinarily high. HBC members regard their inability to compose their differences as an indication of the difficulty of the decisions they are forced to face in each resolution. A senior Republican who had served on both HBC and House Appropriations regularly dissented in the Budget Committee while joining the majority in Appropriations:

> There's a big difference between the two committees. [On Budget] we have to face up to the totals and we can't vote just on the line items. The Budget Committee has to make priority decisions while the Appropriations Committee avoids that problem by handling one bill at a time in separate subcommittees.

This explanation goes to the heart of budgetary conflict within the House Budget Committee. The committee must decide the parts and the whole, the budget's totals as well as its functional allocations. Members have to be satisfied with both the aggregates and the components in order to be satisfied with the budget. This has not been an easy task for HBC because the parts and the whole have generated contradictory pressures. Almost half of HBC members have been dissatisfied with the budget because of what they regard as unacceptably high deficits, while some Democrats have deplored what they consider inadequate spending for social programs. Yet larger outlays for such programs would force overall expenditures and deficit totals higher, further alienating Republicans and conservative Democrats. Lower spending totals could limit the funds available for the programs favored by liberals. There simply is no way for HBC to harmonize these differences.

THE HOUSE DIVIDED: FLOOR FIGHTS AND PARTY CLEAVAGES

Because the resolutions of the House Budget Committee are accompanied by so many dissenting opinions, easy sailing cannot be expected on the floor. HBC cannot assure the House that it is con-

Table 15

NUMBER OF CHANGES BETWEEN HBC MARK AND COMMITTEE REPORT, BY FUNCTION, SIZE, AND DIRECTION OF CHANGE, FIRST RESOLUTIONS, FISCAL YEARS 1976-80

				Increases		
Function		*Decrease*	*No Change*	*Less than 2%*	*2%-4.9%*	*5% or More*
National Defense	BA[a]	2	2	1	1	0
	O[b]	1	3	2	0	0
International Affairs	BA	2	2	0	1	1
	O	2	3	1	0	0
General Science, Space,	BA	0	4	2	0	0
and Technology	O	0	4	1	1	0
Energy	BA	0	2	0	0	0
	O	0	2	0	0	0
Natural Resources and	BA	0	3	2	1	0
Environment	O	0	4	2	0	0
Agriculture	BA	1	5	0	0	0
	O	0	5	1	0	0
Commerce and Housing	BA	2	2	1	0	1
Credit	O	2	3	1	0	0
Transportation	BA	0	2	0	0	0
	O	0	1	1	0	0

Community and Regional Development	BA	2	1	1	1	2
	O	2	1	1	1	1
Education, Training, Employment, and Social Services	BA	0	1	3	2	0
	O	0	1	3	2	0
Health	BA	1	3	2	0	0
	O	0	5	1	0	0
Income Security	BA	1	1	4	0	0
	O	3	1	2	0	0
Veterans' Benefits	BA	1	4	1	0	0
	O	1	4	1	0	0
Administration of Justice	BA	1	3	1	0	1
	O	1	3	1	1	0
General Government	BA	3	3	0	0	0
	O	2	3	1	0	0
General Purpose Fiscal Assistance	BA	0	5	1	0	0
	O	0	6	0	0	0
TOTAL [c]		30 (17%)	92 (52%)	38 (22%)	10 (6%)	6 (3%)

NOTE: Table includes third resolution for 1977.

[a] BA = Budget authority.

[b] O = Outlay.

[c] Total excludes interest, allowances, and offsetting receipts.

Source: Tabulated on the basis of the chairman's recommendation for the first resolutions 1976-79, the third resolution for 1977, and the Democratic recommendation for the first fiscal 1980 resolution.

Table 16

NUMBER OF ADDITIONAL OR DISSENTING VIEWS FILED IN HOUSE BUDGET COMMITTEE REPORTS BY MAJORITY AND MINORITY COMMITTEE MEMBERS, FISCAL YEARS 1967-80

	Supplemental and Additional Views (Majority)		*Dissenting Views*		*Minority Views*		*Supplemental and Additional Views (Minority)*			
Resolutions	*No. of Stmts.*	*No. of Signers*	*No. of Stmts.*	*No. of Signers*	*No. of Stmts.*	*No. of Signers*	*No. of Stmts.*	*No. of Signers*	*Total Stmts.*	*Total Signers*[a]
Fiscal 1976										
First	6	7	2	2	1	8	1	1	10	17
Second	4	5	1	1	1	8	1	1	7	14
Fiscal 1977										
First	5	7	1	1	1	8	3	3	10	16
Second	3	4	0	0	1	8	1	1	5	12
Third	7	8	0	0	1	8	1	2	9	16
Fiscal 1978										
First	9	10	0	0	1	8	4	6	14	18
Second	6	7	0	0	1	8	2	2	9	15
Fiscal 1979										
First	7	10	1	1	1	8	4	4	13	18
Second	5	5	2	2	1	8	1	1	9	15
Fiscal 1980										
First	5	6	0	0	1	8	3	3	9	14
								Average	9.5	15.5[b]

[a] Members who signed more than one statement are only counted *once* for purposes of this column.
[b] This represents approximately 60 percent of the membership of the committee.

Source: Author's tabulations.

tent with its own product or that disputes have been satisfactorily settled in committee and need not be reopened on the floor. With the committee fractured into warring parties, it can expect many of its decisions to be fought over again. Thus members of both parties have offered many floor amendments during consideration of each HBC report.

Through five years of budget making, the voting alignment in the House has closely resembled that of the committee: steadfast Republican opposition combined with Democratic factionalism. Although all of the required resolutions have been passed, several have squeaked through with only a few votes to spare. (The roll calls are displayed in table 17.) In one instance (the first resolution for fiscal 1978), the House rejected the resolution but approved a revised version a week later. In another (the first resolution for

Table 17

REPUBLICAN AND DEMOCRATIC VOTES ON ADOPTION OF THE BUDGET RESOLUTIONS IN THE HOUSE

	Vote[a]		*Democrats*		*Republicans*	
Resolutions	*Yes*	*No*	*Yes*	*No*	*Yes*	*No*
Fiscal 1976						
First	230	193	225	55	5	138
Second	225	191	214	67	11	124
Fiscal 1977						
First	221	155	208	44	13	111
Second	227	151	215	38	12	113
Third	239	169	225	50	14	119
Fiscal 1978						
First (First Round)	84	320	82	185	2	135
First (Second Round)	213	179	206	58	7	121
Second	199	188	195	59	4	129
Fiscal 1979						
First	201	197	198	61	3	136
Second	217	178	215	42	2	136
Fiscal 1980						
First	220	184	211	50	9	134

[a] These votes are on passage of the resolution in the House, not on adoption of the conference report.

Source: *Congressional Record*, various issues.

1980), the conference report was rejected but a slightly modified one was adopted the next day.

The Republican "No"

Republicans started with a strong incentive to support the new budget process because they initially perceived it as an opportunity to control budget deficits and slow the growth of federal spending. When the House took up its first resolution in the spring of 1975, conservative Delbert Latta, HBC's ranking Republican, warned that "it would be disastrous for us to defeat this resolution . . . we have to have a budget resolution." [2] But the very next day, Latta voted with 137 party colleagues against the resolution; only 5 House Republicans voted for passage. Forced to choose between their fiscal ideology and the budget process, most Republicans could not go along with the $70 billion deficit recommended by the Budget Committee. Prior to the vote on the resolution, 113 Republicans had supported a Latta substitute that would have trimmed the deficit to $54 billion, and when this failed, they all opposed the resolution.

Voting "no" on the HBC resolution has become a habit for all but a few House Republicans. Since the Democrats took control of the White House in 1977, House Republicans have become even more united in opposition to the budget resolutions produced by the majority party and, by 1979, on average, only 1 of 20 Republicans voted for a budget resolution.

Clearly, the sizable budget deficits have been the main sticking point for most of the Republicans. Although the size of the deficit has been whittled down, Republicans have not abandoned their negative posture. Only two House Republicans supported fiscal 1979's second resolution, although its projected deficit was barely half of the deficit initially set for fiscal 1976. Moreover, as the size of the deficit was reduced, Republican support for Rep. John Rousselot's perennial "balanced budget" proposal increased. Rousselot's first try at a balanced budget (for fiscal 1976) attracted 75 Republican votes, but 128 Republicans supported his balanced budget proposal for the 1980 fiscal year.[3]

---

2. 121 *Congressional Record* (daily ed., April 30, 1975) H3463.
3. Rousselot also became more successful in attracting Democrats to his cause. Only 15 Democrats voted for a balanced budget for 1976; 58 supported his balanced budget amendment for 1980. But despite the additional support from both Democrats and Republicans, the balanced budget amendment has not yet passed.

House Republicans view the budget resolutions as the great divide between the two parties, as one of the few contemporary issues on which there ought to be a clear-cut demarcation between Republican and Democratic positions. They regard the budget as a political statement about the reach and purpose of the federal government, its economic role, and the national priorities of the United States. For House Republicans, the budget resolutions sum up the essential differences between the two parties; the dollar disputes, accordingly, do not merely reflect conflicts over money but go to the heart of the American political process.

This Republican conception of the budget resolutions has been clearly articulated by Barber Conable, a leading member of both the Ways and Means and Budget Committees. After the House rejected the first resolution for fiscal 1978, Republicans were pressed to supply some of the votes needed to win majority support for the new version. When most Republicans persisted in their opposition, Conable took the floor to defend his party against charges that it would be responsible should the budget process fail. Reminding the Democrats that they had a two-to-one lead in the House, Conable admonished, "You are the ones who control the legislative program for the next 2 years, and you are the ones who should properly be held accountable to the people for the overall performance of the Congress." [4] The budget, he contended, was too basic an issue for the Republicans to submerge their differences just for the sake of reaching legislative agreement:

> On many issues Republicans and Democrats agree: we all understand the wide areas of consensus which are possible and appropriate in the moderate climate of American politics. But the more basic the issue—and what issue is more basic than the setting of the year's priorities?—the greater the obligation on those charged with the decisions of government to consider a range of options rather than to try to force a consensus.[5]

In line with their conviction that the two parties should diverge on budget policy, Republicans have regularly offered an across-the-board cut (sometimes with selected functions excluded) as an alternative to HBC's resolution, but they have never been able to overcome the Democratic majority (see table 18). The first of these—Latta's substitute for the fiscal 1976 resolution—lost by

---

4. 123 *Congressional Record* (daily ed., May 5, 1977) H 4066.
5. *Ibid.*

almost 90 votes (159-248), a margin that was exceeded in a similar vote during consideration of the first resolution for fiscal 1978. The Republicans modified their strategy for the 1979 budget, coupling tax and spending reductions in a single amendment. This effort carried the Republicans close to success. All but one of the voting Republicans, as well as 60 Democrats, supported the substitute for the first 1979 resolution. When the 15-minute voting period had expired, the electronic scoreboard in the House showed the substitute in the lead. However, the Speaker prolonged the roll call, giving party whips additional time to persuade recalcitrant Democrats to change their votes. The final count was 197 to 203 against the substitute, after which only 3 Republicans voted for the resolution. The Republican alternative for fiscal 1980 concentrated on a reduction in the size of the deficit, but it too went down to defeat, by a 191-228 vote.

Since the Republicans as a group have not tried for piecemeal revisions in the resolutions (although individual Republicans have proposed changes in particular functions), the defeat of their all-or-nothing substitute has left them without a significant voice in congressional budget policy. From the start of markup in HBC through the completion of floor action, House Republicans have been outsiders, rarely courted or consulted by the Democratic majority. Whether self-imposed or dictated by the majority, this alienation of House Republicans from the budgetary process has proved as formidable a barrier to support of the resolutions as has the ideological distance between the two parties. Because they have not been able to point to anything in the resolutions that was truly their own, Republicans have not voted for them.

If this explanation is correct, the price for Republican support need not be radical concessions such as a balanced budget or even the cuts called for in the substitute resolutions. While most Republicans would persist in opposition, modest concessions (for example, a little more money for defense or a little less for social programs) might secure sufficient additional votes to assure passage of the resolutions in the House. This happened in the fiscal 1978 budget, when 29 Republicans voted for the conference report on the first resolution. In conference, Republican Marjorie Holt repeatedly suggested that her party would supply the necessary votes if defense spending (the principal issue in dispute between the House and Senate) were set at a higher level than the level that House Democrats wanted. The Democrats reluctantly accepted her offer only after they were unable to reach agreement among them-

Table 18

PARTY VOTING PATTERN FOR THE REPUBLICAN ALTERNATIVE TO THE HOUSE BUDGET COMMITTEE'S RECOMMENDATIONS

	Vote		*Republicans*		*Democrats*	
Resolutions[a]	*Yes*	*No*	*Yes*	*No*	*Yes*	*No*
Fiscal 1976						
First	159	248	113	22	46	226
Second	159	257	113	23	46	234
Fiscal 1977						
First	145	230	110	17	35	213
Second	Rejected by voice vote					
Fiscal 1978						
First (First Round)	150	250	126	9	24	241
First (Second Round)	150	240	122	7	28	233
Fiscal 1979						
First	197	203	139	1	58	202
Second	201	206	140	1	61	205
Fiscal 1980						
First	191	228	148	6	43	222

[a] The Republicans did not offer alternatives to the third resolution for fiscal 1977 or to the second resolution for fiscal 1978.

Source: *Congressional Quarterly*, various issues.

selves. Holt then appealed to fellow Republicans to live up to the bargain, even though "many minority Members of the House are appalled at the idea of voting for a budget with a $65 billion deficit":

> I think if we are going to be part of setting the priorities of this country, we have got to get in here and be active in it. We cannot sit back and vote "no"; that is easy, that is beautiful, but we have got to participate if we are going to have any effectiveness in it at all.[6]

The 1978 budget turned out to be a special case. The Democrats offered concessions for Republican support because they had no alternative. In all previous and subsequent resolutions, the

6. *Ibid.*, H4560.

Democrats proceeded alone and most Republicans were content to vote "no."

It should be noted that some Republicans supported the 1978 resolution not only because of concessions offered by the majority party, but also because they did not want the budget process itself destroyed by failure to pass the necessary resolution. As much as they complained that the process had not curbed the growth in government or ended deficit spending, many Republicans believed that matters would be worse in the absence of budgetary controls. As we have seen, some Republicans have provided "bail-out" votes when a resolution was threatened with defeat—in 1976 when the initial resolution was stalled in HBC, on this occasion in 1978, and again in fiscal 1980, when the conference report was attacked by liberals for inadequate funding of education programs. In the last case, a record number of Republicans (36) voted for the conference report, although their support was not sufficient to rescue the resolution from defeat. To be sure, the "yes"-voting Republicans also were spurred by a feeling that the conference report was the best deal they could get, and that its defeat would only lead to higher domestic spending. When the report was voted on again, it had more funds for education, and Republican support for it declined.

The Democrats' Dilemma

With the Republicans united in opposition, the closeness of the vote in any budget turns on the number of Democratic defectors. The first resolution for 1976 passed with only 4 votes to spare because 68 Democrats joined the opposition; the second resolution for 1978, however, enjoyed a 76-vote margin because only 38 Democrats defected. This voting pattern has compelled Democratic leaders to take an active role in moving the resolutions through the House. They have not been able to sit back and rely on the Budget Committee because defeat of a resolution might be interpreted as a rejection of Democratic budget policy. The leadership's involvement has extended beyond the customary whip counts to ascertain how rank-and-file Democrats expect to vote. Democratic leaders have effectively superseded the HBC chairman as floor managers of the budget resolutions.

Democratic rejectionists come from both the conservative and liberal wings of the party. The more conservative or liberal a Democratic Member of the House is, the greater the likelihood that he or she will be dissatisfied with the results. Table 19 cate-

Table 19

CONSERVATIVE COALITION SUPPORT SCORES OF HOUSE DEMOCRATS WHO VOTED AGAINST MORE THAN HALF OF THE FISCAL 1976-79 RESOLUTIONS

Liberals	*Score*	*Moderates*	*Score*	*Conservatives*	*Score*
Ottinger	4	Jacobs	40	McDonald	97
Dellums	5	Hughes	42	Flynt	96
Conyers	6	Fithian	44	Satterfield	95
J. Burton	7	Santini	51	Waggonner	90
Carr	13	Mottl	53	Hall	90
Lundine	14	Evans	60	Montgomery	89
Schroeder	19	Davis	64	Lloyd	88
Keys	28			Runnels	88
				Fountain	88
				Ichord	86
				Brinkley	84
				Chappell	83
				Mathis	79
				Byron	78
				Andrews	73
				Bennett	71
				Levitas	71
				Mann	69
				Hefner	68

Source: Tabulations of voting records; the conservative coalition scores are from the 1977 *Congressional Quarterly Almanac.*

gorizes the defectors between 1976 and 1979 (Members who opposed more than half the resolutions) according to their "conservative coalition" scores for 1977. The table indicates that alienated conservatives outnumbered liberals by about two to one, a ratio that reflected the tilt of Democratic leaders toward the liberals. Because of the polarization of House Democrats, party leaders have acknowledged that they cannot woo both factions; nor can they tilt so markedly to one side as to risk further loss of support from the other. Although a move to the right might win back some conservatives and pick up some Republicans, the Democratic leadership has deliberately avoided this course. It has not wanted to become dependent upon Republican votes to pass the resolutions or to aggravate liberal disaffection with the budget process. The Democratic strategy has been to hold down liberal desertions while appealing to the large number of "swing" Democrats in the House. The latter category includes about a dozen members who opposed four of the resolutions, a slightly larger number who voted against three resolutions, and approximately 30 Democrats who were recorded against two resolutions.

The difficulty of satisfying all wings within the Democratic Party was demonstrated by the voting on the first resolution for 1980. Although they did not solicit Republican support, Democratic leaders were pulled by demands for balanced budgets and spending limitations into a more restrictive budget posture. The HBC resolution displeased many House liberals, but their efforts to provide more funds for domestic programs were defeated on the floor. To make matters worse, the House adopted an across-the-board cut that further reduced funds for the programs in which the liberals were interested. As a result, 30 northern Democrats deserted their party and voted against the resolution. Unlike prior years when conservatives led the Democratic opposition, this time the bulk of the "no" voters came from liberal quarters. Although the resolution passed by 36 votes, liberal frustration boiled over when additional program cuts were made in conference, and the resolution had to be salvaged by restoring some money to education.

The Democrats have been as willing as the Republicans to cast the budget as a contest between the two parties. This approach was enunciated by Majority Leader Jim Wright in a "Dear Democratic Colleague" letter after the House had rejected the initial 1978 budget resolution:

> The majority party has the responsibility to act—to ratify this document and proceed with the important business of the Congress. We can expect *no help from the Republicans.* They have the luxury of criticizing without assuming responsibility.
>
> So it is up to us. We must produce enough *Democratic* votes for the resolution to pass it—just as we have done in each of the last two years. This is the only way Congress can fulfill its constitutional responsibility to control and direct spending. And that's what it means to be the majority party.[7]

Democratic leaders, in their attempts to make the resolutions more palatable to party liberals, have written off the possibility of attracting Republicans or conservative Democrats. At first the leadership relied on floor amendments to attract liberal votes. Majority Leader O'Neill sponsored successful spending increases

7. Letter from Rep. Jim Wright, May 4, 1977.

to the first and second resolutions for 1976. But this strategy had an obvious drawback: it put House Democrats in the position of openly promoting higher spending and larger deficits. (Significantly, both the O'Neill amendments took advantage of late reestimates to allocate additional funds for favored programs without raising the overall spending level or the deficit.)[8] Accordingly, in subsequent years Democratic leaders concentrated on working their will in HBC. During markup of the first resolution for 1977, as already noted, O'Neill headed a move to add funds for job programs and for start-up of national health insurance and the Humphrey-Hawkins full employment legislation. Similarly, near the close of the markup of the first 1979 resolution, HBC—on the motion of Majority Leader Wright—added $2 billion for an accelerated public works program favored by party liberals. Democratic leaders have preferred, however, to influence budget outcomes through behind-the-scenes consultations with the HBC chairman and committee Democrats. Even before the Budget Committee switched to a Democratic rather than a chairman's mark, the leadership had become the dominant force in putting together a resolution that could command sufficient Democratic support to win House approval.

Because of the schism in the party and the Democratic leadership's unwillingness to try for Republican support, the prospects for passage of budget resolutions cannot be significantly improved by committee or floor amendments. Some liberals regularly oppose the resolutions despite the leadership's concessions. Their price for voting "yes"—a substantial shift from defense to domestic spending—probably would result in the loss of many more votes than it would gain. Approximately 20 conservative Democrats have been intractable opponents of the resolutions, and paying their price for support—reductions in federal spending and the deficit—also would cost Democratic votes. The leadership's task has been to retain a sufficient number of "swing" votes (Democrats who sometimes vote "no") so as to secure passage of the resolutions. Because it has been reluctant to propose spending increases, the leader-

8. The O'Neill amendment for the first 1976 resolution offset the $2.7 billion outlay increase with about $2 billion in reductions because of reestimates and about $500 million for a program not expected to be reported by the relevant House committee. O'Neill's amendment to the second 1976 resolution anticipated a reestimating amendment by a Democratic colleague which recouped all but a small part of the spending increase.

ship has relied on exhortation rather than budgetary inducements. "Vote the process, not the numbers" has been the argument used time and again to whip lukewarm Democrats into line. The message to Democrats is that they will be held culpable for the failure of budget reform and that they therefore must vote for the resolutions even if they are unhappy with the budget's priorities. The leadership's repertoire includes a lot of old-fashioned arm twisting ("elbow breaking is what it's like," attested one House Democrat who had experienced the treatment) as well as intensive lobbying by Democratic whips and HBC members during the weeks prior to floor action. In 1978, the Speaker set up a 25-member task force (headed by Butler Derrick, a second-term Congressman on the Budget Committee) to round up Democratic votes.

The "vote for the budget process" theme has become explicit during floor debate on the budget resolutions. "Today, once more," Majority Leader Wright told the House as it approached a final vote on the first resolution for 1979, "I am asking Members of this body to set aside what may be their own personal preferences and predilections and cast a yea vote for this resolution." [9] Democrats have been told the numbers are the best they can get without losing majority support. As Wright said in the 1978 debate: "I plead with my colleagues to look at this budget resolution on balance and recognize that it is the best that we collectively have been able to do." [10] Voting for the process also has meant voting against floor amendments, even attractive ones, which might lose votes for the final resolution:

> Members should not be vying with one another, each attempting to make this entire budget over in his own individual image. We must recognize that the task of the Committee on the Budget and the task of Congress in this resolution is not to try to imprint the stamp and stain of each individual personality upon the budget.[11]

Most House Democrats have voted for the budget process. "I am going to vote for the budget resolution," Appropriations Chairman George H. Mahon announced in 1978. "It is important that we

9. 124 *Congressional Record* (daily ed., May 2, 1978) H3439. Similar floor statements were made by Wright half a dozen other times during House debate on the resolution.
10. *Ibid.* (May 10, 1978), H3735.
11. *Ibid.* (May 3, 1978) H3485.

support the budget process."[12] But Mahon provided a clue as to why Members of Congress can vote for a budget resolution even though they might not be quite satisfied with its contents: "Fortunately, this resolution only sets a target and does not actually provide the spending itself. That will be done in later actions through various appropriations and other spending bills." [13]

Many Democrats—including those who support every resolution as well as those who swing with the pressure or times—have voted for the budget process because they believe that the numbers in the resolution are not all-important. "This proposal," party loyalist Jack Brooks said of 1976's first resolution, "is not binding. What will be done will be done by the legislative committees and the Committee on Appropriations and approved by this Congress."[14] Rep. Clifford Allen switched to the "yes" column in the first resolution for 1978 after opposing two of the preceding year's resolutions:

> Bear in mind that the figures that we set in this first budget resolution are merely tentative target figures. . . . as we progress over the next four months we will come back and set the final figures. We will hear further from the President. We will hear further from the different agencies of the Government. We will hear further from the committees. At that time we will have the flexibility to change the budget document in accordance with the light that we may have at that time, as it reflects upon the various items in this resolution.[15]

Evidently, not all Democrats have been persuaded by the "vote for the budget process" argument; some have refused to vote for numbers not in line with their own budget priorities. This position was well stated by liberal John Conyers who has opposed most budget resolutions:

> I will say this to all of the Members who think that we cannot support the budget process if we vote against the budget resolution. . . . There are only two things we can do with a budget resolution. We can vote it up or we can vote it down. If we vote it down, it does not mean that we are against the budgetary process in the Congress. It means that we do not like what went into the budget.[16]

12. *Ibid.* (May 10, 1978) H3721. Similar sentiments were expressed by Mahon during prior year's budget debate: for the 1976 budget, see 121 *Congressional Record* (April 29, 1976) H3652.
13. 122 *Congressional Record* (April 29, 1976) H3652.
14. 121 *Congressional Record* (May 1, 1975) H3565.
15. 123 *Congressional Record* (May 5, 1977) H4090.
16. 122 *Congressional Record* (April 28, 1976) H3521.

The House has managed to pass budget resolutions because most Democrats (including most of the liberals) have been willing to vote for the process even when they have not liked everything in the budget. But "vote the process" is an appeal that loses force in repetition. Members cannot be expected to forgo their substantive interests endlessly, just to keep the budget process alive. As budgeting becomes less novel on Capitol Hill, Members may become less willing to vote for resolutions that do not reflect their budget priorities. The long-term health of the congressional budget process cannot be secured by frantic, last-minute appeals to vote against one's political interests or views.

The House's Dilemma: The Parts Versus the Whole

Why does the House have so much difficulty formulating a budget with which it is genuinely satisfied? Why does it have an all-or-nothing choice, the "only two things" that Representative Conyers suggested can be done with a budget resolution? Why can it not amend the resolutions to suit the preferences of a House majority? Actually, the House has been unusually permissive in its handling of the budget resolutions, admitting floor amendments at any stage of consideration.[17] Yet the House makes few significant changes; the resolution it approves has been very similar to the one sent to it by the Budget Committee. Most of the functional allocations are untouched by the House, and the budget aggregates are hardly changed at all.

In five years of congressional budgeting, the House approved 30 amendments—less than one-quarter of those offered (see table 20). But most of the approved amendments had special features that accounted for their success:

—Three were sponsored by the HBC chairman to reflect changes (such as legislative or executive actions) that occurred after the committee completed its work. HBC accomplished on the floor that which it ordinarily would have done during markup.

—Two were promoted by the Democratic leadership. As discussed earlier, these O'Neill amendments were contrived to provide funds for some programs without raising the spending totals.

—Seven were for increased allocations to veterans. The House

17. Generally the House permits amendments only when the portion of the bill (usually a section or paragraph) is being considered.

simply cannot vote against more money for veterans, even when the chairman of the House Veterans' Affairs Committee openly opposes the action.[18]

—Five were "symbolic" actions which had no significant effect on budget amounts. One of these put the House on record against spending to implement certain aspects of the Panama Canal treaties; another sliced $7 million for congressional pay increases from the budget; three called for adoption of a tuition tax credit. In all of these cases, the actual legislative decisions could not be made through the congressional budget process.[19]

—One was a reestimate (no policy change was involved) and another was nullified by a subsequent vote.

—One dealt with procedures for handling appropriations bills, a second dealt with funds for the fiscal year already under way, and a third excised $1 billion from the allowances category as a prod to reduce waste in government.

On average, the House approved for each budget resolution one substantive amendment not sought by HBC or House leaders and not involving veterans' programs.

The simple requirement that the budget's components and totals must be arithmetically consistent limits the ability of the House to satisfy its members by responding sequentially to their diverse interests. As a result, when the House amends a resolution to provide additional funds for particular programs, it risks increasing Member disaffection with the final product. This lesson is clear from the debacle of the first resolution for 1978. The House adopted four amendments to increase expenditures, including one that was endorsed by HBC and another that was a bitterly contested allocation for defense programs. But then, having apparently tailored the resolution to its specifications, the House rejected it by an 84-320 vote, compelling the Budget Committee to work out a compromise version. Liberals deserted the resolution because of the higher defense spending; conservatives (and many middle-of-the-roaders) rejected it because of the $4.5 billion rise in the projected deficit. When the House took up a revised resolu-

18. See 122 *Congressional Record* (April 28, 1976) H3521, remarks of Rep. Ray Roberts, chairman of the House Veterans' Affairs Committee.

19. The House passed a tuition tax credit in 1978, but it failed to become law when the House and Senate were unable to resolve differences in conference.

Table 20

DISPOSITION OF HOUSE AMENDMENTS TO BUDGET RESOLUTIONS

Resolutions	Number of Amendments Approved	Rejected	Explanation of Approved Amendments
Fiscal 1976			
First	3	3	Tax reform and removal of limitations on federal pay and retirement
Second	2	2	Reestimates and leadership's increase for certain social programs
Fiscal 1977			
First	2	12	Increase for veterans
Second	0	3	
Third	1	1	Increase for countercyclical program
Fiscal 1978			
First (First Round)	6	9	Two committee amendments plus increases for defense, law enforcement, and veterans. Reduction of $7 million to eliminate legislative pay raises

First (Second Round)	1	6	Increase for veterans
Second	4	3	Committee amendment, tuition tax credit, and increases for agriculture and veterans
Fiscal 1979			
First	4	22	Veterans' increase, tuition tax credits, and limitation on Panama Canal spending
Second	1	4	Reduction in Comprehensive Employment and Training Act (CETA) manpower program
Fiscal 1980			
First[a]	6	35	Increase in "third" resolution for fiscal 1979 to provide for supplemental appropriations; increase for veterans; revenue increase by curbing foreign tax credits; provision concerning handling of appropriations bills deleted; decrease in allowance function in order to reduce governmental waste; and 0.5 percent across-the-board cut
Total	30	100	

[a] Includes amendments relating to fiscal 1979 attached to the first resolution for fiscal 1980.

Source: Author's analysis of amendments reported in *Congressional Record*, various issues.

tion in a second round of votes, it held the line against all amendments except the increase for veterans. With the need to "vote the process" brought home by the near collapse of the budget system, the House approved the second version by 213 to 179.

The 1978 experience revealed another danger to the ability of the House to marshal majority support for its budget decisions. The fact that they can vote for spending increases and then oppose the budget totals because they are too high gives Members a double political advantage: They can simultaneously show themselves responsive to important interests and concerned about the growth of government. Rep. Edward Pattison explained how the process works:

> The games goes like this: Many of my colleagues, who have voted for various specific budget increases, and have also voted for across-the-board reductions, will now vote against the whole budget.
>
> To each of the special interest groups will go a letter explaining how that Member voted to advance their particular interests. To the public in general will go a news release proclaiming that the Member voted against a swollen budget—in an effort to reduce the ever-expanding big Government that everyone has come to despise. It is all pleasure and no pain; the politician's heaven.
>
> Sadly, the game is played with equal vigor by both Democrats and Republicans, "liberals" and "conservatives." And almost everyone gets away with it. The budget process is probably the only casualty.[20]

Rep. David Obey has described the practice this way:

> Nothing in the last 2 years of my service here has stunned me more than seeing the number of Members walking off this floor last night, taking the elevators down and going over to the Rayburn Building and saying, "My God, that budget process doesn't work any more." I am surprised to hear Members say, "My God, all that budget process does is to give the irresponsible among us the chance to cheap shot it. It requires the chairman of the Budget Committee to ask people to be responsible on amendment after amendment after amendment when you know that the political payoff is on the other side. Why should we keep the process?"[21]

Considering the temptation to "cheap shot" the budget process, Members have engaged in remarkably little of this practice. Few budget-raising amendments (other than those for veterans) have

20. 124 *Congressional Record* (May 10, 1978) H3736-7.
21. *Ibid.*, H3717-8.

passed, and in every case the House has managed to pull together a majority for the totals. Members do not want to be tagged as big spenders, responsible for a bigger deficit.

If spending increases have been hard to push through, proposed reductions have had an even more difficult time. Only one substantive reduction has been passed, and that action occurred after the House had previously reduced authorizing levels in the affected program below the level anticipated in HBC's resolution. Proposed reductions encounter a formidable coalition of opponents: Budget Committee members who defend their recommendations; authorizing committee members interested in their programs; and Appropriations members bent on keeping as much room as possible for future needs. Proposed reductions also run into the argument already mentioned that the House should leave its options open for the legislative process to work its will. If the money is not needed, the argument runs, it can be cut later by the authorizing and appropriating committees.

The best bet for budget cutters, therefore, has been across-the-board reductions which both avoid singling out particular programs for reductions and appeal to Members who feel that the numbers are too high. This argument was used by Rep. Joseph L. Fisher in sponsoring an across-the-board reduction for fiscal 1979:

> Each one of us will have a program or a function in the budget that he or she is particularly fond of. That goes without saying. I think that at this stage of the game, after we have spent 3 days discussing, debating, arguing about different programs in the budget, it is time for looking at the aggregates.[22]

At the beginning of the 96th Congress, the House—at the instigation of the Democratic Caucus—banned across-the-board amendments unless they allocated the reductions among the various budget functions.[23] The expectation was that once its effects were specified, an across-the-board proposal would antagonize so many

---

22. *Ibid.* (May 9, 1978) H3684.
23. Some Republicans have advocated a two-step budget approach to circumvent this problem. First, the House would commit itself to budget totals, after which it would allocate the totals among the functions. This method undoubtedly would generate much budgetary tension in the House—with functions forced to compete against one another—and one cannot be sure that the initial totals would survive later challenges from a House bent on assuring adequate funds for the various functions.

Members as to thwart its passage. Nevertheless, the House adopted one such amendment to the first resolution for fiscal 1980. By a 255-144 vote, the House sliced 0.5 percent from each function, for a total reduction of about $2.5 billion.[24]

Like many of the other approved amendments, this action was essentially symbolic. It gave Members an opportunity to do something about the size of the budget and the deficit without taking a significant amount from any category. A majority of Members of Congress were able to vote for it, confident that a 0.5 percent reduction could be absorbed without injuring any of their interests. In the same budget round, the House took a similarly symbolic action, deleting $1 billion for allowances without identifying the programs to be cut. The amendment garnered overwhelming approval (402-3) because it enabled Members to do something about waste in government without directly harming any programs.

Much of the debate in the House has concerned symbolic actions that use the budget resolution as a "vehicle" for expressing sentiment on essentially nonbudgetary matters. In the course of making budget decisions, the House has gone on record with respect to legislative pay increases, the Panama Canal treaties, and tuition tax credits. A congressman who sought to curtail Korean aid because that government had not cooperated with a congressional investigation of corruption answered his own question, "Why the Budget Act?" "The Budget Act, and only the Budget Act is an instrument to express our disapproval without directly affecting the diplomacy, the appropriation, or the program itself."[25]

Not only in their votes on extraneous issues, but even in deciding the budget, House Members see themselves as engaged in symbolic actions. They view themselves as voting on basic political issues, not on specific programs or legislation. And political symbols can be more divisive than concrete numbers on which bargains can be struck.

---

24. One of the most forceful statements against across-the-board cuts was made by Senator Muskie in opposing one such attempt on 1978's first resolution: "It goes to the very heart and the very life of the congressional budget process. . . . It is the kind of approach to budget cutting that we tried many times before the establishment of the congressional budget process. It never worked. It never succeeded because it never identified the areas where real cuts were possible and where cuts could be achieved without damaging essential and vital areas of governmental activity. 124 *Congressional Record* (April 25, 1978) S6271.
25. *Ibid.* (May 10, 1978) H3724, remarks of Rep. Bruce Caputo.

SBC'S BUDGET RESOLUTIONS: VOTING FOR THE NUMBERS

The formulation of a budget resolution has followed a markedly different course in the Senate from that in the House. The Senate has demonstrated little of the strident partisanship or heated opposition to the budget decisions that have characterized House action. Many issues provoke controversy, some in committee, a few on the floor; but at no time has a Senate resolution been in danger of defeat. Most resolutions have passed the Senate by better than a two-to-one margin, with many Republicans joining in support. Table 21 shows the roll call patterns in the Senate.

Table 21

REPUBLICAN AND DEMOCRATIC VOTES ON ADOPTION OF THE BUDGET RESOLUTION IN THE SENATE

	Senate		*Democrats*		*Republicans*	
Resolutions [a]	*Yes*	*No*	*Yes*	*No*	*Yes*	*No*
Fiscal 1976						
First	69	22	50	4	19	18
Second	69	23	50	8	19	15
Fiscal 1977						
First	62	22	45	6	17	16
Second	55	23	41	5	14	18
Third	72	20	55	3	17	17
Fiscal 1978						
First	56	31	41	14	15	17
Second	63	21	46	8	17	13
Fiscal 1979						
First	64	27	48	8	16	19
Second	56	18	42	6	14	12
Fiscal 1980						
First	64	20	44	5	20	15
Second	62	36	45	14	17	22

[a] These figures are votes on passage of resolution in the Senate, not on adoption of the conference report.

Source: *Congressional Record*, various issues.

The Markless Markup

SBC members receive voluminous briefing materials before the start of a markup. These documents are prepared by the majority's core staff in consultation with Republican staff representatives. Like the Democratic mark prepared for HBC members, the Senate markup materials begin with an extended review of economic conditions and revenue alternatives, which is followed by an examination of each function. The documents prepared for SBC use, however, have tended to have more analytical and program content. On many issues, SBC staffs have provided in-depth discussions of program options and performance.

The SBC markup has lacked a chairman's mark. Nowhere did the documents reveal Senator Muskie's budget preferences. In SBC, the chairman has been first among equals, pressing his views with the advantages of the chair, superior access to staff and data, and a more comprehensive grasp of the budget situation than anyone else, but he has not given the committee his own recommendations in advance of markup. Muskie eschewed this role at SBC's initial markup when Sen. Ernest F. Hollings prodded him to take a commanding lead in committee deliberations. "If the Chairman says here is where we are, and we are going to go no higher, I would feel good."[26] This puzzling invitation from a Senator who often has taken an independent stance on budget policy and other legislative issues drew an immediate rejection from Muskie:

> I know that the worst thing to try to do is for me to set targets in advance, and then try to pull all of you together to those targets. I think it would be counterproductive at this point. You may well persuade me my own tentative judgments are wrong.[27]

To understand Hollings's suggestion and Muskie's demurrer, it is useful to recall that in HBC the mark has served as a constraint on committee action. HBC can exceed the recommended totals, but has not often done so by very much. Nor has it often strayed far from the functional marks established by the chairman or by the caucus of Democrats. Hollings, who feared that an unguided Budget

26. Senate Budget Committee, markup of the first concurrent resolution for fiscal 1976, transcript, p. 11.
27. *Ibid.* Muskie further explained his aversion to a chairman's mark: "If I was the only member of this committee, I could put my numbers in right now, but I am not the only member of this committee. This committee is representative of the whole Senate."

Committee might load the resolution with costly spending proposals, sought a similar premarkup constraint on SBC. "We need some discipline," he cautioned. "I would hope on the budget we would be far more conservative than the Senate is, generally, or we are a dead duck. We have to cut back."[28] Muskie drew exactly the opposite conclusion, that a chairman's mark would be a sitting duck for Senators bent on pursuing their own budget objectives. "All of us have our own targets in mind and I have mine. . . . Whether or not I can get there by the means I would prefer depends upon how I can con the majority of you in following my invisible lines."[29]

Muskie was not reticent about exercising the power of the chair; at the same session in which he refused to disclose his preferences, Muskie tried to get the SBC to start its markup with his new countercyclical proposal rather than with the individual budget functions. But he believed that SBC could develop a budget resolution with broad appeal in the Senate only if his colleagues were free to pursue their own interests, unconstrained by the chairman's likes and dislikes.

Muskie also had a political reason for avoiding a chairman's mark. At the time the budget process was launched, he was preparing for an election campaign and did not want to be regarded as the person who led SBC to a big deficit. He preferred that SBC itself adopt the deficit after examining the options facing it.

There were additional gains for Muskie in not having his own mark, a matter noted by a close staff assistant:

> There were lots of individual causes where Muskie wanted more or less money than the majority of the committee wanted. It was a good reason not to have a chairman's mark. It enabled him to vote for the number that he really wanted without being repudiated as chairman. I don't know that we conceived it that way, but that is the way it worked out. He is a very effective chairman precisely because he is able to operate in that kind of consensus fashion. He gets about what he wants and he gets to vote the way he wants, even if he loses. He can afford to lose under those circumstances; if he had a hard mark, he couldn't afford to.

In lieu of using a chairman's mark, Muskie opted for a procedure that would give him an opportunity to intervene more ac-

---

28. *Ibid.*, p. 12.
29. *Ibid.*, p. 463. Sen. Joseph Biden, an SBC member, suggested, "All of us probably have done what I have done or my staff. I have got my own budget here. Everybody around the table has their own budget on every item that is in here. . . ." *Ibid.*, p. 122.

tively after the committee had made tentative budget decisions. He put the committee through two rounds of functional decisions, a procedure similar to that used in HBC but with a different purpose.[30] "The first round we get all our impressions out in the open, and then, the second round nail them down."[31] Muskie expected that SBC members would use the first round to advance their particular causes and that expenditures would total more than a majority wanted. Subsequently, they would be more receptive to his leadership.

Muskie was willing to signal his preference on noncontroversial matters that could be disposed of quickly, usually stable functions that account for comparatively small shares of the budget. For example, at the beginning of the fiscal 1978 markup, Muskie offered four motions and Bellmon three, all of which were adopted by voice vote.[32] In a similar arrangement, for the first fiscal 1979 resolution, Bellmon sponsored six motions and Muskie four, all of which passed without objection. Muskie sometimes signaled his expectations via staff aides who dealt with other SBC members and could suggest possible budget levels without committing their chairman to a fixed position. This approach was formalized for SBC's markup of the second resolution for fiscal 1979. The briefing book provided a "suggested ceiling" for each function which it identified as the amount "that the Senate Budget Committee staff suggests as a beginning point for Committee discussion. . . ."[33] Although some staff officials regarded this as a step toward a chairman's mark, they did not expect Muskie to move further in this direction if such action would have jeopardized bipartisanship on the committee.[34]

---

30. In HBC, the second round often is used to add items excluded in the first round so as to make the resolution more palatable to liberal Democrats; SBC uses it to shave down the totals to make them more acceptable to a committee majority.
31. Senate Budget Committee, markup of the first concurrent resolution for fiscal 1979, transcript, p. 12.
32. See S. Rept. No. 95-90, pp. 106-8 for the fiscal 1978 markup, and S. Rept. No. 95-739, pp. 170-72 for the fiscal 1979 decisions.
33. Senate Committee on the Budget, *Markup Materials for the Second Concurrent Resolution on the Budget, Fiscal Year 1979*, August 7, 1978 (processed), p. III-1.
34. These persons note that (1) the suggested ceilings were used for a second concurrent resolution where SBC generally limits its work to ratification of other congressional actions and (2) the suggested ceilings were useful because many of the appropriation bills had not cleared the Senate before the markup and hence the committee needed some guidance from staff as to what Congress was likely to do.

Although it has lacked a starting mark, SBC has been unwilling to use the President's request as the baseline against which committee decisions are measured. Initially, Muskie oriented the markup to "current policy" estimates that adjust all programs for inflation. "This means," he announced at the start of committee deliberations on the fiscal 1977 budget, "we can have more objectivity about the policy assumptions of the executive branch."[35] This approach had several advantages for Muskie and many of his SBC cohorts. First, it treated all programs alike, regardless of whether an inflation adjustment was provided for by law. With current policy numbers, a program indexed to the cost of living would not be pegged to a higher base than one for which Congress has discretion in adjusting for inflation. For this reason, Muskie regarded current policy as a more neutral baseline than either the President's budget or estimates that adjust for inflation only when mandated by law.[36]

Second, when President Ford was advocating severe cuts in existing programs for fiscal 1976 and 1977, current policy provided a much higher baseline than the President's budget. If SBC had marked up the resolutions in terms of the President's estimates, the committee would have appeared to be on the side of higher spending and bigger deficits. But by basing its decisions on current policy, SBC could claim that it was restraining rather than raising federal expenditures. Thus, when the White House was berating Congress for its spending proclivities, SBC was boasting that it had held federal spending some $9 billion below the current policy level.[37]

Third, the current policy baseline enabled SBC to produce acceptable budget resolutions without delving into program details. The committee could be confident that if it pegged spending for a particular function at or close to current policy, sufficient funds would be available for the programs in which Congress was interested. Accommodation could thus be easily achieved, without de-

35. Senate Budget Committee, markup of the first concurrent resolution for fiscal 1977, transcript, p. 3.

36. See statements by Muskie and Sidney Brown, the SBC staff aide responsible for preparing the markup materials in *ibid.*, pp. 67-8.

37. These claims were more than public relations boasts. When Bellmon complained that "the budgeting process isn't doing its job if we make all the money available that everybody says they need. We have been doing that and extra," Muskie retorted, "We haven't been doing that altogether. We cut about $8 billion in current policy." Senate Budget Committee, markup of the first concurrent resolution for fiscal 1978, p. 175.

tailed program negotiation with the affected congressional committees. SBC used current policy in this way when it decided the fiscal 1978 allocation for the natural resources function, which covered water projects (on which Congress and the President were divided) among many other programs. After the committee approved an allocation for natural resources, Senator Johnston inquired whether the figure included the disputed water projects.

Muskie: It was not discussed explicitly, so there was no figure in mind.
Johnston: Does it just imply current policy where we don't mention it?
Muskie: I would think so.[38]

But after a few years many SBC members became uneasy about this approach. The first complaints came from conservative Republicans who saw it as an inducement to sizable spending increases and big deficits. McClure criticized current policy as "a universal hold-harmless position"[39] which "assumes that Congress is incapable of making any decision except that we will shield everyone in society from any consequences of the recession to the extent that it is possible for us to do so by passing more laws and appropriating more money."[40]

By the fiscal 1978 markup, the protest had spread to middle-of-the-roaders who felt helpless in the face of current policy projections showing why next year's spending had to be much higher than this year's. Current policy conveyed the message that the only way to cut spending was to cut programs. Bellmon complained about the implication that increases for inflation "are built in and you can't do anything about them."[41] Because of current policy, there was a failure "to put any pressure on programs . . . that we might be able to squeeze down a little bit."[42] As already noted, one of the conveniences by which Congress controls spending is to provide a growth rate below that of inflation, thereby restraining expenditure increases without incurring the political onus for cutting programs. But defining increases below current policy as program cuts made it more difficult for Congress to use this option.

---

38. Senate Budget Committee, markup of the first budget resolution for fiscal 1978, transcript, p. 588. Muskie then directed the staff to indicate that current policy was implied in the committee report accompanying the resolution.
39. Markup of the first concurrent resolution for fiscal 1977, p. 69.
40. *Ibid.*, p. 67.
41. Senate Budget Committee, markup of the first budget resolution for the fiscal year, transcript, p. 185.
42. *Ibid.*, p. 174.

SBC members were unsure of what current policy meant or how the figures had been derived. They saw it as a hypothetical projection, put together on the basis of complicated models and assumptions, in contrast to the actualities of past spending and the authoritative estimates of the President. No matter how patiently Muskie and his aides explained the method for estimating current policy, skeptical SBC members could not be persuaded that the numbers were objective and reliable. Discontent over current policy was aggravated by persistent spending shortfalls during the early years of the new budget process. When they marked up a resolution, SBC members were pressured to support hefty increases in order to allow programs to continue uncurtailed. Months later, they learned that billions of dollars would not be needed after all. Although they did not fully understand the reasons for these shortfalls, SBC members could not avoid the suspicion that the original numbers had been too high. "The budget," Senator Hollings insisted, "is always starting off with an inflated figure to begin with. That's what bothers me."[43] Muskie could not hold out against his SBC colleagues: "Clearly, there is the growing impression around this table that the current policy number represents an inflated figure that . . . contains some water."[44]

The markup materials were redesigned for the fiscal 1979 and subsequent budget cycles to distinguish between adjustments mandated by law (current law estimates) and the additional cost of adjusting all programs for inflation (current policy). Moreover, the documents now show the spending adjustments attributable to changes in workload. With these modifications, SBC has alternative baselines for marking up its resolutions. It can use the higher current policy numbers or the lower current law levels. It can provide only for workload increases or it can add funds to account for inflation or to improve programs.

The dispute over current policy is an indication of tension and frustration within SBC. Despite the commanding bipartisan majorities that have been marshaled for the budget resolutions, the committee has not been united on substantive budget policy. Members have been concerned about current policy because they sense that it influences budgetary outcomes. Current policy also has become a target for frustration over the committee's perceived inability to gain satisfactory control over the budget. The sizable year-to-year

43. *Ibid.*
44. *Ibid.*, p. 170.

increases in spending and the big (though declining) deficits have not been matters of pride for most SBC Senators. Republicans especially have demonstrated a growing impatience with the trend of federal budgeting. Those who have supported the resolutions have had to defend deficits not of their own making. Current policy is a symbol of their frustration, and although the tensions have been papered over with a pluralism of baselines, they could break through again to divide the committee.

One Member, One Vote

SBC's voting pattern has been more varied and complicated than that of the House Budget Committee. Party identification appears to have been relevant, but there has been much less bloc or party-line voting in SBC. Table 22 shows that more than half of the roll calls have been partisan, with a majority of Republicans opposing a majority of Democrats. The fact that only 42 percent of the votes have been nonpartisan belies the claim that SBC operates in a consensual, informal fashion.[45]

Yet party identification is a weaker explanation of how SBC members vote and which side wins than it is for the House committee. Table 23 reports the percentage of votes in which SBC members have sided with their party and have been part of the winning coalition. It indicates that although the committee has no "100 percent" Democrats or Republicans, neither have there been sharp cleavages within the parties. Each party has had only one SBC member who has deserted it on more than half of the roll calls. Most Democrats and most Republicans vote with their parties from 75 percent to 90 percent of the time. If fact, the two parties have virtually identical cohesion records, 80 percent for the Republicans, 77 percent for the Democrats.

With SBC Democrats commanding a four-vote margin in committee and neither party exhibiting significantly more cohesion than the other, one would expect the Democratic majority to prevail on most of the partisan votes. As of 1979, the SBC's Democrats held a 67-57 lead in votes contested along party lines, but this margin fell far short of the dominance achieved by HBC's Democratic majority. Although the Democrats have won more contests than have the Republicans in the Senate committee, the Republican

45. ". . . whereas HBC's decision-making process was formal and methodical, SBC's was informal and consensual, as in the manner of a Quaker meeting." Kotler, *op. cit.*, p. 18.

Table 22

SENATE BUDGET COMMITTEE VOTING RESULTS, BY POLITICAL PARTY, FISCAL YEARS 1977-80

	Democratic Majority Prevailed		*Republican Majority Prevailed*		*Nonpartisan Majority Prevailed*	
Resolution [1]	*Number*	*Percent*	*Number*	*Percent*	*Number*	*Percent*
Fiscal 1977 [2]						
First	8	20.0%	15	37.5%	17	42.5%
Third	3	75.0	0	0.0	1	25.0
Fiscal 1978						
First	16	47.0	7	21.5	11	32.4
Second	1	25.0	3	75.0	0	0.0
Fiscal 1979						
First	20	42.6	8	17.0	19	40.4
Second	0	0.0	3	50.0	3	50.0
Fiscal 1980						
First	19	24.0	21	26.6	39	49.4
Total	67	31.3%	57	26.6%	90	42.1%

[1] For purposes of this table, the "Democratic Majority" is determined to have prevailed when the position taken by half or more Democrats voting on a roll call prevails over the position taken by half or more Republicans voting on the same roll calls, and vice versa for the prevalence of the "Republican Majority." A "Nonpartisan Majority" is determined to have prevailed when the same position is taken by a majority of both Democratic and Republican members. It should be noted that the categories are mutually exclusive. For purposes of the table, a tie vote is considered as a vote in which those members voting "no" prevailed.

[2] There were no roll calls on the second resolution for fiscal 1977.

Source: Author's tabulations from committee reports.

record has been respectable there. Abstention or defection by just a few Democrats can bring victory to Republicans in those instances when the latter are united.

While any Democrat is a potential defector and the Republicans do not usually maintain unanimity, there has been a definite pattern to SBC's voting behavior. When the Republicans are united, the most likely Democratic defections are from its Southern contingent. Thus, by a 10-4 vote the committee rejected a proposal by Walter Mondale to increase federal spending on temporary economic programs in the first fiscal 1976 resolution. In that instance,

Table 23

VOTING RECORDS OF SENATE BUDGET COMMITTEE MEMBERS IN MARKUP OF RESOLUTIONS, FISCAL YEARS 1977-80

	Voted With or Against Party Majority			*Voted With or Against Committee Majority*		
Member	*Number With*	*Number Against*	*Percent With*	*Number With*	*Number Against*	*Percent With*
Democrats						
Muskie	170	36	82.5%	134	74	64.4%
Chiles	109	89	55.1	139	52	72.8
Hollings	113	52	68.5	115	54	68.0
Johnston	81	60	57.4	94	49	65.7
Cranston	111	14	88.8	84	41	68.3
Magnuson	103	12	89.6	74	43	63.2
Sasser	73	15	82.9	78	23	77.2
Abourezk	85	12	87.6	63	34	64.9
Biden	75	20	78.9	72	24	75.0
Anderson	75	7	91.5	62	20	75.6
Hart	51	19	72.9	54	21	72.0
Moynihan	59	4	93.7	53	17	75.7
Riegle	53	8	86.9	40	27	59.7
Exon	41	18	69.5	38	24	61.3
Metzenbaum	42	7	85.7	29	23	55.8
Mondale	32	6	84.2	20	18	52.6
Nunn	15	20	42.9	26	9	74.3
Moss	22	3	88.0	12	13	48.0
Total	1,310	402	76.6%	1,187	566	67.7%
Republicans						
Bellmon	169	34	83.3%	148	58	71.8%
Domenici	179	28	86.5	129	72	64.2
McClure	103	17	85.8	58	62	48.3
Dole	77	16	82.8	54	39	58.1
Hayakawa	72	8	90.0	37	43	46.3
Heinz	36	42	46.2	48	30	61.5
Boschwitz	54	15	78.3	55	16	77.4
Packwood	52	14	78.8	49	21	70.0
Kassebaum	57	7	89.1	49	18	73.1

(Continued)

Table 23

VOTING RECORDS OF SENATE BUDGET COMMITTEE MEMBERS IN MARKUP OF RESOLUTIONS, FISCAL YEARS 1977-80 (Cont.)

	Voted With or Against Party Majority			*Voted With or Against Committee Majority*		
Member	*Number With*	*Number Against*	*Percent With*	*Number With*	*Number Against*	*Percent With*
Armstrong	42	18	70.0	36	27	57.1
Hatch	36	15	70.0	26	27	50.0
Pressler	34	10	77.3	35	12	74.5
Beall	10	6	83.8	30	7	81.1
Buckley	30	6	83.3	25	11	69.4
Lugar	3	1	75.0	2	2	50.0
Chaffee	3	1	75.0	0	4	0.0
Total	957	238	80.0%	781	449	63.5%

Source: Author's tabulations of roll call votes of the Senate Budget Committee for the first and third budget resolutions of fiscal 1977 (there were no roll calls during markup of the second); the first, second, and third resolutions of fiscal 1978 and 1979; and the first resolution of fiscal 1980.

all six Republicans were joined by the three Southern Democrats (Lawton Chiles, Ernest Hollings, and Sam Nunn) plus another defector from the majority. In another contested vote on the fiscal 1976 resolution, the six Republicans and three Southerners outvoted all the other Democrats in a 9-6 decision on defense spending.[46]

This voting pattern explains why budget resolutions emerging from SBC generally have had a less Democratic tint than have those advanced by the House committee. On the basis of the traditional differences between the two chambers on spending matters and the different markup procedures in committee, one might have expected SBC's budget to be consistently higher and more liberal than HBC's. Historically, the Senate has favored higher appropriations than has the House. Moreover, HBC gives close attention to the President's request, while SBC marks up the frequently

46. S. Rept. No. 94-77 (1975), pp. 107, 109.

higher current policy (or current law) numbers. Nevertheless, SBC has usually offered a more conservative first resolution. Until the first resolution for 1980, it proposed lower outlay totals and a smaller deficit target in every first resolution. Interestingly, this pattern has not held for the second resolution, in which SBC usually has had higher spending and deficit ceilings. It is possible that in its second resolution SBC has had to allow for the later (and often higher) spending actions of the Senate.

The comparative conservativeness of SBC has been reflected in the allocations to particular functions. SBC has always provided more for defense in the first resolution than HBC has; the House committee has usually allocated more for the social programs contained in the community development, income security, and education, training, employment, and social services functions.

With this pattern, SBC has risked alienating both conservatives and liberals, the former because spending and deficit levels still are quite high, the latter because of the relatively large amounts allocated to defense compared with those for social programs. SBC might have faced the same shaky predicament that has chronically beset the House committee. A divided Senate committee would have sent a resolution that really pleased nobody to an uncertain fate on the floor.

Muskie tried to avert this possibility when SBC neared the end of its very first markup for fiscal 1976. Muskie had been on the losing side of half the roll calls, including those concerning some of the items that mattered most to him, such as defense spending and his new countercyclical spending ceiling. Nevertheless, he urged his colleagues to back the resolution even though it did not contain everything they wanted.

> There is no point in sending something that is fruitless to the Floor. If we send something to the Floor and end up with 15 members of the Committee for one reason or another deciding that they can't support it, we are really going to be in a tough box.[47]

Senator Bellmon proposed the same action for the Republicans. He cautioned against "this Committee going in 15 different directions on the Floor. I don't think anyone here has gotten what he really wanted."[48] Most SBC members fell into line, subordinating their

---

47. Senate Budget Committee, markup of the first budget resolution for fiscal 1976, transcript, p. 743.
48. *Ibid.*, p. 745.

substantive interests to the needs of the budget process. As a result, SBC mustered a broad coalition for its budget decision; in that precedent-making case, all of the Democrats were joined by three Republicans in a lopsided (13-2) vote to report the resolution. All subsequent resolutions have been approved by similar margins in committee. Moreover, SBC members have filed fewer dissenting or separate statements than have HBC's members. On average, one-third of SBC's members have expressed their displeasure with the committee's product, in contrast to almost two-thirds on the House side.

How can the near-consensus in the final vote be reconciled with the fractious markups? Most SBC members fight over the numbers but lay aside differences when all is done. One possible explanation, considered in the next section, is that SBC members can agree on the numbers because they are not compelled to agree on the line items. But other explanations warrant consideration.

First, nobody on SBC has lost everything; everyone has come away from the battle with important victories. Consider the individual success scores computed in table 23. There is a noticeable bunching of Democratic and Republican SBC members within a "success zone" of between 60 percent and 80 percent. If SBC's temporaries (Richard G. Lugar and John H. Chaffee) are excluded, almost two-thirds of SBC members are within this zone. Because SBC members apparently see their resolutions as mixed bags which give them what they want on some matters of importance but deny them on others, few are provoked to opposition by the feeling that they have lost all the important fights. The budget outcomes in SBC thus resemble much Senate legislation in which the final product is fashioned through give and take by collegial bargainers rather than by complete victory for one side and defeat for another.

As a result, SBC's budget resolution has not been mired in the standard schisms of American politics. It has not been a Democratic or a Republican budget; despite their majority, the Democrats' success ratings (67 percent) have averaged only four percentage points higher than those of the Republicans. Nor has SBC's resolution been a liberal or a conservative budget; in fact, ideologues on both sides have tended to be among the least successful voters in committee. Since the resolution is not stamped with an unacceptable label, most SBC members can comfortably support it.

Second, controversy within SBC has been constrained rather than passionate. With few exceptions, Democrats and Republicans have not spoken with the sense of urgency that has affected HBC deliberations. Within SBC, one rarely hears impassioned pleas for the cities, the poor, or unemployed youth. Nor do most Senate conservatives speak in doomsday tones about the sins of deficit spending. For most of the Democrats and Republicans, voting has been an expression of each member's program interests rather than of conformity to an ideological position or a party line. Republicans and Democrats alike have voted with their respective majorities most of the time because members of the same party usually have similar policy orientations. However, a member's defection from the party has not been regarded as a breach of loyalty or as an abandonment of an ideological commitment.

Third, the markup methodology has had a pacifying effect on members. By beginning with a current policy (or law) base, the committee has sensitized Republicans to the fact that the budget cannot be balanced or substantially cut without severe effects on government programs. Yet Republicans have been able to take some satisfaction from the indication that total spending is below current policy. Democrats also have been satisfied by the same approach, for they have seen that their programs can continue without serious disruption.

Fourth, the permanence of SBC membership gives its members some incentive to support the committee and its work. This matter was fully discussed in chapter IV. It should be remembered that members banded together during a period when their tenure on SBC was uncertain. Although most SBC members would have left the committee if they had been forced to give up any other assignments to remain on it, they still were willing to vote for the committee's budget resolutions. On balance, the stability of SBC membership should be regarded as only a reinforcing factor, not one that could have held the committee together if it had been torn apart by ideological or political strife.

Fifth, bipartisanship on SBC, especially the extraordinary relationship between Chairman Muskie and the ranking Republican, Bellmon, fostered cooperation and consensus. Republican staff aides have participated in the preparation of markup materials as well as in the stream of memoranda flowing from SBC staff to members throughout the year. John McEvoy, SBC's staff director saw an explanation for the unusual cooperation between Muskie and Bellmon in their early political careers:

> Senator Bellmon, as it turns out, was the first Republican Governor in Oklahoma history and Muskie was the first Democratic Governor in the

history of Maine, and there was a convergence of experience between those two senators. . . . Muskie had a [state] legislature of about eight to one Republican and Bellmon had basically the same problem with the Democrats. So, those guys learned before they got here to get along with the opposition, to find as little to fight about as you could, to find as much to agree about as you can.[49]

On SBC, bipartisanship has done more than mitigate interparty conflict. It has cemented trust among committee members, encouraging them to work hard for agreement.

Finally, various institutional differences between the House and Senate have contributed to SBC's harmony at the end of markup. Senators have wider electoral bases and thus more heterogeneous constituencies than do Representatives. In addition, by their long terms, Senators are sheltered from quick voter retribution for unpopular stands, such as toleration of high deficits. Moreover, Senators are accustomed to operating under unanimous consent, a practice that depends on a good deal of bipartisan cooperation. SBC members leave markup in concord because they enter it disposed to reach agreement. In between, they fight for the best deal they can get, but most do not let roll call defeats sway them from endorsing the committee's budget.

Line Items and Numbers

SBC officially eschews line-item decisions, insisting that the only numbers with legal effect are the budget aggregates and the amounts allocated to each function. One can surmise that the avoidance of line itemization helps to cool the budgetary debate within SBC by focusing on negotiable numbers. It is hard to get passionate about small differences in big numbers. SBC demands of its members only that they support the figures in the resolution, not the programs or policies assumed by these amounts.

Senator Muskie adamantly avoided line items; he frequently interrupted committee proceedings to castigate members who had discussed specific programs:

I strongly resist line iteming. If we are going to start doing that then we are all going to want to start implying a line item here, there, and everywhere . . . and we will slip into the function of trying to write line items. That is not our business. It is the business of the authorizing

49. Transcript of meeting of Senate Budget Committee staff, December 5, 1978, p. 69.

committees including the Appropriations Committees. That is where these specific issues ought to be raised.[50]

Avoidance of line items can lower the threshold for agreement on SBC. Members can disagree as to the specifics but still vote for the overall number. Two informed observers of the congressional budget scene have suggested that this decisional pattern is a major explanation for SBC's success in developing broadly supported resolutions:

. . . the Senate Budget Committee's deliberations are very vague. They do not specify the spending levels for each account and do not specify the accounts in the proposed functional totals. Frequently, a pool of money is created that can be divided among a number of programs. . . . by being so vague, the Senate Budget Committee minimizes the possibility of partisan differences in that both sides can simultaneously think that their programs will be funded within the pool of expenditures.[51]

On occasion, members attribute different meanings to their votes or seek to maintain the ambiguity of the decision. After one SBC roll call, James A. McClure intervened with a deliberately vague interpretation of the vote: "I think each of us will independently of the action here express how we feel in various ways that amount ought to be divided. . . . I don't think we have to explain it here, or be foreclosed from expressing those opinions later."[52]

Muskie, who had voted against McClure on thta issue, added, "I completely agree with that." After another vote, Sen. Robert Dole sought assurance that "we are not bound by any line items approach," and the following brief exchange ensued:

Chiles: No, there is no line item.
Muskie: Individual members will make their own arguments.
Chiles: I will tell you next week what it meant.[53]

50. Senate Budget Committee markup of the first budget resolution for the fiscal 1978, transcript, p. 589.

51. John W. Ellwood and James A. Thurber, "The New Congressional, Budget Process in the House of Representatives: Some Hypotheses," presented at the 1976 Annual Meeting of the Southwestern Political Science Association, April 7-10, 1976, pp. 36-7.

52. Senate Budget Committee markup of the first budget resolution for fiscal 1976, transcript, p. 298. Muskie also noted that "it has been clear all day that we rationalize our own numbers."

53. Senate Budget Committee, markup of the first concurrent resolution for fiscal 1977, transcript, p. 880.

With the committee restrained from "line iteming," it often appears to decide budget numbers as if they had no program content. "In the defense area," one observer suggested, "SBC in effect auctioned off figures until one gained broad acceptance." [54] Freshman Sen. S. I. Hayakawa was bemused by the manner in which billion-dollar figures were bandied about by committee colleagues:

> I found that being on the Budget Committee isn't as hard as it looks. You don't have any complicated decisions to make because you are not dealing with specific appropriations. . . . What you are dealing with are overall totals.
>
> The numbers you work with on this committee turned out to be very simple. You are always dealing in hundreds of millions or billions. Therefore, when we say 1.0, that means $1 billion. Then we have .1; that means $100 million—and that's the smallest figure we ever deal with in the Budget Committee.
>
> A member of the committee will say, for instance, "Here's an appropriation for such-and-such. It was 1.7 for 1977. So for the 1978 budget we ought to make it 2.9." So all we do is add 1.2; that's not hard.[55]

Yet it would be truly startling if SBC members were interested only in the totals and not the parts. Such behavior would be the reverse of that of other legislative committees which make distributive decisions. They would be allocating billions of dollars without caring about which program got what, without trying to assist the programs they believed in or the constituencies they served. It also would be remarkable if deciding on the totals brought more budgetary peace than dividing up the pieces. The opportunities for logrolling would be greatly circumscribed, as would the possibility of buying budgetary agreement by offering line-item inducements to reluctant committee members. It will be recalled that HBC has used line items to obtain support for resolutions from liberals who do not like some of the functional totals. The liberals have cooperated with the majority because funds have been specified for some of the things they care about.

SBC's comparative silence about line items needs explaining. It should not be assumed that SBC members are ignorant or indifferent about the program consequences of their decisions. Al-

54. Neil G. Kotler, "The Politics of the New Congressional Budget Process: Or, Can Reformers Use It to Undo the System of Privilege," in Marcus G. Raskin, *The Federal Budget and Social Reconstruction* (New Brunswick, N.J.: Transaction Books, 1978), p. 18.

55. S. I. Hayakawa, "Mr. Hayakawa Goes to Washington," in *Harper's*, January 1978, p. 39.

though SBC's attention is not so narrowly focused as the markup in the House committee, SBC members have a lively interest in programs, and they want to know what is likely to be precluded or facilitated by their functional decisions. They spend hours in heated debate over the numbers, cognizant that they are deciding the fate of programs. When they vote on a number, it is usually with shared expectations about programs. But they do not always have to talk about line items to protect their program objectives.

The sharing of expectations explains why Senators who are deeply interested in programs need not articulate their interests. When they vote on a function, members have a strong sense of what the amount means. "If it's at current policy," one of them explained, "it tells us that programs are going to continue, not much new and not much pressure for cuts." What happens, the member was asked, when the decision deviates from current policy? "We know the issues," he said, pointing to the markup materials. What about when members disagree on the issues? "Then," he replied, "we talk about the line items." In other words, members can afford to avoid line-item debate only when they are sure that their program interests will not be prejudiced thereby. When failure to itemize programs offers inadequate protection, however, the decision breaks out into line-item debate. In the typical case, this happens when a member is arguing for a higher functional level than the committee seems to favor. In such a situation, a listing of the programs that might be priced out of the budget by an inadequate total may be an effective tactic. When he wanted more money for education in 1976, Senator Mondale itemized all the pending legislation that might be stopped if the total were not raised.[56] Similarly, Senator Hollings gave his colleagues a lengthy shopping list of coveted weapons when he sought additional funds for the 1978 defense budget.

Members also itemize when they want to develop legislative history in support of their programs. Shortly after admonishing SBC members to "avoid specifically endorsing any line item or any program here,"[57] Sen. Alan Cranston urged the committee to include a few million dollars for a laboratory in his home state: "All I am asking is that there is report language at the appropriate places."[58] In a case mentioned earlier, Senator Johnston pressed

56. Senate Budget Committee, markup of the second budget resolution for fiscal 1976, transcript, pp. 332-33.

57. Senate Budget Committee, markup of the first budget resolution for fiscal 1976, transcript, p. 111.

58. *Ibid.*, p. 297.

the committee to declare that the allocation for the natural resources function would cover funds for water projects which President Carter sought to eliminate.

SBC members like to have it both ways; they avoid line-item review unless discussion of program particulars helps their case. In the markup of the first resolution for fiscal 1976, supporters of a multibillion-dollar anti-recession drive were challenged by opponents to specify the programs they intended to fund. These programs, however, cost more than the total amount the committee was likely to approve; this dilemma led Mondale to urge adoption of an overall ceiling:

> There are people on that Public Works Committee, Appropriations subcommittee and staff that have worked with these issues for years, that are familiar with it. They spent all year hearing about public works projects. . . . There are other subcommittees that have dealt with public service employment, other committees that have dealt with highways, and so on. They have quite the ability and competence and structure for focusing on the details of these proposals which we do not have, cannot have in the limited time within which we must operate. What I would propose is to . . . let the Appropriations Committee, based upon their expertise, decide among them, provided only that they live with . . . the overall counter-cyclical spending ceiling.[59]

The "pool of expenditures" hypothesis can account for the avoidance of conflict only when members have competing program preferences and are constrained by a fixed total from satisfying both sets of preferences. If one set of preferences prevails, the other must be squeezed out of the budget. In this circumstance, silence can produce harmony by allowing all members to pursue their legislative interests regardless of the functional decision. A review of the transcripts of eight SBC markups did not reveal a single conflict in which Senators, having agreed to the total for, but not the composition of, a budget function, then resolved the differences by remaining silent as to the particulars. Most strife in both Budget Committees has been between members in disagreement about funding levels, not about programs.[60] No amount of silence could induce HBC Republicans to vote for the resolu-

59. *Ibid.*, pp. 107-8.

60. The avoidance of line items can, however, lessen conflict in two forums where congressional budget policy is made: on the floor, when members are constrained to support the Budget Committee's numbers without assurance that their programs are included; and in conference where the House and Senate have to reconcile differing numbers as well as divergent program assumptions. Both of these situations are discussed later in this chapter.

tions reported by their committee. Nor could silence purchase support of SBC members who strongly oppose either the totals or the programs. Despite the fact that it abstained from program decisions, SBC needed three roll calls in order to settle the anti-recession spending issue. On the last of these, members split seven to seven on a motion to make further cuts in the totals.

The evidence is clear that avoidance of line-item discussion does not by itself secure budgetary peace for SBC. Each first resolution occasions numerous roll calls, many of which are decided by one or two votes. In each of the first resolution markups for the 1977-79 fiscal years, there were more than two dozen contested votes, more such votes in fact than were taken by HBC during its work on these resolutions. Evidently committee members do not cavalierly support the totals because they have not been pressed to subscribe to the particulars. SBC members are deeply divided over budget policy, but most have been willing to lay aside their differences and support the committee's decisions.

If avoidance of line items has not ameliorated intracommittee conflict, it has helped to ease relations with other committees. When SBC distributes new budget authority and outlays among Senate committees—a task required by the Budget Act—the committee must have firm information about the programs which it expects to be funded. Especially when a budget function falls under the jurisdictions of several committees, SBC must understand clearly the function's programs. Although staffers prepare the "crosswalk" from functions to committees, SBC members are interested in these allocations. The committees on the receiving end also have an interest in maximizing their budget share as well as their legislative discretion. Committees do not want to be locked into SBC's line-item expectations. At one point in the fiscal 1978 markup, Senator McClure wondered about the status of SBC's program assumptions. "I do not believe that the authorizing committees are bound by our assumptions, nor is the appropriations committee bound by our assumptions. They probably are not even aware of them." SBC Staff Director McEvoy responded with appropriate vagueness: "It is one of those continuing mysteries, Senator, that perhaps unraveling could destroy the process. There is a certain element of flexibility in the way the committee proceeds that it might be to the benefit of the committee not to fully define." [61]

61. Senate Budget Committee, markup of the first budget resolution for fiscal 1978, transcript, p. 265.

SBC has proved tactfully inconsistent in its treatment of line items. It has made specific program assumptions, sometimes spelling these out in the reports on its budget resolutions, but it has not insisted that other committees accept those assumptions. The staff director of a major authorizing committee provided a sympathetic appraisal of SBC's problem: "They've been schizophrenic because they want to line item in order to come up with a reasonable basis for developing the total numbers, but they don't want to get themselves into a big fight with the appropriations or authorizing committees either."

Selective attention to line items suits the committee's decisional style. Since SBC marks up the budget resolution from a current policy base (supplemented with current law estimates), the committee would have to specify numerous program curtailments if it adopted line-item review. In contrast to HBC, which builds up from the President's budget and can advantageously add line items, SBC would have to subtract programs if it were consistently open about its program decisions. For example, SBC would have had to disclose the programs for which reductions were intended when it set a fiscal 1977 spending target $9 billion below current policy levels. Silence about line items enabled the committee to claim a sizable spending reduction without drawing an outcry from the interests whose programs might have been jeopardized.

Senators and Their Numbers

SBC members have program interests that are not always articulated during markup. They can afford silence, it has been observed, when their expectations are shared by colleagues or secured by the numbers in the resolution. Members can feel confident that they have selected the right numbers when colleagues whom they regard as specialists in particular legislative areas indicate their satisfaction. Budget Committee members habitually take the lead on matters relating to their other legislative interests. "Now I volunteer something," Moss said at an early SBC markup, "because I'm on Post Office, and he does because he sits on Finance, and we put these little bits and pieces in. We haven't made any real study on it; we just happen to know something about it." [62] What lead members usually communicate is not program knowledge but rather intelligence about the expectations of Congress and in particular of the committees with jurisdiction over the relevant programs.

62. Senate Budget Committee, markup of the first budget resolution for fiscal 1976, transcript, p. 694.

Behavior of this sort has occurred on both Budget Committees. Often, one can correctly surmise the committee attachments of HBC and SBC members merely by observing them during markup. Members become more animated when the discussion touches on matters they deal with in other committees; they talk more about program details and are more likely to offer amendments when "their" programs are being decided. Colleagues seem to be more attentive, although not always more supportive, when program specialists take the lead. "We know where they're coming from; it's not someone just mouthing his own biases," is the way an SBC member explained the cue taking that goes on in committee.

But "opinion leaders" have played somewhat different roles in the two committees. HBC Democrats usually have influenced the outcome by persuading the chairman to incorporate their preferences in his mark. Private understanding might be more effective than public debate in assuring that the figures in the resolution are adequate to protect one's favored programs. SBC members do not have this option; they must make their case in the open, and hence leaders appear to have more actively intervened during markup.

Moreover, SBC has a number of Senate "notables" in its ranks, such as committee and subcommittee chairmen and ranking minority members, who can speak authoritatively about the expectations of other committees.[63] HBC has few members who are leaders on other committees. Its members, therefore, appear to represent only their individual views rather than the expectations of their other committees. There have been some exceptions, however, such as James C. Wright who has "represented" Public Works; Parren J. Mitchell, who has spoken for the Black Caucus; and Barber Conable (though a Republican), who has sometimes conveyed Ways and Means' expectations. Nevertheless, SBC is more deferential to its leading members. It has delayed consideration of the veterans' function until Senator Cranston has made his appearance, and it allows members to put a temporary "hold" on a matter until they can attend the session.[64]

Warren Magnuson provides the clearest example of a Senator who dominates a policy area by virtue of his standing on another committee. As ranking Democrat on Appropriations (until 1978 when he became chairman), and head of its Labor-HEW subcommittee, Magnuson is regarded as the Senate's specialist on health

63. See chapter IV for a discussion of the memberships of the two Budget Committees.

64. HBC, by contrast, considers functions according to a predetermined sequence.

expenditures. His practice has been to send Muskie a letter prior to markup specifying the amount he wants for the health function. He has usually gotten exactly what he wanted, even when he has been absent from the markup. Here is the way health spending was set by SBC for fiscal 1976:

Muskie: Now Senator Magnuson's letter—where is that—on this function is to recommend [$]31 billion in total health outlays.

Beall: [$]31 billion?

Muskie: [$]31. That is [$]100 more than mine.

Mondale: I move that Magnuson figure. . . .

Beall: What does that suggestion include?

Muskie then read a paragraph from the letter, which expressed Magnuson's concern "that the President's budget does not reflect the high priority Congress has given to the health needs of our citizens."[65] After rejecting a Chiles motion for a lower target, the committee voted 11 to 2 to accept Magnuson's figure. The pattern was repeated two years later, this time with Magnuson present; he told the committee that he wanted $48.2 billion in budget authority and $44.6 billion in outlays:

Muskie: Are you proposing that?

Magnuson: Yes, I am proposing that. That is a little lower than the Appropriations Committee wants to go.

Hollings: Old Silas Marner.

Chiles: You had to talk to yourself on that.

Muskie: It is the most effective one-man negotiation I have run into in a long time.[66]

Once again, after the committee turned down Chiles's try for a lower figure, it adopted Magnuson's recommendation.

Magnuson has been eager to volunteer his preferences, but the committees sometimes must prod reluctant members to take the lead. For example, when SBC was wrangling over the 1977 spending target for defense, several members turned for leadership to Sam Nunn, the junior Democrat on Armed Services, and its only SBC member, but a Senator who had already acquired a reputation as the Senate's expert on defense manpower.

---

65. Senate Budget Committee, markup of the first budget resolution for fiscal 1976, transcript, p. 342.

66. Senate Budget Committee, markup of the first budget resolution for fiscal 1978, transcript, p. 472

McClure: Sam, could you respond on the cut in the reserves, the National Guard?

Nunn: Well, our subcommittee has not met yet, and anything I say is my personal opinion. . . .

Beall: Are you willing to give an educated guess as you go through as to what the action of the subcommittee might be?

Nunn: I am reluctant to do that, Glenn. I am in a position where I would be speaking for the subcommittee, and we have not met and decided these things now. I could get quoted as predicting what my subcommittee is going to do, and it is not a good position to be in. . . .

Chiles: He knows, but he does not want to tell you.

Nunn: I do not run my subcommittee in the autocratic fashion like some of our fellow Senators.

Beall: It would be interesting to know what the subcommittee is going to do if we are going to make cuts here . . . if we had some idea of what the experts think, we would better know what to do with these figures.[67]

In this case, Nunn was cross-pressured by his Armed Services and Budget Committee roles. As chairman of an Armed Services subcommittee but of low rank on the full committee, Nunn was obviously reluctant to suggest what the full committee might do, but he also realized that his silence might bring about a lower budget target for defense than he preferred. Nunn finally wriggled out of this predicament by talking about what Armed Services might do, but without recommending a specific budget target.

The Magnuson and Nunn episodes should not be interpreted as evidence that SBC blindly follows its leaders. If it did, and all representatives of other committees got their way, the budget resolution probably would add up to much more than SBC was prepared to allow. Budget members usually test the recommended figures against other data in their possession, particularly the current policy baseline. If a program advocate were to press for an amount deemed excessive, perhaps because it was out of line with the current policy level, SBC might unite in opposition. Senator Cranston learned this lesson when he tried to win SBC approval of the amounts recommended by the Veterans' Affairs Committee (of which he became chairman in 1977). Terming his recommended level "reasonable and responsible," Cranston listed some of the program benefits that would be made possible by spending almost

67. Senate Budget Committee, markup of the first budget resolution for fiscal 1977, transcript, pp. 122-26.

$1 billion more than current policy. Senator Chiles, however, was not persuaded: "It just seems that what we have is just a very good rundown from you of everything the authorizing committee says they want."[68] Over Cranston's opposition, SBC voted 11 to 3 to maintain the veterans' function at the current policy level.

Cranston tried again the next year, but with no more success. Again, he tried for an amount well above the current policy level, asking for full funding of the amount sought by the Veterans' Affairs Committee in its March 15 report:

> I want to stress that you should not view the committee's recommendation as inflated requests that include any nonessential items. They do not. If you look at the membership of the Veterans' Committee, you will see that it represents a spectrum of the Senate including several quite conservative senators on both sides of the party aisle, and we are unanimous in feeling that.[69]

With pressure from Cranston, SBC had a difficult time settling on funding for the veterans function. It took seven roll calls before a compromise was reached on a figure approximately midway between the current policy level and the amount Cranston wanted.

If SBC members willingly followed "lead" colleagues or consensually set the budget targets at or above current policy levels, they probably would be able to reach agreement without much contention. Such has not been the case, however. The figures have occasioned much conflict, as each year's number of roll calls attests. Some budget functions (the small, stable ones such as general science, law enforcement, and general government) usually have been decided with dispatch, sometimes by voice vote. But for the contested functions—those for which there is neither an opinion leader nor general agreement on the appropriate spending level—the outcome has been determined through a voting process that has continue until a majority has been found for a particular level.

GOING ALONG: THE BUDGET IN THE SENATE

Just as the cliffhanging experience with budget resolutions in the House has reflected the schisms within HBC, Senate action has

68. *Ibid.*, p. 666.
69. Senate Budget Committee, markup of the first budget resolution for fiscal 1978, transcript, p. 719.

mirrored the relative calm within its Budget Committee. Muskie and Bellmon have recognized that the surest way to prevail on the floor is to present a united front. They hoped that with the committee solidly behind its product, the Senate would see the resolution as a rational and fair budget policy, not just as a bundle of compromises or as the personal preferences of those who happened to be on the committee. The two SBC leaders were not concerned about a few defections—no budget could satisfy the full range of political views in the Senate—and they were pleased that only two committee members voted against the inaugural resolution for fiscal 1976. But they wanted to stamp SBC members as the Senate's budget experts, not in the sense of their being knowledgeable about all government programs, but in terms of the committee's ability to anticipate Senate interests. Muskie and Bellmon therefore decided to support all committee decisions on the floor, including those that were contrary to their own preferences or to the positions they had taken during markup. They would not back any SBC colleague who sought to reopen an issue decided in committee. They would, in short, seek adoption of the budget resolution without amendments.

The first test came on a motion by SBC liberal Walter Mondale to add $9 billion to fiscal 1976 spending for temporary anti-recession programs. Muskie had strongly supported the scheme in committee, but subsequently he was committed to support the committee's decision:

> Senator Mondale has referred to some of my votes in committee and some of the positions I took. He challenges me to be consistent with those positions here in the vote on his amendment. I feel compelled to make my position clear.
>
> I have this perception of the budget process. The committee is made up of 16 members. For months and weeks we worked toward the committee objective of reaching a consensus as to how much we should spend, what our deficit should be, and at least a tentative decision as to what the budget priorities ought to be . . .
>
> At that point all the votes were in. The committee had voted to send the resolution to the floor. Each member of the Budget Committee then faced this challenge: "Do I go to the floor in support of the new budget process and its discipline or do I go pursuing my own individual priorities?"
>
> I felt fairly certain that whatever lead I set in the committee, members would follow: that if I came to the floor pursuing my priorities, every member of the Budget Committee would come to the floor pursuing his

priorities, and we would, therefore, not have a joint committee consensus. We would simply have some numbers put together by 16 Senators who would then blend into the 100 Senators who are members of this body, all fighting all over again as though there were no budget process to influence the final results.[70]

If Muskie's floor role has been to protect SBC's resolution against proposed increases, Bellmon's task often has been to defend it against proposed reductions. Bellmon's first test also came in the fiscal 1976 budget when SBC colleague Robert Dole moved for a small reduction in expenditures. Bellmon was in the forefront of the opposition:

. . . having sat through the literally months of deliberations of the Budget Committee in trying to understand the responsibilities of our Government in these difficult times and in looking at the functional breakdown of the budget figure we have recommended, I cannot agree that making an additional reduction across the board is defensible.[71]

Bellmon has consistently voted for the resolutions even when he has been disturbed by the level of spending and the deficit. In a typical endorsement he balances concern about excessive spending with support of the budget process. "I felt, as a member of the committee, that I needed to go along and support the final result of the committee, but it is not a result I personally would have crafted had I been able to do so on my own authority."[72]

Muskie and Bellmon have been motivated by more than a desire to win Senate approval of their budget resolutions. They believe that, although Congress has established a new budget process, it has not fully accepted the discipline and constraints of that process. Accordingly, they decry the tendency of Senators to load the resolution with costly amendments, as they preach the need for budget control but continue their business-as-usual practice of spending for favored programs. Muskie and Bellmon fear that the Senate might routinely pass the required resolutions without committing itself to genuine budget control; in their view, approval of a resolution bloated by floor amendments would be an empty victory. Because they believe the budget process to be incapable of surviving the rough and tumble of floor action, they have vigorously challenged all but a few noncontroversial floor

70. 121 *Congressional Record* (daily ed., April 30, 1975) S7200.
71. *Ibid.*, S7177.
72. 124 *Congressional Record* (daily ed., April 24, 1978) S6133.

amendments. At the beginning, they took the position that any substantive floor change endangered the budget process. Muskie used the "we must back SBC for the good of the budget process" argument in resisting an attempt by Edward Brooke to restore housing and community development funds cut by SBC, another instance in which Muskie had been on the losing side in committee:

> Since he [Brooke] has now faced me with my votes in committee, I have to explain why I have to support the Budget Committee resolution. . . . I do believe in those two programs, but if the budget process is to work, the chairman of the Budget Committee has to recognize that he has to yield some of his priorities from time to time in order to avoid the accusation that he brings a prejudiced view to the budget process.[73]

Muskie was most concerned that the budget resolution might be whipsawed in the Senate by the same conflicting pressures that have beset it in the House, when members have voted for increased spending but rejected the final product because the deficit was too high. Muskie felt that to avert this ever-present danger, SBC members would have to take the lead in budgetary restraint. When SBC colleague Alan Cranston tried to get more funds for veterans than had been allocated by the committee, Muskie admonished him:

> If we are to have budgetary restraints, if we are to control spending, every one of us must be willing to restrain our requests for programs we feel deeply about, because other Senators with different priorities feel deeply about other programs . . . and if the Senate is to be moved by that kind of appeal, there will be no budgetary restraints and we will be going down the road to higher and higher deficits.[74]

Other Senate leaders have shared Muskie's belief that the fledgling budget process had to be protected against the preferences of individual members and possibly against the will of the Senate. When the Senate opened debate on the first resolution for 1977, it faced a number of amendments, including the popular increase for veterans that Cranston advocated. Majority Leader Mike Mansfield, however, dampened the prospects for these amendments with an unexpected announcement:

> I do not intend to vote for any amendment, no matter how meritorious or how nice it is, or how politically palatable it may be. . . . I intend to support fully what the Budget Committee has recommended because if

73. 123 *Congressional Record* (daily ed., May 4, 1977) S7048.
74. *Ibid.*, S7060.

we do not then I think we might as well abolish it, and go back to our old ways.[75]

Mansfield was joined by the Democratic Whip as well as by Republican leaders in the Senate, all of whom announced that they would oppose any effort to amend the budget resolution. Cranston defended his amendment against the implied charge that he was undermining the new process. "We have had a year of successful experience," [76] he noted, suggesting that the budget process no longer needed the "kid gloves" treatment demanded by Muskie and Senate leaders. Other sponsors of amendments took care to voice their support for the budget process. Birch Bayh reminded the Senate that it was adopting "a congressional budget . . . not merely a budget formulated by the committees thereof."[77]

As a result of the insistence that the Senate take the budget resolution "whole," SBC had extraordinary success during its first two years (see table 24). It rebuffed all but two of the amendments on the five budget resolutions adopted for the 1976 and 1977 fiscal years. The only successful amendments were those Muskie accepted: the deletion of contingency language concerning fiscal 1976 revenues and a noncontroversial shift of $200 million from one function to another. The budget aggregates approved by the Senate were exactly those recommended by its Budget Committee.

This unnatural state of affairs could not persist beyond SBC's honeymoon period. The Senate could not indefinitely give carte blanche to one of its committees, certainly not to a committee whose legislation spans the full range of government programs. No matter how faithfully SBC tried to anticipate the preferences of the Senate, policy differences were bound to arise between the committee and the chamber as a whole. Although SBC and the budget process benefited in the short run from the informal closed rule, the practice entailed a long-term risk that the Senate would not regard the budget decisions as its own. Muskie recognized this possibility in welcoming efforts to amend the budget resolution on the floor:

I am anxious to see the Senate make whatever changes it must to make this resolution its own—because I am also anxious to see the Senate

75. 122 *Congressional Record* (daily ed., April 9, 1976) S5538-9.
76. *Ibid.* (daily ed., April 8, 1876) S5311.
77. *Ibid.* (daily ed., April 12, 1976) S5477.

Table 24

DISPOSITION OF SENATE AMENDMENTS TO THE BUDGET RESOLUTIONS

Resolution	*Number Adopted*	*Number Rejected*	*Explanation of Adopted Amendments*
Fiscal 1976			
First	1	4	Deletion of contingency provision regarding revenues
Second	0	1	
Fiscal 1977			
First	1	1	$200 million shift; accepted by Muskie
Second	0	0	
Third	0	0	
Fiscal 1978			
First	3	2	Increases for veterans, housing, and community development
Second	3	3	Tuition tax credit; deletion of reconciliation provision for agriculture; disaster relief
Fiscal 1979			
First	0	13	
Second	0	3	
Fiscal 1980 [a]			
First	5	12	Increases for Social Security, food stamps, nutrition programs, and disaster relief. Across-the-board cuts for travel and film making

[a] Includes revision to second resolution for fiscal 1979 attached to the first 1980 resolution.

Source: Author's analysis of amendments reported in *Congressional Record*, various issues.

accept the discipline of decisions it finally makes. Let us make our changes now, in a conscious and orderly fashion, so that we can then enforce the result as we pass our separate spending and taxing bills during the rest of this session.[78]

78. *Ibid.* (daily ed., April 8, 1976) S5292.

The situation changed with the first resolution for fiscal 1978. The Senate adopted three spending increases, those Cranston sought for veterans and those Edward W. Brooke and William Proxmire sought for housing and community development. Three more amendments were added to the second resolution for fiscal 1978, two for unbudgeted spending increases and one to accommodate a tuition tax credit in the revenue totals. Although as of 1979 the Senate is still reserved about tampering with SBC's resolutions, it has amended them when the budget allocations fail to accommodate important programs. The Senate adopted both the first and second resolutions for fiscal 1979 without change, rejecting various floor proposals for across-the-board and targeted spending cuts, as well as a balanced budget amendment, a proposed increase in defense spending, a transfer amendment to shift funds from defense to domestic programs, and an effort to enlarge the tax cut. But five amendments were adopted for the first 1980 resolution, four of which restored funds cut by the SBC from existing programs.

Muskie continued to vigorously resist all but a few attempts to change the budget figures set by his committee, but he came to recognize that SBC sometimes deviates from Senate preference, and that when this happens, the parent body is likely to overrule the committee. Muskie's main interest was not to stop all amendments, but to keep his bipartisan coalition and mainstream budget policy intact.

SBC's floor success cannot be accounted for merely by the novelty of the budget process. This explanation might have sufficed for the first year or two, but after five years other factors appear to be at work. Perhaps SBC's greatest asset is its confidence that the budget resolutions will win overwhelming support from the Senate regardless of the disposition of particular floor amendments. SBC does not have to trade for votes; nor do most Senators decide whether to vote for or against a resolution on the basis of floor outcomes.

Every budget resolution has carried in the Senate by at least 25 votes; only 1 of the 10 resolutions for fiscal years 1976-80 failed to win by better than a two-to-one majority. (The single exception was the first resolution for fiscal 1978, which drew 31 votes in opposition.) The two main differences between the voting patterns in the Senate and the House have been a stable majority for the budget resolutions and the absence of solid Republican opposition in the Senate. Senate Republicans are almost equally divided between regular supporters and regular opponents of budget resolutions. In fact, a majority of Republicans voted in favor of 6 of the 10 resolutions.

Senators' voting behavior may be divided into four categories as follows:

1. **Consistent Supporters.** Half of the members of the Senate have always voted for the resolution; they might oppose SBC on a particular amendment but regardless of the outcome, they have voted for final passage. This bloc has included about one-third of the Republicans, two thirds of the chairmen of Senate committees, and two-thirds of the members of the Senate Appropriations Committee. With this assured support, SBC has had no worry about losing on the floor. The only unknowns have been whether any amendments will be adopted and what the winning margin will be.

2. **Frequent Supporters.** A second, but less reliable, category of supporters encompasses Senators who have strayed from the fold once or twice but can be expected to vote for the budget resolutions most of the time. This list has included a handful of SBC Democrats and perhaps a dozen liberal Democrats. The members of this group have not held swing votes or voted as a bloc. A Senator might defect one year only to revert to form the next, while a colleague who previously had a consistent record in support of the resolutions might break ranks for the first time. The number of defectors appears to have been important only in determining the size of the winning margin.

3. **Frequent Opponents.** Some moderately conservative Senators have vacillated between support and opposition. These have included a few SBC Republicans and some Southern Democrats. These "switchers" have accounted for swings in the number of opposition votes, from a high of 31 in the first resolution for 1978 to a low of 18 in the second resolution for that year.

4. **Consistent Opponents.** Approximately 18 Senators have consistently voted against all budget resolutions. Most of these are conservative Republicans from the Midwest and Far West, but several Democrats (DeConcini, Proxmire, and Edward Zorinsky) are included. These opponents have been most likely to vote for floor amendments that called for a balanced budget or for steep cuts in federal spending.

This voting lineup explains the safe passage of budget resolutions in the Senate. Consistent supporters have outnumbered consistent opponents by three to one, and frequent supporters have outnumbered frequent opponents. Moreover, support for the budget resolutions has come from most committee chairmen, including the chairmen of the Appropriations and Finance Committees. Finally, most SBC members have stood by their committee on the floor, with three-quarters providing consistent or regular support on final passage.

While past voting patterns suggest a trouble-free future for the budget process in the Senate, several factors could lead to closer votes on final passage as well as to more difficulty in repelling floor amendments. Much depends on the extent and durability of Republican support. Participants from both parties doubt that the coalition established by Muskie and Bellmon could survive a Republican drift to the right or that more than half of the Senate's Republicans will long continue to vote for the resolutions. If moderate Republicans were to feel that they could no longer endorse sizable budget deficits, resolutions could still carry in the Senate, but by a slimmer margin. There might be as many as 40 votes in opposition, perhaps more if some Southern Democrats were to switch to the "no" side. Another potential source of opposition comes from Senators who have voted for budget resolutions while also supporting lower federal spending and smaller deficits. Twelve Senators who voted for the second 1979 resolution had previously supported a $10 billion across-the-board cut in total outlays for that fiscal year. When the $10 billion reduction failed (by a 35-38 vote) these Senators supported the higher spending total in the resolution. Perhaps this voting pattern only shows that some Senators want to be recorded as supporting both lower spending and the budget process, and that as long as members can have it both ways, budget resolutions will continue to command sizable majorities in the Senate.

THE BUDGET IN CONFERENCE

Although the House and Senate procedures and political circumstances differ both in committee and on the floor, when the two Budget Committees go to conference, their budget figures do not appear to be far apart. The variance between the two sets has always been less than 1 percent for total revenues and total outlays and has exceeded that amount for each only once, when the spread was 1.1 percent. The House-Senate difference has been greatest for the budget deficit, averaging about 7 percent for the 10 resolutions covered in table 25. The extraordinary 39 percent gap for the first 1980 resolution derived from differing economic assumptions, not from major policy disagreements.

An examination of the functional allocations made by the two bodies reinforces the finding that they generally are not far apart on the numbers. During fiscal years 1976 through 1980, each chamber made 300 functional decisions (not including the amounts

Table 25

HOUSE AND SENATE DIFFERENCES ON BUDGET TOTALS
(dollars in millions)

Resolutions	*House*	*Senate*	*Differences*	
Fiscal 1976				
First				
Revenues	$298,181	$297,800	$ 381	0.1%
Budget Authority	386,831	379,537	7,294	1.9
Outlays	368,249	365,000	3,249	0.9
Deficit	70,068	67,200	2,868	0.5
Second				
Revenues	301,800	300,800	1,000	0.3
Budget Authority	408,004	406,200	1,804	0.4
Outlays	373,891	375,600	1,709	0.5
Deficit	72,091	74,800	1,709	3.8
Fiscal 1977				
First				
Revenues	363,000	362,400	600	0.2
Budget Authority	454,071	454,900	829	0.2
Outlays	415,435	412,600	2,835	0.7
Deficit	52,435	50,200	2,235	4.5
Second				
Revenues	362,500	362,000	500	0.1
Budget Authority	452,583	447,500	5,083	1.1
Outlays	413,240	412,800	440	0.1
Deficit	50,740	50,800	60	0.1
Third				
Revenues	348,800	346,800	2,000	0.6
Budget Authority	477,921	467,000	10,921	2.3
Outlays	419,130	415,000	4,130	1.0
Deficit	70,330	68,200	2,130	3.1

(Continued)

Table 25

HOUSE AND SENATE DIFFERENCES ON BUDGET TOTALS (Cont.)

(dollars in millions)

Resolutions	*House*	*Senate*	*Differences*	
Fiscal 1978				
First				
Revenues	398,094	395,600	2,494	0.6
Budget Authority	502,267	504,600	2,333	0.5
Outlays	464,477	459,200	5,277	1.1
Deficit	66,383	63,500	2,883	4.5
Second				
Revenues	397,930	394,800	3,130	0.8
Budget Authority	508,000	501,400	6,600	1.3
Outlays	459,570	459,900	330	0.1
Deficit	61,640	65,100	3,460	5.6
Fiscal 1979				
First				
Revenues	443,000	443,300	300	0.1
Budget Authority	569,500	566,100	3,400	0.6
Outlays	500,900	498,900	2,000	0.4
Deficit	57,900	55,600	2,300	4.1
Second				
Revenues	450,000	447,200	2,800	0.6
Budget Authority	561,000	557,700	3,300	0.6
Outlays	489,800	489,500	300	0.1
Deficit	39,800	42,300	2,500	6.3
Fiscal 1980				
First				
Revenues	509,000	503,600	5,400	1.1
Budget Authority	605,081	600,300	4,781	0.8
Outlays	529,863	532,600	2,737	0.5
Deficit	20,863	29,000	8,137	39.0

Source: Conference Committee Reports.

for interest and undistributed offsetting receipts).[79] Although fewer than one-third of the allocations were identical, the gap usually was narrow, as table 26 reveals. Two of every three differ-

79. These categories have been excluded because they are primarily estimates rather than policy decisions, though, of course, the estimates are sometimes influenced by policy considerations.

Table 26

RANGE OF HOUSE AND SENATE DIFFERENCES AMONG FUNCTIONAL CATEGORIES, FISCAL YEARS 1976-80

Resolution	*Total*[1]	*No Difference*[2]	*Less Than 5% Difference*	*5%-10% Difference*	*Greater Than 10% Difference*
Fiscal 1976					
First	30	9	13	2	6
Second	30	14	12	0	4
Fiscal 1977					
First	30	5	14	5	6
Second	30	12	13	0	5
Third	30	16	10	3	1
Fiscal 1978					
First	30	5	18	3	4
Second	30	14	10	3	3
Fiscal 1979					
First	34	6	17	6	5
Second	34	8	21	2	3
Fiscal 1980					
First	34	2	20	5	7
Total	312	91	148	29	44
Percent of Total	100.0	29.2%	47.4%	9.3%	14.1%

[1] Expenditure functions excluding interest and undistributed offsetting receipts. Includes both budget authority and outlay differences for each resolution.

[2] This column includes any House-Senate differences of $50 million or less.

Source: Author's tabulaitons.

ences were less than 5 percent. All told, nearly 80 percent of the decisions were the same or within a 5 percent variance. When the two Houses diverged by more than 10 percent, the spread often was due to different estimation procedures rather than to policy disagreements. As budget-estimating techniques have become more reliable within Congress and CBO's capabilities have improved, the incidence of these wide discrepancies has diminished. In the 1976 and 1977 resolutions, almost one of every four differentials in the House and Senate functional allocations was more than 10 percent; in the 1978 and 1979 resolutions, only one of every seven differentials was above the 10 percent mark. But in fiscal 1980 there was an increase in the major differences that may have reflected growing tension over budget policies and priorities.

In view of the small gap between the House and Senate figures concerning most budget items, one might expect a quick and easy conference in which the two sides expediently gloss over programmatic and political disagreements and compromise on the figures. Moreover, the path toward agreement in conference is eased by two features of the budget process. First, the Budget Committees enter conference with a common format; they do not have to decide on the categories to be used, only on the figures to be filled in. Second, both committees regard the resolutions as "must" legislation for which the Budget Act's deadlines furnish a powerful push toward agreement.

Nevertheless, even seemingly small differences can arouse the passions of conferees determined to uphold the positions of their respective Houses. The conferees do not always define the differences in numerical terms; rather, they fight over the policy or procedural disagreements that led to their different budget allocations. At least once a year the conference has been stalemated by an issue that threatens to block final agreement on a budget resolution. In 1975, the two sides fought over whether Congress should adopt a budget resolution for the "transition quarter," the three-month period during which the beginning of the fiscal year was shifted from July 1 to October 1. The next year they were stymied by "earned income tax credits," payments to low-income persons in excess of the taxes they had paid. The committees were not disputing the worth of the program, which had already been enacted by Congress, but the manner in which these credits were to be accounted for in the budget. The House committee wanted to treat these payments as direct expenditures, while the Senate committee argued that they should be computed as revenue losses.[80] In 1977, the Budget Committees warred over defense spending. In 1978, the issue was "soft" public works, federal grants to local governments to employ low-income persons on labor-intensive projects. In this instance, Senator Muskie took the extraordinary step of obtaining a Senate resolution backing his committee's stand in conference. In 1979, the conferees were bitterly divided over education spending.

80. Earned income credits which offset tax liability were not in dispute; all sides computed them as revenue losses.

Eventually all these disputes were resolved, although sometimes only after conferees had threatened to abandon the process rather than to approve an unacceptable resolution. As might be expected, each settlement gave the parties some of what they wanted or blurred the differences between them. The transition-quarter problem was solved by treating the figures for that period in the second ("ceiling") resolution for fiscal 1976 as targets, and the transition-quarter figures in the first ("target") resolution for fiscal 1977 as a ceiling. The earned income credit issue was resolved when SBC, alarmed by various proposals for refundable tax credits, adopted the House position that any such credits should be computed as direct expenditures. The heated dispute over defense spending was settled by splitting the difference, with a slight tilt toward the House position, presumably in recognition of the difficulty of securing passage of budget resolutions in that body. The fight over "soft" public works ended with acceptance of the Senate's figures but with a compromise on report language that left open the possibility that some funds might be available for the program. The flareup over education was calmed only after House rejection of the conference report and subsequent Senate agreement to increase funding for this purpose.

Several Budget Committee conferees who have participated in conferences on appropriations bills believe that disputes over budget resolutions have been more strained and protracted than those involving appropriations. One put his experience this way: "On Appropriations, we work down the list of disagreements and we usually find a place in the middle that both sides are happy with. One or two items sometimes give us trouble, but except when we have those riders, it usually is wrapped up in a single session." Budget conferences are seen as unusually bitter and divisive: "It always starts off pleasant as we get the easy numbers out of the way, but then we get stalled on one item and one side or the other starts posturing or threatening."

Some of the initial haggling in conference was attributable to start-up anxieties as each side tried to protect its distinctive ways of doing business. Originally, each committee feared that any concession would become a precedent and lead to a weakening of its position in conference. One of the first fights was over "undistributed offsetting receipts," a budget category that includes income from the sale of offshore oil leases. The dispute involved estimating assumptions rather than budget decisions, but the two sides fought as if the outcome would determine the amount of oil exploration in coastal waters. Although the Budget Committees had other reasons for taking the matter seriously (the different estimates affected the targets for the budget deficit), the Budget Committees were arguing over whose dollar figures were superior. The fracas over the transition quarter also showed each committee's determination to maintain its particular approach to congressional budgeting. As a committee that has been willing to challenge legislation on the floor, SBC was eager for transition-quarter ceilings it could use to enforce substantive budget decisions. HBC, with its more conciliatory approach, was concerned that the House had not acted on the transition-quarter figures. It preferred not to be on record in a way that might later propel it into a needless confrontation with another committee.

Lines Versus Numbers

There have been recurring flareups in conference over House line items versus Senate figures, with each side insisting that its markup procedures be used to settle disputed allocations. In accord with its official avoidance of line items, SBC has tried to ward off commitments on specific programs in conference. This policy was stated in an internal document prepared several months after the committee was organized: "The Concurrent Resolution must be reconcilable with the House version, suggesting much more emphasis on negotiable numbers than on non-negotiable philosophy."[81] The House committee prefers to carry its line-item habits into conference. For HBC Democrats, a conference agreement on undefined numbers would devalue the program concessions used to win liberal support for the resolutions. At the very least, HBC wants the conference to decide the major disputed issues.

The first time the conferees gathered, they had to decide how to reconcile the exact figures presented by the House with the rounded (to the nearest $100 million) numbers in the resolution passed by the Senate. Despite the small sums at issue (never more than $50 million), the two sides battled as if great principles and budgetary decisions were riding on the outcome. HBC feared that if the conference rounded off the functional allocations, its action would be interpreted as a rejection of specific line-item commitments. SBC was concerned that a conference agreement on exact

81. Senate Budget Committee, "Congressional Budget Process" (November 18, 1974).

allocations would imply its endorsement of the programs assumed in those numbers. SBC has come out ahead on this issue, because conferees have tended to submerge differences by being less, rather than more, precise.

The conference has posed precisely the kind of situation in which avoidance of line-item decisions has often been a precondition for agreement. Unlike markups in the Budget Committees, where the basic disagreements are over budgetary and functional totals rather than over specific programs, conferees tend to be close on the figures even when they disagree on the program components. In many instances, the House and the Senate make different program assumptions which add up to similar functional levels. In one year, for example, the two bodies came to conference with virtually identical targets for the veterans' function. Both provided funds for new programs, but the House assumed that the new money would go for pensions to World War I veterans and their survivors, while the Senate assumed it woud go for reform of the pension system. Had the two sides tried to compose their differences by logrolling—with each House embracing the program preferences of the other—the conference outcome would have been much higher than either wanted, and the increase in spending and the deficit might have jeopardized final passage of the conference report.

When they have disagreed on programs, the conferees have used two methods for achieving agreement: (1) silence, which enables each side to interpret the numbers as it prefers; and (2) negotiated ambiguity, which is the careful formulation of report language to preserve the options of each House. Each committee retains its preconference assumptions and interpretations unless the conference specifically changes them. When Senate conferees refused to endorse a $50 million item the House sought to begin a national health insurance program, the House settled for no mention of the issue. Rep. Robert L. Leggett then indicated how the House would interpret this silence:

> As long as we can have it understood that there is nothing in the compromise figure that detracts from the positions taken by the respective Houses, we are perfectly authorized then to go ahead and move for an authorization bill for start-up costs and nobody can make a point on our side that the budget precludes taking it up.[82]

---

82. Conference on the first budget resolution for fiscal 1977, transcript, p. 105.

In another instance, when the House and Senate were $3.5 billion apart on their assumptions concerning construction grants for a water pollution control program, Senator Bellmon wondered aloud how the two sides could agree on the spending level for the particular function. Again, silence supplied the answer:

Function 300 is one of the functions where the two budget committees have tactitly agreed in a sense to disagree over the assumptions as to what comprises a number. . . . Because the imperative has always been to reach agreement between the two bodies on the numbers, we have been able to not highlight these different assumptions and reach agreement on the numbers.[83]

Sometimes, however, the conferees have not been satisfied with silence. At the beginning of the conference on the first resolution for fiscal 1978, Representative Mattox, a member of the House delegation, demanded "that each of the specific compromises that we make . . . be reflected explicitly in the statement of the managers of the conference."[84] He was supported by Democratic colleagues who pointed to the precarious status of the budget resolution in the House. Giaimo was candid about his need to bring back line-item concessions: "We have had some rocky roads with this conference in the House, and some of our people want to have some assurance that their program is included."[85] Responding for the Senate group, Muskie suggested that some past conflicts had been resolved when "we have agreed to leave an ambiguity, and that has served our purposes."[86] This approach was used for the commerce and transportation function. When Giaimo wanted to know how much money would be available for Small Business Administration loans, Bellmon suggested that silence would be an appropriate way of handling the situation: "As I understand it, the House goes back to the floor and says anything they like and the Senate does the same. It is very simple."[87] But Giaimo needed stronger assurances:

. . . it isn't that I want to quibble over a couple of hundred million, but in this particular function I am very hesitant to cut this, because one of the charges being made [by liberals in the House] is that we are holding the line and cutting back on programs which affect people.[88]

83. *Ibid.*, p. 81.
84. Conference on the first budget resolution for fiscal 1978, transcript, p. 5.
85. *Ibid.*, p. 6.
86. *Ibid.*, p. 7.
87. *Ibid.*, p. 26.
88. *Ibid.*

The conferees finally negotiated language stating that the functional allocation would permit an increase in SBA loans above current policy level.[89] The statement did not, however, specify the amount of funds that would be available for this purpose.

Because silence and ambiguity are convenient ways of bridging differences, it is unlikely that a conference would end in dispute over particular programs. Nevertheless, a breakdown almost occurred when the two sides could not agree on funding for "soft" public works in the second resolution for fiscal 1979. On that occasion, the conferees agreed to allow each side to go its own way. The members' statement accompanying the conference report said, "The House conferees assume that within these amounts $0.7 billion in budget authority is available for public works. The Senate conferees assume the amounts agreed to are necessary to fund existing legislation."[90]

In soft public works, however, the path toward compromise was obstructed by an institutional problem that has posed perhaps the greatest threat toward conference agreement: The conferees do not always represent their respective chambers, so they have been constrained in the concessions they can offer. Let us consider why conferences on budget resolutions are faced with this unusual predicament.

The Constrained Conferees

A budget conference is the only occasion in which House and Senate representatives meet to iron out differences on the full scope of federal revenues and expenditures. The conference covers issues that are handled by 30 House and Senate committees in the course of each year. This across-the-board approach diminishes the common interests of the conferees and increases their dependence on their parent chambers.

A comparison with traditional conferences may be useful at this point. When parallel committees exist in the House and Senate, they are likely to hold similar values about the policy areas in which they operate. The two Armed Services Committees, for example, might differ on the value of particular weapons, but both support a strong defense policy. The House and Senate Agriculture

89. The manager's statement on the conference report stipulated that the amount provided for the commerce and transportation function "permits increases in funding above current policy for . . . Small Business Administration credit assistance programs." S. Rept. No. 95-134 (1977), p. 7.
90. H. Rept. No. 95-1594 (1978), p. 7.

Committees can be expected to work in support of farm interests, even when they disagree on the level of price supports for commodities. The Education and Labor Committee in the House and the Labor and Human Resources Committee in the Senate both advocate an expanded federal role in education, although they do not always see eye to eye on program priorities. In conference, congressional committees usually are brought together by their similarities rather than their differences. They meet in conference because they want to build defense programs, support farm prices, aid education programs. To achieve these common objectives, they must overcome differences in the legislation emanating from the House and Senate. With common program interests, they are predisposed toward reconciliation of the matters on which they disagree.

When budgetary conferees have faced each other across the table, however, they have been united by a desire to make the budget process work, not by substantive interests. When they battled over defense spending for fiscal 1978, the two sides were represented by members with disparate legislative backgrounds. The House contingent included a moderate Democrat and a conservative Republican from Armed Services, a Democratic member of the Defense Appropriations subcommittee, and an assortment of liberals and conservatives from various "domestic" committees. The Senate side had two Southern Democrats from the Defense Appropriations subcommittee and members of nine standing committees, but none from the Senate Armed Services Committee. Thus nonspecialists were in a position to make budgetary decisions affecting the committees of jurisdiction.

The same situation appears to confront each of the Budget Committees in markup. But the conference differs in one crucial way. In markup, each committee produces a resolution by accommodating to the interests and expectations of the committees of its chamber. In this manner, the Budget Committees can make decisions about matters on which they are not legislative specialists without risking floor opposition from the affected committees. But the disagreements brought to the conference often concern matters on which other interested House and Senate committees disagree. The Budget Committees cannot merely settle such matters among themselves; they have to reckon with the wants of other committees. Sometimes they must consult other committees; sometimes deep divisions develop between the Budget Committees.

One possible way out of these conflicts is the subordination of substantive differences to the budget process, the one matter on which the conferees are united. Muskie tried this approach when the fiscal 1978 conference was deadlocked on defense spending:

I understand the difficulty of reaching agreement on a defense number. I will tell you in advance I will support that defense number, whatever it is, recognizing it may not be one I would consider ideal. But I will support it, whatever it is, because I think, above all, in the long run, our priorities, no matter what they are, will be best served if we begin to harness them and control them within the context of this budget process.[91]

But Muskie was not willing to accept *any* number in the interest of preserving the budget process. He wanted a figure that would satisfy the relevant Senate committees:

I have no desire to go back to the Senate and force those who believe that we need these kinds of defense numbers to the line, to the wall. I want to get a number that I can enforce with John Stennis and John McClellan [then chairmen of the Senate Armed Services and Appropriations Committees].[92]

The House Budget Committee has had an even greater need than the Senate committee to accommodate to the interests of its committees. Loss of a few votes can doom the prospects for House approval of a conference report. Paradoxically, HBC's weakness in its own chamber has forced the House committee to act tough in conference. HBC has a compelling need to "keep faith" with House committees, as the following remarks by Representative Wright during the conference debate over the transition-quarter dispute show:

I do have a very strong feeling about the relationships which our Budget Committee must maintain with our regular authorizing committees of the House. If we, in our action, mandate the House Public Works Committee to abandon its position and accept the Senate Committee's position, it seems to me we are overstepping the rightful bounds of our authority.

You see, we, too, have worked with our committees, including the Public Works Committee. . . . I just don't want to preempt the House committees. I don't want to be in the position of breaking faith with them and going back and saying, "Well, the Budget Committee has de-

91. Conference on first budget resolution for fiscal 1978, transcript, p. 151.
92. *Ibid.*, p. 153.

creed that you are going to have to recede from your position and agree to the Senate position. I don't think that is our function as a budget committee.[93]

The same theme was expressed by Giaimo, as he voiced apprehensions about the fate of a Budget Committee that challenged its House peers:

I get awfully nervous as a member of this Committee, having assured the legislative committees in the House that we were going to protect their prerogatives at all times, and now I am going to be forced to go back and tell them that I have made some sort of arrangement with the Senate on highways and on that function that I really don't know much about. . . .

[We] then have every legislative committee in the House breathing down the backs of this Budget Committee which has to get along with them.[94]

The most difficult confrontations in conference are those in which the bargaining freedom of conferees is restricted by their loyalty to other committees. In the earned-income-credit dispute, for example, Muskie initially felt he had to back the preferences of Senate Finance which had the greatest stake in the matter.[95] Another example was the fight over "soft" public works in which the authorizing committees of the House and Senate were moving in opposite directions and the conference was trapped in the middle.

Yet the conferees have managed to reconcile their differences in every case because they have been unwilling to go back to their chambers without a budget resolution. To avoid failure in conference, they conduct parallel negotiations within conference and among the Budget Committees and other interested parties in each House. "Giaimo can't agree to anything without running to the telephone," a Senate aide complained. But if this is the only way to get agreement, it is the one the conferees take again and again. The alternative is for the Budget Committees to sacrifice the budget process to the interests of other committees.

93. Conference on the second budget resolution for fiscal 1976, transcript, pp. 256-57.
94. *Ibid.*, pp. 258-59.
95. Although Muskie has repeatedly clashed with Senate Finance Chairman Russell Long over budget matters, he used a letter from Long to support the Senate's position on the credits. See transcript of conference on the first budget resolution for fiscal 1978, pp. 221-22.

Although both committees want to reach agreement in conference, they have not resolved disputes by splitting the differences. As table 27 shows, virtually every contested functional allocation has been decided by tilting toward one side or the other. (In a few cases, the conference allocation was below or above the amounts set by the two Houses.) Over the entire five-year period, the Senate has "won" more than half of the disputes compared with less than 40 percent for the House. But this overall record is almost an exact reversal of the pattern at the start. During the first two years of the budget process, approximately 55 percent of the settlements favored the House position compared with only 38 percent for the Senate. During the 1978-80 fiscal years, however, the conference decision was closer to the position of the Senate in 65 percent of the disputes and to that of the House in less than 25 percent.

House and Senate Budget Committee members have offered different explanations for this turnabout. HBC members consider themselves bullied by Senate conferees, who have used their permanent tenure on SBC to get their way. Representative Leggett used this argument in calling for a longer term for HBC members:

> The fact of the matter is that the members on the Senate committee are constantly and continually gaining in stature and posture and aggressiveness, and this makes it extremely difficult for us to bargain with them when we are junior members and they have this high degree of seniority which they are continually gaining.[96]

SBC members regard the House Budget Committee as unbalanced, because of its partisan cleavage and the domination by liberal Democrats. One Senator who has participated in most of the budget conferences offered this explanation:

> The Republicans on the House Committee never vote for the resolution. So they force that committee to go to the left every time in order to get a majority. That is why they are way out of balance when they go to conference. Our committee is representative of the Senate as a whole, so we don't have a lot of our actions changed.

Both explanations fit the facts. The downturn in HBC's fortunes began in 1977, when almost half of its Democrats were replaced. All of the replacements were liberal Democrats, turning HBC's membership into a less representative slate than it had previously

96. 123 *Congressional Record* (September 7, 1977) H8957.

been. A third explanation is that the House Budget Committee usually marks up its resolution first; SBC emerges from conference with a better success rate because it enters conference with a more timely and politicially sensitive position.

But SBC can not push its advantage in conference to the point of overriding the interests of the House. When HBC recedes, it is retreating from the positions taken by its parent chamber. Accordingly, when the conference report is taken to it for final approval, the House must feel that its important interests have been protected. A glance at table 27 offers striking explanation for the House's rejection of the fiscal 1980 conference report. Four of every five conference compromises favored the Senate. Many House Democrats felt that the conference had cheated them of the things that mattered most, and although it was too late to recoup most of their losses, they extracted a token concession from the Senate, a small increase in education funds.

BUDGET PROCESS OR BUDGET ROUTINE?

After five cycles of budget making, congressional practices have begun to harden into routines. The Members of the House and Senate and the Budget Committees now know what to expect. Theirs is no longer a new process, for which *ad hoc* arrangements must be improvised each year. One can anticipate continuing adaptation in budget-making features such as the role of the chairman, markup approaches, and floor debate. The Budget Committees are likely to move toward multiyear budgeting, though its exact form is yet to be determined. SBC already has officially embraced a multiyear perspective, but HBC remains somewhat apprehensive.

In both chambers, the political conditions that have prevailed thus far are unstable. This is clearly the case in the House where the resolutions have been imperiled by partisan and liberal-conservative rifts. The extreme polarization of the two parties there is unusual, though it might become a more prevalent pattern in American politics. In the Senate, the Muskie-Bellmon alliance also was unusual, and might not survive the change of SBC's leadership.

Over time, the one constant in congressional budget making is likely to be the striving of the Budget Committees for resolutions

Table 27

CONFLICT RESOLUTION: DIRECTION OF CONFERENCE COMMITTEE DECISIONS, FISCAL YEARS 1976-80

Resolution	*No Significant Conflict*[a]	*Closer to House*	*Closer to Senate*	*Split the Difference*	*Above Both House/ Senate*	*Below Both House/ Senate*
Fiscal 1976						
First	9	12	4	3	2	0
Second	14	6	9	0	0	1
Fiscal 1977						
First	5	15	8	0	0	0
Second	12	11	7	0	0	0
Third	16	7	7	0	0	0
Total 1976-77	56 (37.3%)	51 (34.0%)	35 (23.3%)	5 (3.3%)	2 (1.3%)	1 (0.7%)

Fiscal 1978						
First	5	8	17	0	0	0
Second	14	3	10	0	0	3
Fiscal 1979						
First	6	6	17	2	3	0
Second	8	6	15	0	2	3
Fiscal 1980 [b]						
First	2	6	23	1	0	0
Total 1978-80	35 (21.9%)	29 (18.1%)	82 (51.3%)	3 (1.9%)	5 (3.2%)	6 (3.8%)
Total 1976-80	91 (29.4%)	80 (25.8%)	117 (37.7%)	8 (2.6%)	7 (2.3%)	7 (2.3%)

[a] No significant difference is considered to have occurred when the House and Senate allocations diverged by $50 million or less.

[b] The data for the first 1980 resolution reflect the original conference agreement, not the amount later added after House rejection of the conference report.

Source: Author's tabulations from transcripts of conference committee.

that can gain majority support in the House and Senate. In so doing, these committees will have to seek accommodation to the dominant political interests in their respective chambers. As these interests change, so too will the orientation and output of the Budget Committees. An understanding of why and how the Budget Committees seek accommodation is essential for studying the making of budgets in Congress. This is the subject addressed in the next chapter.

VIII The "Accommodating" Budget

In formulating their resolutions, the Budget Committees cannot operate *ex parte,* as if they were the only ones in Congress with a legitimate interest in what is decided. At all stages of congressional budgeting, the House and Senate Budget Committees must be sensitive to the wants and expectations of other committees. This chapter analyzes the accommodations of the budget process to congressional expectations and the limiting effects of this practice on the ability of the Budget Committees to effect radical change in the budget priorities and the fiscal policies of the United States.

The making of a congressional budget consists of more than just markup procedures, voting patterns in committee and on the floor, success rate of amendments, and party politics. The numbers in each resolution affect the legislative plans of committees and the future course of federal programs; each resolution, therefore, must be made with attention to its legislative and program implications. In short, the budget must accommodate the legislative and political interests of Congress.

It might be useful to begin with the question, What must the Budget Committees know when they produce a budget resolution? The obvious answer is that they should have "program" knowledge, that is, an understanding of the expenditures and activities of federal agencies. Committee members should be informed on the administration of programs, on the groups served, and on spending and workload trends. They should be able to assess the effectiveness of federal programs and expenditures.

Despite the magnitude of this undertaking, the Budget Committees seem to have succeeded. Staff analysts are knowledgeable about federal programs and budgetary practices. They produce an unending stream of internal memoranda and issue papers covering the matters likely to be considered during markup and floor consideration of the resolutions. Although they may not be familiar with every detail of every program, they usually can hold their own in discussions with counterparts from the Appropriations Committees and authorization committees. They are also assisted by the staff of the Congressional Budget Office, discussed in chapter V.

Yet, program knowledge is an insufficient form of intelligence for the Budget Committees. To produce defensible resolutions, Budget Committee members and staffs must be informed concerning the intentions and expectations of Congress and its committees. In the hectic period preceding the markup of a resolution, the members and staffs of the Budget Committees must concentrate on knowing Congress, its interests and concerns, the status of and prospects for legislation, and the legislative lineup on critical issues.

The need for knowledge about Congress goes far beyond the obvious fact that Congress has the final say on budget resolutions. The Budget Committees' resolutions touch on the interests and jurisdiction of every legislative committee. Hence the Budget Committees cannot make substantive judgments about programs without knowing what other committees think or want.

There is yet another reason for the urgent need for knowledge about Congress: The first budget resolution must anticipate later legislative action on revenue and expenditure bills; the second resolution must accord with the actions Congress has already taken. These resolutions are not the only budget decisions made by Congress; nor do they preempt the more established decision-making processes. Claims also are decided when Congress makes appropriations, allocates tax burdens and benefits, and legislates entitlements into law. Moreover, because the budget resolutions do not have the force of law they cannot be used to levy taxes or appropriate money. Their limited status makes the resolutions something less than full-fledged budgets but more than declarations of intent. Congress cannot be certain of what it is deciding when it makes a budget resolution; nor can it make these decisions totally independent of its other processes for allocating federal resources.

No matter how well Budget Committee members understand federal programs, they cannot establish themselves as program experts on Capitol Hill. They can strive for special standing with respect to fiscal policy and the budget's aggregates, but they cannot achieve recognition on Capitol Hill as specialists concerning any of the budget's parts. For this reason, the Budget Committees are always vulnerable to having their recommendations and competence challenged by the committees of jurisdiction. The committees that make the "real" decisions also are the claimants in the process, and the Budget Committees can ignore these committees only at the risk of having their resolutions rejected or disregarded.

THE FIRST RESOLUTION: EXPECTATIONS, ACCOMMODATIONS, AND INDICATIONS

Much of the premarkup activity of the Budget Committees has been aimed at improving their understanding of congressional intentions. Each committee begins with a quick staff analysis of the President's budget. This exercise orients the committees to prospective budget issues, identifies the programs that have been cut or added, and examines the extent to which funding for programs has been adjusted for inflation or allowed real growth. The purpose of this exercise is not to acquire program knowledge; it is much too superficial for that. Rather, the Budget Committees are seeking clues about the likely concerns and reactions of other committees. Budget Committee members ask the same questions as other committees: Will a reduction proposed by the President stick? What are the odds of getting a particular program through Congress? What will the mood be on Capitol Hill concerning defense spending and other contentious issues?

Shortly after they get the President's budget, the Budget Committees launch hearings on economic and budget policies.[1] In the House, the full Budget Committee addresses fiscal issues while issues relating to the various budget functions are parceled among the task forces. Because SBC task forces have withered away, all of SBC's hearings are conducted in full committee. Neither committee tries to cover all of the budget; each concentrates on the issues it expects to be most pertinent. Except for providing the Budget Committees with a range of opinions on economic issues, however, the sessions are more ritualistic than informative. In depth of detail, these hearings do not match the hearings of the appropriations and authorization committees; nor do they give the Budget Committees an adequate base of information on which to make program decisions. Yet the hearings serve two important purposes: They make the committees aware of some of the key issues of the year and they demonstrate to Congress that the committees have done their "homework" before putting together the resolution. "The hearings are something we have to go through," an HBC aide explained. "They eat up a lot of time that might be better used for

1. The Congressional Budget Act (Section 301[d]) requires the Budget Committees to conduct hearings before reporting the first budget resolution.

staff work, but we don't dare come up with a resolution that hasn't been blessed by hearings."

Congressional Input

After the hearings come the March 15 reports from other committees which are intended to alert the Budget Committees to the full range of congressional interests. But, as was pointed out earlier, the value of these submissions is diminished in many cases by unrealistic expectations and by the reluctance of committees to commit themselves on legislative issues before they have made definite legislative plans for the year. Nevertheless, budget staffers, with the help of their counterparts on other committees, have become adept at "reading" these reports to differentiate between the wish lists and the real numbers. Budget staffers consult with their counterparts on other committees about which items are really wanted. The relationship is one of negotiation rather than education. "Nobody in the process," a participant suggested, "wants to be blindsided by developments which could have been foreseen at the start. The Budget Committee does not want to make the mistake of neglecting something which really matters to the other side. The authorizing committee doesn't want its intentions misconstrued." In the hectic weeks prior to markup, representatives from the Budget Committees and other committees try to hammer out informal understandings—"ballpark figures" is the way an interviewee described them—so that the resolution will be a reasonably accurate statement of congressional expectations.

Each Budget Committee has the chore of tending to the interests of its own chamber, not of worrying about Congress as a whole. By the time markup starts, the Budget Committees have a fairly clear idea of what can be expected in their respective Houses. As one SBC staffer explained the situation at markup, "We have a pretty good fix on what will move and what won't. Of course, things don't always work out that way, but the problem usually comes from events over which we have no control."

Discussions in markup are peppered with queries and comments about what the affected committees want. Most members of the Budget Committees do not go looking for a fight. They would rather produce a budget that the affected committees can live with. Tough talk about the excessive demands of other committees often is countered by conciliatory efforts. Thus when Senator Muskie urged a reduction in defense spending for fiscal 1976, to "send the Appropriations Committee a message," Senator Hollings shot back,

> Why don't we send them a different message that we are sort of going along with them? This damn Budget Committee, it is like bone fishing. You have to get the Senate and Congress unbolted first. By gosh, now is the time to get established and get support and get this thing going.[2]

As we have seen, the two Budget Committees have accommodated in different ways. HBC's line-item review has guaranteed that the allocation for each function is sufficiently generous to provide for all wanted programs. HBC knows exactly which programs are assumed in its resolutions, what program initiatives it expects, and which cutbacks are proposed. These expectations are tested in consultations with affected committees and Democratic leaders, on the basis of which the HBC chairman or the Democratic majority present recommendations to the Budget Committee. The Democratic mark makes little effort, however, to take into account Republican expectations because they are not crucial to the fate of the resolution in the House. The switch to a Democratic—in contrast to the chairman's—mark for the first 1980 resolution was an adjustment spurred by the increasing polarization of the majority party. With Democrats split between those who wanted to moderate federal spending and those committed to social programs, the Democrats decided to accommodate by broadening the preparation of the mark to all HBC Democrats, thereby increasing the likelihood that the mark would reflect an intraparty consensus.

The success of the mark as an accommodating statement has been reflected in the relatively few changes made in markup. While HBC usually modifies the mark to reflect the budgetary preferences of committee Democrats, it rarely cuts programs already assumed in the budget.

Because SBC's accommodations have been linked to current policy (or current law), the committee can be confident about funding levels without undertaking a line-by-line review of the budget. When it has deviated from current policy (or current law), SBC has known the prospective impact of that deviation on Senate committees and federal programs.

Budget Committee members have defined their committee's role in terms of congressional expectations. "Our function," Muskie advised the Senate, "is to try to reflect a consensus of the Senate on issues insofar as evidence of a consensus is available to us." [3] Senator Dole expressed a similar view:

2. Senate Budget Committee, markup of the second budget resolution for fiscal 1976, transcript, p. 628.
3. 122 *Congressional Record* (September 9, 1976) S15490.

> The Budget Committee should not pass spending targets that force the adoption of program changes that have not even been contemplated. It has been and should continue to be the Budget Committee's practice to reflect in its spending targets and its scorekeeping the budget effects of pending legislation that appears to have some possibility of enactment.[4]

Despite the best preparations, budget figures change all the time. Fresh requests from the White House, reestimates of spending rates, changes in economic conditions, or shifts in committee sentiments, all can require last-minute adjustments. The Budget Committees are willing to make these adjustments until the very end of floor action; in some years, for example, the HBC chairman has offered floor amendments to account for items that were unknown when the resolution was reported. Accommodations also have been made at the conference stage, when late news has swayed the bargain in favor of one of the Budget Committees. Giaimo interrupted a conference on the third resolution for fiscal 1977 with the announcement, "I am told the Appropriations Committee has just marked up some numbers that might be of interest here."[5] He then proposed a level consistent with the Appropriations Committee's action. Peter Domenici, one of the Senate conferees, was not convinced: "What are we doing here marking up these functions if we are just waiting for Appropriations to give us the figures?"[6] When all the talking was over, however, the conference accepted the numbers implied by the Appropriations Committee's decision.

In an accommodating environment, a tight budget resolution is one that provides only the amounts Congress is reasonably expected to require. Although the Budget Committees want to exert downward pressure on the budget, discretion has dictated hedging somewhat in the first resolution, on the ground that if the funds are not needed later in the year, they can be excised from the second resolution. When SBC debated the international affairs function for fiscal 1978, Sen. J. Bennett Johnston (who wanted a lower allocation for that function) urged a delay because the authorizing committee had not completed hearings on related legislation. In response, Muskie acknowledged that "it is just not possible for all of the authorizing committees to have in-depth hearings prior to March 15." He added:

4. 121 *Congressional Record* (November 19, 1975) S20494.
5. Conference committee on third concurrent resolution for fiscal 1978, transcript, p. 78.
6. *Ibid.*, 79.

But what we are about here is setting targets. Those targets are adjustable between May 15 and September 15. By that time, hopefully, we will have had the hearings. . . . In the meantime, we have to set targets which give committees of the Congress room to operate, which give the administration room to operate.[7]

"Giving room" is an essential feature of accommodation in the Budget Committee. It means not cutting to the bone or below the amount that Congress is expected to spend. When attempting to use the budget process to pressure Congress for a reduction in food stamp expenditures, Sen. Orrin Hatch said, "I do not think the Budget Committee is just an adding machine. It has the ability to put pressure on these committees . . . I think it is a very powerful committee and if it exerts its pressure and power, it can do an awful lot. . . ." SBC's Bellmon, however, was unwilling to take up the gauntlet:

. . . at the present time, the mood in Congress is not to cut back in food stamps. But now the Budget Committee has to take this into account. We cannot come in with a budget that flies in the face of the votes of the Senate and the laws that are on the books. . . . All the Budget Committee and budget process can do is make room for the entitlement programs that are on the books.[8]

In almost a hundred interviews with Members of Congress and staffers, no one expressed the view that the allocations in budget resolution had been knowingly set below legislative expectations. "We got all that we needed," one committee staff director exulted. The chief clerk of an Appropriations subcommittee complained, however, that the target figure in the resolution was too high: "We were faced with pressure to spend up to the full budget allocation. It's almost as if the Budget Committee bent over backwards to give Appropriations all that it wanted and then some."

For the Budget Committees, a restrictive budget is one that does not exceed congressional needs. Speaking of the SBC's role, Muskie said, "One way that we try as a committee to exert pressure upon tendencies to expand spending is to try to hold these total numbers down to what we reasonably believe is going to happen."[9]

Although Budget Committee members understand the need for

7. Senate Budget Committee, markup of the first concurrent resolution for fiscal 1978, transcript, pp. 525-26.
8. 123 *Congressional Record* (September 9, 1977) S14509.
9. 122 *Congressional Record* (September 9, 1976) S15489.

accommodation, occasionally they yearn for more independence. In response to a suggestion during SBC's markup of the first 1978 resolution that more money be set aside for the Postal Service, Muskie acknowledged "quite a deal of frustration allowing all these programs and agencies leeway to cover what they might or might not do later on in the year. What is wrong with forcing them to prove their case later in the year? . . . . Why should we allow everybody this leeway and swallow the deficit here without having a case made?"[10]

The Budget Committees usually opt for accommodation because they cannot choose the forum in which disgruntled claimants make their case. If committees that felt shortchanged were willing to wait until the second resolution to show the Budget Committee that they needed increased allocations, there would be no pressure for early accommodations. Such committees are more likely, however, to take their cases directly to the House or Senate when the first resolution is debated. Once this has been done, the issue is transformed from a matter of budget allocations into a challenge to the Budget Committee's competence. HBC member Omar Burleson, who persuaded the House to add billions of dollars to the 1978 budget for defense programs, issued one such challenge:

The Defense Task Force of the Committee on the Budget, on which I serve, held only three formal hearings of about 6 hours in all. It made no recommendation to the chairman nor to the Committee on the Budget. It had absolutely no input, and there was no discussion with respect to this matter.

On the basis of the chairman's recommendation and only his recommendation, really, the level of $116 billion is included in this resolution for national defense. You will search in vain for any valid rationale for this action because there is none. The recommendation of the Committee on the Budget is totally inconsistent with recommendations of the congressional committees of the Congress which bear the primary responsibility for national defense. Without exception, the House and the Senate Committees on Appropriations and the Committees on Armed Services of both Houses recommended increases, not decreases, in the defense budget, after extensive hearings. These conclusions were reached covering days of study, line by line items. There was no such action in the Committee on the Budget. If we are compelled to completely ignore the recommendations of the responsible committees of this Congress and establish an arbitrary budget on defense, I fear for the integrity of this committee.[11]

---

10. Markup of first concurrent resolution for fiscal 1978, transcript, pp. 347-48.
11. 123 *Congressional Record* (April 27, 1977) H3627.

The fact that committee chairmen have been among the most consistent supporters of budget resolutions attests to the Budget Committees' accommodating role. In the House, where most resolutions have encountered strong opposition, the chairmen of 19 of the 22 standing committees never voted against adoption of a resolution.[12] Moreover, chairmen have rarely complained about the allocations made to their committees or offered amendments to raise the budget levels for the functions in which they are interested.

Budgetary accommodation cannot be accomplished merely by satisfying the legislative interests of other committees, because satisfying these interests might require budget totals in excess of congressional preferences. The Budget Committees must anticipate the actions of Congress—and this anticipation involves reading the mood of Congress as much as sizing up the prospects for particular legislative proposals. When the first resolution for a fiscal year is being formulated, it is much too early for the Budget Committees to foresee what will develop in the course of a legislative session or fiscal year. But although they cannot be certain of how legislation wanted by committees will fare in the House or Senate, the Budget Committees must act as if they know what Congress is likely to do. These committees, however, can sense whether Congress is in an expansive or parsimonious mood, whether it is bent on program expansion or reluctant to endorse initiatives that would add to the deficit.

Mood changes in Congress can broaden or narrow the accommodating discretion of the Budget Committees. When Congress is in an expansive mood, it is hard for the Budget Committees to hold the line or to cut corners in accommodating to the legislative interests of other committees. Committees are in a strong position to make a case for more money. Under these circumstances, one can expect some slack in the spending allocations.

During the first four years of the budget process, Congress was in an incremental mood, willing to authorize some initiatives and hesitant to curb existing programs. However, the fifth (fiscal 1980) congressional budget was constructed under a different set of congressional expectations. Congress was in an economy mood spurred by the Proposition 13 tax cut in California and petitions from more than 25 states for a national convention to place a balanced budget

12. Only one House chairman, John Flynt, was a consistent opponent of the budget resolutions, and his committee—Standards of Official Conduct—has no budget-related jurisdiction.

requirement in the U.S. Constitution. During the four months between the beginning of the legislative session and approval of the first resolution for fiscal 1980, more than one hundred measures were introduced in the House and Senate calling for restrictions on the deficit or on federal expenditures. This mood change affected the terms of accommodation, strengthening the position of the Budget Committees *vis-à-vis* claimant committees.

This cost-conscious mood particularly strengthened the position of the House Budget Committee, whose recommendations have been regularly challenged on the floor. Although HBC produced a tight budget for 1980, with legislative savings pegged at a record high ($6 billion) and many domestic categories held to below-inflation increases, the committee's success against floor amendments was greater than in earlier years when HBC had been more favorably disposed toward the spending plans of fellow committees. In fact, the only significant floor change was an across-the-board pruning of $2.5 billion from the budget.

Savings and Initiatives

Although the first resolution is an anticipatory budget, it is more than just a prediction of things to come. The Budget Committees sometimes prod legislative committees to launch new programs and to scale down some existing ones. In their reports accompanying the first resolutions, HBC and SBC endorse various legislative initiatives (most of which have already been proposed by the President or by the affected legislative committees) by indicating that the program is assumed in a functional allocation or that there is room in the budget for it. The Budget Committees do not assume funding for all of the new programs sought by congressional committees. By implication (and sometimes explicitly), an endorsement of certain programs means that the Budget Committees have withheld their approval from other programs. By picking and choosing among the full agenda of potential legislation, the Budget Committees can influence both the course of legislation and budgetary trends. They also can force legislative committees to make choices of their own, to defer or to moderate some of their wants in order to abide by the budget resolutions.

The Budget Committees can select from a variety of possibilities in deciding what should go into their first resolutions. In addition to the President's request, these committees receive CBO's current policy estimates, reestimates, and cost analyses. Each batch of

March 15 reports conveys parallel recommendations from the appropriations and authorizing committees that reveal different expectations about the funding of programs. Although the estimates and recommendations generally vary by no more than a few percentage points, a tilt in one direction or another by the Budget Committees can mean the difference between having enough room for a program or squeezing it out.

An early budget decision against a proposed initiative can kill a proposal before it has a chance to build legislative support. Significantly, the first resolution has not been regarded in Congress as just the first round in the legislative process, with the real decisions made later in the year. Affected committees keep close watch over the markup and floor action of the first resolution to ensure that their legislative agenda is not curtailed by an adverse budget vote. The Pentagon suffered the costs of neglecting the budget process in the first year and it has not repeated that mistake since. Committees have to be especially protective of their initiatives because the Budget Committees usually have more influence over new than continuing programs.

Yet, when they act on proposed initiatives, the Budget Committees still behave as readers of legislative intent. Outright rejection of a proposal is likely to reflect congressional indifference or opposition rather than just the opinions of Budget Committee members. For example, when the Budget Committees denied funds in their 1980 budget for President Carter's wage insurance program to compensate some wage earners for inflation, the Budget Committees were widely regarded as killing a program that was already destined for defeat on Capitol Hill.

Every resolution has assumed that there would be savings from program curtailments and efficiency improvements. HBC assumed $2 billion in outlay savings in its first resolution for fiscal 1978, $2.3 billion in its fiscal 1979 resolution, and $6 billion in its fiscal 1980 resolution.[13] SBC does not itemize the savings that it expects, but it mentions them in discussing the functions to which they apply. Thus, its fiscal 1979 allocation for the health function assumed "reductions based on the enactment of a hospital cost containment proposal. . . . Further savings are anticipated from improved administration of the Medicaid program."[14]

13. For lists of these savings, see H. Rept. No. 95-189 (report on the first concurrent resolution for fiscal 1978) pp. 121-25, and H. Rept. No. 95-1055 (report on first resolution for fiscal 1979) pp. 164-71.

14. S. Rept. No. 95-739, p. 125.

To avoid conflicts over program issues, the Budget Committees have usually described savings as efficiencies and improvements rather than as program cutbacks. HBC's list of savings in the fiscal 1979 budget included hospital cost containment, changes in the method for setting the salaries of blue-collar workers, and improvements in procedures for determining eligibility for Medicaid. When SBC assumed $1.1 billion for savings in the fiscal 1977 budget for the income security function, Muskie was careful to assure the Senate "that the budget reductions are not intended to hurt the beneficiaries of welfare programs, but rather to recommend that program efficiencies could be realized."[15]

Unlike program initiatives, which usually put the Budget Committees on the side of the legislative proponents, assumed savings often mean a rejection of the recommendations of the committees that would have to propose the changes in order for the reductions to be achieved. Yet savings can be used to force legislative committees to make a choice they might rather avoid: either to produce the expected savings or to forgo the opportunity to implement their legislative initiatives. This dilemma led chairman Russell Long to propose the deletion of savings expected from his Finance Committee from the fiscal 1977 budget:

> . . . this amendment is offered in recognition of what to me is a simple fact of life. We on the Committee of Finance told the Committee on the Budget that . . . they should not expect a net savings because while we would tighten up in some areas affecting programs for the sick or the poor, in other areas Senators would have amendments that would cost us more money . . .
>
> What we should be doing in the budget resolution is bringing in some realistic estimates of something that we think we can do, not be voting for something we do not think we can do.[16]

Paradoxically, although the Budget Committees' proposed savings have usually survived floor action on the first resolution, such savings have rarely been enacted later in the year. The legislative committees have not challenged the Budget Committees on the first resolution because they know that budgeted savings will not be realized unless the legislative committees report implementing legislation. These committees therefore opt for silence when the budget resolution is debated in the expectation that their inaction

15. 122 *Congressional Record* (April 9, 1976) S5324.
16. *Ibid.*, S5323-4.

will force the Budget Committees to restore the funds later in the year.

Although the savings are generally a very small proportion of the budget, they are deemed to be worth fighting for because they show Congress that the Budget Committees are doing something about uncontrollable spending, not just tabulating the costs of past decisions. Moreover, the savings realized in the first year can have a great impact on future budgets. HBC estimated that the $6 billion recommended in fiscal 1980 savings would amount to $55 billion over a five-year period. Savings, thus, are the Budget Committees' attempt to bolster their control over future budgets. A top SBC staff official explained the importance of seemingly small amounts for his committee:

> Now it's true that our input amounts to just a couple percent of the total, but this does not mean that we have no impact on the results. Two percent is the wedge in the budget, the money for new initiatives or the savings that can be plowed back into future budgets. In terms of influencing the future, the 2 percent can be more important than all the rest.

Every first budget resolution is a compound of accommodations to the interests of other committees, expectations of what will happen during the year, and indications from the Budget Committees of the matters they deem important. In every case, the accommodations and expectations account for all but a fraction of the total, a fact that suggests that genuine budget choice almost always is at the margins. But the size of the margin is critical to the place and power of the Budget Committees. For them, the difference between 1 percent or 2 percent can be the difference between shaping the course of the budget or just being carried along.

THE SECOND RESOLUTION: RATIFYING THE PAST

If the first resolution anticipates congressional action, the second resolution confirms it. The Budget Committees do not take a fresh look at the budget when they decide what to put into their ceiling resolution; nor do they reopen issues settled earlier in the year. Even when subsequent events force expenditures above their budget targets, the committees have generally restricted the second resolution to reestimates of permanent appropriations (the expenditures that become available without congressional action), computations of the results of the actions completed by Congress, and projections of what is likely to happen with respect to legislation still pending in Congress.

This limited role was assigned to the second resolution in the first year of congressional budgeting. On the basis of reestimates and completed legislative actions, the Budget Committees were faced with a spending ceiling for fiscal 1976 that was some $6 billion above the budget target set earlier in the year. The committees had two options: They could accommodate to this *fait accompli* by endorsing a $6 billion increase in the spending total; or they could stick with the initial amount and press Congress to reduce anticipated expenditures by $6 billion. Fiscal conservatives on the Budget Committees preferred the latter course; moderates and liberals wanted a more accommodating posture. The following exchange between two Southern Democrats and Muskie illustrates how the lines were drawn within SBC:

Chiles: . . . my concern is if we take that $6 billion that happened without any fault of ours, without any fault particularly of spending programs in the Congress . . . then we are raising our deficit. . . .

Nunn: We are changing our plan.

Chiles: If we change the plan, it ought to be a conscious change rather than inadvertent. We are changing the plan though with the Second Concurrent Resolution. . . .

Muskie: Well, it is nice to speak of our plan, but I would remind members of the committee that this plan involved inputs from a lot of people, from a lot of agencies, whom we don't control, a lot of people and policymakers who did not agree with the plan, a lot of important policymakers who are still fighting the plan. And to sit here and pretend, you know, that we can somehow define all aspects of the plan to whatever the majority of this committee dictates and make it stick for more than a day is unrealistic in the extreme.[17]

Speaking of the additional spending as "the dead hand of the past,"[18] Muskie argued that if SBC were to hold the line on spending, it would have to cut the budget without knowing "what programs could be involved and which ones could be cut, and justify a cut in unidentified programs."[19] After talking about the need for

17. Senate Budget Committee, markup of the second budget resolution for fiscal year 1976, transcript, pp. 266-67.
18. *Ibid.*, p. 269.
19. *Ibid.*, p. 688.

firmer budget control the next year, SBC added the $6 billion. The House Budget Committee, following its own agonizing appraisal, took a similar position in its second resolution for fiscal 1976.[20]

The committees really had no choice. Once the first targets are breached—whether by matters beyond congressional control or because of congressional action—it is too late to insist on the original numbers when the ceiling is adopted. Congress cannot be expected to roll back appropriations or other legislative enactments merely for the sake of meeting its initial budget targets. To do so would invite serious conflict with other congressional committees at a time when most budget decisions have already been made.

The second resolution's ceiling cannot easily be overcome by resort to the reconciliation process authorized by Section 310 of the Budget Act. Under this procedure, congressional committees can be directed to report legislation to change *existing* laws that would cause revenues or expenditures to violate the second resolution.

Barring a radical change in political or economic circumstances during the interval between the two resolutions, the reconciliation process is not likely to offer much opportunity for reconsideration of past actions. The process is modeled after budgeting in the executive branch, in which budget targets are frequently revised prior to publication of the President's budget. But whereas executive decisions can be regarded as tentative—they are made in private and bind no one—legislative decisions have a conclusive character. They represent public commitments, and, especially when they confer benefits on identifiable interests, they are hard to roll back.

If the second resolution does not reexamine the past, neither does it usually mark out new directions for Congress. Although the Budget Committees are willing to accommodate some fresh initiatives in the second resolution, they do not countenance a wholesale consideration of new programs. "We do not want to fight the battle of the budget twice a year," is the way an SBC aide explained his committee's reluctance to consider new budget claims in the second resolution. A staff member of HBC offered another reason for limiting the scope of the fall resolution. "There is a big difference between treating the first resolution as a target or a floor. A target recognizes that circumstances change. Sometimes the changes result in a lower budget; sometimes they mean higher spending. But a floor assumes that the second resolution always will be higher

20. See H. Rept. No. 94-608 (1975) pp. 12 and 57-8.

than the first, regardless of whether economic circumstances warrant it."

Because the second resolution serves as a ratification of past actions, it consumes less time in committee and on the floor than the first resolution. It also stirs less conflict and attracts fewer amendments. Some of the issues that arouse interest during consideration of the first resolution reappear later in the year, but Congress appears to be merely updating its numbers rather than deciding the budget all over again.

THE THIRD RESOLUTION: SOMETHING OLD, SOMETHING NEW

The Budget Act permits Congress to revise its budget decisions any time during the fiscal year by adopting a third resolution. Congress can adopt additional resolutions for any reason, but it is likely to do so either to change the policies set in earlier resolutions or to accommodate to later developments. Congress exercised this option during fiscal 1977, shortly after Jimmy Carter took office. It is unnecessary to consider here whether the third resolution was more a response to political events than to economic changes—both factors spurred Congress to raise spending totals above the levels fixed in the second resolution. Clearly, the additional resolution was more than a confirmation of past decisions. Congress wanted to stimulate federal spending (and to change the tax laws as well), but it did not want a wholly new first resolution for the fiscal year then in progress. The third resolution was a hybrid, more than a second budget, but less than a first.

"We are not in the business here of rewriting the Second Concurrent Resolution,"[21] Muskie told his committee when it convened to develop the third resolution. Democratic leaders in Congress (including the Budget Committee chairmen) had worked out a package of new and expanded programs, and Muskie did not want the third resolution to go much beyond that. Nevertheless, once the door was opened to new programs, the Budget Committee could not preclude additional claims on the budget. "To some extent," Muskie acknowledged, "we may be asked to consider some items that we would not have considered if we didn't write a third reso-

21. Senate Budget Committee, markup of the third budget resolution for fiscal 1977, transcript, p. 182.

lution. . . . That ought not to open the door wide, and I don't have any prejudgments on the eight or nine [nonstimulus items] that we are being asked to consider, but it might affect our judgment on those."[22]

Actually, the House Budget Committee proved more receptive than SBC to additional initiatives. It endorsed more than a dozen such programs, adding $5 billion to the spending level previously sought by the White House.[23] But even for HBC, the third resolution was a limited search for spending opportunities. Although changes were made in most of the functions, most of these were reestimates, while the policy changes were concentrated in a few areas.

A third resolution was again used for fiscal 1979, but this time for a limited purpose.[24] After the second resolution for this fiscal year had been adopted, certain uncontrollable costs (mainly for interest on the public debt) rose above the budgeted level, thereby depleting funds which otherwise would have been available for supplemental appropriations. The Budget Committees were forced to revise the budget authority and outlay ceilings in order to accommodate the supplemental appropriation, but they took pains to insist that they were not to blame for the spending overruns. SBC averred that

> Congress has lived within the budget it adopted last fall in the Second Concurrent Budget Resolution for FY 1979. Since then events beyond the immediate control of Congress have occurred which require adjustments to that budget which do not result from the enactment of new spending legislation. . . . Were it not for these changed conditions, no adjustment to the Second Budget Resolution would be necessary, since Congressional actions on the FY79 budget, in the aggregate, have stayed below the levels estimated in the Second Budget Resolution.[25]

In opting for a revised resolution, the Budget Committees did not even consider the possibility of cutting elsewhere to offset the mandatory increases. Although the additional funds were for an anticipated supplemental appropriation, the Budget Committee had to make room for this congressional expectation in the same way

22. *Ibid.*, p. 132.
23. H. Rept. No. 95-12 (1977) p. 6.
24. The third resolution for fiscal 1979 was attached to the first resolution for the 1980 fiscal year. In this way, it attracted less attention than it would have if it had been advanced as a separate measure.
25. S. Rept. No. 96-68 (1979) p. 265.

that it accommodates the regular appropriation bills in its first resolutions.

AMENDING THE RESOLUTIONS

The Budget Committees have not always accommodated their resolutions to the expectations of their respective Houses. Sometimes they have been unsure of what was wanted or have preferred to go their own way. Sometimes unexpected circumstances have superseded a committee's decisions. In the event of unaccommodating budgets, the House and Senate can amend the resolutions to suit their preferences.

If floor amendments to budget resolutions connote failures in accommodation, the paucity of modifications by the House and Senate indicates that the Budget Committees have been fairly successful in budgeting according to the expectations of their chambers and in defending their recommendations against floor attack. More than 95 percent of SBC's functional allocations have been unchanged by the Senate, and although HBC cannot match this record, more than 70 percent of its recommendations have been adopted by the House. According to HBC staff, the committee's leaders sometimes welcome floor amendments as a means of inducing the sponsors to support the resolutions.

The House and Senate do not amend the budget resolutions merely to improve their bargaining position in conference. As table 28 shows, more than half of the floor changes have narrowed the differences between the two Houses. When a chamber modifies a functional allocation, it appears to be accommodating to the overall mood in Congress; hence it is more likely to move toward rather than away from the position taken by the other chamber.

Accommodating to the Senate

The data in table 28 indicate that the Senate Budget Committee has been more successful at accommodation than has the House committee. SBC's representative slate and bipartisan voting pattern enable that committee to accurately assess what the Senate wants. A revealing glimpse into SBC's accommodating instinct was provided during debate on one of the few changes the Senate made in a budget resolution. In marking up the second resolution for fiscal 1978, SBC had inadvertently failed to provide sufficient funds for

Table 28

CHANGES IN FUNCTIONAL LEVELS ADOPTED BY EACH HOUSE, FISCAL YEARS 1976-80

	House		Senate	
Direction of Change	*Number*	*Percent*	*Number*	*Percent*
No change	214	73.3	279	95.5
Change toward other body	52	17.8	5	1.7
Change away from other body	23	7.9	5	1.7
Same direction as other body	3	1.0	3	1.0
Total	292	100.0	292	100.0

Note: Includes all functional levels (excluding interest, allowances, and undistributed offsetting receipts) for all budget resolutions through the first resolution for fiscal 1980, but does not include changes in fiscal 1979 allocations attached to the first 1980 resolution. Percentages may not add to 100 because of rounding.

Source: Author's tabulations.

disaster relief, so Senator Nunn asked the Senate to add more than $1 billion for this purpose. Muskie was upset that his committee, whose budget decision had been based on OMB estimates, had been caught off guard. He explained that if his committee had been apprised of the situation, it "would have recommended a budget resolution that could accommodate that need."[26]

Sometimes the Senate Budget Committee has chosen not to accommodate. One such instance—SBC's drive for savings in medical and welfare payments in the face of objections from the Senate Finance Committee that the necessary legislation would not be forthcoming—has already been discussed. In that case, Senator Long's attempt to amend the budget resolution was thwarted by the Senate leadership's stand against all floor changes. In the following year, however, when the no-amendments practice fell, the Senate approved two spending increases that were obvious responses to SBC's deliberate failure to accommodate. One amendment restored $500 million in community development funds that SBC had cut in a second round of voting after it had previously allocated the full amount requested by the President. The second amendment provided funding for assisted housing programs at

26. 123 *Congressional Record* (September 9, 1977) S14519.

current policy levels (also the level requested by the President) after SBC had voted for a cutback in the program.

SBC's most blatant disregard of Senate expectations also led to its most stunning defeat. In May 1977, the Senate approved an expensive farm crop support program, overriding Muskie's objections that the legislation would violate the budget targets fixed only a few weeks earlier. When SBC marked up the second resolution several months later, it attached a reconciliation provision that would have compelled the Senate Agriculture Committee to report legislation trimming crop supports some $700 million below the level set in the farm bill (which had not yet cleared Congress, although House and Senate conferees had reached final agreement). The Senate responded to the failure to accommodate by deleting the reconciliation clause and by increasing the budget allocation for agriculture. More than half of the 13 amendments that the Senate had approved as of 1979 had been provoked by intentional disregard of Senate expectations. (See table 27 in chapter VII for a list of floor amendments.) Other amendments resulted from SBC's failure to accommodate to political pressure that could not be resisted by Senators exposed to it on the floor. In one case, SBC refused to allocate the full amount wanted by the Veterans' Affairs Committee, though it gave the veterans more than either the President or the Appropriations Committee had requested and more than the current policy level. In another, SBC refused to endorse tuition tax credits, legislation that had previously passed the Senate but had never been enacted into law.

Making Legislative History

When Members of Congress make budget decisions, they are concerned about funding for particular programs, not just the allocations for functional categories. But with little likelihood of amending the budget on the floor, Senators have devised other ways to accommodate the budget resolution to their program interests: they seek official assurance that the programs can be funded within the relevant functional allocation. Muskie's stock response was that if the Senate wants the program, there will be room for it in the budget, although other programs competing for the same allocation might be crowded out. The following exchange between Senators Ribicoff and Muskie shows how each side played its expected part:

Ribicoff: Is it the view of the chairman of the Budget Committee that there is enough room in the resolution's current health totals to accommodate this child health proposal? . . .

Muskie: Our recommended budget totals for the health function could accommodate this legislation. . . . Now the distribution of these funds will depend on the priorities of the Finance and Appropriations Committees. . . .

Ribicoff: Then, in other words, the committee's first resolution estimates within the total do not preclude any legislative action on the part of the Senate committee.[27]

Senators used Muskie's response to generate legislative support for their programs. When Senator Gary Hart inquired "whether or not the budget resolution we are considering today will be able to accommodate" an energy program in which he was interested, Muskie was noncommittal: "We do not preclude this program or any other program." But Hart managed to twist that reply into an endorsement, arguing that Muskie's response "indicates that the answer to my question is in the affirmative, that this program could be accommodated if, in fact, the authorizing committee so recommends."[28]

With Senators stretching ambiguous responses into firm legislative commitments, Muskie became wary about participating in these exchanges. He opened Senate debate on the 1978 budget with a plea "to avoid colloquies in support of funding for this or that program. . . . This debate should focus on broad totals and on any changes necessary to implement the national priorities of the Congress."[29] But Muskie could not keep silent when queried by interested colleagues; nor could he deny that room can be found in the budget for wanted programs. Moreover, by giving Delphic assurances to concerned Senators, Muskie could secure their support for SBC's budget resolutions without facing floor challenges that might escalate the federal deficit. The making of legislative history is thus an important part of the Senate's accommodation of the budget to its expectations.

Accommodating to the House

If one judges by the number of budgetary changes made by the House, HBC has proved less successful than SBC in accommodating to the interests of its chamber. Not only has the House ap-

27. 123 *Congressional Record* (May 4, 1977) S7037.
28. 124 *Congressional Record* (April 25, 1978) S6285.
29. 123 *Congressional Record* (May 3, 1977) S6916.

proved three times as many amendments to budget resolutions, but also it has added substantial amounts to spending on veterans' programs, as well as smaller increases for other functions.

This pattern needs explanation. One would expect the House Budget Committee to be quite solicitous for the preferences of its parent body. After all, budget resolutions encounter difficulties in the House, and it would seem logical for the committee to draft a budget with majority appeal. The explanation for the pattern that has developed, however, comes in three parts: one pertains to the makeup of the committee, another to the budget preferences of the House, and a third to the types of amendments that have been approved.

Committee Makeup. Except for conservative Democrats, voting in HBC has always been dominated by party identifications. In the first two years of the budget process, the majority party was not always able to get satisfaction in committee because defectors frequently voted with the other side. O'Neill's amendments to the 1976 budget were accommodations that could have been made in committee had it not been for the defections. In the following year, O'Neill won his accommodation in committee, but by only a one-vote margin. HBC was not representative of the 95th Congress (1977-78), for the committee's Democratic members were significantly more liberal than were most other Democrats in the House. The liberal majority was able to write its preferences into the budget resolutions even when sentiment in the House appeared to be leaning the other way. For example, in 1977 HBC targeted $4 billion less for defense than the figure the Democratic President had recommended.

The only legislative committees that can afford to be long out of step with their chamber are ones that have no legislation to pass or are willing to lose a vote on the floor in order to advance other objectives. HBC cannot afford to lose; it must get its only legislative product passed, at least twice a year. It is not surprising, therefore, that after the problems in the 95th Congress, HBC became more accommodating in the 96th Congress.

An indication of this change was HBC's success in defending its first resolution for fiscal 1980 against floor attack. Although every functional allocation was altered by an across-the-board cut of 0.5 percent, HBC's basic posture survived intact. What made its feat most impressive was the sheer number of amendments bombarding the resolution from every direction. With the election of the 96th Congress, almost half of the committee's Democrats were replaced, and because most of the newcomers came from the broad center of the party, the committee's balance was improved and the group became more representative of the House. Moreover, HBC itself was affected by the growing budgetary conservatism in the House. As a result, some HBC members such as Chairman Giaimo took a more moderate position during markup. In sum, HBC produced a less liberal budget for fiscal 1980 than some of its members wanted, and in so doing it accommodated itself to the majority of the House.

House Budget Preferences. Legislative committees—even unrepresentative ones—usually try to anticipate House reactions. Thus, Giaimo offered a committee amendment to add $500 million for defense to 1978's second resolution, to make it conform to the defense appropriation bill. In the same year, HBC abstained from contesting an amendment by the chairman of the House Agriculture Committee increasing budget outlays to accommodate the controversial farm bill. When the House Ways and Means Committee recommended a tuition tax credit that Giaimo had vigorously opposed in the past, Giaimo advised the House

> that the Budget Committee position is no longer a valid one, in my opinion. . . . Since we formed this majority conclusion [against the tuition credits] in the Committee on the Budget, events have superseded us, as I stated, and we could accommodate ourselves . . . to what I think is the will of the House and the will of the Committee on Ways and Means.[30]

HBC's problem has been that it cannot always discern the will of the House. In voting on budget resolutions, the House has consistently split into four overlapping camps: a liberal minority that wants more domestic spending, a conservative minority that yearns for a balanced budget, a near-majority that seeks to slash spending, and a slight majority that supports HBC's effort to accommodate the program interests of the House. One reason for the comparative frequency of House amendments is that the last group is not sufficiently powerful to ward off appealing floor changes.

Types of Amendments That Have Been Approved. Some amendments are not responses to "unaccommodating" budgets but have other purposes. Perhaps one-third of the successful amendments, including the amendments by committees, symbolic amendments, and reestimates, have been of this kind. In the other two-

---

30. 124 *Congressional Record* (May 4, 1978) H3599.

thirds, HBC's expectations were close to those of the committee of jurisdiction, but HBC lost the vote on the floor because the budget process gave Members an opportunity to force a vote on issues long bottled up in committee. A floor amendment to the second resolution in fiscal 1978 was the first House vote on tuition tax credits, a measure previously barred by closed rules. In the previous year, the House had augmented veterans spending, with 13 of the 28 members of the Veterans' Affairs Committee, including the chairman and ranking minority member, in opposition.

The voting on tuition tax credits and veterans programs in the House (and in the Senate as well) indicates that the budget process is not neutral with respect to the expectations of Congress. By enabling claimants to bypass closed legislative channels and forcing recorded votes on popular issues, the budget process can give a boost to previously suppressed aspirations.

Rejecting the Resolution

The ultimate sanction for nonaccommodation is for the House or Senate to withhold its approval of the resolution. Even with an opportunity to amend the resolution on the floor, the chamber might be dissatisfied with the final product because, as has often been noted, Members have to be satisfied with respect to two discrete and sometimes conflicting matters: the budget's totals, including the projected deficit, and the mix of expenditures among the various budget functions. Members may simultaneously be pleased that their programs are provided for in the budget, but chagrined at the size of the deficit; or they may consider the spending total acceptable but disapprove of the amounts allocated for particular programs. In either case, Members might express their discontent by voting against adoption of the resolution.

Although the Senate has not faced this predicament, the House has twice rejected resolutions which it subsequently approved once comparatively minor changes had been made in particular functions. Both rejections resulted from failures in accommodation, but the circumstances were quite different. In the rejection of the first resolution for fiscal 1978, the House voted significant program increases for a number of categories, but the increases made the deficit unacceptably high for some Members and the expenditures for various programs too high for others. The 1978 episode shows that the best road to accommodation is not always through concessions to each program or interest.

Another instance occurred in the final stages of the first resolution for 1980. The conference on the resolution had produced a compromise tilting slightly toward the Senate on one of the major disagreements between the two chambers—the allocation for education. After heavy lobbying from liberal quarters, the House rejected the conference report by a lopsided margin. The House was piqued not only by the timidity of its negotiators, but also by the likelihood that the education allocation would be too little for the education appropriation expected to be reported by the House Appropriations Committee. The failure to accommodate the needs of the Appropriations Committee was remedied by the addition of a small amount ($350 million in budget authority), after which the House approved the resolution.

Although there have been only two outright rejections of Budget Committee resolutions in the House, the numerous close calls attest to the difficulty of accommodating to a chamber that is so deeply divided on budget policy. If the budget process is to survive, either the House membership will have to become more cohesive on budget policies or the House will have to lower its expectations concerning the budget process. Cohesion or reduced expectations would simplify the Budget Committee's task of producing an accommodating budget.

PATTERNS OF ACCOMMODATION

Accommodating budgets are made in distinctive ways and have distinctive outcomes. They treat budget decisions in distributive terms—how much should be allocated to particular programs and functions—thereby avoiding the redistributive issues latent in every budget process. Rather than explicitly pitting programs against one another in open competition for scarce funds, they compartmentalize the budget into discrete segments, handling each part as a separable policy issue. Accommodating budgets rely on the "growth dividend" from an expanding economy to change national priorities and they are not likely to veer radically from previous patterns of expenditure. The result is a budget more anchored in past decisions than in future opportunities, but a budget that mitigates conflict within Congress and between the legislative and executive branches.

Avoiding Overt Congressional Priorities

When the Budget Act was being written, many reformers hoped that the new process would occasion an annual "priorities debate" within Congress. The various budget functions would compete for limited resources, with more for one category portending less for others. The House Rules Committee endorsed this concept in its version of the budget reform legislation. Congress, it argued,

> should have the opportunity to determine spending priorities by comparing the relative value of each program area within a comprehensive budget process. Because the present system is fragmented, with decisions stretching over many months, Congress has no real opportunity to decide spending priorities. It would be given this opportunity if the initial budget resolution set forth the appropriate target for each category.[31]

Despite these expectations, the budget process has not triggered a fresh examination of national priorities. In fact, Congress did more reordering of budget priorities before it had a budget process than it has since. Table 29 reveals that between 1969 and 1975, there was a massive shift in the relative shares of national defense and income security, the largest categories in the budget. Defense dropped from almost one-half to one-quarter of total outlays. Income security took over first place, growing from one-fifth to fully one-third of the budget, and accounting for half the total increase in outlays from 1969 through 1975.

The post-1975 shifts have been on a much smaller scale. Energy has doubled its budget share but is still one of the smaller categories. Agriculture's portion also has climbed, but it has not regained the share it held in 1972. Fiscal assistance (revenue sharing) and international affairs have declined, although the absolute spending levels for each of these categories have been relatively stable. The shares of commerce and housing have slipped more as a result of accounting practices than of legislative policy.[32]

People who have wanted the congressional budget to be a contest over national priorities and a means to change existing priorities have been greatly disappointed. Accommodating budget

---

31. H. Rept. No. 93-658 (November 20, 1973) p. 33.
32. For example, receipts from the sale of participation certificates and mortgages by the Government National Mortgage Association fluctuate substantially from year to year. Since these receipts are treated as negative expenditures, they cause wide swings in budgeted outlays, even when program levels are stable.

makers avoid explicit trade-offs among the functions, preferring instead to treat each as a discrete policy choice. The Budget Committees compartmentalize spending decisions as they work through the roster of functions until they have completed the list. At no time in the first five years of budgeting did either committee explicitly vote to take money from one area to give more to another, though package deals negotiated in private reckoned with the relative allocation among functions. Although the Budget Committees begin with an overview of economic conditions and have a general idea of what they expect the totals to be, neither decides the aggregates until it has made the functional allocations. Senator Muskie explained SBC's markup procedure in resisting a floor move to shift funds from defense to domestic programs. The committee, he said, goes "through each of the 19 functions of the budget carefully, without carrying any total target for spending. . . . Each function's total and, indeed, the missions within each function, are addressed in that fashion. There is no arbitrary ceiling imposed on domestic spending. There is an honest attempt to address legitimate needs in each function."[33]

A similar procedure was outlined by HBC's Robert Giaimo in responding to Republican proposals to make functional decisions only after the budget's totals have been determined. He explained that "if we attempt to set overall budget limits without going into the specific functional categories and taking into account programs and activities which may be funded, we will be proceeding in a factual vacuum. . . . there is no way for us to know what the implications of such a procedure would be for various programs.[34] Members of the Budget Committees are careful to avoid structuring their decisions in ways that might be construed as shifting funds among the functions. Thus, when Sen. J. Glenn Beall suggested adding funds for social programs after SBC had cut funds for defense, he took pains to divorce his proposal from the previous action: "I am not doing this with the idea we are making a trade-off between defense and other parts of the budget. I think that that is very dangerous . . . I do not want to associate this increase with any cut in the defense budget."[35]

Accommodating budgets are made piecemeal because Congress does not have a single or homogeneous interest that it seeks to

33. 124 *Congressional Record* (April 25, 1978) S6243.

34. *Ibid.*, (May 2, 1978) H3418.

35. Senate Budget Committee, markup of the first concurrent resolution for fiscal 1976, transcript, p. 538.

Table 29

DISTRIBUTION OF FEDERAL BUDGET OUTLAYS BY FUNCTION, SELECTED FISCAL YEARS
(dollars in millions)

	Actual Budget Outlays						*Second Budget Resolution*	
Function	*1969*	*Percent of Total*	*1972*	*Percent of Total*	*1975*	*Percent of Total*	*1980*	*Percent of Total*
National Defense	$ 79,418	43.0	$ 76,550	33.0	$ 85,550	26.2	$129,900	23.7
International Affairs	4,573	2.5	4,674	2.0	6,861	2.1	8,400	1.5
General Science	5,016	2.7	4,174	1.8	3,989	1.2	5,700	1.0
Energy	1,001	0.5	1,270	0.5	2,179	0.7	7,250	1.3
Natural Resources	2,848	1.5	4,195	1.8	7,329	2.2	11,900	2.2
Agriculture	5,779	3.1	5,279	2.3	1,660	0.5	2,550	0.5
Commerce and Housing Credit	553	0.3	2,206	0.9	5,604	1.7	2,850	0.5
Transportation	6,531	3.5	8,395	3.6	10,392	3.2	18,600	3.4

Community Development	1,545	0.8	3,413	1.5	3,692	1.1	8,350	1.5
Education, Training, Employment, and Social Sciences	7,538	4.1	12,519	5.4	15,870	4.9	31,000	5.7
Health	11,758	6.4	17,471	7.5	27,647	8.5	54,450	9.9
Income Security	37,281	20.2	63,911	27.5	108,605	33.3	190,000	34.7
Veterans' Benefits	7,640	4.1	10,730	4.6	16,597	5.1	20,800	3.8
Law Enforcement and Justice	761	0.4	1,650	0.7	2,942	0.9	4,400	0.8
General Government	1,649	0.9	2,466	1.0	3,089	0.9	4,200	0.8
Fiscal Assistance	430	0.2	673	0.3	7,187	2.2	9,050	1.7
Interest	15,793	8.6	20,582	8.9	30,974	9.5	58,100	10.6
Allowances	—	—	—	—	—	—	6,200	0.1
Offsetting Receipts	−5,545	−3.0	−8,137	−3.5	−14,075	−4.3	−19,700	−3.6
Total	$184,548	100.0	$232,021	100.0	$326,092	100.0	$554,000	100.0

Note: Percentages may not total 100 because of rounding.

Source: *Budget of the United States Government, Fiscal Year 1977,* and S. Rept. No. 96-399.

maximize in the budget process. Congress is itself a coming together of diverse interests; the Budget Committees satisfy Congress by satisfying particular interests. They accommodate by breaking the budget into its parts and deciding how much to allocate to each. While the piecemeal approach progresses with an eye on the totals and concern as to how the partial decisions add up to the budget, claims are not openly pitted against one another. The competition is ever present, but usually muted.

The budget process is neatly structured to facilitate this accommodation to the parts. Each function covers a portion of the interests at work in Congress. Some of the functions (defense, agriculture, and veterans, for example) correspond to distinct interests within Congress; some (such as income security and the education, training, employment, and social services category) are groupings for a number of interests, each of which must be watchful that the allocation covers its wants. A few important national interests—housing is the leading case—are submerged in the categories, and affected parties have to sift through various parts of the budget to assure that they are tended to.

When Members of Congress address the question "How much priority should be accorded to a function?" they are not referring to the function's relative value but to its particular needs, that is, the programs budgeted within it. They want to know whether an allocation will cover existing programs or force cutbacks, whether it will allow real growth or only an adjustment for inflation. They make priority decisions by comparing the allocation for a function with the allocation made to the same function in the previous year. Their most important calculations are within, not between, functions.

Yet Congress does not consider itself inactive with respect to budgetary priorities. It defines priorities in terms of giving each function its due, more or less than it got last year, more or less than the President wants, more or less than current policy. Priority setting is usually at the margins, a little more versus a little less for each function. Members who seek to reorder budget priorities tend to be impatient with marginal changes. But marginal change is a way of containing conflicts by accommodating to past decisions while responding to new claims.

The House and Senate have rebuffed all proposals to reorder the budget's priorities by taking from one function and giving to another. The first such "transfer" amendment was proposed by HBC liberal Elizabeth Holtzman for the 1977 budget. "I am deeply disturbed," she protested to the House, "that the budget we are presented with this time fails to carry out the essential promise of the Budget Act—to set congressional priorities and to address the serious problems facing this country."[36] Another House liberal, Richard Ottinger, exulted:

> I believe for the first time in the history of this body, we have an opportunity to present this body with a choice of real priorities, in one motion. We have a chance to weigh in this amendment a cut in the fat and waste in the Defense Department against badly needed social programs at home. . . .
>
> Many of us have talked for years about reordering priorities; this is our chance to do it.[37]

The House did not take the bait. It gave the transfer amendment fewer votes than any other floor amendment to that year's budget. The 85-317 rejection had all but one Republican and a majority of the Democrats lined up in opposition. This outcome has been repeated in subsequent years. In 1978 HBC's Parren Mitchell carried the ball for the transfer amendment: "I wanted to get on the Budget Committee—I was anxious to serve on it . . . [but] this Budget Committee has produced a first budget resolution which does not establish priorities."[38] This time the transfer scheme was rejected by a 102-306 margin, with the voting pattern similar to the previous year's. The House had an additional opportunity in the 1979 budget, but again (by a 98-313 vote) it decided against shifting funds from defense to domestic programs.

In fiscal 1980, Mitchell abandoned the transfer route and sought more funds for domestic programs through increased revenues, but the outcome was no different; the House rejected his proposal by a 130-277 vote.

Transfer has fared no better in the Senate. George McGovern attempted to redistribute $4.6 billion in the fiscal 1979 budget from defense to several domestic functions: $2 billion for education, employment, and social services; $1.9 billion for energy; and lesser amounts for transportation and community development. McGovern's ploy was quite obvious: By voting for the transfer, Senators would be able to add funds for cherished projects without increasing the deficit. But the plan did not work; McGovern's

---

36. 122 *Congressional Record* (April 27, 1976) H3455.
37. *Ibid.*, (April 29, 1976) H3558.
38. 123 *Congressional Record* (April 26, 1977) H3558.

amendment was overwhelmed, 14 to 77, receiving fewer votes than any other Senate amendment to the 1979 budget.

For fiscal 1980, McGovern sought to shift half the funds that would be cut from defense to various domestic categories (energy, transportation, and education), and the other half to a reduction in the budget deficit. But this move also failed by a wide margin, 24 to 69.

Congress has no tolerance for the conflict that would be generated by open competition among functions. Precisely because the budget process reminds Congress of the fact that more for one function can mean less for others, it prefers to decide each function in turn, thereby playing down the inevitable tensions of budgeting. The budget that emerges from this process is nobody's ordering of preferences. It does not conform in all its particulars to any Member's comparative preferences, let alone to those of a congressional majority. It does not have to be anyone's budget because most Members have strong feelings about only a few of the items in it. If they are satisfied about these, and not deeply disturbed by the total spending and deficit levels, they can be persuaded to vote for the budget resolutions.

Consensual priorities are acceptable to Members who strongly favor some parts of the budget and are indifferent about the others. Their price for going along with the budget is to have their priorities satisfied, leaving others to take care of matters on which they are indifferent. It was on this basis that Muskie prodded the stalled House-Senate conference on the 1978 budget to resolve its disagreements, saying, "I have learned in this key spot of chairing the Senate Budget Committee that if I want to advance those budgetary objectives in which I am interested, I have got to recognize the budget priorities that others entertain, and I have got to be willing to support the final product." [39] When the conferees finally reached agreement on the 1978 budget, Muskie rallied support for it as a "careful and delicate balance of priorities . . . the budget process is built upon the balancing of needs, upon flexibility and compromise." [40] It was a consensual budget in which no side got all that it wanted and there was no announced reordering of national objectives.

Consensual budgets, however, do not appeal to Members of Congress who strongly oppose certain programs. Those who would

39. Conference committee on the first concurrent resolution for fiscal 1978, transcript, p. 151.

40. 123 *Congressional Record* (May 13, 1977) S7537.

take from defense not only want more for domestic needs; they also want less for the military. Such people make accommodation difficult because the programs they want to cut have strong advocates within Congress.

Accommodating Through Budgetary Growth

Accommodating budgets mitigate conflict by limiting competition for funds. Instead of reshaping priorities by cutting budgets, Congress sets different rates of growth for the various parts of the budget. A function's priority thus hinges on its share of the growth portion of the budget. Over time, the relative values of the functions change because they grow at different rates. Between 1972 and 1975, defense spending rose by $10 billion, but this category's share dropped because other parts of the budget had higher growth rates. During the same years, outlays for income security rose by 70 percent. About half the increase in federal outlays went to income security, compared with only 10 percent for defense.

Table 30 shows the growth rates set in the first resolutions for

Table 30

PERCENT DEVIATION OF FUNCTIONAL ALLOCATIONS FROM CURRENT POLICY (OR CURRENT LAW) ESTIMATES, FIRST BUDGET RESOLUTION, FISCAL YEARS 1977-80

Function		*1977*	*1978*	*1979*	*1980*
National Defense	BA [a]	2.8%	0.1%	1.7%	3.8%
	O [b]	−1.3	−0.1	0.7	0.4
International Affairs	BA	−2.1	24.3	26.7	9.5
	O	−5.7	4.7	−2.8	8.2
General Science	BA	−6.1	3.0	NC [b]	7.6
	O	−4.2	1.4	NC	5.7
Energy	BA	—	—	23.8	334.8
	O	—	—	6.5	−11.7
Natural Resources	BA	58.9	3.3	−0.7	−3.1
	O	3.3	3.7	−0.8	−0.8
Agriculture	BA	−4.2	−20.4	66.2	+2.0
	O	NC	41.1	25.8	+3.8
Commerce and Housing	BA	20.5	4.7	3.5	−4.2
	O	−4.8	−0.5	2.9	NC

(Continued)

Table 30

PERCENT DEVIATION OF FUNCTIONAL ALLOCATIONS FROM CURRENT POLICY (OR CURRENT LAW) ESTIMATES, FIRST BUDGET RESOLUTION, FISCAL YEARS 1977-80 (Cont.)

Function		*1977*	*1978*	*1979*	*1980*
Transportation	BA	—	—	27.7	+3.5
	O	—	—	0.4	−2.7
Community and Regional	BA	−9.8	11.1	27.5	+4.7
Development	O	−9.3	0.8	1.1	1.3
Education, Training, and	BA	14.4	−1.8	7.8	−0.1
Social Service	O	8.5	−0.3	4.0	−3.2
Health	BA	−2.2	0.8	−0.3	0.3
	O	−2.3	−1.2	−1.2	−3.1
Income Security	BA	−13.4	2.8	−0.8	−2.8
	O	−3.9	−0.8	0.9	−0.4
Veterans' Benefits	BA	0.5	4.9	3.9	1.9
	O	−1.0	4.4	4.0	1.5
Administration of Justice	BA	−5.5	NC	4.9	2.3
	O	−5.4	2.2	2.4	NC
General Government	BA	−7.8	4.1	−2.1	2.3
	O	−10.3	4.0	−2.4	2.4
Fiscal Assistance	BA	0.7	0.2	6.6	−4.7
	O	−6.8	−0.4	5.5	−4.7

[a] BA = Budget authority.
[b] O = Outlay.

Source: Reports of the House and Senate Committees on the Budget on the various budget resolutions. The percentages for 1977-79 are computed in terms of current policy; the percentages for fiscal 1980 are based on current law. Current policy adjusts every category for inflation, regardless of whether an adjustment is provided for in law or whether the program is scheduled for termination. Current law allows adjustments for inflation only when provided for by law.

1977 through 1980. The rates are computed as percentage deviations from the current policy baseline, thereby revealing the instances where Congress has provided less or more than inflation adjustments. A zero growth rate usually means that Congress has provided the amount necessary to maintain programs without policy change; a negative rate usually occurs when Congress adjusts spending at less than the expected increase in program costs; a positive growth rate usually allows real growth in the function. (Sometimes, however, a change in growth rate takes place with no overt decision. For example, a recession will automatically increase outlay growth for programs tied to the unemployment rate, such as unemployment insurance.) The importance attached to energy programs in the second half of the 1970s is reflected in the high growth allowed the natural resources and energy functions; agriculture's growth stemmed from enactment of major farm legislation in 1977 and 1978. Although there have been numerous negative real growth rates, in most cases, the allocation for the budget category has increased, but not enough to keep pace with anticipated inflation.

Changes in growth rates mirror shifts in public opinion. Defense has been the prime illustration. In the first year of the budget process, Congress made steep cuts in the President's defense request, continuing the pattern that had begun with the U.S. disengagement from Vietnam. But in the second year, Congress allowed for real growth in defense spending, reversing eight years of uninterrupted decline in the purchasing power of the defense budget. Congress was signaling a turnabout in its budget priorities, even though the modest real growth did not halt further erosion in defense's share of the budget. This congressional shift was consistent with a change in public attitudes toward defense. Potomac Associates' 1976 survey of public opinion reported that "the nationwide extent of increased approval for military and defense spending [compared with its survey two years earlier] . . . is little short of phenomenal."[41] The survey also found more public support for expenditures to develop self-sufficiency in energy than for any other sector of the budget, a consensus reflected in the high growth for energy programs.

Because Congress has long shaped national priorities by controlling growth rates rather than by forcing a head-on contest for funds, it could redistribute budgetary shares even before it had a comprehensive budget process. The 1972-75 shifts did not come about accidentally but reflected congressional intent to lower real defense spending and expand income transfers. Conversely, the activation of a budget process has not necessarily significantly changed spending patterns. Indeed, it is arguable that the budget process has stabilized the distribution of budget shares, and that by focusing attention on budget priorities, it has complicated the task of reordering them. In the past, Congress reordered budgetary

41. Edwin L. Dale and others, *Priorities in an Uncertain Economy: Inflation, Recession, and Government Spending* (Washington, D.C.: Potomac Associates, p. 21.

priorities by fragmenting its budget decisions. Congress never had to vote on redistribution; nor were the overall effects of its actions on budget shares known until after decisions were made. Under the old system, redistribution was facilitated by the ignorance of the losers. Often they did not know how their programs' growth rates compared with those of other parts of the budget, or whether the increases provided for individual programs would protect current policy levels. Congress was able to vote budget increases while diminishing a particular program's share of the budget.

By forcing simultaneous decisions on all parts of the budget, the new process has made all participants aware of distributive outcomes. Before the budget resolution is voted on, information is made available on current functional allocations and on deviations from current policy levels. It is not hard to find out who is winning and who is losing. The March 15 views and estimates give program supporters a convenient procedure to seek support for their interests. With budget priorities cast through a comprehensive budget process, the shifts are more likely to be marginal than radical.

By bringing all budget-related decisions within its orbit, the budget process has impeded the rearrangement of priorities through nonbudgetary actions such as entitlements and other types of backdoor legislation. The steep growth in income security from one-fifth of the budget at the beginning of the 1970s to one-third at mid-decade resulted, in substantial part, from legislative action establishing new entitlements such as the Supplemental Security Income program, food stamps, and payments to black-lung victims as well as discretionary expansion of existing programs such as Social Security. These actions were taken without a judgment by Congress on the relative value of income security *vis-à-vis* other claims on the budget and usually without full knowledge of the impact of these programs on future budgets. Income security escalated because it was not constrained by budgetary information or controls. But all legislative actions affecting revenues and expenditures are now related to the budget by scorekeeping reports and cost projections. The effect has been to inhibit legislative ventures that vest programs with high growth rates.

Accommodating to Economic Conditions

In order for accommodating budgets to shift the relative emphasis of the budget without reducing functional allocations, Congress must have a growth dividend that it can "spend" on favored functions and programs. If it had no dividend, Congress's only redistributive options would be to transfer funds among budget categories (opening up the legislative conflicts that accommodating budget makers seek to avoid) or to finance growth through deficit spending (a course of action permitted by the Budget Act for which Congress must take explicit responsibility). Economic growth is an essential condition for peaceful redistribution of budget shares.

Since 1975, Congress has acted as if it lacked a growth option. It has been afflicted by a sense of scarcity, of a need to cut back or at least slow the rise in government costs. These low-growth expectations preceded the Budget Act. It will be recalled from chapter II that talk about the need to set priorities entered budgetary discourse in the late 1960s when the federal government was confronted by the escalating costs of the Vietnam War and pressures to fund its Great Society initiatives. Alarmed by the spiraling spending, chronic deficits, and growth in uncontrollable programs, Congress accepted a budget process that made Congress more responsible for its actions. The effect of the 1974 Act on budgetary growth has depended more on the conditions under which it had operated than on the procedures written into it.

Congress has not reverted to high-growth expectations because the economy has not produced "fiscal dividends" and because political pressures have constrained its appetite for spending. This section examines the economic conditions under which congressional budgeting has been practiced; the purpose is to assess the impact of the economy on Congress, not the impact of Congress on fiscal policy. The following section looks at one of the political constraints on budgetary growth, the budgetary policies of Presidents Ford and Carter.

The budget process was launched in a period of economic adversity. When the Budget Committees set their targets in early 1975, 8 million Americans were out of work, more than at any time since the Great Depression. The unemployment rate was still climbing; it had reached 8 percent in February 1975 and would peak at 8.9 percent three months later. Economic output had suffered a real decline (—7.5 percent) in the last quarter of 1974 and an even steeper drop (—9.6 percent) in the first quarter of 1975. Most indicators of economic activity were depressed: the duration of unemployment was up while real wages dropped; one-third of the manufacturing capacity of the United States was idle; housing starts were barely half of what they had been two years earlier.

By any measure, the nation was in the throes of its worst postwar recession.

The economic tailspin had come with devastating suddenness. Through 1974, most economists had concentrated on the double-digit inflation (a 12 percent annual rate) ignited by critical food and fuel shortages. In September 1974, President Ford announced an anti-inflation drive, proposing a 5 percent surtax on individual and corporate incomes and a $300 billion limit on federal spending. In November, he sent Congress a list of $4.6 billion in proposed outlay reductions and renewed his plea for fiscal restraint. As the economy deteriorated, however, Ford was compelled to shift to a stimulative policy. In his fiscal 1976 budget (issued in February 1975), Ford acknowledged that "the economy is now in a recession," and asked for a $16 billion tax cut. Yet he also spoke of the need "to keep the budget from perpetuating inflation," and therefore proposed about $17 billion in spending reductions in the budget. The budget projected a $51.9 billion deficit; this amount was raised to $59.7 billion a few months later after Congress had passed a larger-than-requested tax cut, and reestimates had raised spending for certain programs above their budgeted levels.

Both Budget Committees wanted a budget that would be more stimulative than the President's. SBC pronounced the recession "the most serious since the 1930's and the trend is mostly down. Unemployment . . . is likely to get worse in the months ahead."[42] The Senate's budget makers forecast that the President's proposals would yield an unemployment rate of 8.5 percent by the end of calendar 1976. HBC warned that "unless Congress acts decisively, it is extremely unlikely that the economy can correct itself without undue human suffering."[43] Yet Congress's budgetary response was restrained; Congress did not throw fiscal caution to the wind in an effort to put millions of Americans back to work. The resolution adopted in May 1975 targeted a $68.8 billion deficit, with outlays approximately $12 billion above the latest presidential estimates. Most of this increase resulted from congressional rejection of Ford's budget reductions, but about $7 billion was targeted for public works and public service employment. Budget experts outside Congress estimated that this legislative stimulus might shave 0.5 percent off the unemployment rate: "Thus the anticipated

42. S. Rept. No. 94-77 (April 15, 1975) p. 7.
43. H. Rept. No. 94-145 (April 14, 1975) p. 5.

economic recovery set in motion under the congressional budget is still likely to be modest."[44]

The Budget Committees responded to the fiscal crisis by accommodating to the program expectations of Congress. They rejected the program cuts that Congress was not inclined to enact and promoted the programs that Congress appeared ready to accept. By its own account, HBC "attempted to produce a counter-recessionary plan by providing spending authority for nearly every stimulative program that has been passed by a House committee, passed by the House, or recommended by the House leadership."[45] For the most part, HBC endorsed programs that had already been approved by the House (such as the emergency jobs appropriation bill passed by the House) or appeared on their way to approval. HBC added its support for Democratic public service employment programs, but it did not launch an all-out drive to promote economic recovery. The committee wanted more stimulation than the President sought, but not much more.

SBC's budget was even less stimulative. It rejected Mondale's plea for a $12 billion anti-recession program and retained the $4.5 billion set aside for economic recovery by a seven-to-seven vote. The Senate committee urged Congress "to go slow in this area," expressing "skepticism that programs that are designed to be temporary will in fact prove to be temporary."[46] SBC insisted that there is "little room for expanding the level of permanent government programs . . . this fiscal discipline is important in order to insure an appropriate fiscal policy when full employment is achieved."[47] To discourage program expansion under the guise of aiding economic recovery, SBC adopted a two-budget approach, separating temporary recovery activities from the fiscal base. SBC alerted the Senate to the value of countercyclical budget policy, though the amount targeted for this purpose was quite limited.

The Budget Committees were restrained in their response to the perceived economic crisis because unemployment was not their only concern; they also had to wrestle with inflation and the deficit. Although inflation had subsided from its 12 percent peak, it still troubled many Members. SBC insisted that "the fiscal 1976 budget

44. Barry M.. Blechman and others, *Setting National Priorities: The 1976* Budget (Washington, D.C.: The Brookings Institution, 1975), p. 236.

45. 121 *Congressional Record* (April 30, 1975) H3456, remarks of Representative Adams.

46. S. Rept. 94-77 (April 15, 1975) p. 19.

47. *Ibid.*, p. 17.

should be planned with both recession and inflation in mind . . . in combating the one problem, Congress must avoid actions that could lead to major inflation in the years ahead." [48] It therefore urged policy restraint in those areas which would commit the nation to new spending programs.[49] HBC was confident that the slack economy could handle the stimulus without provoking more inflation, but it was nonetheless reluctant to advocate additional expenditures that would enlarge the deficit.

The size of the deficit was the biggest obstacle to providing more economic stimulus. The $70 billion deficit was a peacetime record, though less than what some private economists had endorsed and many fiscal conservatives had feared.[50] Both Budget Committees took pains to assure Congress that the deficit was caused by the recession, not by legislative actions. HBC widely advertised its estimate that each 1 percent rise in unemployment would increase the deficit by $16 billion. On this basis, the committee claimed, the deficit was not the product "of profligate federal spending, but of deteriorating economic conditions." [51] According to HBC's calculations, its budget would have had a very small deficit if the economy had been booming. SBC specifically "built its budget on the principle that the fiscal base [permanent programs] should not exceed the revenues that existing tax laws would produce if the employment rate were at 4 percent." [52] With this policy, the Budget Committees had to rely on the "automatics" in the budget—falling tax revenues, rising unemployment compensation, and rising welfare payments—plus the previously passed tax cut to provide the bulk of the stimulus.

The deficit alarmed not only conservatives who opposed the first resolutions, but also middle-of-the-road Democrats whose votes were essential for passage of the budget targets. SBC's Joe Biden admitted "the inevitability, even desirability, of a deficit under present economic conditions," but added, "I do not believe

48. *Ibid.*, p. 26.
49. Muskie and SBC economists tried to educate committee members to countercyclical fiscal strategies, in which temporary programs would be triggered or terminated by changing economic conditions, rather than permanent programs which would continue after the economy has recovered.
50. With off-budget agencies added, the deficit was about $80 billion, near the upper range suggested by many of the economists testifying before the budget committees.
51. H. Rept. No. 94-145 (April 14, 1975) p. 6.
52. S. Rept. No. 94-77 (April 15, 1975) p. 17.

that we can literally spend our way out of a recession through massive 'temporary' spending programs without risking serious secondary effects."[53] HBC's Jim Wright voted for the budget resolution but argued that the deficit "could and should be reduced by prudent economies."[54] His colleague, Thomas Ashley, also supported the committee's work, but expressed "serious concern . . . over the size and composition of the anticipated deficit."[55] Robert Giaimo used stronger language, registering "profound concern over the unqualified optimism with which the effect of the recommended deficit has been presented."[56] All these Democrats voted for the budget resolution but their concern about the deficit dampened the congressional response to economic crisis.

Budget Committee liberals who wanted more money for economic recovery also were hemmed in by the deficit. They wanted a reordering of priorities to shift funds to domestic needs without enlarging the deficit. HBC's Elizabeth Holtzman voted against reporting the first resolution:

> I do not agree that we need a deficit of $73.2 billion in order to fight the recession or that the country can easily afford deficit spending of this magnitude . . . the deficit should be reduced without requiring cuts in spending on human needs or impairing our ability to fight the recession.[57]

SBC's Cranston voted for the resolution despite his concern that the "temporary programs in the Committee budget will not be enough—either to promote a rapid reduction in the rate of unemployment, or to bring about a prompt recovery from our deep recession."[58] He nevertheless urged the Senate to hold the line on the deficit, but he asked for a $4 billion cut in defense spending. A majority in Congress, however, was not prepared to reduce defense spending beyond the sizable cuts the Budget Committees had already recommended. Since there was great reluctance to increase the deficit, Congress was limited to a modest antirecession budget.

The 1976 congressional budget was voted on during the trough in economic activity. As economic conditions improved, the size

53. *Ibid.*, p. 124.
54. H. Rept. 94-145 (April 14, 1975) p. 70.
55. *Ibid.*, p. 71.
56. *Ibid.*, p. 75.
57. *Ibid.*, p. 114.
58. S. Rept. No. 94-77 (April 15, 1975) p. 132.

of the deficit was reduced, but legislators' apprehensions persisted. In the face of continuing high levels of unemployment (still above 7.5 percent), Congress approved a 1977 budget with total spending below the current policy level for the fiscal year. Although the anticipated $50 billion deficit was lower than the previous year's, it still troubled many Members. Conservatives once again condemned congressional profligacy and warned about inflationary pressures; liberals renewed their pleas for transfers from defense to domestic needs that would aid recovery without raising the deficit. Moderates expressed concern about the deficit while acknowledging that Congress had no choice but to go along with economic realities.

The deficit thus defined the boundaries of congressional debate. With few exceptions, permanent programs could not be established because they would either raise the deficit or compel Congress to rearrange priorities by cutting existing programs. The Budget Committees became the guardians of future budgets, projecting budgetary balance some years ahead if the economy were restored to full health. But they could promise future balanced budgets only by constraining program initiatives, and limiting budget expansion to temporary spending increases that would phase out with economic improvement.

Under these circumstances, some liberals came to see the budget process itself as the cause of Congress's limited response to economic adversity. The AFL-CIO reasoned that the new process had focused congressional debate on the size of the deficit rather than on the economic needs of the nation:

> The new budget process adopted by Congress threatens to undermine the ability of Congress to lead the nation out of recession and provide for the needs of the American people . . . In the final analysis, if the congressional budget process is to have real meaning for the nation, it must place human needs above dollar deficits.[59]

One can certainly conjecture that without a budget process Congress might have been moved to bolder economic decisions. It would not have been so directly challenged concerning the deficit, and it might have been willing to take various incremental actions without worrying about their total cost. On this basis, one might argue that because of its focus on the deficit, the budget process

59. AFL-CIO, *Platform Proposals Presented to the Democratic and Republican National Conventions*, 1976, p. 55.

will tend to be most constrictive when economic expansion is needed, and most expansive when constraint is appropriate. When the economy is strong, Congress may be expected to invest the fiscal dividend in program growth. When the economy is weak, however, low-growth expectations might lead Congress to freeze budget priorities and refrain from program initiatives.

Accommodating to the President

Before embracing this gloomy conclusion, one must reckon with another constraint that sharpened congressional sensitivity to the deficit and fostered a low-growth outlook. During the thick of the recession and the beginning of the presidential election campaign, President Ford was preaching budgetary retrenchment and charging Congress with budgetary irresponsibility. His 1976 budget was predicated on $17 billion in program curtailments and he followed this proposal with a spirited attack against congressional budget policies. In a nationwide television address March 29, 1975, during which he signed tax-cutting legislation, Ford accused Congress of heading for a $100 billion deficit. "I am drawing the line right here," Ford challenged Congress, pointing to a $60 billion deficit as being "as far as we dare to go." He then added, "I will resist every effort by the Congress to add another dollar to this deficit by new spending programs." [60] The $100-billion-dollar deficit label was pinned on Congress shortly before the Budget Committees reported their first 1976 resolution. Inevitably, "the Budget Committees and the Congress fell victim to Administration rhetoric and allowed the size of this recession-induced deficit to become the central issue of debate." [61] President Ford continued on the attack during work on the 1977 budget, demanding that expenditures be kept some $28 billion below current policy levels.

With Ford in the White House, Democratic Members frequently cited the Budget Act as a declaration of independence from presidential influence. Senator Moss called the first resolution for 1977 "the Federal budget":

> It is not just a congressional budget. . . . It is the Congress' exercise of its exclusive power of the purse. . . . [The President's proposal] represents one important, but not decisive, input in the continuing evolution of the Nation's fiscal year 1977 budget.[62]

---

60. 11 *Weekly Compendium of Presidential Documents*, April 7, 1975, p. 321.
61. AFL-CIO, *op. cit.*
62. 122 *Congressional Record* (May 12, 1976) S7060.

Congress used the budget process to defend its priorities against those of the President. In urging the House to override Ford's veto of an education appropriation bill, Adams said, "Congress, not the Administration, must be responsible for federal spending and for the setting of priorities in federal programs." [63] Muskie used a similar argument in supporting the override of Ford's veto of a Labor-HEW appropriations bill:

> When the country is told by the President that a bill such as this exceeds the budget, Congress and the country should always bear in mind that the President is speaking of his budget. The congressional budget represents a different set of priorities. . . . This bill is a reflection of congressional priorities which are different in a significant way from those of the President.[64]

During the Ford years, the priorities argument was useful as a rejoinder to White House accusations that Congress was "busting" the budget by appropriating more for social programs than the President had recommended. For a Democratic Congress that wanted to go its own way on some controversial budget issues, the priorities argument became a declaration of independence.

When Carter became President, congressional Republicans assumed a mantle of independence. Sen. Henry Bellmon warned against turning the congressional process into "a rubber stamp of the administration":

> The challenge now . . . is to insure that the congressional process does work and continues to work as a separate, independent process, with an integrity of its own, a policymaking potential of its own, a data-accumulation base of its own. . . . Only in that way can we serve the purpose for which the congressional budget process was created.[65]

Bellmon's appeal was occasioned by the third resolution for 1977 which conformed in most respects to preinauguration agreements between Democratic leaders in Congress and the incoming Administration. Congress was able to raise the fiscal 1977 deficit from the $50.6 billion previously set in the second resolution to $69.7 billion because the new President was willing to go along with the higher level. The fact that economic conditions appeared to be worsening—GNP growth had slowed to 1.2 percent com-

63. 121 *Congressional Record* (September 9, 1975) H8484.
64. 122 *Congressional Record* (January 28, 1976) S725.
65. 123 *Congressional Record* (February 21, 1977) S2804.

pared to 8.8 percent earlier in the year—was not a sufficient cause for raising the deficit. A change in political conditions also was necessary. Several months later (in April 1977), the political winds shifted again when the President withdrew his support for tax rebates, and Congress returned the deficit to its $50 billion level. This docile congressional response prompted HBC Democrat Robert Leggett to protest the surrender of budgetary independence:

> . . . our budget process must be capable of producing sound, independent judgments about the appropriate action which Congress should follow, regardless of which political party occupies the White House or for that matter which party controls Congress.[66]

The Budget Act, however, did not insulate Congress from presidential influence. When a President announces a deficit or attacks Congress for deficit spending, he is shaping political expectations about the size of the deficit. Congress must accommodate to the President because the way a deficit is perceived politically depends on how the President defines it. Congress could have safely produced a $60 billion deficit for fiscal 1976 because Ford had given it his stamp of approval. Although Congress decided against that amount because it would have required unacceptable program cutbacks and barred discretionary expenditures to stimulate the faltering economy, Congress was limited in how far it could stray from the President's position. Congress added a little stimulus to the economy—and several billions more to the estimated deficit—but its options had been narrowed by the President.

Even when it squeezes more deficit into the budget, Congress tries to show that its numbers are not so different from the President's as they appear to be. It thus tries to accommodate both presidential and congressional demands. SBC's 1977 deficit was $6 billion above Ford's, but Muskie proclaimed:

> Despite any rhetoric to the contrary, no significant difference exists between the deficit set forth in our committee's report and that proposed by the Ford Administration. When put on the same basis—that is, when nonpolicy differences in accounting and projections are factored out—the difference . . . is less than a billion dollars.[67]

Giaimo used the same theme in playing down the $6.5 billion deficit increase his committee recommended for fiscal 1978: "The

66. *Ibid.*, (April 26, 1977) H3571.
67. 122 *Congressional Record* (April 8, 1976) S5293.

committee's recommendations . . . differ only moderately in real terms from those proposed by the President." [68]

One would expect a Democratic Congress to be more attentive to Democratic than Republican Presidents. Table 31 seems to support this expectation. With respect to 11 of the 14 functions for which comparisons are appropriate,[69] Congress made smaller adjustments to Carter's budgets than to Ford's. Two-thirds of the congressional allocations were within 5 percent of Carter's requests, while only one in seven strayed more than 10 percent from his budget. When Ford was President, however, one-third of the functional allocations diverged 10 percent or more from his estimates. Half of the allocations were within 5 percent of the budget, but most of these were concentrated in the stable functions (general government, general science, law enforcement and justice, etc.) concerning which there has been little budgetary controversy. Congress, however, allocated substantial increases for the social functions (community and regional development, education, training, employment, and social services) which Ford wanted to cut.

Yet these figures do not give the whole picture. Ford, in fact, had a restraining influence on congressional budget allocations, perhaps more so than did his Democratic successor. As shown earlier in table 29, more than two-thirds of the functional allocations for fiscal 1977 were *below* current policy, about the same proportion as were *above* Ford's budget. Congress accommodated to Ford's budget-cutting campaign by keeping expenditures below current policy levels. When the presidential constraints were relaxed by Carter, Congress responded by pegging two-thirds of the allocations above current policy.

Accommodating at the Margins

Because an accommodating budget responds to presidential and congressional expectations, it has disappointed those who expected the congressional budget to be written from scratch, with a new slate of priorities and unencumbered adaptation to fiscal conditions. Such a budget could not possibly pass legislative muster.

The beginning of success for the Budget Committees is the realization that they are not the only ones within Congress inter-

---

68. 123 *Congressional Record* (April 26, 1977) H3553.

69. Comparisons are not appropriate for five of the functions: energy and transportation because they were not used prior to the 1979 budget; interest, allowances, and undistributed offsetting receipts because the differences do not directly represent policy disagreements between Congress and the President.

ested in budgetary outcomes. Every committee has a stake, and while all interests cannot possibly be satisfied, the Budget Committees have to accommodate to a sufficient number of interests to pull together a majority. And as has been discussed, the committees also have to reckon with the President's budget, for he too has a stake in what Congress does and he actively shapes congressional expectations with respect to the budget's totals and its allocations. "The whole budget process," Muskie has said, "is a reaction." "Congress," he explained, "reacts to the country's reaction to the President."[70] The result is a congressional budget not all that different from the President's budget. "The truth is," Rep. Henry Gonzalez told the House during its euphoric first budget cycle, "the President's budget has a kind of life of its own . . . As it turns out, our budget estimates are about the same as those of the President, and almost exactly the same as our unscientific appropriations system projected . . . it seems not to make much of a difference in the way things turn out."[71]

It is tempting to conclude that Congress merely accommodates to what would have happened if there had been no budget process. But if this were the case, there would be little or no budgetary conflict within Congress. As we have seen, however, vigorous disputes have occurred within the Budget Committees and on the floor over the content of the budget resolutions, and over budget-related legislation developed by other committees. Conflicts have flared up over savings sought by the Budget Committees or legislative initiatives thwarted by the budget resolutions. Although the amounts at issue cannot be quantified, they surely amount to no more than a small percentage of the total. The Budget Committees have discretion at the margins: to deviate from the President's numbers, to squeeze committees for program savings or to prod them to initiate programs, to tilt the composition of the budget one way of another, to allocate somewhat more or less than current policy. One of the House liberals frustrated by attention to the margins protested this conservative bias of the budget process:

> In the end, we will undoubtedly decide on a final budget for next year which deviates little from the committee recommendation, which itself deviates little from the recommendations and budgets of the Presidents before him. . . .

70. Jack W. Germond, "Congress and Carter: Who's in Charge?" in *The New York Times Magazine*.
71. 121 *Congressional Record* (November 11, 1975) H10957-8.

Table 31

PERCENT DIFFERENCE BETWEEN FIRST BUDGET RESOLUTION AS ADOPTED AND PRESIDENT'S BUDGET REQUESTS, FISCAL YEARS 1976-80

		Ford Budgets		Carter Budgets		
Function		*1976*	*1977*	*1978*	*1979*	*1980*
National Defense	BA [a]	−6.5%	−0.7%	−1.3%	0.2%	−1.2%
	O [b]	−3.5	−1.0	−0.8	−1.8	−1.4
International Affairs	BA	−61.2	−6.2	−9.7	−2.3	−7.4
	O	−23.5	−4.3	−6.4	−4.2	−3.7
General Science	BA	0.3	−6.1	NC [a]	NC	NC
	O	0.4	NC	NC	−2.0	NC
Energy	BA	—	—	—	9.5	−3.6
	O	—	—	—	−0.1	−13.9
Natural Resources	BA	12.9	75.3	1.0	8.7	−2.3
	O	9.7	13.8	−2.4	−0.8	+1.7
Agriculture	BA	0.6	NC	−18.5	70.8	+2.0
	O	−0.9	5.3	89.1	53.7	+25.6
Commerce	BA	54.2	1.6	3.6	−10.6	−16.9
	O	13.3	7.9	−2.5	20.0	−5.9

Transportation	BA	—	—	—	9.1	−5.6
	O	—	—	—	0.1	3.4
Community and Regional Development	BA	113.0	25.4	−12.8	−2.6	−21.2
	O	46.1	36.8	6.9	NC	+9.5
Education, Training, Employment, and Social Services	BA	38.8	53.7	0.4	−7.0	0.2
	O	20.6	30.7	2.6	3.2	1.0
Health	BA	6.7	3.4	0.2	−0.3	0.8
	O	9.3	6.8	−0.4	−0.4	0.4
Income Security	BA	4.4	1.0	0.6	0.9	0.3
	O	5.5	2.0	0.7	0.2	2.2
Veterans' Benefits	BA	11.4	13.6	6.0	11.5	0.9
	O	8.0	13.4	5.8	8.8	0.9
Law Enforcement and Justice	BA	4.1	0.9	−2.6	2.4	−2.3
	O	3.4	0.9	−1.3	NC	NC
General Government	BA	−0.1	2.9	NC	2.5	−2.2
	O	3.8	2.9	−1.3	2.5	−2.3
Fiscal Assistance	BA	NC	0.8	−8.4	−35.8	−8.0
	O	−0.1	−0.8	NC	−2.0	−8.0

[a] No change.

Sources: Reports of the Committees on the Budget, United States Senate and House of Representatives, and the Conference Reports for the respective budget resolutions.

We have an expensive system to make sure that . . . no radical departures are taken to improve or reorient public policy. Nothing more, nothing less.[72]

Accommodating budgets are passable budgets, and for this reason, congressional budget makers have to settle for marginal—though potentially significant—influence on budgetary outcomes.

72. 123 *Congressional Record* (April 27, 1977) E2524-5, Remarks of Representative Harrington.

IX Enforcing the Budget: Process and Policy

A budget restrains people who are governed by it from doing what they might do in its absence. When important interests are at stake, affected parties can be expected to attempt to circumvent budgetary restraints or to break the rules of the process. For this reason every budget process—legislative and executive alike—needs controllers to guard against violations. In the executive branch, the Office of Management and Budget reviews thousands of agency actions and communications each year to assure compliance with presidential policies. In Congress, the Budget Committees are the principal guardians of the budget process. They monitor legislative activity in committees and on the floor, keeping score of the many bills that affect the budget. These congressional monitors busy themselves with both procedure and substance; they defend the rules prescribed for legislative budgeting as well as the fiscal decisions made in the periodic budget resolutions.

This chapter examines how the Budget Committees and Congress have enforced the budget process. Although the principal concern here is with the internal workings of Congress, the chapter also considers the impoundment controls prescribed by the 1974 Budget Act. The impoundment procedures were intended to enforce congressional budget priorities against executive rescissions and deferrals; hence they form an important part of the process by which Congress assures compliance with its budget decisions

SPENDING RESULTS: A SPURIOUS TEST OF BUDGET CONTROL

Before turning to the specific enforcement activities of Congress, one must come to grips with what seems to be the "bottom line" test of the budget process, the extent to which actual revenues and expenditures conform to the final congressional resolution for the fiscal year. If spending exceeds the budget ceilings, it is arguable that Congress has failed to enforce its budget decisions, that the Budget Committees have not been able to protect the budget against the spending inclinations of Congress. Conversely, if expenditures stay within the budget, a case can be made that the budget process has worked, that whether by self-discipline or enforcement Congress has abided within its own spending decisions.

The latter claim was trumpeted by the chairmen of the two Budget Committees on July 1, 1976, the day after completion of the first year of the congressional budget process. At a joint press conference, Representative Adams and Senator Muskie boasted that actual spending for the just-concluded fiscal year was billions of dollars below the amounts allowed in the budget resolution. A House Budget Committee press release exulted in this signal accomplishment of the budget process:

> Fiscal year 1976 ended at midnight yesterday and for that year Congress lived within its spending ceiling and is below its deficit target. . . . The successful operation of this new budget process is historic. . . . It shows that Congress has recaptured from the Executive its constitutional role in controlling the power of the purse.[1]

Several months later, when the books were closed on fiscal 1976, the numbers showed that outlays had been $8.4 billion below the budget. Concern about "shortfalls" began to enter budgetary debate as analysts tried to explain why outlays had been so far below earlier estimates. The experience was repeated in the succeeding fiscal years. Fiscal 1977 outlays fell $7.3 billion below the final congressional budget, and outlays for fiscal 1978 were more than $6 billion below congressional budget decisions.

Before these numbers are certified as conclusive evidence of congressional budget success, other budget numbers also have to be accounted for. Although outlays receive the lion's share of public notice, budget authority is a more valid measure of congressional impact. The outlays incurred during a year depend primarily on the rate at which funds authorized in the past and newly authorized funds are spent. Congress thus had limited say over actual

---

1. House Budget Committee press release, July 2, 1976.

outlays, though it influences them when it makes budget-authority decisions.[2]

Actual budget authority for fiscal 1976 turned out to be $7.3 billion above the aggregate Congress set in its second budget resolution for the fiscal year. By this measure, Congress failed to live within its budget or to enforce its financial decisions. Rather than showing the success that Adams and Muskie claimed, the actual data seem to indicate failure. Not only was total budget authority above the ceiling but the budget authority levels for almost half the functions were exceeded. Having voted its budget resolution, Congress would appear to have gone on its spending way without concern that it was violating its own decisions.

This conclusion, however, would be as invalid as the first. The fact is that when Congress makes a budget resolution, it does not deal with or control actual budget outcomes for a fiscal year. It makes decisions that govern its own actions, not those of the executive branch or the performance of the economy. The fiscal 1976 discrepancy between projected and actual budget authority, as well as the unexpected shortfall in outlays, resulted from external factors over which Congress had little control. The timing of executive actions, for example, can result in multibillion-dollar shifts over which Congress has no say. Swings in the economy can automatically raise or lower federal spending without any intervention by Congress. Changes in accounting practices can add or subtract billions of dollars from the budget's totals. In fiscal 1976, outlays for national defense were $1.9 billion below the congressional budget; new budget authority for defense, however, was $2.8 billion above budget. This discrepancy between the two numbers was due partly to the long lead time between the procurement and acquisition of major weapons systems and partly to the method used for computing certain military transactions. Regardless of the reason, it should be clear that neither the excess in budget authority nor the shortfall in outlays justifies any firm

2. Although Muskie understandably credited the budget process with holding expenditures below the budget ceiling, he acknowledged on occasion that Congress does not exercise meaningful control over outlays. One such instance occurred during Senate debate on the first budget resolution for fiscal 1979: "We control the budget by controlling budget authority. . . . there is no way of controlling deficits by simply controlling outlays. There is no way of controlling spending by controlling outlays. We control spending by controlling budget authority." 124 *Congressional Record* (daily ed., April 25, 1978) S6282.

conclusion with respect to the effectiveness of congressional budget controls.

When Congress makes its budget decisions, it is estimating what the executive branch and the economy will do. If Congress's decisions vary widely from the mark, the problem is apt to lie in faulty expectations rather than congressional breaches of the budget. When Muskie and Adams held their happy press conference on July 1, 1976, they estimated that budget authority for the already ended fiscal year totaled $406.7 billion. In fact, budget authority was $8.6 billion higher. There is no reason to believe that the Budget Committees deliberately underestimated budget authority. They merely used the latest CBO numbers. If Congress had appropriated an additional billion dollars before June 30, 1976, it would not have violated its budget rules because it was guided by the estimates at hand, not by the final figures which only became known months later.

In sum, actual budget authority and outlays are substantially determined by factors over which Congress exercises little direct control. Neither the outlay nor the budget auhority results are sufficient tests of congressional budget operations. A proper test must be based on what Congress itself does in the course of the year as it acts on the numerous measures that affect the budget. Enforcing the congressional budget is much less a matter of protecting the "bottom line" than of continuous monitoring of the revenue, spending, and authorizing legislation produced by committees and considered on the floor. It is with these individual activities that this and ensuing chapters are concerned. This chapter considers overall enforcement processes, while chapters in Part Three deal in detail with the enforcement of revenue and spending decisions through appropriations and tax legislation.

THE ROUTINES OF ENFORCEMENT

Occasionally an enforcement issue blows up into a contest between one of the Budget Committees and another congressional unit. During the years covered by this study, there have been many major confrontations. Several are presented in this chapter as case studies of how Congress enforces its budgetary rules and decisions.

It is tempting to score the public fights as measures of how well the budget process is faring in Congress, but the public confrontations can provide a distorted view. A budget's greatest successes are not won through open warfare but through routine obeisance to its dictates. For a budget process to be effective, constrained parties must accede to it much more often than they challenge it. If congressional committees regularly break the budget's rules and limitations, the process could not succeed, no matter how vigilantly the Budget Committees guard against infraction. A Congress bent on circumventing its own budget controls is not likely to be stopped by appeals to uphold the process or by the various points of order implanted in the Budget Act. Voluntary compliance must be the basis of budgetary regularity in Congress.

The big fights are aberrant cases, deviations from the pattern of compliance that generally prevails within Congress. They are important because of the insight they provide on how Congress copes with budgetary conflict when the controls break down. But the fact is that most committees have tried to work within the budget's rules. For every confrontation, there have been dozens of legislative decisions routinely made with fidelity to the budget process. For every issue blown up into a public contest, there have been several quietly settled by the affected parties. The workings of the congressional budget process are to be found in the unexciting routines of budgeting as much as in the few conflicts that receive public notice.

Most congressional committees have accepted the requirements of congressional budgeting. On procedural matters, most make honest efforts to clear their bills by May 15, and most wait until adoption of the first budget resolution before pushing their spending programs. Most do not knowingly place "backdoors" into their bills, and most try to live within the dollar limits of the budget resolutions. Most committees have educated themselves about the budgeting process, and most have added budget specialists to their staffs. Most maintain regular contact with the Budget Committees, checking to assure that their legislation conforms to the Budget Act and soliciting advice when a violation is found.

The term "most committees" is deliberately vague, for not all committees have internalized the budget's norms. For some, the task has been quite easy because their legislation is not the sort that normally runs afoul of the Budget Act. For others, compliance has been more difficult because they deal with matters (such as entitlements) that are more likely to have budgetary problems. Some committees cooperate with the process; others try to find ways of neutralizing the budget controls without overtly violating them. Clearly the revenue committees have been more troublesome than the Appropriations Committees, and the Senate Finance Committee has been more recalcitrant than the House Ways and Means Committee.

It is tempting to attribute differences in committee behavior to the styles and personalities of their leaders. Hence, it can be argued, Ways and Means has cooperated because Al Ullman is committed to making the budget process work; Finance has rebelled because Russell Long is determined to sabotage the process. This facile explanation misses the main reason: committee cooperation with the budget process depends on the legislative interests involved. Given the propensity of the Senate to load tax measures with revenue losses, the Finance Committee could not have an easy relationship with the Budget Committee, no matter who was in charge. The two Agriculture Committees were initially among the most cooperative congressional committees, working closely and informatively with their respective Budget Committees. They turned into reluctant adversaries when shifing interests compelled them to abandon the easy cooperation that had prevailed in the beginning.

Self-interest drives committees toward compliance with the Budget Act. No committee wants to risk derailment of its legislative plans by an avoidable violation of budget rules. On the floor, a point of order is a formidable weapon in the hands of adversaries; it can either block legislation or force the reporting committee to accept unwanted changes. When the budget process was new, committees frequently violated its terms through ignorance, not because they preferred to play fast and loose with the rules. Now that the requirements have become familiar, committees guard against violations. "It is one of the costs of doing business," the staff director of a House authorizing committee explained. "Sure it can be a nuisance, and I sometimes wish that it would go away, but it is far better to make sure that everything is in order than to get caught unawares later on." After the House Budget Committee blocked some key legislation that had been sponsored by his Ways and Means subcommittee in 1976, Rep. James Corman instructed his staff to clear everything with HBC before it was reported. "Clearing it with the Budget Committee" has become standard procedure on many committees.

But even with cooperation from its committees and Members, Congress cannot expect absolute fidelity to its budget rules and decisions. Some breaches occur because committees are unaware of the requirements of the budget process. Others result from changing circumstances that cause financial or program pressures different from those that had prevailed when the initial budget decisions were made. Sometimes a committee tries to get its way without regard to the budget decisions made by Congress. The Budget Committees try to head off violations by maintaining close contact with other committees. They assist committees in meeting Budget Act requirements and in allocating the shares of each budget resolution among their subcommittees and programs.[3] When a violation occurs or appears imminent, the Budget Committees frequently suggest ways of overcoming the problem.

In the course of a year, Budget Committee staffers spend more time enforcing Budget Act requirements than on any other committee activity. "There is no such thing as a slack season," an HBC staff leader protested, in response to a question about what the committee does during the long interval between budget resolutions. HBC, he noted, reviews every bill reported by House committees or scheduled for floor action to assure compliance with the budget process. HBC's enforcement strategy is geared to intervention at the earliest possible stage. To begin with, HBC has arranged for each House committee to designate someone as its staff person on Budget Act issue. HBC uses these contacts to find out what is happening in each committee and to communicate its concerns. If it spots a Budget Act problem, HBC tries to work out a solution before the legislation is reported. It often takes a problem to the House Parliamentarian, and uses the informal ruling to bolster its behind-the-scenes bargaining position. According to HBC staff members, once a committee is informed of a problem, it usually makes the necessary changes in its legislation. Inevitably, however, some Budget Act violations are not detected until a committee has completed its work and reported a bill. Most such problems are settled through negotiations in which the offending committee agrees to offer a floor amendment removing the violation. Moreover, as will be discussed later, HBC uses support from the leadership and the House Rules Committee to persuade recalcitrant committees to modify their legislation. In this way, HBC can accomplish most of its enforcement objectives informally and without public notice or conflict. It can afford to be silent or

3. Section 302(b) of the Budget Act requires each House and Senate committee to report on its suballocation of new budget authority and outlays among its programs or subcommittees.

accommodating on the floor because it has already obtained what it wants, or all that it is likely to get, through private dealings.

HBC conducts weekly "early warning" meetings at which it reviews legislation scheduled for floor consideration. A staff report compares the amounts in revenue and spending bills with the assumptions in the latest budget resolution. The report also deals with unusual financial arrangements and with violations of Budget Act procedures. The early warning sessions are sometimes used to plot floor strategy, but because most violations have already been resolved, HBC has rarely had to prepare for floor combat. Indeed, HBC's enforcement policy has been based on the belief that open fights are a sign that it has not been effective. "The floor," a Budget Committee member suggested, "is the last place to stage a battle and expect results."

Although the Senate Budget Committee has been more willing to confront violations on the floor, it too has elaborate routines for handling Budget Act problems before they blow up into public issues. In fact, SBC's enforcement activities are more extensive and formal than those of the House committee. A weekly legislative activity report covers all budget-related measures on the calendar, including authorizing legislation. SBC also tracks bills still being marked up in committee, and staff members prepare detailed memoranda for the chairman on major legislation or on matters that might become floor issues. The legislative report covers prospective issues—what might happen—not just the actions already taken by committees.

As enforcers of the budget process, the Budget Committees are not free to do entirely as they will. Most violations are by-products of the legislative work of other committees. In a collegial setting, the Budget Committees cannot ignore the interests of their peers. They cannot adamantly insist on a procedural point without taking into account the substantive effects. They must weigh their interest in budget control against Congress's other legislative interests. To the extent that Budget Committee members have substantive interests of their own, these interests are likely to affect how the budget process is enforced. Once a budget matter becomes a public issue, the burden of enforcement shifts to the House or Senate as a whole, and the Budget Committee can prevail only if it persuades a congressional majority to uphold its position. The Budget Committee can use the Budget Act as a talking point, but if a majority of Members take a different view, the Budget Committee will lose. Thus, the ultimate arbiters of the budget process are the House and Senate and each body must balance budget control against competing interests.

PROCESS VERSUS POLICY

As long as enforcement of a budget rule or limitation is within the custody of the House or Senate Budget Committee, HBC or SBC can elect to treat the issue as a procedural question. Once an issue spills over into the House or Senate, however, the outcome often depends on whether the matter is perceived as one of policy or procedure. Congress can pursue its policy objectives by brushing aside Budget Act impediments, or it can uphold the budget requirements even at the cost of prejudicing substantive interests. The way an issue is perceived makes a difference. If it is cast in process terms, the Budget Committees are likely to get their way; if the matter is deemed to be substantive, the Budget Committees are likely to be abandoned by a congressional majority.

The contrast between policy and process was illustrated in two Senate floor disputes that took place in 1977. The protagonists were the same in both cases, Sen. Edmund Muskie speaking for the budget process and Sen. William Proxmire favoring housing programs, but the results were quite different.

In June 1977, the Senate Banking, Housing, and Urban Affairs Committee produced legislation which (among other things) would have altered the way in which new budget authority was computed for federally subsidized housing programs. Although it would not have directly affected the level of program operations, the committee's proposal would have lowered the amount of new budget authority for housing by many billions of dollars each year by redefining budget authority to exclude the future costs of current housing programs.[4] Senator Proxmire, Chairman of the Banking Committee, opposed the measure on policy grounds; he held that housing would be prejudiced by the manner in which future costs were computed because other programs were charged only with one-year costs. "What this means is that housing will be the first

4. The Budget Act defines budget authority as authority "to enter into obligations which will result in immediate or future outlays involving Government Funds." Pursuant to this definition, the new budget authority for subsidized housing programs was computed on the basis of full runout costs (up to 40 years).

program to be cut and the last program to be restored or funded."[5]

Just a month earlier, SBC had suffered a public defeat at the hands of Proxmire when the Senate restored $6.2 billion in new budget authority that the Budget Committee had cut from the first concurrent resolution for fiscal 1978. These funds were for the same subsidized housing program for which Proxmire was now seeking a redefinition of housing costs. The same powerful coalition of interest groups—labor unions, bankers, home builders, and government organizations[6]—which had successfully campaigned for more housing money in the first budget resolution was now prodding Senators to back Proxmire again. The issue gave Senators an easy way to show their support for housing without spending more money or raising the deficit. But despite SBC's earlier loss, Muskie carried the fight to the floor, castigating Proxmire's move as a "dangerous precedent that could lead other special interest groups to develop new ways to disguise the budgetary impact of programs under their jurisdiction."[7] He was joined by Bellmon, who insisted that the issue is a "truth-in-budgeting matter of great importance and impact far beyond a mere technicality."[8] Sen. Joseph Biden, an SBC colleague, emphasized the distinction between process and policy:

> What faces us today is another process or procedural sort of issue. The question is not do we favor housing programs. . . . The question today is how can we best present the budget authority for housing programs in the budget so that everyone will know how much we propose to spend.[9]

When the votes were counted, it was clear that the Senate had treated the redefinition of costs as an issue altogether different from the addition of $6.2 billion for subsidized housing. While Proxmire had prevailed by a 57-39 vote in his first confrontation with Muskie, he was on the losing end of a 18-70 verdict in the dispute over budget definitions. In the latter vote, fewer than half of the Banking Committee's members backed their chairman. The defectors included the two Senators (Alan Cranstan and John Heinz) who had seats on both the Budget and Banking Committees.

5. 123 *Congressional Record* (daily ed., June 7, 1977) S9086.
6. *Ibid.*, S9085.
7. *Ibid.*, S9081.
8. *Ibid.*, S9082.
9. *Ibid.*, S9092.

Muskie, by contrast, was supported by all but one of his committee colleagues,[10] and he was backed by nearly three dozen Senators who had sided with Proxmire on the earlier vote.

The Senate treated the first vote—how much should be spent for subsidized housing—as a policy issue concerning which the Budget Committee had no special expertise or status. The policy specialists to whom Senators defer are members of the committees with substantive jurisdictions over the programs. However, it treats the second vote as a procedural question: What does the Budget Act require? When it comes to process questions, the Budget Committees are regarded as the experts, and their views tend to receive greater weight than do those of the substantive committees.

In the two disputes between Proxmire and Muskie, the Senate drew a fairly obvious distinction between what constitutes budget authority (the process question) and how much should be spent for housing programs (the policy question). But any issue can be defined one way or the other; there is nothing inherent in any issue that compels Members to perceive it only one way. Even "How much should be spent?" questions can be cast as cut-and-dried procedural matters to be decided without considering substantive impacts.

This is exactly what happened in July 1975 when the Senate Budget Committee scored its first major floor victory in enforcing the budget targets set by Congress. Sen. George S. McGovern had proposed an amendment to expand the popular school lunch program which benefits every state and district in the nation. The amendment was not deemed controversial until Muskie made a last-minute effort to challenge it. No "Dear Colleague" letter had gone to other Senators asking them to join in opposition; all Muskie had was a staff memo explaining the budgetary impact of McGovern's proposal and its political appeal. After reading the memo and deciding on his course of action, Muskie wondered, "Am I going to be the only one voting against this?" [11] Less than two hours later, the Senate rejected McGovern's amendment by a 29-61 vote. Muskie won because he persuaded the Senate to disregard

---

10. One committee member (Abourezk) voted with Muskie but then paired with a Senator who would have voted the other way.

11. Quoted in Bernard Asbell, *The Senate Nobody Knows* (New York, N.Y.: Doubleday & Company, 1978) p. 159. Asbell followed Muskie in the Senate and in Maine for more than a year. His book provides an interesting account of the school lunch conflict and Muskie's reaction to it. See pp. 146-63.

the emotional issue of lunches for poor youngsters and, instead, to see the issue as one of upholding the new budget process:

. . . if we were to breach the budget on this, we would simply be opening the door to further breaches on other programs as we go down the line. . . .

If the budget reform legislation is to mean anything, it has to mean that we are willing to accept its discipline, not only with respect to those programs which we may not be enthusiastic about, but also the programs that have real, heart-plucking implications such as this one.

Discipline is discipline. It cannot be directed only at the defense budget or only at the space budget or only at those programs that have no relevence to our own States and our own needs.[12]

One liberal Democrat voted against the amendment after a chat with Muskie on the floor. "I just told him that it was a budget-buster," Muskie later explained to an observer. [13] Muskie did not have go into program details to persuade a Senate majority.

Muskie had one clear advantage in the school lunch debate. Because he was known to be a supporter of liberal programs, his opposition to the McGovern amendment could not be interpreted as an effort to use the budget process for substantive advantage. Muskie was sacrificing his own policy interests for the sake of the budget process, and he was able to prevail upon many colleagues to do likewise. The situation was markedly different several weeks later when Muskie took the floor in opposition to the conference report on the defense authorization bill. Although Muskie was not identified as an enthusiastic supporter of defense programs, he was nevertheless able once again to cast the issue in process terms by linking the defense and school lunch bills.[14] Both bills, he noted, have major implications for the new congressional budget:

I am compelled, as a Member of the Senate and as chairman of the Senate Budget Committee, to vote against both. I will vote against the

12. 121 *Congressional Record* (daily ed., July 10, 1975) S12359.
13. Asbell, *op. cit.*, p. 163.
14. After the Senate rejected the McGovern amendment, it passed the school lunch bill and sent it to conference with the House. McGovern's proposal was restored in conference, with the result that the total cost of the bill was well above the amount contemplated in the budget resolution. Although Muskie linked the conference reports on defense and school lunch, the latter was considered by the Senate in September, more than a month after it rejected the defense authorization bill.

military procurement conference report because it authorizes military expenditures which translate into appropriations which exceed our congressional budget targets.

I will vote against the school lunch conference report because it is automatic spending legislation which, as it comes back from the conference, would result in 1976 spending almost $430 million in excess of our budget target. I hope other Senators will vote likewise. . . .

These bills test whether we are serious about the budget reform process. . . . They test whether we are going to deal even-handedly in holding the line, both for defense and domestic spending.[15]

Muskie was demanding nothing less than the subordination of policy objectives to the requirements of the budget process. Rather than a balancing of process against policy in which the outcome depends on the strength of the competing interests, he wanted the budget process to be accorded a preferred position in Congress. But although the defense and school lunch votes represented the triumph of process over policy—both of the conference reports were returned to committee [16]—this dominance of the budget process could not be long sustained. Budget control is not the only aim of Congress and the budget process cannot, except in special cases, be the only test by which legislation is measured. When the process was new and Members were proud and protective of their handiwork, they could defer to the special claims of budgeting. Once the novelty wore off, the budget process no longer had a preferred claim on congressional loyalties or a veto over program ambitions. The budget process became just another consideration in the balancing of congressional interests.

PATTERNS OF ENFORCEMENT: HBC VERSUS SBC

The balancing of congressional interests begins in the Budget Committees. Although they can take a hard line and try to block legislation that runs afoul of the budget's rules, the Budget Com-

15. 121 *Congressional Record* (daily ed., August 1, 1979) S14719.
16. The conference report on the defense authorization bill was rejected by a 48-42 vote. Congress subsequently approved a second conference report with lower spending levels. The school lunch legislation was recommitted to conference by a unanimous 76-0 vote, after which a bill with slightly scaled-down levels was passed.

mittees have reason to accommodate the budget process to the legislative interests of other committees. When Congress itself is disposed toward balance, the Budget Committees would risk repeated defeat—and possibly the loss of their prized process as well—if they were always to insist on their prerogatives. After the school lunch and defense bills were recommitted, Muskie decided to accept scaled-down measures that still were above the levels "assumed" in the budget resolution. Even as he preached the sanctity of the budget, Muskie was willing to strike a balance between his committee's process and peer committees' program concerns.

The trick for the Budget Committees is to accommodate without surrendering all meaningful enforcement. If they consistently turn the other cheek and allow legislative committees to have their way, the Budget Committees will buy peace but lose the opportunity to influence legislative outcomes. The two Budget Committees have sought balance in strikingly different ways. Each has specialized as an enforcer of a different aspect of the budget process. The House committee has emphasized the procedural rules of budgeting; the Senate committee has concentrated on the dollar limitations in the budget resolutions. Neither committee has completely disregarded the other committee's concerns—SBC has guarded certain budgetary procedures and HBC has been interested in some substantive issues—but each has accorded priority to a different facet of budgeting. However, as the budget process has matured, the sharp distinctions in enforcement styles has narrowed, and the two committees have become more alike in their attitudes toward the Budget Act.

The substantive side of budgetary enforcement is reflected in the defense and school lunch fights. In both cases, legislation was challenged on the ground that expenditures would exceed the levels targeted in budget resolutions. Both battles were waged in the Senate after legislation carrying high price tags passed the House without comparable challenge from the Budget Committee. HBC does not intervene on conventional authorizations (such as the defense bill that drew Muskie's ire). HBC rarely has found serious fault with an appropriation bill, although it has occasionally vigorously contested entitlement bills on cost grounds. HBC has concentrated on the technical requirements of the Budget Act. Legislation to compensate black-lung victims, which was brought to the floor in March 1976, is a case in point. As an entitlement, the measure was subject to special provisions of the Budget Act.

HBC Chairman Adams did not like the bill because although costs would be small the first year, they would rise substantially the next year. Moreover, the bill, which was to take effect at once, was being considered prior to adoption of the first budget resolution for the next fiscal year. Adams voted against the rule providing for consideration of the black-lung measure but he did not make an issue of it because the bill was not in technical violation of the Budget Act:

> I rise to comment on the pending rule . . . from the standpoint of the Budget Act not on the merits of the bill. The report of this bill was filed in calendar year 1975 to be effective in fiscal year 1976. Thus, under section 401 of the Budget Act, there is no statutory bar to House consideration of the measure at this time. . . .
>
> From the point of view of the congressional budget process, it would be more appropriate to consider this bill after Congress establishes budget targets for fiscal year 1977 in the first budget resolution this Spring, but there is no legal bar to considering it.[17]

Yet HBC does take an active stance on legislation that offends Budget Act procedures. As guardian of the procedures, HBC has quite actively enforced four Budget Act provisions:

—Section 303, which prohibits floor consideration of revenue, spending, or entitlement legislation for the next fiscal year prior to adoption of the first budget resolution for that year.[18] The purpose of this provision is to assure that financial decisions are made through the budget process, and that budget options for the next year are not foreclosed by prior congressional decisions.

—Section 401(a), which stipulates that new contract or borrowing legislation must carry a proviso making the funding effective only to the extent provided in appropriation acts. This provision closes the backdoor for contract or borrowing authority, except for certain types of programs.[19]

—Section 401(b), which provides that new entitlements cannot become effective before the beginning of the next fiscal year.

17. 122 *Congressional Record* (daily ed., March 2, 1976) H1425-26.

18. Section 303(b) exempts advance revenue legislation and advance appropriations—that is, bills that take effect after the next fiscal year—from this prohibition. Significantly, there is no exemption for advance entitlements.

19. Backdoor status may, however, be continued for contract or borrowing authority financed through a trust fund or for a government corporation.

Its purpose is to give Congress the option of reviewing entitlements in the context of the second budget resolution for a fiscal year.[20]

—Section 402, which requires authorizing legislation to be reported by May 15.

Each of these provisions entails close examinations of "fine print" to determine whether a particular measure meets the requirements. These provisions can be effective only if someone vigilantly reviews legislation as it comes out of committees to assure compliance with the required budgetary procedures. The House Budget Committee staff closely monitors all bills coming to the House, and HBC insists that Budget Act rules not easily be waived. Although it has been compelled to retreat from the "no exceptions" policy it initially adopted, HBC has endorsed waivers in only a few cases. However, the committee frequently supports waivers for "technical" violations, that is, instances in which there is prior agreement to remove the violation through a floor amendment.

HBC emphasizes procedure to gain adherence to congressional budget policy. One staffer spoke of the irritations for committees which face Budget Act challenges and make substantial concessions to avert HBC opposition. In the 1976 black-lung legislation, for example, the version brought to the floor was less costly than the one originally promoted by the House Education and Labor Committee. HBC believes that in the long run, the success of the Budget Act depends on even-handed enforcement of its provisions. According to one staffer, "We do not play favorites; by treating everybody the same way, we can demand strict compliance with the budget procedures." The implication here is that a substantive orientation on the part of HBC would require selective enforcement, that is, looking the other way in order to advance certain programs or to avoid conflict with powerful congressional interests. Moreover, substantive issues are more likely to grow into angry confrontations than are procedural questions. Thus, HBC's enforcement style is compatible with its preference for quiet diplomacy.

A focus on procedural rules requires that the budget's numbers not be repeatedly challenged. If other committees were to regularly breach the budget allocations, HBC would be compelled to intervene in substantive issues. To remain passive would risk discredit-

20. In addition, Section 401(b) provides for the referral of entitlement legislation to the Appropriations Committee if it would cause the amount of new budget authority to exceed a Section 302 allocation.

ing the whole budget process. But of the three types of substantive legislation, HBC has been troubled only by entitlements. It has taken the view that authorizations which require appropriations do not matter, and it has been blessed by the House Appropriations Committee's fidelity to the budget. As we shall see, HBC has become more active with respect to entitlements, but it still deals with them more cautiously than does the Senate Budget Committee.

SBC has had a more relaxed attitude toward Budget Act procedure. With few exceptions, it has not held committees to the May 15 deadline for reporting authorizations; nor has it accorded high priority to guarding against backdoor contract and borrowing authority. SBC, however, has taken a tough stance with regard to entitlements because of their effect on future budgets.

SBC has distinguished between procedure for its own sake and procedure that affects policy. For example, in deciding whether to recommend a waiver of a Budget Act deadline, SBC will examine whether the spending authorized in the legislation was assumed in the budget resolution. If passage of the measure would not cause any major difficulty, the committee would be inclined to support a waiver. If SBC has problems with the legislation, however, it uses the waiver requirement to hold up the legislation or exact more favorable terms.

Day Care: A Study in Budgetary Contrasts

The different enforcement styles of the two committees led to sharp conflict in 1976, shortly after the Budget Act was fully activated. The provocation was a bill dealing with federal regulation and support of day care centers. The bill that the House originally passed had no effect on the budget; it merely delayed implementation of federal standards for these centers. The Senate version, however, added a $250 million entitlement to assist states in upgrading their day care facilities. This added provision clearly violated Section 401(b) of the Budget Act, inasmuch as the entitlement would have taken effect before the beginning of the next fiscal year.

Muskie was alerted to this problem by his staff, which advised him neither to ignore the procedural violation—"it would be 'embarrassing' if the issue is raised by someone else"[21]—nor to block

21. Memorandum to Senator Muskie from Marc Lackritz, "Senate Consideration of H.R. 9803, a Bill to Provide Additional Federal Funds for Child Care Centers," January 27, 1976.

passage of the bill. A staff memorandum pointed out (1) that the day care funds were contemplated in the most recent budget resolution, hence there would be no substantive violation, and (2) that Muskie had previously gone on record as saying that the bill was consistent with the congressional budget. Accordingly, if he were to raise a point of order, Muskie "could be accused of inconsistency and possibly bad faith in implementing the procedures of this [Budget] Act."

Muskie opted for a third course suggested by his staff. He notified the Senate of the Budget Act problem, but dismissed it as a "technicality" that "ought not to be raised on the Senate side at this point."[22] But Muskie warned the Senate that the House Budget Committee has "a different problem in connection with this legislation," and he inserted an HBC staff memorandum to Brock Adams into the record. The HBC document strongly disputed SBC's interpretation and argued "that there are substantial policy reasons for abiding by the letter, as well as the spirit, of the law."[23] The extraordinary maneuver of placing an adverse House interpretation in the Senate record did not avoid an impasse on day care, or ease the strained relationship on the matter between the two Budget Committees.

When the day care bill went to conference, Congress was under great pressure to agree quickly because the stringent federal standards that were about to take effect threatened the closure of numerous child care facilities throughout the country. Nevertheless, the conference was stalemated for more than five weeks because HBC refused to endorse a bill in violation of Budget Act procedures. HBC took the view that a single infraction could become a precedent for future breaches of the budget process; it also feared that if committees got their own way without challenge, the Budget Act would soon become a dead letter. Only recently HBC had blocked floor consideration of an unemployment compensation bill reported by Ways and Means (the same committee that handled the day care bill) and it was still holding firm to a "no waivers" rule.

The House Budget Committee was perturbed by what it regarded as the Senate Budget Comimttee's laxity in enforcing the rules of the budget process. HBC believed that it was being forced into a position of protecting Congress against Senate violations,

---

22. 122 *Congressional Record* (daily ed., January 29, 1976) S873.
23. *Ibid.*, S872.

usually at the conference stage when legislation is most vulnerable to pressure. HBC staffers began to screen Senate legislation to detect Budget Act problems; in some instances, they found bills that the Senate had approved without removing or waiving obvious Budget Act violations.[24] On some matters pending before the Senate, HBC staffers pressed for points of order to stop the legislation.[25]

SBC staffers had a different view. They argued that substantive outcomes were more important than budgetary technique and that no advantage would accrue from upholding a point for its own sake. Moreover, SBC argued that the allocation for day care fit within the latest budget ceilings. SBC did not appreciate HBC's surveillance of Senate activity and insisted that it would be unwise to try to stop legislation so late in the process. SBC summed up its differences with the House committee in a staff memorandum to Muskie:

> The Senate Committee has focused on the priority decisions in the concurrent resolutions and how to make them stick once adopted, highlighted by the successful floor fights and increasing activity within other committees to enforce the resolution. . . .
>
> The House Committee has assumed a different course. It has . . . assumed the posture that it must be the principal enforcer of all provisions of the Budget Act without regard to the consequences, including section 401, the backdoor closing provision, which was included in the legislation largely to accommodate the Appropriations Committee.[26]

Another staff memorandum urged Muskie to maintain the Senate position because "we believe that the Budget Act is not well served by exalting technicalities which obstruct the legislative process where legislation is consistent with that process and with the Budget Resolutions."[27]

24. One such example cited by HBC staff in internal memoranda was S. 521, the Outer Continental Shelf Management Act of 1975. Passed by the Senate, the bill provided backdoor borrowing authority, but no objection was raised to this provision on the floor.
25. The leading case was food stamp legislation which would have changed eligibility standards, thereby providing new entitlements. HBC staffers vigorously urged enforcement of Budget Act rules, but SBC staff took the position that the food stamp legislation was explicitly contemplated in the second budget resolution for the fiscal year.
26. Memorandum for Senator Muskie from John McEvoy, "Budget Resolution Enforcement by the Two Houses," March 5, 1976.
27. Memorandum for Senator Muskie from John McEvoy, Conversation with Linda Kamm, general counsel of HBC, March 2, 1976.

Muskie and Adams tried to iron out differences at a meeting during which each pledged staff cooperation in developing common positions on enforcing the Budget Act. The already strained relationship was brought to the breaking point, however, by the intrusion of another bill that was working its way through the legislative process. The measure to provide supplemental appropriations for the new ConRail system was emergency legislation, but the problem was that funds were to be provided for the next fiscal year before passage of the first budget resolution. HBC was in a quandary: It did not want to endorse a waiver, but neither did it want to block the legislation. The House Appropriations Committee circumvented the problem by providing funds for fiscal 1976 and the transition quarter (both of which were covered by existing budget resolutions), no funds for fiscal 1977 (the year with the Budget Act problem), and advance appropriations for 1978 and 1979. But rather than viewing this skipped-year technique as a weakening of budget control, Adams (a strong supporter of the railroads) applauded the solution: "The Appropriations Committee has . . . shown that the congressional budget and appropriations process can be flexible enough to meet special and unusual needs."[28]

SBC saw matters differently, and it opted for a waiver of the Budget Act without a lapse in funding. In an official committee report, SBC argued "that the approach . . . passed by the House of Representatives is inconsistent with the Budget Act." SBC protested that if the House precedent

> were to become commonplace, the discipline of the Congressional budget process would be eroded. Congress could be confronted with a considerable number of bills providing budget authority for future fiscal years without any consideration of the Congressional budget for those years or how the bills compared to one another or to the national priorities and fiscal policy which the Budget Act intends Congress shall control through the budget process.[29]

Adams, enraged by SBC's attack on the House, instructed a key staff aide to inform SBC of his "displeasure at the Senate's failure to enforce the Budget Act." Nevertheless, Adams could not persist in his absolute objections to day care funding. His committee members were receiving letters from constituents protesting HBC's blockage of critical legislation. The Speaker ordered the partici-

---

28. 122 *Congressional Record* (daily ed., February 18, 1976) H1180.
29. S. Rept. No. 94-650 (February 25, 1976).

pants to work out a solution and at one time, four House committees (Appropriations, Budget, Rules, and Ways and Means) were involved in the negotiations. One proposed solution was to convert day care from an entitlement to an authorization, but this suggestion was vetoed by Ways and Means, which would have lost effective jurisdiction over the program to Appropriations. The negotiators found themselves in a web of Budget Act problems; for example, a proposal to solve the Section 401 problem by delaying funds until the next fiscal year would have opened up a Section 303 issue. With no way of avoiding a budget violation, HBC was forced to retreat from its no-waiver rule. The compromise solution provided for funding limited to the current fiscal year and the transition quarter. By a 15-10 vote, HBC recommended a waiver on the convenient ground that the temporary arrangement preserves "the opportunity to consider funding of this program for fiscal year 1977 and beyond in the context of the first budget resolution for the upcoming fiscal year."[30] All parties to the compromise expected the additional funding to be continued in the next fiscal year, but as long as the *appearance* of budget control was maintained, HBC was willing to accept this face-saving compromise.

Day care and ConRail demonstrate that the two Budget Committees differ not only about what constitutes a problem but also about what is an appropriate remedy. In both cases SBC applied a substantive test to its solutions; it accepted revised defense and school lunch bills because spending had been lowered in the second conference. HBC applied a procedural test; it approved day care and ConRail funding because the funding had been timed in a way that overcame the technical problem.

Why the Committees Differ

The Budget Act seems to give SBC a much more direct role in enforcing budgetary procedures than HBC has. Section 303(c) of the Act vests in the Senate committee jurisdiction over waivers of the rule against revenue or spending legislation before the first budget resolution has been adopted. Section 402(c) gives it similar jurisdiction over waivers of the May 15 deadline for authorizing legislation. The House Budget Committee has no statutory role in enforcing the rules or in granting waivers. This responsibility is lodged in the House Rules Committee which has broad jurisdiction

30. Letters from Brock Adams to Rep. Ray J. Madden, Chairman of the Rules Committee, March 11, 1976.

over the terms and conditions under which most legislation is considered on the floor. Shortly after the Budget Act took effect, however, HBC formally injected itself into the process by requesting Rules to notify it of any waiver request. "In such cases, the [Budget] Committee will make known to you its views on the waiver request as promptly as possible."[31] HBC also wrote to every House Committee asking each "to bring to the attention of the Budget Committee any request you plan to make for such a waiver." Rather than regarding HBC's involvement as a trespass, Rules welcomed it. By relying on HBC expertise and judgment, Rules has not become ensnared in the complications of the Budget Act. Every time a waiver has been requested, Rules has gotten a recommendation from HBC, either by a letter from the HBC chairman or through personal contact. With few exceptions, Rules has accepted HBC's recommendations.

With comparable vigor, HBC has seized the House lead in guarding against backdoor legislation. "Backdoors" involve the legislative interests of the Appropriations Committees, and SBC has taken the view that these committees should bear the main responsibility for guarding against contract and borrowing authority abuses. HBC regards backdoors as a Budget Act issue and therefore a matter concerning which it must have an active role.

The House and Senate Budget Committees differ in their roles, their enforcement strategies, and their solutions to problems. Neither committee is entirely consistent; congressional pressures necessitate expediency and exceptions. The differences are rooted in (1) the compositions of the two committees and (2) House and Senate attitudes toward legislative rules.

Composition of the Committee. Because HBC members have limited terms, they do not develop strong attachments to the committee. Rather, they try to use their Budget Committee connection to pursue their more permanent substantive interests. All members bring their own policy outlooks to the committee; all try to stamp those views on the budget resolutions. This behavior results in the partisanship and cleavages discussed in earlier chapters. Because HBC members are so divided on substance, they cannot unite in enforcing the substantive outcomes of the budget process. As partisans, most are more interested in getting their way on particular programs than in assuring adherence to the dollar levels in budget

---

31. Letter from Brock Adams to Representative Madden, March 21, 1975, printed in 121 *Congressional Record* (daily ed., March 24, 1975) H2231.

resolutions. Procedure is one budgetary issue on which HBC members can unite, although not necessarily for the same reasons. HBC Republicans tend to support budgetary procedures as controls on spending; committee Democrats see them as a means to preserve the budget process.

Procedure unites Republicans and Democrats, conservatives and liberals, and one generation of HBC members with another. The rituals of the budget process give the committee continuity and roots. Rather than being reborn every time its membership turns over, HBC has developed a body of tradition that links one Congress to the next.

In contrast, with permanent attachments, Senate Budget Committee members have given substantive support to the budget process. They have a recognized group advantage in assuring that the budget resolutions are complied with. The bipartisan bond between Muskie and Bellmon has been built on their willingness to subordinate program interests to congressional budget decisions. Of course, all SBC members have other committee assignments and loyalties, which sometimes take precedence over budgetary matters, and rank-and-file members cannot be expected to have the same stake and commitment as the SBC leaders. But committee cohesion has been strengthened by efforts to enforce the substantive requirements of the process.

House-Senate Attitudes on Procedure. The House and the Senate have different attitudes toward legislative procedure. The House is more inclined to stick to its rules, and it has special procedures—"rules" devised for the floor consideration of particular measures and "suspensions"—for deviating from its permanent rules.[32] When the House debates a "rule," it usually is informed of the permanent rules which are being temporarily set aside, and it often makes the decision by roll call vote. Controversy over the "rule" has sometimes overshadowed debate on the legislation itself. Several early Budget Act waivers demonstrated House concern for

32. A "rule" in the form of a simple resolution is necessary before most legislation can be considered in the House. For example, a rule can specify that no floor amendments may be considered ("closed rule") or that only certain amendments may be considered ("limited rule"). Also it may specify the amount of time for debate, and other conditions for floor consideration. The House must approve the "rule" before it can take up the bill. "Suspension" is a procedure under which a bill is called up without a "rule." In order to pass, a bill considered under suspension must be approved by a two-thirds vote.

sticking to the new budget procedures. On March 20, 1975, the House took up a "rule" waiving the Section 401 prohibition against backdoor spending for a housing bill which had borrowing authority. The violation of the Budget Act was purely technical because the House committee responsible for the legislation had agreed to an amendment removing the backdoor provision. Because of a ruling by the House Parliamentarian,[33] however, it was necessary to waive Section 401 before the House could consider the housing bill. Rep. John Anderson immediately raised a point of order that the Budget Act does not provide for waivers in the House. After he was overruled, House Republicans launched a spirited attack against the "rule." Minority Leader Rhodes called the issue "probably the first test of the Budget Act, and to have a bill come out which immediately waives points of order seems to me to do violence to the act itself."[34] Although House Republicans undoubtedly were provoked as much by opposition to the housing bill as by an interest in upholding budget procedure, they based their case on House respect for its rules.

The issue was renewed less than a week later when the House considered a school lunch bill. Once again, the House was asked to adopt a "rule" waiving the Section 401 ban against backdoors. This time, however, the violation was more than technical. Rep. Richard Bolling announced that "there is no apparent attempt on the part of the chairman of the committee or the majority of the committee to heal . . . a wound in the enforcement of the Budget Act."[35] But the House would not let budget procedure stand in the way of a popular program, and it approved the "rule" for consideration of the school lunch bill. Nevertheless, the floor debate showed widespread unease over violation of the budget's rules; as a result, the floor manager of the bill offered a substitute that eliminated the backdoor financing:

> . . . the lengthy discussion . . . has made it apparent that many Members are in disagreement with certain features of the bill. . . . Further concern has been expressed by the members of the House Budget Committee that certain provisions of the bill could be considered as by-

---

33. As a technical matter, when a committee reports a bill along with an amendment to "cure" a Budget Act violation, it first takes up the bill and then proceeds to the committee amendment. The Parliamentarian has ruled that since the bill itself has a violation, it cannot be considered without a waiver.
34. 121 *Congressional Record* (daily ed., March 20, 1975) H2078.
35. 121 *Congressional Record* (daily ed., March 24, 1975) H2231.

passing the appropriations procedure. In view of this concern, the substitute amendment is designed to meet the objections of the members of the Budget Committee.[36]

The Senate has had a more relaxed attitude toward its rules. Because absolute compliance with the rules would probably prevent the Senate from passing much legislation, most Senate business is processed under "unanimous consent" agreements that preempt the permanent rules and set time limits and other conditions for the consideration of particular measures.[37] Senate leaders negotiate most unanimous consent agreements in private with the members directly involved in the legislation, and such measures are often approved without floor debate.

The Budget Act created special procedures for the waiver of budget rules in the Senate. Sections 303 or 402 can be waived in the Senate by a recommendation of the committee with jurisdiction over the affected legislation. The waiver recommendation is referred to the Senate Budget Committee, which has no more than 10 days to make its own recommendations, after which the Senate itself decides whether to approve the waiver. In addition, Section 904 of the Budget Act authorizes the suspension or waiver of any of the budget procedures by majority vote or unanimous consent in the Senate. There are no special provisions for Budget Act waivers in the House, though the "rules" discussed above are available for this purpose.

The House and Senate face different enforcement problems. Spending bills usually carry higher price tags in the Senate than in the House; an appropriation that breaks through a budget target in the Senate might have cleared the House with room to spare. Revenue measures often are "Christmas treed" in the Senate; even if they are in compliance with the revenue floor in the budget resolution when they come out of the House, they are likely to be loaded with money-losing provisions in the Senate. Some bills that

36. 121 *Congressional Record* (daily ed., March 25, 1975) H2279, remarks of Representative Perkins.

37. Every unanimous consent agreement waives one or more Senate rules, though the rule which is being waived, or even the fact that one is to be waived, is rarely mentioned. The use of such agreements has changed substantially in recent years. Where once they were used for routine purposes (such as to waive the reading of the journal or to permit staff persons on the floor of the Senate) or to bring debate already underway to a close, during the 1970s, unanimous consent agreements were worked out to establish time limits for legislation prior to floor consideration.

pass the House with no budgetary impact are turned by the Senate into "vehicles" for costly programs. The House version of day care, for example, had nothing to do with the budget; the Senate, however, added several hundred million dollars for an expanded program.

SBC, therefore, has had to be more concerned about substantive violations of the budget process. When major breaches of the budget levels have occurred in the House, HBC has been active, but most legislation going through the House has not presented substantive problems.

THE BUDGET ACT AS A BARGAINING CHIP

Whether their interests are substantive or procedural, the Budget Committees seem to be in a strong position to enforce the requirements of the budget process. The Budget Act permits points of order to be raised against legislation at variance with the terms of the second budget resolution or not in accord with any of the procedural rules. Yet the Budget Committees cannot persistently block legislation advanced by other committees. It would be unthinkable for the House or Senate to permit one of its committees to hold a veto over wanted legislation or to apply a single, unbending yardstick—fidelity to the budget—to legislative decisions. As a practical matter, the Budget Committees cannot prevent Congress from doing what it wants to do; nor can they unilaterally rewrite legislation to suit their terms. The Budget Act gave them the power to bargain, not the power to legislate. By threatening points of order or floor challenges, they can try to get other committees to remove or modify offensive provisions. The bargaining power of the Budget Committees does not depend solely on the "chips" they hold. The other parties have levers of their own, not the least of which is their ability to line up votes in support of legislation. Bargaining outcomes often turn on the success of the contesting parties in attracting allies or on the perceived importance of the issue. The Budget Committees cannot prevail if they stand alone or if they do not deem the matter worth a fight.

Allies

Whether they strive to uphold budgetary procedure or policy, the Budget Committees can win only if they attract others to their cause. These committees have found it easier to get procedural support than substantive allies. In most cases, the House Rules Committee has refused to grant waivers that lack HBC's endorsement. The exceptions have occurred when the issue was posed in substantive rather than procedural terms. One such instance was the controversy over funds for the B-1 bomber. As part of his decision to cancel the bomber program, President Carter asked Congress to rescind funds previously appropriated for the B-1 and to provide new funds for alternative weapons systems. The new funds were included in a supplemental authorization bill that needed a Section 402 waiver because it had been reported by the Armed Services Committee long after the May 15 deadline. HBC refused to support the waiver; its chairman advised the Rules Committee to wait until the House acted on the President's request to rescind the previous appropriation for the B-1.[38] Rep. Melvin Price, chairman of the Armed Services Committee, protested, "I don't believe that there is anything in the Budget or Impoundment Control Act which justifies the proposal to hold one bill [the supplemental authorization] hostage for action on another program in another committee on funds for another fiscal year." [39] Once the waiver had been linked to a substantive cause, HBC surrendered its preferred position. The Rules Committee treated the case as a substantive dispute in which the Budget Committee had no special expertise and voted for a waiver.

Although the Rules Committee has the lead role in determining floor procedure, that committee is influenced by the attitudes of the Parliamentarian and the Speaker. If the Parliamentarian finds no problem, legislation can move to the floor without a waiver. During the early, precedent-setting years of the budget process, the Parliamentarian worked closely with the HBC staff and was sympathetic to its strict interpretation of the Budget Act. In view of the fact that the House rarely overturns a ruling of the chair, the Parliamentarian's support has bolstered HBC's enforcement of budgetary procedure. The role of the Speaker with respect to floor ac-

38. Letter from Chairman Giaimo to Rep. James J. Delaney, Chairman of the House Rules Committee, September 29, 1977.

39. Letter from Representative Price to Representative Giaimo, September 30, 1977. Giaimo replied the same day, agreeing with Price "that the Budget Committee ought not to get involved in 'line-item' program decisions," but insisting that since a number of the items in the authorization bill "were proposed as alternatives to the B-1 Bomber, it would be impossible to determine the emergency nature of these items until the matter of the B-1 has been resolved."

tion, which has always been important, has been magnified in recent years by the effective conversion of the Rules Committee into an arm of the leadership. Now the Rules Committee usually writes the "rules" according to the Speaker's preference, and is unlikely to refuse a waiver for legislation that the Speaker wants to bring to the floor. HBC cannot expect the Rules Committee to uphold its position when the latter is being urged by the leadership to bring legislation to the floor. In the day care case, Speaker Carl Albert pressed both HBC and Rules to find an acceptable solution. Even though Albert regarded the Budget Act as his cardinal achievement and he enthusiastically backed HBC, he could not permit budget procedure to impede the legislative interests of the House. But Albert did not impose his own day care solution; rather, he instructed HBC to work with the other parties to hammer out an agreement.

When Rep. Tip O'Neill became Speaker in 1977, he had already served as the leadership representative on the Budget Committee. O'Neill is not a stickler for the rules; his interests run more to substantive results. One of his major innovations as Speaker has been a substantial increase in the number of measures considered under suspension of the rules.[40] This expediting procedure can weaken HBC's ability to enforce the budget rules, not only because of time pressures—suspensions often are considered shortly after they have been reported and are rushed through the House—but because the up-or-down vote on suspensions denies HBC the opportunity to bargain for floor amendments that might produce more favorable legislation.

In the Senate, the Majority Leader has cooperated with SBC by "holding" legislation until it has been cleared by the Budget Committee.[41] As a *quid pro quo*, however, SBC is expected to act quickly on waiver requests. The "hold" occurs when the bill is already on

40. During the 95th Congress, there was a sharp increase in the use of the suspension calendar in the House. This practice poses great threats to HBC's control over budget procedure because an item brought up under suspension cannot be amended on the floor and is given only brief consideration. Thus the House can pass a bill that violates Budget Act procedure and Members have no opportunity to raise a point of order or to remedy the problem.

41. An example of this process at work occurred on May 13, 1977. The Senate was about to proceed to the consideration of a minor bill when Majority Leader Byrd announced, "I will have to wait to be sure that this has clearance with the Budget Committee. I think that can be done in a short time." The matter was cleared quickly and the Senate then passed the bill. See 123 *Congressional Record* (daily ed., May 13, 1977) S7550.

the calendar, often no more than a day before the Majority Leader intends to call up the measure. Thus, Muskie prodded his committee the very first time it met to consider a waiver, saying, "Now the Highway Act is on the calendar. The leadership would like to move it today, as early today as possible."[42] Even though they had some qualms about the waiver and the legislation it freed for floor action, SBC members took it for granted that they would approve the waiver without delay. This hurried pace has not encouraged SBC independence; it usually has swept the committee along in the rush to get the legislation through.

With support from House Appropriations, the HBC has been successful in guarding against backdoor contract and borrowing authority. In the House, the Budget Committee has usually gotten the authorizing committee to correct the backdoor violation and the problem has been resolved without public controversy. SBC has cooperated with the Senate Appropriations Committee (there is considerable overlapping of membership), to thwart efforts to curb the discretion of the Appropriations Committee and resist attempts to expand the use of refundable tax credits.[43] The two committees have common substantive interests because legislative actions that improve Appropriations Committee control over federal programs also are likely to enhance the ability of the Budget Committee to control the course of spending.

Although the Budget Committees have constant allies on procedural issues, they normally must settle for transitory support on substantive matters. Each issue brings its particular configuration of allies and adversaries, depending on the interests that would be affected by budgetary discipline. During the 1977 session of Congress, for example, the Senate Budget Committee's leaders took positions on nine bills and floor amendments "which clearly involved significant budget-related issues."[44] Only 14 Senators sided

---

42. Transcript of executive session of the Senate Budget Committee, December 11, 1975, p. 5. The Senate did begin work on the bill on the same day, immediately after approving the requested waiver.

43. Refundable tax credits are refunds in excess of taxes paid to the government. There have been disputes in Congress as to whether these payments should be treated as reductions in federal revenues or as budget outlays. There also has been conflict over the extent to which refundable credits should be subjected to the appropriations process.

44. See Senate Committee on the Budget, Hearings on *Can Congress Control the Power of the Purse?* January 17-19, 1978, 92nd Cong., 2nd Sess., pp. 7-10. SBC listed 13 roll call votes, but 4 pertained to the budget resolutions rather than to enforcement and have been disregarded for purposes of this discussion.

with SBC on more than half of the roll calls, although all but a handful backed it on one or more of the votes. Two-thirds of the Senators supported the SBC position on at least two of the roll calls. This pattern suggests that hardly anyone voted for or against SBC just because the particular issue was budget related. Virtually every Senator outside SBC voted in accord with his stand on the substantive issue. Several who consistently sided with the committee against tax credits favored more spending for particular programs. Some fiscal conservatives who backed SBC against higher spending parted company on revenue issues. Those who supported SBC on a majority of the votes were almost equally divided between Republicans and Democrats, though the list tended toward fiscal conservatives. These supporters did not view their votes as expressions of support for congressional budget decisions, but as opportunities to take sides on particular issues. Significantly, 6 of the 14 who voted with SBC in a majority of the cases voted against final adoption of the first budget resolution for the fiscal year and another 2 opposed the resolution sent to conference by the Senate. Thus, some of the most avid enforcers of the congressional budget were opposed to its adoption, an anomaly that can be explained only by regarding their votes as expressions on substantive policy, not as support for the budget resolutions.

Because each of the Budget Committees has to put together a new coalition every time it wants to combat a substantive violation, each is understandably cautious about the fights it picks. Even with caution, both can expect to lose a good portion of their floor confrontations. SBC lost two-thirds of the enforcement votes on which it took a stand in 1977. The prospects for winning are obviously much improved when the Budget Committee can hold the support of its members. Such support not only gives the Budget Committee a head start toward a majority, but also it indicates that the committee's position enjoys substantive support in the chamber (because, as has been emphasized, most Budget Committee members see the issue in substantive rather than budgetary terms). Only three SBC members took the committee's side on a majority of the votes. Bellmon alone had a perfect pro-committee record and he clearly subordinated some of his own interests to those of the committee. (Muskie missed a considerable number of the votes because of illness.)

The ability of the Budget Committees to recruit congressional allies depends not only on the provisions of the Budget Act but on the political conditions prevailing at a given time. As these conditions change, so too does the enforceability of the budget process. After a losing record in 1977, SBC was victorious (by its own count) on 14 of the 17 enforcement issues it contested in 1978. Its performance was the more impressive because it chose to fight a number of popular authorizations on which Congress could be expected to vote high amounts in anticipation of lower appropriations. Thus, SBC won a floor amendment cutting approximately $5 billion from a housing authorization bill; a second amendment deleted a new billion-dollar mass transit subsidy; a third tightened eligibility standards for public service employment programs. A series of amendments scaled down spending for "impact" aid to school systems and education for handicapped and talented children. SBC also was active on the procedural side, winning floor battles on tax legislation, backdoor spending, and tuition tax credits.

Why did a disappointing record one year turn into a successful one the next? The explanation has already been given. In June 1978, California votes approved Proposition 13 which set limits on the state's taxes. In the wake of this "message," an economy mood swept Washington, reinforced by a national drive for a constitutional amendment to require a balanced federal budget. Under these circumstances, many Senators allied themselves with the Budget Committee in support of spending restraint and fiscal discipline. Three-quarters of the Senators sided with SBC on half or more of the enforcement votes. Significantly, SBC prevailed in a number of instances without a roll call, as its preference was incorporated into the legislation by voice vote.

This mood emboldened the House Budget Committee to be more insistent on substantive issues; the committee also became more successful in drawing key allies to its side. Two 1979 legislative issues illustrate how HBC, while continuing its quiet ways, challenged substantive legislation. In one, the House Small Business Committee reported a bill (H.R. 90) dealing with (among other things) the disaster loan program managed by the Small Business Administration. A similar bill had sailed through the House under suspension in 1978 but had been vetoed by the President. The new measure was sent to the Rules Committee, which was asked to clear it for floor consideration. But when HBC communicated its strong opposition to the legislation, Rules Chairman Richard Bolling decided not to bring H.R. 90 before his committee. The only way the Small Business Committee could get legislation was by coming to terms with HBC. After private negotiations, the committee produced a new bill (H.R. 4011) which gave HBC the concessions it wanted.

In a second instance, HBC was successful because of timely support from the Speaker. A child nutrition bill reported by the House Education and Labor Committee had been placed on the suspension calendar. The only budget problem was that the legislation did not implement any of the savings anticipated in the first budget resolution. Although its past record on legislative savings targeted in the budget resolutions had been dismal, HBC knew that this probably would be the only opportunity to bring the issue before the House during 1979. It thereupon persuaded Speaker O'Neill to withdraw the child nutrition bill, and to return it to the Education and Labor Committee for substantive changes. O'Neill cemented HBC's triumph with an announcement from the chair that he would "not recognize Members for bills under suspension that violate the Budget Act without the concurrence of the Budget Committee."[45]

Although they seek congressional support, the Budget Committees also have the potential of working with the White House to bolster their control over the budget. This option was not open, however, during the Ford Administration. The Democratic-controlled Budget Committees could not make a deal with a Republican President bent on retrenching the federal government's role in social policy. These committees could not permit themselves to be cast as enforcers of a budget policy that accepted high levels of unemployment and redistributed public funds from domestic programs to defense. The advent of the Carter Administration has brought opportunities for cooperation, but the Budget Committees have found the White House to be an unreliable ally. In early 1977, President Carter proposed a $50 tax rebate plan, which the Budget Committees supported. He later abruptly withdrew his support of the plan without informing the committees. That same year, Carter also suddenly changed signals on farm legislation, dropping his opposition to an expansive measure that the committees had opposed. The Budget Committees were then defeated in the House and Senate.

The White House cannot be more than a sometime ally because it must work with other interests and congressional committees. It cannot sacrifice its legislative and political ambitions on the altar of budgetary control any more than the House or Senate can. The Budget Committees can expect to retain presidential support when

---

45. 125 *Congressional Record* (daily ed., June 5, 1979) H4038.

their position already enjoys substantial support in Congress. They cannot expect the President to valiantly go down to defeat with them.

In sum, therefore, the enforcement powers of the Budget Committees are directly related to the support they can draw in the House and Senate. Alone, the Budget Act gives them little advantage; with allies, they have a good chance of winning.

The Bargaining Chips

The Budget Act gives the Budget Committees bargaining chips to use in enforcing substantive decisions as well as in meeting procedural requirements. Substantive enforcement is legally centered on the second budget resolution adopted by Congress each year. Section 310 of the Budget Act establishes an optional reconciliation process for directing legislative committees to report legislation consistent with the second budget resolution. Under this procedure, the Budget Committees can ask Congress to change *existing* laws that would cause revenues or expeditures to violate the second resolution. Section 311 rules out congressional consideration of *new* legislation that would cause revenues to drop below or expenditures to exceed the levels set in the second resolution.

These provisions indicate that the Budget Act links enforcement to the second resolution. Compared with its revenue floor and expenditure ceilings, the first resolution figures are only targets. No point of order can be raised against a bill that breaches the levels fixed in the first resolution; the resolution only provides a budgetary context within which Congress makes its own decisions. When the Budget Act was first proposed, the first resolution was cast as a ceiling; many regarded the subsequent switch to a target as a dilution of budget control in Congress.

Once Congress has adopted a target, it must bear political costs in raising the total; at the same time, no ceiling can withstand the pressures of changing circumstances or a change in congressional attitudes. Muskie was able to enforce the first budget resolution against a defense authorization bill by raising political rather than legal objections: "Congress can change its mind about budget targets after they are adopted. But . . . if Congress decides to breach a spending target, it is actually making a judgment to increase the deficit."[46]

Muskie's argument implies that the second resolution, with its associated reconciliation procedure, is an ineffective enforcer of

46. 121 *Congressional Record* (daily ed., August 1, 1975) S14719.

budgetary discipline. He feared that if the first targets were breached, it would be too late to hold the line when the ceilings are adopted. If Congress disregards the budget targets during the summer, it will not roll back its earlier decisions in September when the second resolution is adopted. This expectation is consistent with the finding in chapter VII that the second resolution has tended to ratify the decisions made by Congress in the course of the year. If circumstances change, Congress moves to a third resolution, as it did in 1977 after Carter's election.

The Budget Act also vests the Budget Committees with "chips" in the form of points of order against legislation in violation of one or another procedural rule. While either of the Budget Committees (or any Member of Congress) can raise a point of order, the Senate Budget Committee has a more direct enforcement role by virtue of its jurisdiction over waivers. Paradoxically, however, the House Budget Committee probably is in a stronger bargaining position than SBC. Because it has no formal role in the enforcement of budget procedures, HBC can "hide" behind the Rules Committee. As long as Rules is willing to accept its recommendations, HBC can remain in the background and defend the budget procedures without bearing the brunt of attack. When HBC refused to support a waiver for the day care bill, it received letters and telegrams from "grass roots" interests urging the committee not to block the needed legislation. Its standard reply was, "The bill is being handled by another committee; we have no jurisdiction over it."

SBC is directly involved in Budget Act waivers; it reviews all waivers recommended by other committees. SBC, however, cannot control the disposition of waivers. If it rejects a waiver, the Senate still has the final say; if it tries to pigeon-hole the matter, SBC is automatically discharged after 10 days and the Senate determines the outcome. The Senate Budget Committee is cognizant of its weak position:

> We can't block the Senate from considering legislation . . . simply by refusing to grant a waiver. No point of order lies against such legislation unless the *Senate* refuses to adopt a waiver resolution. . . . The opinion of the Budget Committee is simply stacked up in any case against the opinion of the authorizing committee, and the Senate determines the issue on a vote on the resolution. If the Senate votes against the Budget Committee and in favor of the authorizing committee, no point of order lies against the legislation.[47]

47. Memorandum to Senator Muskie from John McEvoy, March 5, 1976.

The Case of Social Security: The Chip as a Liability

SBC's vulnerability was displayed in November 1977 when the Senate passed legislation that raised Social Security taxes and made other changes in the program. The bill had a problem related to Section 303 because it changed revenues for fiscal 1979 before that year's first budget resolution was adopted. In the House, Section 303 was waived by "rule," a move endorsed by a 13-9 vote of the House Budget Committee. In the Senate, the Finance Committee reported the bill on November 1, only three days before the scheduled adjournment. Finance also reported a waiver of Section 303 which was referred to the Budget Committee in accord with the Budget Act. Senate Finance Chairman Long took the floor to argue that inasmuch as the Social Security bill would produce additional revenue, SBC could have no reason for opposing a waiver, "I do not think those budget conscious Members of the Budget Committee or any other committee would want to object to the Committee on Finance helping balance the budget." [48]

With Social Security already docketed as the pending business of the Senate, Majority Leader Robert C. Byrd looked for quick action, and obtained unanimous consent to take up the waiver immediately after it came from SBC. Pressured to act at once, the committee met on the afternoon of November 1, but the members instinctively rebelled against the hurried pace forced upon them. Sen. Ernest F. Hollings, acting as chairman in place of the hospitalized Senator Muskie, led the protest parade: "We had no chance, as a Budget Committee, to do very responsible and very much required analysis and give judgment to the Senate itself." [49] Two days later as the Senate pressed for action on Social Security waivers, Hollings told the Senate more bluntly, "This is a stinking way to proceed." [50]

McClure saw grave danger to the budget process:

> . . . the budget resolution, the Budget Act procedure itself, both are in danger of being trampled and destroyed, and the tendency on the part of the Finance Committee to leave measures of this nature to the waning hours of the session are becoming so apparent that they no longer need to be whispered about. . . . If this procedure is permitted, the budget resolution means nothing.[51]

---

48. 123 *Congressional Record* (daily ed., November 1, 1977) S18321.
49. Transcript of Senate Budget Committee meeting, November 1, 1977, p. 14.
50. 123 *Congressional Record* (daily ed., November 3, 1977) S18631.
51. Transcript of Senate Budget Committee meeting, November 1, 1977, p. 19.

Bellmon had "seven good reasons for not granting this waiver," [52] and he urged postponement of Social Security legislation until the next session of Congress. Sen. Lawton Chiles wanted SBC to take advantage of the 10 days allotted to it for waiver resolutions, but he recognized that the committee could not prevail without backing from the leadership. The Budget Act "is just not worth the paper it is written on if the leadership won't support you in a move to uphold the point of order." [53] The leadership was represented by Majority Whip Cranston, who doubled as a member of the Budget Committee: "I am torn in both directions. I am very interested in preserving the budget process [but] . . . I am concerned about the hangups that are involved in this." [54]

SBC was only letting off steam, for it had little choice but to approve the waiver. The Leadership had made Social Security "must" legislation during the final days of the session and it had no patience for procedural delays. With the leadership pressing for action, SBC did not relish the prospect of being blamed for delaying the tax measures. Moreover, Finance had made its bill consistent with the second budget resolution by deferring the tax increase until 1979 and subsequent years. In another concession, Finance had modified a refundable tax credit after SBC objected to it.

But if SBC basically approved Finance's bill, it was deeply concerned about some of the floor amendments waiting in the wings. Some amendments offered fresh tax credits, while others would have liberalized Social Security benefits; as a group, the amendments would have had a multibillion-dollar impact on future budgets. The Finance Committee's request for a waiver (which could not be modified, but only approved or rejected in whole by SBC) covered five expected amendments. If Finance's waiver were to be approved, it would give the green light to consideration of these as well.[55]

Hollings met with Long on the night of November 1, and Long attended an SBC meeting the next morning. Majority Leader Byrd

---

52. *Ibid.*, p. 20.
53. *Ibid.*, p. 24.
54. *Ibid.*, p. 26.
55. SBC explained its anti-amendment position in its first Section 303 waiver: "The purpose of the prohibition against such amendments to legislation upon which a waiver has been granted is to assure that, in adopting such waivers, the Senate does not open the door to amendments which would increase the levels of budget authority or new spending authority beyond those levels contained in the bill upon which a waiver was granted. . . ." S. Rept. No. 94-535 (December 11, 1975).

twice recessed the Senate on November 2 to await the outcome of the negotiations. The parties finally agreed to a modified waiver, covering the Finance bill and a Republican substitute, but none of the other amendments. SBC's troubles were far from over, however, as the waiver issue ricocheted between the Budget Committee and the floor for the next two days. Four Senators whose amendments had been excluded from the waiver approved by SBC introduced their own waiver resolutions. SBC met a third time as it wrestled with the closed-rule effect of giving Finance a waiver while denying it to individual Senators. Senator Domenici pinpointed SBC's predicament:

> I don't think substantive committees, and in particular the Finance Committee, need any additional leverage to get their position through the United States Senate, and I believe that is what we are doing through this process. . . . It gives them [the Finance Committee] tremendous added leverage to get their way and no one else's way. This is a bad position for the Budget Committee to put the Senate in.[56]

On the floor, SBC was railed against by Senators who threatened to filibuster the Social Security bill unless their amendments obtained waivers. Senator Dole, a member of the Budget Committee and one of those whose amendment had been blocked, blasted his SBC colleagues for voting "in a way to influence the outcome of certain legislation. . . . Unfortunately, it is not the Budget Act they are concerned about; they are opposed to the amendment." [57] While he blamed SBC for the impasse, Senator Long admitted that "I sort of like the idea that the Budget Committee can sometimes protect the Finance Committee and help us defend against an amendment that is going to cost a great deal of money." But he concluded that it would be best "to see that every Senator has a chance to offer his amendment." [58] SBC finally discharged itself from the debacle, splitting seven to seven on the waiver issue, and the Senate promptly approved the four waivers en bloc. Right on deadline, the Senate passed the Social Security bill on November 4, after approving several of the challenged amendments.

In a formal defense of his committee's role (inserted for him in the *Congressional Record*), Senator Muskie pointed to SBC's will-

56. Transcript of Senate Budget Committee meeting, November 2, 1977, pp. 68-69.
57. 123 *Congressional Record* (daily ed., November 3, 1977) S18613.
58. *Ibid.*, S18618.

ingness to work within impossible time constraints. Muskie credited SBC with contributing to "sound, orderly debate on matters of significant budgetary and economic impact," although he expressed the hope "that when a bill of this magnitude comes to the Senate . . . the Budget Committee will be permitted to review it in more deliberate fashion." He warned, however, that if SBC were not free to operate "without undue pressure from other members of this body," then the committee's role would be "subject to serious question." [59]

A pressure-free environment is exactly what SBC cannot expect in its role as budget enforcer. Not only must it bear the brunt of pressure for waivers, because it applies a substantive test to these exemptions, but also it is vulnerable to the charge that it is meddling in the affairs of other committees and trying to force its views upon the Senate. Such a charge was made in the Social Security episode, and it can be expected to be made again whenever SBC insists on a hard line against wanted legislation.

Bargaining Outcomes

Bargaining has rarely resulted in one side's getting all that it wants and the other party's getting nothing at all. One-sided bargains have usually indicated great inequality in the importance of the issue to the contestants or in the contestants' political power. HBC has gotten its way on most Section 402 waivers; SBC has usually given in without a fight. One committee cares about the procedures at stake, the other does not. SBC, however, does care about Section 303 (which bars floor action on revenue and spending bills until passage of the first budget resolution) and it usually has gotten something in exchange for a waiver.

It should be clear by now that the outcome is affected by the support the Budget Committee has (or expects) in its chamber. For example, in February 1976, HBC blocked an unemployment compensation bill which Ways and Means wanted considered before adoption of the first budget resolution; such consideration would have violated the Budget Act's Section 303. When HBC refused to endorse a waiver, the bill was shelved for several months. That same month, HBC also refused a waiver for the day care bill already discussed. The issue and the contestants were the same as in the unemployment legislation case, but in the latter instance, the Budget Committee receded and a waiver was issued.

59. 123 *Congressional Record* (daily ed., November 4, 1977) S18843.

In the unemployment case, HBC sensed that the bill (which called for a tax increase) was not overly popular and it felt little pressure from the House to move quickly on the legislation. In fact, when unemployment compensation was called up several months later, the House rejected the "rule." This rejection was unusual for legislation coming from the Ways and Means Committee. Day care, however, presented a different situation. Without taking a vote on the matter, HBC knew that it could not hold up day care for months until the first budget resolution was cleared.

When the Budget Committee has had to yield on something it considers important, it has tried to get concessions in return. On the day care matter, HBC got the bill's supporters to accept temporary funding, even though all parties understood that permanent funds would be provided for the next fiscal year after the Budget Act problems had passed. In the case of Social Security, SBC won the removal of certain refundable tax credits to which it had objected. When the other party bows to the procedural constraints of the budget, it also can be expected to seek something in return. *Quid pro quo* thus has been a recurring feature of the congressional budget process.

What a committee gets and what it gives up depend on what it values most. When the House Budget Committee is interested in procedural enforcement but its adversary wants substantive results, the typical exchange upholds the budget rules while giving the other most (or all) of its substantive objectives. The first application of this formula occurred in April 1975 when the House rushed through a bill already approved by the Senate providing funds for a summer school food program. The Senate version had a "backdoor" provision which provoked a standard objection from HBC. With summer approaching, however, supporters of the backdoor provision feared that a requirement that funds be provided through the appropriations process would effectively kill the program. Accordingly, a deal was arranged to remove the backdoor provision in exchange for a firm commitment to expedite the funds through the appropriations process. Floor manager Perkins spelled out the terms of the deal:

> We have agreed to include in our amendment an elimination of backdoor spending on the assurance that funding—consistent with the Senate provision requiring $52,700,000 in Section 32 moneys—would be provided through the appropriations process. More specifically, we discussed the possibility of adding such an amount to the pending supple-

mental appropriations bill or if this was not possible, providing for funding in a special resolution.

Our agreement, Mr. Speaker, which is responsive to the sensitive feeling of the House regarding of "backdoor spending," represents a commitment as firm as the Senate's to financing this program at an adequate level and in a timely manner.[60]

Give and take also governed the outcome of entitlement legislation for the Corporation for Public Broadcasting. The bill developed by the House Commerce Committee both authorized and appropriated federal funds to match private contributions made for educational radio and television. The legislation covered a five-year period, and was in response to pressure for long-range financing of public broadcasting.[61] The bill was referred to the House Appropriations Committee, which objected to the entitlement as well as to the advance commitment of funds. The Appropriations Committee was backed by HBC which was in a position to block the measure by raising a Budget Act objection. But pressure from the broadcast industry for "politics-free" financing induced the HBC to compromise. A satisfactory arrangement was negotiated by converting the entitlement to an authorization combined with an explicit promise by Appropriations to provide advance funding for three years at a time.[62]

Time pressure and constituency influences converged in the 1976 extension of the revenue-sharing program, with HBC once again conceding to the substantive interests. The House Budget and Appropriations Committees tried to convert revenue sharing from an entitlement into a conventional authorization financed through the appropriations process. The House, however, voted to continue the entitlement, thereby showing wide support for the program.[63] When the bill came back from conference, however, it provided for

60. 121 *Congressional Record* (daily ed., April 9, 1975) H2609.

61. See H. Rept. No. 94-245, Pt. 1 (May 22, 1975).

62. Daniel J. Flood, chairman of the House Appropriations subcommittee with jurisdiction over the program made this commitment to the House: ". . . when authorizing legislation is enacted, the [appropriations] committee will recommend appropriations for fiscal year 1976, and advance appropriations for fiscal years 1977 and 1978, and would expect that Congress would consider additional advance appropriations in the course of the annual appropriations process each year." 121 *Congressional Record* (daily ed., November 10, 1975) H10872. The Appropriations Committee has honored its commitment, and the Corporation for Public Broadcasting is the only entity to which a three-year advance appropriation is made.

63. The move by Adams would have extended revenue sharing as an entitlement for 21 months but subjected it to the annual appropriations process thereafter. This amendment lost by a 150-244 vote.

modest spending increases in each of the years covered by the legislation. HBC Chairman Adams objected to these increases as a Section 303 violation and his point of order was sustained by the Speaker.[64] Because no remedy had been worked out in advance, HBC seemed to be in a good position to drive a hard bargain, but such was not the case. Congress was scheduled to adjourn in barely another day and would not return until the existing revenue-sharing program had expired. The pressure thus was on HBC to find a solution to *its* Budget Act problem. HBC had to swallow a formula which was deemed to preserve the procedural letter of the Budget Act while providing the additional funds sought by the Senate. But rather than specifying the additional funds in the legislation, revenue sharing was "indexed" to federal income tax receipts. As the latter climbed, so too would revenue-sharing payments, but the formula was "capped" to limit each year's increase to $200 million, exactly the amount provided in the conference report. HBC had its procedural victory, but in terms of substantive control over expenditures, it gave away more than had been conceded by the version to which it had objected. With revenue sharing now tied to federal tax receipts, congressional control over future spending could be weakened merely by removing the cap.[65] HBC had traded away something of substantive value in order to retain its hold over budget procedure.

Because it is more interested in budget substance than in procedure, SBC exacts a different *quid pro quo* than HBC does for going along with a bargain. If the problem is substantive, such as the amount of spending, SBC tries to negotiate a reduction in expenditures to bring them closer to the level anticipated in the congressional budget. SBC is particularly active when entitlement legislation is proposed, as the next section shows.

THE ENTITLEMENT PROBLEM

Whatever their differences on budgetary enforcement, both Budget Committees have reason to take a hard line on entitlements,

64. 122 *Congressional Record* (daily ed., September 30, 1976) H11860.
65. Rep. Jack Brooks, an opponent of revenue sharing, objected to the remedy: ". . . even though the provisions may technically qualify within the words of the Budget Act, the effect of this effort is no different from the provision in the conference report . . . there is no way that it can be of any value other than to serve as a vehicle for raising entitlements and, therefore, effectively breaching and thwarting the purpose of the Budget Act." *Ibid.*, H11877.

legislation that obligates the federal government to make payments to individuals or other governments. Not only have entitlements been the fastest-growing part of the federal budget, but they account for more than two-thirds of all uncontrollable spending. When Congress establishes a new entitlement, the Budget Committees are the big losers. Their discretion over future budgets is diminished, because once established in law, entitlements are not easily taken away. The fact that entitlements are sometimes rolled back (as in 1976 when the Budget Committee successfully campaigned to eliminate a 1 percent bonus in cost-of-living adjustments to pensions of retired federal workers) should not obscure the entrenched position that most of these statutory benefits have in the federal budget.

The Budget Committees have tried to discourage the spread of entitlements into new program areas. To do so, they have used two weapons, the procedural rules of the Budget Act, and publicity about the cost of entitlements. The Budget Act prescribes special rules for entitlements, but these are not so stringent as those governing backdoor contract and borrowing authority. Thus, while new contract or borrowing authority is available only to the extent provided in appropriation acts, new entitlements can be funded by authorizing legislation. But entitlements must wait until adoption of the first budget resolution and cannot take effect prior to the start of the next fiscal year. Moreover, if an entitlement would cause an authorizing committee to exceed its allocated budget authority, the legislation is referred to the Appropriations Committee, which has the option of offering an amendment to reduce the amount of entitlement.

In effect, the Budget Act makes the Appropriations and Budget Committees partners in the control of entitlements. These committees have a common interest; both suffer a loss of budgetary control when entitlements are established or expanded. But, as with other aspects of the budget process, these committees have the right to bargain, not the right to block legislation.

These committees were caught off guard and prevented from using their bargaining power in 1977 when the Senate converted a small ($28 million) nutrition education program from an authorization to an entitlement. The bill reported by the Agriculture Committee was a straightforward authorization and SBC gave it a routine Section 402 waiver. The entitlement bill was added by floor amendment and approved by voice vote. After the bill was adopted, Senator Chiles, a member of both the Budget and Appropriations

Committees, moved for reconsideration, protesting that "for the first time we have an education grant program to the States that would become an entitlement program."[66] Senator Muskie rushed to the floor to rebuke the Agriculture Committee for not informing SBC of the prospective development when it asked for a waiver. "I believe that the Budget Committee might have responded unfavorably [to the waiver] if they had known the new program would be converted into an entitlement two days later."[67]

But it was too late for SBC to play its chip, and the bill was approved unanimously by the Senate. One year later, the Senate took up another nutrition bill with an entitlement feature. This time the stakes were much higher; the aggregate cost over the four years of the legislation was $3.2 billion. Before floor action, the bill was sent to the Senate Appropriations Committee, which had the option of proposing a scaled-down version of the program. But Appropriations wanted to do more than merely to adjust the spending level in the bill; it also wanted to cast the legislation into a conventional authorization by eliminating the entitlement provision. SBC was concerned about the cost as well as the entitlement feature of the bill, and it participated in the bargaining. The compromise worked out by the affected parties gave something to everyone, as the following data show:

	Agriculture Committee Bill		*Compromise Bill*	
Fiscal Year	*Amount (in millions)*	*Status*	*Amount (in millions)*	*Status*
1979	$600	Entitlement	$550	Entitlement
1980	800	Entitlement	800	Entitlement
1981	900	Entitlement	900	Authorization
1982	950	Entitlement	950	Authorization

The Budget and Appropriations Committees won a small reduction in first-year expenditures and a return to authorizations in the last two years of the program.[68] The Agriculture Committee how-

66. 123 *Congressional Record* (daily ed., June 30, 1977) S11202.
67. *Ibid.*, S11219.
68. Although he went along with the compromise, Senator McGovern, the bill's manager, insisted that the Appropriations Committee had exceeded its authority under the Budget Act. That is, rather than merely proposing a change in spending level. Appropriations made a substantive change in the program. See 124 *Congressional Record* (daily ed., July 21, 1978) S11472.

ever, seems to have gotten the better part of the bargain. It garnered a steep increase in the second year's funds when the program still would be an entitlement. It thus has a solid base for high spending levels in future years, even though the program would be turned into an authorization. Although its bargaining chip brought some gain, the Budget Committee was not able to stem the congressional inclination to provide assured funding to powerful interests.

The Budget Committees have an additional lever that applies to all budget issues but is especially advantageous in entitlement matters. Many entitlements are open-ended; they do not restrict, or even identify, the amount to be spent. In these circumstances, actual spending is determined by factors that cannot be foreseen with precision, principally the number of beneficiaries and the payments to which they are entitled. Prior to the Budget Act, Congress could conveniently disregard or underestimate the prospective cost of this type of legislation, but it is no longer so easy to legislate in ignorance.

As required by the Budget Act, CBO estimates the future cost of all entitlement bills reported by House and Senate committees. These cost projections have become formidable instruments of budgetary control. During 1977, congressional debate over food stamp legislation centered on the estimated cost of competing reform proposals. All parties seemed committed to a program that would not exceed the budgeted level. The Budget Committees can sensitize Congress of the cost of legislation that appears on its face to be "costless." In one of its most satisfying victories, HBC thwarted "sleeper" legislation that would have entitled federal employees to retirement pay after 30 years of service, regardless of the employee's age. Although the bill did not carry a price tag, HBC estimated that it would cost $3 billion over the lifetimes of the current population of federal workers. When the chairman of the sponsoring committee was apprised of this unexpected estimate, he quietly withdrew the measure from the calendar.

The creation of new entitlements definitely has slowed down since the Budget Act was enacted. One telling statistic is the percentage of the federal budget taken by uncontrollable "open-ended programs and fixed costs" (the term used by the Office of Management and Budget). Leaving aside interest costs, which are not directly subject to budget determination, these payments grew an average of 9 percent a year in fiscal years 1977-79, compared with an 18 percent annual growth rate in the first half of the decade. Virtually all of the 1977-79 increase was due to the mandatory rise in existing entitlements rather than to congressional action. It is hard to ascertain whether the pronounced slowdown in new entitlements has been due primarily to the operations of the Budget Act or to the fiscal temper in Congress, but it seems reasonable to conclude that both factors have been relevant.

IMPOUNDMENT CONTROL: LEGISLATIVE DOMINATION VERSUS EXECUTIVE DISCRETION

The Budget Act concentrates on the internal operations of Congress, but in coupling impoundment control to the budget process, Congress recognized that it must enforce its budget decisions against executive deviations from its spending priorities.[69]

Title X of the Budget Act is known as the Impoundment Control Act. It establishes procedures for congressional review and control of executive actions that prevent or delay the expenditure of funds appropriated by Congress. Impoundment controls are predicated on a distinction between rescissions and deferrals, with different procedures applied to each category. When the President does not anticipate any current or prospective need for funds, or when withheld funds would lapse before they are scheduled for release, he must ask Congress to rescind the appropriation. Deferrals are to be proposed when the President anticipates future but not current need for the funds. The President must notify Congress of all proposed rescissions and deferrals; he must also provide certain required information concerning each action.

In the case of rescissions, the funds must be released unless Congress passes a rescission bill within 45 days of continuous session (as defined by the Impoundment Control Act) following notification by the President. Deferrals, however, may continue in effect unless either the House or Senate disapproves them by an impoundment resolution. There is no time limit for congressional veto of a deferral, but a deferral cannot extend beyond the

---

69. Representative Bolling, floor manager of the budget reform legislation, argued that "budget reform and impoundment control have a joint purpose: to restore responsibility for the spending policy of the United States to the legislative branch. One without the other would leave Congress in an ineffective and weak position. No matter how prudently Congress discharges its appropriations responsibility, legislative decisions have no meaning if they can be unilaterally abrogated by executive impoundments." 119 *Congressional Record* (daily ed., December 4, 1973) H10577.

end of a fiscal year. The Comptroller General is responsible for overseeing executive compliance with the impoundment controls. He must inform Congress if the President has failed to report an impoundment or if an action has been improperly classified. The Comptroller General also is empowered to bring suit to enforce the impoundment controls.

The Impoundment Control Act has not put an end to impoundments; more than $60 billion in rescissions and deferrals were submitted to Congress during the first five years of impoundment control. Nor has the Budget Act ended all controversy over impoundments, although the passions have abated. Except for occasional problems, impoundment control has settled into a three-stage process involving presidential recommendations and reports, Comptroller General review, and congressional action or, in most cases, inaction. At each of these stages, Congress has been bombarded with documentation and paperwork, much required by the law itself, some growing out of the manner in which the law has been implemented. In 1974 Congress opted for a broad definition of impoundments, on the ground that excessive paperwork is preferable to excessive strife. Section 1011 of the Act defines a deferral as any "(A) withholding or delaying the obligation or expenditure of budget authority . . . provided for projects or activities; or (B) any other type of Executive action or inaction which effectively precludes the expenditure of budget authority."

This provision can be read to cover many thousands of routine administrative actions that affect the rate and level of expenditure. Sensibly, however, the Comptroller General has ruled that the Impoundment Control Act "does not purport to invalidate the exercise of reasonable administrative discretion in the adoption of program provisions and regulations."[70] He also has held that failure to spend the full amount of an appropriation does not by itself constitute an impoundment: "There must be sufficient evidence of behavior on the part of responsible Executive agency officials that demonstrates an intention to refrain from obligating available budget authority."[71]

Even with a narrow interpretation of impoundment, more than six hundred proposed rescissions and deferrals, packaged into

70. *Decision of the Comptroller General of the United States,* June 11, 1975, Reprinted in General Accounting Office, *Review of the Impoundment Control Act of 1974 After 2 Years,* June 3, 1977, p. 173.

71. Letter of the Comptroller General to Representative James J. Florio, September 28, 1976, printed in *ibid.,* p. 217.

numerous presidential messages, have been forwarded to Congress, along with numerous supplementary submissions. Since 1974 the General Accounting Office has sent more than a hundred communications to Congress, many in response to legislative complaints about executive actions. Congress has considered a dozen rescission bills, more than a hundred impoundment resolutions have been introduced, and 50 have been passed.

The Routines of Impoundment Control

Table 32 reports on nearly five years of impoundments.[72] During this period, deferrals totaled almost $50 billion compared with $10.3 billion for the rescissions; in each of the years, the dollar value of the deferrals was at least three times greater than the amount proposed for rescission. The executive branch can be expected to favor deferrals because they continue in effect if Congress fails to act. Rescissions, however, must cease if Congress fails to complete action during the 45-day period. Nevertheless, the preponderance of deferrals has more to do with the purposes for which impoundments are made than with presidential exploitation of the Impoundment Control Act. A routine impoundment occurs when a program or project can be completed without full use of available funds or when the funds cannot be used until a later date. A policy impoundment occurs when the President decides that he does not want the program or project, or wants it on a smaller scale than that authorized by Congress. Most deferrals have been routine administrative actions; with many billions of dollars appropriated for long lead-time construction and procurement activities, it is not surprising that the executive branch would routinely defer the use of large sums of money. Rescissions, however, are more likely to have policy motives. President Ford tried to cancel billions of dollars added by Congress for social programs; President Carter persuaded Congress to rescind funds it had appropriated for military weapons.

Overall, impoundment has been a declining activity, with the total volume of both rescissions and deferrals much lower under President Carter than under his predecessor. Most of the drop has been in policy impoundments; after all, there is no reason to expect routine deferrals or rescissions to steadily decline. Policy impound-

72. The data are drawn from the files of the House Appropriations Committee and differ from statistics compiled by the General Accounting Office. Most of the differences are minor, but several might affect the conclusions drawn in the text.

Table 32

RESCISSIONS AND DEFERRALS, FISCAL YEARS 1975-79
(dollars in thousands)

Rescissions					
Year	*Number*[a]	*Amount Proposed*	*Amount Approved*	*Percent of Dollars Rescinded*	*Percent of Proposals Approved (in whole or part)*
1975	91 (4)	$ 3,328,500	$ 391,295	12%	43%
1976[b]	50 (1)	3,608,363	138,331	4	14
1977	21 (1)	1,835,602	1,271,040	70	48
1978	8 (0)	644,055	55,255	9	38
1979[c]	10 (0)	908,692	723,609	80	80

Deferrals						
Year	*Number*[a]	*Amount Deferred*	*Amount Disapproved*	*Number of Deferrals Disapproved*	*Percent of Dollars Disapproved*	*Percent of Deferrals Disapproved*
1975	159	$24,574,236	$9,318,217	16	38%	10%
1976[b]	119 (2)	9,209,780	393,081	24[d]	4	20
1977	68 (4)	6,831,194	25,600	3	0.4	5
1978	66 (0)	4,910,114	69,531	6	1.4	9
1979[c]	58 (1)	4,393,328	13,852	2	0.3	3

[a] The GAO notifications of unreported impoundments indicated in parentheses are included in the tabulations of rescissions and deferrals. Thus the 91 rescissions in fiscal 1975 include 87 reported by OMB and 4 reported by GAO.

[b] Fiscal 1976 data include the transition quarter. A proposal to rescind funds in both fiscal 1976 and the transition quarter July-September 1975 is counted as a single proposal.

[c] Data provided through June 1979.

[d] Two fiscal 1976 deferrals were disapproved by both the House and Senate; they are counted only once here.

Source: Tabulated from House Appropriations Committee data.

ments (mostly rescissions) have declined for two reasons. First, when President Ford sought to eliminate funds appropriated in excess of his budget requests, Congress generally refused to give him a second chance to accomplish via the new impoundment process that which it had denied to him earlier in the course of the appropriations process. The more than 90 percent rejection rate for Ford's rescissions indicates that he was repeatedly rebuffed in his efforts to use impoundment control to overturn the budget priorities voted by Congress. After getting the message that Congress would not go along with wholesale policy impoundments, the executive branch cut down its resort of this practice. Second, the changeover from a Republican to a Democratic White House contributed to a drop in policy impoundments. A President of the same party as Congress is unlikely to engage in protracted dispute over the level or purposes of expenditure, or to carry a conflict to the impoundment stage. Moreover, when Carter entered office, he promised congressional leaders not to use impoundments for policy purposes.

Party relationships also explain congressional responses. Carter has had a much higher success rate with regard to both rescissions and deferrals than his predecessor had. In dollar terms, less than 10 percent of Ford's rescissions were approved by Congress, while approximately two-thirds of Carter's rescissions have been enacted. Because of common party identifications, Carter has been reluctant to propose rescissions and Congress has been reluctant to disapprove those proposed. Carter also has been more successful in defending his deferrals against congressional veto. Only about 5 percent of his deferrals have been overturned, compared with 15 percent of Ford's. If one measures deferred funds in dollars, Ford was compelled by Congress to release 20 percent of his deferrals while Carter has had to release less than 1 percent of his deferrals.

Regardless of who is in the White House, however, Congress is much more likely to uphold a deferral than a rescission. Most deferrals are sustained by congressional inaction; most rescissions proposed by the President have been "disapproved" by congressional inaction. Over the five-year span, only 10 percent of the deferrals were disapproved by Congress, while 65 percent of the rescissions were disallowed by congressional unwillingness to approve the necessary legislation. In dollar terms, the level of disapprovals was inflated by a single action forcing the release of $9 billion of highway reserves accumulated over the years. With the highway deferral excluded, Congress disapproved less than 2 percent of the dollars deferred by the President; it disapproved 75 percent of the funds proposed for rescission.

Just as they have adjusted to a shift in political conditions, the impoundment controls have survived a change in the uses to which they have been put. More than 90 percent of Ford's rescissions were from domestic programs; only 5 percent were related to defense. The proportions were reversed during the Carter years; almost 90 percent of the rescissions have been proposed in defense programs while hardly any dollars have been taken from domestic activities. Under both Presidents, Congress has been willing to go along with policy rescissions from defense programs. Congress approved both Ford's cutoff of production of F-111 aircraft and Carter's cancellation of funds appropriated for the B-1 bomber. All told, Congress has repealed two-thirds of the defense dollars proposed for rescission but only 8 percent of the nondefense dollars. Congress has approved (in whole or in part) 88 percent of the defense-related rescission proposals; it has enacted 26 percent of the nondefense proposals.

Why have defense interests been unable to hold on to appropriations that they won only months earlier? Why have they been less successful than domestic interests in warding off presidential impoundments? The impoundment controls do not appear to be inherently biased against defense expenditures. It is possible that because liberal Members of Congress pushed for the Impoundment Control Act in order to prevent the President from curtailing their programs, they have been especially vigilant to assure that the Act is not turned against their programs. Conservative Members of Congress who tend to favor defense programs might be willing to accept cutbacks on economy grounds.

Impoundment Control as the Containment of Budgetary Conflict

The Impoundment Control Act has established a workable, if burdensome, procedure for review of executive impoundments. It does not resolve basic constitutional questions of legislative-executive relations and the extent of presidential power, but it offers a method of settling these disputes without addressing more contentious issues. Congress has been able to prevent the President from unilaterally withholding funds, and the executive branch has been able to manage its financial affairs without undue rigidity. The impoundment battles have not ended, but now they usually are fought through agreed-upon means. In contrast to the contests of the Nixon era, impoundment control means limited warfare and, in most cases, resolution of the dispute within a limited period of time. Very few of the impoundment conflicts since 1974 have spilled over into the courts.

The executive branch has generally conformed to the procedures of the 1974 Act. GAO has brought to Congress's attention few unreported impoundments and few serious misclassifications of rescissions or deferrals. Both Ford and Carter expeditiously released funds when required by the law. Yet a President bent on overriding the policies of Congress might disregard the impoundment controls as well. One can only speculate about what might have happened if the impoundment law had been in operation during the early 1970s when a willful President unilaterally cut off funds for programs favored by Congress. But it should be noted that Nixon exploited the absence of law—the fuzzy demarcation of power between the two branches—to take power into his own hands. A future impounder would have to reckon with statutory constraints and an enforcement procedure involving Congress, GAO, and the courts.

Although Congress has gained the upper hand, it is not completely satisfied with the impoundment controls. The volume of paperwork has bothered some Members of Congress and there have been suggestions to eliminate or to simplify the control of routine impoundments.[73] A more disturbing problem has been delay in the reporting of impoundments. It often takes weeks for an agency's withholding of funds to work its way up through the bureaucracy, OMB, and the White House. In addition, because OMB prefers to group a number of impoundments into a single presidential message, it sometimes delays their submission to Congress. Although GAO is supposed to monitor executive compliance, it cannot inspect every administrative action affecting the availability of funds. GAO cannot always distinguish between delays caused by prudent management and delays prompted by policy motives. Even when it is vigilant, GAO ordinarily becomes aware of an executive action only after it has taken effect.

Moreover, GAO has adopted a reactive posture toward executive branch impoundments. Rather than initiating investigations, it gets involved only after the President has filed an impoundment report or a third party has complained about executive action. This

73. The Comptroller General has proposed numerous modifications of the Impoundment Control Act. See General Accounting Office, *Review of the Impoundment Control Act of 1974 After 2 Years*, pp. 10-18.

procedure does not always protect congressional interests. Thus, when President Carter decided to terminate the B-1 bomber, he ordered the cancellation of construction contracts three weeks before notifying Congress. Although Congress could have disapproved the rescission proposal and compelled the Defense Department to resume work on the airplane, reopening the program would have entailed considerable costs.

The delay problem is compounded by the way in which the 45 days for acting on rescissions are computed. Because periods during which Congress is in recess are not counted and because the period begins anew after Congress has adjourned *sine die,* the 45 days can stretch to a much longer period of time. During the 1975 and 1976 fiscal years, the interval between the submission of a rescission proposal and the end of the 45-day period averaged 80 calendar days. Because impoundments do not have to be reported until after the 30 days allowed by law for the apportionment of funds, the actual time between appropriation and termination of the rescission averaged more than a hundred days. As a consequence of these delays, Ford used the impoundment process to put unwanted programs into cold storage for much of the fiscal year, thereby frustrating congressional intent and impairing program effectiveness. Delay sometimes has been sought for its own sake and, possibly, for political advantage as well.

Executive tardiness has been exacerbated by Congress's tendency to wait until the last moment to act on rescission bills. When Congress fails to give the executive branch an early indication of its intentions, funds are tied up while rescission legislation is pending. Foot dragging by Congress has led to an anomaly in impoundment control: some rescissions are approved after the 45-day period has expired. The B-1 bomber is a case in point. After the President proposed a rescission, the 45-day clock started to run, but time ran out before Congress completed action on a rescission bill. Months later—148 days after Congress had been notified—a rescission of B-1 funds was attached to a supplemental appropriations bill. Under strict application of the impoundment controls, the President should have ordered the immediate release of impounded funds and resumption of work on the cancelled contracts. Instead, the Defense Department released the funds without actually obligating them. The money was not impounded, but it was not used either.

In one instance, Congress fashioned its own remedy while a

rescission was being considered. After President Carter announced his opposition to certain water projects, Congress attached a rider to the Public Works Employment Act of 1977:

Sec. 201. Congress hereby finds and declares that . . . such projects should not be discontinued except by following the legislative process provided by . . . the Congressional Budget and Impoundment Control Act of 1974.

Sec. 202. Notwithstanding the deferral and rescission provisions of Public Law 93-344, all appropriations provided in Public Laws 94-355 and 94-351 [fiscal 1977 appropriations for public works and agriculture] for construction projects or for investigations, planning, or design related to construction projects shall be made available for obligation by the President and expended for the purposes for which the appropriations are made. . . .

Although the language of the two sections appears to be contradictory—Section 201 seems to uphold impoundment control procedures while Section 202 seems to bypass them—the intent was to avert a possible rescission or deferral by announcing in advance that Congress would disapprove any such action. If this remedy were applied across the board to all appropriations, it would effectively negate the Impoundment Control Act.

Legislative Control Versus Executive Discretion

Congress has tried to apply the Impoundment Control Act in ways that limit executive discretion in the use of appropriated funds. The executive branch, often aided by sympathetic rulings from the Comptroller General, has tried to confine impoundment control to overt withholding of funds. The controversy has taken a number of forms; the two that have provoked explicit congressional reactions are the reprogramming of funds and administrative ceilings on personnel. Reprogrammings occur when funds are shifted from one purpose to another within the same appropriation account. GAO has ruled that these transfers do not violate the Impoundment Control Act—that is, the fact that funds are being underspent for the activity from which funds are taken does not constitute an impoundment—so long as there is no *net* withholding of funds. The issue arose when President Carter sought to apply funds appropriated for development of the Clinch River breeder reactor to the termination of the project. In a June 23, 1977, letter to Sen. Henry M. Jackson, the Comptroller General held that this diversion of the funds did not violate the impoundment controls:

The Act is concerned with the rescissions or deferral or budget authority, not the rescission or deferral of programs. Thus, a lump-sum appropriation for programs A, B and C used to carry out only program C would not necessarily indicate the existence of impoundments regarding programs A and B. So long as all budgetary resources were used for program C, no impoundment would occur even though activities A and B remain unfunded.[74]

Congressional response to reprogramming has been to extend impoundment controls to particular programs and projects. Thus, Section 304 of the second supplemental appropriation for fiscal 1977 had the following prohibition:

None of the funds appropriated or otherwise made available in this act shall be obligated or expended for the termination or deferral of any project, activity, or weapons system approved by Congress, except specific projects, activities, or weapons systems for which, and to the extent, budget authority has been rescinded or deferred as provided by law.

Although its sponsor insisted that this provision would not bar reprogrammings, the effect seems to have been otherwise. If a similar provision were extended to all programs, appropriations would, in effect, be converted to a line-item basis and most, if not all, reprogrammings would be proscribed.

Congress also has moved toward line-item controls in response to ceilings on agency personnel. These ceilings—established by OMB or the agencies themselves—can affect the level of expenditure in two ways: First, the amount of money spent on salaries is likely to be less than the amount provided by Congress; second, personnel shortages can slow down administrative operations and reduce the level of expenditure below the amount appropriated for programs. For example, an agency might be unable to process all eligible loan applications because OMB ceilings prevented it from hiring needed personnel.

Congressional concern over impoundment by means of personnel

74. In another part of this opinion, the Comptroller General held that use of the funds to terminate the Clinch River project violated federal law which prohibits expenditure of funds for unauthorized purposes. Having reached this conclusion, the Comptroller General might have reasoned that since the money should not be spent on termination, failure to spend it for intended purposes violated the Impoundment Control Act.

ceilings was reflected in the agriculture appropriations bill for fiscal 1979. The House Appropriations Committee protested

> the tendency of the executive branch to establish arbitrary personnel ceilings to slow down or stop various programs . . . in violation of the spirit, if not the letter, of the Impoundment Control Act.
>
> On several occasions, funds have been appropriated for additional staff deemed essential by the Congress, and then used as additional funds for travel or equipment and supplies.[75]

The Appropriations Committee restructured the 1979 budget accounts for several agriculture programs to prevent these practices:

> . . . to avoid such de facto impoundments in the future, the committee has recommended in many instances separate appropriations for "personnel compensation and benefits" and "for other expenses". As a result of this bill language, any attempt to withhold funds for salaries must be reported to Congress for its consideration under the law.[76]

In effect, the committee moved to "line-itemize" certain appropriations, thereby bringing them under the scope of the Impoundment Control Act.

Impoundment control is the contemporary version of a battle that has been waged between the legislative and executive branches since the origin of American nationhood: line-item control by Congress versus executive discretion. The main difference between this and earlier confrontations is that whereas Congress once asserted line-item controls in order to prevent the executive branch from spending funds, now it uses the controls to compel the executive branch to spend funds against its wishes. For two hundred years, power over the line items has seesawed between the two branches. Congress was dominant through much of the 19th century; with the conversion to lump-sum appropriations in this century, the executive branch gained supremacy. The Impoundment Control Act represents an effort by the legislature to tilt the scales back in its favor, but it is unlikely that the Act will settle the issue. In the matter of spending power, gray areas will continue to exist in the relationship between the two branches, and these will be breeding grounds for future controversy and confrontation.

---

75. H. Rept. No. 95-1290 (June 13, 1978) p. 30.
76. *Ibid.*

THE LIMITS OF ENFORCEMENT

Congress has been successful in guarding its budget decisions against presidential impoundment. By using the impoundment controls, it has compelled successive Presidents to spend money against their wishes. While the controls have not been absolutely problem-free, the results thus far justify a finding that unilateral impoundment has been effectively curtailed.

The same finding cannot be made with respect to the congressional budget process. The Budget Committees have had limited success in protecting Congress from itself. Congress has, in fact, passed just about all the legislation it has wanted, though not always in the preferred form. On process issues, Congress often has deferred to the requirements of the Budget Act, but it has not been willing to let procedure get in the way of its substantive goals. Congress has been willing to negotiate with its Budget Committees; it has not been willing to give them an absolute check against legislation. On contentious issues, the parties usually have compromised, with the Budget Committees preserving what they regard as the essentials of their process and Congress getting the essentials of its legislation.

PART THREE

IMPACTS ON SPENDING AND TAXING COMMITTEES

X The Subdued Guardians: The Appropriations Committees and Their Process

The appropriation of funds is the oldest spending power exercised by Congress and the only one specifically anchored in the Constitution: "No money shall be drawn from the Treasury but in consequence of appropriations made by law." The Appropriations Committees have commonly been regarded as among the most powerful units in Congress, with the House committee generally more esteemed than its Senate counterpart by virtue of its initiative in money bills.[1] Members have coveted places on Appropriations; many have surrendered their seats on other committees in order to get this prized assignment.[2]

Yet during the late 1960s and early 1970s, a series of changes in the structure and internal operations of the Appropriations Committees weakened their status and diminished their power as guardians of the treasury. As pointed out in chapter II, these changes were major factors leading to enactment of a congressional budget process as a new form of spending control. Their cumulative effect was diminution of the role of the appropriations process as a check on government spending.

Congressional budgeting was a response to the weakness—not the strength—of the appropriations process. Congress felt a need for spending control that was not being adequately satisfied by the

1. The Constitution requires that revenue bills originate in the House. By tradition, the House also initiates action on appropriation measures.
2. During the 80th through the 89th Congress, only 1 Congressman transferred from, and 27 transferred to, the House Appropriations Committee. See Richard F. Fenno, *Congressmen in Committees* (Boston: Little, Brown and Company, 1973), p. 17.

Appropriations Committees. Paradoxically, however, these committees were weak because Congress preferred it that way, not because of default by the Appropriations Committees. In order to understand why Congress looked for a new source of spending control, one must first consider the changes in the Appropriations Committee in the years prior to the Budget Act.

THE APPROPRIATIONS COMMITTEES VERSUS CONGRESS

The traditional purpose of the appropriations process has been to counter the spending pressures within Congress and from the executive branch. With the authorizing committees generally cast as program promoters or claimants of resources, the Appropriations Committees have served as Congress's guardians of the treasury. For generations, budget cutting has been branded into new members of the Appropriations Committees as a mark of distinction and the yardstick by which those committees measure their effectiveness. Year after year, the Appropriations Committees have produced figures showing that they have cut the budget. These arithmetic rituals provide concrete evidence that the committees have maintained their guard in the face of spending demands.

In his magisterial study of the appropriations process, Richard Fenno identified budget cutting as the foremost operational goal of the House Appropriations Committee.[3] In this process, the Senate committee has a moderating role; it hears appeals from executive agencies and restores some of the funds cut by the House. (Because the House committee has long had prime responsibility for guarding the budget, that committee has been much more affected by change than the Senate committee has been, and hence is more closely examined in this chapter.)

Budget cutting via the appropriations process has served two basic legislative expectations: that Congress should guard against waste and extravagance and that it should control executive actions and expenditures. But the Appropriations Committees have had another legislative purpose, one directed at Congress itself rather than at the executive branch: to function as guardians against the spending interests of Congress. They deterred Congress from

3. Richard F. Fenno, *The Power of the Purse: Appropriations Politics in Congress*, (Boston: Little, Brown and Company, 1966).

spending as much as it might otherwise have preferred on favored programs. Over the past century, Congress has bolstered the Appropriations Committees when it has been willing to abide by their discipline; it has weakened them when it has preferred a freer rein to spend as it wills.

The conflict between the Appropriations Committees and the rest of Congress has been a Capital Hill fixture since the committees were established in the 1860s. The fortunes of these committees have varied with the climate in Congress for spending control. But even when it has wanted effective guardians, Congress has not unleashed the Appropriations Committees to cut a broad swath through the federal budget. Guarding the treasury can be but one of the goals pursued by Congress. Congress has also wanted to spend on its preferred programs, even if it must weaken the appropriations process in order to get its way. Unchecked power over money would give the Appropriations Committees the potential to dominate their respective chambers and to override the program interests of Congress. If the Appropriations Committees were not constrained, they could interfere in everybody's business, for almost everything done by government entails the expenditure of funds. The Appropriations Committees would be able to nullify authorizing legislation by denying money for programs they did not favor.

The main constraint on the Appropriations Committees has been their awareness that they must satisfy the expectations of their parent bodies. No legislative committee can ignore the desires of the chamber in which it operates. It is not merely a matter of being challenged on the floor or having its jurisdiction trimmed, though these formidable sanctions have been applied against recalcitrant Appropriations Committees in the past. Rather, a committee—even one as powerful as Appropriations—is part of a legislative system and shares the dominant objectives of that system. House Appropriations, long the bastion of fiscal conservatism, experiences the same tensions that beset Congress. As Fenno notes, "the Committee is subject to two sets of expectations—one holding that the Committee should supply money for programs authorized by Congress and one holding that the Committee should fund these programs in as economical a manner as possible."[4]

Caught between their guardianship role and the broader program interests of Congress, the Appropriations Committees have adapted

4. *Ibid.*, p. 410.

to the problem by concentrating their budget-cutting efforts within a narrow "safe" zone. They have cut the budget but in most cases still allowed an increase over the prior year's appropriation. Three-quarters of the 575 House Appropriations Committee decisions that Fenno examined were below the budget estimates; in just about the same proportion of the cases, the appropriation was higher than the previous year's level. "On the whole," Fenno concluded, "the Committee supports programs and effects economies—*both at the same time.*" [5] The zone of discretion within which the Appropriations Committees have operated has normally been bounded by the current year's appropriation and the next year's budget request. Within this range, the Appropriations Committees have dominated the spending process on Capitol Hill. Over the years, accordingly, most of their influence has been marginal, to shave the amounts somewhat, to slow down the rate of growth, to add or to subtract a little from the budget.

Fenno's study was published in 1966 (although most of the research was completed several years earlier), shortly after the chairmanship of House Appropriations passed from Clarence Cannon to George Mahon. Cannon had been a domineering chairman who tried to thrust his conservative views on the committee and vigorously guarded Appropriations against raids on its jurisdiction; in contrast, Mahon was conciliatory and accommodating during his 15-year term as chairman which ended with his retirement in 1978. Fenno noted Mahon's "temperamental distaste for conflict." [6] a disposition that deterred Mahon from vigorously opposing inroads on the appropriations process but also enabled him to survive as chairman during a period in which several other House leaders were dethroned.

When Mahon became chairman during fiscal 1965, federal outlays were $118 billion; when he retired in fiscal 1979, expenditures were approaching $500 billion. For a committee that has historically defined its purpose as guarding the purse, this budget spiral was a difficult experience. Of course, some Appropriations Committee members welcomed the increased spending, particularly for programs they favor. For others, the clear indication was that control had slipped away, that the Appropriations Committees no longer had the will or authority to withstand the pressures. One manifestation of this feeling came at the conclusion of an

5. *Ibid.*, p. 355.
6. *Ibid.*, p. 261.

interview with the veteran clerk of a Senate Appropriations subcommittee. He thrust into the interviewer's hand a letter he had written to the chairman of the full committee comparing the national debt on the day he entered Appropriations Committee service with the twice-as-large debt less than 10 years later. The letter attacked deficit spending as "a narrow dead-end street" and appealed for "a resounding vote of encouragement . . . to those who would control spending."

The vote of encouragement was not forthcoming because in the decade before enactment of the Budget Act, dedication to budget cutting had already begun to fade in Congress. Congress could not in this circumstance permit itself to be beholden to a process that regarded expenditure control as its prime mission. Therefore, Congress engineered a change in the spending process that weakened Appropriations Committee control over the budget.

Through the first half of the 1970s, the Appropriations Committees managed to produce budget cuts each year. From fiscal 1970 through fiscal 1975 (the last year before the Budget Act took effect), some $30 billion was said to be pruned from the budget through appropriations decisions. These official statistics appeared to provide evidence that the guardians were vigilantly patrolling the federal budget against the big spenders. But the numbers cannot be properly interpreted without differentiating among various types of appropriations. Much budget cutting was achieved by means of fiscal legerdemain—time-honored accounting practices that often veil the true effects of congressional actions. The Appropriations Committees sometimes produced budget "cuts" without taking anything out of the budget by shifting funds backward to the past fiscal year or forward to the next fiscal year, by juggling the estimates for mandatory expenses, or by deferring items for supplemental consideration at a later date. Only by a painstaking, account-by-account examination could one distinguish between real and apparent budget cuts.

Appropriations ingenuity seems to have peaked when Congress wanted to increase spending in opposition to presidential preferences. In fiscal 1975, for example, Congress "reduced" appropriations for the Departments of Labor and Health, Education, and Welfare (HEW) by lowering the estimates for mandatory public assistance programs by $1.2 billion. While this was a legitimate action by Congress (its budget estimates often are more accurate than those of the executive branch), the effect was to provide a distorted picture of legislative impact on the budget. Whether that $1.2 billion would be spent depended on external factors, not on Appropriations actions.

Although Appropriations still boasts in public of its accomplishments, insiders privately acknowledge the paucity of real budget cuts. One experienced committee staffer summed up the attrition of budget control this way:

> Clarence Cannon used to say that the appropriations process is the saucer in which the legislative brew is cooled. But that no longer fits today's world of big spending. The Appropriations Committees have been living off a claim to past glory. It might have been true in the past that the committees really cut the request of the President, but it certainly hasn't been true in recent times. Most of the cuts are picked up in supplemental appropriations or in the next budget. Nowadays, true cuts are so seldom that it would be newsworthy to have a big one.

To appraise the impact of the appropriations process on federal spending, it is useful to divide appropriations into three categories, each of which has a distinctive pattern: housekeeping bills, defense and international programs, and client-oriented programs. Although most appropriation bills do not fall neatly into one of these categories, even at this high level of aggregation, it is possible to distinguish among the three types of bills, as the data presented in table 33 reveal. The percentage cut from or added to the budget differs markedly among the three categories.

Housekeeping appropriations for the continuing operation of federal agencies tend to attract line-item review, with the Appropriations Committees concentrating on proposed increases for new staff, travel, and other items of expense. Housekeeping requests usually are cut, but rarely by more than a few percentage points. For programs in this category, the Appropriations Committees excel in providing "half a loaf," allowing some fraction of the proposed increase but not all of it. Housekeeping appropriations are a declining portion of the federal budget, however, and the cuts in this category are not large. All but 5 of the 30 housekeeping appropriations during the 1970-75 fiscal years were below budget, but the cuts never reached 7 percent. In the average bill, the reduction amounted to only 1.5 percent of the funds requested by the executive branch.

Defense and international programs experienced deep cuts in the first half of the 1970s. Each year, Congress appropriated substantially less than had been requested for defense, foreign assistance, and atomic energy. In fact, only 1 of the 18 bills in this category escaped reduction between 1970 and 1975. On average, each bill suffered a cut in excess of 10 percent, significantly higher than the fraction cut from housekeeping appropriations. The more than $30 billion pruned from these bills accounted for the net total of all appropriations reductions during the years under review. In other words, although Congress increased total "domestic" spending through the appropriations process, it was able to claim a reduction because of the enormous cuts in defense and international programs. One analyst who methodically reviewed every defense appropriation between 1971 and 1976, however, classified more than half the "savings" reported in these programs as financial adjustments and postponements of procurement and construction rather than as genuine program cuts.[7]

Client-oriented programs usually receive more money from Congress than the executive branch has requested for them. These programs include the appropriations for the Departments of Labor, HEW, Housing and Urban Development (HUD), and Agriculture; for the Veterans' Administration and for rivers and harbors. Congressional increases for these programs were constrained by presidential vetoes during the years under review. In a number of instances (such as the fiscal 1971 appropriations for HUD and Labor-HEW and the fiscal 1975 appropriations for Agriculture) Congress responded to a veto by passing a scaled-down appropriation with a smaller increase than it had initially preferred. Nevertheless, more than three-quarters of the enacted appropriations for client programs carried more funds than the President had requested.

At least during the years just preceding enactment of the Budget Act, the Appropriations Committees functioned more as rearrangers of national priorities than as guardians of the treasury. Their effectiveness certainly challenges the oft-repeated assertion that Congress was unable to make priority decisions before it was forced to do so by the new budget process. Nevertheless, the Appropriations Committees' role as claimants and promoters for a sizable and growing portion of the federal budget marked a departure from their traditional role as protectors of the purse.

It can be argued that, during the period under review, the

7. See Richard P. Cronin, *An Analysis of Congressional Reductions in the Defense Budget; Fiscal Years 1971-1976* (Multilith, Congressional Research Service, September 16, 1976).

Table 33

CONGRESSIONAL ACTION ON THE PRESIDENT'S BUDGET REQUESTS, REGULAR APPROPRIATIONS BILLS, FISCAL YEARS 1970-75

Bill	*Number Reduced*	*Number Increased*	*Average Percent Change*	*Range of Percent Change*
Housekeeping				
Transportation	4	2	− 2.14	− 6.88/+ 2.55
Interior	2	4	+ 0.96	− 0.75/+ 3.07
State, Justice, Commerce	6	0	− 3.05	− 4.90/− 0.50
Treasury	6	0	− 2.11	− 5.83/− 0.17
HUD (other than Veterans Administration and Dept. of HUD)				
Independent Agencies [1]	6	0	− 1.67	− 3.88/− 0.63

Defense/International				
Defense	6	0	− 5.26	− 7.49/− 3.13
Military Construction	6	0	−10.03	−18.61/− 4.35
Atomic Energy	5	1	− 3.05	− 6.01/+ 0.24
Foreign Assistance	6	0	−24.26	−31.94/−11.90
Client-Oriented				
Agriculture	1	5	+ 4.19	− 0.44/+ 9.68
Labor-HEW	2	4	+ 1.40	− 1.45/+ 3.59
Public Works	0	6	+ 8.42	+ 1.40/+37.62
Veterans' Administration[1]	1	5	+ 0.74	− 0.07/+ 1.78
HUD[1]	3	3	+ 4.76	−13.39/+28.06
Education	0	2	+ 5.78	0.13/+11.43
Public Service Employment	no change		—	— —
Energy and Research	0	1	+ 1.47	1.47

[1] These three items appear in one regular appropriations bill, "HUD and Independent Agencies." They have been separated for this analysis.

Source: U.S. Congress, House and Senate Committees on Appropriations, *Appropriations, Budget Estimates, etc.*, selected years.

Appropriations Committees were compelled to behave as claimants because of presidential attacks on client-oriented spending. A good case can be made that President Nixon submitted unrealistically low Labor and HEW budgets in anticipation of increases by Congress. But even if such were the case, it merely adds weight to the contention that the Appropriations Committees were changed from guardians and budget cutters into claimants and spenders. Moreover, the behavior of the Appropriations Committee cannot be explained solely as a response to executive retrenchment. Important changes in congressional operations also eroded the will and capacity of these committees to guard the budget.

GUARDIANS INTO CLAIMANTS

On the surface, the appropriations process has not changed much over the years. Each agency appears before its Appropriations subcommittee with voluminous "justification" books detailing its activities, past and current expenditures, and its budget requests for the next year. These documents tend to be less bulky than they once were, and many (depending on the subcommittee) now contain less line-item detail and more program information than once was the case. But much attention still is given to item-by-item comparisons of current and proposed expenditures, and to the factors accounting for requested increases over the current level. The subcommittee can question any matter within its jurisdiction or interests, from the specifics of a trip by an employee to an agency's basic policies and long-range plans. Each subcommittee independently marks up its bill (one regular bill for each subcommittee) and sends the bill to the full committee which usually makes few or no changes. For each account the committee report makes a statistical comparison of current spending, the President's request, and the committee's action. Then come explanations of changes by the committee and (in many cases) expressions of concern with regard to particular issues, coupled with instructions as to how the money should (or should not) be spent.

Although the appropriations process has kept its traditional facade, other developments have wrought significant changes in the role and operations of the Appropriations Committees. In the years just prior to the Budget Act, the principal changes were (1) shrinkage in the effective scope and jurisdiction of these committees; (2) opening the Appropriations Committees to spending pressures; and (3) liberalization of the memberships of the House and Senate committees.

Limiting the Scope of the Appropriations Process

The shift from permanent to limited-term authorizations was considered in chapter VI from the vantage point of the authorizing committees. The trend to annual and multiyear authorizations also imposed formidable constraints (informal but nonetheless potent) on the Appropriations Committees. In the normal sequence, Congress makes appropriation decisions after it has cleared the authorizing legislation. As a consequence, as Fenno showed, "every authorization bill expresses the expectation . . . that the Appropriations Committee should provide support for the activity specified therein." Inasmuch as most fixed-term authorizations (unlike the permanent ones) specify a spending level, Congress's expectations have been clearly delineated before the appropriations are considered. Fenno explained the limitations on the Appropriations Committees:

> The [Appropriations] Committee's money decisions are expected to conform broadly to expenditure patterns established by authorization statutes. And any particular authorization is expected to circumscribe the Committee's decision-making freedom. . . . The Committee is not expected to appropriate every last nickel requested. But it is not expected to vote so little money that the program, as conceived by the House, cannot survive. . . .
>
> One can only generalize that when a majority has declared support for a program, the Appropriations Committee is expected to appropriate most of the money authorized or requested for it. A vastly larger portion of a request is expected to be beyond the reach of the Appropriations Committee than is expected to lie within its area of discretion. The Committee's independent influence is expected to be marginal or incremental. Such is the dominant demand of every authorization statute.[8]

Authorizations are powerful claims for federal dollars. The extent of their influence was admitted by the House Appropriations Committee in its reluctant approval of a special public works employment appropriation bill for fiscal 1977. In reporting the bill, committee members felt bound to finance a program already authorized by Congress:

> The accompanying bill is recommended in response to the mandate of the House of Representatives of July 22, 1976, when by a vote of

8. Fenno, *The Power of the Purse*, pp. 7-8.

310-96, the President's veto of the Public Works Employment Act of 1976 [the authorization bill] was overridden. The action of the Committee honors the clear intention of an overwhelming majority of the Members of the House of Representatives that prompt consideration be given to providing appropriations to implement the provisions of the Act.[9]

A similar position was taken by Appropriations Chairman George Mahon who supported the appropriation even though he had earlier voted to sustain the veto of the authorization bill:

As chairman of the Committee on Appropriations and as members of the Committee on Appropriations, we regard the vote of the House as a mandate . . . to implement the authorization bill which was passed over the President's veto. Therefore, we have faithfully brought before the Members today an appropriations bill providing funds for employment. . . .

I personally am deeply concerned about this antirecessionary revenue-sharing provision and about some of the other provisions in the bill, but in view of the mandate of the House and the overwhelming will of the majority, we have brought this bill before the Members. . . .[10]

Congress sometimes does more than signal its expectations to the Appropriations Committees; it bypasses them althogether by providing funds through the backdoor. As discussed in chapters VI and IX, backdoor spending comes in a variety of forms, the common element of which is that the effective decision is made outside the appropriations process. On many backdoors, the Appropriations Committees, put up no fight at all, but bow to the tide of events within Congress. Backdoor spending is much more than a technical deviation from standard legislative procedures. As indicated earlier, it represents a congressional determination to shelter certain programs from appropriations review and control, giving such programs an advantage in the competition for federal dollars.[11]

Many backdoors are permanent appropriations that become available each year without any current action by Congress. While the primary justification for permanent appropriations is to assure funds for mandated obligations of the United States (such as

9. H. Rept. No. 94-1475 (1976).
10. 122 *Congressional Record* (daily ed., August 25, 1976) H9031.
11. There is little doubt, for example, that the $18 billion water pollution control program enacted through a backdoor maneuver in 1972 would have been scaled down if it had been processed through the Appropriations Committees.

interest on the debt and Social Security), permanent appropriations also are valued because they protect preferred programs against the possibility of adverse decisions in the appropriations process. The combined effect of backdoors and permanent appropriations has been to remove more than half of the federal budget from Appropriations Committee control. Only 44 percent of the fiscal 1974 budget, the Joint Study Committee estimated, was "associated with the items to be considered in the appropriations bills. Even some of these funds are approved on what for all practical purposes is a *pro forma* basis because the authorizing legislation in effect required the appropriations."[12] In other words, some expenditures handled by the Appropriations Committees are mandatory, and in such cases, the committees have no choice but to provide the funds required by law.

In sum, by the early 1970s the Appropriations Committees were not able to stem the spending tide because they lacked effective jurisdiction over the fastest-growing portions of the budget. Appropriations Committee control shrank not by happenstance but as a result of a deliberate effort by Congress to unshackle itself from its fiscal guardians. If the Appropriations Committees took a hard line on certain spending matters, Congress was willing to circumvent them through the backdoor. If these committees had maximum discretion when programs had permanent, indefinite authorizations, Congress responded by turning to limited-term legislation. If the Appropriations Committees had a free choice when expenditures were controllable, Congress's response was to make an increasing portion of the budget "uncontrollable."

Exposing the Appropriations Committees to Spending Pressures

In order for the Appropriations Committees to guard against the spending inclinations of Congress, they have to shelter themselves from some of the pressures to which Congress is subjected. Otherwise, the Committees' budgetary preferences probably would not be much different from those of Congress itself. Over the years, the capacity of the Appropriations Committees to restrain Congress was protected by various arrangements that enhanced

12. Joint Study Committee on Budget Control, *Recommendations for Improving Congressional Control Over Budgetary Outlay and Receipt Totals*, April 18, 1973, p. 10. The data were derived from the now extinct Joint Committee on Reduction of Federal Expenditures, which functioned as a staff arm of the Appropriations Committees.

their ability and will to say "no" to spending pressures. The protective features were concentrated in the House Appropriations Committee which (as explained earlier) carried the main burden as guardian of the treasury.

House Appropriations Committee members were carefully selected from relatively "safe" districts. Because their reelection prospects were favorable, these members could afford to resist pressure from interest groups. Turnover on the committee was low and new members went through a prolonged apprenticeship before they gained positions of authority. By the time they became subcommittee chairmen or ranking minority members, most Appropriations Committee members had learned to conform to the group's norms, including banding together to resist outside pressures. On occasion, the committee applied sanctions against members considered to be unduly supportive of programs within their subcommittees' jurisdiction. These sanctions included abolishing the subcommittees, changing their jurisdiction, or altering their membership. Committee and subcommittee meetings were almost always held behind closed doors, beyond the easy reach of interest groups. Committee members rarely filed dissenting opinions, although they sometimes "reserved" the option of reopening an issue on the floor. Floor consideration in the House was in the Committee of the Whole, where the individual votes of members were not recorded. As a consequence, Members of Congress were able to hide their opposition to spending proposals in the anonymity of voice or other unrecorded votes. As Fenno found in his review of appropriations decisions, comparatively few recommendations of the House Appropriations Committee were overturned on the floor.[13]

Many of these protections were attenuated by the reform movement that swept through the House of Representatives in the early 1970s and weakened the ability of the Appropriations Committee to withstand congressional spending demands.

Open Meetings. Traditionally, the Appropriations Committees and their subcommittees conducted most of their business in executive sessions.[14] Every one of the more than 700 meetings of the

13. Fenno, *Power of the Purse*, p. 448ff.
14. According to Fenno, House Appropriations "members believe . . . that closed, executive sessions are necessary to protect Committee deliberations from pressure generated through publicity which would, in their view, increase appropriations and prevent them from protecting the Treasury." *Ibid.*, p. 113.

House Appropriations Committee in the 91st Congress (1969-70) was closed; the Senate committee closed about three-quarters of its meetings. Then in a rapid series of moves, the House and Senate chipped away at rules permitting or mandating closed sessions. By the mid-1970s, the rule was firmly established in both chambers that committee meetings must be open except when the committee formally voted to meet in executive session. Thus within the space of a few years, House Appropriations was transformed from a cloistered into a public group. From a 100 percent closed rate in the 91st Congress, it slipped to a 92 percent closed rate in the next Congress, and to only 11 percent in the 93rd Congress. The percentage of closed meetings dropped still further to 6 percent in 1975 (the last year for which the *Congressional Quarterly* published the rate). Most of the closed meetings related to national security matters; virtually all sessions dealing with domestic issues were open to the public. All markups of the full House Appropriations Committee were opened in 1975, as were many of its subcommittee markups. A similar pattern prevailed in Senate Appropriations, which shifted from a largely closed to a predominantly open committee in the course of just a few years.

For the first time, there is an audience at Appropriations meetings—an informed, alert audience, deeply interested in the proceedings and prepared to swing into action to promote its causes. Appropriations members are aware of the audience, and they now must be cautious in opposing politically attractive ideas advanced in open session. The chilling effect on opposition to spending proposals was described by a subcommittee clerk who clearly was not happy about the results:

> The House Appropriations Committee is weaker now. The members seem to be playing to the audience. They are not prone in an open markup or conference to say what they want to say. This year we had five or six members who showed up at our conference and some of the projects they wanted were dogs. But our members are not likely to criticize another member's feelings, so you don't have the kind of exchange we used to have when markups and conferences were closed.

Some of the subcommittees have gone "underground," with major decisions made in private discussions rather than formal meetings. These decisions are then formalized at perfunctory markups which occasion little or no discussion among the members.

Selection of Committee and Subcommittee Chairmen. For many years, House Appropriations had a tradition of strong chairmen who had been schooled in the budget-cutting norms of the group and thrust their views on committee colleagues. Along with other House committees, the chairmanship of Appropriations was invariably determined by seniority. With few exceptions, the same was true of the selection of subcommittee chairmen. In 1971, however, the Democratic Caucus breached the seniority rule by establishing a procedure under which it could select chairmen on grounds other than seniority. The seniority rule was further eroded at the opening of the 94th Congress when the Democratic Steering and Policy Committee was given the role of recommending committee chairmen and assigning members to committees. The deposing of three long-time Democratic chairmen [15] in 1975 signaled that the caucus was willing to use its new muscle against senior members who were out of touch with rank-and-file Democrats or party policy. Chairman Mahon was reelected by the caucus probably because of his permissive leadership of Appropriations the members' respect for him. As chairman, Mahon rarely tried to force his views on other committee members and, like a good team player, he usually went along with the majority when he was outvoted. Mahon survived because he posed no obstacle to the spread of liberal budget views on the Appropriations Committee.

The Democratic Caucus broke new ground in 1975 by extending its election process to the House Appropriations subcommittee chairmen. The caucus justified this extraordinary intrusion into the internal affairs of a committee, the only one so treated, on the ground that Appropriations subcommittees are virtually autonomous and function almost as if they were full committees. But there was another, unstated motive behind this move. The subcommittee chairmen were among the most conservative members of the House Appropriations Committee. In the 93rd Congress, only 1 of the 13 subcommittee chairmen had an American for Democratic Action (ADA) score above the average for all Democrats on the committee. By reserving the power to dismiss chairmen, the caucus was putting the conservatives on notice that they would risk losing their posts if their subcommittees blocked liberal spending proposals. Here, too, the result was a weakening of Appropriations Committee control, as explained by a veteran staffer:

15. The chairmen unseated by the Democratic Caucus were Herbert of Armed Services; Poage of Agriculture; and Patman of the Banking, Currency, and Housing Committee.

All of a sudden, the subcommittee chairman is playing to an audience and that audience has to vote on him every two years to put him back in his chair. That has a great deal to do with how the committee is reacting to the fiscal situation. There doesn't seem to be a tendency in the committee to cut so much anymore because they are doing what the Democratic Caucus wants them to do.

Independence in the Ranks. Although election by caucus was undoubtedly a restrictive influence on some Appropriations Committee chairmen, the decline in the role of the chairman resulted more from changes within the committee than from pressures without. During the Mahon era, the full committee chairman became little more than just one among equals, certainly less influential with regard to particular spending areas than the relevant subcommittee chairmen. Mahon probably had a greater say in Appropriations decisions by virtue of his chairmanship of the Defense subcommittee than because of his leadership of the full committee. Before Mahon became chairman, one of the levers held by the chairman had been the power to periodically restructure subcommittees, which had enabled each chairman to reward cooperative colleagues (those who cut the budget) and penalize recalcitrant ones. During the Mahon years, however, the number of subcommittees stabilized at 13 and jurisdictional shifts became increasingly rare. One of the few such changes was the transfer of environmental programs from conservative Jamie Whitten's Agriculture subcommittee to the HUD subcommittee headed by Edward Boland, the subcommittee chairman with the most liberal voting record. Thus, rather than using internal sanctions to dampen spending pressures, Appropriations used those sanctions to assure that liberal programs were not blocked by fiscal guardians.

A further weakening of committee leadership resulted from a change in the procedure for allocating subcommittee seats among Appropriations members. For many years, the chairman and ranking minority member had the final say in deciding who got on which subcommittee. On occasion, members were deliberately placed on subcommittees in which they had little political interest.[16] Since the early 1970s, however, members have been allowed to pick their subcommittees in accord with a seniority-based pro-

---

16. ". . . in pursuit of the Committee's budget-cutting goal, the Chairman and ranking minority member have employed a . . . countervailing pattern of subcommittee selection. That is, they have deliberately appointed individuals to subcommittee membership where no clientele interest exists." Fenno, *The Power of the Purse*, p. 141.

cedure. Inevitably, this self-selection process has led to a predominance of program advocates on subcommittees. A staff assistant to Chairman Mahon explained the result:

> What we find is that the city and inner-city guys are all on Labor-HEW, all of the hawkish guys go to Defense, and the big [full] committee chairman no longer has the power to take the guy who has a defense interest and say, "you serve on the Agriculture subcommittee and do the public some good."

Even in the heyday of fiscal control, Appropriations subcommittees tended to be dominated by program supporters; the forced placement of "indifferents" on subcommittees was an exceptional practice used to bring members (or subcommittees) into line with with overall committee expectations. But the switch to self-selection spelled a serious decline in group identifications and the rise of individualistic, disintegrative values on House Appropriations. Members have always used their positions on Appropriations to advance their interests, but their individualism was tempered by consensus on the committee's role as protector of the purse. Without shared values about the need to cut the budget, the Appropriations Committee surely would have been just another logrolling committee, subservient to each member's spending wishes. If House Appropriations succeeded in cutting the budget, it was because members occasionally moderated their wants in order to achieve that collective objective.

The triumph of individualism has been reflected in the abandonment of the tradition against public dissent in committee reports. During the 16 years from 1947 through 1962, only 12 minority reports were issued by members of the House Appropriations Committee. According to Fenno's computation, 94 percent of the appropriations bills reported by the committee received unanimous endorsement.[17] This tradition no longer prevails. Three-quarters of the regular appropriations bills reported by House Appropriations for the 1975 and 1976 fiscal years carried a separate expression of opinion by one or more committee members. More additional and dissenting views were filed during these two years than in all the years covered by Fenno's study.

The decline of the chairmanship went hand in hand with the rising independence of members to erode the Appropriations Com-

17. Fenno, *The Power of the Purse*, p. 203.

mittee's control of the purse. Mahon and other fiscal conservatives were frequently outvoted in committee, but went along with the majority when the appropriations bills reached the floor. Mahon endorsed a conference report on a Labor-HEW bill even though he was unhappy with the high spending level: It "troubles me a great deal because it is far above the President's budget and in my judgment is too high." [18] Bob Michel, the ranking minority member on the Labor-HEW subcommittee, responded with an explanation of why spending control had diminished on Appropriations:

> . . . under the old rules under which we were operating I felt much more confident that when we really got to the nitty-gritty, the committee chairman would stand up with some of us and really keep these figures limited to what he and I both would, as a matter of personal philosophy, prefer. The fact is, though, that there is a process on that side of the aisle of electing chairmen and subcommittee chairmen from among the whole membership, and that has had the very kind of effect that I am talking about here.
>
> That effect is that we do not have any more of that "College of Cardinals" that was in a position where chairmen could take a traditional hard stand on spending by the Federal Government.

With characteristic modesty, Mahon responded with his own explanation for the loss of control:

> Mr. Speaker, the committee chairman has never had the ability to dictate the policy of the committee. . . . Certainly the chairman of a committee has more clout than a nonchairman, but all one can do is his best under the circumstances. I have wrestled with these problems through the years, just as the gentleman from Illinois has. The gentleman from Illinois has seen new Members come, and, generally speaking the new Members are more liberal than the ones they replaced.[19]

Membership of the House Appropriations Committee

Structural changes alone do not explain the attenuation of budget cutting as the guiding objective of the House Appropriations Committee. If fiscal conservatives, convinced that their course was correct and determined to hold the line against big spenders, had continued to dominate the committee, Appropriations would have had a difficult time adjusting to new budgetary attitudes. The

---

18. 122 *Congressional Record* (daily ed., August 10, 1976) H8624.
19. *Ibid.*

reorientation of the committee has been facilitated by the liberalization of its membership.

Between 1967 and 1977, the House Appropriations Committee experienced a markedly greater turnover among Republicans than among Democrats. Less than 25 percent of the Republicans on the committee in 1967 were still on it 10 years later. Among committee Democrats, the retention rate was better than 50 percent. Despite the fact that the Democratic contingent was twice as stable as the Republican, significant ideological changes were concentrated in the Democrats. For the most part, conservative Republicans were succeeded by conservatives; the two Republicans (Silvio O. Conte and Joseph M. McDade) with the most liberal ADA/ACA (Americans for Democratic Action/Americans for Constitutional Action) scores in 1967 still were at the top of their party's list in the 1977 rankings. In both periods, all but a few of the Republicans on the House Appropriations Committee were identified with the very conservative wing of their party.

On the Democratic side, critical changes came about through the addition of liberals, not by the displacement of old members. In 1977, senior Democrats on the Appropriations Committee were clustered near the top of the longevity list in the House of Representatives. Eight of the 23 Democrats with the longest service in the House were on Appropriations. More than half of the subcommittee chairmen in 1967 were still holding their posts a decade later. The senior Democrats also happened to be among the most conservative members of the Appropriations Committee. As a group, the Democratic members of House Appropriations were not more liberal in 1977 than in 1967 (see table 34). The average ADA rating for the 10 "oldest" Democrats in 1977 was below the average for all committee Republicans in the same year.

Nevertheless, a change in the party ratio between 1967 and 1977 weakened the influence of conservative Democrats on Appropriations. In 1967, the committee's composition was 30 to 21, a Democratic margin of only 9, which enabled conservative Democrats to combine with Republicans to dominate the committee. By 1977, the majority's advantage had been stretched to 37 to 18, more than double the earlier margin. This shift was due primarily to a Democratic Caucus decision that Appropriations, along with other key House committees, should have at least a 2-1 party ratio. This change in the composition of Appropriations vitiated the conservative Democrat-Republican coalition. Even when conservative Democrats sided with committee Republicans, they were outvoted

Table 34
ADA AND ACA SCORES OF DEMOCRATIC MEMBERS OF THE HOUSE APPROPRIATIONS COMMITTEE

	1967			1977	
Members [1]	*ADA* [2]	*ACA* [3]	*Members* [1]	*ADA* [2]	*ACA* [3]
Mahon	27	24	Mahon	5	70
Kirwan	67	5	Whitten	10	56
Whitten	7	67	Sikes	10	60
Andrews	0	96	Boland	65	11
Rooney	80	5	Natcher	30	52
Sikes	0	63	Flood	40	16
Passman	0	68	Steed	20	28
Evins	47	20	Shipley	30	19
Boland	87	4	Slack	30	40
Natcher	40	28	Flynt	5	78
Flood	73	7	Smith	55	8
Steed	33	25	Giaimo	60	24
Shipley	53	19	Addabbo	80	4
Slack	73	11	McFall	65	8
Flynt	7	70	Patten	55	11
Smith	53	4	Long	55	30
Giaimo	73	11	Yates	95	11
Hansen	73	4	Evans	70	25
Joelson	87	7	Obey	85	0
Addabbo	80	4	Roybal	85	0
McFall	73	4	Stokes	90	0
Hull	27	64	McKay	25	41
Cohelan	87	4	Bevill	15	56
Morris	33	25	Chappell	5	75
Patten	80	7	Burlison	45	11
Long	60	7	Alexander	25	24
Marsh	0	69	Koch	35	7
Yates	100	0	Burke	85	4
Casey	20	44	Murtha	20	27
Pryor	27	30	Traxler	60	22
Average	48.2	26.5	Duncan	50	25
			Early	80	20
			Baucus	65	23
			Wilson	25	26
			Boggs	30	15
			Benjamin	50	26
			Dicks	50	9
			Average	46.1	39.1

[1] Members are listed in order of seniority.
[2] Americans for Democratic Action.
[3] Americans for Constitutional Action.

Sources: Americans for Democratic Action and Americans for Constitutional Action.

by the liberals. Equally important, the Democrats extended their better than 2-1 edge to the subcommittees, where the bulk of appropriation decisions are made. In 1967, for example, the Democrats had a bare 5-3 edge on Labor-HEW; in 1977, they enjoyed an 8-3 advantage.

The addition of liberal Democrats not only changed the political complexion of the committee; it also undermined socialization and cooptation of new members. With many newcomers joining the committee in each Congress, it was not possible for the slow "learning" process to successfully educate the recruits in the traditional committee norms. Moreover, a number of the new Democrats joined the committee to subvert its traditionally conservative approach on spending issues.

Although the Senate Appropriations Committee has not had the budget-cutting role associated with the House committee, between 1967 and 1977 it, too, underwent a membership shift that had the effect of liberalizing its budgetary attitudes. Although two-thirds of the Democrats were replaced during this period, the party continued to have a "representative" slate on the committee, with the overall tilt somewhat more liberal in 1977 than 10 years earlier. But the composition of the Republican group changed dramatically over the decade. In 1967, only two of the committee's nine Republicans had liberal voting records; in 1977, more than half the Republicans could be classified as liberals. As a group, the Republicans on Senate Appropriations were unrepresentative of their party in the Senate; as measured by ADA ratings, five of the seven most liberal Republican Senators were on the Appropriations Committee (see table 35).

APPROPRIATIONS DECISIONS ON THE FLOOR

In order for the House Appropriations Committee to succeed as fiscal guardian for Congress, its recommendations must have a high acceptance rate by the chamber as a whole. This outcome is far from assured, however, because the committee's role with respect to Congress's spending interests can place it in an adversary relationship *vis-à-vis* its parent body. Even if its members stuck together, the committee might come out second best in a floor confrontation between restrictive budget levels and popular programs. The legislative inhibition against "writing" legislation

Table 35

ADA AND ACA SCORES OF REPUBLICAN MEMBERS OF THE SENATE APPROPRIATIONS COMMITTEE, COMPARED WITH AVERAGE SCORE OF DEMOCRATS

	1967			*1977*	
Member	*ADA* [a]	*ACA* [b]	*Member*	*ADA* [a]	*ACA* [b]
Young	0	81	Young	5	79
Mundt	15	85	Case	90	12
Smith	23	39	Brooke	80	4
Kuchel	38	45	Hatfield	60	36
Hruska	0	100	Stevens	20	50
Allott	8	90	Mathias	75	14
Cotton	23	81	Schweiker	15	56
Case	100	11	Bellmon	20	64
Javits	77	17	Weicker	60	39
Republican average	31.6	61		47.2	39.3
Democratic average	36.2	32.7		48.1	31.9
Difference between Republican averages and Democratic averages	−4.6	+28.3		−0.9	+7.4

[a] Americans for Democratic Action.
[b] Americans for Constitutional Action.

Sources: Americans for Democratic Action and Americans for Constitutional Action.

on the floor would be unlikely to deter a Congress determined to generously endow its favorite programs over the objections of the House Appropriations Committee.

Longtime participants in the appropriations process invariably point out that there has been a sharp upsurge in the number of floor amendments. Some of the increase is accounted for by riders to appropriation bills (such as those relating to the Vietnam War in the early 1970s and abortion policy late in the decade) rather than by amendments proposing to change dollar levels.

The floor record of appropriation bills cannot be divorced from the experiences of other types of legislation. Between 1966 and 1976, the number of roll calls tripled in the House of Representatives (from 193 to 661) and grew by nearly the same rate in the

Senate (from 235 to 688). Part of the increase in the House was undoubtedly attributable to a change in voting procedure in the Committee of the Whole, where Appropriation bills are initially considered. Until the 1970s, individual votes were not recorded in the Committee of the Whole, but the Legislative Reorganization Act of 1970 provided for recorded votes, at the request of 20 or more members, during this stage of floor action.

Perhaps more important than this procedural change has been the relaxation of informal inhibitions against floor challenges to committees. The steep spiral of roll calls in both the House and the Senate suggests that the customary deference accorded committees no longer restrains Members from trying to get their own way on the floor. The legislative norms (apprenticeship, reciprocity, and specialization) that held the independence of Members in check and enabled committees to steer their work through Congress without much floor opposition have been eroded by the "democratization" of the House and Senate and the determination of junior Members to seize a greater share of legislative power.

Short of restrictive rules that limit floor action, the best policy for a committee determined to avoid serious challenge is to produce a bill that satisfies the expectations of the parent body. No committee wants to lose a vote in public or to have wholesale changes made in its handiwork. Accordingly, when Congress has become more generous with respect to spending demands, the Appropriations Committees have tilted in the same direction. An examination of floor amendments to appropriation bills in the 91st and 92nd Congresses (1969-72) suggests that the House Appropriations Committee was fairly successful in anticipating the "floor." All told, the committee faced 200 financial amendments (not counting those dealing with legislative issues), an average of 50 per year and only 3 or 4 per appropriation bill. As might be expected, proposed increases outnumbered amendments calling for reductions. Also as might be expected, demands for higher spending were more successful than proposed decreases. Less than 10 percent of the reductions were passed, but 40 percent of the increases received majority support. Overall, the House committee had a success rate of almost 75 percent, slightly better than the long-term average computed by Fenno for the period from 1947 to 1972. Although almost half of the proposed increases were adopted, the picture that emerges is not one of a remote Appropriations Committee ambushed on the floor by predatory Members of Congress. Most of the committee's recommendations passed without drawing a single amendment. By rough estimate, amendments were offered for fewer than 10 percent of the appropriation accounts; the rest were accepted without challenge.

The committee "succeeded" because it was not a stern guardian, bravely turning down demands for more money even at the risk of floor defeat. It anticipated what the House wanted and produced numbers accordingly. Its ability to foresee House preferences was improved by the changes that had made the committee both more representative of the parent chamber and more open to outside influence. In the floor exchange with Michel over the Labor-HEW appropriation quoted earlier, Chairman Mahon alluded to his committee's subservience to congressional interests:

> We do need to impose greater discipline on ourselves. . . . But when we deal with all of the 435 Members of this body and the Members of the other body, then we have to do the best we can under the circumstances. The Congress and the country must come to the position of supporting a greater degree of restraint than we have now.[20]

The clear implication of this statement is that despite its reputation for power, the Appropriations Committee is beholden to the House. The committee cannot be a more restrictive guardian than Congress wants it to be. As Congress became more favorably inclined toward spending, so too did its Appropriations Committees. Even as they defended the appropriations process with statistics showing how much had been cut from the budget, conservatives on Appropriations knew that their committee had lost effective control. The report of the Joint Study Committee in 1973, which called for new budget controls, was a veiled indictment of the appropriations process. In its unanimous report, the joint committee (almost half of whose members were among the most conservative and senior members of the House and Senate Appropriations Committees)[21] opened with an attack on deficit spending:

> The constant continuation of deficits plus their increasing size illustrates the need for Congress to obtain better control over the budget . . . The present institutional arrangements in many cases appear to make it impossible to decide between competing priorities with the result that

20. *Ibid.*, H8625.
21. The 1973 average ADA score for the House Appropriations members of the Joint Study Committee was 6, compared to a 36 average for the full committee; Senate Appropriations members averaged 33 on the ADA scale, compared to 50 for all committee members.

spending is made available for many programs where the preference might have been to make choices among the programs rather than providing for spending in all cases.[22]

Although the appropriations process is not mentioned in this statement (it does figure prominently in other sections of the report), there can be no doubting the Joint Study Committee's conviction that appropriations controls were inadequate to withstand spending pressures within Congress. Conservative interests disturbed over persistent budget deficits also endorsed this appraisal of the appropriations process. One of the reasons "the financial circles in this country wanted the Budget Act," a Senate Appropriations staffer argued, "was because the appropriations process had been penetrated by liberals to a point where they were able to get funding for a lot of their programs." This interpretation overstates the extent to which outside interests were active in the development of the Budget Act, but it accurately captures the prevailing view that appropriations control had diminished within Congress.

The 1974 Budget Act sought to compensate for the weakening of fiscal guardianship in the Appropriations Committees by centering new controls in the congressional budget process. The impact of this process on the Appropriations Committees is the subject of the next chapter.

22. Joint Study Committee, *op. cit.*, p. 1.

XI Ambivalent Claimants: The Appropriations Committees in the Budget Process

The Budget Act distinctly separated the budget and appropriations processes. Budget allocations are made by "function," the 19 "macro" categories into which all federal programs are classified. Appropriations are structured into more than a thousand accounts which correspond (in most cases) to federal organization units. Each process is supposed to operate within its own sphere, with an informational "crosswalk" linking them together. If everything worked according to plan, the budget resolutions would address national priorities while appropriations would decide specific spending issues.

The Budget Act also redefined the roles of the Appropriations Committees. No longer are these committees regarded solely as the protectors of the purse; they are now seen as claimants whose spending inclinations must be policed by the budget process. Thus the Budget Act prohibits appropriation decisions until the first budget resolution has been adopted. Before they report any of their bills, the Appropriations Committees must allocate their share of the budget among their subcommittees. Before it brings a single bill to the floor, the House Appropriations Committee must mark up all its regular bills and report to Congress on how all these actions compare with the allocations in the congressional budget. Every appropriation measure comes to the floor with a scorecard showing its relation to the figures in the congressional budget. The actions of the Appropriations Committees are monitored by controllers from the Budget Committees to assure that the budget targets and ceilings are protected. When an appropriation bill is debated in the House or Senate, the chairman of the Budget Committee usually takes the floor to announce whether the Appropriations Committee has complied with or violated the budget controls.

These procedures are built on the expectation that the Appropriations Committees cannot be trusted to abide by the congressional budget unless their actions are watched and controlled. To put the matter bluntly, the budget process exists to prevent "budget busting" by the Appropriations Committees (as well as other congressional spenders). This casting of the former guardians as claimants is the logical culmination of the transformation of the Appropriations Committees during the decade preceding the Budget Act.

THE RELUCTANT CLAIMANTS: THE PROBLEM OF MARCH 15

The Appropriations Committees are forced to behave as claimants early in the budget process, when they prepare their March 15 views and estimates. They must submit this annual report before they have completed the legislative work on which their bills will be based. Although this problem afflicts many committees, it is particularly troubling for the House Appropriations Committee, which has a reputation for voluminous hearings and detailed examination of budget requests. The loose and premature estimates for March 15 have disturbed committee members who were accustomed to precise decisions derived from methodical review of agency spending plans. A typical complaint came from a subcommittee aide:

> We really aren't ready to make the report by March 15. If we get our hearings started by the first of February we are very lucky. The hearings usually run through the middle of April. Then we have a markup in early May, so the quality and usefulness of the March 15 report is not very great.

As was discussed in chapter VI, the March 15 process induces committees to peg their requirements above the amounts they expect to recommend later in the year, and probably above the President's estimates as well. The Appropriations Committee cannot ask for less than they might want in subsequent appropriation bills; nor can they calculate their needs so closely as to risk a possible breach of the budget targets later in the year. To be safe, they must err on the high side, even if this means a further weakening of their control over federal expenditures. This is the way the process has worked from the vantage point of a Senate participant:

> The President's budget comes up in January and you barely have the opportunity to examine it in any detail. So what you do is get your best reading possible of the budget request and you make certain assumptions that there undoubtedly will be certain reductions in that request and certain increases reflecting congressional priorities. Then you toss in a ballpark estimate of what you think upcoming supplemental appropriations will be which is looking ahead even into the next session. There may be reason to anticipate certain budget amendments by the President. So it is quick and dirty and there is a lot of guessing in it. Although you can normally expect a certain pattern of increases, you come out with a figure which is necessarily going to be a bit large at this point. You don't want to cramp yourself into too tight a ceiling, because there is one thing you know for sure—there is always going to be something coming up that nobody even is talking about at that point, a disaster or something. That is probably one of the bad characteristics of the budget process, everyone comes up with a little more ceiling than they really need. In effect, the committee comes out with an inflated estimate.

The prematurity of the March 15 deadline reinforces the autonomy of Appropriations subcommittees and impels even those which have retained a frugal fiscal posture to behave as claimants for a share of next year's budget. Each subcommittee has a strong incentive to claim a fair share of total appropriations; each must assure that its needs are adequately covered when the full Appropriations Committee allocates its total among the various subcommittees. Rather than being concerned about the full committee, each subcommittee must take a parochial view of its interests. Moreover, the full committee cannot effectively exert downward pressure on its subcommittees at this early date. By March 15, the full committee is in no position to challenge the wants of the individual subcommittees. Both House and Senate participants concurred that the full committee does little more than put its stamp of approval on subcommittee recommendations. As one observer noted, the Senate Appropriations action is "essentially a stapling operation. You have to have more analysis at the full committee level if you are going to question the judgments of the subcommittees." An observer of the House Appropriations Committee action commented that "theoretically, we mark it up at the full committee, but there isn't a lot that is going to be done at that point since the subcommittees have already had an opportunity to mark up their individual pieces of it. No substance is added at the full committee."

As might be expected, the House Appropriations Committee has been more troubled than the Senate Committee has been by its claimant role, because many old-timers still see their committee as guardian of the treasury and yearn for a return to that role. The House committee makes a practice of introducing its March 15 report with general comments on the budget and appropriations processes. Its report for fiscal 1977 was prefaced with the reminder that

> . . . for years the Committee on Appropriations has consistently appropriated less than the amounts requested by the President and far less than advocated by many Members of Congress and numerous groups of the public in general. This has not been an easy task, and each year it seems to grow increasingly more difficult.[1]

The difficulty was especially acute for fiscal 1977 because, as discussed earlier, President Ford's budget had called for massive cutbacks in domestic spending. The committee could not recommend less than the President; to be realistic, it had to ask for many billions more. House Appropriations tried to ease this predicament by labeling its deviations from the President's budget as contingencies rather than as recommendations. For each function, the committee listed the budget authority and outlays sought by the President and identified contingencies which might lead to higher (and in a few cases, lower) spending. In a cautionary note which has become boilerplate in subsequent March 15 reports, it stressed that

> . . . these contingencies should not be interpreted as recommendations of the Committee on Appropriations. It should also be pointed out that the Committee has only begun the fiscal 1977 budget process. Hearings during which hundreds of witnesses from the Executive Branch, the Congress, and the public will be heard, have not been completed and much information remains to be developed before any recommendations can be made. Thus, it is not possible at this time to make recommendations in this report. However, the Committee has identified areas

---

1. House Committee on the Budget, *Views and Estimates . . . on the Congressional Budget for Fiscal Year 1977*, Committee Print, March 22, 1976, p. 64.

and contingencies that may possibly lead to changes in the budget and they deserve further consideration. . . .

The Committee emphasizes that the contingencies identified herein in no way reflect an overall recommendation on the Federal budget as to its size or priorities.[2]

With the contingencies included, the House Appropriations Committee estimated that fiscal 1977 expenditures would exceed the President's budget by $20 billion. This big "overrun" was conveniently displayed in a summary table that conveyed the clear impression that a committee which once boasted of its budget-cutting prowess now was advocating a hefty increase in spending. The disclaimer about the difference between contingencies and recommendations did not deter others from treating the figures as authoritative recommendations of the House Appropriations Committee. (In fact, aggregate spending proposed by the House Budget Committee in its first budget resolution for the fiscal year was almost identical to the total, including contingencies, estimated by Appropriations.) To avoid a repetition of this "misunderstanding," the subsequent March 15 reports issued by House Appropriations have eliminated the tally of contingencies, although such items appear in the discussions accompanying the various functions.

The Senate Appropriations Committee has been less concerned about statistics showing that it expects to appropriate more than the President has requested. Inasmuch as program advocacy has openly displaced budget cutting as the guiding principle of several of its subcommittees, the March 15 process is a welcome opportunity for the claimants to announce their preferences without tipping their hands on particular items. The Senate committee's reports are less detailed than those issued by House Appropriations and are organized by subcommittee rather than by functional categories. The March 15 document represents each subcommittee's hedged projection of what it expects to do with its appropriation bill.

THE COERCED CLAIMANT: HOUSE APPROPRIATIONS VERSUS THE BUDGET PROCESS

When they behave as claimants, the Appropriations Committees ordinarily do so by choice, without overt pressures being applied

2. *Ibid.*, p. 58.

by other legislative participants. Because the House Committee is still ambivalent about its spending attitudes, it sometimes adheres to a guardian ethic, but the budget process does not always allow it a free choice in determining its spending policy. In a direct clash between the Appropriations and Budget Committees early in 1977, House Appropriations was compelled to abandon its budget-cutting stance in favor of a spending role. Although the incident occurred behind the scenes and was resolved in a face-saving manner for the Appropriations Committee, it demonstrates the extent to which the committee was forced into a claimant role by the budget process.

Shortly after President Carter took office in January 1977, he proposed various budget increases for the fiscal year already underway. Most of the recommendations had been worked out in preinauguration negotiations with Democratic leaders in Congress. To accommodate this economic stimulus program, Congress passed a "third" budget resolution for the fiscal year, but with more jobs and public works money than the President had requested. After adoption of the third resolution, House Appropriations reported a supplemental bill that was hundreds of millions of dollars below the amounts allowed by the resolution. In effect, the House committee was merely fulfilling its old role as guardian of the purse by cutting the budget. When Chairman Giaimo of the House Budget Committee became aware of this action, he protested to Speaker O'Neill that the Appropriations Committee was undermining the jobs program. The Speaker summoned Rep. George H. Mahon and others from House Appropriations to his office, where they were told to restore the funds cut from the stimulus package. The Appropriations Committee was given two options: to propose restoration of the funds on the floor (it was too late to do so in committee) or to have an amendment to this effect offered on behalf of the Democratic leadership and the Budget Committee. Appropriations Committee leaders took the first course of action when the bill reached the floor on March 15, 1977. Referring only obliquely to the heated confrontation, Chairman Mahon said, "Now, we are going to have a rather awkward operation this afternoon."[3] One by one, the chairmen of the relevant Appropriations subcommittees dutifully sponsored amendments adding about $700 million to the supplemental bill. Everything went according to script and not a public word was uttered about the

3. 123 *Congressional Record* (daily ed., March 15, 1977) H2079.

showdown in the Speaker's office. Rep. Robert N. Giaimo complimented

> the various subcommittee chairmen for their willingness to offer these amendments in order that the economic stimulus package we have agreed upon can be promptly implemented. . . . I urge their adoption, and once again commend the Appropriations Committee for its responsiveness to the needs of the economy as expressed through our budget process.[4]

After it was over, participants from the Budget and Appropriations Committees insisted that the economic stimulus proposal had been a special case. It was exceptional, they explained, because that appropriation bill was in response to a just-adopted "third" resolution in which Congress had made an explicit decision as to the amount of stimulus that should be pumped into the economy. Moreover, the budget process was purposely set up to enable Congress to make overall fiscal decisions. They suggested that the Appropriations Committee would have more leeway in making "micro" decisions than in setting spending levels. But even as a special case, the incident shows how the new budgetary rules have changed expectations about the appropriations process.

RECONCILING THE BUDGET AND APPROPRIATIONS PROCESSES

Congress passed more than 75 regular and supplemental appropriation bills during the first five years of the budget process. Only one of these—the stimulus package—provoked a "to the brink" confrontation between the Budget and Appropriations Committees. On some matters, differences were successfully negotiated before they ballooned to significant proportions; on others, one of the parties chose to look the other way rather than make an issue of the problem. When the budget process was launched, the Appropriations Committees were understandably wary of the new budget makers. After all, it was their turf that was being challenged, their actions that were being watched. Even in the absence of specific provocation, tension existed between the two sets of committees. "It's more a general view of the world than any specific instance," a Senate staff member explained. The relationship usually was correct, but rarely comfortable. The two sides could

4. *Ibid.*, H2085.

not be at ease while each was testing the other's intentions and behavior.

The burdens of the budget process have nettled the Appropriations Committees, which resent being required to divert time from their crowded hearings schedule to prepare the March 15 reports. They view much of the budget process as makework, lacking the purpose and precision of their own appropriations activities. They also dislike the attention lavished on appropriations bills by the Budget Committees, viewing this as a biased application of the new budget controls. They would prefer that equal attention be directed at the revenue side of the budget which, many on the Appropriations Committees believe, share responsibility for high budget deficits. Nevertheless, after several years of experience in working together, the Budget and Appropriations Committees have forged solid ties. While a clash is always possible, both parties make strenuous efforts to avoid one. The budget process, one who has participated from the appropriations side suggested, "illustrates the great capacity of members to submerge conflict and avoid confrontation with each other. A politician of necessity learns how to make accommodations; it is one of the things that goes on around here."

The ingredients of the peaceful coexistence have included the determination of participants to avoid strife and the fortuitous convergence of appropriations and budget interests. No matter how committed they might be to peace, the committees would have made war if their interests had pulled them in opposite directions.

The Peacemakers

The path toward peace has been easier in the House than in the Senate. From the beginning, the chairmen of the House Appropriations and Budget Committees have worked for a smooth relationship. As an early advocate of budget control and a leading fiscal conservative on the House Appropriations Committee, Representative Mahon welcomed the discipline of the budget process. On a number of occasions, he openly expressed the hope that the budget process would lead to a more restrained attitude toward spending by Congress. Mahon's distaste for intramural conflict and his gracious demeanor were matched by the quiet, conciliatory style of Rep. Brock Adams as first chairman of the House Budget Committee. One Member who served concurrently on the Budget and Appropriations Committees credited Adams with a major role in harmonizing the two processes:

> Initially, perhaps, members of the Appropriations Committee had some apprehension. It was based on the fear that the Budget Committee might encroach upon their area of jurisdiction and limit the function of the appropriations process. To a large degree the way that Brock Adams began maintaining his relationship with all the committee chairmen and particularly the Appropriations Committee chairman and chairmen of the subcommittees has allayed the fears that the Appropriations Committee had. It has worked out well even to the point where the Appropriations Chairmen became dependent on Brock to come on the floor and help with their bills.

Overlapping membership has not been a significant factor in the cooperative relationship between the House Budget and Appropriations Committees. Because the House Appropriations subcommittee structure is so fragmented, it is difficult for any person to speak for the whole committee or to serve as a bridge from it to other committees. A member of both committees who tried to act as a go-between might be regarded as a trespasser rather than an honest broker. An Appropriations Committee member who also belonged to the Budget Committee can inject his or her own interests or expertise into the budget proceedings, but such a member has no special advantage over colleagues who permit their other legislative interests to intrude on their budget work.

Relationships between the two House Committees did not improve when a member of Appropriations became head of the Budget Committee in 1977. Although the cooperative pattern had already been established by the time Robert Giaimo became chairman, tension increased somewhat. Despite his longevity on Appropriations (he joined it in 1963), Giaimo still did not chair any of its subcommittees. He was regarded as an outsider, more liberal than most of his colleagues on the Defense subcommittee, his principal appropriations interest. Giaimo has been offended by the efforts of many Appropriations Committee (and subcommittee) members to act as if the budget process had not been established. Nevertheless, except for occasional strain, relations have continued to be friendly and cooperative.

Intercommittee harmony has been strengthened by close relationships at the staff level. One of Budget's top staff officer previously served as Mahon's key aide on Appropriations. The staffs of the two committees regularly exchange information and keep each other informed of their activities. The two committees share a common data base and rely on the same computerized information system. An Appropriations staffer crisply summed up the relationship: "They talk to us about the budget resolution and we talk to them about what we are putting in the appropriation bill." With neither side fearful of surprise attack, both can work to ward off possible trouble.

In the Senate, relationships between the Budget and Appropriations Committees got off to a contentious start. Even before the Budget Act was passed, Chairman John L. McClellan of Appropriations was displeased by the direction that the reform had taken. During early consideration of the legislation in the Senate Government Operations Committee (which he chaired for two decades before assuming the Appropriations chairmanship) McClellan advanced his pet scheme for a joint Budget Committee.[5] When this was rejected, he lost interest in the legislation and withdrew from the proceedings. Despite Senate Appropriations' enormous stake in the outcome, the committee limited itself to "observer" status as the budget bill was developed. When the measure came before the Senate, McClellan waited until the final moments of the four-day debate to issue a skeptical prognosis:

> I am convinced that this bill in its present form will fall far short of the goals it professes to achieve. . . . this measure places such a burden on the legislative and appropriations processes that it is impractical and maybe impossible for Congress to comply with its terms and conform to its directives.[6]

Once the budget legislation became law, McClellan decided to cooperate fully with the new committee. "He put out the word," one of his aides recounted, "that whatever it takes, we are going to follow the Budget Act. Whatever we have to change on the Appropriations Committee, we'll do it. It's the law; I'm not going to resist it." This compliant posture was very much in line with McClellan's stern, legalistic character, and enhanced his committee's influence over the new process. Again, one of his aides explained the strategy:

> The power relationships in the Senate were in the process of change. We could all see that and we felt that if we didn't become part of it, it would happen in any event. The net result, if we were uncooperative,

5. During the 1950s and 1960s, Senator McClellan repeatedly sponsored legislation to establish a joint committee on the budget. This legislation was passed by the Senate several times (the earliest was in 1952), but it never passed the House which was concerned about the potential loss of initiative in appropriation bills.
6. 120 *Congressional Record* (daily ed., March 22, 1974) S4314.

is that we would have had a more diminished role than if we took part in the budget change and tried to cooperate.

Despite McClellan's determination to live at peace with the budget process, conflict erupted within months after the Act took effect. The provocation was the Senate Budget Committee's insistence that it share jurisdiction over the new impoundment controls established by Title X of the Budget Act. The Senate Appropriations Committee was equally insistent that under the rules, impoundment matters were exclusively within its scope. (The House Budget Committee did not evince any jurisdictional interest, so the House Appropriations Committee had the field to itself.) After several months of angry dispute during which Senate action on several pending impoundment measures was delayed, the deadlock was broken by a unanimous consent agreement to refer impoundments jointly to the Budget and Appropriations Committees, as well as to any authorizing committee with jurisdiction in the affected area.[7]

Sen. Edmund S. Muskie was convinced that his Budget Committee would not have a strong budget role unless it vigorously defended its interests against those of older and more entrenched Senate committees. Because impoundment was the first substantive feature of the Budget Act to be implemented, it became a test case of the Senate Budget Committee's intentions and clout. As one SBC staffer explained, "Muskie wasn't sure what the Budget Committee was going to do, whether there was going to be much of a role. So he was trying to get just about anything he could."

At the time, the importance of impoundment was inflated by the very large number of rescissions and deferrals President Ford had proposed. In retrospect, all the combatants appraise it as a minor fracas that left no lasting imprint. The confrontation, however, alerted staff persons on both committees of the need to establish lines of communication and to consult on a regular basis. In the aftermath of the impoundment fight, both sides developed harmonious working relationships and information sharing became standard practice.

The Allies

The peacemaking activities of Budget and Appropriations leaders have been reinforced by the concrete benefits from working to-

7. S. Res. 45, 94th Congress. See 121 *Congressional Record* (daily ed., January 30, 1975) S1280 and S1302.

gether. The House Budget Committee has earned considerable credit with the Appropriations Committee as a result of its resolute stand against backdoor spending.

Backdoors are a less compelling issue for Senate Appropriations because its members are cross-pressured by their service on authorizing committees. Occasionally, SBC and Appropriations have aligned themselves on the same side of an issue, as when the Senate Finance Committee wrote a "refundable tax credit" into a 1977 energy bill. Although it was to be a cash payment from the treasury—recipients were to be eligible for "refunds" in excess of their tax liability—the payments were to be made without going through the appropriations process. Muskie joined Senate Appropriations leaders in a floor attempt to require annual appropriations for the tax credits, but he and his allies were outvoted by Senate Finance's large coterie of supporters.[8] The next year, however, Sen. Lawton Chiles, a member of both the Appropriations and Budget Committees, led a quiet, but successful, move to require all future refundable tax credits to go through the appropriations process.

This alliance of the Budget and Appropriations Committees with respect to the refundable energy tax credit was a transitory matter. It was held together by each side's reading of its own interests, not by a lasting commitment to work together for a common cause. Only months before, SBC had taken a different stance on a similar issue. It insisted that the "earned income credit" for low-income persons should be computed as a loss of tax revenues rather than as an expenditure. In that instance, SBC found the Finance Committee to be a convenient ally. HBC, however, sided with its Appropriations Committee and insisted that the earned income credit be treated as a direct expenditure.[9]

The opportunities of the moment affect the relationship between the Budget and the Appropriations Committees. In one noteworthy budget victory, SBC and HBC took identical positions but had rather different relationships with their Appropriations Committees. The case involved a joint effort by leaders of the Senate Budget and Public Works Committees to include a limitation on highway trust fund obligations in a transportation appropriation bill. The move caught Sen. Birch Bayh (chairman of the Trans-

---

8. Senator Magnuson offered an amendment to require an appropriation for the refundable tax credit. Senator Long's tabling motion lost 38-41, but the amendment was then defeated 20 to 47. See 123 *Congressional Record* (daily ed., October 28, 1977) S18037-52.

9. SBC ultimately agreed to treat these credits as outlays.

portation Appropriations subcommittee) by surprise and he initially resisted it as a "legislative impoundment." But Senator Muskie had planned well and Bayh, conceding the futility of his cause ("I have a pretty good command of the process of addition"), accepted the ceiling.[10] Similar objections to legislative impoundment were raised in the House but this time a coalition of Budget and Appropriations Democrats won approval of the highway spending limitation in the face of strong opposition from the authorizing committee.[11]

The constantly shifting coalitions suggest that Budget and Appropriations are less allies than committees in need of allies. An Appropriations aide concluded, "Members see the two committees operating in separate spheres and they do what they have to do to make peace."

Budget Functions and Line Items: Information Links and Conflicts

The budget and appropriations processes can retain their autonomy because they operate within distinct information frameworks. The former is anchored in a small number of budget functions; the latter is built on a large number of appropriations accounts. This informational differentiation is a prerequisite for budgetary peace in Congress. Without it, the two sets of committees would be unavoidably intruding on each other's jurisdiction. Yet this dichotomy also generates budgetary confusion and strife. The problem is rooted in the cross-walk between functional and appropriation categories.

Some functions closely match their corresponding appropriations categories. Almost all the funds in the national defense function are provided in the defense and military construction appropriations bills. In these cases, the conversion from one informational dimension to the other poses no difficulty. Some functions, however, are split among a considerable number of appropriations bills, while some appropriation bills derive from numerous functions. The greater the number of functions contributing to a single bill, the greater the difficulty of reconciling it with the functional allocations. On occasion, the problem has produced intercommittee bickering. In one such case when Senator Muskie apologized for

10. 121 *Congressional Record* (daily ed., July 25, 1975) S13774.
11. *Ibid.*, (daily ed., November 11, 1975) H10924-29.

the fact that the fiscal 1976 Labor-HEW bill cut across a half-dozen functions, Senator McClellan exclaimed:

> Why did the Committee on the Budget find it necessary to make the process so confusing? I do not understand how it works. Why could the committee not follow the appropriation bill so its analysis would be simple, understandable, and we would all know what we are doing and what we are expected to do? [12]

The confusion dragged through six pages of the *Congressional Record* with Muskie patiently but unsuccessfully explaining how the budget process works and McClellan demanding a straightforward answer as to whether each appropriation was consistent with the budget targets.

This problem of translating functions into appropriations proved to have no enduring effect on the budget process. Once a computerized scorekeeping process was installed, the translation became routine. Moreover, with experience, the Appropriations Committees learned that the separation of functions and appropriations secured more flexibility and discretion for them than would a perfectly synchronized information system. Because the two sets of figures do not always match, the Appropriations Committees can shift funds among functions without violating the budget allocations. Once the Senate Appropriations Committee sensed this advantage, its members insisted that they not be officially informed as to how the functional allocations relate to its appropriations bills, although its staff does get details from SBC counterparts. The Senate Appropriations Committee does not want its share of the budget resolution allocated by function. "We take the position," an Appropriations Committee expert confided,

> that to do so would make the allocations too detailed. To do a perfect allocation by function and subcommittee, you really get down to the account level. So we don't do it by function in the Senate. We only allocate by subcommittee. We do not take the report of the Budget Committee and look into each item—what did they assume?—and make ours conform. We make sure that the total is in line and that's good enough.

House Appropriations has gauged its interests differently and opted for functional allocations. One of its information specialists explained the committee's reasoning:

---

12. 121 *Congressional Record* (daily ed., September 17, 1975) S16128.

The fact that the Budget Committee gives us functional targets is compatible with our own thinking. We were very conscious of the difference between the way the Senate wanted to deal with it. We just felt that as long as the budget process is going to be focused upon functional objectives, it was meaningful to set up targets along functional lines. As a matter of fact, we set up a whole computer system just to be able to do that. We are the only ones who really set that thing up and we did because we wanted to help work along these functional allocations.

Obviously, the two Appropriations Committees have seen their interests quite differently on this issue. One can more readily understand the Senate Committee's objection to being tied to precise budget allocations. House Appropriations has had a different preference because the interests of the two committees *do* diverge. In marking up its appropriations bills, the House committee is accustomed to precise comparisons with baseline numbers (last year's spending, the President's request, etc.). Moreover, functional targets pose much less threat to the House committee than to the Senate committee. Most appropriation bills passed by the House are substantially below the comparable amounts in the bills passed by the Senate; consequently, House bills are much less likely to exceed functional targets.

The House Appropriations Committee has another reason for accepting functional allocations: it wants to maintain a clear distinction between its spending jurisdiction and that of the Budget Committee. From the beginning of congressional budgeting, House Appropriations has been apprehensive about "line iteming," the setting of functional targets by estimating the cost of each line in the budget.[13] So great was its concern that Appropriations castigated its fellow committee in its March 15 report for fiscal 1978:

With respect to the content of the reports on the concurrent resolutions on the budget, the Committee notes with concern the tendency to identify and to make recommendations for specific appropriation line items. While these line item recommendations have no actual effect, they do tend to obscure the overall macro-economic responsibilities of the Budget Committee and to needlessly duplicate much of the hearings and deliberations that are the responsibility of the authorizing and appropriating committees. There has been some evidence that there is increasing pressure to fragment the functions into more detailed aggregations of Federal activities. This fragmentation should be avoided since it will only serve to focus the overall debate on the "means" and

13. The problem has not arisen in the Senate because SBC generally avoids line-item detail in marking up its budget resolutions.

mechanics of Federal programs, not the broad-based macro-economic objectives of the Federal budget.[14]

Resentment over the Budget Committee's attentiveness to line items has not reached the point of damaging relations between the two committees. HBC has become more sensitive to the fears of the Appropriations Committee and more cautious to avoid the appearance of trespass on the older committee's turf. By permitting the Budget Committee to give it functional allocations, Appropriations has delineated the respective boundaries of the two committees. Line items are the Appropriations Committee domain, in contrast to functions, which (in its judgment) are the only proper concerns of the Budget Committee.

Speeding Up the Appropriations Process

Perhaps the principal reason for the generally harmonious coexistence of the Budget and Appropriations Committees is that surprisingly little has been changed in the day-to-day operations of the appropriations process. While the place of the Appropriations Committees in the overall congressional scheme has been altered, the committees' internal procedures continue much the same as before. These tradition-bound committees have been more willing to suffer a decline in legislative importance than to revamp their own operations to meet contemporary congressional expectations.

The Budget Act has brought one noticeable change, a speedup in the movement of appropriations bills through Congress. Before 1976, action on regular appropriations bills was scattered throughout the year. The Appropriations Committees considered each bill separately, after the relevant subcommittee had finished its work. After House Appropriations marked up a bill, it sent the measure to the floor, without regard for the status of the other appropriations. Under this arrangement, many months usually passed between floor consideration of the first and the last appropriations bills. Some appropriations lagged because they had to await congressional action on authorizing legislation; others because they were controversial and agreement was difficult to secure; still others were held "hostage" to other legislative interests.[15] The net

14. House Committee on the Budget, *Views and Estimates on the Congressional Budget for Fiscal Year 1978*, March 15, 1977, p. 41.

15. For example, the military construction appropriation bill which earmarks funds for military bases in the United States and overseas usually was

result was that most appropriations were enacted after the beginning of the fiscal year to which they applied. In a few extreme cases, Congress did not enact the regular appropriations, and funding for the entire fiscal year was provided by continuing resolution.

The Budget Act calls for Congress to complete action on all regular appropriations early in September, before the opening of the fiscal year. The Act further requires the House Appropriations Committee to report all its regular bills concurrently, and to show how all of these actions fit into the first budget resolution. In order to meet this timetable, the Appropriations Committees have been compelled to accelerate their work. House Appropriations subcommittees move into the hearings stage within weeks after the President's budget is submitted. Senate subcommittees follow on their heels, and there now is considerable overlap in the hearings schedule. Because House Appropriations must report all the bills concurrently, some bills are held up until the laggards have been cleared. The House then sets aside a period in June for the appropriations bills, when it tries to dispose of them at the rate of about one a day. Rather than wait for the House to complete its work, the Senate Appropriations Committee marks up some of its bills before the final outcome in the House is certain. Senate floor consideration usually occurs within a couple of weeks after the House has acted, and the bills are processed at breakneck speed. On one Saturday in 1976, the Senate took up and passed three appropriations bills.

The evidence of this extraordinary pace is contained in table 37, which shows the schedule for fiscal year 1978. All of the regular appropriations for 1977 were enacted no later than the first day of the fiscal year, the first time this feat had been accomplished in three decades. The results were less spectacular in the following years as numbers of the regular bills had to be rescued by continuing resolutions. Not even the time pressures of the budget process could overcome protracted controversy on substantive issues (such as abortion policy) that increasingly intrude on the appropriations process. Nevertheless, overall performance continues to be much speedier than once was customary.

Members of the Appropriations Committees have taken great pride in this accomplishment. They perceive it not only as a

---

one of the last regular appropriations to clear Congress even though it was one of the smallest. The bill allegedly was used to hold members in line or to extract favorable treatment for projects.

Table 36

MOVEMENT OF FISCAL 1978 APPROPRIATIONS BILLS THROUGH CONGRESS

Bill	*Passed House*	*Reported in Senate*	*Passed Senate*	*Conference Report Approved*	
				House	*Senate*
Treasury, Postal Service	June 8	June 14	June 20	July 14	July 14
Transportation	June 8	June 15	June 23	July 18	July 20
Interior	June 9	June 16	June 17	July 12	July 13
State, Justice, Commerce	June 13	June 21	June 24	July 19	July 19
HUD, NASA, Veterans' Administration	June 15	June 21	June 24	July 19 Sept 23 [a]	Sept 23
Labor-HEW	June 17	June 21	June 29	Aug 2 Oct 12	Aug 4 [c] Oct 12
Public Works	June 14	June 25	July 13	July 25	July 25
Agriculture	June 21	June 23	June 29	July 27	July 29
Military Construction	June 21	June 23	June 29	Aug 5	Aug 5
Foreign Aid	June 23	July 18	Aug 5	Oct 18 [b]	Oct 19
Legislative Branch	June 29	July 13	July 18	July 26	July 26
Defense	June 30	July 1	July 19	Sept 8	Sept 9
District of Columbia	Sept 16	Sept 19	Oct 4	May 16 [c]	

[a] HUD bill was returned to conference because of Senate-House disagreement on a rider.
[b] Foreign Assistance bill recommitted by House on October 12.
[c] Labor-HEW and District of Columbia funded by continuing resolution.

measure of their compliance with the Budget Act but as an indication of the vigor and adaptability of the appropriations process. The first time the process was accelerated, Chairman Mahon boasted of his committee's logistical *tour de force*:

> During the next two weeks, the Committee on Appropriations will be presenting 12 of its 13 regular major appropriations bills. These 12 bills will cover every agency and department of the Federal Government. . . . Hundreds of hearings[,] 4,276 witnesses, 64,762 pages of printed hearings in 75 volumes and uncounted hours of work on the part of the members and the staff of the committee have all taken place in order to get to this point.[16]

Mahon's statistical summation was his way of telling the House that there had been no slackening of appropriations review because of the speed-up. His committee was just as thorough and vigilant as in the past; its hard work and dedication had made up for the lost time. Others, however, were not so sure. Before the first accelerated cycle was launched, the ranking Democrat on Appropriations warned the House:

> I do not see any way in the world we can live up to that short schedule. . . . I do not see how our committee can do a good job on the budget in the short period allowed . . . because to do the regular job we must have time to study these bills. . . .[17]

House Appropriations met the truncated schedule because it was more efficient in processing its legislation and because it cut corners in scrutinizing agency submissions. The full committee developed a master schedule of subcommittee hearings, and substantially reduced delays. But one cannot scan the thousands of pages of printed testimony without concluding that the hearings have become shallower and more hurried because of time pressures. Each agency sends its retinue of witnesses (adding up to the thousands, as Mahon reports) but a substantial portion of the published hearings is taken with photocopies of agency justifications and submissions. Occasionally members admit that the quality of appropriations review has been impaired by pressure to get the bills out on schedule. The problem has been more severe for subcommittees that handle big, controversial bills than for those that deal with routine

16. 122 *Congressional Record* (daily ed., June 14, 1976) H5768.
17. 121 *Congressional Record* (daily ed., December 15, 1975) H12537, remarks of Representative Whitten.

housekeeping measures. When the mammoth defense appropriations bill for 1977 came to the floor, Rep. Daniel Flood spoke of the compromises necessary to meet the timetable:

> The subcommittee did not have time to hold a detailed hearing which has customarily been held in the past. We covered the entire budget request. Much of our deliberation was more general and less detailed than has been the case in recent years. . . . The printed hearings are less voluminous than they have been and you will note that the report is less lengthy. The subcommittee streamlined its procedures in order to meet the requirements of the Budget Control Act.[18]

A similar complaint was voiced the next year by the ranking Republican on the Defense subcommittee:

> Due to the time constraints imposed by the Budget Control Act, we did not hold detailed hearings on each account as we have in the past. Instead we focused on key issues and problem areas such as tanks, shipbuilding, and strategic programs. Although I feel we did the best we could under the circumstances, I would have preferred to spend more time on some of the more complex issues.[19]

The time pressures also have affected Senate Appropriations, but in a different way. Its hearings normally have not been so detailed or intensive as those conducted by the House committee. As an appellate body, the Senate committee concentrates on items brought to its attention by federal agencies. But the Senate committee has experienced difficulty in getting its members (all of whom serve on other committees and numerous subcommittees) to find time for appropriations hearings on their crowded schedules. One subcommittee's solution was to publish voluminous proceedings for hearings that never took place. Dialogue was scripted to substitute for real discourse, and the volumes were stuffed with backup material supplied by executive agencies. This practice was publicized in news reports and led to the departure of Harley Dirks, the subcommittee's chief clerk.

Most Senate participants aver that the appeals process has not been significantly curtailed by shrinkage of the interval between House passage and the report of the Senate committee. The Senate report on the 1978 defense appropriation was filed just one day after the House acted; in a few instances, House action and the

18. 122 *Congressional Record* (daily ed., June 17, 1976) H6068.
19. 123 *Congressional Record* (daily ed., June 24, 1977) H6484, remarks of Representative Edwards.

Senate report have occurred on the same day. For the average bill, there has been only one week's lapse between the House and the Senate actions. Nevertheless, agencies have been able to partly compensate for this compression by maintaining close tabs on the work of the Appropriations Committees. Often they are informed of what the House committee will do long before the report is filed and can thus carry their appeals to Senate Appropriations before the House completes its work.

The Appropriations Committees have been willing to compress their work into a narrow time span because they benefit from the avoidance of continuing resolutions. If continuing resolutions once again become commonplace, the Appropriations Committees might lose their main incentive for speeding up the process and the timetable of the Budget Act might not be sufficient constraint against returning to a more leisurely schedule.

Even if they wanted to hurry the process, the Appropriations Committees might not be able to do so if they lost the "no continuing resolutions" leverage. Because of the accelerated timetable, most appropriation bills come to the House with some items lacking authorizations but with a special rule waiving points of order. The authorization committees have grumbled about this usurpation of their role, but thus far without success. When Rep. Richard Bolling referred to the waiver of points of order for one appropriation bill as "routine," a disgruntled Member protested against "the bankruptcy of the budget system. . . . The fact of the matter is that all year long we have been passing rules that waive the rule against having appropriations without authorization bills."[20] More vivid was the explosion of Rep. Walter Flowers when the House granted a waiver for the 1978 Interior appropriations bill:

> Get your bags packed and hold on to your hats, because you are getting ready for the ride on the appropriations choo-choo. It is going to be moving through here fast. Whether or not your authorization bills are ready, it matters not. The Appropriations Committee is ready and they are coming at you full speed ahead.[21]

Flowers went on to protest the "squeezing to death" of the authorization process by the budget and appropriations processes. With waivers becoming standard procedure, the complaints of authorizing committees are likely to increase. Demands have al-

20. *Ibid.*, June 22, 1977, H6297, remarks of Representative Bauman.
21. *Ibid.*, June 9, 1977, H7636.

ready been heard for a relaxation of the budget timetable;[22] if continuing resolutions once again become an annual routine, such demands may prove to be irresistible.

IN COMMITTEE: APPROPRIATING TO THE PRESIDENT'S NUMBERS

The Appropriations Committees now make their decisions earlier, but they do not make them much differently. The most important "nonchange" is their continuing reliance on the President's budget estimates rather than on the congressional budget allocations. The internal decision-making processes of these committees have not been significantly altered by the new budget process. The executive budget continues to be starting point and yardstick for the Appropriations Committees.

The Appropriations Committees are among the most executive-oriented committees in Congress. They rarely initiate legislative business, but instead usually act only in response to a presidential budget request. They are dormant except when roused by a presidential request. Every appropriations bill is formulated pursuant to a presidential action. Far greater than any other possible change, a shift from a presidential to a congressional perspective would have wrenched the Appropriations Committees from their traditions and disoriented them.

No such shift has occurred. From the moment the executive budget is released through the end of the appropriations process, these committees direct their attention to the President's figures. When they get the executive budget, Appropriations Committee members and staff comb through the documents to find out what the President has cut or added. This orientation to the presidential budget continues during the hearings process. "We are still dealing with the President's budget," an Appropriations Committee member admitted. "We are hearing the President's budget and that is what we are scoring against." At every turn, the questioning relates to what the budget includes or fails to include. One can read thousands of pages of appropriations hearings without encountering a single mention of the congressional budget process or of the amounts allocated in budget resolutions.

22. See, for example, House Committee on the Budget, Hearings on *Oversight of the Congressional Budget Process*, 95th Cong., 1st Sess., October 5 and 6, 1977, statement of Rep. Jack Brooks, p. 43.

The primacy of the President's numbers persists during the markup of appropriations bills. "I attend a lot of markups of the various subcommittees," a senior member boasted, "and we rarely even refer to the fact that the Budget Committees exist." This "benign neglect" was confirmed by a fellow committee member who also had had a leading role in the budget process. "They [Appropriations] are always talking about the President's budget. They hate to acknowledge the existence of the congressional budget." An important staff aide who has participated in hundreds of markups recalled that "the budget resolution numbers were mentioned at most once or twice during markup and that was by staff dragging it up. Afterwards, there was stony silence and they went on to other stuff."

As appropriations levels approach congressional budget targets, attentiveness to the congressional figures increases. But these numbers are used selectively, not as an absolute veto against proposals that might "bust" the target. A staff assistant explained that "subcommittee clerks and members added the Budget Act to the armament of reasons for stiffing a request that they don't want to fund." One of the clerks described how the process works:

> The budget resolution has given the subcommittee and the full committee a tool to resist increases over and above what the committee would otherwise recommend. We've used it this year saying, "Gee whiz, we'd like to put that in but we've got the budget ceiling and it would take us over." It has given the committee a crutch to resist what they might want to resist anyway.

When Appropriations members want something, however, they can just as well look the other way, disregarding the budget constraints. This is the way the process has been used by Warren Magnuson, the powerful chairman of the Labor-HEW Appropriations subcommittee (and chairman of the full Senate Appropriations after McClellan's death in 1977):

> It doesn't disturb Maggie if he wants to add another $90 million to the cancer budget above the House totals, way above anything. He will do that, and then will stiff Cannon on two or three million for ACTION. Maggie will then go through the bill and fund major increases in the things he wants with no regard at all for the budget resolution.

Even if they consider the congressional numbers during markup, the Appropriations Committees return to an executive focus in their reports. For each appropriations account, the report compares the committee's recommendation with the amount requested by the President (as well as with the amount appropriated for the prior year). The committee then discusses the major differences between the budget estimate and its recommendation, usually concentrating on proposed increases that it has disallowed, the items added, and restrictions it has placed on use of funds. Each appropriations report also contains a "comparative statement of budget authority," a tabular comparison of the budget estimates and the committee's recommendations. The only concessions to the Budget Act are a short table comparing the total in the bill with the funds available pursuant to the most recent budget resolution, and estimates of the outlays to be spent from each bill.

The continuing dominance of presidential figures results chiefly from habit. The Appropriations Committees simply would not know how to tackle the mammoth federal budget if they were bereft of the decision-making methods that served them so well in the past. Their customary line-by-line review works well with the line-item budget and justifications submitted by the executive branch. They could, of course, devise new methods but the budget process offers them meager incentives to do so. They can comply with the requirements of congressional budgeting while holding on to their traditions. Moreover, the new budget process encourages the Appropriations Committees to continue using the President's figures chiefly because the highly aggregated budget resolutions are not directly relevant to the discrete choices facing the Appropriations Committees. These committees mark up their bills item by item, delving into the lines that constitute the various appropriation accounts. "The Budget Committees," an Appropriations staffer explained, "are dealing in macroeconomic policy, in billions of dollars; we are usually dealing in 5 or 50 million-dollar issues." Another staffer put the matter quite succinctly: "The budget numbers are just a bunch of big numbers." For committees that have to make thousands of little decisions each year, the functional allocations in the budget resolutions are not useful guidelines.

The discrepancy between budget functions and appropriations accounts gives the Appropriations Committees license to disregard the budget's numbers. Someone who has viewed the process from the vantage point of the Appropriations Committees commented:

> Questions about the relationship between the appropriation bill and the budget are raised during markup. But here's the rub: If the ques-

tion is answered truthfully, it doesn't make any difference what the Budget Committee has in the resolution because we can reallocate the thing any way we want.

Thus, the demarcation between budget functions and appropriations lines turns out to be much more than a technical issue in data classification. With congressional budget decisions lumped into functional categories, the Appropriations Committees can continue their fixation on the President's figures and ignore the budget allocations except when they choose to use them. The Appropriations Committees can seek clarification with respect to the assumptions that go into each function, but this action might be construed as an open invitation to the Budget Committees to infringe on the appropriations process. The risk is greater in the House, where the Budget Committee composes its spending targets by anticipating the amount for each account. An information specialist from House Appropriations has insisted that "we don't have, or want to get, numbers from the Budget Committee on what's assumed in each account. They have a system where they put down an amount for each account and put it into a computer. We have discouraged them from doing that. We don't want to know what the Budget Committee thinks unless it is a multibillion-dollar item."

This last comment suggests that the Appropriations Committees cannot completely disregard the budget's dictates. Big-ticket items cannot be ignored; nor can smaller programs concerning which Congress has expressed a special interest. Moreover, the Appropriations Committees prepare March 15 views and estimates and they cannot be indifferent to how their spending preferences are faring in the budget process. They also have to parcel the appropriations share of each budget resolution among their subcommittees, and this compulsory exercise reminds the Appropriations Committees of the budget's expectations and constraints.

ON THE FLOOR: THE ADVANTAGES OF SELECTIVE ATTENTION

There is more talk about the congressional budget when an appropriations bill is on the floor than when it is in committee. The floor manager (the subcommittee chairman) usually introduces the bill by comparing it to the President's budget, indicating how much it is over or under the request. Many managers also discuss the relationship between the appropriations and the congressional budget allocation, although such discussion is not yet standard procedure.

The political situation on the floor differs from that in committee. Having decided how much they want spent, the Appropriations Committees have to defend their recommendations against challenge. They must guard against both cuts and additions, but the latter are a more formidable threat on the floor. Amendments to increase spending outnumber proposed decreases and have a much higher success rate. In rallying support for their preferences, Appropriations are willing to use the budget process to their advantage.

Silence about the congressional budget often is not an available option because the Appropriations Committees know that the budget numbers will be introduced into the debate by a spokesman for the Budget Committee. Rather than allow the Budget Committees a clear field to interpret the figures their own way, the Appropriations manager might want to use the budget numbers to show that his committee has acted responsibly, in accord with congressional budget decisions. In sum, the Appropriations Committees have three main reasons for injecting the congressional budget into floor debate on their bills: to justify their actions; to defend Congress against criticism of its spending decisions; and to resist floor amendments.

Justifying Appropriations Actions

The Appropriations Committees want to demonstrate that they have abided by the budget decisions of Congress. When one of their bills is within the amount set aside for it pursuant to the budget resolution, the committees want Congress to know about it, particularly if the spending level is controversial. In recent years, the two most contentious appropriations bills (in terms of spending) have been those for the Defense Department and Labor-HEW; in bringing these bills to the floor, their managers have declared their compliance with the congressional budget. Senator McClellan expressed his pleasure that the conference report on the fiscal 1977 defense appropriation was

> $405 million below the ceiling set for budget authority and $44 million below the outlay ceiling as reported by the Senate Budget Committee. I am very pleased that the conferees were able to bring this bill in an amount that is both reasonable from the standpoint of the needs of our

military forces and responsible in terms of our own congressionally mandated budget ceilings.[23]

Attentiveness to the congressional figures is especially useful when an appropriations bill exceeds the President's budget request. Rep. Daniel J. Flood defended the fiscal 1978 Labor-HEW bill by pointing to the budget resolution:

Although the bill is higher than the President's budget requests, it is well within the congressional targets of the congressional budget resolution. Well within that. Do not forget that. It is your budget resolution.[24]

But when they have exceeded the congressional numbers, the Appropriations Committees still sometimes find it useful to mention the budget resolution. They know that the Budget Committee will have its own floor statement, so they would rather portray the excess spending in the most favorable light than to let Members get the news from the budget's policemen. There are several ways to "game" the overrun, depending on how the Appropriations representative feels about the issue. Sen. Gale W. McGee pleaded innocence, explaining that his Agriculture subcommittee had complied with the budget target—"we lived up to our responsibility"—but that the full committee added $100 million for "an extremely valuable program, good, needed, desperately needed. But we were trying to meet our responsible commitment and we exceeded it because of full committee action."[25] McGee pledged his fidelity to the budget process while hinting that it would be a good idea to accept the extra $100 million.

Appropriations Committees can defend their excess spending by talking about the imperfections of the congressional scorekeeping procedures. When the 1977 defense bill failed to produce the spending cutbacks assumed in the budget resolution, an Appropriations Committee member urged the House not to make an issue of it because "it is becoming very clear that the application of the first budget resolution to the various appropriation bills is by no means an exact science." He termed the discrepancy between the defense bill and the budget's expectations "only a rough estimate,"[26] something the House should not worry about.

---

23. 122 *Congressional Record* (daily ed., September 13, 1976) S15684
24. 123 *Congressional Record* (daily ed., June 16, 1977) H6033.
25. 122 *Congressional Record* (daily ed., June 23, 1976) S10222.
26. Ibid., daily ed., June 17, 1976) H6065, remarks of Representative Edwards.

Another defense is to admit the excess spending but to assure members that total appropriations will be kept within budget limits. Sen. Robert C. Byrd coupled a statement that the 1978 Interior bill "is significantly above the budget" with an assurance "on behalf of the chairman of the Appropriations Committee . . . that the committee expects to stay within the full allocation from the first budget resolution for fiscal 1978."[27] This is an effective way of defusing concern over excess spending without opening the door to other deviations from the congressional budget.

Defending Congressional Priorities

The Appropriations Committees are most enthusiastic about congressional budget numbers when they want to justify spending in excess of the President's request. Rather than pleading guilty to a violation of the executive budget, they can claim that the additional expenditures actually uphold congressional budget priorities. Byrd defended the increases for Interior as "a conscious effort to respond to congressional priorities as well as the priorities established by the President."[28] Representative Flood, the floor manager for the Labor-HEW appropriations bill declared that the President's budget only "represents one reference point to be considered along with other sources of advice and guidance."[29] Senator Chiles, a member of both the Appropriations and the Budget Committees, regarded 1978 spending for Labor-HEW as too high, but he insisted on a congressional test for the expenditure level:

> . . . it is essential that we use congressional targets, rather than the President's budget, as our guideline for whether any spending bill puts too much of a strain on the budget. The Budget Act of 1974 was both a reassertion of Congress' constitutional responsibility for spending decisions and a challenge to develop a new sense of fiscal discipline. . . . To keep the process credible we must keep it whole, and not pick out any one bill because it exceeds the President's budget proposal.[30]

The Budget Committee chairmen have supported the use of the new process as a defense of congressional budget priorities. For Brock Adams, "the President's budget request is no longer the critical question. The critical question is the relationship of the appropriation bill to the amounts provided in the budget resolu-

27. 123 *Congressional Record* (daily ed., June 17, 1977) S10131.
28. *Ibid.*, S10125.
29. 122 *Congressional Record* (daily ed., September 30, 1976) H11847.
30. 123 *Congressional Record* (daily ed., June 29, 1977) S11077.

tion."[31] For Ed Muskie, "Congress expresses its own preference on how federal spending is allocated among the functions of government. This process is independent of what the President proposes to Congress in his annual budget message and appropriation requests."[32]

These vigorous assertions of congressional priorities should not be taken as evidence that the budget targets have superseded the President's figures as the key reference points for the Appropriations Committees. Appropriations still are dominated by the executive budget, but when Congress wants to spend more than the President has requested, Budget Committee numbers offer a convenient and satisfying justification.

Warding Off Floor Amendments

The congressional budget provides fresh arguments for opposing unwanted floor amendments that would cause spending to exceed budget targets. Thus, even when he defended an Interior Department appropriation that exceeded congressional targets, Senator Byrd urged "those who are interested in additional funding in one area or another to exercise restraint."[33] The plea sometimes gets immediate results; for example, Hubert Humphrey withdrew an amendment after being told that it would breach the spending allocation. "I bow to the constraints of the budget . . . the distinguished Senator from Maine . . . has disciplined me in this matter."[34] On the basis of several years of grappling with the new budget controls, a spending advocate from the House Education and Labor Committee argued that "the budget process makes it less likely that you can go to the floor and roll the Appropriations Committees for more money."

The record does not clearly support this statement, however. During the first two cycles of congressional budgeting, 40 of the 68 amendments seeking increased appropriations were passed in the House and 80 of the 89 increases proposed in the Senate were approved. Although it cannot be known how many additional increases might have been promoted and passed in the absence of budget constraints, a reasonable conclusion is that the congressional targets are not an insuperable barrier to popular amendments. An Appropriations clerk supplied a clue to his committee's

31. 122 *Congressional Record* (daily ed., September 30, 1976) H11850.
32. 123 *Congressional Record* (daily ed., June 28, 1977) S10860.
33. 123 *Congressional Record* (daily ed., June 17, 1977) S10125.
34. 121 *Congressional Record* (daily ed., November 20, 1975) S20714.

lack of success against amendments. "We go out on the floor and usually have so much slack left over that it is hard to make a case against the amendment." Seldom does a single amendment take total spending over the top; if an amendment pushes spending above a functional target, its supporters can argue that funds can be drawn from the overall allocation to the Appropriations Committees. The Appropriations Committees frequently make this claim when a bill is above the budget; a similar argument can be used with equal effect against the Appropriations Committees by Members sponsoring floor amendments.

Budget Committee representatives frequently comment on pending amendments, but a desire to avoid line-item review usually induces them to settle for a general warning that adoption of the proposal might crowd out later spending initiatives rather than to directly oppose the amendment. When a floor amendment is defeated, it is more likely to be the work of an adept floor manager and a unified Appropriations Committee than that of a persuasive Budget Committee chairman.

THE BUDGET COMMITTEES IN THE APPROPRIATIONS PROCESS

The Budget Committees have another reason for avoiding vigorous opposition to floor amendments. The numerous amendments that pass obviously have substantial support within Congress. If they were to regularly oppose floor increases to appropriations bills, the Budget Committees would be trying to deny Congress the opportunity to overrule its Appropriations Committees. In these circumstances, the Budget Committees might find themselves on the losing end of a lot of floor votes.

The Budget Committees have to pick their issues and their fights. They cannot complain about every spending measure that they dislike. Not only on floor amendments, but also in their stance on appropriations bills, the Budget Committees must be reserved in their use of "budget-busting" arguments. They must be supportive of the Appropriations Committees, limiting their opposition to blatant abuses of the budget process. With 15 or more appropriations bills reaching the floor every session, the collegiality of Congress would be strained by recurring conflict between two sets of committees.

Almost every time an appropriations bill is on the floor, the chairman of the House or Senate Budget Committee issues a formal statement on behalf of his committee assessing the budgetary impact of the bill and its degree of compliance with congressional budget decisions. The HBC chairman has a much easier task than his Senate counterpart. Almost every appropriations bill taken up by the House provides less funds than the bill considered by the Senate. It is a rare House Appropriations bill that runs afoul of the budget targets; trouble is much more likely to arise in the Senate where the higher numbers confront the Budget Committee with the problem of avoiding challenges to the bills without risking loss of credibility. In the House, the Budget Committee chairman has been consistently supportive of the Appropriations Committee. When President Ford vetoed the 1977 Labor-HEW appropriations, Chairman Adams was in the forefront of a successful override: "I can advise the Members that the Labor-HEW appropriation bill is entirely consistent with congressional budget goals and allocations which we have adopted."[35] When House Republicans launched a floor drive to trim the next year's Labor-HEW bill, Bob Giaimo vigorously defended the Appropriations Committee:

> . . . when the committee comes in with amounts over the targets, then I am going to be down in this well screaming and pointing out that they are over the budget targets. But the Committee on Appropriations has been coming in on every bill, and certainly in this bill, with figures well below our budget targets.[36]

Despite the spending increases incorporated into many appropriations bills in the Senate, Muskie has been able to endorse most bills and to stop short of opposing all but a few of those that have exceeded budget targets. A favorite tactic—repeated numerous times each year—is to limit his remarks to appropriations totals, sidestepping comment on specific appropriations issues. "The Budget Committee is not a line item committee. It is for the Appropriations Committee to establish those line items."[37] Still another way out is the "let's take it to conference" approach, which is used in expectation that the lower House figures will prevail. Muskie adeptly applied this solution to the health portion of the 1978 Labor-HEW bill, which was well above target; he noted that "the

35. 122 *Congressional Record* (daily ed., September 30, 1976) H11850.
36. 123 *Congressional Record* (daily ed., June 16, 1977) H6041.
37. 122 *Congressional Record* (daily ed., June 23, 1976) S10233.

House levels are below the target, so I think we must see the results of the various appropriations conferences before a definitive judgment on health spending can be reached."[38] Muskie has ignored minor infractions of the budget target, exercising the chairman's prerogative to decide whether an overrun is of sufficient consequence to evoke his protest:

I do not want to be an annoyance in the Senate Chamber. My job as chairman of the Budget Committee is to highlight what I think are the significant issues in order to keep us within the functional targets. I am not going to try to pick up every nickel and dime that I take issue with. I think that would be disruptive of the whole process.[39]

As this first-year pronouncement indicates, Muskie's original intention was to hold the Appropriations Committee figures to the functional targets. But strict adherence to this position would have forced Muskie into opposition to the Appropriations Committee whenever it exceeded its subcommittee or functional allocations. Hence Muskie adopted a formula that permits the Senate Appropriations Committee to shift funds among functions as long as it abides by the total allocation for the committee:

It is certainly a prerogative of the Appropriations Committee to divide the funds allocated to it under the budget resolution among its subcommittees as it sees fit. This is true even if that division among subcommittees is at some variance with the targets in the budget resolution.[40]

Muskie also has acknowledged the Appropriations Committee's discretion to shift funds among its subcommittees: "It is the prerogative of the full Appropriations Committee to exceed its subcommittee allocation . . . as long as the full committee remains within the total allocation."[41] This permissive attitude has avoided conflict between the Budget and Appropriations Committees, but it also has permitted early bills to sail through Congress with excess budget authority that must either be diverted from later appropriations or accommodated by higher ceilings in the second budget resolution. Muskie's first approach to the problem was to admonish the Senate that "if we vote in favor of the bill before us today,

38. 123 *Congressional Record* (daily ed., June 28, 1977) S10860.
39. 121 *Congressional Record* (daily ed., September 17, 1975) S16136.
40. 123 *Congressional Record* (daily ed., June 17, 1977) S10131.
41. 122 *Congressional Record* (daily ed., June 24, 1976) S10705.

some other high priority items may be crowded out later."[42] McClellan responded "that the full Appropriations Committee expects to be able to stay within the full allocation made to this committee under the first budget resolution, including all possible later requirements known at this time."[43]

The Budget Committee chairmen have taken care to keep separate their roles as spokesmen for the Budget Committees and as individual Members of Congress. If their every pronouncement on an appropriations bill were to be perceived as the authoritative position of the Budget Committee, the chairmen would not be free to oppose or to support spending measures on nonbudgetary grounds. Every time they took the floor to attack an item, the issue would be regarded as a contest between the two committees; every time they supported increased spending, they would be vulnerable to charges of using their budget positions to advance favored programs. As things have worked out, the chairmen have not had to announce whether they are wearing their Budget Committee or Member's hat. The style in which the statement is made has usually signaled the role that is being filled. As Budget Committee spokesman, the chairman usually has provided a straightforward accounting of the financial impact of the appropriation; as a Member with particular interests, the chairman usually has addressed the substance of the legislation.

Sometimes the chairman has blurred the two roles. As a result he has been able to use his Budget Committee position without creating an issue between the Budget and Appropriations Committees. In one such instance, Giaimo, enraged by a supplemental appropriation for disaster loan programs, stopped short of opposing an appropriations bill as HBC chairman. The program's cost, when coupled with that of an earlier supplemental bill, had soared from $20 million in the initial budget request to $2.3 billion—with the possibility of additional funding before the fiscal year was out. Giaimo went into the financial details of the program, conveying the impression that he was speaking as HBC chairman, but he did not introduce the usual scorekeeping considerations into the debate (how much margin remained in the budget resolution), thus signaling that he was not asking the House to reject the bill as a violation of the budget process.[44] When Giaimo lost the vote 23 to

42. 122 *Congressional Record* (daily ed., March 23, 1976) S4084.
43. 123 *Congressional Record* (daily ed., June 30, 1977) S11277.
44. 124 *Congressional Record* (daily ed., May 8, 1978) H3648-50.

346, his defeat was not regarded as a defeat for the Budget Committee.

FLOORS AND CEILINGS: THE IMPACT OF BUDGETING ON APPROPRIATIONS

Has the congressional budgeting process changed appropriations outcomes? Observers differ in their interpretations of apparent changes. For fiscal 1976 Congress cut more from defense ($5.9 billion) than in any prior year during the decade, although the percentage reduction was in line with appropriations patterns during the post-Vietnam era. Looking at that year alone, one could have concluded that the new budget process had forced the Appropriations Committees to prune more from defense than they might have done in the absence of pressure from the budget resolutions. This interpretation was widely circulated at the time in the media, on Capitol Hill, and in the Pentagon. In each of the next three years, however, Congress cut a much smaller percentage from defense than in any other year since Vietnam. The opposite conclusion—that the budget process pushed defense spending higher than it otherwise might have been—now appears logical.

The zigzagging fortunes of defense are mirrored in the conflicting interpretations and perceptions of Budget and Appropriations Committee members and staff. The two words used repeatedly during interviews are "floors" and "ceilings"; they nicely sum up the differences of opinion about the budget process. Some participants perceive the budget resolutions as exerting downward pressure on appropriations. One described them as "psychological restraints"; another contended that the budget targets had "forced the Appropriations Committees to look at the totals first, and this necessarily had a limiting effect on their discretion to add in separate Christmas-tree items." A third thought that the "pain level" had gone up in appropriations markups because of the budget constraints. Several pointed to specific instances in which the budget process resulted in lower appropriations: "We had a real problem with Labor-HEW in the second concurrent resolution. They wanted about $3 billion more in outlays and we just didn't have it and we told them we didn't have it." A committee clerk speculated that some amendments that had been rejected by one or two votes in the whole committee "probably wouldn't have been rejected before the Budget Act."

Conversely, quite a few participants have argued that the budget resolutions have served as floors on appropriations—that rather than constraining the Appropriations Committees, the resolutions have stimulated additional spending. This line of thinking was prevalent during interviews with an Appropriations staffer: "We have members who don't understand why we don't appropriate up to the level allowed in the budget resolution." Another tried to explain why "the so-called ceilings become floors. You have $20 million left in the budget and a member is pushing hard for something in particular—especially if he is up for reelection and needs a little help here. You've got plenty of room under the congressional budget, so you don't worry about it. The budget sort of legitimizes these things that you wouldn't ordinarily fund."

The notion that the budget process has spurred higher spending was forcefully argued by the clerk of a client-oriented Appropriations subcommittee that has consistently reported appropriations bills above the President's figures:

I think you can argue that we're spending more instead of less. If you look at what the Appropriations Committees will do this year, in contrast to what they ordinarily do, you might find that the Budget Control Act is working in just the opposite direction than it set out to work. The principal reason why it's working well is because the Budget Committees and the Congress have agreed to spend more than the President asked for. In fact, we've said why don't we spend $17 billion more than the President's budget.

You know under this new system, where we have a ceiling, the ceiling will also become the floor. In other words, recipients of federal funds, under education or health programs or any other programs, are going to expect to receive the full amount of the ceiling. And the pressure will build against the Appropriations Committee, and the appropriations process, not to provide less than the ceiling. My point is that lobby groups, organizations, associations, people who represent other people with human needs, are going to figure out how this new process works. First they're going to figure out how to get up to the ceiling, and then they're going to figure out how to bust the ceiling.

Members of the Appropriations Committees also attribute high spending to the budget process. The following from a conservative on the House Committee reflects this view:

We are now using the new congressional budget process as a means to justify substantial increases in spending—spending which had previously been held pretty well in check, at least the "nonbackdoor" items, by our appropriations process.[45]

A leading liberal on the House Appropriations Committee who has also served as a member of the Budget Committee expressed much the same view during a House-Senate conference on the first budget resolution for fiscal 1978. Rep. David R. Obey tried to reduce the allocation for health programs and was opposed by Senator Muskie:

Muskie: If we come to regard budget resolutions as mandates for spending, then that would change the whole character of the process. I certainly do not regard it as such. If we can get spending below the ceiling, that is fine with me. But we have to provide room for the authorizing committees to make their priority decisions. . . .

Obey: I am speaking in practical terms, and I know because I serve on the subcommittee that deals with it, that we will wind up with this appropriations bill right at the ceiling.[46]

Those who argue that the budget ceilings have stimulated higher appropriations point to the costly supplemental appropriations bills enacted for the 1977 and 1978 fiscal years. The new budget authority provided in these supplementals exceeded $60 billion dollars. Congress, the argument runs, was encouraged to supplement its regular appropriations because it had room for additional appropriations in its budget resolutions.

Appropriations results for the first years of the budget process are inclusive on the ceilings versus floors issue. As required by Section 302 of the Budget Act, after adoption of each budget resolution, the Appropriations Committees have been allocated their share of budget authority and outlays. Table 37 shows the actual appropriations for the 1977 and 1978 fiscal years were significantly below the allocations made to the Appropriations Committees. On the basis of these results, the Appropriations Committees appear to have kept within the budget in spending federal dollars. More to the point, they sought to avoid spending the full amount available to them, and in fiscal 1978 embarked on a strategy that held down the amount of funds provided by supplemental appropriations. Nine supplemental bills were enacted for fiscal 1978, more than for any year during the preceding two decades. But the total

45. 122 *Congressional Record* (daily ed., August 10, 1976) H8625.
46. Conference on the first concurrent resolution on the budget for fiscal 1978, transcript, p. 209-10.

Table 37

BUDGET ALLOCATIONS TO THE APPROPRIATIONS COMMITTEES AND ACTUAL APPROPRIATIONS, FISCAL YEARS 1977 AND 1978

(millions of dollars)

Allocations and Appropriations	*Fiscal 1977*	*Fiscal 1978*
First Resolution Allocation	$299,278	$328,889
Second Resolution Allocation	291,388	327,950
Third Resolution Allocation	323,897	—
Fourth Resolution Allocation	320,697	—
Total Appropriations	314,548	322,791
Amount Below Last Resolution	6,149	5,159

Sources: Section 302 reports of the House Appropriations Committee and CBO scorekeeping reports.

amount appropriated in these bills was less than that for any year since fiscal 1974 and a smaller percentage of the total budget than that for any year since 1970. By devising separate bills for various emergency needs (for example, $13 million for railroads, $57 million for the Department of Agriculture, and $254 million for the black-lung disease program—each in its own bill), the Appropriations Committees assured that these bills would not be "Christmas treed" on the floor by the addition of funds for other items. In this way, they successfully deterred Congress from using all the money allocated in the latest resolution.

The data in table 38 also show that the second resolution allocations were lower than those made pursuant to the first resolution. These reductions are significant because the first allocations were made before enactment of the regular appropriations bills for each of the fiscal years, while the second allocations occurred when congressional work on these bills was nearly completed. Although the appropriations allocation was raised after adoption of the third resolution for 1977, this increase was the result of policy decisions to stimulate the economy, not a result of a failure of the Appropriations Committees to live within their limits.

Yet there is another way of looking at the performance of the Appropriations Committees. Approximately one-fourth of the annual appropriations made by Congress are mandated by existing law; the amount spent in a particular year depends on factors over which the Appropriations Committees have no direct control. Virtually all of the shortfall in appropriations has been in the mandatory items, not in the spending over which the Appropriations Committees (and Congress) have discretion. In both fiscal 1977 and 1978, the second resolution allocations for discretionary budget authority were higher than the comparable first resolution allocations. For fiscal 1977, the second allocation was almost $10 billion lower for mandatory items and $1.2 billion higher for discretionary spending. For fiscal 1978, there was a $2 billion drop in the mandatory accounts and a $1 billion increase in the discretionary ones (see table 38).

This pattern suggests that by making liberal assumpitons concerning mandatory appropriations, the Budget Committee resolutions have provided room for the Appropriations Committees to increase discretionary spending without breaching the budget limits. Both sides win through this arrangement. The Budget Committees can claim that their decisions have been enforced, and the Appropriations Committees can raise spending levels without running afoul of the budget process.

The question of whether the budget targets and ceilings dampen or stimulate appropriations can be argued both ways because any

Table 38

BUDGET ALLOCATIONS TO THE APPROPRIATIONS COMMITTEES, MANDATORY AND OTHER ITEMS, FISCAL YEARS 1977 AND 1978
(millions of dollars)

Allocations and Appropriations[1]	*Fiscal 1977*	*Fiscal 1978*
Mandatory Appropriations		
First Resolution	$ 87,032	$ 73,546
Second Resolution	77,654	71,711
Reduction in Second Allocation	−9,378	−1,835
Nonmandatory Appropriations		
First Resolution	212,495	255,343
Second Resolution	213,734	256,239
Increase in Second Allocation	+1,239	+896

[1] The data in this table are based on allocations made to the House Appropriations Committee; the allocations to the Senate Appropriations Committee differ, but not significantly.

Sources: Section 302 reports of the House Appropriations Committee and CBO scorekeeping reports.

budget process does both things at the same time. Although some Appropriations Committee staffers with long memories "cannot recall a single difference because of the budget process," there undoubtedly have been instances where an appropriation has not been made (or the amount provided has been lower) because of pressure from the budget resolution figures. The congressional budget process has its greatest effect when an amendment is not offered or an idea is quashed before it comes up for a vote in committee or on the floor.

But there is another side to every budget process. The same way it legitimizes claims on government—a conclusion discussed in chapter VI—a budget licenses expenditures. It would be folly for program supporters not to rely on budget arguments to justify additional spending when the money is there. Several of the supplemental appropriations enacted by Congress under its new budget regimen have been loaded with costly programs that might have been deferred had it not been for the availability of a margin in the budget. Especially during periods of high unemployment, members can adroitly exploit the budget process to win additional funds for their programs.

In 1977, for the first time in memory, Congress appropriated more money for a fiscal year than the President had requested. Undoubtedly President Ford's unrealistic budget (which proposed cutbacks of more than $20 billion for existing social programs) left Congress with little choice but to restore much of the money the White House had cut. But Congress clearly used the budget process in 1977 to legitimize this extraordinary deviation from the President's budget.

In some cases, funds have been "assumed" for a particular program in a budget resolution and the assumption then is used to claim funds in the appropriations process. An Obey amendment to help low-income families meet their high heating bills was added to a supplemental appropriation for fiscal 1977 on the claim that the money had already been included in the recently adopted third resolution.[47]

Every budget is an exercise in anticipation and accommodation, a bilateral process in which both the Budget Committees and other committees subject to budget control form expectations about the future. In the congressional budget process, the Appropriations

---

47. 123 *Congressional Record* (daily ed., March 16, 1977) H2165, remarks of Representatives Brademas and Giaimo.

Committees must anticipate the budget and the budget makers must anticipate the appropriators.

As we have noted, the fact that the congressional budget process is rarely mentioned during appropriations hearings and markups or in the committee reports does not mean that the Appropriations Committees are unaware of or do not care about the spending decisions made in the budget process. The congressional budget is very much an unarticulated fact of the appropriations process. The Appropriations Committees work behind the scenes to get budget numbers compatible with their preferences and with the appropriation bills they expect to report in the months ahead. Silence is the Appropriations Committee members' way of coping with the traumas of this new process, an effort to preserve a maximum of autonomy for their committee.

Silent accommodation works because the Appropriations Committees generally have lived within their budget allocations, not only with regard to spending totals but for individual bills as well. Although Appropriations Committee members rarely cite the budget numbers as justification for what they do, they usually make an honest effort to comply with the congressional budget. Even though the work of Appropriations subcommittees is well advanced by the time the first budget resolution clears Congress, the resolution's basic shape is known long before final congressional action. Appropriations members know (or can deduce without great difficulty) what is assumed to be included in or excluded from the budget resolution. They know when appropriations bills are approaching the budget targets and they know whether programs that are being discussed can be fitted into the budget.

Silent accommodation is facilitated by the stability and predictability of the appropriations part of the federal budget. Except for events that cannot be foreseen when the budget is submitted, experienced participants can project total regular appropriations for the next fiscal year with a margin of error of only a few billion dollars. After a quick examination of the President's requests, Appropriations veterans can predict which cuts are likely to be restored and which increases to be disallowed or scaled down. These expectations are transmitted to the Budget Committees, which do their own anticipating, and the staffs of the two committees cooperate to develop a budget resolution that holds few surprises for the Appropriations Committees. Because they know what the congressional budget holds in store for them, the Appropriations Committees do not have to talk much about it.

In budgeting for an uncertain future, the Budget Committees influence the spending actions of Congress by establishing tight or slack targets. The overwhelming consensus on Capitol Hill is that the Budget Committees have bent over backward to accommodate what they expect the Appropriations Committees to do. Senator Muskie's phrase "we have to provide room" expresses a central, if unwritten, decisional rule of the Budget Committees. "The budget ceiling is quite generous," an Appropriations clerk averred, going on to explain, "that's the principal reason why the Budget Control Act is working." When questioned, not a single person associated with the appropriations process thought that it had really been pinched by the budget ceilings. Their perceptions may well have been colored by the fact that the interviews were conducted during fiscal 1977. With spending that year well above the level requested by the President, it was difficult to convince Appropriations old-timers that the Budget Act had brought much spending control.

The Appropriations Committees give selective attention to the budget process, and the Budget Committees give selective responses to Appropriations Committee actions. Both parties try to accommodate to each other's interests and usually find themselves on the same side of the issue. They can operate in this manner because their substantive interests (as opposed to jurisdictional ones) do not greatly diverge. The Budget Committees could not be conciliatory on the floor if their resolutions were ravaged by the Appropriations Committees; the Appropriations Committees could not silently conform to the budget process if their preferences were foreclosed by what they viewed as unreasonable budget targets. The politics of accommodation has not required either side to bend very much.

XII Tax Policy: From "Nondecisions" to Benefits

Before it passed the Budget Act, Congress already had an established system for legislating tax policy, one centered in two of its most powerful committees—House Ways and Means and Senate Finance. This system functioned as a virtually self-contained component of the legislative process. The system treated tax policy largely as a "nondecision" rather than as a recurring matter of legislative choice. The term *nondecision* refers to informal rules and behavioral patterns which assure that a policy already in place will continue in effect without new explicit decisions being made. *Nondecision making* is not merely legislative indolence or inertia but systematic bias (though often veiled and informal) against active consideration of certain issues. "Some issues," Schattschneider wrote in *The Semisovereign People,* "are organized into politics while others are organized out."[1] Congress cannot reopen every issue each year or all issues at once. To do so would overload both its organizational capacity to process legislation and its political capacity to forge agreements. "Nondecision making" reduces the legislative agenda "to a limited range of 'acceptable' issues and political demands."[2] General consideration of the tax system is one issue accorded such treatment by Congress.

Between 1948 and 1974, Congress passed 14 major tax bills, not including Social Security tax measures (see table 40).[3] This legislative output—an average of one tax bill every two years—appears to suggest that Congress has been an active tax policy maker since

1. E. E. Schattschneider, *The Semisovereign People* (New York, N.Y.: Holt, Rinehart, and Winston, 1960), p. 71.
2. Matthew A. Crenson, *The Un-Politics of Air Pollution* (Baltimore, Md.: The Johns Hopkins Press, 1971), p. 23. Crenson's introductory chapter provides a lucid statement of nondecision making and its relationship to pluralist politics.
3. See Joseph A. Pechman, *Federal Tax Policy,* 3rd ed. (Washington, D.C.: The Brookings Institution, 1977), p. 34, for a compilation of these enactments.

Table 39

MAJOR TAX LEGISLATION, 1948-74

Type and Name of Act	*Initiator*	*First Full-Year Revenue Effect (billions of dollars)*
Wartime Tax Increases		
Revenue Act of 1950	President	+ 4.6
Excess Profits Tax Act of 1950	Congress	+ 3.3
Revenue Act of 1951	President	+ 5.7
Revenue and Expenditure Control Act of 1968	President	+10.2
Limited Tax Changes		
Excess Tax Reduction Act of 1954	Congress	− 1.0
Federal Aid Highway Act of 1956	President	+ 2.5
Revenue Act of 1962	President	− 0.2
Excise Tax Reduction Act of 1965	President	− 4.7
Tax Adjustment Act of 1966	President	no change
Recodification of Tax Laws		
Internal Revenue Code of 1954	President	− 1.4
Broad Reductions in Tax Liabilities		
Revenue Act of 1948	Congress	− 5.0
Revenue Act of 1964	President	−11.4
Tax Reform Act of 1969	Congress[a]	− 2.5
Revenue Act of 1971	President	− 8.0

[a] President Nixon recommended tax changes in April 1969, two months after Congress had commenced work on the legislation.

Source: Adapted from table 3-1 in Joseph A. Pechman, *Federal Tax Policy*, 3rd ed. (Washington, D.C.: The Brookings Institution, 1977), p. 34.

the end of World War II, and that it had not permitted the tax system to function on a "nondecisional" basis. Yet this record of activity does not mean that Congress has frequently undertaken a comprehensive review of the tax laws. Four of the enactments were wartime tax increases (three during the Korean War, one during Vietnam), two were reductions in excise tax rates, one was an increase in gasoline taxes to finance the interstate highway system, one was an adjustment to the withholding system that did not alter tax rates. Congress recodified the Internal Revenue Code in 1954;

it passed a small tax reduction in 1962 and a truly major one in 1964. It also produced tax reform legislation in 1969 and another reduction in 1971. With the exception of wartime, special, and limited actions, Congress passed only five major tax bills during this 26-year period.

In the years just preceding enactment of the Budget Act in 1974, however, far-reaching changes in the system for handling tax legislation required Congress thereafter to take a more active role in making tax policy. Moreover, significant changes in economic conditions have spurred Congress to give more frequent consideration to tax policies. To assess the impact of the Budget Act on Congress, one must comprehend the legislative process for making tax decisions and the overall economic and political context within which such decisions are made. This chapter thus begins with a consideration of tax making prior to 1974. It then surveys changes that caused Congress to assume a more active role in the process. Finally, it examines the tax-related provisions of the Budget Act.

THE CLOSURE OF TAX POLICY

Before the enactment of the Budget Act, Congress did not make tax policy every year. In most years, revenues were the "givens" of federal budgeting, and budget activity was concentrated on the spending side of the ledger. The President's budget estimated the revenues expected from existing sources; Congress did not have to produce estimates of its own, although it normally did so as part of the annual adjustment of the public debt limit.[4] In "nondecision" years, Congress often made some minor changes in the tax code, affecting only a small number of taxpayers and small amounts of money. Occasionally, however, Congress made tax policy a prime item on its legislative agenda and produced a multibillion-dollar package affecting virtually every taxpayer. Such was the case in 1964, when Congress lowered individual and corporate income tax rates, and in 1968, when it imposed a surcharge on these taxes.

"Nondecision making" provided a relatively stable tax structure, which was widely regarded as desirable for business investment

4. The permanent public debt limit is hundreds of billions of dollars below the actual indebtedness of the United States. Consequently, Congress must enact a temporarily higher limit, usually of 6 to 12 months' duration, to accommodate the borrowing needs of the federal government.

and capital formation. A zigzagging tax policy would not have given investors clear signals as to the prospective profitability and risk of their actions. By accepting the tax structure as it was, Congress did not have to undertake an arduous reconsideration of the Internal Revenue Code every year or two.

Congress could afford to simplify its legislative workload in this manner because of the elasticity of federal revenues. Because receipts have grown faster than the gross national product, Congress has been able to finance budgetary expansion with incremental revenue from existing sources, thus satisfying its program interests without having to explicitly allocate the costs among taxpayers. Moreover, the federal government was not pressed to balance its budget; it could absorb a deficit without tampering with the tax laws.

"Nondecision making" was a welcome strategy because it avoided political and economic liabilities associated with active tax policy. When it takes up broad tax issues, Congress has three options: (1) It can raise taxes; (2) it can lower them; (3) or it can redistribute the tax burden. The understandable political distaste for higher taxes militates against the first course of action except under special circumstances. Since World War II, Congress has raised broad-based taxes only in time of war or to finance Social Security expansion. The second option—to lower taxes—is almost always politically attractive but opens up the possibility of a "raid" on the treasury by Members responsive to taxpayer pressures. The federal government simply could not afford a fight every year over the size of the tax burden; the outcome would usually be a loss in federal revenues. The government's ability to tolerate a deficit actually whets the legislative inclination for tax reduction. By foreclosing large-scale action on taxes in most years, the President and Congress have protected the treasury against a potential loss in revenues. With policy made by nondecision, Congress can sidestep the persistent pressures for tax cuts.

The third form of tax action is redistribution, to shift the burden of taxation from one group to another without significantly altering the overall yield to the treasury. But redistribution is among the most contentious issues faced by Congress, which excels as a distributor of public benefits. Congress has, in fact, redistributed the tax burden from time to time, but usually as part of an overall reduction in tax liabilities. Everybody gains, but not equally. Potential conflict is defused, although some taxpayers may be relatively worse off as a consequence. "The United States tax system," Pechman and Okner reported in *Who Bears the Tax Burden?*," is essentially proportional for the vast majority of families and therefore has little effect on the distribution of income." [5] Although nobody is enthusiastic about paying federal taxes, proportionality does make it easier for Congress to practice "nondecision making."

Congress was able to respond selectively to pressures on the tax structure by approving various "Members bills," items of interest to no more than a few Members of Congress. These measures did not threaten the treasury with significant revenue losses, and they usually were rushed through Congress without any hearings in committee or much debate on the floor. They did not breach the pattern of "nondecision making" in Congress.

"Nondecision making" is widespread in American politics. There are numerous dormant public issues concerning which few people care or complain; the relevant interests are satisfied and established policies continue in effect without reexamination. This, however, does not seem to be a plausible explanation for Congress's relative inactivity in the field of tax policy. Too much is at stake. Americans often express dissatisfaction with their tax bills and actively campaign against taxes at state and local levels of government. Why should taxpayers be less agitated about their most burdensome taxes—the federal ones—than about the property and sales taxes that are the principal sources of local revenue? [6]

Part of the answer lies in the federal government's comparative remoteness, the convenience of its withholding tax system, and the government's noted ability to produce higher revenues with constant or even lower tax rates. Another part of the answer is rooted in the ideology of federal taxation. By portraying Social Security as an insurance plan and a payroll tax as a contribution, the federal government has been able to impose high (and regressive) Social Security taxes without incurring taxpayer wrath.[7] In time of war, the government has been able to exact huge tax payments in the name of national defense. (Because Vietnam was an unpopular

5. It should be noted that this finding covers the entire U.S. tax system—all federal, state, and local taxes. See Joseph A. Pechman and Benjamin A. Okner, *Who Bears the Tax Burden?* (Washington, D.C.: The Brookings Institution, 1974), p. 10.
6. Federal income taxes tend to be the most burdensome taxes for high-income taxpayers; property, sales, and payroll taxes generally are more burdensome for low-income groups.
7. This has been true since passage of the Social Security Act in 1935, but there are signs of change in the public's passive acceptance of this growing burden. See Martha Berthick, *Policy Making for Social Security* (Washington, D.C.: The Brookings Institution, 1979).

war, enacting a tax increase for defense was more difficult in the Vietnam era than it was in other wars.)

For this study, the best explanation for Congress's relative inactivity in tax policy lies in the institutional structure of Congress for tax legislation. In its basic form, Congress is a highly permeable institution. Each of its Members can introduce bills and sponsor amendments; dozens of its committees prepare legislation for floor action. Of course, only a tiny fraction of the proposals make it through the legislative process,[8] a fact that suggests that Congress has its own "nondecisional" routines. For most legislation, the main bottleneck is in committee; all but a few of the bills referred to committee are filed and forgotten. Yet for tax matters, Congress has additional means of closing off the legislative process and assuring a "nondecisional" outcome.

Congress rarely takes the initiative when major tax changes are at issue. Rather, it usually moves into action only if the President has proposed significant changes in the tax laws. Both the 1964 and the 1968 revenue laws were prompted by presidential initiatives launched more than a year before the legislation was finally passed. If the President does not advance any tax proposals, Congress is not likely to consider major tax legislation. One exception to this pattern was the 1969 tax reform.

Interestingly, even though Congress normally concedes the initiative on tax policy to the President, once Congress becomes involved, it is likely to act independently and to formulate a legislative package significantly different from the executive's proposal. Once the "nondecisional" constraints are removed, Congress is exposed to the many interests clamoring for changes in the tax laws.

Within Congress, the tax-writing process is circumscribed in various ways that limit the opportunity for action. Although the constitutional requirement that revenue measures originate in the House (Article I, Section 7) does not shut off Senate initiative, it definitely restricts the flow of tax legislation through Congress. The Senate is adept at attaching extraneous tax amendments to minor bills.[9] but the 1968 surcharge was the only comprehensive tax enactment in recent times initiated in the Senate rather than

8. In a two-year Congress, only about 600 bills are enacted into law.

9. This does not mean, however, that "as a constraint on Senate behavior in the face of the Senate majority, Article 1, Section 7, might as well never have been written," as John F. Manley claimed in *The Politics of Finance* (Boston, Mass.: Little Brown, and Co., 1970), p. 253.

the House. In that instance, political stalemate, not senatorial usurpation, dictated the unusual sequence of events.[10] Without the constitutional restriction, there probably would be significantly more tax activity in the Senate and in Congress as a whole. The Senate frequently attaches "special interests" provisions to bills passed by the House, but it rarely considers comprehensive legislation *de novo*.

As the congressional point of origin for major tax legislation, the House Ways and Means Committee is in a dominant position to determine whether tax policy will be actionable in a particular year. During Wilbur Mills's long tenure as chairman (1958-74), Ways and Means functioned without any subcommittees; tax matters, along with its other legislative business, were handled by the full committee. The jurisdiction of Ways and Means during those years was extraordinarily broad. In addition to revenue measures, Ways and Means was responsible for more than one-third of the direct expenditures of the federal government, a massive concentration of power for a legislative body in which power is supposed to be widely shared.

A lack of subcommittees compelled Ways and Means to process major legislation on a "one at a time" basis. By forgoing the conventional legislative division of labor among subcommittees, Ways and Means was able to restrict its output. If Chairman Mills decided that the main item of business during the next year would be Social Security, he could foreclose consideration of income tax legislation. There was no subcommittee to challenge his agenda or to take the initiative on its own. Of course, Mills was not impervious to pressures from other committee members or from the House, and he sometimes adjusted the agenda to accommodate fellow Members of Congress or the President. Nevertheless, the overall effect was to close off major tax action in most years.

When Ways and Means chose to act, it maintained effective control over floor action by insisting that its tax bills be considered under a "closed rule." The rules of the House accord privileged status to tax measures; they can be called up for floor action without first being cleared by the Rules Committee. But such a procedure would have opened up tax bills to an unlimited number of

10. As recounted in chapter II, the President's surtax proposal was stalled in the House by the Ways and Means Committee's insistence that it be combined with a ceiling on expenditures. The deadlock was broken on the Senate floor by an amendment which added a spending limit to a tax bill.

floor amendments and would have threatened the ability of Ways and Means to control the final product. By obtaining a closed rule, Ways and Means limited the House to two options: to approve the bill as reported by committee or to reject it.[11] With rare exceptions, the House approved tax legislation exactly as Ways and Means recommended. (Minor tariff and tax bills generally are considered under suspension of the rules, another procedure that bars floor amendments.) To assess the restrictive impact of the closed rule, one need only compare the controlled action on tax bills in the House with the free-for-all in the Senate, where major tax bills sometimes provoke an avalanche of floor amendments.

"Nondecision making" was fostered by the centralization of tax information and expertise within Congress. Neither Ways and Means nor Finance had its own tax staff; lacking subcommittees, they also lacked the specialized staffs often associated with these units. Since 1926, the two committees have shared a single tax staff—the Joint Committee on Taxation,[12] a group renowned for its nonpartisanship and professional competence. In 1973, half the House committees had larger staffs than Ways and Means, and 13 of the 17 standing committees in the Senate had larger staffs than Finance. Although these statistics do not take into account the Joint Tax Committee staff, they indicate that both Ways and Means and Finance were modestly staffed compared with congressional committees with much narrower jurisdictions. Although its staff serves all the members of Ways and Means and Finance, the joint committee is most responsive to the chairmen of its parent committees. Wilbur Mills and Russell Long owed a great deal of their acknowledged mastery of tax law to their preferential access to the joint committee's tax experts. Taxation is an unavoidably complex subject but the man-made obscurantism of the Internal Revenue Code

11. Richard Fenno and John Manley have contended that the House Ways and Means Committee's success with the closed rule manifests the confidence of that committee and its chairman. They argue that if Ways and Means were to formulate legislation unacceptable to the majority of the House, the closed rule would not stand in the way of floor rejection, something which rarely occurred during Mills's chairmanship. Manley, *op. cit.*, and Richard C. Fenno, *Congressmen in Committees* (Boston, Mass.: Little, Brown and Company, 1973). Yet one cannot avoid the conclusion that the terms of accommodation between Ways and Means and the House were markedly different under the closed rule from what they might have been if the chamber had had an unrestricted choice.

12. Until 1977, this group was known as the Joint Committee on Internal Revenue Taxation. The committee has no legislative jurisdiction of its own and merely functions as the tax staff for Ways and Means and Finance.

worked to the advantage of the few Members who controlled the flow of information.

If tax information was controlled within Congress, it was substantially lacking outside. Because Ways and Means and Finance marked up tax legislation in executive session, only special interest groups with privileged access to Members of Congress were in a position to influence the process. Usually the legislative aides of committee members were not permitted in the meeting room, although Treasury Department tax experts sat at the staff table with specialists from the joint committee and actively participated in the markup. Outsiders did not have timely reports of committee deliberations; nor could they rely on tax groups (comparable to the numerous associations active on the state and local levels) to represent their interests. Of course, many interest groups monitored congressional tax activity and lobbied on behalf of legislation favorable to their constituents, but virtually all confined their interests to the particular matters in which they specialized—agriculture, business, labor, and so on. By selectively responding to these special interests, Congress could deflate pressure for a comprehensive review of the tax laws.

TAXATION AS AN ACTIVE LEGISLATIVE ISSUE

Congress passed major tax legislation in each of the first four years of operation under its new budget process. This sustained activity clearly indicates that Congress is not now practicing "nondecision making" with regard to tax policy. Two factors have impelled Congress toward a more active role: (1) the economic and political objectives of tax policy, and (2) changes in the tax-making structure of Congress.

Tax Policy Objectives

Taxation does more than merely produce revenues to finance government operations. The purposes and effects of taxation spread to many other areas of public policy. During the 19th century, for example, tariffs were not only the principal source of federal revenues but also a barrier against the importation of foreign goods. In recent times, the tax system has become a central instrument of U.S. economic policy. Congress cannot fail to act with respect to tax policy, when taxes serve economic or political objectives for which decisions have to be made.

The role of the federal government as economic manager evolved over a period of decades but it was not until the advent of the "new economics" of the 1960s and attempts at "fine-tuning" of the economy by the federal government that the budget's economic potential was officially recognized.[13] Both the successful 1964 tax cut and the too-little, too-late surtax in 1968 were measures to achieve economic growth and stability. The notion that the federal government can fine-tune economic performance by adjusting spending and revenue levels is no longer so confidently held as a decade ago, but when the economy lags, the government still uses tax policy to stimulate economic improvement. Neither Congress nor the President can be sure of what will work, but in the face of high unemployment rates both have supported a succession of tax reductions.

Much of the fiscal stimulus or restraint sought in the budget must be accomplished through tax rather than spending policy. Short-term fiscal adjustments can be made more precisely and speedily by manipulating tax rates than by expanding or contracting federal expenditures. There is a lag of uncertain duration between the initiation of an expenditure policy and the onset of its economic effects.[14] Tax changes made for fiscal purposes are apt to be temporary; there is thus likely to be a recurring need for tax action in order to keep the economy on a desired course. The temporary tax relief enacted in 1975 set the stage for additional actions in 1976 and 1977. Among the advantages of a temporary action is that it preserves the future budgetary options of the government. Regardless of the motivation, short-term fiscal adjustments require active rather than "nondecisional" tax policy.

The federal government also has become active as a redistributor of income. The government has sought redistribution through cash assistance to the poor, but there are compelling economic reasons for relying on tax policy as well. When assistance is based exclusively on direct subventions, beneficiaries are likely to be faced with unacceptably high benefit reduction rates—well above 50

---

13. For differing views of the origins and applications of the "new economics" by two former chairmen of the Council of Economic Advisers, see Walter W. Heller, *New Dimensions of Political Economy* (New York, N.Y.: W. W. Norton Co., 1967), and Herbert Stein, *The Fiscal Revolution in America* (Chicago, Ill.: The University of Chicago Press, 1969).

14. For an explanation of why short-term fiscal adjustments are more appropriate through tax policy, see Barry M. Blechman and others, *Setting National Priorities: The 1976 Budget* (Washington, D.C.: The Brookings Institution, 1975), pp. 197-210.

percent—if they consider exchanging welfare for work. These benefit reduction rates are implicit tax rates from the point of view of the recipient whose total income is diminished by loss of welfare benefits.[15] At the heart of the negative income tax scheme is the realization that every graduated form of assistance (in which the more one earns, the less one receives from government) has an implicit tax rate. By tying redistribution to the tax structure, the government is able to take into account the tax effects of its welfare policy.

Taxation also is implicated in redistribution, because tax cuts aimed at fiscal stimulation can have unintended, regressive results. Tax relief accorded only to taxpayers does not directly benefit the very poor who pay no taxes at all. The 1964 tax reduction was grounded on the expectation that the poorest segments of the population would benefit from an overall improvement in the economy. Now, however, there is wide acceptance of the view that general tax relief does not necessarily trickle down to those who are cut off from the benefits of economic growth. The earned income credit introduced in 1975 compensates partially for this deficiency in the tax system by providing cash payments to people who do not pay taxes. It thus employs an active tax policy in order to achieve a more desired distribution of income than would be possible if the tax system were not deliberately used for this purpose.

A third economic objective of the tax system is to encourage income earners—corporations and individuals—to make a portion of their earnings available for investment. The forms and rates of taxation influence the spending and saving habits of businesses and individuals. The federal tax structure is a jumble of numerous incentives and disincentives for capital formation; one cannot be certain of the tax structure's net effect on savings. But in the 1970s, various public officials and economists warned of a possible capital shortage in the future.[16] This concern has reopened basic questions with regard to the federal tax system, such as the relationship between corporate and individual income taxes.

Interest in tax policy also has been stirred by apprehensions about the future energy supply of the United States. Tax incentives have been proposed (and some have been passed) to promote con-

15. U.S. Congress, Subcommittee on Fiscal Policy, Joint Economic Committee, "Income Transfer Programs: How They Tax the Poor," Studies in Public Welfare, Paper No. 4, Dec. 22, 1972.

16. See Barry Bosworth, James Deusenberry, and Andrew S. Carron, *Capital Needs in the Seventies* (Washington, D.C.: The Brookings Institution, 1975).

servation and the development of new energy sources, while tax penalties have been advocated to combat wastefulness. Although there is nothing new about using the tax laws to influence a particular sector of the economy—the Internal Revenue Code is riddled with preferential provisions for numerous industries—energy policy requires broad tax action because it affects virtually all facets of economic life.

"Nondecision making" is apt to be an acceptable policy only if the tax burden remains relatively stable, that is, if taxpayers are not significantly harmed by government inaction. But the tax burden has not remained stable, because a progressive tax structure requires proportionately more money from taxpayers as their real income grows and as inflation propels them into higher marginal income tax brackets. Inflation is the more serious problem, because taxpayers can suffer a decline in real disposable income when taxes rise faster than their income.

Over the years, however, individual income taxes have been a remarkably constant percentage of total personal income in the United States. From 1951 through 1974, these taxes ranged between 9.2 percent and 11.6 percent of personal income.[17] In all but five of these years, individual taxes were between 9.5 percent and 10.5 percent. This stability resulted from periodic congressional action to adjust taxes for the effects of inflation and economic growth.

Congress could respond to inflation-induced tax increases by indexing the tax rate to changes in the price level, which is a "nondecisional" method. Indexation has been adopted by a number of countries, but thus far Congress has opted for discretionary action rather than a "nondecisional" procedure to counter the effects of inflation. Such adjustments have a number of advantages. Congress can take the credit for lowering federal taxes, an advantage which would be lost if taxes were reduced automatically. Moreover, discretionary adjustments enable Congress to redistribute the tax burden while holding income taxes to a relatively constant share of personal income. Low-income taxpayers generally have benefited more from legislative action than they would have from indexation. Congress has, in effect, used the "revenue dividend" from inflation to shift the tax burden to higher-income taxpayers. Finally, indexation would deny Congress the option of using these revenue increases to finance desired programs. By

17. See Pechman, *op. cit.*, table B-5, p. 326.

deciding when and how to make tax adjustments, Congress retains discretion to chart the future budgetary priorities of the federal government.

High rates of inflation during the 1970s induced frequent legislative adjustments to prevent the tax burden from rising markedly above its normal peacetime level. Thus inflation and the contemporary economic objectives of the federal government ruled out "nondecision making" as acceptable tax policy.

"Nondecision making" often arises from a "satisficing" (the term is Herbert Simon's combination of *satisfaction* and *sufficing*) acceptance of the status quo. There probably never has been a time when most taxpayers felt that they were paying only their fair share and no more, but during the 1970s chronic complaining was supplemented by an organized drive for tax reform. It is one thing to have a vague sense of being cheated but quite another to have an organized effort, backed up by sensational news stories of millionaires who pay no federal taxes as well as by analytical probings of numerous preferences and special provisions built into the tax laws. Awareness of the incidence and effects of taxation was much more widespread at the end of the decade than at the beginning.

The movement for tax reform first bore fruit in 1969, when Congress passed a Tax Reform Act imposing a minimum 10 percent tax on certain sources of income excluded from regular income taxes. But the minimum tax was less effective than originally expected,[18] and Congress later established new tax preferences for the sheltering of income. Consequently, reformers intensified their campaign against the inequities and complications of the tax code. Their persistence was reflected in the establishment of public interest groups to lobby and litigate with regard to federal tax policy. Three important groups were organized in the 1970s; their activities included the publication of timely materials on tax policy, close monitoring of the work of the Ways and Means and Finance Committees, and legal actions.[19] Perhaps their most notable success to date has been changing the structure of Congress, a development to which we now turn.

---

18. See George F. Break and Joseph A. Pechman, *Federal Tax Reform* (Washington, D.C.: The Brookings Institution, 1975), p. 78ff.

19. The groups and their years of establishment are: Tax Analysts and Advocates (1970) which publishes *Tax Notes*, a weekly report on federal tax policy; Taxation with Representation (1970), an advocacy group which claims thousands of members; and the Public Citizen Tax Reform Research Group (1971), associated with Ralph Nader and very active on Capitol Hill.

Impacts of Congressional Reform

Congress abandoned "nondecision making" as a result of dramatic changes in its tax-making apparatus. In the space of just a few years, the ability of the Ways and Means Committee to control tax legislation in the House of Representatives was substantially weakened. Some of the changes that affected Ways and Means were specifically directed at this powerful committee, but others emanated from a broader reform movement in the House.[20]

In December 1974, the Democratic Caucus expanded Ways and Means from 25 to 37 and changed the party ratio on the committee from 15 Democrats and 10 Republicans to 25 Democrats and 12 Republicans. (Democrats got all but 2 of the 12 new seats on the committee.) When Ways and Means was organized at the start of the 94th Congress (in January 1975) almost 60 percent of its members were newly appointed to the committee. This upheaval was particularly remarkable because during the preceding dozen years, turnover on Ways and Means had averaged 20 percent per Congress. The enlargement of the committee compelled Ways and Means to relax its preference for members with substantial congressional service. In the preceding three decades, members had averaged more than three terms in the House before appointment to Ways and Means; those appointed to the committee in 1975 had served less than two terms in the House. The new members included several freshmen (virtually unprecedented on Ways and Means), one black, and one woman. In the past, Ways and Means had recruited members from "safe" districts, but half of the 1975 appointees had a winning margin of 55 percent or less in their most recent election. The new Democrats on Ways and Means were slightly more liberal and voted more consistently with their party's majority than their counterparts on the committee had done in the past.[21]

---

20. Perceptive analyses of these developments are provided in Catherine E. Rudder, "The Reform of the Committee on Ways and Means: Procedural and Substantive Impact, 1975," presented to the Southwestern Political Science Association, April 1976; and M. Kenneth Bowler, "The New Committee on Ways and Means: Policy Implications of Recent Changes in the House Committee," presented at the 1976 Annual Meeting of the American Political Science Association.

21. In the 93rd Congress, the median "conservative coalition opposition score," the percentage of votes by Ways and Means Democrats in disagreement with the conservative coalition (as computed by the *Congressionial Quarterly*) was 51; in the 94th Congress, the median op-

Another aspect of congressional reform affected the composition of the Ways and Means Committee. Prior to 1974, Democratic members of Ways and Means served as the Democratic "committee on committees," making membership assignments to all House Committees. In 1974, the Democratic Caucus shifted this selection power to the party's Steering and Policy Committee. Once Ways and Means no longer had the appointment power, it was less important that its Democratic members be senior, well entrenched, and geographically representative. There were thus fewer constraints on assigning junior Members to the committee. Ways and Means now attracts activists with an interest in tax policy and legislation. The new members wanted a major role in legislating and they put heavy pressure on the chairman to make certain that they had an opportunity to play that role.

Expansion of Ways and Means and its changing membership broke the pattern of consensual decision making that had been practiced by the committee during the long chairmanship of Wilbur Mills. When the committee was divided on an important issue, Mills generally tried to develop a middle ground that could accommodate both Democrats and Republicans and attract overwhelming support. He preferred to avoid close votes in committee, fearing that they would spell trouble for Ways and Means legislation on the floor. But consensus has been much more difficult to secure in the 37-member committee, not only because of the larger size but because many of the newcomers have been unwilling to follow the leader. Some of the new recruits have been among the most active committee members, particularly with regard to tax reform issues. In 1975, the roll call replaced consensus as the predominant decision-making mode of the committee.

In a move clearly aimed at Ways and Means, the Democratic Caucus in 1974 ordered all House committees to establish at least four legislative subcommittees. Ways and Means responded by establishing six subcommittees, but it continued to handle major tax legislation in the full committee. (The Senate Finance Committee also created a large number of nonlegislative subcommittees, but it, too, reserved tax matters for the full committee.) Along with creating subcommittees, Ways and Means more than doubled its

---

position percentage to conservative positions was 70. The median "party opposition score" by Ways and Means Democrats, the percentage of votes against the majority of Democrats dropped from 14 in the 93rd Congress to 9 in the 94th Congress. For the derivation of these statistics see the annual *Congressional Quarterly Almanac.*

staff size. No longer constrained by a one-big-bill-at-a-time approach, the full committee was able to deal with tax legislation while its subcommittees were working on other measures.

In 1973, the Democratic Caucus established a procedure to break the closed rule. Upon petition of 50 or more Democratic Members, a Democratic Caucus majority can instruct the Rules Committee to write a rule allowing a floor vote on a particular amendment. This "appeals" procedure has enabled Ways and Means Democrats to get floor votes on some amendments rejected in committee.

Rather than face defeat in caucus, Ways and Means has adopted the practice of seeking "modified" rules allowing floor consideration of a limited number of hotly contested amendments. This procedure preserves a modicum of control for Ways and Means over tax legislation and avoids direct challenges to its judgment. Sometimes, however, the committee supports an open rule. The 1975 energy tax bill (H.R. 6860) was taken to the floor under a rule that permitted consideration of more than two hundred amendments. Most of these amendments were not actually voted on, but the legislation that finally passed the House was but a shadow of the bill reported by Ways and Means. Virtually all of its major tax provisions were gutted or eliminated on the floor.

The opening of Ways and Means bills to floor amendments has enabled the House to substantially modify much of the legislation coming out of the committee. But the House is not likely to relish the free-for-all that attends Senate action on major revenue legislation. Its experience with the 1975 energy bill convinced House leaders (and many rank-and-file Members as well) that restrictions must be placed on the floor considerations of controversial revenue bills. When the House voted on energy legislation again in 1977, it acted under a modified rule that opened the bill only to specified amendments.

Both the House and Senate have opened most of their committee meetings to the public. In March 1973, the House mandated open markups unless a majority voted in open session to close the meeting. In the same month, the Senate authorized its committees to make their own rules with regard to markups, thereby repealing the old rule requiring most sessions to be closed. In 1975, the Senate adopted a resolution requiring open meetings unless closed by majority vote and providing for open conferences unless the House or Senate conferees voted to close them.

The effect of these new rules obviously has been greatest on those committees that once conducted most of their business behind closed doors. Both Ways and Means and Finance have moved from substantial closure to almost complete openness, but many major decisions still are made in private, informal sessions. Barely a handful of sessions are now closed by either committee. The open meetings have enabled staff aides to attend committee markups and this practice, in turn, has encouraged members to participate more actively and independently.

Several actions have contributed to a weakening of the position of Ways and Means. In the wake of personal tragedy, Wilbur Mills resigned as chairman in 1974, thus ending his legendary domination of the committee and tax policy in the House. Al Ullman (who served briefly as the first chairman of the House Budget Committee) has not dominated committee deliberations, and it is unlikely that any future chairman can rule over Ways and Means with the same authority that Mills had. There has been too much diffusion of power for a single legislator to control committee members and their output. In 1974, the House also stripped Ways and Means of some of its vast jurisdiction by transferring legislative authority for revenue sharing, renegotiation, Medicaid, and the work incentive program to other committees. Although these jurisdictional losses were less severe than those initially recommended by the Select Committee on Committees,[22] the changes demonstrated that the committee no longer dominated House politics. Between 1973 and 1976, the House defeated three debt ceiling bills reported by Ways and Means, equaling the number of defeats during all of Wilbur Mill's 18 years as chairman.

The various developments recounted in this section diminished the ability of Ways and Means to maintain tax policy as a "nondecision." As one scholar commented, ". . . there are more opportunities for more people and groups to register their positions on issues considered by the Ways and Means Committee. . . . The committee is more porous, more open to diverse influences,"[23] and not so beholden, therefore, to "nondecisional" routines. The new members of Ways and Means proved to be significantly more reform-minded than committee old-timers. The Democrats who joined the committee in the 94th Congress had a mean "pro-

22. See Roger H. Davidson and Walter Oleszek, *Congress Against Itself* (Bloomington: Indiana University Press, 1977).
23. Rudder, *op. cit.*, pp. 30-31.

reform" score of 68 percent on roll call votes in Ways and Means, compared with a mean score of 49 percent for the holdovers.[24] At the same time, committee members were almost evenly divided on tax reform proposals. Ways and Means could no longer shut off tax reform issues with a bipartisan coalition of conservative Democrats and Republicans, but liberals in favor of tax reform could not consistently marshal a committee majority behind their position. The pro-reform position was in the majority on exactly half the roll calls, a statistical indication of the divisions within Ways and Means on contemporary tax issues.

Ways and Means remains one of the most powerful congressional committees, if only for its still-enormous jurisdiction which encompasses virtually all federal revenues, most of the Social Security system, and much foreign economic policy. One should not leap to the conclusion, expressed in the *National Journal* after the 1974 caucus actions, that this committee "now is no more than one among equals." [25] Ways and Means, along with its Senate counterpart, remains an active guardian of its tax jurisdiction.

REVENUE PROVISIONS OF THE BUDGET ACT

At the same time that Congress was revising its procedures for handling tax legislation, the Congressional Budget Act was separately progressing toward enactment. The two movements were independent of each other, although some reformers were active in both.[26] At first, most Members viewed budget control as a means of curbing expenditures and deficits; hence, comparatively little attention was paid to the revenue side of the budget. The Joint Study Committee's statement of principles in its interim report hardly mentioned revenues at all. Eight of the principles pertained solely to expenditures, two mentioned revenues as part of the process, and one dealt with procedural issues. But as the Budget

24. The pro-reform scores were computed by Taxation with Representation, a private organization which keeps a close watch on tax legislation in Congress.
25. Michael J. Malbin, "New Democratic Procedures Affect Distribution of Power," *National Journal* 6 (December 14, 1974): 1881.
26. Representative Bolling, for example, was chairman of the House Select Committee on Committees which tried to strip Ways and Means of a portion of its jurisdiction. Professor Stanley Surrey, a leading tax reformer, was influential in getting the Budget Act to deal with tax expenditures.

Act was accommodated to a wider range of congressional interests, it gave a fuller and more balanced treatment to tax policy. As enacted, it contains numerous provisions relating to the budgetary status of revenues.

The central provision is in Section 301, which requires each concurrent resolution on the budget to set forth "the recommended level of Federal revenues and the amount, if any, by which the aggregate level of Federal revenues should be increased or decreased by bills and resolutions to be reported by the appropriate committees." Like many other provisions of the Budget Act, this one was a product of legislative compromise. The JSC bill did not have a provision concerning changes in the amounts of federal revenues.[27] The House Rules Committee's version distinguished between the first and second budget resolutions. Only total revenues would be included in the first resolution, but the second resolution could "call for adjustments in tax rates . . . and direct that legislation to implement such adjustments be reported" by the Ways and Means and Finance Committees. The Senate Government Operations Committee went a step further, providing for the budget resolutions to itemize the "major sources" of revenues plus recommended changes in aggregate revenues. The Rules and Administration Committee introduced a reconciliation process, tied to the second budget resolution, by means of which Congress could direct its tax-writing committees to report legislation changing the total amount of federal revenues. In its report, the committee stressed the need to consider revenues when making budgetary decisions:

> Perhaps the most significant weakness in the bill referred to the Committee was the failure to give sufficient attention to the revenue aspect of Congressional budgeting . . . a sound Congressional budget policy cannot be based on the assumption that control of spending levels is sufficient to achieve desirable economic results.[28]

As enacted, the Budget Act struck a balance between the demands for more versus less budgetary control over revenues. The

27. JSC, however, proposed that if the amount of surplus or deficit specified in the budget resolution could not be attained with the revenues estimated to be received under existing law, Congress would be required to adopt a surcharge (or a substitute measure producing an equivalent increase in revenues). This mandatory surtax was struck from later versions of the legislation.
28. S. Rept. No. 93-688 (1974) pp. 18-19.

first resolution concentrates on aggregate revenues and recommended changes and is supplemented by Budget Committee reports allocating the total recommended revenues "among the major sources of such revenues." The second concurrent resolution can "specify the total amount by which revenues are to be changed and direct the committees having jurisdiction to determine and recommend changes in the revenue laws." Two ambiguities in the operation of the congressional budget process have resulted from this compromise: One concerns the respective jurisdictions of the Budget and Tax Committees; the other concerns the relationship between the revenue totals in the budget resolution and the revenue details in the Budget Committee reports. By opening itself to conflicting interpretations, the Budget Act set the stage for later battles over the boundaries between the tax and budget processes on Capitol Hill.

The Act made a similar compromise in its groundbreaking definition of tax expenditures—the various exclusions, deductions, and tax preferences in the tax laws.[29] By defining tax expenditures, the Budget Act converted these "preferences" into actionable features of the legislative process, not merely loopholes against which critics of the tax system could rail. The term itself conveyed the message that tax preferences ought to be treated in the same manner as direct expenditures of the federal government. In an assortment of provisions, the Act converted tax expenditures from hidden benefits into publicized details of the federal budget.

The Budget Act requires only the publication of information on tax expenditures, but this matter was much debated in the development of the legislation. The bill developed by the Senate Government Operations Committee would have required the inclusion of a "tax expenditure budget"—a listing of tax expenditures by major categories—in each concurrent resolution. The Rules and Administration Committee, however, proposed that information on tax expenditures be moved from the budget resolution to the Budget Committee's report, and the legislation incorporated this proposal.

This requirement is one of several in the Act dealing with tax expenditures. The President's budget must list existing and

29. Section 3(a)(3) of the Budget Act defines tax expenditures as "revenue losses attributable to provisions of the Federal tax laws which allow a special exclusion, exemption, or deduction from gross income or which provides a special credit, a preferential rate of tax, or a deferral of tax liability."

proposed tax expenditures (Section 601); CBO has to consider tax expenditures in its annual report on the budget (Section 202); the Budget Committees are directed to study and devise methods of coordinating direct and tax expenditures (Sections 101 and 102); legislation providing new tax expenditures must be accompanied by five-year projections as well as comparisons with the amounts assumed for the most recent budget resolution (Section 308[a]); CBO must produce a five-year projection of tax expenditures (Section 308[c]). The cumulative effect of these provisions has been an outpouring of data on tax expenditures. But here, too, the division of power between the Budget and Tax Committees is uncertain, and the Act increases the prospects for strife within Congress.

Despite the Budget Act's stress on revenue decisions, the budget staffs within Congress have few tax specialists. When it was organized, the Congressional Budget office contemplated an 18-member tax analysis staff; its actual size has been about 12 professional and clerical persons, in comparison to the more than 50 staff members of the Joint Committee on Taxation. In the first years under the Budget Act, the new committees and CBO have been reluctant to duplicate the established and respected work of the Joint Tax Committee. That committee, however, has not been actively concerned about the link between direct and tax expenditures, so this subject could become a fertile area for analysis by CBO and various congressional committees.[30]

The provisions of the Budget Act allow but do not compel congressional activity with regard to tax legislation. Whenever it produces a budget resolution, Congress can estimate or legislate: it can set the revenues in its resolutions at the amounts expected from existing laws, or it can decide to rewrite the tax laws to change federal revenues or redistribute the tax burden. It can, in other words, budget by "nondecision" or by active policy making. Yet the Budget Act intended that Congress take action on taxes only in the context of its budget process, not as an independent policy determination. This is the clear purpose of Section 303's prohibition against the consideration of tax legislation before the first

30. For example, CBO in May 1977 issued a report on *Real Estate Tax Shelter Subsidies and Direct Subsidy Alternatives.* The report was jointly requested by the chairman of the House Budget Committee, and the House and Senate committees with jurisdiction over housing programs.

budget resolution has been adopted and Section 311's prohibition against tax legislation not in accord with the second resolution.[31]

Thus, in two major ways—by calling public attention to tax expenditures (preferences) and by setting congressional revenue targets to be met by the tax system—the congressional budget process impinges on the tax-writing committees and their freedom.

CONFERRING BENEFITS THROUGH TAX LEGISLATION

Tax legislation gives Congress an opportunity to provide benefits to political interests. When Congress considers such legislation, it ordinarily does so for the purpose of reducing tax burdens. This view of taxation is different from that of state legislatures and city councils which usually exercise taxing power to increase the revenues of their governments.

For years, "nondecision making" restricted congressional opportunities for conferring benefits through tax legislation. The absence of subcommittees, limited and safe membership, the closed rule, and its privileged possession of tax information all enhanced the role of Ways and Means as a control committee, one set up by Congress as a restraint on its own legislative freedom. The extraordinary reach of this committee resulted not only from self-aggrandizement but also from the willingness of the House to abide limitation on its own legislative power. In the same manner that the House Appropriations Committee functioned as a guardian against the spending inclinations of the parent body, Ways and Means served as a bar to greater use of tax legislation to distribute benefits.

The abandonment of "nondecision making" was much more than a change in legislative procedure or in the fortunes of congressional committees. The policy shift opened Congress to previously bottled-up pressures to benefit various interests which were clamoring for use of the tax laws to their advantage.

The abandonment of "nondecision making" exposed Congress to all sorts of pressures for tax relief. Congress needed a new con-

31. Section 303 has an escape clause: before adoption of the first resolution, Congress can take up revenue measures which become effective after the next fiscal year. Section 311 excludes only revenue legislation which would lower federal revenues below the amount in the second resolution; it does not bar revenue increases at variance with the second resolution.

trol mechanism to regulate the amount of benefits provided through tax legislation. The revenue provisions of the Congressional Budget Act serve this purpose; in an era of activist tax policy, the Budget Act is intended to discipline the benefit-conferring appetite of Congress.

The next chapter deals with the effects of the budget process on tax legislation.

XIII Tax Turbulence in Congress: Revenue Legislation Under the Budget Act

In the four years following enactment of the Budget Act in 1974, Congress passed seven major tax bills; an eighth passed in the House but died in the Senate. This extraordinary productivity added up to the most far-reaching restructuring of the tax system in more than a generation. This spurt of legislative activity significantly changed the tax burdens of most Americans, redistributed tens of billions of dollars, and curtailed many tax expenditures while starting some new ones. If ever there was an opportunity for the congressional budget process to influence tax policy, that chance came when the process was new.

This chapter reviews the legislative history of these bills in terms of their relationship to the budget process. One bill—the Tax Reform Act of 1976—is examined in some detail because the Senate Budget Committee exerted considerable effort to influence it. The eight actions are few enough to permit the telling of each story, but they add up to a definite pattern with regard to the relationship between tax and budget policy in Congress. After the legislative cases have been presented, it should be possible to define the limitations and potential of the budget process in shaping tax legislation.

The effect of budget decisions on tax outcomes appears to depend on the kind of revenue action taken by Congress. The eight bills fall into three categories: special tax legislation, that is, the use of the tax laws to make substantive policy; changes in total federal revenues; and changes in the distribution of the tax burden.[1] Each category of bills has had a different relationship to the

1. These are not "pure" categories but reflect the major aims of the legislation considered in this chapter. The Tax Reform Act of 1976, for example, provided both reform and tax reduction, just as the 1975 Tax Reduction Act had some reform provisions. Nevertheless, the categories are useful because Congress appears to deal somewhat differently with each type of measure.

budget process. Special tax measures have had the weakest link to congressional budgeting; measures affecting total revenues, the strongest.

SPECIAL TAX LEGISLATION

The special tax legislation category covers the 1975 and 1977 energy tax bills and the 1977 legislation to boost Social Security revenues. Despite the enormous potential impact of these bills on revenues, Congress, in determining both the substance and the disposition of the bills, acted as though the budget resolutions were virtually irrelevant.

The 1975 Energy Tax Bill (H.R. 6860)

When the House Ways and Means Committee filed its first March 15 report under the Budget Act, the energy bill still was in tentative form. The committee understandably hedged with regard to the revenue implications of the pending legislation; in its report, the committee assumed that the bill would "produce no net revenue increase" because the additional gas taxes would be offset by decreases in other federal taxes, but also acknowledged that there could be as much as $1.5 billion revenue gain "to the extent that any portion of the gasoline tax is not offset by tax credits."[2] The committee tried to protect its options and to keep the budget process at a safe distance.

The Senate Finance Committee was even less precise and more cautious in its March 15 report, commenting only that "the Committee does not feel . . . that any reasonable estimate is possible, at this time, of the likely effects of further revenue legislation to be considered later this year. Accordingly, the Committee's estimates do not reflect increases or decreases under subsequent revenue legislation."[3]

In its action on the first budget resolution for fiscal 1976, the House Budget Committee remained on the sidelines concerning the energy legislation. It rejected the President's $30 billion tax package—a proposal already doomed on Capitol Hill and all but aban-

2. Report of the House Ways and Means Committee, March 13, 1975, no pagination. Four days later, Chairman Ullman introduced a draft bill (H.R. 5005), which was superseded by H.R. 6860 reported on May 12 and passed by the House on June 19.
3. Senate Finance Committee report, March 15, 1975, p. 5.

doned by the Administration—but it did not even mention the bill being marked up by Ways and Means.[4] The Senate Budget Committee was less reticent, but no more decisive: "The Committee makes no recommendation at this time on energy taxes. . . ." To accommodate all possibilities, however, SBC placed two revenue figures in the resolution, one based on existing tax law, the other contingent on energy tax legislation (as well as an extension of temporary tax cuts).[5]

Despite the fact that the dual set of numbers protected the options of the Finance Committee, Senator Long opposed the hedge and successively moved for its deletion. Long argued that assumptions about the revenue effects of energy legislation were premature: "We will have a second budget resolution in the fall, and we will have an opportunity to consider the effects of further tax legislation in the light of economic circumstances at that time."[6] Senator Muskie accepted Long's amendment without a fight, explaining the SBC had provided two revenue marks for informational purposes:

> . . . We felt that we should indicate the possibility of some energy tax revenues accruing to the Treasury in the later part of the fiscal year. . . . However, our point having been made, and the information having been conveyed to the Senate with all Senators understanding the possibility, I see no reason to insist upon inclusion of the language of the resolution.[7]

Senator Long's maneuver had two objectives, both of which were intended to restrict the scope of the budget process. First, he put the Budget Committee on notice that its resolutions should deal only with revenue totals. This position might have been compromised by the reference to energy and other tax legislation. Second, Long wanted to deter SBC from expressing any assumptions with regard to future revenue actions by his committee. Even though the resolution allowed two different revenue outcomes, Long believed that it trespassed on the Finance Committee's sphere of interest. By acting the first time that a budget resolution reached the floor, Long demonstrated that he would not passively accept intrusions into his committee's domain.

---

4. H. Rept. No. 94-145 (April 14, 1975) pp. 12-13.
5. S. Rept. No. 94-77 (April 15, 1975) p. 22.
6. 121 *Congressional Record* (daily ed., April 29, 1975) S7108.
7. *Ibid.*

Bereft of budgetary guidance, the House gutted the energy bill when it reached the floor in June 1975. Without even a mention of the recently adopted budget resolution, the House voted to delete both the basic 3 cents per gallon tax and the standby 20 cents per gallon tax. It then passed the remainder of the energy tax bill, only to have the measure killed by the Senate Finance Committee's inaction.

The 1977 Energy Tax Legislation

When Congress considered the 1977 energy tax proposals, its budget process was fully in place, but once again the tax decisions were made independent of the budget decisions. By the time President Carter had unveiled his national energy program on April 20, the budget process for fiscal 1978 was well underway. Congressional committees had submitted their March 15 reports, the Budget Committees had framed their first resolutions for the fiscal year, and floor action was imminent. The Ways and Means Committee noted that energy tax recommendations were expected, but because "there is no information now available regarding the tax components and revenue effects," it took no position on the matter. The Senate Finance Committee opted for complete silence on prospective energy legislation, although it took care to urge the Budget Committee to provide a $100 million margin in its resolution for miscellaneous tax bills. The Budget Committees deferred action on energy taxation until the second resolution for fiscal 1978, in the hope that by then the legislative outlook would be clearer.

Under an arrangement formulated by Speaker O'Neill, the various parts of President Carter's omnibus national energy legislation were first parceled among the several House committees of jurisdiction, after which they were reviewed by an *ad hoc* committee on energy. Ways and Means worked on the tax sections, reporting a measure that would have resulted in a fiscal 1978 revenue loss of about $1 billion, although it would have yielded substantial additional revenues in future years. But the *ad hoc* committee proposed a new tax on gasoline, which would have proposed a net revenue gain of about $800 million in fiscal 1978. Accommodating the budget to the position of House Democratic leaders, the House Budget Committee incorporated this revenue increase in its second resolution. On the day that HBC reported the second resolution (August 5), however, the House struck the gas tax from the energy bill, thereby converting the anticipated gain into a loss. Consequently, when the House acted on the budget resolution one month later, HBC had no choice but to offer a committee amendment reducing the revenue levels to make the resolution conform to the previous House decision on energy legislation.[8]

When SBC marked up the second resolution for fiscal 1978, the Finance Committee had not begun its consideration of energy taxes. In recognition of Finance's preference for new tax credits rather than additional levies, SBC's resolution assumed a $900 million revenue loss in 1978. After the second resolution was adopted, Finance tackled the energy bill, rejecting virtually all of the revenue-producing provisions included in the House bill, and loading a variety of revenue losers on the measure. The Finance Committee's energy bill would have meant a cumulative revenue loss of $40 billion by 1985, compared with a projected revenue increase of $30 billion in the bill passed by the House. The budget process was sufficiently versatile—or irrelevant—to accommodate a $70 billion swing in revenues. Of more immediate concern for the budget process was the potential first-year revenue loss of $1.9 billion, some $800 million more than the amount allowed in the second resolution adopted one month earlier. To avert a point of order against its energy tax bill, the Finance Committee added a directive to the Secretary of the Treasury to postpone any of the effective dates for tax credits until such time as necessary to maintain fiscal 1978 revenues at the floor set in the second budget resolution.[9]

This extraordinary surrender of legislative power to the executive branch was not a mindless circumvention of the budget process. Finance simply was trying to secure an advantageous position for its conference with the House. The bill passed by the House was heavily weighted in favor of tax penalties to encourage energy conservation. Senator Long and other Finance members favored tax credits to stimulate energy production. Finance was willing to accept legislation that plowed back the additional revenues from the House bill to energy producers, but to strengthen its bargaining position in conference, Finance loaded its bill with an assortment of costly tax credits. In conference, it would be prepared to trade away many of the credits in exchange for tax benefits to producers. The Finance bill openly signaled this desired outcome with a "sense

8. 123 *Congressional Record* (daily ed., September 8, 1977) H9019.

9. H.R. 5263, Section 1056(b), directed the Secretary of the Treasury to "postpone (but not later than October 1, 1978) any of the effective dates . . . to assure that revenues for fiscal-year 1978 will not be less than $397,000,000,000."

of the Senate" clause, expressing the intent to hold the fiscal 1978 revenue loss within the amount of the second resolution.[10]

Finance's "wait for the conference" strategy put SBC in an exceedingly difficult position. The energy bill was President Carter's prime legislative priority for the year, and at the top of congressional leaders' "must" list before adjournment. "I do not think we can swim against the tide of the entire Senate wanting to get this to conference,"[11] Senator Hollings advised his colleagues at an emergency SBC meeting held only hours before the Senate was scheduled to take up the energy bill. An SBC challenge not only would slow down the legislative process but also might appear to other Senators as a needless response to a phantom threat. "One of our problems," Chiles noted at the meeting, "is that we are dealing with this provision [the discretion given to the Secretary of the Treasury] as if it is a legitimate provision with rationale behind it, and I don't think you can deal with it on that basis."[12]

Nevertheless, SBC feared that if it did nothing but wait for the conference, it could be establishing a precedent that would seriously weaken the budget process. Muskie was worried that if SBC were permitted to delegate its legislative power to the executive branch, "from here on we can expect similar provisions in revenue laws that would make them completely outside the budget process . . . if such a device is used to evade the discipline of the current fiscal year, then, in effect, the budget process would have no impact on future revenue legislation."[13]

Despite this perceived threat, SBC had reason to be cautious. This was not the first time it had locked horns with Finance over the conformity of a tax bill to the revenue level of a budget resolution. The earlier battle (detailed later in this chapter) left scars and bruised relationships, and many Budget Committee members simply were not in the mood for another fight. SBC opted, therefore, not to make a point of order against the bill at the start; nor would it offer its own amendment to make the measure conform to the budget resolution. Rather, the Budget Committee would inform the Senate that the Finance Committee's energy tax bill vio-

10. Section 1057 of the energy bill read, "It is the sense of the Senate that the conferees on the part of the Senate on this Act shall, to the extent practicable, reduce the revenue loss from this Act for the fiscal-year 1978 to $972,000,000."

11. Senate Budget Committee meeting on Energy Production and Conservation Tax Incentive Act, October 25, 1977, p. 33.

12. *Ibid.*, p. 26.

13. *Ibid.*, p. 2.

lated the congressional budget. It would monitor Senate action, and only at the end of floor consideration decide whether to offer any amendments.

Hollings represented SBC on the floor because Muskie was ill and did not participate in the debate. Hollings presented Muskie's prepared statement expressing sympathy "with the problems the Finance Committee has faced in producing this bill," but urging the Senate not "to sacrifice the budget process as a matter of one committee's convenience, even for the highest of motives." It warned that if Finance's "artifice" were upheld, other committees would follow suit and the budget process would have become a "dead letter."[14] Long defended the Finance Committee's circumvention, stressing that "we have complied with the budget resolution . . . and we intend that we will remain within the budget resolution. . . . We have committed ourselves to it and we are going to do it."[15] Long reviewed the problems facing his committee in producing a bill and readying itself for the conference, concluding: "In the last analysis, this bill will either pass or not pass, because the Senate either likes the bill enough to advance it or because it does not want to do anything about what the President is urging us to do."[16] In other words, the fate of the legislation would be decided by Senate preferences with regard to energy policy, not by applying the strictures of the budget process.

This was exactly what happened. SBC withdrew from the debate and the Senate took up numerous amendments, some to add tax credits, others to trim them. When the legislative work was done, the Senate had passed a bill with a smaller breach of the budget process ($300 million instead of $800 million), but it had made its decision on energy not budgetary grounds. The "point of order" weapon of the budget process was not used.

Following the Senate's approval of the energy tax measure, it took Congress almost a full year to complete action on the legislation. During that time, Congress adopted the first and second resolutions for fiscal 1979, both of which had to take account of the possible gain or loss of revenues from the energy legislation. With the House and Senate so far apart on this issue and with the conference stymied by conflict over other portions of the energy program, it was not easy for the Budget Committees to decide what to do. Moreover, by the time they were considering the 1979 reso-

14. 123 *Congressional Record* (daily ed., October 25, 1977) S17679.
15. *Ibid.*, S17681.
16. *Ibid.*, S17683.

lutions, the Budget Committees were more concerned about the size of general tax reduction than the specifics of energy taxation. The House Budget Committee resolution supported the bill passed by the House, which had a small first-year revenue loss that could easily be absorbed within its overall revenue target for 1979.[17] The Senate Budget Committee had a greater problem because of the size of the revenue loss in the bill the Senate had passed. SBC stalled, making "no assumption in the First Resolution . . . with respect to the effects of energy tax legislation." It noted, however, that "an appropriate adjustment to the [revenue] floor can be made in the Second Resolution, if progress toward a fiscally appropriate settlement of the current situation occurs before September."[18]

By the time the second resolution was being formulated, the major revenue provisions had been stripped from the energy measure and it was apparent that if anything was to emerge from conference, it would be an assortment of comparatively minor tax credits. Neither of the Budget Committees paid much attention to the energy tax issue; they were chiefly concerned with the tax reduction bill pending in Congress. In the waning days of the 95th Congress, the conference finally reported an energy tax bill but the measure had been stripped not only of provisions that had disturbed the House and Senate more than a year earlier, but also of the features that had once made it relevant to the budget process.[19]

Social Security Financing

After decades of accumulating surpluses, the Social Security system began to sustain sizable deficits during the mid-1970s. From a peak balance of $48 billion in fiscal 1975, the main trust fund was estimated to decline to $37 billion by the end of fiscal 1978, with the prospect of depletion of its reserves by the early 1980s. In his 1977 budget, President Ford proposed an increase in Social Security taxes to bring in $3.5 billion during the fiscal year. Both the tax committees and the Budget Committees rejected this request and Congress took no action. Senate Finance worded its rejection (in its March 15 report) in a manner that once again advised SBC to limit its concern to revenue aggregates: ". . . should the [Fi-

17. H. Rept. No. 95-1055 (1978) p. 25.
18. S. Rept. No. 95-739 (1978) pp. 36-7.
19. As finally approved by Congress, the energy tax measure provided credits resulting in a $1 billion revenue loss during the first year. In voting for the conference report, Senator Muskie merely noted that this would leave less room for a general tax reduction. See 124 *Congressional Record* (daily ed., October 14, 1978) S18834.

nance] Committee subsequently decide to enact some or all of this proposal, the income tax reductions could be increased by an equivalent amount to fit with the overall revenue target."[20] In other words, Finance advised the Budget Committee not to get involved in Social Security financing because even though the budget authority amounts might require modification, the revenue total might not be affected.

President Ford renewed his request for a Social Security tax increase in his 1978 budget, but this was withdrawn in President Carter's revised budget for the fiscal year. The new Administration announced its own Social Security plans on May 9, too late to influence the first concurrent resolution for fiscal 1978, which was approved a few days later. Carter's proposal involved the transfer of general revenues to the Social Security fund and a higher tax on employers than on workers. Both features encountered stiff opposition on Capitol Hill, and the legislative outlook was uncertain when Congress acted on the second resolution for the fiscal year. During September, at about the time that Congress was completing action on the resolution, Ways and Means and Finance started to mark up Social Security legislation.

The two Budget Committees took different approaches to the Social Security problem. SBC constructed its second resolution on the assumption that there would be no increase in Social Security revenues in fiscal 1978, a position it advocated on the grounds that reserves were adequate for the short term and that new taxes would adversely affect the economy.[21] HBC, however, provided for $6.4 billion in budget authority for Social Security, but it did not adjust the revenue numbers in the resolution.[22] This seemingly inconsistent behavior had the virtue of permitting a tax increase without committing Congress to such action.[23] It did not, HBC reported,

20. Senate Finance Committee Report to the Senate Budget Committee, March 4, 1976, p. 8.
21. S. Rept. No. 95-399 (August 4, 1977) p. 35. "The Committee believes that there would be adverse economic effects associated with a substantial tax increase at this point in the economic recovery."
22. The receipts of the Social Security trust fund are automatically appropriated. When Congress changes Social Security taxes, it also changes budget authority by an equivalent amount. Thus, a raise in Social Security taxes would appear in the budget as increases in total revenues and in budget authority.
23. This two-sided approach was necessary because, as noted, the receipts of the Social Security system are accounted for in the federal budget both as revenues and as new budget authority. Even though a revenue increase would not violate Section 311, an increase in total budget authority above the amount budgeted in the second resolution would.

"imply an endorsement of the administration's financing proposals; instead, it simply retains the option for the House to approve additional financing within the budget authority ceiling which will be imposed under the second budget resolution."[24]

This hedge did not survive the conference. SBC insisted that the resolution should not open the door to a tax increase, and the House conferees settled for a statement urging "the responsible committees [to] report legislation putting Social Security on a sound financial footing for both the short term and the long term," but emphasizing that the resolution "does not assume an increase in Social Security taxes during fiscal year 1978."[25] But this was not the final word on the subject. Responding to widespread anxiety about the solvency of the Social Security system, the Ways and Means Committee disregarded the second budget resolution and developed a Social Security measure that would have raised additional fiscal 1978 revenues, and liberalized some benefits while contracting others. When informed that these actions might violate the budget resolution, the chairman of the Ways and Means Social Security subcommittee is reported to have declared that these changes would be made "regardless of whether the budget committee likes it or not."[26]

Ways and Means proposed a hugh infusion of revenues, building up from $1.3 billion in the first year to $14.9 billion in the fifth year, a cumulative increase of $40 billion during these years alone. Because the revenue level in the second resolution constitutes a floor, not a ceiling, the first-year increase was not subject to a point of order even though it was inconsistent with the resolution. As for the "out-years" the budget process could not have a bearing until it would be too late to do anything about them.

The Social Security bill came to the House during the preadjournment rush. The House waived its requirement that fiscal 1979 revenue legislation had to wait until the first resolution for that year had been adopted, and it approved the massive Social Security bill without even a single mention of the budget process and without HBC participation in the discussion.

The result was the same in the Senate, though the legislative route was embarrassingly different. Finance reported the bill on November 1, immediately after the Senate had completed action on the energy bill and only three days before the scheduled adjourn-

24. H. Rept. No. 94-582 (August 5, 1977) p. 64.
25. H. Rept. No. 95-601; S. Rept. No. 95-428 (September 13, 1977) p. 9.
26. *Washington Post*, September 15, 1977, p. A-1, article by Spencer Rich.

ment. The bill was called up the same day, before a written report was available. But before floor action could commence, the bill needed a waiver of the Budget Act, because it provided for a tax increase in 1979, the next fiscal year. SBC was thrust fully into the debate because it has jurisdiction over waivers of the Section 303 prohibition against the consideration of money legislation before the first resolution has been adopted. The waiver fight was chronicled in chapter IX; here we need only note that the Senate approved the Social Security bill after SBC was forced to retreat on the waiver issue, which was SBC's only means of influencing the legislation.[27]

Summary

In the two energy bills and in the Social Security legislation, the Budget Committees (and their resolutions) hedged or kept silent, and were largely disregarded in the final outcomes. The Budget Committees' impotence was exacerbated by problems of timing. Carter's energy and Social Security proposals reached Congress after the first budget resolution had been framed; Congress took somewhat unexpected action on these matters after the second resolution had been developed. Yet the budget process in Congress might be inherently unsuited for the making of special tax decisions. Substantive policy questions rather than tax level questions tend to be overriding in special legislation. The ostensible purpose of energy taxation is not to raise (or lower) federal revenues, but to influence the use and development of energy resources. When substantive concerns are dominant, the budget process has no special claim on Congress; rather, the particular interests relevant to each issue determine the outcome.

It is to the advantage of the Budget Committees to cast substantive issues in fiscal terms. They tried to do this in the Social Security case by stressing the adverse effects of a tax increase on the economy. Congress, however, preferred to treat the matter in programmatic terms—replenishment of the trust fund—and it, therefore, bypassed the budget process in making its Social Security decisions. Although Section 303 waivers might be regarded as only a

27. After the Social Security tax was enacted, the two Budget Committees reversed their positions. In reporting the first resolution for the next fiscal year, HBC called for a $7.5 billion cut in Social Security taxes, while SBC urged that Congress not reduce these taxes. The conference report on the resolution made no mention of Social Security taxes and Congress took no subsequent action.

technical matter, they represent nothing less than the making of important fiscal decisions outside the congressional budget framework. By granting waivers on the Social Security bill, SBC was allowing itself to be excluded from that legislation. To the extent that SBC had any influence over the outcome, as Senator Muskie claimed, it was because of the leverage gained by its waiver power, not because of its role in tax policy.

Even when an issue is perceived to be fiscal in character, the role of the budget process in special legislation is weakened by the fact that the revenue impact tends to be slight in the first year—the year for which budget decisions are made—with most of the revenue changes occurring in later years. Thus, the energy bill passed by the House in 1977 would have resulted in a net loss of less than $1 billion in the first fiscal year, although it would have brought in tens of billions of dollars over the next decade. Similarly, in Social Security, the tax increases were graduated so as to produce much more new revenue in the "out-years" than in the budget year.[28]

CHANGING THE REVENUE TOTALS

The relevance of the budget process to tax legislation increases when a tax measure concerns primarily fiscal rather than substantive issues and when the short-term revenue impact is significant. Both conditions applied to the four tax reductions Congress enacted between 1975 and 1978. Congress passed a tax reduction bill early in 1975, another one late in that year, a third shortly after President Carter took office in 1977, and a fourth in 1978. The first three of these measures are reviewed here; the 1978 legislation is detailed in a later section.

The 1975 Tax Reduction Act

On October 8, 1974, President Ford proposed a 5 percent sur-

28. The first-year impact of the Social Security legislation on federal revenues was substantially diminished by the manner in which new revenues were to be raised: by an increase in the wage base on which the tax is levied rather than in the tax rate itself. (Social Security taxes are levied each year, starting in January, on the full amount of wages; the taxes stop at that point in the year when a worker's total earnings exceed the taxable wage base.) As a result, little additional revenue was received until late in the calendar year, when taxable wages exceeded the previous wage base.

charge on most individual and corporate income taxes. Three months later, Ford reversed his position and called for a $16 billion tax cut, consisting of a rebate on the previous year's taxes and a temporary credit for business investment. On March 29, 1975, President Ford signed the $22.8 billion Tax Reduction Act into law. Once the President had come out in favor of a sizable tax cut, there was no doubt that Congress would follow. The brief interval between presidential request and enactment made this one of the swiftest legislative tax actions in recent history. The 1971 tax reductions had taken 4 months from initiation to passage, the 1969 reforms 8 months, the 1968 surtax 11 months, and the 1964 reductions, 13 months.

Despite this rapid action, the 1975 reductions provoked a number of controversies—one related to the size of the cuts, another to their distribution, and a third to certain tax expenditures.[29] These are perennial issues in tax legislation; unless the Budget Committees have a hand in their resolution, they cannot be an influential force in tax policy. But 1975 was the "optional" year under the Budget Act, with full implementation not required until the next year. Section 906 of the Act authorized the Budget Committees to selectively implement features of the new process "to the extent and in the manner" they deemed appropriate. Although they decided to activate major components of the process, the committees could not delay tax legislation until they were ready to produce the first budget resolution. In their implementation plan, filed in early March when Congress was just beginning to produce a tax reduction bill, the Budget Committees prudently opted not to apply the Section 303 bar against revenue action before adoption of the first resolution, "Due to the critical need to take quick action on the Nation's deteriorating economy, the Budget Committees believe that implementation of this provision may unduly delay necessary action on the economy."[30]

One can only guess what might have ensued if the budget process had been in operation before the 1975 reductions were initiated. The Budget Committees might have had some role in the de-

29. The enacted tax cut was $6 billion more than the President requested but $8 billion less than the Senate's bill. Ford proposed an across-the-board rebate, but Congress concentrated the tax among lower-income taxpayers.

30. S. Rept. No. 94-27 (March 5, 1975) p. 7.

cision, but it is unlikely that they would have tried to block action until passage of the first resolution.

The 1975 Tax Cut Extension

The Tax Reduction Act was a temporary measure effective only for the 1975 calendar year. If these cuts had not been extended, most taxpayers would have faced an automatic increase in the amounts withheld from their earnings at the start of the next year. HBC based its revenue targets in the first fiscal 1976 resolution on the expectation that Congress would continue the tax relief beyond the scheduled expiration date. SBC adopted a wait-and-see attitude, commenting that the decision can "be made as late as September when it can be based on careful reading of the latest economic indicators."[31] Nevertheless, as noted earlier, it specified alternative revenue levels in the resolution in order to account for possible action on energy taxes and the tax cut extension. The "contingency" estimates were removed at the insistence of Senator Long, who preferred not to have on record any intimation of his committee's future course of action. In conference, Senator Muskie reiterated the Finance Committee's view that the extension "was not a foregone conclusion"; when he was informed that withholding rates would substantially rise, however, he acknowledged "that it is not likely to be allowed to happen,"[32] and accepted the House position.

The second budget resolution for fiscal 1976 directed the Ways and Means and Finance Committees to report legislation extending the tax cuts.[33] These committees readily complied with this instruction: Ways and Means incorporated the extension in a tax reform bill but subsequently dropped it in favor of a six-month extension reported by Finance. The extension, Muskie explained, was "a result of a deliberate, rational process of discussion which has included the Finance Committee, the Ways and Means Committee, [and] the Budget Committees of both Houses."[34] It seemed to be a straightforward, noncontroversial continuation of a law already in effect.

31. S. Rept. No. 94-77 (April 15, 1975) p. 21.
32. Conference on first concurrent resolution for fiscal 1976, transcript, p. 23.
33. This was the first formal use of the "reconciliation" procedure provided in Section 310 of the Budget Act. However, it was not a real test of reconciliation, since the affected committees would have reported the legislation even without the budget directive.
34. Remarks of Senator Muskie to the Senate Democratic Conference, in 121 *Congressional Record* (daily ed., December 15, 1975) S22099.

Such was not the case, however. Before Congress completed action on the temporary legislation, President Ford dropped a political bombshell into the new budget process. On October 6, 1975, Ford demanded that Congress enact a $28 billion tax cut along with a $395 billion ceiling on expenditures for fiscal 1976. On the basis of current services estimates by the Office of Management and Budget, this limitation would have required a $28 billion reduction in federal spending. Ford threatened to veto any tax cut that was not matched dollar for dollar by a spending reduction.[35] He wanted Congress to completely bypass its new budget process, to revert to the *ad hoc* procedures used between 1967 and 1972, and to impose arbitrary ceilings without prior consideration of their fiscal or programmatic effect. The call for a spending limit came almost a full year before the beginning of the fiscal year to which it would apply and more than seven months before the deadline for adoption of the first budget resolution.

Ford's intervention converted the extension from a tax issue into a fight over budget procedures, and it moved the Budget Committees from the periphery of legislative action into the center of the battle. These committees quickly gained recognition within Congress as the guardians of the new process, and they understandably saw the President's action as a direct challenge to their position. The conflict was waged over the proposed linkage of tax and spending action, with virtually all attention directed at the spending side of the issue. Most congressional Democrats viewed the President's move as a bid to gain political advantage for his forthcoming election campaign, and they conveniently used the budget process to thwart his demands. Republicans wanted to support their President's political and economic objectives, but without subverting the new process.

The controversy raged for several months, until the last day of the legislative session. House Republicans tried to attach a spending limit to both a debt ceiling bill and tax reform legislation but were rebuffed both times.[36] Barber Conable, a leading Republican

35. In his address, the President noted that "there will be a temptation to overwhelmingly approve the tax cuts and do nothing on the spending cuts," but he promised that he would "not hesitate to veto any legislation" that did not match tax and spending reductions. *11 Weekly Compilation of Presidential Documents* (1975), p. 1128.

36. The debt ceiling bill (H.R. 10585) was brought up under a closed rule which precluded a Republican amendment setting a $395 billion outlay limit for fiscal 1977. The rule was adopted 221 to 185, with only one Republican breaking party ranks to vote for it. The vote was much closer on the tax reform bill (H.R. 10612), with a modified rule upheld by a 219-197 margin.

on the Ways and Means and Budget Committees, defended his party's tactics this way: "Far from downgrading the budget reform procedure . . . if we want the Budget Committee to function properly, then we have to know what level of spending the House would like to see us establish for fiscal 1977."[37] This line of reasoning was rejected by Rep. Brock Adams: "Let us not play games with the Budget Act by going . . . with a [$395 billion] figure that at the present time nobody can support."[38]

Senate rejection of the linkage of spending reductions to tax cuts was less partisan, with Senator Bellmon, the ranking Republican on the Budget Committee, joining his Democratic colleagues in defense of the budget process:

> We pleaded with President Ford to accept the fact that we now have a better system than the arbitrary ceiling he has asked us to accept. I, personally, seriously doubt that President Ford understands the changes that have been made since he was a member of Congress. . . . I believe it would be a mistake for us to abandon the budget process in the first year of its infancy and agree upon an arbitrary spending limitation without prior judgment as to its effects and method of enforcement.[39]

Congress ultimately prevailed in this contest with the executive —not because of its budget process, however, but because of the President's political disadvantage. When Congress refused to link tax and spending reductions but instead passed a six-month extension of tax cuts, the President vetoed the bill. The veto came near the close of the legislative session, barely two weeks before withholding rates were scheduled to rise. Cast in the unfavorable position of promoting a tax increase, the White House (after the House had sustained the veto) embraced a face-saving compromise. With Republican approval, the Senate passed a new six-month extension along with a "sense of the Congress" resolution endorsing the principle of dollar-for-dollar tax and spending cuts, but asserting the right of Congress to adopt whatever spending level it deemed to be warranted by economic conditions or other circumstances.[40] The House (with the Budget Committee playing a role) modified the

37. 121 *Congressional Record* (daily ed., November 12, 1975) H11026.
38. 121 *Congressional Record* (daily ed., November 13, 1975) H11060.
39. 121 *Congressional Record* (daily ed., December 15, 1975) S22183.
40. The resolution was developed by Democratic and Republican members of the Finance Committee with little input from the Budget Committee. For a discussion of the way the language was developed, see 121 *Congressional Record* (daily ed., December 19, 1975) S22998, remarks of Senators Muskie and Long.

resolution to emphasize that future decisions about spending levels would be made through the congressional budget process.[41] Months later, after the issue had abated, Congress ignored the linkage of tax and spending reductions and passed a budget resolution for fiscal 1977 that set spending at more than $15 billion above the President's budget and called for $17 billion in tax reductions.[42]

The 1977 Tax Stimulus

Congress made some of the tax cuts permanent in 1976, as part of the tax reform legislation to be discussed in the next section. But this did not end the series of reductions, for in January 1977, the incoming Carter Administration proposed tax relief as part of an economic stimulus program worked out in preinauguration conferences with congressional leaders. Congress concentrated on the spending side, enacting more costly jobs and public works programs than the Administration had initially proposed.

The stimulus package necessitated a third resolution for fiscal 1977; both its revenue and spending components were at variance with the second resolution adopted before the presidential election. As presented to the House Budget Committee on January 27, 1977, the plan called for $13.8 billion in tax reductions during the fiscal year, consisting of $11.4 billion for one-shot rebates and payments and $2.4 billion in other cuts. HBC Chairman Giaimo expressed concern about the "adequacy and sufficiency" of the program;[43] the committee itself acknowledged "widespread skepticism that rebates and reductions can spur sufficient economic activity" to ameliorate unemployment. It also had reservations about the inequities of the President's program and its expanded use of tax credits.[44] Nevertheless, HBC went along with the Administration's tax package, although it left the components to be decided by the Ways and Means Committee.[45] Ways and Means (acting before the third

41. As adopted, the resolution affirmed the linkage of taxes and spending, but did not commit Congress to dollar-for-dollar reductions.
42. The $17 billion in tax reductions were based on an extension of the temporary tax cuts through all of fiscal 1977. The $413 billion spending level in the first resolution was $19 billion above the President's budget, but some of the difference was accounted for by reestimates and amended budget requests.
43. House Committee on the Budget, Hearings on *The Economy and Economic Stimulus Proposals*, 95th Cong., 1st Sess. (1977), p. 223.
44. H. Rept. No. 95-12 (1977) pp. 16, 18.
45. As reported, the third resolution "does not assume the exact components of the President's tax recommendations; those components will be determined by the Ways and Means Committee and the Congress in the next several weeks." *Ibid.*, p. 18.

resolution was adopted) recommended tax reductions somewhat different from those of the Administration, so HBC offered a floor amendment to make its revenue figure the same as the amount reported by the tax committee.[46]

SBC also had doubts about the Administration's approach, but it, too, fell into line. During its markup of the third resolution, committee Republicans strongly attacked the temporary rebates and called for permanent tax cuts instead. Senator Muskie, however, took the position that SBC should specify only total revenues and not decide whether the tax cuts should be temporary or permanent. Muskie wanted to avoid offending the Administration (which wanted temporary cuts), the Finance Committee (which wanted SBC to deal only with total revenues), or the Republicans on his committee. SBC thus straddled the issue in its report on the third resolution, recommending an amount that would permit either "the tax relief as proposed by the Carter administration, or enactment of permanent tax rate reductions or other forms of temporary tax relief of comparable amount."[47]

Having dutifully complied with the Administration's tax preferences, the Budget Committees were understandably upset in April 1977, when President Carter withdrew the rebate proposal. This action could not have come at a more embarrassing time for the Budget Committees. Congress had already passed the third resolution for fiscal 1977 (which was developed primarily to accommodate the rebates) while both Budget Committees had already reported the first resolution for fiscal 1978 (with economic assumptions predicated on the tax stimulus) and scheduled it for floor action in the near future. Neither Giaimo nor Muskie had been consulted on or informed of the Administration's decision in advance of the public pronouncement; both, however, had to reconvene their committees and decide what to do about the reversal. The Budget Committees could have opted to do nothing, but inaction would have left the revenue floor for fiscal 1977 billions of dollars below estimated receipts. This course not only would have spotlighted the irrelevance of the budget resolutions for tax policy, but also might have invited the tax committees to produce their own versions of tax cuts.

HBC capitulated with a retroactive adjustment (appended to the

46. 123 *Congressional Record* (daily ed., February 23, 1977) H1328, remarks of Representative Giaimo.
47. S. Rept. No. 95-9 (1977) p. 5.

first fiscal 1978 resolution) to the revenue level for fiscal 1977.[48] Giaimo conceded that "it was not the desire of the committee to eliminate the $50 payment . . . but we are now faced with the realities of life, in that the President has said he is not going to pursue the rebate. The other body [the Senate] obviously is not going to implement it."[49]

The Senate Budget Committee decided to stick with the rebates, reaffirming "its judgment about the advisability of tax stimulus in some form in 1977. . . . The committee is not persuaded that significant changes in economic prospects for 1977 and 1978 have taken place since adoption of the third budget resolution for fiscal 1977."[50] Muskie, who only weeks earlier had been the most vigorous congressional advocate of rebates at a time when the scheme was losing favor on Capitol Hill, accused the Administration of undermining the credibility of the budget process.[51] In conference, however, he recognized the futility of fighting for the abandoned rebates, and the third resolution was modified to delete them.

Summary

The budget process appears to have been somewhat more relevant to tax reductions than to special revenue legislation. Decisions about the size of these reductions are clearly within the province of the Budget Committees, which can call for reductions in their budget resolutions and provide stimulus and support for quick action by the revenue committees.

The Budget Act—through Section 311's asymmetrical prohibition against tax reductions, but not tax increases—has cast the Budget Committees as bulwarks against unbudgeted tax reductions. Constraining congressional temptations to treat revenue legislation as an opportunity to provide benefits through tax reductions has not proved an easy or popular role to play on Capitol Hill, but the Budget Committees have stuck to it.

In playing this role, the Budget Committees have generally reacted to tax cuts proposed by others; they have not reached for the

48. When the House took up the first resolution for fiscal 1978, Giaimo offered a committee amendment adding a new section to amend the levels set in the third resolution for fiscal 1977. 123 *Congressional Record* (daily ed., April 26, 1977) H3569.

49. *Ibid.*, H3571.

50. 123 *Congressional Record* (daily ed., May 3, 1977) S6916, remarks of Senator Muskie.

51. Senate Budget Committee, transcript of meeting on tax rebates (April 1977), pp. 13-14.

initiative. Thus, they remained on the sidelines in late 1977 when there was talk of the need for new tax cuts to stimulate a faltering economic advance and to offset Social Security tax increases. Again in 1979, when some economic indicators pointed to a recession, the Budget Committees were unwilling to call for tax reductions that had not been proposed by the President; thus they avoided blame for increases in the deficit while accommodating to congressional pressures for tax cuts.

DISTRIBUTING TAX BENEFITS AND BURDENS

When Congress cuts taxes, it is apt to be less concerned about how much the reduction amounts to than about who gets it. The Budget Committees have a weaker voice concerning tax distribution issues than they have concerning distribution of federal expenditures. In the budget resolutions, the Budget Committees make functional allocations and distribute the spending shares to various congressional committees, but they have no equivalent role in tax decisions.

Efforts to redistribute the tax burden generally accompany legislative consideration of major tax bills. Redistribution may be accomplished by giving unequal tax reductions to various income classes (or by changing the relative burdens of corporate and individual income taxes) or by providing preferential tax treatment—"tax expenditures"—to particular groups. Curiously, the Budget Committees have not played a role in attempts to redistribute general tax burdens, but in several instances they have sought to reduce, or to restrict the enactment of, tax expenditures.

Tax reform, that is, reducing or eliminating tax preferences, was an early budget issue.[52] In 1975, the Ways and Means Committee developed legislation (H.R. 10612) that ultimately became the Tax Reform Act of 1976. This measure stimulated more active participation by the Budget Committees that had been the case in the special revenue and tax reduction legislation described earlier; it also provoked an open and protracted clash between the chairmen of the Senate Budget and Finance Committees.

As the newest Senate committee, SBC did not start out looking for a fight with one of the oldest and strongest committees. During SBC markup of the first resolution for fiscal 1976, Chairman

52. Some tax reform was achieved in the Tax Reduction Act of 1975, which repealed the oil depletion allowance.

Muskie warded off consideration of tax reform proposals by pointing out that "a lot of additional tax reform would not yield any additional revenue in 1976."[53] He knew that legislation repealing tax subsidies ordinarily takes months or years to work its way through Congress. Moreover, because the tax and fiscal years do not coincide—most taxes are levied on a calendar-year basis—even if Congress had acted promptly, additional revenues would not flow into the treasury until the second half of the fiscal year.[54] Muskie pressed his viewpoint on the floor in opposing an amendment sponsored by Sen. Walter Mondale to raise $2.5 billion in new revenues through tax reform. Muskie agreed that Congress "sooner or later (should) get into the tax reform business," but cautioned that "to rest our revenue assumptions for 1976 upon the enactment of some of these tax reform proposals that have not been able to generate majority support in the Congress . . . is extremely unrealistic." [55] The Mondale amendment (which also would have added $9 billion in expenditures for economic stimulus programs) was defeated, 20 to 64.[56]

The outcome was different in the House where the Ways and Means Committee projected a first-year revenue gain of $500 million from reform in its March 15 report. The Committee warned, however, that it was "highly speculative to estimate the revenue effect of a tax reform bill." [57] In its first resolution for fiscal 1976, HBC did not account for a revenue increase through tax reform. On the floor, Brock Adams acknowledged that "greater attention has been devoted to the expenditure side of the budget while not dealing with and developing the revenue side as much as may be desirable."[58] Adams voted for an amendment offered by Rep. Henry S. Reuss to raise $3 billion in additional revenues by closing tax preferences. One reformer expressed the hope that the budget would become "an instrument through which we can call attention to . . . tax expenditures." [59] With strong support from Democratic

53. Senate Budget Committee, markup of the first concurrent resolution for fiscal 1976, transcript, p. 8.
54. In fiscal 1976, the tax year started six months after the fiscal year; beginning with fiscal 1977, the tax year starts three months after the fiscal year.
55. 121 *Congressional Record* (daily ed., April 30, 1975) S7207.
56. Interestingly, Senator Long voted in favor of the Mondale proposal, though he did not participate in the debate.
57. Committee on Ways and Means, report to the House Budget Committee, March 13, 1975.
58. 121 *Congressional Record* (daily ed., May 1, 1975) H3358.
59. *Ibid.*, H3563, remarks of Representative Ottinger.

members of the Budget Committee, the Reuss amendment carried by a wide margin, 277 to 128.

In conference, Muskie read a lengthy letter from Senator Long insisting that "inclusion of such a substantial revenue increase in a concurrent resolution would be highly unrealistic" and might damage efforts to stimulate the economy. After some wrangling, Muskie endorsed a $1 billion target as "reasonable enough so that it is worth trying." He was joined by Senator Mondale, who declared that "the matter of principle may be the most important thing we do because it brings the Ways and Means and Finance Committees into the picture."[60]

By the time the Budget Committees turned to the second resolution for fiscal 1976, only limited progress had been made on tax reform. HBC retained the goal of a $1 billion revenue gain, but SBC dropped the provision because it was too late to expect significant new revenues from reform in fiscal 1976[61] This position prevailed in conference and the first year of the budget process ended with the tax committee free to move on reform without guidance or encumbrance from the budget resolutions.

Ways and Means produced its tax reform bill (H.R. 10612) in November 1975, coupling it to an extension of the temporary tax cuts voted earlier in the year. The reported version would have yielded an estimated first-year revenue gain of $752 million, far less than the $2.6 billion increase set in the original draft bill marked up by the committee. But Ways and Means asked for a modified rule in order to allow floor decisions on a number of amendments sought by reformers. Three revenue-raising amendments were adopted while two others were rejected by narrow margins. As passed by the House, H.R. 10612 would have generated about $1.5 billion in new revenue.

Senate Finance separated the tax reduction and reform sections of the bill, passing a six-month extension of tax cuts but deferring the reforms until the next session of Congress. Chairman Ullman of Ways and Means had previously resisted proposals to separate the two matters—"if we don't hold this measure together, we probably won't get a reform bill,"[62]—but he was compelled to accept the Finance Committee's maneuver because inaction would have brought an automatic tax increase.

60. Conference on the first concurrent resolution for fiscal 1976, May 7, 1975, transcript, pp. 16 and 19.

61. The committee's reasoning was similar to that used against it by Senator Long in the following year. See S. Rept. No. 94-453, p. 18.

62. Quoted in *Congressional Quarterly Almanac*, p. 151.

With House action on tax reform completed, the critical next step was in Senate Finance, a committee that has been much less favorably disposed to tax reform than Ways and Means has been in recent years. In the 94th Congress, for example, the reform position prevailed in less than 30 percent of the roll call votes in Finance, while it won on half of the votes in Ways and Means.[63] Finance did not even mention tax reform in its March 15 report for the 1977 budget, despite the fact that it was actively working on tax legislation at the time.

The Senate Budget Committee could not remain on the sidelines in 1976 so easily as it had a year earlier. For one thing, it could not argue so convincingly that tax reform would not yield substantial first-year revenues. After all, the House had already acted and because of the scheduled change in the beginning of the fiscal year, nine months of increased revenues would spill over into the fiscal year compared to six months under the old fiscal calendar. For SBC to claim that significant first-year revenues could not be forthcoming would have virtually eliminated it as a meaningful participant in congressional tax reform decisions. If the excuse could be used when one Chamber had passed the legislation, it could be used again and again to thwart efforts at tax reform through the budget process. SBC was prodded to a pro-reform stance by Senator Hollings, who vigorously challenged Long's argument that additional first-year revenue could not be secured through tax reform. According to one participant, SBC also was influenced by its staff which was "anxious to impose the discipline of tax expenditures that we were imposing on other expenditures . . . one of the tests of the budget process was whether or not by imposing a squeeze we could produce some tax reform. We, I think, got used to the idea at the staff level, that this was a good thing to do." As a committee heavily reliant on its staff for direction, SBC, in this instance, deferred to the staff's "good thing to do."

But there was another compelling reason for SBC to jump into the fray. Tax reformers were determined to use the budget process to force reform on an expectedly recalcitrant Finance Committee. For years they had been frustrated in their efforts to stimulate pro-reform sentiment in the Senate. They had little prospect for

63. The House and Senate scores pertain to different votes and, therefore, cannot be strictly compared. In view of the Senate's open rule, one would expect Senators to have lower tax-reform scores than Representatives who operate under a different set of incentives.

success on the floor where an open rule and "Christmas tree" behavior had made it difficult to block enlarged tax preference for favored interests. Nor could they expect sufficient support in the Finance Committee, which was consistently more generous than Ways and Means in providing tax subsidies. Accordingly, the band of tax reformers looked to the budget process as an opportunity to compensate for their weakness in the Senate.

Working through the budget process promised a more favorable outcome than using the standard tax route in Congress. When Congress legislates tax policy, it deals with each issue separately, section by section, tax expenditure by tax expenditure. For each preference built into the tax law, there is an interest that would lose by its removal. Taxpayers benefiting from the threatened provision can be expected to rally behind their cause and press Congress to retain their advantage. For this reason alone, it is hard to take away a tax expenditure, perhaps as hard as it is to eliminate a direct expenditure from the budget.

The balance of interests is substantially different, however, when Congress tackles tax reform through the budget process. Rather than item-by-item consideration, the issue is how much total reform should be targeted in the congressional budget. Congress can vote for a $1 billion tax reform without deciding which preferences are to be ended and without knowing which interests would be the losers. Potential losers are not directly threatened, for reform might be achieved at the expense of other unknown (and unknowing) taxpayers. In an environment open to intense pressure to retain existing tax advantages and to add new ones, Members of Congress can more freely vote for tax reform than for changing the tax laws. Reformers hoped that once the Senate had committed itself to a dollar target for tax reform in the budget resolution, it would be easier to get Members to make the hard decisions on individual items.

Sen. Edward Kennedy unveiled this strategy in appearances before both the Finance and Budget Committees. Though he was not a member of either committee, Kennedy had made tax reform one of this major legislative interests and he became the unofficial spokesman for hard-core reformers in the Senate. On March 16, 1976, Kennedy described the Budget Act as "an imaginative and useful way of dealing with the impact of the tax laws on the overall budget process." Kennedy told SBC, "My purpose here is not to propose specific tax reforms," but he urged the committee to include a $2 billion reduction in tax expenditures in its first resolution for 1977.[64] Two days later, Kennedy furnished a shopping list of tax reforms to the Finance Committee, declaring that "the Budget Reform Act is bringing the same long overdue discipline to tax expenditures as it has already brought to direct expenditures. The Senate looks to this committee and the Budget Committee for responsible fiscal leadership in controlling tax expenditures. . . ."[65]

Senator Long reacted to this attempt to outflank his committee on tax reform by making an extraordinary appearance at the Senate Budget Committee's mark up of its budget resolution. "In light of his position," Muskie told the Budget Committee "we owe him that courtesy and that opportunity." Long's first words set the terms of confrontation between the two committees: "I am simply here to urge that the Budget Committee stay within its jurisdiction . . . and that we stay within our jurisdiction."[66]

Long was prepared to do battle over the thing that mattered most to him: not a provision of the tax code—there are many ways to resolve that kind of dispute—but the position of his committee and what he saw as an effort to chip away at its power. "Finance," an observer of the committee remarked, "has a chairman who is jealous of his prerogatives; he is the most jurisdictional-territorial man in the Senate." Long often has boasted that there are few tax provisions for which he can claim credit. Except for the few matters in which he has a strong interest, Long is willing to accept almost any tax item preferred by his committee or the Senate. As one observer noted, "Precisely because he is not locked into any numbers, Long is not constrained in the deals he can make and can retain command of the process." But Long did not see this as a tax issue for which deals could so readily be contrived. By defining the issue as a jurisdictional squabble, Long shifted the terms of the argument from fidelity to the new budget process to an invasion of his committee's role in the Senate.

Long did more than hoist a warning flag. He specified how the lines between the Budget and Finance Committees must be drawn in order to avoid a conflict:

Now, what we fully expect to do is to tailor the tax bill that will be reported to whatever figure this Budget Committee arrives at. You tell us

64. Senate Committee on the Budget, Hearings on *First Concurrent Resolution on the Budget—Fiscal Year 1977*, p. 10.
65. Senator Kennedy's statement appears in 122 *Congressional Record* (daily ed., March 18, 1976) S3755.
66. Senate Budget Committee, markup of the first concurrent resolution for fiscal 1977, transcript, pp. 551-52.

how much revenue you expect and how much spending you expect, and we will undertake to tailor our activities to meet that. . . . We on the tax committee can live with whatever figure you recommend here, as long as you put a figure on it.[67]

Muskie sought to ease the tension by claiming that SBC was doing nothing more with regard to taxes than what Congress had already accepted as its proper role on the expenditure side of the budget:

I agree that we are not a tax-writing committee. Neither are we an appropriations committee. Neither are we an authorizing committee. Our jurisdiction is an overall one . . . [but] we have responsibilities beyond simply adding up the numbers dictated by current law.[68]

"Beyond simply adding up the numbers," in Muskie's judgment, meant that the Budget Committee should indicate how it derived the revenue total and the reductions in tax expenditures that should be achieved:

. . . if you really want to influence the Finance Committee and the Congress on the question of tax expenditures . . . we have some obligation . . . to indicate what proportion of that revenue number is expected to be achieved by reform in the tax law, with whatever detail it pleases the [Budget] committee to include.[69]

Battle lines, thus, were drawn between Long, who would have restricted the budget resolution to a single revenue figure, and Muskie who wanted SBC to specify some of the details of tax policy as well. Long realized that the higher the revenue gain projected in the budget resolution, the more difficult would be the task of his committee in meeting it. Revenue gainers, he argued, generally are made effective at the start of the next calendar year, while losers are often given retroactive effect. He warned, therefore, that even if changes in tax expenditures would produce long-term revenue increases, they might show a first-year loss.

SBC disregarded Long's argument and voted for a $2 billion reduction in tax expenditures, the amount fixed by the House committee in its resolution. "This motion," insisted Senator Hollings, who vigorously supported the $2 billion figure, "is one really of

67. *Ibid.*, pp. 553-54.
68. *Ibid.*, p. 555.
69. *Ibid.*, p. 901.

restraint." In his view, it was "realistic and easily obtainable."[70] Muskie downplayed the issue of whether the amount was achievable by "urging the Finance Committee to look to a $2 billion yield from tax expenditures as a target. We can't mandate it in any case. I think if we set that number that generates pressure to achieve as much as they can."[71]

With Long promising a tax bill consistent with the revenue level in the budget resolution and Muskie conceding that the resolution's revenue target would not be mandatory, one might have expected a quiet end to the differences between the Finance and Budget Committees. Long, in fact, did not challenge the $2 billion reduction in tax subsidies when the budget resolution was debated on the floor, though he vigorously disputed some of the other targets affecting his committee. Nevertheless, when the Finance Committee reported the tax reform bill in June 1976—less than one month after final passage of the resolution—bitter fighting broke out between Muskie and Long over Finance's fidelity to the budget process and Budget's jurisdiction in tax policy.

Perhaps without realizing it, SBC was seeking to force an abrupt change in the role of the Finance Committee and in the relationship between the House and Senate tax committees. On every major tax bill over the past 20 years, the legislation reported by Finance would have produced less first-year revenue from reform (or lost more revenue because of new tax subsidies) than the bill passed by the House. Senate Finance (like Senate Appropriations) had functioned as a "court of appeals," trimming back some of the reform-induced tax gains voted by the House. In 1969, for example, Finance's tax reform bill would have generated $300 million less than the measure passed by the House. But the 1976 tax reform bill approved by the House was itself at least $400 million below the $2 billion reform target set in the first budget resolution. In order for the Finance Committee to conform to the budget target it would have had to take a harder line on tax subsidies than the House had, something Finance had not done in many years.

Both participants and observers attest that Long guided Finance's markup of the tax bill in such a way as to minimize deviation from the budget target. Despite his reputation for supporting whatever his colleagues suggested, he opposed subsidies endorsed by some committee members and promoted stronger reform provisions than some had expected. Long used the $2 billion target to advantage;

70. *Ibid.*, p. 891.
71. *Ibid.*, p. 903.

he expressed sympathy with those who sought new credits but reminded them of the constraints in the budget resolution. Nevertheless, the traditional role of Finance as a provider of tax relief, combined with the structure of the tax laws, made it difficult for Finance to conform to the revenue target.

Long thus was wedged between his commitment to conform to the "bottom line" in the budget resolution and the prospect that Finance's bill would be substantially below target. He realized that outright rejection of the budget resolution would pose a dangerous threat to the jurisdiction of his committee. Long sensed that the best way to protect Finance's interests would be through nominal adherence to the requirements of the budget resolution.

Finance, therefore, contrived to meet the revenue target arithmetically by (1) extending the temporary tax cuts through only nine months of the fiscal year, and (2) "front-loading" revenue gainers and deferring the effective dates for revenue losers. It did, in other words, exactly the opposite of what Long had told SBC about tax legislation. As a consequence of this tampering with effective dates, the bill reported by Finance conformed to the overall revenue level of the budget resolution, even though the first-year revenue gain from tax expenditure reductions was less than half the $2 billion target.

The Finance Committee's action presented Muskie and SBC with a dilemma. SBC could simply agree that Finance had met at least the letter of the budget resolution while expressing the hope that a better deal would emerge from conference. If SBC had taken this way out the committee might have been able to align itself with Long in opposition to floor amendments providing additional tax subsidies. But this option posed some difficulties of its own. For one thing, the small core of Senate tax reformers (no more than 15 to 20 members in all but including Senators Mondale and Hollings, active SBC members) had prepared a package of loophole-closing amendments and they were contemplating use of the budget argument to persuade others to join their cause. Muskie could have allied himself first with the reformers and, after they were defeated, he could have joined Long to ward off further inroads on federal revenues. An arrangement (to which he was not a party) had been worked out to enable Muskie to play both roles,[72] but it

72. The tax bill was more than a thousand pages, so rather than consider its provisions in sequence, Long and the tax reformers agreed to take up a number of reform amendments at the start. But this approach was discarded when SBC asked for an immediate consideration of the budget impact on the tax bill.

broke down when SBC launched a frontal attack against Finance's bill.

At an SBC meeting called shortly before the tax bill was scheduled for floor debate, Muskie strenuously objected to Finance's legerdemain and argued that it violated the spirit of the budget process. "We have an obligation as a committee to make clear . . . that the Finance Committee bill does not meet the requirements, at least the clearly stated policy direction of the first concurrent resolution."[73] One can only guess what pushed Muskie and SBC to confrontation. By some accounts, the committee's staff played a key role in seeking new successes to demonstrate the effectiveness of the budget process one observer speculated:

> Budget was beguiled by the success it had had with Stennis on the defense bill the year before. Staff figured that if they could take Stennis, they could take Russell Long. They wanted to show the Finance Committee that it couldn't be free of the discipline of the budget process, and here was a perfect opportunity to show they could take on Russell Long. They really did look upon it that way.

But this is only a partial explanation. SBC's pugnaciousness stemmed from an earnest conviction that the Finance Committee was doing real injury to the budget process. SBC knew that Finance's bill was a revenue loser, not the revenue gainer it purported to be. By back-dating the reductions in tax expenditures and leag-frogging the next fiscal year for some new credits, Finance had concealed the fact that the bill actually would have lost revenue in the "out-years," those beyond the reach of the budget resolution. If Finance could satisfy the dictates of a budget resolution merely by manipulating the effective dates, it could nullify the budget process.

As a result, Muskie and Bellmon circulated a "Dear Colleague" letter to all Senators, announcing that they would challenge the tax bill when it reached the floor. "This is not a contest between the Budget and Finance Committees. . . . The question before the Senate is whether to sustain the congressional budget."[74] Once SBC had attacked Finance's handiwork, however, the fight could not avoid becoming a contest between the two committees. Long—in his own "Dear Colleague" response—exploited this inevitability by broadening the jurisdictional issue to cover all congressional committees.

---

73. Senate Budget Committee, transcript of meeting on June 15, 1976, p. 11.
74. Printed in 122 *Congressional Record* (daily ed., June 16, 1976) S9569.

> . . . the Senate will have to decide whether the function of the Budget Commitee is to recommend target figures within which each committee will live, or whether the Budget Committee, in addition, is to write the specifications for the bills of other committees within the area of their jurisdiction. This is not an issue involving the integrity of the congressional budget process. That process is secure and we firmly support it. Instead, this is an issue involving the proper jurisdictional functions of the Senate's committee. . . .
>
> Is the Senate to respect the right of each committee to make its recommendations? Or is the Senate to expect a single committee to tell all other committees in advance what they would do, in detail, and police them to see that they do precisely that? [75]

When the fight reached the floor, it turned into a contest between two willful chairmen. Muskie tried to force an early vote on a full-year extension of the tax cuts in order to show the likely effect of Finance's bill on federal revenues; Long responded by accusing Muskie of being a "budget buster." Through four days of sharp exchanges, punctuated by procedural maneuvers, Long insisted that the budget process had been complied with and Muskie argued that it had been breached. After Long's position was upheld by floor votes, Muskie withdrew his amendment, noting, "I get messages pretty clearly. I got two within the last 45 minutes."

Yet the messages allowed multiple interpretations, at least with respect to senatorial attitudes toward the budget process. The votes did not mean explicit rejection of the budget process. If Long won the floor battle, it was largely because he enabled Senators to have their budget process and their tax preferences as well. Most Senators knew that Muskie's arithmetic was correct, but they still voted the other way. Many undoubtedly saw the Budget Committee as a threat to their own jurisdiction. One observer commented, "Russell Long effectively used the winning argument, 'If this can happen to my committee, it can happen to yours, too.' " In a key vote that Muskie lost 42 to 49, committee chairmen backed Finance by a two-to-one ratio. Members probably understood that if SBC won this battle, they would be stopped from offering their own tax preferences, not only on this measure but on other tax legislation as well. Strictly enforced, a revenue target could have turned into a virtual closed rule on tax bills.

With the jurisdictional issue out of the way, the Senate devoted seven weeks (intermingled with other business) to the tax bill. It took 129 roll call votes, many of which favored additional tax

75. *Ibid.*, S9570.

expenditures. Whatever discipline might have been provided by the budget process was dissipated by the jurisdictional loss. Long selectively opposed some amendments on the ground that their revenue loss would violate the budget but he supported others with comparable revenue-losing effects. Muskie rose again and again to oppose added tax credits, usually unsuccessfully. On one particularly popular and costly tax subsidy—for college tuition tax credits—Muskie carried the full burden of floor opposition: "I simply cannot, as chairman of the Budget Committee just silently let this process continue as it has. . . ."[76] The tuition credit was then approved by an overwhelming majority.

Just before final passage of the tax bill, Long offered an amendment expressing the "sense of the Senate" that its conferees should produce legislation holding the fiscal 1977 revenue loss to $15.3 billion, the exact amount specified in the first resolution. This was another way of reminding the Senate that Finance would live up to the revenue level in the congressional budget provided that SBC did not try to dictate the details. The revenue figure binding on the Senate, he once again admonished his colleagues, is "what the budget resolution said, not what the fine print inside the budget committee report said."[77] Long might have had another purpose in his "sense of the Senate" amendment, to signal to the Senate that the real tax bill would be the one worked out in conference, not the one marked up by Finance and dotted with floor amendments. As he was to do one year later on the energy tax bill, Long was willing to load the tax reform legislation with costly provisions that would have to be abandoned in conference. These "bargaining chips" would help produce an outcome more in conformity with his own preferences than one that could be achieved in the Senate.

From a statistical perspective, the Senate complicated the task of producing a conference agreement. It converted the bill from a $350 million revenue gain over a five-year period into a $3.5 billion revenue loss over the same period. Furthermore, it stretched the five-year disparity between the House and Senate bills to more than $13 billion. Yet, the conference succeeded in bridging these

76. 122 *Congressional Record* (daily ed., August 5, 1976) S15366. Muskie's motion to "indefinitely postpone" consideration of the tuition tax credit lost 20 to 68.

77. 122 *Congressional Record* (daily ed., August 6, 1976) S13785. Long incorporated a similar resolution in the 1977 energy tax bill discussed earlier in this chapter.

differences and in producing a measure substantially in compliance with the requirements of the budget resolution. The new bill had a first-year revenue gain of $1.6 billion, the amount incorporated into the second budget resolution for fiscal 1977.[78] A sizable portion of this increase was due to the retroactivity of certain reforms (such as reduction of the sick-pay exclusion), and Congress was later pressured to surrender about half of the gain by postponing some of the effective dates. Nevertheless, the legislation was much more than a numbers game; it produced genuine tax reform. The tip-off was its impact on future revenues: over a five-year period, the bill projected a $10 billion revenue gain, much of it the result of higher minimum tax levels and a curtailment of tax shelters, two of the primary goals of reformers.

The conference outcome stimulated a round of cheers from the Budget Committees. As usual, Brock Adams was all positive, calling the final bill "a substantial victory for the congressional budget process," and a demonstration "that Congress is willing to live within its budget and begin the lengthy and arduous task of instituting responsible reform in sensitive areas such as tax expenditures."[79] As usual, too, Muskie mixed criticism with applause, praising Long "for a conference report so much improved over the Senate-passed version of the tax reform bill," but castigating "the prevailing attitudes exhibited in the Senate toward tax legislation." He added, "Changing this attitude will take strong discipline that will have to be applied by the Senate itself. The Senate cannot abdicate its sense of fiscal responsibility and rely on its appointed conferees to modify tax legislation to provide appropriate tax policy."[80]

The 1976 result did not conform to the pattern of past House-Senate conferences. Although the conference often drops or scales back provisions added in the Senate, John Manley's study of 20 tax bills between 1947 and 1966 found that the final level usually was closer to the Senate's version. He attributed the success of the Senate primarily to two factors: It acts on revenue bills after the House and, therefore, can take later developments into account; and it is more open and responsive to the interests affected by tax

78. The Senate's version of the second resolution anticipated only $1.1 billion from tax reform, compared to $1.6 projected in the House's resolution. In accepting the House number, the conferees had solid information on the likely outcome of the tax bill.

79. 122 *Congressional Record* (daily ed., September 10, 1976) H9718.

80. 122 *Congressional Record* (daily ed., September 16, 1976) S16018.

legislation.[81] Both these factors have been weakened by the budget process, at least with regard to reform issues. An earlier budget mark can have more influence on the outcome than a later Senate action; and the conferees may be more willing to fend off powerful interests when they are armed with revenue targets.

When the conferees convened in 1976, they were provided with revenue estimates for each of the 250 items in dispute. This was the first time that all conferees had such detailed budgetary information in advance of their deliberations. In addition, the conference met in open session, though all the important deals were negotiated in private. The conferees, and especially the chairmen of the tax committees, knew that their performance would be measured in terms of how close the final bill came to the revenue markup in the budget resolution. By this standard, the budget process was successful in influencing the tax reform in 1976.

A staff leader on the Finance Committee explained why the budget process was more effective in conference than on the floor. "Voting on the floor is issue by issue, whereas conferees have to fashion something which is overall in line with the budget." This pattern put SBC in a quandry: If it should disregard noncompliance in the expectation that the problem will be remedied in conference, it would be in the position of tolerating violations of the budget process; if it were to protest such violations, it would probably be rebuffed by the "wait for the conference" argument which Finance adroitly used for the 1977 energy bill. But after the conference is over, it may be too late to do much about tax measures still at variance with the budget resolution.

THE REVENUE ACT OF 1978: ACCOMMODATING TAX AND BUDGET POLICY

When the 1976 confrontation was over, an SBC staff leader said, "We lost every battle and won the war." But it was a limited, costly victory at best, and perhaps a pyrrhic one. The Budget Committees had established a jurisdictional foothold in the tax field, but they were still outsiders pressing for recognition against the superior positions of Ways and Means and Finance. The committees had deterred Congress from more tax reduction than was available in the budget resolution, and they had won some tax reform; but they

81. John F. Manley, *The Politics of Finance* (Boston: Little, Brown and Company, 1970), pp. 269-94.

lost on the principle of whether the amount of reform can be dictated in the budget process. Clearly, the 1976 pattern could not be repeated for every major tax bill. Neither the Budget Committees nor the revenue committees welcomed another round of combat with attendant risks and tensions. On the Senate side, where most of the fighting had occurred, both sides saw advantage in avoiding open confrontation, although neither wanted to retreat on its jurisdictional claim. As the major power holder in the tax process, Finance had the most to lose; as the newest participant in tax legislation, the Budget Committee did not want its nascent role nipped in the bud. Finance did not relish being regarded as an uncooperative committee bent on subverting the budget process; Budget did not want to be viewed as an interloper meddling in the business of other committees. Though their differing interests and perspectives would provoke unwanted clashes, both sides were determined to seek accommodation.

Fresh opportunity for conflict came with the tax reduction and reform package President Carter sent Congress in January 1978. Acting on one of his principal campaign pledges, Carter called for more than $5 billion in tax reform, including the repeal or scaling down of numerous preferences. This time if the Budget Committees chose to fight, they would have an ally in the White House.

From the outset, however, tax reform was a lost cause. The mood in Congress favored tax reduction, not legislation raising taxes for some persons. Neither the House Ways and Means nor the Senate Finance Committees discussed the President's reform proposals in their March 15 reports; instead, both emphasized their "bottom-line" recommendations for total revenues. The Budget Committees indicated general support for the cause of tax reform in reporting their first resolutions for fiscal 1979, but neither set aside a specific amount for this purpose. HBC made "no recommendations with respect to the President's specific tax reform proposals," although it expressed "continuing strong support for such reform as an integral part of budget policy."[82] SBC also "made no specific assumptions with respect to the elimination or reduction of existing tax expenditures. However, the Committee believes it is as important to control the growth of tax expenditures as it is to control the growth of direct spending programs."[83] The lack of interest in tax reform persisted on the floor; not a single amendment was offered for this purpose in the House or Senate.

82. H. Rept. No. 95-1055 (1978) p. 26.
83. S. Rept. No. 95-739 (1978) p. 36.

Despite their seeming inattention to tax reform, the Budget Committees influenced congressional action on tax expenditures by using the size of the tax cut as a constraint against enactment of new tax expenditures and as pressure for elimination of some old ones. The Budget Committees scaled down the amount of tax reduction from the $25 billion originally requested by President Carter to about $15 billion.[84] This reduction was barely sufficient to offset the tax increases expected as a result of inflation and the Social Security tax increases scheduled to take effect in 1979. By not leaving room for additional tax cuts, the Budget Committees were able to squeeze out most proposed tax expenditures, and they alerted Congress to the trade-off between tax expenditures and tax reductions. "A larger amount of gross general tax reductions," the Budget Committees noted in their conference report on the first resolution, "could be enacted in fiscal 1979, provided the additional reduction were offset by an appropriate amount of tax increases."[85]

In order to influence the particulars of tax policy by constraining overall tax reduction, the Budget Committees had to ward off efforts to authorize larger reductions. HBC rebuffed a Republican move to provide an additional $10.3 billion in tax reduction; SBC successfully defended its recommendations against a proposal to enlarge the tax cut by making it effective earlier.[86] In fact, the tax reduction targeted by the conference on the first resolution was lower than the reduction either the House or Senate had previously agreed to.

But in order for this strategy to be successful, it had to comport with the tax legislation being developed by Ways and Means and Finance. This posed no problem in the House, which approved a tax reduction bill several billion dollars below the available amount. This House action meant that Finance could add its own reductions without breaching the revenue level set in the budget resolution. But it also invited the Budget Committees to tighten their pressure in the second resolution by further scaling down the amount of reduction to the House-approved figure. To protect his committee's interest and to avoid a fight over revenue reduction, Senator Long

84. The reduction was negotiated in meetings between Giaimo, Muskie, and the President, and in consultation with the chairmen of the Ways and Means and Finance Committees.
85. S. Rept. No. 95-866 (1978) p. 4.
86. The House rejected the Republican move by a 163-239 vote. 124 *Congressional Record* (May 3, 1978) H3516. The Senate rejected the larger tax cut by a 22-65 margin. 124 *Congressional Record* (April 25, 1978) S6294.

made an informal agreement with the Senate Budget Committee: If the Budget Committee gave Finance a reasonable amount of reduction—equivalent to the amount pegged in the first resolution—Long would bring in a bill consistent with the revenue level.

The deal was struck during SBC's markup of the second resolution, in another of Long's remarkable appearances before the committee. Long noted that the House had not used "the full authority in the first budget resolution for tax deductions." But this did not mean that less should be set aside for reductions, he said. "The way I remember hearing it from the House Ways and Means Committee people was that they fully expect we on the Senate side will use the full amount of tax cut authority available to us in the bill that we send to them."[87] Long left no doubt that his committee would "recommend a tax cut by as much as we have budget authority to recommend it."[88] When doubt arose over the amount needed by Finance, Muskie suggested that "our staffs could work those numbers out," and Bellmon added his own conciliatory words, "We ought to try to see eye to eye as much as we can."[89]

SBC lived up to its part of the bargain, producing a second resolution that retained the full reduction targeted earlier in the year. Long delayed Finance's markup of the tax bill until the amount of reduction was confirmed by the House-Senate conference on the second resolution. He then used the budget constraint to argue against many of the schemes advanced by his colleagues. Time and again, Finance members were warned about the "budget squeeze,"[90] and although they reported a bill that exceeded the budgeted reduction, they understood that the final amount would have to be in accord with the second resolution's revenue floor.

The Senate handled the tax bill in its customary fashion, adding dozens of amendments and billions of dollars in tax reductions. Muskie repeatedly took the floor to decry the violation of the congressional budget, and he was sometimes joined by Long, who voted against various proposals to enlarge the reductions. With Long's backing, the Senate sustained the elimination of one of the most popular tax expenditures, the federal tax deduction allowed

87. Senate Budget Committee, markup of the second budget resolution for fiscal 1979, transcript, August 9, 1978, p. 306.
88. *Ibid.*, p. 323.
89. *Ibid.*, pp. 315, 319.
90. See *Congressional Quarterly Weekly Report*, (September 30, 1978) pp. 2608-09.

for payment of state and local gasoline taxes.[91] But in a bitter floor battle, the Senate explicitly rejected Muskie's attempt to bar amendments that would reduce future-year taxes, and the tax bill approved by the Senate contained billions of dollars' worth of such reductions. Yet most of these amendments were eliminated in the ensuing conference, and Congress—on the last day of the session—gave final approval to tax legislation consistent with the budget resolution.

The 1978 events point to a jurisdictional demarcation between the tax and the Budget Committees, with the latter concentrating on the revenue aggregates, the former on the particulars of tax laws. This differentiation of roles would enable the Budget Committees to apply indirect pressure for tax reform rather than the direct pressure that was tried two years earlier. The Budget Committees may not be content with this role, for the link between cause and effect usually is not so obvious as to enable them to take credit for particular outcomes. Nevertheless, if the Budget Committees stray to the particulars, they risk future confrontations with the tax committees, with no assurance that they will be any more successful in influencing the final results.

LIMITATIONS OF THE BUDGET PROCESS

Why have the Budget Committees had to strain so hard to gain a role in tax policy? These committees appear to have a weaker position with respect to tax issues than they have when spending measures come before Congress. Part of the answer lies with the Budget Act, for the Act made fewer changes concerning revenue decisions than concerning spending issues. In contrast to their itemization of expenditures into functional categories, the budget resolutions deal only with the total for revenues; they do not identify the sources from which revenues are to be derived nor the manner in which the tax burden is to be distributed among various economic classes. Although the Budget Act requires the House Ways and Means and the Senate Finance Committees to file March 15 reports and it imposes various time requirements on revenue measures, it does not compel the Budget Committees to do more

91. The vote came on a point of order against an amendment to restore the gasoline tax reduction. The ruling that the amendment violated the Budget Act was upheld 49 to 42, with Senator Long voting with the majority. 124 *Congressional Record* (October 10, 1978) S17993.

than estimate the revenues expected to be received under existing law. But the Budget Act is not the only limiting influence. A number of factors peculiar to revenue legislation complicate the task of making tax decisions through the Budget process.

Timing of Tax Activity in Congress

The timing of tax action vitally affects the congressional budget and revenue legislation. When a government has a budget process, its decisions are supposed to be made in accord with a fixed schedule; in the absence of a budget process, financial actions can occur at any time during the year. The scheduling of decisions is not merely a matter of administrative convenience but a prerequisite for fiscal control. When decisions are made out of cycle, the usefulness of the budget process is diminished.

The congressional budget process would be facilitated if presidential proposals were submitted before consideration of the first budget resolution and completion of legislative action, during the interval between the first and second resolutions. This is the arrangement contemplated in the Budget Act for appropriations bills. But unlike appropriations, which recur with a great deal of regularity—Congress expects to have 13 regular appropriations measures plus at least one early and one late supplemental measure each year—tax activity is uncertain. The Budget Act does not prescribe the period during which Congress should take up revenue measures or the frequency of tax actions.

Table 42 confirms the irregularity of the tax process in Congress. The President usually submits major tax proposals in conjunction with his annual budget, but this was not the case with regard to the energy and Social Security actions initiated in 1977. Ways and Means reported several tax measures before the first resolution was adopted, two between the resolutions, and another two after Congress had completed action on the second resolution. The time spread was equally large in Senate Finance, which pigeon-holed one bill, reported two before the first resolution, another during the May-September interval, and four more after the second resolution had been adopted. Congressional action was least likely to occur during the period between the two resolutions. The period of time between the report from Ways and Means until final congressional action ranged from 35 days for the 1977 Tax Reduction Act to more than 300 days for the 1976 Tax Reform Act.

Because the process is so irregular and unpredictable, the Budget Committees cannot effectively plan for congressional action in their budget resolutions. They either find themselves rubber-stamping decisions already made or being swept aside by legislative actions.

Table 40 provides an additional clue to the limitations of the budget process. Five of the enactments cleared Congress during the preadjournment rush; four were passed by the Senate during the final days of the session. Late consideration strengthens the ability of the tax committees to control floor action on their legislation. Senator Long has often endeavored to have "the last train out of the station," a practice that shows his keen understanding of the importance of timing in the legislative process. Late in the session, Congress does not want to be tied up by intramural wrangling over budget figures; it is willing to bend its rules a bit in order to get its work done. It regards tax reductions as "must" legislation, and does not want to be held up by points of order or technical discussions over the requirements of the Budget Act.

Particulars Versus Totals

As noted earlier, the Budget Committees' role with regard to revenues is more limited than their expenditure role. Revenues are budgeted in the aggregate, with the particulars (sources of revenue and tax expenditures) consigned to backup reports. If the Senate Budget Committee had been content to deal with total revenues, the 1976 tax reform fight would not have occurred. When SBC tried to dictate some of the specifics of tax policy, it was challenged for trespassing on the tax committee's jurisdiction.

Budget Committees confined to aggregate revenue decisions cannot directly address the distributive tax policy issues: how much is to be extracted from each class of taxpayer and how much retained by each through tax subsidies. These are more contentious political questions than is the marginal decision of whether one year's tax cuts should total $18 billion or $20 billion. As the Budget Committees have found out, a resolution restricted to aggregate revenues gives the Tax Committees ample discretion to change the tax laws without violating the congressional budget. The ingenuity with which Finance has manipulated effective dates demonstrates that the budget process, by itself offers little impediment to the enactment of its chief preferences. Almost any tax policy can be made to fit within the revenue mark of one year's budget resolution. The same revenue total can accommodate either an increase or a reduction in tax expenditures, depending on when particular provisions are scheduled to take effect.

Table 40

LEGISLATIVE HISTORY OF MAJOR TAX BILLS, FISCAL YEARS 1975-78

Legislation	*Presidential Initiation*	*House Ways and Means Committee Report*	*House Considera-tion and Passage*	*Senate Finance Committee Report*	*Senate Considera-tion and Passage*	*Congress Completes Action*	*Days Be-tween First Report and Completed Congres-sional Action*
P.L. 94-12 Tax Reduction Act of 1975	Jan. 15, 1975	Feb. 19, 1975	Feb. 27, 1975	Mar. 27, 1975	Mar. 18-22, 1975	Mar. 26, 1975	37 days
P.L. 94-168 Tax Cut Extension	Oct. 6, 1975	Nov. 12, 1975	Dec. 19, 1975 [a]	Dec. 12, 1975	Dec. 19, 1975	Dec. 19, 1975	38 days
P.L. 94-455 Tax Reform Act of 1976	[b]	Nov. 12, 1975	Dec. 3-4, 1975	May 27, 1976	June 16-Aug. 6, 1976	Sept. 16, 1976	310 days
P.L. 95-30 Tax Revision Act of 1977	Jan. 27, 1977	Feb. 17, 1977	Mar. 8, 1977	Mar. 28, 1977	Apr. 18-29, 1977	May 16, 1977	89 days

H.R. 6860 Energy Tax Bill of 1975	Jan. 15, 1975	May 15, 1975	June 9-19, 1975	—	—	—	—
P.L. 95-617 Energy Tax Act of 1978	Apr. 20, 1977	July 13, 1977 [c]	Aug. 3-5, 1977	Oct. 21, 1977	Oct. 25-31, 1977	Oct. 15, 1978	459 days
P.L. 95-216 Social Security Financing Amendments of 1977	May 9, 1977	Oct. 6, 1977	Oct. 26-27, 1977	Oct. 31, 1977	Nov. 2-4, 1977	Dec. 15, 1977	69 days
P.L. 95-600 Revenue Act of 1978	Jan. 21, 1978	July 27, 1978	Aug. 10, 1978	Sept. 27, 1978	Oct. 10, 1978	Oct. 15, 1978	80 days

[a] The House passed a different version of its original bill after a Ford veto.

[b] The House Ways and Means Committee resumed consideration of a tax reform bill it had considered in the previous Congress.

[c] House Ways and Means reported the tax provisions of the energy bill on this date. The bill then was considered by the Ad Hoc Committee on Energy which reported it on July 23. The energy bill was divided into separate bills in the Senate.

Source: *Congressional Record*, dates indicated.

Restricting the Budget Committees to revenue totals would seem to have the virtue of encouraging them to concentrate on the fiscal implications of tax policy. Meddling in the details of the Internal Revenue Code would only distract these committees from the macroeconomics of taxation. Yet, fiscal policy depends on much more than a single revenue number, independent of its composition. The same "bottom line" can affect the economy in a variety of ways, depending on how it is derived. When President Carter initially advocated tax rebates in 1977, the Republicans countered with a proposal for permanent tax cuts. There was little dispute over how much revenue should be pared from the budget; the issue was whether permanent cuts would stimulate the economy more than a one-shot rebate. The following exchange shows SBC's predicament in trying to formulate tax policy without offending the Finance Committee:

Senator McClure: . . . when the only option we have in the Budget Committee is to vote for a revenue figure, then it really masks or hides the real function of the Budget Committee in trying to establish economic policy. . . .

Senator Muskie: Would you like to make this the Finance Committee?

Senator McClure: . . . I certainly don't suggest that what we will do will bind the Finance Committee but I think we ought to try, at least, to indicate to the Congress . . . when we adopt a resolution whether or not it's a temporary tax cut, we are suggesting within the context of these figures or a permanent tax cut within the context of these figures. . . .

Senator Muskie: . . . if we have the time and want to go into it and actually take a vote that will be binding on nobody, including ourselves, on what our preference is, if there is a consensus on the temporary tax cut versus the permanent tax cut, to meet our immediate problem, I am willing to do that.[92]

SBC finally got out of its dilemma by reporting a resolution with enough room for either "temporary tax refunds or permanent tax rate reductions of a comparable amount." The committee did not stray over the line between totals and particulars; it secured budgetary peace by forgoing an opportunity to influence fiscal policy.

The Budget Committees have devised two strategies to compensate for their weak role with respect to particular tax issues. First, by constraining the total revenue reduction, they have tried to

92. Senate Budget Committee, markup of the third concurrent resolution for fiscal 1977, transcript, p. 82.

"crowd out" new tax expenditures and prod the tax committees to do something about existing ones. This strategy was helped in 1978 by an improving employment picture and a rising concern over inflation—the type of economic condition that calls for less tax reduction. The Budget Committees might have to allow for more slack in their revenue targets when the economy needs stimulation. Furthermore, the 1978 revenue totals were accepted by Ways and Means and Finance. One doubts whether the outcome would be the same if these committees were to insist on a larger reduction. The ability of the Budget Committees to use tax reduction as a distributive policy lever depends on the willingness of the tax committees to go along with the Budget Committees revenue numbers.

The Budget Committees' second tactic also was introduced in 1978, when there was strong congressional sentiment for tuition tax credits and strong presidential support for expanded loans and grants to college students. The Budget Committees took advantage of this situation to encourage a trade-off between helping students through tax credits and helping them through direct expenditure programs. The committees made it clear that only a limited amount of money would be available for student assistance, and that money spent on tax credits would reduce the funds for loans and grants. This approach broadened the contest between the Budget Committees and the tax committees to involve the committees with legislative jurisdiction over education programs as well. In this larger group, the Budget Committees had allies who helped sway the final outcome in favor of loans and grants rather than tax credits.[93]

Direct Versus Tax Expenditures

The strategy used in 1978 appears appropriate for all tax expenditures. The Budget Committees could try to align tax and direct expenditures in a way that would make Congress choose between the alternative forms of governmental assistance. But it should be noted that tax reformers were more successful in incorporating tax expenditures into the Budget Act than in persuading Congress to treat these subsidies as the budgetary equivalent of direct expenditures. This mismatch between the reach of the budget process and the perspectives of Members of Congress has been a

93. Senator Kennedy has proposed that legislative committees be given concurrent jurisdiction over tax expenditures related to their programs. If this were implemented, it would strengthen the possibility of Budget Committee-legislative committee alliances against the tax committees.

source of budgetary strife. Many Members either do not understand the concept of tax expenditures or are not convinced that these subsidies ought to be treated as if they were cash payments from the treasury. The grant of dollars through the tax system is not widely perceived in Congress as a disbursement of public funds.

The problem extends beyond tax expenditures to the revenue side of the budget as a whole. In the eyes of most Members, budget control means control over expenditures. They want the budget process to concentrate more on spending policy than on altering the tax system. When SBC appeared reluctant to grant a waiver for the consideration of Social Security legislation, Sen. Charles Curtis complained: "I always had the idea that the prime responsibility of the Budget Committee was to hold down expenditures, to balance the budget."[94] While this partisan view from the ranking Republican on Finance might have overstated legislative sentiment, it does reflect congressional imbalance in the treatment of revenues and expenditures. No one in Congress argues that the "prime responsibility" of the budget process is to change the tax system.

In trying to influence tax policy, the Budget Committees can exploit the Budget Act's mandate "to devise methods of coordinating tax expenditures, policies, and programs with direct budget outlays." In the long run, the Budget Committees might secure more tax reform by educating Congress than by leading a reform movement. They surely would attract less outright opposition from the tax committees if they concentrated on studies of areas in which tax subsidies are comparable to direct expenditure programs than if they tried to force Ways and Means and Finance to produce billions of dollars of additional revenues by the immediate elimination of tax preferences.

The Budget Year Versus Future Years

The Budget Act bars floor action on money legislation until the first budget resolution has been adopted, but places no time restriction on a revenue measure "which first becomes effective in a fiscal year following the fiscal year to which the concurrent resolution applies." In other words, budgetary control relates only to the current and forthcoming fiscal years, not to any "out-years."

This exemption applies equally to revenue and spending bills, but in practice it opens a much bigger escape clause for revenue

94. 123 *Congressional Record* (daily ed., November 2, 1977) S18419.

legislation. Although the Appropriations Committees generally have been reluctant to approve advance appropriations, the tax committees have been adept at leap-frogging the budget year with revenue provisions that become effective in future years. This practice has given the tax committees the flexibility they need to meet the letter of any budget resolution without subscribing to the particular revenue policies intended by the Budget Committees. Even if the tax committees did not manipulate the effective dates, revenue actions of Congress (except for temporary tax cuts) would tend to affect the out-years more significantly than the year covered by the budget process. "We have learned," Senator Muskie told his committee during the heat of the 1976 struggle,

> that the calendar year or the 12-month fiscal year is a very inadequate period within which to change the direction of this government. Here if you start treating revenue changes . . . as a 12-month exercise, you are really going to create problems for the Congress as we try to put our budget into shape moving, it in a direction five years down the road that we want to go.[95]

The one-year-at-a-time perspective makes it difficult for the Budget Committees to influence future revenue policy without intruding on the work of the committees of primary jurisdiction. But they cannot be endlessly at war with other committees, so in most budget seasons, the Budget Committees go along with the tax committees and settle for a single-year perspective.

Senator Muskie challenged the single-year perspective in 1978 and lost. The issue was a Republican proposal to phase in substantial tax cuts over a three-year period. Muskie invoked Section 303 of the Budget Act which bars the consideration of revenue (or spending) measures before adoption of the first resolution for a fiscal year but permits the consideration of such measures for future years. While the debate focused on the technicalities of the Budget Act, the Senate knew that the real issue was the relative power of its Budget and Finance Committees. Muskie was blunt in pointing to the consequences of multiyear revenue legislation: "We endanger the [budget] process for revenues altogether, because I see no point in trying to protect the budget from January 1 to May 15 if, prior to that time, Congress is free to enact any tax cuts for any fiscal year that it chooses."[96] Senator Long argued

95. Senate Budget Committee meeting, June 15, 1976, transcript, p. 21.
96. 124 *Congressional Record* (daily ed., October 5, 1978) S17240.

equally vehemently that Muskie's interpretation would thwart the will of the Senate:

> . . . anybody in this body has a right to offer an amendment providing a tax cut or a tax increase in the year following the year to which the budget resolution applies. Otherwise, Senators would not be able to offer a tax cut affecting their people after the end of the budget year without the consent of the Budget Committee. . . .[97]

When the presiding officer (on the advice of the Senate Parliamentarian) upheld Muskie's point of order against the three-year tax cut, Long appealed the ruling and won on a close 48-38 vote. Muskie then took the floor to "accept the Senate's will as a direct interpretation of the Budget Act. . . . [These] are my new orders and I shall follow them."[98]

Where did these orders leave the Budget Committees? Less influential with respect to revenue legislation than they would like, but not feeble. Having rebuffed Muskie on the future-year issue, the Senate loaded the tax bill with amendments that raised its future—fifth-year—cost from $32 billion in the measure passed by the House to $56 billion. But Long then negotiated a conference agreement that not only held the first-year cost within the revenue floor of the budget resolution, but also reduced the fifth-year cost to $34 billion. Long had his own reasons for not wanting to commit Congress in advance to future tax cuts. "Think of all the joy you would lose," he was quoted as saying, "by not being able to vote for tax cuts in the future. There wouldn't be anything left to cut."[99] Sooner or later, premature tax cuts would have a confining effect on Finance, forcing it to forgo additional cuts or, worse yet, compelling it to vote tax increases that might have otherwise been avoided.

What Long sought in enabling the Senate to deal with future-year tax cuts was a safety valve, not an escape hatch. Hemmed in by congressional pressure for more tax reductions on one hand, and the constraints of the budget process on the other, Long needed some room for maneuver, some way of responding to the pressures without violating the terms of the process or "giving away the store." Limited concessions concerning future revenues enabled him to assemble a powerful coalition in support of his tax bills and

---

97. *Ibid.*, S17238.
98. *Ibid.*, S17245.
99. Quoted in *Congressional Quarterly Weekly Report*, (September 23, 1978) p. 2583.

thus to buy legislative peace in the Senate. By dealing in this manner, Long has controlled the tax process in the Senate.

Where do Long's maneuvers leave the Senate Budget Committee? Long provided part of the answer shortly after the Senate overturned Muskie's point of order in 1978. Muskie, he urged, should continue to do what he has done: ". . . when I have brought in an amendment for a tax cut in a future year, even though it did not run counter to the budget resolution. I hope he will speak out strongly and say, 'The Budget Committee has considered this matter and we find we cannot stand the revenue loss. . . .' "[100]

Long would like the Senate Budget Committee to serve only as an independent source of information on tax policy, and to leave the decisions to the Finance Committee. Muskie, while not wanting to delimit his committee's role in this way, also recognized SBC's usefulness in providing the Senate with timely information on the short- and long-term effects of its tax decisions. During one of his floor entanglements with Long over tax policy, Muskie defended his intrusion into the debate: "We have only one discipline in the budget committee, . . . the discipline of information. If I do not have that responsibility, I do not have any."[101] But SBC has tended to mix information with confrontation, fearful, perhaps, that the facts by themselves would not deter the Senate from doing what it was determined to do. But the record suggests that facts supported by budget controls have not always deterred the Senate either.

TAXATION WITH BUDGETING: AN UNBALANCED RELATIONSHIP

The work of the Budget Committees intrudes on the interests of every other congressional committee. The extent to which the Budget Committees have a secure role on Capitol Hill largely depends on the extent to which the committees of primary jurisdiction (authorizations, appropriations, and tax) accept the new committees as legitimate participants in the legislative process. Because congressional committees are protectors of their legislative territory, it would have been unthinkable for Ways and Means and Finance to welcome the new budget entities unreservedly and give

100. 124 *Congressional Record* (daily ed., October 5, 1978) S17245.
101. 123 *Congressional Record* (daily ed., April 12, 1977) S6213.

them a substantial part of the tax power. But the kind of *modus operandi* that has developed between the Budget and Appropriations Committees might have emerged in the tax field as well. Such has not been the case. Even the House Budget Committee, which has maintained a cautious and deferential posture, has had, in the opinion of one of its top staffers, "more fights with Ways and Means than we will ever have with Appropriations. Every time we turn around, we have an issue with the Ways and Means Committee."

On every tax issue in Congress, the Budget Committees and the tax committees have a choice of confrontation or accommodation. If the Budget Committees had a voice in the 1976 outcome, it was by confrontation. They had to fight for what they got, HBC through quiet pressure, SBC through sounding the battle cry. But no successful legislative committee could function on these terms for long. On Capitol Hill, success comes not through confrontation but through deference accorded to committees (and members) by virtue of their status as specialists in particular areas of legislation. A committee that has to keep score to know whether it is making a difference is a committee uncertain of its position in Congress. At least in the tax field, the Budget Committees cannot survive by merely going along with what others would do without a budget process. A committee that has to repeatedly battle its peers is a committee with no sure jurisdictional claim of its own, no uncontested piece of the legislative process.

Victories won by such committees have no halo effect. The Budget Committees were not enriched in will or resources by their 1976 accomplishment. Perhaps partly because of Muskie's absence due to illness, the Senate Budget Committee put up a dispirited fight when the energy and Social Security bills were rushed through the Senate in the final days of the 1977 session. When Senator Long engineered an evasion of the budget process in the 1977 energy tax legislation, many Senators just were not interested in hearing any more about the problems and prerequisites of the budget process. SBC paid a price for its 1976 triumph; it had acquired a reputation as an overreaching, combative committee, not merely as the guardian of the congressional budget.

In most situations, the Budget Committees have chosen accommodation rather than confrontation. On all three tax bills produced in the year after the great tax reform battle, the committees offered only token resistance to the legislative tide. On tax rebates, they backtracked after the Administration withdrew its endorsement. On energy, they were whipsawed between the $30 billion tax increase voted by the House and the $40 billion tax reduction passed by the Senate. On Social Security, their counsel against a tax increase was brushed aside by a Congress eager to restore the huge system to financial health. In 1978, the Senate Budget Committee cooperated with Finance on the size of the tax cut, SBC accommodating to the tax committee's interest in exchange for an understanding that the budget figures would be adhered to. But even this conciliatory arrangement did not avert acrimonious outbursts on the floor.

In taxation, as in other facets of the budget process, the House Budget Committee has favored accommodation, while the Senate Committee has been more willing to confront. Statements from key participants in the tax process indicate HBC's limited role. A member of HBC's tax expenditure task force said:

> There's some delicacy because obviously we don't want to start moving in on other people's territory. . . . We might make an assumption that Ways and Means has to raise X billions of dollars, but we don't have to tell Ways and Means how to do it. We'll leave that up to Al Ullman.

A member of both Ways and Means and HBC commented:

> The role of the Budget Committee has been mostly estimating what the economy will bring in. Its role has been very modest. For instance, the kind of thing that comes up is Ways and Means asked for a $100 million cushion for tax expenditures, the right to enact small tax adjustments that might add up to as much as $100 million in lost revenues. Now that is the level of confrontation we've had, not the Budget Committee saying to Ways and Means, "We want you to convert personal exemptions to credits," or anything like that.

An HBC staff leader said:

> We have been deficient in the tax area. I can't give you a good reason why. In the very first year, 1975, we did practically nothing with tax expenditures. . . . The second year we had a pretty good impact, but it was not an impact that we really initiated. We developed a $2 billion number by talking quite a lot to the Ways and Means staff—it looked like that figure was about what they would get.

When the budget process was launched, both the House Budget Committee and the Ways and Means Committee were deeply divided over tax reform. Thirteen of 25 HBC members supported reform on at least half of the tax reform votes in the 94th Congress, while 18 of 37 of the Ways and Means members supported reform

Table 41

TAX REFORM SCORES FOR
MEMBERS OF THE BUDGET AND TAX COMMITTEES,
94th CONGRESS

	House Budget Committee	*Ways and Means*	*Senate Budget Committee*	*Finance*
Mean	54.4	53	41.1	34.5
Median	53	47	40-46	22
Percent of Members Scoring 100	4	8.1	0	0
Percent of Members Scoring 75 or more	44	43.2	6.3	11.1
Percent of Members Scoring 50 or more	52	48.6	31.3	22.2
Chairman's Score	94	76	77	22

Source: Taxation with Representation.

more than half of the time (see table 41). Not only were the two committees similarly divided on tax reform, but their median and mean voting scores were almost identical. The sharp division within each committee inhibited reformers from using HBC as a launching pad for their legislative aims and inhibited HBC from pressuring Ways and Means to take a stronger pro-reform position. The result has been a fairly harmonious relationship with HBC ratifying the amount of reform that Ways and Means leaders considered appropriate.

Tax reformers on Ways and Means have not looked to HBC for support; nor have the members who serve on both committees encouraged the Budget Committee to take an active role in tax policy. One reason is that tax reform means quite different things to each committee. In a budgetary context, reform means reducing the more than $100 billion of tax subsidies provided by the federal government. For Ways and Means, however, reform is not a single issue but a large number of internal revenue provisions, each of which has to be separately decided on its political and economic merits. Ways and Means (and Finance) members deeply resent the fact that the Budget Committees can support tax reform without taking hard stands on particular issues. One participant described the problem this way:

It's easy enough for the Budget Committee to say we have to achieve $2 billion in budget reform, but they really don't have to go through and see what that does to people or take it on an item-by-item basis. It's just too easy to make a decision like that. That shouldn't be a legislative decision. Legislative decisions should follow due legislative process, not just the budget process.

Tax reformers on Ways and Means and Finance do not look to the budget process for support or guidance. A Ways and Means member with a perfect pro-reform score rejected the notion of an alliance between reformers on the two sets of committees:

The budget resolution doesn't affect the vote of any member on Ways and Means. Does a member have to say, "Well, yes, I'll vote to tighten up the loophole on real estate taxation because the Budget Committee says we've got to find $2 billion?" I've never heard any of that reasoning by individual members and that's what counts.

At best, Ways and Means is an occasional ally of the Budget Committee, using the budget process for advantage on particular issues, but abandoning it when the politics of the situation dictates a different strategy. Referring to the conference on the 1976 Tax Reform Act, a staff aide close to Al Ullman admitted to this opportunism:

Ways and Means used the budget process in that instance the same way that a lot of committees seem to be using the process, as a reason not to do or to do things that otherwise would be very difficult for them. Things, in other words, that you want to do but that you could not find a way to justify politically.

Even Ullman, who is openly committed to the budget process, has occasionally abandoned that process for political reasons. The 1975 dispute over President Ford's linkage of tax and spending cuts forced Ullman into opposition to the budget process. Republicans, it will be recalled, wanted to attach a spending limitation to the debt-ceiling bill. Such bills almost always come to the floor under a closed rule, but Ullman wanted to report a bill that had some Republican support. Consequently, he agreed not to oppose a rule that would allow a floor vote on an expenditure ceiling—disregarding Brock Adams' impassioned plea, "I beg of you not to destroy a process that we're just trying to get into gear."[102] Ullman did not

102. Quoted in *Congressional Quarterly Almanac 1975*, p. 119.

want to harm the budget process, but he had to put his own committee's interests above those of the Budget Committee.

In the Senate, the relationship between the Budget Committee and the tax committee has been much more strained than has been the case in the House. The Senate Finance Committee has conducted more formal and extensive markups of its March 15 reports than most Senate committees have, but Finance has provided little more than summary information in its annual "letter" (the format it uses for the report) to SBC. For example, Finance's staff prepared an 80-page print for its markup of the fiscal 1978 budget, while its letter to SBC totaled 12 pages, with only 2 pages devoted to revenues. By complying with the bare minimum of the Budget Act, Finance has signaled SBC that it should not stray into the details of revenues or other matters within Finance's jurisdiction.

Reform sentiment does not dominate either Finance or SBC, but it is stronger in the latter. Senators who favor the reform side on more than 50 percent of the votes have less than one-third of the SBC seats and barely one-fifth of the Finance positions. In view of SBC's apparent lack of enthusiasm for tax reform, how can its active role in the 1976 tax conflict be explained? At least three factors go into the answer: (1) SBC's median and mean reform scores are much higher than Finance's, even though it has few fully committed reformers. (2) Chairman Muskie had the highest reform score on SBC and he effectively influenced the committee's proreform decision on the first budget resolution for fiscal 1977. (Chairman Long, by contrast, had a much lower reform score; he was exactly in the middle of his committee on this issue.) (3) When Long appeared before SBC to oppose the $2 billion reform target, some SBC members took it as a challenge to their budgetary role and rallied behind the reform cause. The issue was thus defined in terms of the role of the Budget Committee rather than reform of the tax laws. The revenue target was approved unanimously, with virtually all of the discussion devoted to SBC's role in tax legislation and the reachability of the target. Hardly a word was said about the substance of tax policy or about particular tax reforms.

The 1976 tax reform conflict ended SBC's illusions about what it could achieve on Capitol Hill, but the conflict also demonstrated that a defeat would neither destroy the budget process nor prevent SBC from establishing normal ties with other Senate committees. Long's attitude and performance have been summed up in a remark often attributed to him: "Show me the rules and I'll play the game as well as the next feller." Playing by the rules means not to openly subvert the budget process, nor to bend more than necessary to its dictates. Yet, Long has sometimes turned friendly to the budget process and used the revenue levels in the budget resolution to oppose costly tax credits. Someone who has observed Long's dazzling use of legislative skills explains:

> Long would be happy not to take many of the floor amendments and he would want to avoid losing in conference. It is clear that Long would prefer to avoid that if he could; he would rather head it off on the floor. He is pleased to have this budget process so he can say, "Look fellows, it's not me, it's those fellows on the Budget Committees."

In 1977, Muskie and Long tried to avoid a repeat of the tax reform battle. SBC tried to anticipate Finance's intentions when it prepared the third budget resolution, and Finance tried to schedule the Social Security tax increases in a manner compatible with the revenue level in the budget resolution. Muskie loyally advocated the Finance Committee's treatment of earned income credit (payments to individuals in excess of their tax liability) as a reduction in revenues rather than as a direct expenditure because it was a matter in which Long had a strong interest.[103] For his part, Long agreed to attach an extension of countercyclical revenue sharing (Muskie's number one legislative priority) to the 1977 tax reduction bill, even though Finance had not held any hearings on the legislation. Despite these mutual efforts at accommodation, SBC and Finance fought three times in 1977—over tax rebates, energy taxes, and Social Security. Reciprocal efforts at conciliation could not avert renewed conflict in 1978 when the tax bill was on the floor. Muskie sought to enhance SBC's influence over future tax decisions; Finance wanted to be free of budget controls concerning future years. In separate pursuits of self-interest, each committee was propelled to action that infringed on the other's sphere of operations.

It is easy to portray SBC as excessively belligerent in its pursuit of a tax role. A top SBC staffer defended his committee's posture: "We have to fight for every bit of jurisdiction, other than reporting the budget resolutions. The Budget Act was written this way; it puts us in an adversary position *vis-à-vis* Finance."

---

103. With prodding from several SBC members, Congress added a provision to the second supplemental appropriation bill for 1978 requiring future refundable credits to go through the appropriations process. SBC changed its mind on this issue after it realized that refundable credits are entitlements.

SBC is stronger in the tax field than it would have been in the absence of confrontation. Finance has conceded SBC's legitimate role in aggregate tax policy, and has committed itself to work within the revenue floor set by the budget resolution. One might argue that the House Budget Committee has achieved comparable prominence without antagonizing peer committees. But the fact is that Ways and Means usually offers low tax-reduction figures (as it did in 1978) and the House (because of a closed or modified rule) has little opportunity to sweeten the pot. Finance plays the role of providing more benefits, with open season on the floor for more revenue-losing amendments. HBC can get budgetary control through quiet negotiation, while SBC has to fight from the ramparts.

By the same token, Finance is playing its historical role, not just trying to undercut the budget process. Senator Muskie prefaced the Senate's debate on the first 1978 resolution with an unusually open attack on committees and colleagues who disregard the budget process. Finance was one of his favorite targets, and its manipulation of the effective dates in the 1977 energy legislation was one of his telling exhibits:

> During the debate last year on the energy tax bill we witnessed again this eagerness to sacrifice budget reform . . . when political opportunity becomes more attractive for the moment. . . . the Committee on Finance included a gimmick in its bill to create a new loophole in the discipline of the budget process.[104]

This interpretation of Finance's—or its chairman's—motives is incomplete. Although it is reputed to be the most powerful committee in Congress, Finance has the most on the line in the budget process. Its congressional role could be threatened by controls that would prevent it from increasing the tax reductions set by the House, and its position in conference *vis-à-vis* Ways and Means could be seriously weakened. If the House were to approve a tax bill that consumed all the margin available in the budget resolution, Finance would have only two distasteful options: to accept the House bill without substantial change, or to rearrange the tax benefits without violating the budget numbers. The first option would reduce Finance to a rubber stamp; the second would require it to take benefits from some taxpayers in order to give to others. It is not surprising that Finance has opted to schedule tax reduc-

---

104. 124 *Congressional Record* (daily ed., April 24, 1978) S6100.

tions in such a way that it can add benefits without exceeding the budget level. Significantly, Finance was able to be cooperative in 1978 because the House did not "spend" all the tax reduction available under the budget resolution.

Finance has also opted for unfettered floor action. Far from viewing such a course as a breach of budget discipline, Long views it as strengthening his committee's, and the Senate's, bargaining position in conference. Long can buy support for his tax bill by allowing Senators to add their amendments; at the same time he fulfills his commitment to abide by the budget's limits. If this requires some manipulation of effective dates, the purpose is for the Senate's advantage. There is some evidence that Muskie understands Finance's predicament. After the Senate had tackled the 1978 tax reduction and added tens of billions of dollars to future-year cuts, Muskie decided to vote for passage of the legislation:

> I would be gravely concerned about the impact of this bill on the 1980 budget if I thought that this bill would be enacted into law in its present form. Fortunately, however, I doubt very much that that will be the case. The chairman of the Finance Committee . . . has given us his word . . . that he will be back from conference with a tax bill consistent with the fiscal year 1979 budget, and with very greatly reduced later-year tax cuts.[105]

Muskie's attitude put SBC in a very difficult position, for if extended to future legislation, it would have spelled acceptance of the "wait for the conference" argument that SBC rejected in the 1977 energy bill. SBC would have to settle for informal understandings coupled with formal evasions of the budget process, but perhaps this deal is the best that SBC can make with the Finance Committee.

CONCLUSION

The Budget Committees cannot be expected to forge a relationship with the tax committees that is comparable to the easy relationship the Budget Committees have worked out with Appropriations. The Appropriations Committees need allies, both to defend their recommendations on the floor and to guard against backdoor raids on their jurisdiction. Their relationship with the Budget

105. *Ibid.*, (daily ed., October 10, 1978) S18037.

Committees arises from a shared need and a commonality of interest. Without the Budget Committees' support, the Appropriations Committees might not be able to uphold the spending levels set in their bills; without the Appropriations Committees' support, the Budget Committees could not gain adoption of the spending amounts in their resolutions.

The tax committees, which rank among the truly powerful congressional committees, both in terms of scope of jurisdiction and ability to move their bills on the floor, do not generally need budgetary allies. There is very little that the Budget Committees could do for Ways and Means and Finance to cement their relationship or to foster a sense of interdependence.

Chapter XIV. AN ASSESSMENT OF THE CONGRESSIONAL BUDGET PROCESS

Expectations and Reality

The Accomplishments of Congressional Budgeting

XIV An Assessment of the Congressional Budget Process

Since enactment of the Budget Act in 1974, Members of Congress, budget watchers on Capitol Hill, and journalists have "kept score" of congressional budget actions on a continuing basis. They have interpreted these actions almost as if the survival of the new process turned on each outcome. Victories and defeats have been tallied frequently, with observers switching moods in accord with the latest results.

The Senate Budget Committee was judged on its way to success in 1975 when the Senate sent the military procurement and school lunch bills back to conference with the claim that they were inconsistent with the approved budget resolution. The committee seemed to be in eclipse the very next year when the Senate passed a tax measure that did not fit SBC specifications. The process was declared doomed in the spring of 1977 when the House rejected the Budget Committee's first budget resolution, but observers proclaimed a resurrection some days later when the same body passed a new resolution with only minimal changes. Both Budget Committees were judged to be losers when farm legislation was passed against their wishes in 1977 but were acclaimed winners when Congress passed a farm bill more to their liking in 1978. It was "A Good Year for the Congressional Budget Process" according to a *National Journal* headline in September 1978 after the Budget Committee scored a few successes.[1] But a few weeks later it was a "bad time for the process" as the House passed a highway bill vigorously opposed by HBC's chairman and the Senate overturned a point of order concerning one of the critical budget controls.[2]

1. See Joel Havemann, "A Good Year for the Congressional Budget Process," 10 *National Journal*, September 23, 1978, pp. 1501-03.
2. On October 5, 1978, the Senate voted to overturn a ruling that barred it from considering an amendment to cut federal taxes in future years. The point of order was based on Section 303 of the Budget Act which prohibits consideration of revenue, expenditure, or debt legislation before the first resolution for the fiscal year to which the legislation applies has been adopted. See 124 *Congressional Record* (daily ed., October 5, 1978) S17244.

Members themselves have not been immune to this roller-coaster reaction. In the throes of defeat or disappointment they have often denigrated the budget process as just a bookkeeping exercise, an "adding machine" that does not really make much policy difference. In triumph, Members have hailed the process as the means by which Congress has recaptured the power of the purse, set the economy on a stable and productive course, and established the public priorities of the United States. Judgments vacillate whenever Congress takes up budget resolutions, authorization bills, appropriations bills, and tax measures.

EXPECTATIONS AND REALITY

These widely varying views of the congressional budget process stem from uncertainty concerning its purpose, impact, and durability. Congress is not quite sure what it wrought in 1974, nor the extent to which it can abide its new discipline. Past failures of legislative budgeting are etched into the institutional memory, inflating the importance of each victory or defeat. The budget process, developed amid tense impasses between the executive branch and Congress over money, has been implemented in a goldfish bowl. Each major confrontation has been viewed as a test of the staying power and potency of budget reform, and because the conflicts have usually been fought in the open, the episodic outcomes have assumed an importance far beyond their real meaning.

Controversy about the effects of congressional budgeting has also risen from a tendency to test the process in terms of expectations that were not inscribed in the 1974 Act. People who sought stern budgetary discipline and spending cutbacks have been discouraged by continuing deficits and spiraling expenditures; they have disregarded the fact that the Budget Act permits Congress to adopt any budget policy it deems appropriate. People who sought to extensively revamp national priorities to match their own preferences have been disappointed by the slow pace of change, as if a budget process alone could uproot interest group politics in the United States or change the basic political function of Congress in resolving conflicts among claimants on the public purse.

Some critics view budgeting as a complex but straightforward technical exercise; they profess themselves appalled at the pulling and hauling Congress seems to go through to adopt a resolution and to legislate consistently with it. They denigrate Congress's efforts in comparison with the executive budget process, often hailed as an example of rational budgeting.

Congressional budgeting has been afflicted by inflated expectations formed during a half-century of executive budget practices. As the federal budget has grown, its preparation has come to be regarded as the principal instrument for deciding America's programs and policies. The first volume in the highly successful Brookings *Setting National Priorities* series celebrated the President's budget as "the vehicle for the most important and comprehensive collection of priority decisions which our society makes in the course of a year."[3] This claim has been widely accepted at face value although it provides a misleading view of the federal budget process.

The President's budget records priority decisions that are reached within executive agencies and in the White House through as difficult a political process as the process Congress goes through in public. In the development of that document, as in the development of the congressional budget, past decisions are major determinants of the final outcome. Claimants struggle over marginal amounts prior to release of the budget.

Many Members of Congress and others expected the congressional budget process to do for Congress what the executive budget process seemed to have accomplished for the President—control over federal programs and priorities. In addition, many expected the process to free Congress from dependence on the President's budget, as if an institutional change could displace decades of budgetary habit.

A serious appraisal of congressional budgeting must be grounded, however, on realistic expectations rather than unreal aspirations. Congress does not have an all-purpose budget process that meets the conflicting and exaggerated expectations of those who have promoted it. The budget process is only one, and not always the most powerful, of the tools Congress has for making financial and program decisions.

This concluding chapter assesses the accomplishments and limitations of the congressional budget process. Both are substantial. There are significant limitations to what any budget process can achieve, and the congressional budget process is subject to those applicable to the executive branch, plus some unique to a collegial

3. Charles L. Schultze et al., *Setting National Priorities: The 1971 Budget* (Washington, D.C.: The Brookings Institution, 1970), p. vii.

body. But there are also clear accomplishments to report. When measured against realistic expectations, the process has been successfully implemented. Much that has been written and spoken about its implementation both by participants and observers, however, has used an implicit set of criteria of success that no real-world budget process could meet, or should be expected to meet.

What the Budget Process Does Not (and Was Not Intended To) Do

Before assessing the accomplishments of the budget process, it is necessary to consider some of the criteria applied (or assumed) by critics who declare the process a failure. The bill of particulars against the budget process can be summarized as follows: The process has failed because it has not curbed the growth in federal spending or produced a balanced budget. All of the budget resolutions approved from fiscal 1976 through fiscal 1980 authorized deficit spending, with the cumulative deficit during these years totaling $240 billion. Federal spending soared from $326 billion in fiscal 1975 (the last year before the process was implemented) to more than $560 billion in fiscal 1980, only five years later. Moreover, uncontrollable spending continued to dominate the federal budget. Uncontrollables amounted to 72.8 percent of total expenditures in fiscal 1975 and an estimated 76.1 percent in fiscal 1980. Another charge is that the budget process has not induced a significant realignment in federal priorities. Spending, critics allege, is not significantly different from what it might have been in the absence of congressional budget controls.

These criticisms reflect certain assumptions about what the budget process was supposed to do, but it is not clear that the Budget Act was framed to satisfy these assumptions. It will be recalled that the Act was approved by overwhelming majorities in the House and Senate. This broad support reflected consensus within Congress that the legislative branch needed its own budget process. The support also reflected the Act's framers' successful reconciliation of divergent views about the type of process to be established. Conservatives wanted stern limits on congressional discretion, while liberals preferred a permissive process that would enable Congress to budget as it willed. Liberals and conservatives alike joined in endorsing the budget process, each group for its own reasons and each with its own expectations of what would be accomplished. In the bargaining that led to the Budget Act, people who wanted a permissive process got targets in the first resolution, while the hard-liners got ceilings in the second resolution. All parties to the compromise recognized that the actual meaning and effect of the budget process would be determined by the way it was implemented. The give-and-take of marshaling a consensus on budget reform, however, generated a number of misconceptions about the purposes of the new process. Even though they accepted compromise language in the Budget Act, many Members of Congress retained their original expectations concerning what an effective budget process should do. When these objectives were not realized, disappointed observers and participants charged the process with failure.

The principal misconceptions about the budget process are that it would—

—curb the growth in federal spending,
—bring an end to uncontrollable expenditures, and
—change federal budget priorities.

The Budget Process Should Constrain Federal Spending

Perhaps the most persistent complaints about the budget process are that it has not curtailed the rise in government spending and that it has not produced balanced budgets. These views are widely held in Congress. During the 96th Congress (1979-80), more than two-thirds of the Members introduced or sponsored restrictions on Congress's budget powers. More than 70 constitutional amendments requiring a balanced budget or limiting total federal outlays were proposed and more than 100 statutory limitations were introduced. Senator McClure, a former member of the Senate Budget Committee and a vigorous sponsor of restrictions on Congress's power of the purse, charged in 1980 debate on a proposed spending limitation that "the Budget Act has not worked as I conceive it was intended . . . by the time we reported our first congressional resolution, it was clear that although we had created a new budget process, we were still unwilling to control spending."[4]

In fact, however, the Budget Act neither prescribes a balanced budget nor imposes a fixed limit on federal spending. As chronicled in chapter III, most of the proposed constraints on congressional discretion (such as a rule of consistency and early ceilings) were eliminated before final passage of the Budget Act. Indeed, the

4. 126 *Congressional Record* (daily ed., March 25, 1980) S2932.

Budget Act expressly authorizes deficits in budget resolutions. Critics who charge that the budget process has failed to curb expenditures or deficits really are arguing that Congress passed the wrong legislation in 1974. Their complaint ought to be directed at what transpired before 1975, not at subsequent events.

The issue is not merely a question of what the Budget Act's framers intended; the issue is central to the budget role of Congress. Should Congress have free rein to take any budget action it deems appropriate, or should its budget powers be fettered in order to secure some predetermined outcome? Congress opted in 1974 for full power of the purse. Inasmuch as the Budget Act was provoked by White House intrusions on Congress's power, it would have been unseemly for Congress to rebuff presidential encroachments only to impose fresh restrictions on its own role.

Proposals for constitutional or statutory spending limitations are aimed at restricting Congress's exercise of its budget powers. The various schemes would proscribe certain budget outcomes, such as deficits or expenditures in excess of fixed limits. The Budget Act, however, arose from the conviction that Congress ought not be constrained in the exercise of its constitutional powers. People who favor restrictions would be on safer ground in resting their case on a particular ideology or economic theory, not on the claim that the Budget Act has failed.

It is erroneous to regard a budget process as a means of limiting the government's size or expenditures. Sixty years of presidential budgeting did not produce this result, and it is not likely to ensue from congressional budgeting. A budget process can generate pressure for higher expenditures or provide a mechanism for restraining the growth of government. These conflicting possibilities are rooted in the twin functions of a budget process as an opportunity for claiming resources and as a procedure for rationing limited resources among claimants. The congressional budget process both invites legislative committees (and the interests they represent) to ask for more money and provides a means for saying "no" to these claimants. Whether the articulation of claims or the rationing of resources is dominant depends on the political environment within which the budget process operates. A political climate that favors program expansion is not likely to coexist with restrictive budget policies. As political conditions change, so, too, will the results produced by the budget process. The balance between the claiming and rationing functions of budgeting will vary, therefore, from year to year. The same congressional budget process that provided opportunities for stimulative spending during the 1975 recession and after Carter's election also was the forum for approving a balanced budget, along with the revenue and spending policies consistent with balance, for the 1981 fiscal year. The budget process is neutral; the side that has the most votes decides what gets into the budget.

Congress Should Control All Federal Spending

A second complaint about the budget process is that it has not eliminated uncontrolled spending. As noted earlier, the percentage of the budget officially classified as "relatively uncontrollable under existing law" is higher in 1980 that it was before the process was inaugurated.

Yet the record is not so disappointing as a simple perusal of the uncontrollability statistics might lead one to believe. During the first five years of congressional budgeting, there was little real or discretionary growth in entitlement programs, the largest and fastest-growing category of uncontrollables during the five years before the budget process was implemented. The continuing growth in uncontrollables has been due almost entirely to growth in the populations covered by entitlement programs and the indexing of major entitlements to cost-of-living increases.

Moreover, "uncontrollability" is not an accident or an inadvertence of the legislative process but a willful decision by Congress to favor nonbudgetary values over budgetary control. As this chapter argues later, the balancing of budgetary and competing values is one of the major successes of the congressional budget process. To understand why Congress has voluntarily yielded some of its controls over expenditures, consider how a "perfect" budget system in which Congress retained complete, annual control would operate.[5] Each year's budget decision would be unencumbered by past actions; no commitments would spill over from one year to the next. Annually, Congress would decide how much should be spent on pensions, interest payments, and other entitlement categories. Contractual obligations would extend only until the end of the fiscal year, so that when the next year's decisions were made, Congress would have a free choice. Such a system would be perfect in the sense that it would accord Congress complete control over the budget. All spending proposals would have

5. This paragraph is adapted from U.S. Congress, House Committee on the Budget, *Congressional Control of Expenditures*, Committee Print, 95th Cong., 1st Sess., pp. 5-7.

to compete on equal terms and go through the same authorizations-appropriations-budget processes. There would be no entitlements with preferred claims on expenditures. Everything would be controllable each year.

But this "perfect" budget system would be a legislative nightmare. Each year's budget would be an uncertain, raucous affair, with the sheer magnitude of the task obstructing the way to agreement. Everything would be up for grabs and the scope of conflict would be vastly expanded. The tension level within Congress would escalate in proportion to the uncertainty of program beneficiaries. With everything reopened every year, retired persons, bondholders, and other claimants would besiege Congress merely to assure continuation of their benefits.

Congress settles the budget by limiting the use to which its budget power is put. It surrenders control over major portions of the budget in order to have an opportunity to decide the rest. "Uncontrollable" is the *cordon sanitaire* of budgeting, a way of making budgets by limiting their reach.

This is not to say that every uncontrollable item deserves its special status or that the Budget Committees ought to accept all uncontrollables as an uncontested part of the budget. One of the key responsibilities of the Budget Committees is to speak for budget control, to challenge not all of the uncontrollables every year, but some. They have to be especially vigilant against proposed new uncontrollables, but Congress has the final decision with respect to further inroads into the controllable sector of the budget.

The Budget Act Should Change Federal Spending Patterns

People who are disappointed with budget outcomes commonly complain that the process has not reordered national priorities. In recent years, liberals have criticized the process for failing to transfer funds from defense to human resource programs. Whether or not this is an accurate perception of budgetary results, it should be clear that the process neither compels a particular set of priorities nor requires that functions (or programs) be explicitly traded off against one another in the competition for funds. Congress, as was argued in chapter VIII, prefers to set priorities by allocating budget authority and outlays to the various functions, not by open competition among functions. By providing different increments or (occasionally) decrements to the various functions, the budget process leads to marginal changes in priorities, even when it does not formally shift funds from one category to another.

The spending pattern that emerges from the congressional budget process might not be significantly different from what would result from the piecemeal arrangements that prevailed before the process was introduced. Whether through a comprehensive budget scheme or fragmented choice, congressional decisions are likely to reflect majority preferences. The budget process probably has speeded up congressional response to changing public sentiment concerning federal programs. By offering a focal point for debate, the budget process enables a program's supporters to campaign for higher allocations. The process also prods Congress to take distasteful actions—such as curtailing programs, reducing benefits, or deferring a tax reduction—which it might otherwise avoid. At the margins, budget outcomes can be changed by the process, but dramatic shifts should not be expected from a process that vests stakeholders with multiple opportunities to make their cases.

THE ACCOMPLISHMENTS OF CONGRESSIONAL BUDGETING

A truly neutral budget process cannot be properly assessed with substantive criteria. The relevant tests are essentially procedural: Has Congress lived up to the requirements of the Budget Act? Has Congress passed the prescribed budget resolutions and legislated in accord with their terms? This chapter and book conclude with an examination of three criteria for assessing the budget process:

1. Adoption of budget resolutions
2. Balancing of budgetary and other interests
3. Management of budgetary conflict within Congress.

The Institutionalization of Congressional Budgeting

The first measure of budgetary success must be procedural: the ability of Congress to adopt the spring and fall budget resolutions. If Congress failed to adopt these measures, the Budget Act would quickly become a dead letter.

Thus far, Congress has succeeded in adopting all of the required resolutions. Legislators have been willing to subordinate policy goals to budgetary peace. Several of the "close calls" demonstrate that while Members of Congress may be willing to carry budgetary conflict to the brink, they have not been willing to risk destruction of their process. It will be recalled that two Republicans supplied the necessary votes to report the first 1976 resolution out of HBC. Two years later, many Representatives switched to support a revised resolution after the first version was defeated in the House. HBC's Marjorie Holt explained "that when the resolution was defeated, everybody in the House who wants to have the process succeed reevaluated what we were doing."[6] Members, of course, are sometimes willing to threaten the budget process as a means of extracting more favorable terms. This posture was taken in the conference on the first resolution for 1978 when SBC's Peter Domenici insisted that he would rather have no budget than one that failed to provide the allocation he wanted for defense:

> . . . if this is the time to bust the budget process, there is no better one. If we need time to say "It just won't work," then I think this is as good a one as any. . . .
> If there ever is an issue when this senator will opt out of the budget process, it is this situation. I would not vote for a House figure that they have submitted to us for military preparedness and use as a defense that I am trying to preserve the budget process.[7]

After the deadlock had been broken, Domenici changed his tune and voted for the resolution. Now he insisted that there is no process

> more important to our institutions, to the House of Representatives and the Senate, and to the prosperity of America, than the budget process. . . . Because of that, I felt that the stalemate in the conference was probably going to end up with the real probability of no Budget Act at all. . . . if we had come back without resolving it, then I think the Budget Reform Act and its tremendously important qualities for credibility in this democratic process could very well have gone by the board.[8]

One cannot be certain that members will always be willing to compromise for the sake of the budget process. Sooner or later, this argument may lose force and the process will then survive only if it satisfies the expectations of congressional majority. Yet there is throughout Congress a conviction that the congressional budget process is the correct, responsible way to make financial decisions. Most Members like the sense of order the process has brought to legislative work and regard the process as the keystone of legislative responsibility. This attitude is shared by Members

6. Transcript of conference on first concurrent resolution for fiscal 1978, p. 171.
7. *Ibid.*, pp. 155-56.
8. 123 *Congressional Record* (daily ed., May 13, 1977) S7541.

who served in Congress before the budget was enacted as well as those who came after 1975 and have never known any other procedure. "I feel as if we have always had a budget process," said an old hand. "I can't even imagine how we managed without one in the past." Much the same sentiment was expressed by a newcomer: "Maybe Congress was able to make do without a budget process when the federal government was small; nowadays, there is no other rational way to operate."

These feelings sometimes translate into a take-it-for-granted attitude toward the budget process. When the House rejected the conference agreement on the first resolution for fiscal 1980, everybody knew that another version would be promptly submitted. The fact that the May 15 deadline for the resolution had already passed only stimulated congressional leaders to act quickly so as not to delay other legislative business. They did not consider proceeding to other matters (such as appropriations) without first passing the necessary resolution.

The budget process has become a regular, accepted feature of the congressional landscape. Its routines have been fixed in the House and Senate calendars and in the minds of Members. The annual cycle of committee and floor work is oriented to the budget schedule. Budget events no longer come as a surprise or as an unexpected intervention. Senators know that SBC spokesmen will take the floor to comment on the budgetary impact of pending legislation. They know that bills and amendments will be scored in terms of the assumptions in the latest budget resolution and that proposals that were not taken into account when the budget was adopted generally will have a harder time making it through Congress than those that were accounted for.

The Balancing of Legislative Interests

The budget is only one of a number of interests that Congress has to take into account. The full range of program interests compete with the budget for congressional attention. The peer controls on which the budget process is grounded cannot abide use of the budget as the checkpoint through which all other legislation must be gauged—the sole yardstick for measuring the worth of the bills produced by legislative committees.

If the budget process is to survive, it will have to coexist with other legislative interests and activities. This means that a successful budget process requires the balancing of budgetary and other values. If the budget process were an all-reaching, consistent, critical decision process as it has often been credited with being, command over the budget would bring control over the political system as well. Instead, the budget is only one—and not always the most important or decisive—arena for public choice. Congressional committees make budget decisions when they develop legislation; administrators make budget decisions when they promulgate regulations; the President influences the budget when he hits the campaign trail.

It can be said that the budget process serves two rather different functions: It is at once the process by which some decisions are made and the process by which some decisions are accounted for financially and recorded. Some program decisions are made in the budget; others are merely translated into dollar terms when the budget is assembled. For example, legislation mandating the payment of black-lung benefits is accounted for in each year's budget, but the decision was made at the legislative stage, when the entitlement was conferred. Congress has been repeatedly urged to use its budget for making policy; otherwise, it has been argued, the process would become only an accounting tool. In truth, both types of budgets coexist in the same process. Perhaps the best recognition of this dual process is the budget's statement that most expenditures are "uncontrollable under existing law." This does not mean, however, that three-quarters of the budget is completely uncontrollable, because for most items Congress can revoke or revise the law mandating the expenditure. Congress can repeal or roll back the black-lung program if it so desires. But Congress cannot change the level of black-lung spending by budgetary action alone; no matter what amount is contemplated in its budget resolutions (or appropriations), the expenditures will be determined by laws already on the books or commitments already made. To substantially reduce the portion of the budget that is uncontrollable, Congress would have to extend the effective scope of the budget into the jurisdictions of its legislative committees. Whatever virtues there might be in such a far-reaching budget process, it certainly would cause an escalation in budgetary conflict and impair the ability of Congress to balance the many interests pressing for satisfaction.

The institutionalization of the budget process has contributed to a perceptible shift in the focus of congressional debate on important programs from substantive issues to financial considerations. Members often argue over the cost of a weapons system or of changes in food stamp eligibility as if finance were the only relevant consideration. The President unveils a welfare reform proposal or a national health insurance program and the discussion immediately narrows to budgetary concerns. In the early 1970s, each year's defense authorization bill occasioned great debate in the Senate on one or another aspect of national policy. At the end of the decade, the discussion was cast in fiscal terms—the rate at which defense spending should grow, the relative budget shares of defense and civilian program, the amount assumed in the latest resolution for defense. When a measure is in line with the budget, it is likely to speed through the House and Senate, as if the critical test had already been met and the basic decisions had already been made. A measure with a budget problem often finds itself stalled, as the debate opens into an examination of financial accounts.

The Management of Budgetary Conflict

Conflict is inherent in the budget process because the contestants have one-sided views of their legislative responsibilities. The role of the Budget Committees is to speak for the budget process, not to represent the many other interests pressing upon Congress. Program committees' interests are defined by jurisdictional assignments; these committees cannot make the budgetary process their principal concern. With the Budget Committees tending to the budget and other committees looking after their special interests, budgetary conflict is sometimes unavoidable.

The sources of budgetary conflict antedate the Budget Act. It will be recalled from chapter II that before 1974 Congress experienced protracted strife over spending ceilings and committee jurisdictions. These altercations were incited by clashes between demands for more spending and concern over the financial condition of the United States. At the very time that Congress was becoming more open and vulnerable to budgetary pressures, it was becoming more sensitive to budgetary scarcity. In the years before the Budget Act was passed, the guardianship norms of the House Appropriation Committee and its control over federal spending were weakened by changes in its composition and structure. Spending demands were increasingly expressed through limited-term authorizations and satisfied through backdoor schemes. These changes within Congress were matched by the growing attentiveness of interest groups to budgetary matters. The federal budget became an open book, its secrets and potential plumbed by the numerous interest groups stationed in Washington.

Congress might have tried to extricate itself from these cross pressures by erecting institutional barriers to the articulation or satisfaction of budgetary demands. It might, for example, have required balanced budgets or made it difficult for Members to approve budget-increasing amendments to appropriations bills. But in the Budget Act Congress rejected these and other proposed restraints on its discretion. Congress elected instead for an open process; it encouraged legislative committees to press their views and estimates and enabled the House and Senate to approve any budget satisfactory to their majorities. Rather than quashing budgetary conflict at the source, the Budget Act assured that conflict would be in the open. In deciding not to bottle up the budgetary pressures but to allow a free fight over spending, taxes, and deficit, Congress institutionalized its own ambivalence over budget policy. Because it could not foreclose any substantive outcome in 1974, Congress left to each year's budget cycle a fight over what the decisions should be.

It is not surprising, therefore, that there has been so much budgetary conflict within Congress or that the process has experienced bruising defeats and resounding successes. All that Congress decided in 1974 was that the disputes would be resolved through a process in which the majority rules. The Budget Committees win when they have the votes; they lose when Congress brushes aside budget protests in order to advance some other interest.

No system based on cooperation among peers could long survive if one side won or lost all the time. So it is in Congress, with the Budget Committee winning some and losing some. The President's Office of Management and Budget also loses dozens of big and small fights each year, but most of its defeats are hidden from public view. OMB is sheltered by the President because it is to his advantage to foster the belief that he has a powerful budget office. Because most congressional battles occur in public, their importance is magnified. If the budget process in the House appears to be less contentious than in the Senate, one reason is that HBC's behind-the-scenes approach has shielded the results from the public eye. SBC, by contrast, has won and lost big because so much of its activity is open to public view.

The competition between budgetary and other values is affected by the mood of the moment. Sometimes, when Congress is eager to push ahead with spending plans, expansionist fever overwhelms the budget controls; at other times, when Congress is more concerned about stock taking and retrenchment, it might favor strict budget control over competing interests. Congressional budget makers cannot expect to be equally powerful every year. Sometimes there will be a strong congressional market for their point of view, at other times, a weak one. The Appropriations Committees have lived with these swings in congressional sentiment for 120 years; the Budget Committees also will have to ride out the ups and downs in their legislative esteem.

The Budget Committees need congressional allies in order to carry the day, but a pattern that emerges from this study is that the committees can only hold transitory allies who make common cause for a particular issue and for their own advantage.

Although conflict cannot be eliminated, it must be restrained if the budget process is to survive. Congress would be torn apart if every legislative action prompted a major battle. Rather than wondering why budget fights have occurred, one might marvel at how few there have been. Basically, the budget and program committees alike understand that a collegial body can hold together only if it restrains its tendency toward conflict. Thus, most congressional committees try to abide by the Budget Act's procedural and substantive terms.

But more than good intentions are needed to contain budgetary conflict. The process also must be engineered to assure a peaceful outcome in most situations. The Budget Act, however, seems to entrench conflict within Congress by positioning the Budget Committees as the adversaries of other legislative committees. If they do the job for which they were established, the Budget Committees cannot avoid stepping on legislative toes. Intramural strife can erupt when the Budget Committees review the March 15 claims, when they pressure other committee for savings or resist their proposed initiatives, or when they police the budget-related activities of other committees. Budget conflict also can occur when Congress has to formulate resolutions that set forth the priorities and fiscal policy of the United States. These stress points are essential features of the budget process, not peripheral or accidental occurrences. The Budget Act expects conflict and organizes Congress for it.

In sum, when Congress fights over the budget, it is fighting over each year's margins: The bulk of the budget is, with general agreement, determined by prior years' legislative decisions. In a budget the size of the federal government's, the disputes over margins might cover a few billion dollars. This is a large enough stake to stir the combatants to battle, but it is a sufficiently manageable amount to enable them to negotiate budgetary accord. The budget process provides them with a useful legislative tool for conducting this necessary business.

Appendix

DEFINITIONS OF BUDGETARY TERMS[1]

Appropriation

An authorization by an act of the Congress that permits federal agencies to incur obligations and to make payments out of the treasury for specified purposes. An appropriation usually follows enactment of authorizing legislation. An appropriation act is the most common means of providing budget authority (see **Budget Authority**), but in some cases the authorizing legislation itself provides the budget authority. (See **Backdoor Authority**.)

Appropriation Act

An act under the jurisdiction of the Committees on Appropriations which provides funds for federal programs. At this time there are 13 regular appropriation acts. Supplemental appropriation acts are also enacted from time to time.

Authorization (Authorizing Legislation)

Basic substantive legislation enacted by Congress, which sets up or continues the legal operation of a federal program or agency either indefinitely or for a specific period of time or sanctions a particular type of obligation or expenditure within a program. Such legislation is normally a prerequisite for subsequent appropriations or other kinds of budget authority to be contained in appropriation acts. It may limit the amount of budget authority to be provided subsequently or may authorize the appropriation of "such sums as may be necessary." In some instances budget authority may be provided in the authorization (see **Backdoor Authority**), which

1. Adapted from a more detailed document by the Comptroller General of the United States, *Terms Used in the Budgetary Process*, Washington, D.C.: U.S. General Accounting Office, July 1977.

obviates the need for subsequent appropriations or requires only an appropriation to liquidate contract authority or reduce outstanding debt.

Authorizing Committee

A standing committee of the House or Senate with jurisdiction over the subject matter of those laws, or parts of laws, that set up or continue the legal operations of federal programs, agencies, or particular types of obligations within programs. The authorizing committee also has spending responsibility in those instances where the budget authority ("backdoor authority") is also provided in the basic substantive legislation.

Backdoor Authority

Budget authority provided in legislation outside the normal (Appropriations Committees) appropriations process. The most common forms of backdoor authority are borrowing authority, contract authority, and entitlements. In some cases (e.g., interest on the public debt), a permanent appropriation is provided that becomes available without any current action by the Congress. Section 401 of the Congressional Budget Act of 1974 specifies certain limits on the use of backdoor authority.

Borrowing Authority

Statutory authority (substantive or appropriation) that permits a federal agency to incur obligations and to make payments for specified purposes out of borrowed moneys. Section 401 of the Congressional Budget Act of 1974 limits new borrowing authority (except for certain instances) to such extent or in such amounts as are provided in appropriation acts.

Budget Amendment

A formal request submitted to the Congress by the President, after his formal budget transmittal but prior to completion of appropriation action by the Congress, that revises previous requests, such as the amount of budget authority.

Budget Authority

Authority provided by law to enter into obligations which will result in immediate or future outlays involving Government funds, except that such term does not include authority to insure or guarantee the repayment of indebtedness incurred by another person or government. The basic forms of budget authority are appropriations, contract authority, and borrowing authority. Budget authority may be classified by (a) the period of availability (one-year, multiple-year, no-year), (b) the timing of congressional action (current or permanent), or (c) the manner of determining the amount available (definite or indefinite).

Budget Update

A statement summarizing amendments to or revisions in budget authority requested, estimated outlays, and estimated receipts for a fiscal year that has not been completed. The President may submit updates at any time but is required by the Congressional Budget Act of 1974 to transmit such statements to the Congress by April 10 and July 15 of each year.

Budgetary Reserves

Portions of budget authority set aside under authority of the Antideficiency Act (31 U.S.C. 665), as amended by the Impoundment Control Act of 1974, for contingencies or to effect savings whenever savings are made possible by or through changes in requirements or greater efficiency of operations. Section 1002 of the Impoundment Control Act of 1974 restricts the establishment of budgetary reserves and requires that all reserves be reported to the Congress. (See **Deferral of Budget Authority**.)

Concurrent Resolution on the Budget

A resolution passed by both Houses of Congress, but not requiring the signature of the President, setting forth, reaffirming, or revising the congressional budget for the United States Government for a fiscal year. There are two such resolutions required preceding each fiscal year. The first required concurrent resolution, due by May 15, establishes the congressional budget. The second required concurrent resolution, due by September 15, reaffirms or revises it. Other concurrent resolutions for a fiscal year may be adopted at any time following the first required concurrent resolution for that fiscal year.

Congressional Budget

The budget as set forth by Congress in a concurrent resolution on the budget. These resolutions shall include

(1) the appropriate level of total budget outlays and of total new budget authority,

(2) an estimate of budget outlays and new budget authority for each major functional category, for contingencies, and for undistributed offsetting receipts based on allocations of the appropriate level of total budget outlays and of total new budget auhority,
(3) the amount, if any, of the surplus or deficit in the budget,
(4) the recommended level of federal revenues, and
(5) the appropriate level of the public debt.

Continuing Resolution

Legislation enacted by the Congress to provide budget authority for specific ongoing activities in cases where the regular fiscal year appropriation for such activities has not been enacted by the beginning of the fiscal year. The continuing resolution usually specifies a maximum rate at which the agency may incur obligations, based on the rate of the prior year, the President's budget request, or an appropriation bill passed by either or both Houses of the Congress.

Contract Authority

A form of budget authority under which contracts or other obligations may be entered into in advance of an appropriation or in excess of amounts otherwise available in a revolving fund. Contract authority must be funded by a subsequent appropriation or the use of revolving fund collections to liquidate the obligations. Appropriations to liquidate contract authority are not classified as budget authority since they are not available for obligation. Section 401 of the Congressional Budget Act of 1974 limits new contract authority, with few exceptions, to such extent or in such amounts as are provided in appropriation acts.

Controllability

The ability under existing law to control budget authority or outlays during a given fiscal year. "Relatively uncontrollable" usually refers to spending that cannot be increased or decreased without changes in existing substantive law. The largest part of such spending is the result of open-ended programs and fixed costs, such as Social Security and veterans' benefits, but also includes payments due under obligations incurred during prior years.

Crosswalk

The relationship between one set of classifications and another, such as between appropriation accounts and authorizing legislation or between the budget functional structure and the congressional committee spending jurisdictions.

Current Policy Budget

Projections of the estimated budget authority and outlays for the upcoming fiscal year to operate federal programs at the level implied by enacted appropriations and authorizations for the current fiscal year without policy changes, but adjusted for inflation, changes in the numbers and kinds of beneficiaries, and in some instances to reflect the continuation of certain programs scheduled to terminate.

Current Services Estimates

Estimated budget authority and outlays for the upcoming fiscal year based on continuation of existing levels of service, i.e., assuming that all programs and activities will be carried on at the same level as in the fiscal year in progress and without policy changes in such programs and activities. These estimates of budget authority and outlays, accompanied by the underlying economic and programmatic assumptions upon which they are based (such as the rate of inflation, the rate of real economic growth, the unemployment rate, program caseloads, and pay increases), are transmitted by the President to the Congress when the budget is submitted.

Deferral of Budget Authority

Any action or inaction by any officer or employee of the United States that withholds, delays, or effectively precludes the obligation or expenditure of budget authority, including the establishment of reserves under the Antideficiency Act as amended by the Impoundment Control Act. Section 1013 of the Impoundment Control Act of 1974 requires a special message from the President to the Congress reporting a proposed deferral of budget authority. Deferrals may not extend beyond the end of the fiscal year in which the message reporting the deferral is transmitted and may be overturned by the passage of an impoundment resolution by either House of Congress. (See **Impoundment Resolution**.)

Entitlement Authority

Legislation that requires the payment of benefits to any person or government meeting the requirements established by such law, e.g., Social Security benefits and veterans' pensions. Section 401 of the

Congressional Budget Act of 1974 places certain restrictions on the enactment of new entitlement authority.

Fiscal Policy

Federal government policies with respect to taxes, spending, and debt management, intended to promote the nation's economic goals, particularly with respect to employment, gross national product, price level stability, and equilibrium in balance of payments. The budget process is a major vehicle for determining and implementing federal fiscal policy. The other major component of federal economic policy is monetary policy.

Fiscal Year

Any yearly accounting period, without regard to its relationship to a calendar year. The fiscal year for the federal government begins on October 1 and ends on September 30. The fiscal year is designated by the calendar year in which it ends; e.g., fiscal year 1980 is the fiscal year ending September 30, 1981.

Full Employment Budget

The estimated receipts, outlays, and surplus or deficit that would occur if the economy were continually operating at a rate defined as being at full capacity (traditionally defined as a certain percentage unemployment rate for the civilian labor force).

Function (Functional Classification)

The Congressional Budget Act of 1974 requires the Congress to estimate outlays, budget authority, and tax expenditures for each function. The functional classification is a means of presenting budget authority, outlay, and tax expenditure data in terms of the principal purposes that federal programs are intended to serve. Each account is generally placed in the single function (e.g., national defense, health) that best represents its major purpose, regardless of the agency administering the program. Functions are subdivided into narrower categories called subfunctions.

Government-Sponsored Enterprises

Enterprises with completely private ownership, such as federal land banks and federal home loan banks, established and chartered by the federal government to perform specialized functions. These enterprises are not included in the budget totals, but financial information on their operations is published in a separate part of the appendix to the President's budget.

Guaranteed Loans

Loans for which the federal government guarantees in whole or in part the repayment of principal and/or interest.

Impoundment

Any action or inaction by an officer or employee of the United States that precludes the obligation or expenditure of budget authority provided by the Congress. See **Deferral of Budget Authority and Rescission.)**

Impoundment Resolution

A resolution of the House of Representatives or the Senate disapproving a deferral of budget authority set forth in a special message ordinarily transmitted by the President under Section 1013 of the Impoundment Control Act of 1974. Passage of an impoundment resolution by either House of Congress has the effect of overturning the deferral and requires that such budget authority be made available for obligation.

Obligations

Amounts of orders placed, contracts awarded, services rendered, or other commitments made by federal agencies during a given period, which will require outlays during the same or some future period.

Off-Budget

Transactions that have been excluded from the budget totals under provisions of law, e.g., the Federal Financing Bank. Off-budget transactions are not included in either budget authority or outlay totals, but are presented in a separate part of the budget appendix and as memorandum items in various tables in the budget.

Offsetting Collections

Moneys received by the government as a result of business-type transactions with the public (sale of goods and services) or as a result of a payment from one government account to another. Such collections are netted in determining budget outlays.

Offsetting Receipts

All collections deposited into receipt accounts that are offset against budget authority and outlays rather than reflected as budget receipts in computing budget totals. Under current budgetary usage, cash collections not deposited into receipt accounts (such as revolving fund receipts and reimbursements) are deducted from outlays at the account level. These transactions are offsetting collections but are not classified as "offsetting receipts."

Offsetting receipts are generally deducted at the budget function or subfunction level and from agency budget authority and outlays. In three cases—employer share of employee retirement, intragovernmental interest received by trust funds, and rents and royalties from the Outer Continental Shelf lands—the deductions, referred to as **Undistributed Offsetting Receipts**, are made from budget totals rather than being offset by function and subfunction and by agency.

Open-Ended Programs

Entitlement programs under which actual obligations and resultant outlays are limited only by the number of eligible persons meeting eligibility requirements fixed by law who apply for benefits and the actual benefits received, e.g., Medicaid.

Outlays

The amount of checks issued, interest accrued on most public debt, or other payments; net of refunds and reimbursements. Total budget outlays consist of the sum of the outlays from appropriations and funds included in the unified budget, less offsetting receipts. The outlays of off-budget federal entities are excluded from the unified budget under provisions of law, even though these outlays are part of total government spending. Federal outlays are recorded on the "cash basis of accounting"—with the exception of most interest on the public debt, for which the "accrual basis of accounting" is used.

President's Budget

The budget for a particular fiscal year transmitted to the Congress by the President in accordance with the Budget and Accounting Act of 1921, as amended. Some elements of the budget, such as the estimates for the legislative branch and the judiciary, are required to be included without review by the Office of Management and Budget or approval by the President.

Program

Generally defined as an organized set of activities directed toward a common purpose, objective, or goal, undertaken or proposed by an agency in order to carry out responsibilities assigned to it. In practice, however, the term "program" has many usages and thus does not have a well-defined standardized meaning in the legislative process. "Program" has been used as a description for agency missions, activities, services, projects, and processes.

Reappropriation

Congressional action to restore the obligational availability, whether for the same or different purposes, of all or part of the unobligated portion of budget authority in an expired account. Obligational availability in a current account may also be extended by a subsequent appropriation act.

Reconciliation Process

A process used by the Congress to reconcile amounts determined by tax, spending, and debt legislation for a given fiscal year with the ceilings enacted in the second required concurrent resolution on the budget for that year. Section 310 of the Congressional Budget Act of 1974 provides that the second required concurrent resolution on the budget, which sets binding totals for the budget, may direct committees to determine and recommend changes to laws, bills, and resolutions, as required to conform with the binding totals for budget authority, revenues, and the public debt. Such changes are incorporated into either a reconciliation resolution or a reconciliation bill.

Reprogramming

Utilization of funds in an appropriation account for purposes other than those contemplated at the time of appropriation. Reprogramming is generally accomplished pursuant to consultation between the federal agencies and the appropriate congressional committees.

Rescission

The consequence of enacted legislation which cancels budget authority previously provided by Congress prior to the time when the authority would otherwise lapse (i.e., cease to be available for obligation). Section 1012 of the Impoundment Control Act of 1974 requires a special message from the President to the Congress reporting any proposed rescission of budget authority. These proposals may be accepted in whole or in part through the passage of a rescission bill by both Houses of Congress.

Rescission Bill

A bill or joint resolution that provides for cancellation, in whole or in part, of budget authority previously granted by the Congress. Under the Impoundment Control Act of 1974, unless Congress approves a rescission bill within 45 days of continuous session after receipt of the proposal, the budget authority must be made available for obligation.

Scorekeeping

A procedure used by the Congressional Budget Office for up-to-date tabulations and reports of congressional budget actions on bills and resolutions providing new budget authority and outlays and changing revenues and the public debt limit for a fiscal year. Such reports include, but are not limited to, status reports on the effects of these congressional actions to date and of potential congressional actions, and comparisons of these actions to targets and ceilings set by Congress in the budget resolutions. Periodic scorekeeping reports are required by Section 308(b) of the Congressional Budget Act of 1974.

Spending Authority

As defined by the Congressional Budget Act of 1974, a collective designation for borrowing authority, contract authority, and entitlement authority, for which the budget authority is not provided in advance by appropriation acts. These are also commonly referred to as backdoor authority.

Supplemental Appropriation

An act appropriating funds in addition to those in an annual appropriation act. Supplemental appropriations provide additional budget authority beyond original estimates for programs or activities (including new programs authorized after the date of the original appropriation act) for which the need for funds is too urgent to be postponed until enactment of the next regular appropriation act.

Tax Expenditures

Losses of tax revenue attributable to provisions of the federal tax laws which allow a special exclusion, exemption, or deduction from gross income or which provide a special credit, preferential rate of tax, or a deferral of tax liability.

Trust Funds

Funds collected and used by the federal government for carrying out specific purposes and programs according to terms of a trust agreement or statute, such as the Social Security and unemployment trust funds. Trust funds are administered by the government in a fiduciary capacity and are not available for the general purposes of the government. Trust fund receipt accounts are credited with receipts generated by the terms of the trust agreement or statute.

Unified Budget

The present form of the budget of the federal government, in which receipts and outlays from federal funds and trust funds are consolidated. When these fund groups are consolidated to display budget totals, transactions which are outlays of one fund group for payment to the other fund group (i.e., interfund transactions) are deducted to avoid double counting. Transactions of off-budget federal entities are not included in the unified budget.

Index